D1591360

Cricket in America,
1710–2000

Cricket in America, 1710–2000

P. David Sentance

McFarland & Company, Inc., Publishers
Jefferson, North Carolina, and London

Frontispiece: Robert A. Fitzgerald's amateur England team in America, 1872. This was the only time W.G. Grace played in America (Grace: sixth from left; Fitzgerald: second from left). Source: Lord Beaulieu editor, *British Sports and Sportsmen (BSS)* (London: Longmans, 1907).

LIBRARY OF CONGRESS CATALOGUING-IN-PUBLICATION DATA

Sentance, P. David, 1952–
Cricket in America, 1710–2000 / P. David Sentance.
p.   cm.
Includes bibliographical references and index.

ISBN 0-7864-2040-5 (softcover : 50# alkaline paper)

1. Cricket — United States — History.   I. Title.
GV928.U6S46   2006
796.3580973 — dc22   2006000201

British Library cataloguing data are available

On the cover: Cricket game, Newport, Rhode Island, ca. 1902
(Library of Congress); Cricket bat and ball ©2006 PhotoSpin

Manufactured in the United States of America

*McFarland & Company, Inc., Publishers
Box 611, Jefferson, North Carolina 28640
www.mcfarlandpub.com*

In Memorium

Harry Sentance
Linda Susan Soriano-Sentance

Contents

Preface

RESEARCH FOR *Cricket in America, 1710–2000* started during the Philadelphia Cricket Festival in 1996. New Zealand all-rounder Sir Richard "Paddles" Hadlee, the first bowler to take over 400 test wickets, was guest of honor. While Sir Richard shivered gallantly on the boundary at the historic Haverford College cricket ground, I headed for the warmth of the C. "Christie" Morris Cricket Library. Once in the library, researcher Carol Babb and Amar Singh, curator of the library, became my research allies. The C.C. Morris library has the most complete collections of *The American Cricketer* and *Spalding's Cricket Annual* in the United States.

Many cricket records referred to California. My father had a hunch to turn off Highway 80 after viewing California's Gold Country, and it led to a stop at Penryn Museum located next to a granite quarry eight miles east of Sacramento. The curator of the museum put me in touch with Barbara Pierce. Barbara kindly shared her research on the English colony of Penryn, which had played cricket to a high standard. As I read through the Penryn documents, it became obvious that the California story of cricket was complex.

Donna Howard, the assistant curator of the Lakeport Museum in Lake County, California, directed me to filing cabinets of cricket records that took three days' research to unravel.

Donna then arranged for me to see Herbert Keeling's 100-year-old cricket bat and scrapbooks. Gradually the California cricket picture came into perspective. A quick crash course in southern California history drew my attention to accounts of cricket games in the *Los Angeles Times* and *Santa Monica Outlook* between the Santa Monica and Los Angeles cricket clubs. Two years later I was prepared to write a California cricket history.

Fortunately, I decided to pursue a greater challenge, a history of cricket in America. Carol Babb sent documents for Chicago cricket. Reconstructing Chicago cricket expanded my knowledge of southern California cricketers, many of whom came from Illinois. Trips to New York, Florida and Philadelphia fleshed out the East Coast part of the story. Personal experience with the Los Angeles Krickets in Utah had already brought my attention to the regular playing of cricket in the heart of America's Mormon and Indian country. A trip to Flagstaff, Arizona, and a review of its copper industry at the University of Northern Arizona produced a fascinating insight into how cricket played an important role in the social structure of mining towns near Bisbee. Tom Melville's pioneering cricket research helped me get a feel for cricket in the cold northern climes of Minnesota.

Piecing together the research and getting the right balance or emphasis remains a delicate task for any historian. The Edinburgh University and UCLA African history departments were adept at researching lost cultures utilizing comparative linguistics in preliterate societies. Loan-words from lost cultures were absorbed by the new dominant racial and cultural group. In sport, as baseball increasingly took root in the pop culture of the day, cricket was buried like a lost culture. The cricket historian's job was made easier as there were numerous American records of cricket matches. For clarity, minor changes have been made to the spelling and punctuation of quoted material.

Phrases such as "playing on a sticky wicket," or "playing with a straight bat" were readily understood in America at the beginning of the twentieth century. New York merchant-banker Jack Morgan gained experience at J.P. Morgan's Morgan-Grenfell bank in London. Between 1898 and 1905, Jack and his Boston-born wife Jessie lived in England. In 1901 they leased Aldenham Abbey in Hertfordshire. Jack's father, Pierpont Morgan, already owned a house in London and "in the Anglophile Morgan world, Pierpont Morgan's Dover House staff would meet Jack's Wall Hall crew for cricket matches.... As neighbors, there were Earl Gray and Florence Nightingale; for occasional dinner companions, Rudyard Kipling, Henry James, Sir James Barrie, and Mark Twain."[1]

Jack Morgan was a regular visitor to Scotland in the summer grouse-hunting season.

> Socially, Jack shared his father's snobbery and disdained the hurly burly of American life ... he had a special horror of arrivistes. Summering in Newport might be fine for others, but for Jack the place was "swamped by the horrid vulgar lot who make or rather ruin the reputation of it."[2]

In 1910, Jack Morgan bought Aldenham Abbey, a 300-acre estate, and renamed it Wall Hall. The English mansion complemented a red brick chateau modeled after Denham Palace in Buckinghamshire, which was set on 250 acres called Matinicock Point, on New York's Long Island.[3] Long Island was home to many of New York's most successful people at the turn of the century. Theodore Roosevelt's Oyster Bay home was on Long Island, as were the homes of F. Scott Fitzgerald, Ring Lardner, and Harry P. Whitney. Whitney captained the first U.S. polo team to victory over England at the Meadowland polo grounds on Long Island in 1909.

Though wealthy American families in Long Island and Philadelphia set the tone for cricket as an aristocratic sport in America prior to the First World War, of all America's sports adopted from Britain — golf, tennis, soccer, polo and cricket — cricket remains the only sport in which America has not prevailed over England. This was no accident as America's best cricketers were its professional sportsmen. By focusing on transitional figures in American cricket and baseball, such as Harry and George Wright, one can examine the evolution of sport in America as it first professionalized itself and redefined the aristocratic amateur-sports ethos that had been promulgated in England. Baseball grew exponentially as an easily accessible sport for all immigrants, once the large numbers of English immigrants to America tailed off prior to the First World War.

The logistical demands of the Civil War generated a national consciousness that stimulated a demand for professional sport. Baseball had flourished in both Confederate and Union prison camps, where four games of baseball could be held in the space required for one game of cricket. Cricket, depicted as too English by Arthur Goodwill Spalding, became the touchstone for how sports influenced a nation. Before he became America's second president, John Adams referred to the organization of cricket clubs with their president, treasurer-secretary and recorded minutes as a viable model for the running of the new republic. It is ironic that cricket's democratic governance later became associated with aristocracy's arbitrary, feudal ways. In England, the Corinthian spirit of the gentleman amateur not only permeated the house of J.P. Morgan on both sides of the Atlantic but also resonated in the Long Room of Lord's, home of the Marylebone Cricket Club.

Professional cricket teams from England had visited America regularly since 1859 but it was Fitzgerald's 1872 tour that brought the greatest sports star of his age, the amateur W.G. Grace, to America. As the MCC pursued amateurism America's professional ball players helped craft a new American identity through sport. A rich picture of America's sporting tradition emerges when examining America's cricket heritage — which is longer than that of the republic. Sport, to the weavers, banking clerks, and numerous others composing the middle class, became a serious business starting with the 1869 Cincinnati Red Stockings' tour of America. However, it was not until Babe Ruth — with his self-confident home run swing — rescued baseball from the gambling scandals of 1919 that hitting a home run became part of the everyday American lexicon. It was in the 1920s that cricket in America faced its greatest challenge, as its vocabulary became marginalized by the dominant culture. But then prejudice leant a hand. America's view of itself in the 1920s was largely that of the dominant Anglo-Saxon culture. White Irish baseball players such as Cap Anson (Chicago White Stockings) brought down the Jim Crow curtain on black baseball players by refusing to play against them from 1884 until 1947. Cricket was more racially accommodating. In New York, West Indian cricketers regularly beat the elite white cricket teams, creating an oasis of civility in an era of lynching and hatred. Cricket rediscovered its role as a civilizing agent. This time it was not Kipling's White Man's Burden but a level playing field, where people of all cultures and religions could earn each other's respect through skill at participation.

Cricket as an example of the American melting pot in action for the last century is now on the cusp of change. It has found a new aristocracy of wealth in the Indian immigrant community. Merrill Lynch estimates that there are 200,000 Indian millionaires in the U.S.[4] Indian cricketers, steeped in their own traditions, now have the numerical advantage on the West Coast. Seeking to tap the 5–7 million estimated cricket fan base, in 2004 the United States Professional Cricket League funded evening matches in baseball stadiums throughout the country. Support was weak but the die has been cast. If just 5 percent of America's Indian community pool their money and business acumen, cricket will be placed on a financial footing greater than it has seen since it was patronized by the American aristocracy of wealth at the end of the nineteenth century. The question is whether cricket will use the baseball model of development — a commissioner and competing national leagues—or will go for the world market aimed at by Arthur Goodwill Spalding with his "World Series of Baseball." The future will tell. Baseball already has the markets that cricket wants and it will be cricket that has to adapt to local beliefs in a game that has been marketed as America's National Pastime. Cricket has two centuries of developing local roots. Here's to an exciting future as cricket enters its fourth century in America.

For their participation on my research playing field I would like to thank the MCC librarian Stephen Green, the C.C. Morris Library and the Amateur Athletic Foundation. Other fine institutions also must be recognized: the Huntington Library (San Marino); Bancroft (U.C. Berkeley); the San Francisco, Los Angeles and New York public libraries; the Newberry Library (Chicago); the Public Records Office at Kew; the Foreign Office Library (London); and regional libraries in Nevada City, Grass Valley, Lakeport and Lower Lake in Lake County, California. Institutions rely on people.

Without David Hirst (*The Australian*); Dr. Atul Rai (former president of USACA and the SCCA); Tony Verity, M.D.; Dr. Merrick Posnansky; Dr. Chris Ehret; Dr. Ned Alpers at UCLA; Tom Van Dyke; Mike Miller (Marin County Cricket Club and president of U.S. Junior Cricket); Malcolm Nash (formerly of the Glamorgan County Cricket Club); Karl Stephens; Wazim Mirza, M.D. (Pakistan)—a great swashbuckling batsman with a flawless cutting stroke; computer specialists Sunil Ramienini and Shekar "Chandra" Akiti (India) and my other teammates on the Victoria Cricket Club; Leon Lamprecht of the Hollywood Golden Oldies Cricket Club; Mark and Kemal Azeez of the venerable Hollywood Cricket Club; my wife Carla and sons Jeremy, Cameron and Colin; this fascinating innings would have ended early. Thank you all for helping me prevail at the writing crease.

David Sentence
Silverlake
Los Angeles
January 2006

1. Cricket's Prologue in America

CRICKET WAS AMERICA'S BAT AND BALL GAME for 140 years before baseball became established in America.[1] In *The Secret Dairy of William Byrd of Westover,* William Byrd II recorded a coded entry on February 20, 1710, which declared, "We play at cricket and I sprained my backside ... I could not run."[2] He described seven games of cricket played on his Westover Estate, located on the James River. A distant relative of George Washington's by marriage, William Byrd was born in Virginia in 1674 but was educated in England, where he studied law at the Middle Temple. The Virginia aristocrat returned to America in 1704, the same year England acquired Gibraltar in the War of Spanish Succession.[3] Byrd died in Virginia in 1744. Another planter, William Stephens, educated at Winchester and Cambridge, also played cricket on his estate in Georgia in 1737.[4] Aristocratic slave owners such as William Byrd were playing cricket in colonial America at about the same time as England's great aristocratic patrons such as John Frederick Sackville, third duke of Dorset, took up the game. The duke of Dorset sponsored Hambledon CC (Cricket Club) games at Knole, his country seat at Sevenoaks Vine in Kent, where cricket had been played since 1720 when the first duke of Dorset took up the game. The duke sometimes played for Hambledon CC. When the duke of Dorset later became British ambassador to France, John Adams, liking and trusting him, asked his advice on the protocol involved in being presented to King George III.[5]

Another keen cricketing aristocrat was George Lennox, who later became the fourth duke of Richmond. The duke's country seat was Goodwood in Sussex, where the earliest reference to cricket dates to 1622, when the local magistrate handed down punishment on six people playing cricket on the Sabbath in the grounds of the Boxgrove Priory.[6] The duke of Richmond and Lord John Sackville, sponsored cricket because

> it reflected many of the values central to the aristocracy's conception of itself. Nobility meant the willingness to engage in friendly, "manly" sports with friends and neighbors; to provide leadership and a model of uncomplaining integrity that lesser men might follow; to offer generous hospitality to players and spectators alike. It was through the involvement of great aristocrats that the game was transformed from a peasant sport in an organized, professional

one. It is easy to see how it happened: a nobleman whose team was beaten in a game for high stakes might strengthen it in the rematch which honor required him to demand, by including the gardener or the groom alongside his relatives. It is only one step from this, to the actual employment of the people in the households of the nobility because they were cricketers, whatever their skills at the gardening or care of horses. There were other kinds of professionals—players who were in effect independent contractors and were paid a match fee by the promoter, yet spent most of their time at their own crafts and trades. But these players retained by the great men were the nearest thing to full-time professionals.[7]

Hambledon CC's players were regarded as professionals and paid four guineas per game at a time when agricultural laborers received an average wage of seven pounds a year. The affinity between horses and cricket and their associated space requirements was formally recognized when both sports received their first set of rules at the Star and Garter pub in Pall Mall near St. James.[8] The Star and Garter pub was located near card-playing clubs such as Boodle's and White's in the Strand. Both *The Game at Cricket* (1744) and the *Jockey Club Rules* (1751) were drawn up there by committees of aristocratic gentlemen who were mainly concerned about a fair set of competitive rules for betting on the outcome of games or races.[9] *The Laws of the Game at Cricket* were subsequently published in 1755. Sports rules distinguished Great Britain (then comprised of England and Scotland since the Act of Union in 1707) from its archenemy France, for it was Whig historian George M. Trevelyan's belief that

> In those days, before it became scientific, cricket was the best game in the world to watch, with its rapid sequence of amusing incidents, each ball a potential crisis! Squire, farmer, blacksmith and labourer, with their women and children came to see the fun, were at ease together and happy all summer afternoon. If the French noblesse had been capable of playing cricket with their peasants, their chateaux would never have been burnt.[10]

When war broke out with France again in 1756, William Pitt the elder was prime minister. The French, allied with Huron Indians, attacked British possessions in North America during the Seven Years' War, which lasted from 1758 to 1763. The French made the first thrust of their campaign against the 13 colonies down the Champlain Valley. British major general Braddock countered the French invasion by a move on Fort Duquesne, a French fort that stood astride the three rivers upon which Pittsburgh now stands. Braddock included cricket equipment and heavy rollers for leveling a pitch in his baggage train as he responded with regular troops reinforced by colonial troops led by officers such as Colonel George Washington. George Washington fired the first shot in the Seven Years' War.[11] The rollers were never put to use. Braddock was killed during the campaign, becoming the first British general to lose a battle in America.[12]

When Britain defeated France in North America, Hanoverian George II was king of England. His son Frederick, prince of Wales, was a keen cricketer. To his German speaking mother, Frederick was a beast or monster, the first *wechselbaig* (werewolf) in London.[13] When he died two years later of an infected cyst to the head in 1751 after being beamed by a cricket ball at a match in Surrey, his slightly crazed son was left to inherit the throne. "Farmer" George III preferred England's favorite pastime of gardening to cricket and during his crazed periods spent time at his palace overlooking the gardens at Kew. Benjamin Franklin attended George III's coronation in 1760 and returned to Philadelphia with the latest edition (the 1755 "London method") of cricket's laws.[14]

Another American who had the respect of the British in London was Benjamin West. In 1763 he was elected president of the Royal Academy of Art where he became renowned for his portraits of high society on both sides of the Atlantic. In 1763 he painted The Cricketers (oil on canvas, now in the Brook Club, New York) showing some young Americans, "James Allen, Andrew Allen, and Ralph Wormley, and their equally aristocratic South Carolina friends, Ralph Izard and Arthur Middleton ... posing proudly with their cricket bats."[15]

Weighing five pounds, their bats were at least two pounds heavier than those used today. Shaped more like field hockey sticks, they were curved on the bottom and made from one piece of wood. The cane spliced handle came later. The curved, clublike bat was used to fend off a hard ball aimed at a small goal made of two upright sticks approximately 18 inches high crossed by one bail across the top. In the art record of the middle eighteenth century, sporting subjects became popular among aristocratic patrons.

The fashion of portraying young men and boys holding a cricket bat started in the 1740s and was especially employed by Thomas Hudson, as for instance in his great family group of the third duke of Marlborough at Blenheim, where the duke's eldest son on the far left carries a bat on his shoulder, and a ball in his right hand, a pose loosely based on the Apollo Belvedere.[16]

In British Colonial times, American-born Englishmen were content to emulate the aristocratic pastimes of their English-born cousins. William Byrd's plantation was worked by slaves as was common among Virginia plantations, but there is no mention in his diary of employing slaves as cricketers or for that matter employing the head gardener as the captain of the team as Lord Frederick Sackville did at Knole.[17] Valentine Romney — the duke of Dorset's head gardener — captained "Kent versus England" there in 1744 in a match so closely watched by the big aristocratic punters that the third duke of Richmond kept the score sheets. Cricket had been played in the Finsbury suburb of London at the Honorable Artillery Ground since 1725.[18] According to David Underdown, "The Honourable Artillery Company, the fashionable militia unit for the sons of wealthy London citizens, had owned the field in Finsbury since before the civil wars."[19]

Cricket did well even without George III's royal patronage, as it had deep roots in the English countryside, in the Weald and the South Downs of Hampshire. On Thursday, June 18, 1777, at Sevenoaks in Kent, Tom Aylward batted all day for Hambledon CC. Batting again Friday morning he scored 167 for the first recorded century in cricket. Hambledon CC scored over 403 in the innings, which was also a record for the first innings over 400 runs by one team in an innings. Hambledon CC defeated the "England" side by an innings and 168 runs.[20] Hambledon's success led to regular Artillery Company invitations to London where the pool of aristocratic punters was greater. Games were played at the artillery grounds until 1780.

The best innings in the eighteenth century occurred the same year British redcoats commanded by the corpulent and indecisive Colonel Francis Smith marched on Lexington. According to historian Niall Ferguson, Lexington Green in Massachusetts, where the 77 Minutemen assembled to be mown down by the British regulars, represented the wealthiest citizens of the British Empire. New Englanders were wealthier than Old Englanders. They paid far less tax by a ratio of 26 to 1. They owned bigger farms, raised bigger families, and had better education.[21] In short, Lexington Green was an "ideal setting not for internecine war but for a game of cricket."[22]

In Philadelphia cricket was played near the House of Burgesses. During the American Revolution that hall's name was changed to Independence Hall to suit the revolutionary timbre of the times. In Hartford, the *Connecticut Courant* published a challenge for a cricket game between teams of fifteen to be played near the Grand Bridge. The challenge's proclamation was published in the same newspaper on May 20, 1767, signed by William Pratt.[23]

On Manhattan Island, New York newspapers published advertisements for cricket players as early as 1739. In 1751 the *New York Gazette and Weekly Post* reported, "Last Monday afternoon [May 1] a match at cricket was played on our common for a considerable wager between eleven Londoners against eleven New Yorkers. The game was played according to the London method." The New Yorkers won by 87 runs.[24] Regular games of cricket were also played near the Fulton Fish Market on Manhattan Island, when a "team called New York played another described as the London XI 'according to London method'"[25]

The London Code referred to as laws drawn up as *The Game at Cricket* in the Star and Garter tavern near St. James' Square, London, published 1755.[26] It was not long before Manhattan Island supported at least two cricket teams that played by the London rules. Cricket was still played by the London method when the Declaration of Independence was made in 1776 and New York State's population swelled to 168,000. Cricket continued to expand during the British army's seven-year occupation of Manhattan as the population on the island doubled from 30,000 to 60,000 people.[27] Cricket was also played regularly near the British army headquarters on Fulton and Elm streets in Brooklyn. Cricketers gathered in the Ferry House Tavern and held regular practices "near the Jews burying ground" every Monday during 1780.[28] The Greenwich CC and the Brooklyn CC played at Bowling Green near Cannon's Tavern on Corlear's Hook, overlooking the East River. The strict etiquette for cricket matches mirrored that required in a duel. Invitations extended by the host club required a written acceptance from the opposition. After the British evacuation of New York in 1783, cricket continued to be played near the Ferry House Tavern and near the racecourse at Flatbush. In April 1876 the *New York Independent Journal* carried advertisements selling cricket balls and bats and in 1794, the New York Cricket Club met regularly at Batten's Tavern.[29]

The Continental Army also kept fit by playing cricket. In May 1777, General Washington, with the morale of his troops uppermost in his mind, issued general orders from his headquarters in Morristown, Pennsylvania, which declared that "Games of Exercise for amusement may not only be permitted but must be encouraged."[30] After Washington's troops lost the Battle of Brandywine, Philadelphia was left to the British troops as the Continental Army decamped to Valley Forge. At Valley Forge, First Lieutenant Ewing wrote in his diary on May 4, 1778, that General Washington "did us the honor to play Wicket with us."[31]

Not long after General Washington's game of Wicket, the fortunes of war turned in the American's favor when British major general "Johnny" Burgoyne's relief column for Fort Ticonderoga was defeated resulting in France's entering the American War of Independence. With the young aristocrat General Lafayette leading the French, American enthusiasm for playing cricket was not diminished. In 1782, American lieutenant William Feltman played cricket in South Carolina where cricket was a popular pastime and played frequently.[32]

After America's Revolutionary War victory, at the Constitutional Convention in Philadelphia, the organizational form of cricket was used by the Founding Fathers as a model for the New Republic when "John Adam's preference for 'His Exalted High Mightiness' was shelved in favor of 'President of the United States.' Senator Oliver Ellsworth of Connecticut complained that even fire companies and cricket clubs had presidents, but it was just the type of democratic tone that helped set this government apart from Old World Monarchies."[33]

Cricket's democratic tone suited the fledgling republic, where cricket was played in its modern form though bowling was still done underhand and pitches (the grass playing surfaces) were highly irregular. Engravings of a wicket game appeared in *Massachusetts Magazine* for February 1793. Ten years later George Tichnor engraved a print of cricket being played on the front lawn of Dartmouth College in New Hampshire.[34] By 1800 cricket was played at Yale, and Edward Oliphant, in his *History of America* published in Edinburgh, referred to the healthy diversion of football and cricket as being universally practiced in America.[35]

In England baseball was mentioned for the first time in 1798 by Jane Austen in *Northanger Abbey*. Wells notes that the first rules of baseball were published in Germany under the unprepossessing title *Ball mit Freystaten (Oder Das Englishe Base-ball)*.[36] Local variants of town ball in Boston and New York were taken more seriously following the anti–British feeling caused by the burning of the White House during the War of 1812 between Britain and the United States.[37]

The commercialization of leisure occurred first in London. The British Empire had expanded since the loss of the 13 colonies. Canada had grown more loyal with the immigration of 100,000 loyalists from America, and the West Indies trade was booming. Australia started to be settled in 1776 following Captain Cook's circumnavigation of the globe, and India had become predominantly British following the end of the Seven Years' War. By 1780, London's population had reached 750,000 — more than five times the size of Philadelphia, America's largest city. Ironically, it was English artisans escaping the rigors of the Industrial Revolution in Sheffield and Nottingham who eventually laid the groundwork for the New Republic ownership of its own sport. Modern baseball's foundation was laid in the decade from 1834 to 1844 when increased English immigration gave a new fillip to cricket in America's two biggest cities, New York and Philadelphia. The artisans— weavers and steel workers— were well paid and could afford the leisure time required of organized team sports. These working-class cricketers developed cricket from its status among the aristocrats as an occasional game to that of a regular summer game played with skill, vigor and intensity. The urbanization of New York and Philadelphia, linked by railroads as of the 1840s, enhanced the demand for commercialized sport, and cricket moved from its pastoral phase to the American middle class.

Cricket's pastoral phase was still well represented in the antebellum South where there were 25 cricket clubs before the Civil War. The *Southern Patriot* of Charleston carried an advertisement for cricket in its June 23, 1831, edition.[38]

In Richmond cricket was played from 1857, as well as in Baltimore, Lexington, Mobile, and New Orleans. A recent *Cricinfo* article by Deb Das reports cricket was played at the Crescent Cricket Club in New Orleans as early as 1822.[39]

A detailed study by Timothy Lockley revealed that cricket was played in Savannah by middle-class professionals with an average age of 27. These people were attracted by the low entry cost of cricket compared to racing and yachting. The Savannah Cricket Club offered its presidency to a member of one of Georgia's founding families, namely, Francis Barton. Lockley postulates the Savannah Cricket Club offered the opportunity for Southern youth to show off their manliness just prior to the Civil War. The club died as soon as the Civil War started; many of its 32 members joined Oglethorpe's Light Infantry, commanded by the cricket club's president, Barton. Of the 32 Savannah cricketers that served in the Confederate Army, 14 became officers, seven were killed, and one Moxley Sorrel served with distinction alongside General Longstreet and ended the war as a brigadier general.[40]

On the other side of the continent, cricket in California started in 1852 at Rincon Point in San Francisco, while the Gold Rush was in full swing. The riches from the Gold Rush put the United States on its financial feet and changed the way Americans thought about the acquisition of wealth. Alexander Hamilton's financial plan of securitizing the debt created by the Revolutionary War was supplemented by selling federal land west of the Mississippi. Gold from California stabilized the Union greenback. Slavery could be replaced by wage laborers working machines as the more industrialized North financed the expansion of its industrial base with gold backed currency. The Gold Rush imprinted the idea of the "big hit" on the American psyche. But the big-hit mentality lay dormant in the years following the four years of carnage created by the Civil War. Postbellum American culture evolved a national consciousness following the completion of the transcontinental railroad in October 1869.[41] Harry Wright's Cincinnati Red Stockings took advantage of the improved coast-to-coast communications when they made their unbeaten 57-game baseball tour of the United States in 1869. In their one year of existence, the Cincinnati Red Stockings demonstrated the huge potential for professional sports in the United States, and it was the working-class, professional cricketers on the side that demonstrated the financial potential of professional baseball.

As baseball established its financial viability by attracting crowds of immigrants, university-trained cricketers in Philadelphia took the elitist route. Cricket in its modern round-arm form was introduced at Haverford in 1834. Philadelphia, like Tidewater, Virginia, had an established aristocracy, and it took to cricket. Following the Civil War, Philadelphia's elite clubs were the bastions of Anglo-Saxon superiority. In England, W.G. Grace and the MCC were able to laud the superiority of the amateur over the professional in Gentlemen's versus Players games. In the United States, with the rapid rise in popularity of baseball among the Irish and German immigrant communities, Philadelphia promoted cricket as an exclusive, Anglo-Saxon sport.

Haverford became the heart of cricket resistance. Baseball was a "growing evil," "a trysting place for all sorts of immorality," a "game for boys and ragtags." "Anybody can play baseball," wrote one scholar, "and the result is that anybody does play."[42]

The Intercollegiate Cricket Association, founded in 1874, organized cricket competition between Ivy League colleges such as Harvard, Yale, Brown and Columbia. Ivy League competition perpetuated a genteel tradition both in baseball and cricket. Baseball pulled away from the genteel tradition. E.L. Doctorow captured this change by comparing a Harvard baseball game to a New York Giants match at the Polo Grounds in 1903:

Father remembered the baseball at Harvard twenty years before, when the players addressed each other as Mister and played their game avidly, but as sportsmen in sensible uniforms before audiences of collegians who rarely numbered more than a hundred. He was disturbed by this nostalgia. He'd always thought of himself as a progressive. He believed in the perfectibility of the republic. He thought, for instance, there was no reason the Negro could not with proper guidance carry the burden of human achievement. He did not believe in aristocracy except of individual effort and vision.... But the air in this ball park open under the sky smelled like the back room of a saloon. Cigar smoke filled the stadium and, lit by the oblique rays of the afternoon sun, indicated the voluminous cavern of air in which he sat pressed upon as if by a foul universe, with the breathless wind of a ten-thousand-throated chorus in his ears shouting its praise and abuse.[43]

Cricket was the highbrow sport until 1905 at Harvard. In Philadelphia, cricket was racially exclusive. In 1911, "Haverford cancelled a cricket match against a West Indian team when it was learnt that some of their opponents might be ... black Americans."[44]

As cricketers squandered their player base, golf, polo and tennis supplanted cricket as a highbrow fad just as democratizing influences such as Ford's Model T put the United States on wheels. Baseball learned to communicate with its ever expanding fan base. Writers such as Ring Lardner made baseball easy to understand with their colloquial style. Commenting on a Chicago White Sox victory in 1906, he stated simply, "The score at the time was 4 to 2 — us had the 4 and them the 2."[45] Baseball was

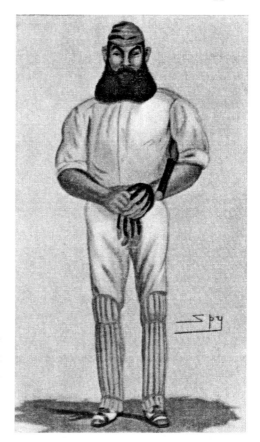

W.G. Grace visited America once in 1872 with Lord Harris. England's greatest player, his first-class career lasted from 1867 to 1905. He was the first sports hero to be used for advertising a product. His tie-in with Colman's hot mustard was appropriate as he had a hot bat and was the first cricketer to score 100 centuries in first-class cricket. He was also a very canny bowler, as John Lister, captain of the Gentlemen of Philadelphia, noted when he played him in England.

A TOUGH GAME played by tough men, yet for all its rudeness it also had humor and innocence. Its players had been raised on Georgia farms, in Pennsylvania coal towns and Chicago alleys, and they brought the individual character of their backgrounds to the game.... In its diversity baseball was ... a reasonably faithful representation of a young nation still too close to its frontier to have lost its rough edge or its folk heritage. It was a nation of only 90 million but only four hundred major-league ballplayers, and to the 90 million the four hundred were demi-gods; not until the nation learned that the 1919 World Series had been fixed would everyone understand that the four hundred were "only men."[46]

Ring Lardner became baseball's most loved sports-journalist, reporting Chicago White Sox and Black Sox games in the *Chicago Tribune*.[47] Baseball excluded Afro-

Americans. John J. McGraw, manager of the Baltimore Club, and Charles Comiskey of the White Sox were the leading proponents of white baseball. Educated Afro-Americans need not apply either, as Harvard educated William Clarence Mathews discovered. Little wonder his schoolmate W.E.B. DuBois, activist and editor of *Crisis* magazine, predicted that "the biggest problem of the twentieth century will be that of the color line."

Despite geographical (there were no professional teams west of the Mississippi) and racial limitations, baseball established a collective government—unlike cricket in the United States—that successfully redeployed income to make the game grow further.

A national commission was organized to govern the game (its members were the presidents of the two major leagues and a chairman chosen by them) and the groundwork for prosperity was laid. A schedule of 154 games was established, and in those cities that had two teams (Boston, Chicago, St. Louis, New York and Philadelphia) schedules were coordinated to avoid direct competition. The wooden ball parks of the late nineteenth century were replaced by steel-and-concrete structures: Sportsman's Park in St. Louis in 1902; Shibe Park in Philadelphia and Forbes Field in Pittsburgh in 1909; League Park in Cleveland and Comiskey Park in Chicago in 1910; Ebbets Field in Brooklyn, the Polo Grounds in New York and Griffith Stadium in Washington in 1911; Fenway Park in Boston, Crosley Field in Cincinnati and Tiger Stadium in Detroit in 1912; Weeghman (now Wrigley) Field in Chicago in 1914; and the Braves Field in Boston in 1915. The parks were privately financed and owned, but they were the colosseums of the New World and the sources of enormous pride for the cities lucky enough to have them.[48]

When the Cubs played Pittsburgh in 1908, Ring Lardner witnessed "the biggest crowd that ever saw a ball game, the world's champion Cubs beat Fred Clarke's Pirates on Pittsburgh's beautiful new field ... 3 to 2. A throng of 30,338, or ninety one more than the former record, paid their good money to Messrs. Dreyfus and Murphy."[49]

Baseball, like golf of this era, was played with a rubber-core ball. A handstitched horsehide cover covered three layers of woolen yarn. Sewn like a cricket ball, it was never changed during the game and frequently got pounded out of shape. By 1911 the rubber-core ball adopted the cork-core ball used in cricket balls.[50] This livelier cork-core ball raised the team batting averages by nine points in 1912. Big-hit baseball arrived with Babe Ruth. The old "scientific" game, which stressed moving players along the bases with carefully crafted hits was pushed aside by the brash new power-hitter, franchise players. Long ball baseball rescued baseball from the World Series fixing scandal of the 1919 Chicago Black Sox.

As baseball found its radio voice and responded to challenges, cricket still mumbled explanations of itself to an increasingly dwindling upper class of spectators. The exception was in California, where cricket had less competition from professional baseball. There were minor league teams in Los Angeles, Sacramento, Fresno and San Francisco, but it was not until the 1958 arrival of the Brooklyn Dodgers in Los Angeles and New York Giants in San Francisco that major league baseball was played in the Golden State. In depicting baseball as central to America's conception of itself, baseball writers occupied the cultural high ground. There were no well known cricket journalists writing for American papers by 1920. British writers and avid cricketers Charles Dickens, Sir James Barrie (Peter Pan), Reverend Hornung (Raffles), Sir Arthur Conan Doyle, Rudyard Kipling, and A.A. Milne generally referred to cricket tangentially in their novels. Kipling deviated from this rule once, in his poem *The Islanders*, when he criticized the British sports ethos as it applied to the debacle of British arms in the Boer War, by referring to cricket's practitioners as the "muddied oafs in the goal and the flannelled fools at the wicket." Kipling's warning was misconstrued by the patriotic press and lost him the poet laureateship, which had been his for the asking until that point.[51]

It is no aberration that C.L.R. James became cricket's most effective communicator in the Depression years of the 1930s. Marxism was in its heyday when he wrote about cricket's importance for the identity of the West Indian. Schooled in Trinidad, James was highly sensitive to colonialism's racial nuances. He effectively communicated cricket's artistry at a time when English cricket writers such as Sir "Plum" Pelham Warner, Sir Neville Cardus and John Arlott depicted cricket as a crucible of Englishness. James' writing transcended class and racial solidarity, putting players of all colors through a thorough technical analysis of their skill to achieve an empathetic understanding of their unique talents and contribution to the game. James was truly an educator when he wrote on cricket. Read James' essay on George Hedley, the first black Jamaican cricket captain, and you become color-blind as the human spirit triumphs over adversity and small-mindedness.

As cricket increasingly became synonymous with the insect in most American libraries, the upper class in Philadelphia took to their yachts, the links or the tennis courts, where women were liberated from spectatorship to activity on the court. Meanwhile, the magnates (Lardner's term) in Chicago built bigger stadiums with parking lots, as cricket was pushed into the public park where cricket's working-class roots reasserted themselves. By playing cricket at Prospect or Cortlandt park, West Indian immigrants strengthened the sinews of their communities against a virulent race prejudice that excluded blacks from high paying jobs in professional baseball and regular jobs. By 1926, with Philadelphia no longer playing the Halifax Cup, cricket moved from its exclusive mode to fighting racial prejudice in the public parks arena.

This book explores the important role cricket played as a catalyst of American identity over the last three centuries. America's oldest sport, now on the cusp of professionalism in the United States, provides a multicultural model, achieved through many transformational experiences on the wicket, that offers hope for a civil future in an uncivil age.[52]

2. How Cricket in New York Helped Establish Baseball as America's National Pastime

NEW YORK'S FIRST MODERN CRICKET CLUB, the New York Cricket Club, was founded on September 20, 1838, by William Jupe, an iron merchant, Thomas Bage, an insurance specialist, and John Taylor, a wool merchant. The New York Cricket Club changed its name to the St. George's Cricket Club at the Bloomindale Tavern in Manhattan on April 23, 1839—St. George's Day in England.[1] At this time Henry Chadwick remembered,

> Among the earliest of the field sports in Brooklyn, which I witnessed, were the most prominent one of cricket matches which were played at the vacant lots adjoining Smith and Bergen streets in 1838.... In one of these contests which took place on September 20th, 1838, the contesting elevens were players, residents of New York and Brooklyn, who were native cricketers of the old English county towns of Sheffield and Nottingham. I had been on one of my fishing jaunts to the Gowanus Creek millponds, and on my return home across the lots, I happened to see quite a crowd of people watching the cricketers on the field, and the game in progress was fixed in memory from a particular incident of play, which was the failure of the wicket keeper to hold a fly-ball which had been hit in the air directly over his head, the dropping ball slipping through his uplifted hands and blackening one of his eyes. In those days they played old-fashioned cricket with a slow under-handed twisting bowling, the swift round-arm bowling of the present being unknown. They began to play early in the morning, about 9 or 10 o'clock and they got through before sundown. In my "American Manual of Cricket" published in 1874, will be found the scores of the two most prominent of these old time contests. The Sheffield eleven in the game I refer to, consisted of Messrs. Thomas Dodworth (the father of the old bandmaster Allen Dodworth, the latter's son now teaching dancing classes in this city), Person, Gill, Stead, Wheatman, Fisher, Bradshaw, Berry, Taylor and Holmes. The Nottingham side contained the Wyvill brothers, old Sam Parker, old Tom Alvey, Tom Dent-all three of whom kept English "Shades" in the city—together with Turton, Hurst, Beecraft, Shelton, Sneath, and Taylor. Mr. Lacey acted as umpire for Sheffield, and James Raynor for Nottingham.[2]

George Stead sailed to California in the Gold Rush and played for the Pioneer Cricket Club at the Union Race Track ground in San Francisco in 1856. George Wheatman and Robert Bage founded the Newark Cricket Club in 1845, establishing a pitch on a New Jersey lot by a chemical factory. The club moved to a new field by the railroad tracks in 1855.[3] Wheatman then founded Lowell CC and Dorchester CC in 1857 in Massachusetts.[4] Respected by cricketers in New York, New Jersey and Massachusetts, Wheatman was invited to umpire the New York games of George Parr's tour in 1859. By this time Newark had become the center of blue-collar cricket in New Jersey. The city's three cricket clubs— the Newark, Mechanics and Essex — were controlled by jewelers, silversmiths and tailors with Newark CC having the most affluent membership. At this stage in American industrialization, shop owners who were master craftsmen toiled alongside their employees. In this sense the cricket clubs were premodern or transitional to today's modern cricket clubs, in which most white collar professions are represented[5]:

> In a few factory towns, leading citizens matched their skills against machine operators. In September 1857 in Waltham, Massachusetts, the Rumford club, composed mostly of the town's elite defeated the United, who were mainly factory workers. An observer viewed the game as an example of cricket's democratic tendencies. He noted that in such matches, "employers and employees meet in friendly strife and intercourse, where all distinction is for the time being entirely removed, promoting as it does the improvement, happiness, and health of all concerned."[6]

When interclubs games were not scheduled, intramural games between Batchelors and Benedicts or left- versus right-handed players were popular: "In October 1858 the best batters at a match between Essex and Mt Washington clubs of Newark won a 'splendid plated cup and a gold mounted chain,' courtesy of the city's jewelers."[7]

American versus English cricketer member games were first held between Newark CC and NYCC clubs in August 1854, when "the Newark Cricket Club organized the first all–Native American match ever played in the United States, as it split a home series with the New York Cricket Club."[8] Similar matches occurred between the Newark and Philadelphia clubs in 1856 and the Newark and Brooklyn clubs in 1860.[9] In upstate New York at Rochester, Albany and Syracuse, cricket was played regularly. The games between artisans from Sheffield and Nottingham had a high standard for their time. Nottingham was home to Wil Clarke's All England Eleven, the world's first professional sports team. Immigrants from Nottingham had watched high level cricket games even if they had not participated in them before sailing to America. Nottingham and Sheffield were two of England's earliest industrial towns with close links to the countryside where farming traditions originated before medieval times. Feast days and religion were closely affiliated in feudal times, and cricket flourished in this world. The lighter attitude towards religion of America's artisan cricketers helped break down the Puritan taboo, held since the times of Oliver Cromwell and the *Mayflower*, toward adults playing sport for its own pleasure. Cricket's traditions proved hard to resist for John Richard, the English-born editor of Porter's *Spirit of the Times*. Richard reconstituted the New York Cricket Club on October 11, 1843, in a meeting at McCarty's Tavern at the Elysian Fields in Hoboken, New Jersey. John Richard's publisher, William Porter, became president of a NYCC, which limited its membership to American cricketers. The English-versus-American dichotomy in New York cricket fueled spectator interest and drew the attention of media magnates such as Oliver of the *New York Clipper* and Porter (and later Wilke) of the *Spirit of the Times.* Ferryboat entrepreneur John A. Stevens, whose son Edward played on the NYCC team, also encouraged the growth of cricket as a spectator sport. The NYCC was the first cricket club to lease a ground at Hoboken in New Jersey. The club paid a nominal $50 ground rent to the founder of the New York Yacht Club, Commodore Stevens, who owned the Elysian Fields. Stevens recouped the low rent in fares made ferrying passengers from Manhattan and Brooklyn to Hoboken to see cricket matches.[10]

Games between the St. George's Cricket Club (SGCC) and the New York Cricket Club attracted large numbers of spectators. In the 1850s Henry Chadwick became a NYCC member, which helped solidify the link between New York's baseball and cricket communities. The NYCC was the successor to the American Cricket Club, founded by Harry Wright, James Creighton, Asa Brainerd, John Whitney, and Thomas Dakin. It was "an organization that encouraged baseballers not only to try cricket but to do so in a way that would inform something of an American spirit to the game. Membership in the club was limited to American citizens or those British intending to become citizens."[11]

Renowned American artist William Ranney became a NYCC founding member. Ranney was born in 1813 at Middleton, Connecticut. After his travels in the West, where he "found the subject matter for most of his art," he returned to New York and "became proficient in illustrating the life of the frontiers.... During the 1840s he was a zealous cricketer, and he kept playing to the age of forty until he was sidelined with illness."[12]

In their first game at Hoboken, the NYCC beat the Union Star Cricket Club. The USCC was Brooklyn's first predominantly Jewish team. It was founded in 1844 by Henry and William Russell, two brothers who played in international matches for the SGCC Dragonslayers against Canada. Despite having quality cricketers on the side, the NYCC and USCC later switched to baseball. Baseball began in New York in 1842, when white-collar workers living near Madison Square and Murray Hill began playing New York style around a diamond of bases. The same year Alexander Joy Cartwright, a shipping clerk who later opened a bookstore and stationery shop, proposed to his friends that they constitute themselves as the Knickerbocker Base Ball Club.[13] The club evoked New York's aristocratic Dutch past to establish a non–English origin for baseball, though Cartwright's team adopted the "Gentleman's etiquette of cricket," replete with formal gatherings and cotillions after the game. More important, the baseball rules developed by the KBC were later adopted by town-ballers in Boston and in other East Coast cities where variants of baseball were played. While baseball still experimented with its format, cricket's tradition was well established and offered a template for organizing team sport that had proven effective for over a century in England. Easier to learn, baseball soon caught on in Brooklyn. Four USCC cricketers played for the Brooklyn Base Ball Club against the New York Base Ball Club at the USCC's Fort Greene ground in 1845.

By 1851 the Knickerbocker Base Ball Club and SGCC moved their grounds to Hoboken where they used the New York Yacht Club facilities provided by Stevens. The SGCC took over the NYCC lease. Cricket and baseball also overlapped at the Long Island Cricket Club in Bedford. From 1854 the Eagles, Empires, and Excelsiors baseball teams regularly competed across the Hudson in South Brooklyn. Most of these baseball clubs were middle-class fraternal organizations. Postgame cotillions were held at local hotels or restaurants and in the winter, suppers, promenades, skating parties, soirees, and an annual ball. Most

Cricket in Hoboken, New Jersey, in 1859. Source: *Harper's Weekly*, October 15, 1859.

of the games were intramural, with only an occasional match, initiated by written challenge, the winner of which got to keep the game ball in a trophy case. The clubs insisted on decorum and gentlemanly behavior, emphasizing their self-control in contrast to working-class raucousness.[14] Gentlemanly behavior remained important to the NYCC, but they gave up on their experiment of using only American cricketers after four years when Henry Sharpe, an accomplished cricketer, became team captain in 1854. Hoboken's Elysian Fields, where both the SGCC and NYCC played from 1856, was

> a beautiful spot and an ideal cricket ground formed in the shape of a saucer, quite level, but rising at the sides slightly. On the other side where the little club house stood, there was a small hill on which was a grove of fine trees. This was called the Fox Hill, and people could sit in the shade all day and see the matches played. The game at the time was a full two-innings game, generally occupying two days. We always commenced play before 11 o'clock each day. Stumps were drawn at half past 6. It was the custom then to have a good lunch every day when the matches were on at 6 o'clock.... At the conclusion of the game the captain of the losing side made the usual speech complimenting the winning side and presenting the cricket ball which they played with as the trophy of victory.[15]

When De Lancey Barclay, the British consul, became president of the NYCC, membership grew to over 400 members. However, baseball drew important converts from cricket including Henry Chadwick and Harry and George Wright, who played their first baseball for the Knickerbockers. Chadwick played shortstop for the Knickerbockers in 1847 and started umpiring baseball games in 1849. At this time mohair caps replaced the straw hats the Knickerbockers wore.[16] Cricketers were wearing caps by this time and Chadwick was still playing cricket for the SGCC. The young, athletic Chadwick started his journalistic career early. He wrote his first article at age 19 for the *Long Island Star*. When he joined the *New York Clipper* he described the day he first witnessed baseball in 1856:

> On returning from the early close of a cricket match, I chanced to go through the Elysian Fields during the progress of a contest between the noted Eagle and Gotham Clubs. The game was being sharply played on both sides and I watched it with deeper interest than any previous baseball match that I had seen. It was not long before I was struck with the idea that base ball was just the game for a national sport for Americans.[17]

Knickerbockers president, Dr. A.L. Adams, speaking of the 1850s SGCC recalled that "The first professional English cricket team that came to this country used to practice near us, and they used to come over and watch us occasionally. They rather turned their noses at it, and thought it tame sport, until we invited them to try it."[18] Adams' pride in his baseball team was deserved but had an edge to it, as cricket remained popular among Americans. In New England, the Reverend Thomas W. Higginson—a Harvard-educated cricket player—fulminated against the Puritan notion that playing sports was useless and immoral

in a series of magazine articles he published in the 1850's. In "Saints and Their Bodies," which appeared in the 1858 issue of the *Atlantic Monthly*, he argued that proper exercise and recreation were of vital importance and were entirely appropriate and necessary for a full intellectual and spiritual life. He practiced what he preached—in 1858 he served as President of the Lincoln Cricket Club of Worcester, Massachusetts. In his later life he distinguished himself as a Union officer in the Civil War, and as a writer and advocate of "muscular Christianity."[19]

"Muscular Christianity" in England was effectively introduced by Thomas Arnold at Rugby School and Benjamin Jowett at Balliol College, Oxford. By 1860 most of England's top public schools insisted on team sport as part of the curriculum, and the movement was popularized in the United States by the widely read *Tom Brown's School Days*. Its author Tom Hughes visited the United States and spoke at Cornell University in 1870, where his remarks inspired the students to form a rowing club.[20] American social commentators such as Walt Whitman, who worked with Henry Chadwick on the *Brooklyn Eagle*, drummed up support from the clergy for team sport's potential of remedying "the many evils resulting from immoral associations boys and young men of our cities are apt to become connected with."[21]

Henry Chadwick came from a staunchly independent English "Dissenting" tradition. His father James fit the Jeffersonian mold in America as a staunch supporter of the French Revolution and a follower of Thomas Paine. Sir Edwin Chadwick, Henry's 27-year-older half-brother, pioneered the interpretation of statistics as a basis for reform of the English Poor Laws in his *Report on the Sanitary Condition of the Labouring Population of Great Britain*, published in 1842. After arriving in New York in the same year as Samuel Wright (father of Harry Wright) during the depression of 1837, Henry Chadwick started reporting baseball when it was first indexed under cricket articles in Frank Queen's *New York Clipper* in 1853. He was hired by the *New York Clipper* in 1856 to cover both cricket and baseball. While working for the paper, Chadwick used cricket's scoring techniques for tabulating local baseball club standings alongside his cricket reports. Henry Chadwick reported the founding of the National Association of Base Ball Players in 1857, which met annually to refine rules. The NABBP's stated mission was "the cultivation of kindly feeling amongst the different Base Ball clubs."[22] Porter's *Spirit of the Times* reported the founding of the association of the Base Ball Clubs of Manhattan Island, which sought to achieve "the same standing which the Marylebone Club of London exercises over the game of cricket throughout the British Isles."[23] While emulating cricket's organization at first, Porter's *Spirit* also remarked on a key difference between baseballers and cricketers, which was the tendency for cricketers to allow ringers on their teams. Baseball players "seemed to place more value on team unity and therefore tried to discourage the recruitment of team 'ringers.'"[24]

Solidarity on the field translated to greater will to resolve conflict off it. In 1858 baseball resolved its conflicts and rule changes at regular annual meetings of the NABBP. Cricketers met annually from 1857 to 1862 but never succeeded in establishing a national organization for the game in America as cricket's traditions were mired in regional concerns.

Entrepreneurial cricketer Harry Wright understood the importance of a national tradition and found it easier to make baseball grow nationally, using cricket's touring tradition established by professional cricketers such as Wil Clarke and his successor George Parr. Wright was born in Sheffield and immigrated to New York with his father when he was one year old. His father Samuel Wright had married Irish nationalist Wolf Tone's niece in England.[25] After immigrating to New Jersey, he secured a job as a cricket professional with the SGCC. His integrity made him a household word in New York's cricket circles.[26] Wright's younger brother George was born in Harlem when the SGCC were based there, before their move to Hoboken. According to author Christopher Devine, Harry Wright helped support his family, dropping out of the New York school system at 14. He played his first game for St. George's in 1842 when he was 15 years old, and supported himself—after an apprenticeship—as a clockmaker at Tiffany's.[27] Later in life, Harry Wright stated, "Cricket was my first love as a school boy[;] it commenced when I was a school boy and I still retain the old love of it."[28] From the age of 17, Harry Wright earned $12 a week as a cricketer skilled at bowling round-arm for St. George's. Despite dropping out of school through necessity, Harry Wright believed that an educated sports person "has a brighter and quicker perception than an unlettered one. His correct habits of life will make him as superior physically as he is mentally."[29]

In his prime, Harry Wright was 5' 9¾" and weighed 157 pounds. The Wright brothers and James Creighton played for SGCC before becoming semiprofessional baseball players. St. George's CC played their first home game against the Toronto CC at their new ground in Manhattan on 42nd Street and Bloomingdale, located near a vegetable garden. When the Toronto Cricket Club visited in 1844, they were driven to and from the ground in a carriage with four horses. Over 3,000 spectators watched the game, which generated over $100,000 in wagering.[30] The match proved so popular with its backers that a second one was arranged between the two clubs near the Red Tavern headquarters of the SGCC, in rural Harlem. Among the 5,000 spectators at the game were ten local politicians including former New York congressman Ogden Hoffman, who saw Canada win.[31] In 1846, the Dragonslayers challenged the Union Cricket Club of Philadelphia to a game that Porter's *Spirit of the Times* claimed was "the greatest ever played in the U.S." One of the UCC batsmen made the first century recorded in New York. Robert Waller, who helped found the UCC in Philadelphia, became a keen advocate of top quality cricket games. When he became president of the SGCC he encouraged a social atmosphere in which "the home-and-home matches of the New York and St. Georges clubs were the cricket features of the season and always drew a large attendance. The games were all hard fought and usually a close finish. Large scores were not easily made, as there were no boundaries and every run had to be run, and the bowling was remarkably good and very few scores reached the 50's."[32]

The *Dragonslayers* remained exclusively English, and

men of commerce comprised more than half of the rolls of New York's St. George's club in 1859, while skilled artisans accounted for only about fifteen per cent. Although Porter's *Spirit* ranked it at the head of all Cricket Clubs in the United States, its membership was not as affluent as that of New York's top social, literary, jockey, or yacht clubs. It was composed of "gentlemen of unexceptionable standing," but with "several of wealth and very high position." The New York Cricket Club drew more of its men from the city's literary, artistic and theatrical circles than from its mercantile community. Its players were also probably less affluent than the Dragonslayers of St. George.[33]

In Manhattan the rivalry between the NYCC and the SGCC boiled over in 1858, when the NYCC refused to finish a game they were about to lose and appealed first to *Bell Life* in London and then to the Albany CC to arbitrate their claim that they had no need to continue the game after a traditional 6 o'clock curfew. The SGCC won the ruling and gave up the ball prize, but the NYCC refused to play at the Dragonslayers' new enclosed ground (where they charged 10 cent admission) from 1860 until 1865. Bad behavior at competitive cricket matches threatened the progress of the game. The *Clipper* reported that

> that acrimonious spirit, resulting from the too general desire to win at all hazards, provided the mere letter of the law is adhered to has been generally creeping into cricket matches, alike to the detriment of the best interests of the game, and the entire prevention of all pleasures in the contests that are marked by it. Cricket is a game designed for the *recreation* of all classes and conditions of men, and is eminently a social game, and one in which the amenities of the social life are of vital importance to its existence.[34]

SGCC players Harry Wright and his younger brother George played in four U.S.-versus-Canada games between 1846 and 1853; this included a seven-year hiatus in the playing of international games after a St. George's player deliberately threw a ball at a Toronto batsman after the fielder was obstructed by the batsman from catching him out. The incident occurred in front of 5,000 spectators. In 1853 the bad blood between the two clubs was set aside and the series was renewed. From 1853, selection for the U.S. team was expanded to include the Newark, Syracuse and Albany cricket clubs as well as St. George's and the Union Cricket Club of Philadelphia.

The 1853 game between Canada and the United States was the first true international game between the two countries. Played at the St. George's ground near Red Hill Tavern in the fashionable resort area of Harlem on 2nd and 106th Streets, 8,000 spectators watched the two days of cricket. Manhattan's total population was 250,000 at the time. Clearly cricket was a big draw. After the United States beat Canada convincingly in a low scoring game by 34 runs, ceremonies celebrating the games were held at New York's most fashionable restaurant, Del Monico's.

In 1854, the U.S. introduced three new players, Sams, Bingham and Gibbes, for the sixth international:

> Sams was a fine opening bat who scored thirty-five for New York v. Germantown in 1860 and who also played for King's County. For Kings County v. St. George he scored 114 in 1855, the first century every scored in New York. The Honorable H. Bingham, apparently connected with English aristocracy but living in New York, played in two games without distinction. He must have been a fairly good cricketer, however, because in 1859 he scored fifty-nine for St. George's against Montreal. A.H. Gibbes was also a member of St. George's, and in 1856 he scored forty-three, the highest innings played in the international series to date. Playing in two matches for XXII of USA v All-England in 1859, he took three wickets for twenty-eight in the first match and scored a valiant twenty out of ninety-four in the second match at Philadelphia.

Gibbes became a Vice-President of the St. George's Cricket Club and served on the committee. [35]

In 1856, Gibbes scored 43 on a difficult pitch at Hoboken to help the U.S. to victory in a match umpired by George Wheatcroft, who played in the first Canada-U.S. game in 1844.[36] Wilby of St. George's was one of the new players introduced to the 1856 U.S. team. He also played against George Parr's tourists in 1859 but had little success. James Higham, the U.S. wicket-keeper, played for the New York CC. He played five internationals averaging 13.60 runs an innings. Higham was

> born at Gravesend, England on June 21st 1827 and was a very popular cricketer. He learned the game in England and emigrated to the United States after getting into financial trouble, apparently because he would rather play cricket than attend to business! Shortly after arriving in New York he went into the tailoring business with his brother. They established themselves in Maiden Lane, later in Cortlandt Street and established a fine business eventually on 293 Broadway. About 1865 he left the business and opened the "the Office," pub.... The pub became headquarters for sports and theatrical people in New York. Higham was a great supporter of the New York C.C. He died suddenly on 9 July 1872.[37]

In the eighth match held in Toronto in 1857, the U.S. introduced three new players to the side. One was Lang, the opening batsman of St. George's, who proved unable to step up to international-level competition. Barry of St. George's also played in the match, scoring 12, and like Lang did not play for the U.S. again. William Crossley of the NYCC did better; this was the first of three internationals in which he represented the U.S.

> Crossley was professional to New York CC and scored twenty-six for New York v. Germantown in 1860. He took twenty-six wickets for 202 runs in the season of 1859. He was a fine medium paced right hand bowler with an amazing off break and probably learned his cricket in England.... He took nine wickets for 6.77 in his three games and played against All England in 1859 but without distinction. He was a notable single wicket player, partnering Tom Senior in one historic match.[38]

In the ninth U.S.-versus-Canada match, William Hallis of Newark, New Jersey, proved a very effective bowler. As the professional for the Newark CC he played against Parr's AEE and was the leading wicket taker. In his four matches against Canada his average of 8.90 was earned by taking 22 wickets.[39] In the last U.S.-versus-Canada match before the arrival of George Parr's AEE in September, the United States won by four wickets in a game that introduced the Reverend T.D. Phillipps to international cricket. The Reverend Phillipps was later to have a great impact on Chicago cricket though on this occasion he was overshadowed in performance by two other great cricket names, Walter Newhall and William Rotch Wister, who were also playing in their first international for the U.S. against Canada. William Hammond of Willow CC in New York and C.H.T. Coles, the St. George's and the U.S. wicket-keeper, rounded out the New York contingent on the U.S. side. When not playing for St. George's, Coles played for the Delphian CC in Philadelphia. Coles attained the rank of brigadier general in the Union Army during the Civil War. [40] The Canada-versus-U.S. match provided a great opportunity for topnotch practice before the main American sporting event of 1859: the arrival of the AEE touring side.

Robert Waller, now president of the SGCC, hosted George Parr's All England Eleven at Hoboken when a New York XXII that included five British-born professionals was easily beaten. Henry Sharpe of the NYCC was one of three principals—the other two were

Waller and James Pickering — involved in organizing the AEE visit. Sharpe ran a successful decorating business.

> [Born] in Derbyshire in 1820, he became a Chartist and immigrated to the United States after the failure of the Chartist movement in 1848. He made the first of his eight appearances for the United States against Canada in 1853 and was elected President of the *New York Cricket Club* during the Civil War. By then he had earned a reputation for being an enlightened employer who sponsored outings to Hoboken for the workers he employed in the house-decorating trade. An excellent cricketer, Sharpe played internationals against Canada and in his sixteen innings against Canada his batting average was 7.42.24.[41]

James Pickering raised the £1,200 in gold required to finance the AEE trip. The Eton educated Pickering lived in Canada and organized the Canadian venues of the six-game tour. He played in two of the games against Parr's team and in two games against Richard Daft's team in 1879 when he was 60 years old.[42] The AEE were captained by George Parr, the "Lion of the North." Leaving Canada via Montreal, Parr's team arrived by rail in the New York state capital, Albany, on September 30, 1859. In Albany Parr's team boarded the paddle-steamer *New World* and arrived in New York the next day. They stayed several nights at Astor House, the best hotel in New York. Each floor offered separate bathing and toilet facilities. Its rooms were gas lit, powered by its own gasworks. High quality food completed the guest's package with a selection of 30 dishes each day, ranging from oyster pie to round of beef. On October 3, when Robert Waller arrived at the Astor Hotel to escort England's best professional cricketers to Hoboken, the cricketers

> were most enthusiastically received, and loudly cheered, by the multitude, as they wended their way down the steps towards the "four-in-hand" prepared for their reception; the horses were beautifully decorated with American and English flags, as well as a multiplicity of flowers. We crossed the ferry without alighting, and soon found ourselves on the ground at Hoboken, where, at that early hour, were upwards of five thousand spectators. The preparations for the convenience of the public were on the grandest scale imaginable, and evidently had involved an immense outlay. The ground had only been newly laid in the spring, and was not therefore in such good order as is requisite to play the game as it should be played. The English party received every courtesy and were immediately conducted to a marquee.[43]

The U.S. XXII was easily beaten by the skilled play of George Parr's team before a crowd of about 25,000 spectators. The American spectators did not get to see great cricket because the sides were unevenly matched and the pitch was poor. According to Lillywhite, "the want of more talent opposed to them ... prevented the eleven from exhibiting the masterly display which they have so frequently shown in all parts of England.... Should the States be fortunate enough to secure a first-class bowler, there will be no difficulty in bringing forward cricketers; but until then, we can offer little hope on that score."[44]

The best amateur U.S. bowler was William Comery of the St. George's CC. A fair round-arm bowler, he "bowled eighteen overs for five maidens, thirty-one runs and no wickets, playing a supporting role to Hallis and Gibbes, the first string bowlers. For the United States he took seven wickets in the 1846 match versus Canada, thirteen wickets in the 1853 game and three in the 1854 encounter. He was one of the leading American bowlers of the period."[45]

No U.S. XXII player reached double figures, as the United States were all out in the first innings for 38 and scored only 54 in the second. The All England Eleven made 156 in their innings. The Cambridge County openers for AEE, Hayward (33) and Carpenter

Four England cricket captains in America. *Top, left:* George Parr, 1859; *right:* Edgar Willsher, 1869; *bottom, left:* Richard Daft, 1879; *right:* Lord Hawke, 1891. Source: *British Sports and Sportsmen.*

(26) scored more runs between them than the U.S. XXII's first innings total of 53. The United States had several English trained professionals on the side including Sam Wright, Tom Senior, William Hammond, Hallis and Gibbes. Hallis and Gibbes took all the AEE wickets, but the game was over so soon that George Parr was persuaded to organize an intrasquad game that resulted in an invitation to Harry Wright and Robert Waller to play on Tom Lockyer's team against Heathfield Harmon Stephenson's side. Lockyer's side won in two innings by a score of 263 to 179, or 84 runs. Harry Wright and Robert Waller were the top run-scorers of Lockyer's side. Wright scoring 10 runs in the first innings and Waller 12 in the second.[46] The AEE spent a week in New York. During this week the *New York Herald* gave its opinion that "even if there were no baseball in existence cricket could never become a national sport in America."[47]

America needed a national sport and not the cosmopolitanism intimated by Robert Waller when, in his capacity as president of the SGCC, he toasted the health of Queen Victoria and the president the United States at a banquet held in Astor House on the Friday before the AEE's departure. Replying to Waller's toast, George Parr offered the following sentiment: "England and America — the mother and the daughter. One race, one language, one interest, one hope. Those whom God hath joined together let not man dare to put asunder."[48]

Parr made his declaration at the peak of cricket's popularity in New York, when 25,000 or 10 percent of New York's population had turned out to see the England's first professional team to visit America. Parr's tour established New York as a cricket capital and demonstrated sport was financially viable as mass entertainment. With the market now clearly defined, the question was which sport would capture the affection and open the wallets of the New York spectator:

> In 1859 Porter's *Spirit of the Times* claimed that about six thousand cricketers lived within one hundred miles of New York City, including Philadelphia. England's national game had also spread to such southern towns as Baltimore, Savannah, and New Orleans. Chicago, Cleveland, Cincinnati, Milwaukee, and even San Francisco were among the two dozen western cities that fielded teams. While many clubs only lasted a brief time, and while certainly many members were inactive, it is possible that there were between eight and ten thousand men and boys in the United States in 1860 who had played cricket for at least one year.[49]

A few months after the visit of George Parr's team, an American cricket team of 18 players defeated an English Eleven selected from local residents, for the first time. The *New York Herald* was optimistic that with Americans proving they could play cricket on equal terms, the "go ahead character of the American people" would deepen cricket's roots in America.[50] But other forces were at work. In 1860, Jim Creighton's "fame spread throughout the state with the Excelsiors' August 4th 1860 tour of New York State. Scores between baseball clubs were high as the Excelsiors beat the Atlantics by a score of 27 to 23 runs to win the U.S. Championship."[51]

Behind Creighton's pitching, the Excelsiors of Brooklyn dominated baseball in New York, Massachusetts and Philadelphia. SGCC cricketer Jim Creighton was 20 when the Excelsiors first won the U.S. baseball championship in 1857. He became baseball's first star attraction. Cricket did not offset Creighton's star appeal but it did, under Sharpe's leadership at the NYCC, actively encourage youth cricket by inviting players under 18 to join the club for a $1 membership that entitled them to same privileges as the regular members: "The Brooklyn Cricket Club followed their example by organizing a 'Junior Class' for youths under eighteen, who paid less than half the regular dues. The St. George club also sponsored a junior eleven, but in general the New York City region lagged far behind both Philadelphia and New Jersey in popularizing cricket among its young."[52]

Creighton's drawing power expanded baseball's appeal beyond New York. His death at 21 after getting injured playing cricket was deeply felt by both cricket and baseball communities in Brooklyn, where a monument was raised to his memory by his fellow cricket and baseball players.

> In 1860 the *New York Times* stated that in Philadelphia, cricket was "as popular with Americans as Base Ball is in New York...." According to the *Times,* native sportsmen deserved the credit for the Philadelphia cricket boom, while Englishmen who dominated the sport in Manhattan had almost "utterly squelched the rising spirit of cricket amongst Americans in New York; and driven it into baseball as a means of outdoor exercise and recreation."[53]

With the outbreak of the Civil War, Union regiments still played cricket in New York, particularly those stationed in New York from Pennsylvania. Wilke's *Spirit of the Times* endorsed cricket as

> a preparatory school for the army.... A quick eye and a ready hand, good stamina, a developed muscle,... the discipline that yields obedience to a glance from the captain's eye, that never questions the umpire decision, all essentials to the true cricketer — are all qualifications and materials from which a good soldier is readily formed.[54]

Kirsch notes that cricket

> was not as prevalent in the camps as baseball but its enthusiasts made bats out of anything. Lieutenant William Moore of the 62nd New York Volunteers, an Englishman, took bats and balls back to his cricket club in the Army of the Potomac. One of the contests ... matched elevens chosen from New York's 32nd and Pennsylvania's 95th regiments, at White Oak Church, Virginia, in April 1863.[55]

The Civil War disrupted both cricket and baseball in Manhattan. Ninety-one players of the Excelsior Base Ball Club joined the Union Army. While baseball players signed up, cricket organizers metaphorically shot themselves in the foot — thereby starting a long tradition in America: "Annual cricket conventions commanded little respect and displayed much less vitality than the gathering of the baseball crowd. Cricket's version of the national organization passed into oblivion after 1862."[56]

Baseball attracted more players, according to Henry Chadwick, because "We fast people of America, call cricket slow and tedious; while the leisurely, take-your-time-my-boy-people-of-England think our game of baseball too fast. Each game, however, just suits the people of the two nations."[57]

What Henry Chadwick did not mention was that baseball proved very popular in prisoner of war camps on both the Confederate and Union sides. These prisoners were certainly not in a hurry, but with time hanging heavy on their hands, playing baseball in the prison yard allowed for more games to be played at once in crowded conditions. When the equivalent density was reached in the urban environment between 1901 to 1916, as America became thoroughly industrialized, baseball exploded in popularity across the nation as ballparks were built in inner cities throughout the United States; Boston's Fenway, Shibe in Philadelphia, Forbes in Pittsburgh, Ebbets in Brooklyn, and Comiskey's Wrigley in Chicago are but a few.[58]

Cricket after the Civil War continued to flourish in the working-class textile towns of Massachusetts such as Lowell, Dorchester, Shelbourne Falls, and in the cities of Cincinnati and Detroit. But baseball showed itself better equipped for modernization to American ideals. Spectators were placed close to the batting action by the simple expedient of eliminating play behind the batsman and reducing the arc of play to 90 degrees from the 360-degree full circle or oval traditionally associated with cricket. Baseball's playing-field configuration made it easier to squeeze fields into receding areas of space. Sponsorship for baseball was more forthcoming than for cricket because American industrialists identified more easily with their local baseball teams than with cricket teams controlled by first generation immigrants seeking to preserve their cultural identity and connection with place of origin.[59] St. George's remained the top cricket team in New York after the Civil War, but they neglected youth cricket and according to *The Clipper* pursued an overly snobbish and exclusive policy even though they had a full treasury made possible by charging spectators to view cricket at the newly enclosed grounds. In another example of Harry Wright's entrepreneurial skill in action, two daguerreotype portraits of Harry Wright and William Hammond, priced at 75 cents each, made in 1863 to promote a cricket game at the Dragonslayers ground, sold at a 2004 New York auction of baseball memorabilia for over $85,000.[60] These portrait cards were made five years after Harry Wright took up baseball professionally in 1858. The *New York Dispatch* has already declared by this time that Harry and George Wright were "the best proponents of base ball as a science in the country. These players know how to strike, when to strike and where to put the ball."[61] In fielding, the *Detroit Post* was impressed with both the skill and humility of the cricketer, noting the "instinctual knack for tracking flyballs. Harry Wright is the finest, safest, best and least showy player in America."[62]

Despite St. George's CC having members of Wright's skill and demonstrated promotional abilities in both sports, it squandered a golden opportunity to expand cricket among youth. The SGCC had no coaches capable of attracting young players to the game. Then not long after the assassination of President Abraham Lincoln, St. George's faced a new challenge after losing its lease in Hoboken. The SGCC sought a new venue for cricket in 1865 when Central and Prospect parks, designed by Frederick Law Olmstead and Englishman Calvert Vaux, were opened to the public. Olmstead spent time in California during the Civil War where he worked as superintendent of John Fremont's gold mines in Mariposa County. After working for Fremont he spent time in Yosemite with John Muir and recommended it become a park; Theodore Roosevelt later ensured this with National Park legislation. In San Francisco, Olmstead mapped out the original designs for Golden Gate Park, Oakland Cemetery and the Berkeley campus of the College of Education. When he returned to New York in 1865, Central Park's 846 acres and Prospect Park's 526 acres were landscaped to create an atmosphere of space and tranquility in the heart of America's most urbanized city. Sheep grazed meadows interspersed liberally with trees in Brooklyn's Prospect Park, and Central Park's 28-acre North Meadow was allocated for cricket.[63] When the parks were complete the commissioners of Central Park delayed St. George's first game there, noting that cricket might damage the turf in the park.[64] Political motivation to position baseball in the park at the expense of cricket was suspected by St. George's CC leadership, which demanded a trial match in the Central Park to determine the relevance of the Park Commission's comments.

Apart from St. George's CC there were five other New York cricket clubs in 1866. They were the Manhattan CC, the NYCC, the Willow CC in Brooklyn, the Satellite CC on Long Island and the Staten Island CC, founded in 1856.[65] After the Civil War, the Staten Island CC secured its own ground by raising $10,000 to pay for Livingston Park on Staten Island.[66] After losing their battle with the Central Park commissioners, St. George's migrated to Hudson City in 1868, where they remained for four years before establishing a new ground at the foot of Ninth Street in Hoboken, New Jersey. The NYCC remained closest to Central Park at they returned to a ground they had leased prior to the Civil War near the park entrance on 92nd Street.[67]

Baseball got the right to play in Central Park, but the sport was becoming far less dependent on public space for its games as it attracted a paying audience following the Civil War. The Civil War effectively put an end to the "Highland Clannish" mentality of states like Virginia in favor of a national spirit. Baseball Americanized itself after the Civil War. The Eagles and Knickerbockers were the best teams in 1865. In 1867 the first baseball players' convention was held in San Francisco. The same year, the Eagles and Stars played paying crowds in enclosed grounds.[68] Sports articles filled the space once used for war reportage. There were eight semiprofessional baseball teams in the New York area by 1870: the Knickerbockers, Gotham, Eagles, Empire, Eclectic, Active, Eureka (Newark) and Union (Morrisania). The New York–based teams competed against a league comprising the Atlantic, Eckford, Excelsior, Resolute, Enterprise, Star, Putnam and Mystics (of Yorkville) baseball clubs.[69] The Atlantic Club beat the Athletics of Philadelphia for the championship in 1865. Two matches were played in the championship series, one in Philadelphia and the other in Brooklyn.[70] The Atlantics dominated New York baseball for five years, winning the U.S. championship five times in a row. When teams attended the meeting of the National Association of Base Ball Players in San Francisco, 202 baseball teams were represented from 17 states.[71]

Cricket's only semiprofessional team in New York at this time was St. George's, though there were 50 amateur teams participating in local competition. New York also attracted English touring teams such as Edgar Willsher's English team of professionals in 1868. Willsher's six-game tour of North America ended at Hoboken, where St. George's hosted a match between XXII of America and Willsher's team on October 13–16. America 70 (Edgar Willsher of Kent CC 11–27) and 65 runs (George Freeman of Yorkshire CC 12–27) lost to England, which scored 143 runs by an innings 8 runs.[72] Willsher's team was less successful in the ten baseball matches they played, failing to win one. The losses were a surprise, as Willsher's team introduced overarm bowling to the America after it was permitted by the MCC Rules Committee in 1864. The English team's failure to win a baseball game highlighted baseball's change in pitching technique, which was done from a stationary position starting in 1863. Cricket bowlers still used the traditional run-up prior to delivering the ball off the front foot. In 1869, the same year Willsher's cricketers toured the East Coast, George Cummings was credited with pitching the first curveball.[73] Fielding had less divergent techniques, as bare hands were used by baseball players until the glove was introduced from 1883. Catchers caught without gloves in California until 1890.[74]

The Wright brothers played both baseball and cricket against Willsher's team just a few months before their historic baseball tour of the United States in 1869. Later Harry Wright would emulate Willsher's effort to combine both baseball and cricket on the same tour when he made his first baseball tour of England in 1874 with his team of baseball professionals. With the return of Willsher's team from New York via Liverpool to England in a rough crossing that took ten days, the New York cricket season returned to its domestic schedule. By 1870, Prospect Park in Brooklyn had become the home of cricket in New York. There were nine cricket teams in New York at this time: St. George's, Albion, King's County, Manhattan CC, New York CC, Staten Island CC, New Bedford CC and Brooklyn CC. New Haven in Connecticut also played against the New York's nine cricket teams. The use of Prospect Park made it possible for amateur cricket to grow. Cheap land or long-term leases aided the expansion of cricket in England. In New York cricket teams — except in the exceptional case of the Staten Island Cricket Club — rarely secured exclusive use of their playing surface owing to the requirement of public access to park land.

Good playing surfaces were required. One player was killed at Lord's when a ball ricocheted off a stone in the pitch and hit the Nottinghamshire County player, George Summer, in the temple. He died four days after the match.[75] Before the leveling of the pitch in 1875, "John Lillywhite enjoyed bowling at Lord's but conceded that it did not resemble a billiard table 'except for the pockets.'"[76] Rolling the pitch improved the playing surface but mowing techniques remained rudimentary; sheep were used until the introduction of the rotary mower in 1899.

Batting went through a revolution in technique once William Gilbert Grace started playing regularly in 1865 at the beginning of the overarm bowling era. According to Kumar Ranjitsinhji in the *Jubilee Book of Cricket*, Grace turned batting from an accomplishment to a science.[77] Crowds grew to enjoy Grace's prolific scoring, and pitches improved with greater preparation from ground staff, who were paid from increased county membership and expanded crowds of spectators that the Champion attracted to cricket in large numbers by his larger-than-life persona. Robert Allan or "Bob" Fitzgerald, the new secretary of the MCC in 1865, was one of the first to spot the young W.G. Grace's potential. Though only 24 himself, he invited the 18-year-old Grace to join the MCC. Fitzgerald was a good batsman, scoring over 1,420 runs in 1,860 in 46 games for the MCC. Educated at Harrow and Cambridge where he played cricket on both first XI's, Fitzgerald was born in Purley House, Berkshire, and played for Middlesex, Buckinghamshire, Hertfordshire, the Cambridge Qudnuncs, the MCC and the I Zingari.[78] As secretary of the MCC, expansion and improvement was Fitzgerald's policy. In 1872 he took the first amateur English side to Canada and the United States.

Bob Fitzgerald's England Amateur cricket team played New York in 1872, entering the United States from Hamilton, Ontario, and stopping on the way to view Niagara Falls, the Niagara Whirlpool, and the monument to the victorious 1812 general Isaac Brooks at Queenstown Heights. The team also took time to "observe trotting races and visit Central Park in New York. While in Boston, a local cricket club arranged a tour of nearby Harvard University ... and the famous baseball brothers, Harry and George Wright, presented each cricketer with a baseball."[79] They played the seventh game of their eight-game tour (the first six games were in Canada) at the St. George's ground in Hoboken against a New York XXII on September 18 and 19. The New York XXII was all out for 66 in their first innings as Arthur Appleby took 12 wickets for 18 runs. New York scored 44 runs in their second innings. W.G. Grace took 11 wickets for 27 runs. Grace scored 68 runs in England's only innings. England won the game by an innings and 39 runs after scoring 249 in their first innings. The eighth game of Fitzgerald's tour was in Philadelphia. The last game of the tour, against a Boston XXII, was the most exciting as both sides got 51 runs in the first innings, George Wright taking 5 wickets for 24 runs on a rain sodden pitch before the game had to be called as a draw.[80] Fitzgerald's tour galvanized the New York and Boston cricketers to action in 1873, when intercity cricket expanded beyond just local East Coast cities to include a match against the St. Louis Cricket Club. St. George's CC, recently settled at their Ninth Street grounds in Hoboken, beat the St. Louis CC by 36 runs.[81] St. Louis CC played well against the Philadelphia clubs, thereby establishing cricket in the Midwest.

The SGCC's next fixture on July 26 was against the Merion CC of Philadelphia. This was followed by games against the Manhattan CC First XI and the local Zingari XI.[82] The SGCC lost to Merion and Manhattan but beat the local I Zingari team. The Staten Island Cricket Club improved their performance on the field in 1874. Their chief strike bowler, Rogers, pitched underhand grounders to get Manhattan's top six wickets as the visitors were all out for 53 runs. The SICC (93) defeated Manhattan CC (50) by 43 runs in a second game that lasted four hours at their Camp Washington grounds.[83] Meanwhile, St. George's played a Prospect Park XI on August 4 at Hoboken followed by a game against Paterson CC at Prospect Park. Clearly cricket was flourishing in New York; the number of sides playing increased from nine to twelve. In 1875 St. George's handed the visiting Germantown CC side two defeats. The scores in the August game were 128 to 79 followed by a more convincing SGCC victory of 114 to 43 runs on October 5.[84] Most New York area teams played less than ten games a season in the 1870s. Staten Island's eight First XI games in the 1878 season were played between June 15 and October 19, in three states. They played the Fall River and Longwood teams in Massachusetts, the Manhattan and St. George's teams in New York and the Germantown team in Pennsylvania.

In 1878 the SICC won only two of their games. They played three in June and one a month thereafter.[85] This was not enough to develop local talent, though the SICC did have enough cricketers to support a Second XI that played three games. St. George's focus was more on Massachusetts. They lost a close game to Waltham of Massachusetts at their Ninth Street grounds in Hoboken on July 18, 1878, by a score of 49 to 56 runs.[86] When the Longwood Cricket Club was founded in Boston in April 1877, cricket in New England took a giant step forward. Harvard played Longwood CC in their first season during 1877, while old New England clubs such as Mystic CC of Medford and the Alpha CC of Salem maintained the quality of cricket in the New England states by employing professionals.[87] The LCC became the dominant team in the Boston area after George Wright joined in 1880 on ending his professional baseball career with the Rhode Island Grays. The Longwood CC joined the Boston Driving and Athletic Association (BDAA) in 1881 which gave it fixtures against Harvard, Fall River, Boston, Lawrence, Staten Island, St. George, St. John (New Brunswick) and Columbia.

The strong connection between the New York clubs such as St. George's and Staten Island and Massachusetts clubs was one founded on social equivalency or education. Kirsch found Philadelphia players were on average seven times wealthier than their New York counterparts. St. George and Staten Island had the wealthiest New York membership. They chose to play in the BDAA as an alternative to the Metropolitan Cricket and District League, founded with eight teams in April 1877. Competitive league cricket improved the standard of cricket in New York and in 1878 the era of international cricket was inaugurated by the visit of the first Australian test side. St. George's hosted the Australians at their Hoboken ground, which they returned to after leaving Hudson City in 1875. On September 15, 1878, the *New York Times* reported,

> Capt. J. Conway, the agent of the Australian cricket team arrived in the city yesterday by the steam-ship the City of Berlin, and is now staying at the Grand Hotel.... He states the cricketers will leave on the steamship the City of Richmond on the 19th inst. On Oct. 1 and 2 they will play the eighteen of New-York and vicinity at Hoboken, and on the 3rd, 4th and 5th an eleven of Philadelphia at Nicetown.[88]

The comparative state of New York and Philadelphia cricket can clearly be seen by the fact that New York put 18 players in the field against the Australians, while Philadelphia played with 11 players. The Philadelphia team had already been selected on September 15 while New York still had to organize their team, though they were to host the first game. An attempt to organize a game against Detroit based on their strong touring performance during the year in which they beat several East Coast clubs was rejected by Mr. Conway on account of the yellow fever scare in St. Louis. Conway earned much of the credit for promoting the success of the 26-game Australian tour of England, which ended with six games in North America. David Gregory's Australians dismissed the New York XVIII at St. George's ground in Hoboken on October 1–2 for 63 runs. Bance and Cashman were the top New York batsmen, scoring 15 and 13 runs each as Demon Spofforth took 8 wickets for 33 runs in 22.2 overs. Brewster — not the Philadelphia William Brewster — took 7 for 24 runs in 37 overs for New York in one of the finest American bowling performances ever made by an American against an Australian test side. Leading by only seven runs after the first innings, Australia limited New York to 98 runs after a spirited middle batting order effort by John Soutter, Anthony Marsh and Gordon Giles, who scored 20, 12 and 25 runs respectively. In the second innings Australia knocked off the remaining runs for the loss of five wickets as they won the game by five wickets. Brewster took another wicket in the Australian second innings, bowling 46 overs for an economy rate of less than one run an over as he took 1 for 43. Joseph E. Sprague, a retired pitcher for Jim Creighton's old team, the New York Excelsiors, also took Australian wickets with his swift, twisting, underarm bowling.[89] New York's performance against Australia was their finest ever against an international team. Baseball players were impressed by what they saw and took up cricket in upstate New York in the towns of Rochester and Utica. Even the New York Knickerbockers joined the act by finishing their baseball season with a cricket game against the Manhattan CC.[90]

The 1878 Australian tour was highly successful financially as each Australian player earned the equivalent of $5,000, 25 percent more than predicted. It was not long before English professional teams tried to emulate the Australians' success in America. Seven international games— not counting the annual Canada-versus-America game — were played in America in 1879, starting with the May stop-over of Lord Harris' England team, on returning from his Australian tour. Although Lord Harris was not present for his team's game against a combined Philadelphia and New York XI team held at Hoboken, his team won by an inning and 114 runs on strong batting performances by George Ulyett and "Monkey" Hornby. In September the Gentlemen of Ireland visited America for the first time, and they won all 12 games they played, including eight of them against the

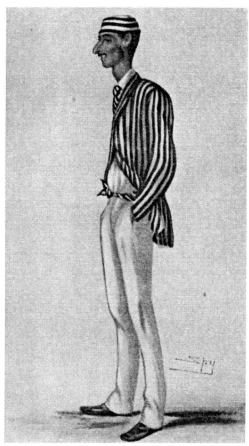

Left: Lord Harris brought visiting teams to America on three separate occasions, once losing to Philadelphia in 1891 at Germantown. This loss galvanized the growth of cricket in Philadelphia. *Right:* "Demon" Spofforth was Australia's premier fast bowler; he played both coasts in New York and San Francisco in 1878. His unplayable bowling on a wet wicket against England, in 1881 at the Oval, resulted in Australia's winning a test series in England for the first time. England's demise resulted in bails being burned, the ashes of which were placed in an urn that became the Ashes Trophy.

odds. (Cricket was started in Ireland by the British army, first in Phoenix Park in Dublin and then in the North with the founding of the Northern Ireland Club in 1859.) GOI team members were selected from the Connaught Rangers, the Irish Guards or from clubs such as the Phoenix CC and Trinity College, Dublin.[91] Once the GOI departed, Richard Daft's Professionals visited America for an extended tour of 13 matches.

> J.P. Ford, a member of the Nottingham Town Council, who had interests in North America, asked Richard Daft, the Notts captain to select and lead a side of professionals.... Daft picked six other Notts players: Alfred Shaw, John Selby, Arthur Shrewesbury, William Oscroft, William Barnes and Frederick Morley, plus five Yorkshiremen: Tom Emmett, George Ulyett, Ephraim Lockwood, William Bates and George Pinder.[92]

For George Ulyett this was the second tour of America within the year, and he returned again with Alfred Shaw's team in 1881. Arthur "Give me Arthur" Shrewesbury was England's best opening batsman. An innovative cricket entrepreneur, he earned his nickname after W.G. Grace was asked who he regarded as the best English batsman besides himself. Daft's cricketers were businesslike and mainly from northern England. Amateur cricketers were found mainly in the Home Counties (Surrey, Middlesex, Sussex, and Kent) of southern England. Shaw's team of 12

> left Liverpool on August 28th and after a rough seven days crossing reached Canada. The programme began with three matches in Toronto.... After two victories at Hamilton and London, the team moved to Detroit, where two Kentish cricketers, Littlejohn and Dale, tended the local ground. Rain caused the match here to be drawn, but as in Canada, the home batsmen made a poor showing. From Detroit, the team moved via Niagara Falls, to New York for two matches, where the batsmen mainly went in for cross-batted swipes of baseball players and Alfred Shaw had another field day.[93]

Daft's team easily beat XXII of Central New York by an innings and 70 runs. The eighth match of the tour was played against a XXII of the United States on Staten Island at Livingston Park. This game marked the replacement of the St. George's CC by the Staten Island CC under Arthur Outerbridge as the new clearing house for cricket in New

Arthur "Monkey" Hornby came to prominence playing for Harrow. He helped steady the England side in San Francisco in 1881 after it lost several quick wickets to a baseball pitcher. He captained England on occasion and played county cricket for Lancashire.

York. Alfred Shaw took 10 for 29 and 11 for 27 as the New York chosen side lost the game by 188 runs. The New York side played five trained English professionals who were tied down by Alfred Shaw's line and length bowling.

After their two victories in New York State, Daft's team traveled to Philadelphia where over 25,000 spectators turned the tour into a remarkable financial success. The team then returned to New York to catch the steamer home. According to Wynne-Thomas, "The tour was successful from all viewpoints and unlike most of its predecessors it was free from any minor disputes and disagreements."[94]

After Daft's tour, New York became a popular venue for international cricket teams, but New York's cricket community was not able to pay for professional teams without incurring a loss. When Alfred Shaw, Arthur Shrewsbury and Lillywhite approached the Staten Island Cricket and Base Ball Club about a proposed tour to New York, Edward Outerbridge, secretary of the club, noted in his refusal, "Cricket does not draw a good attendance in New York and, outside of the gate money, our club could not guarantee anything. In our match with Daft's XI (1879), where they had half the gross gate receipts the amount they obtained was comparatively small and our club was out some 300 to 400 dollars in expenses."[95] Outerbridge's letter also gives some insight into how thinly spread the executive talent was in New York's premier club as he went on to report, "It is a pity to have to say this, but it is unfortunately true. Our season has been a very quiet one and our men all being engaged in business are at that season in the fall very much tied down."[96]

Outerbridge's refusal to host Shaw and Shrewesbury's English team gave St. George's an opportunity to host the England side in their second game of the American part of their 28-game tour. Shaw captained the team in New York as Shrewesbury traveled directly to Australia to finalize arrangements for the remaining 23 matches in Australia and New Zealand. This was the most ambitious tour by an English team to date. The tour party, apart from the three promoters from Nottingham — Shrewesbury, Shaw and Lillywhite — included William Scotton and John Selby of Nottinghamshire; William Bates, Tom Emmett, Edmund Peate and George Ulyett of Yorkshire; R.G. Barlow and Robert Pilling of Lancashire; and William Midwinter, the close teammate of W.G. Grace and a double test player for both England and Australia, from Gloucestershire. The all professional side sailed "from England on 17 September, ... played its first match against the Twelve of Philadelphia and won by an innings. Four other matches were played in America. All of them proved a financial loss."[97] In the match against the XVIII of the St. George's Club held on Oct 5–7, England drew the match after scoring 254 (G. Ulyett 86, W. Bates 63) when St. George's replied with 65 and 46 for 13. The third game against an XVIII of America was held at Miltown on October 7–10. England won by 132 runs before catching the train to St. Louis where, after scoring 144 for 5 wickets, rain stopped play. The last game in San Francisco was played with fit English players who on occasion had run alongside the slow train on its trip across the plains from Chicago to San Francisco.[98]

A year after the visit by Shaw's England team, St. George's CC hosted the 1882 Australians at Hoboken on Oct. 9–10. They defeated England in England for the first time, resulting in the Ashes trophy being created "In Affectionate Remembrance of English Cricket which died at the Oval on August 29th 1882." Demon Spofforth splayed Peate's stumps as the Australians won an amazing come-from-behind victory by seven runs in a game made possible by the organizational skills of Surrey County secretary C.W. Alcock.[99] The team that played St. George's had only lost four of 38 matches played. The Australians' batting improved immeasurably with the stiff competition from England. Pollard notes:

> The rustic, sometimes primitive batting techniques of other Australian teams disappeared in a team that worked skillfully for their runs. In Alick Bannerman they had a stonewalling opener on whom to base long innings, with hitters Massie, McDonnell and Bonnor to follow, and the cultivated Murdoch ready to steady an innings. Horan and Sam Jones provided the ideal middle order aggression before opposing bowlers reached the tail. The bowling included four of the most consistent wicket-takers of all time: Boyle, Spofforth, Palmer and Garrett. They were disciplined, athletic, and alert to every signal from the captain Murdoch or their matchless keeper Blackham.[100]

At St. George's the New York side faced the Australian side that had put international cricket permanently on the map through its memorable victory against England at the Oval, and only lost by seven wickets in two innings. William "Billy" Midwinter, who had toured America the year before with Shaw's team, umpired the match but did not play.

Charles Wilson had the best performance for New York, scoring 35 runs as opener in the second innings before he was bowled by Boyle. New York was all out for 27 in their first innings. Australia replied with 116, the top score being made Murdoch, who scored 54. Charles Lane was the second highest scorer for St. George's, scoring 4 and 10 in both innings. He was also the best bowler, taking 7 wickets in both Australian innings for 33 runs in 40.3 overs, a fine performance for an American-based player at a time when competition in the New York area averaged ten games a season.[101]

After the great cricket event of 1882, New York's domestic cricket seasons in 1883 and 1884 were enlivened by the annual Canada-versus-United States match though few New York players were selected for the U.S. side, as Philadelphia's Newhall family provided the backbone of the U.S. team from 1882 and were more comfortable with a Philadelphia supporting cast of players. The strength of Philadelphia cricket relative to New York was proven again in 1885 when E.J. Sanders arranged a short eight-game tour of North America in September with the help of a re-energized Staten Island CC:

> The players involved were the Reverend R.T. Thornton, A.J. Thornton and T.R. Hine-Haycock of Kent, W.E. Roller and C.E. Horner of Surrey, A.E. Newton of Somerset, H.O. Whitby of Warwickshire, J.A. Turner of Leicestershire, A.R. Cobb of Oxford University, H. Bruen of Ireland and W.E.T. Bolitho of Devon. The team left Liverpool on 20th August.[102]

The Thornton brothers were the two hardest hitting batsmen in England at the time. The Reverend Thornton captained the team, which played its first game against the XII of Staten Island on September 1–2. Sanders' XII scored 91 and 244 runs with John Pool of Staten Island taking 7 for 43 in the first innings. Staten Island scored 62 in the first innings and was 72 for 3 in the second innings before the game ended as a draw. Sanders' second game was against a XV from the Peninsula Club in Detroit. In the third game against Canada in Toronto, Edward Ogden of Chicago was invited to play for the Canadians. After defeating XV of Montreal in the fourth game easily by an innings and 40 runs, Sanders' team had a historic loss to Philadelphia at Nicetown on September 17–19 when they were convincingly beaten by 109 runs. The Philadelphia win was the first time an American cricket team ever beat a top-notch English side. Philadelphia scored 200 and 178 in their two innings, and Charlie Newhall was the hero after he disrupted a well set partnership between the Thornton brothers before capturing the final English wicket with a lob. Attendance at the games in Philadelphia also set records with over 8,000 to 9,000 present on some days; over half the crowd were women. No large crowds were in attendance when Staten Island was defeated by an inning and 125 runs on September 21–22. Sanders' team then returned to Philadelphia where they got a revenge for their loss by making 243 runs. They finished their tour in

The best cricketer in the United States in 1890, George Wright toured England as shortstop for the Boston Red Stockings on his brother Harry's tour in 1874. He introduced tennis to Boston on his return from England. Source: *Outings*, May 1890.

Boston at the Longwood CC against a XV of New England on September 28–29, winning by a mere 16 runs in a game made close by the tough and intelligent bowling of George Wright, 6 for 25, and Chambers, 6 for 34.[103]

In 1885, New York's place as America's second cricket city was threatened by the fine cricket played at Longwood CC and in other parts of New England such as Montpelier and Waterboro in Vermont, St. Paul's in New Hampshire, and in Rhode Island, where the American Thornton brothers played excellent cricket. In New York, on October 22, 1885, John Cuddihy of the New York Zingari took all ten wickets of the Staten Island CC for eight runs. The loss to the local "wandering" team was indicative of how difficult it was to get a cricket side with a solid core of players in New York. In 1888 *Outings* reported that St. George's or Staten Island had no games scheduled for 1888 though Prospect Park had become home to three teams: the Manhattan, King's County and Albion cricket clubs.[104] Sixty matches were scheduled between the nine clubs of the Metropolitan League at a meeting of secretaries that took place at T&H Martin on 335 Broadway. Albion, Cosmopolitan, New Haven, Claremont, Newark, Amateur League, Manhattan and Alma were the nine clubs represented. There was surprise that the Essex and Patterson cricket clubs of New Jersey had not joined the league for the 1888 season.[105] Staten Island CC organized 13 games outside the league in 1889. In 1889 Staten Island scored 113 in their first innings and made it stand up for a convincing victory over the Hamilton CC, visiting from Ontario, by an innings and two runs.[106]

Cricket by 1890 had to vie for spectators' attention with a number of sports and it had success positioning itself as a morally edifying game capable of being played by those of refined taste. The New York Athletic Club and the New York Jockey Club both fielded cricket teams in 1890. Even in this up-market environment, cricket vied for attention in Richmond County with polo. Of Indian (some say Persian) origin, polo was introduced to the United States in 1876 by the Anglophile editor of the *New York Herald*. James Gordon Bennett first saw polo played at the Hurlingham Polo Club in England and was so taken with it that he returned to the United States with polo mallets and balls, determined to introduce it to the Big Apple. The game of polo had been taken up in India

> by English officers in India at first principally because it afforded a pastime better adapted to the climate than cricket.... The time of play was much shorter than cricket; a match could be played out in the cool of the afternoon.... "Polo," the name of the Tibetan form of the game, was the one finally adopted. Gen. G. Stewart, superintendent of Cachar about 1863, started the clubs at Calcutta, Cawnpore and Peshawur. With this start the sport spread rapidly through all India, not only among the officers of the crack light cavalry regiments and the artillery but among the officers of the line regiments as well.
>
> The game soon found its way back to England ... and flourished as sport only can when among Englishmen on English soil. Its headquarters may be said to be the Hurlingham Club, which administers all its affairs in the same way the Jockey Club does those of the racing world.[107]

Polo spread quickly among the American upper class and followed the same template as tennis. The Casino Club in Newport, Rhode Island, became the summer polo headquarters, as wealthy New Yorkers left Manhattan Island for the cooler climate. Polo was also played closer to the Big Apple, in Saratoga Springs, where Artimus Ward recommended the 400-person guest list for Mrs. Vanderbilt's Dance Assembly, held at her mansion on Fifth Avenue in the winter season.

Cricketers playing for New York's cricket clubs in the summer months did not achieve access to the social elite. Having failed as an elite sport in New York, cricket was taken up by the urban middle class. George Wright, writing in *Field and Stream*, noted that by 1886 that there were ten cricket players for every one five years earlier.[108] New York's premier cricket clubs, St. George's, New York, and the Staten Island Cricket and Base Ball Club, drew business expatriates as members. They perpetuated the influence of the British Empire in New York long after the American Revolution. However, it was the social and athletic clubs catering to the leisured urban middle class that provided facilities for expanding cricket, as the members of the clubs did not want to play professional sport and cricket's strict adherence to amateurism from 1870 suited them. In 1884 the American army and navy encouraged the playing of cricket and baseball to relieve the drudgery of life in uniform during peacetime. Both armed services' support lasted until the 1920s, when the articulate, well educated cricketers who promoted cricket's amateur ethic no longer retained the influence on the game they once had. This was partly due to the huge numbers of young men and cricketers lost in the First World War. During the First World War, West Indian cricketers in New York kept the game growing in local parks to the extent that when Indian businessmen settled in New York from 1960 onwards they found their favorite game played in Prospect and Cortlandt parks as a regular part of New York's cultural landscape. Though cricket lost its blue-collar audience to baseball, its upper-class audience to tennis, polo and yachting, and the American middle class audience after the First World War, it continued to be a familiar cultural touchstone for the first generation immigrant and has continued to play a vital role as an agent of modernization within the American mainstream for all immigrants from the cricket-playing countries of the Caribbean, South America, Europe, Africa, India, Pakistan, Australia and to a lesser extent the Middle East. From 1890 on, cricket established itself as an oasis of modernization in the most diverse city in the world. In New York cricket drew on two distinct cricket traditions from 1920 on, the British and West Indian. The Indian subcontinent, which includes India and Pakistan, became a factor after their independence in 1948 though the full influence of subcontinent's passion for cricket really was not felt in New York until the mid 1990s.

India's introduction to cricket occurred with Britain's initial contact with India in 1721. As we have seen, cricket was still in its infancy in England, mainly in the Weald and Downs country of Sussex and Hampshire. India's association with cricket matured along with the game unlike in America, where it was brushed aside in 1920 by the new wireless medium that nationalized baseball and sealed cricket's fate as a cultural anomaly of modernization with no traditional relevance for second generation Americans. Ironically, soccer was more popular than cricket in India prior to its independence from Britain in 1948. Mihir Bose in his magisterial *A History of Indian Cricket* speculates that if the British had been ejected from India through force as occurred in America, soccer, which was a cheaper sport to play, would have become the dominant game in India. Instead, because Gandhi led an astute national movement based around Bombay and was educated in the same school in Rajkot as Kumar Ranjitsinhji, cricket won out.[109] Gandhi would have been familiar with Ranji's achievement, as Indian school children memorized Neville Cardus' essay on Ranji and C.B. Fry putting Yorkshire to the sword. Gandhi was opposed to the annual Pentangular Tournament, as it pandered to communal interests rather than national ones. In this tournament, India's separate cultures and religions, the Parsees, Hindus, Muslims, British, and the rest (comprising Indian Christians, Anglo-Indians and Jews) played each other for a trophy.[110] It had been introduced in Bombay as the Presidency Cup by the presiding governor of Bombay, Lord Harris, in 1890. Gandhi naturally opposed the divide-and-conquer tactics of the colonial British masters that pitted one community against another. But although he agitated for the abolition of the Pentangular Tournament, he saw cricket as one of the good things the British had introduced to India that ought to be retained. "Cricket, without any fuss or much debate, was seen as a part of the British system of which Indians approved."[111]

Indians were secure in their own culture at independence so they simply adopted cricket as a game suited to the Indian temperament — "an Indian game accidentally discovered by the English."[112] America at independence was not secure in its identity and indeed took 40 years before developing its own literature and separate voice. There was no American equivalent to the ancient or sacred Sanskrit texts such as the *Vendanta* or *Mahabharata* in American history. Sport actually became the proving ground of American identity, and as we have seen it took well over a century before Americans beat British sportsmen at any team sport. The efforts that Arthur Goodwill Spalding put into creating the American foundation myth for baseball in 1907, in which Major

Kumar Shri "Ranji" Ranjitsinhji captained the 1899 England team to Philadelphia. He played with Jessop at Cambridge and, playing for Sussex County, became the first batsman to score 3,000 runs in an English first-class cricket season. Drawing by Sir Leslie Ward.

General Abner Doubleday was adjudged the founder of baseball though he has since been proven not to have played it, speaks volumes about the degree to which American identity was based on myth rather than history.[113] This was because, as Nandy posits,

> Sport is a safety valve and helps integrate society. It re-affirms the dominant profile of value in a society and re-socializes the people to the profile. It mirrors the fundamental social concerns of the people and allows them to cope with these concerns at the level of fantasy. Sport is a soaring saga of a battle against the safe, mundane, killing predictability of everyday life which ends up as an ode to the establishment and values achievement, performance, competition, and productive work.[114]

New York by 1890 had become the proving ground for America's sporting profile. The great American baseball writer John Thorn noted the importance of baseball to the

American psyche when he said, "America is about hope and renewal. Baseball meets our occasional need for dependency. It is what Mother England was to us once ... the repository of sustaining legend. Baseball is our home base, replenishing our spirits, restoring our hopes, repairing our losses and blessing us to journey anew."[115] Philadelphia used cricket to replenish its psyche as it beat English and Australians sides at cricket, on occasion, but New York did not. As we have seen, the New York cricket clubs did not put heir heart into training American youth. They had no schools program and their top clubs were not established as country clubs fit for local aristocrats as in Philadelphia. Two leagues of eight teams each, the Metropolitan and District League and the New York Cricket League, organized league competition. Despite having two contending leagues, New York league competition never achieved the stature of Philadelphia's Halifax Cup. This was largely due to the ephemeral nature of New York cricket teams, which relied more on businessmen for their cricketers rather than drawing on the diverse pool of players flowing from local schools, universities, country clubs and the occasional overseas businessman. Philadelphia had the inclination to treat cricket as the craft whereas New York sports spectators were results-oriented. Cricket left room for elegant solutions (a draw after three days) or ambiguity whereas baseball always produced a result. Amateurs in cricket were perceived as guardians of the sportsmanship ethic subsequently inherited by the Olympic movement. Baseball saw their guardians as the spectators, who paid for bigger and better ballparks as they reaffirmed their identity in a democratic society by passing through the turnstile for each game. As baseball drew increasing numbers, cricket on the field in New York from 1890 to 1914 captured a level of interest among its participants not duplicated since. There were two major players in this quarter-century span. They were Maxwell Cobb and Frederick Fitzmaurice Kelly, both expatriates. We will turn to these cricketers later to get an insider's view of New York's Golden Age of Cricket.

3. Philadelphia: The Cradle of Competitive Cricket in America, 1834–1890

CRICKET IN PHILADELPHIA GREW FROM 1834 on with an influx of British immigrants. Englishman William Carvill started cricket at Haverford College, where he became gardener.[1] Apart from college cricket, George Tichnor's team played cricket below Fairmont Bridge, which spanned the Schulykill River near Harding's Tavern in West Philadelphia. Four Tichnor brothers, George, John, Robert and Prior, played on the team along with Thomas Bacon, Joseph Nicholls, William Richardson and Francis Blackbourne. With no dedicated ground of its own, the Tichnor team crossed the Delaware for games in Camden on Mrs. E.S. Sayres' estate. This gave an opportunity for American-born players such as William Rotch Wister to play cricket. Rotch's father "encouraged his six sons to play on his Belfield Estate to keep them out of harm's way. Though he knew little about the game the family patriarch danced for joy on one occasion when his son's team won a game."[2]

William Rotch Wister relates,

> The first cricket I ever saw was on a field near Lyons School on the Old York Road, about the year 1843. The hosiery weavers at Wakefield Mills had formed a club under the leadership of Lindley Fisher, a Haverford cricketer. This club was in the habit of playing a "full match" on Whit Monday and other holidays, and occasionally on Saturday afternoons. Here I played my first game, [and] my brother John, afterwards prominent in cricket, was also taking part. We had played Town Ball, the forerunner of baseball of today, at Germantown Academy and our handling of the ball was appreciated by the Englishmen, who were glad to have us with them. There were some tolerable cricketers among those weavers, and their best bat, Joe Bakerstaff, once made 130 not out.[3]

Robert Waller founded the Union Cricket Club in 1843 by attracting the Wakefield Mill weavers and English mechanics from the Philadelphia suburb of Kensington. Waller had played cricket for the St. George's Cricket Club in New York before moving to Philadelphia. He attracted Edinburgh University–trained Dr. John Mitchell to the game. A respected Philadelphian physician, Dr. Mitchell proved an invaluable link to Philadelphia's elite. Mitchell and Waller hired William M. Bradshaw, a cricket professional, to coach the UCC cricketers. The UCC was the first cricket club in Philadelphia with its own dedicated ground. Bradshaw was a good cricket coach. Within a year of Bradshaw's appointment, three UCC members—two Tichnor brothers and James Turner—were selected by the St. George's Cricket Club of New York to play in an international cricket game against a Canadian team. Canadian cricket benefited from British army support. Cricket having been the official sport of the British army since 1841, garrisons stationed in Halifax, Toronto and Montreal supplied cricketers for the Canadian team.

The first challenge match, for a wager of £100 between teams from the U.S. and Canada, was held in Toronto on August 29, 1840. The U.S. team won the first international game in any sport by an innings. The game proved a great success. After a game won by the Canadians in Toronto, 1844 a second game was arranged the following month at the SGCC ground in Harlem. George Tichnor, his brother John, and James Turner were again selected. All three UCC players were English born. This second match was held on September 24–25, 1844, when the Toronto Cricket Club offered a $2,000 challenge on behalf of Canada to play any side in the U.S. The TCC-selected side was stronger than the first Canadian team, which won by 23 runs. Canada scored 82 and 63 and the United States, 64 and 58.[4] International games helped James Turner to improve his batting skills. He scored 120 runs for the UCC against the SGCC in New York on October 3–4, 1844.[5]

The UCC victory against the most prominent cricket team in America fired Philadelphians' interest in cricket. UCC coach Bradshaw coached new American recruits to the game such as William Rotch Wister. Wister had six brothers and came from a prominent Philadelphia family. While attending the University of Pennsylvania he founded the Junior Cricket Club, which practiced at the UCC ground for a nominal $50 rent. Wister remembered Bradshaw as a stern disciplinarian who "insisted on the proprieties of the game, including obedience to the Captain and submission to the decisions of the Umpire."[6] Wister gave Bradshaw credit for fostering the spirit of obedience in Philadelphia cricket that filtered down to succeeding generations of cricketers and with preserving "the good order that has uniformly prevailed in our Philadelphia matches" throughout the nineteenth century.[7]

After a ten-year hiatus, Haverford College renewed its interest in cricket in 1848. The Lycean and Dorian cricket teams were started by English-born Dr. Lyons, who taught at a nearby boarding school. American schools began included cricket in their curriculum as early as 1843, when St. Paul's in New Hampshire began its cricket program. These American-trained cricketers needed senior teams to play with, and after the collapse of the UCC on Robert Waller's departure to pursue mercantile opportunities in New York, attorney William Rotch Wister briefly revived the UCC with its English working-class, weaver-mill immigrant membership. The UCC stayed in existence until 1856 by which time Wister incorporated the Philadelphia Cricket Club on October 10, 1854, after a meeting in his officers at 47 S. 5th Street[8]:

> A constitution and bye-laws were adopted at this meeting, a Junior organization for those under twenty-one years of age was established and officers elected.

The club adopted the Marylebone Cricket Club Rules for their games and decided that the expense of the matches would be provided entirely by voluntary contributions, and not from the funds of the Club as established by the yearly dues. The first officers of the ... club ... were: J. Dickinson Sergeant, President; William Rotch Wister, Vice President; James B. England, Secretary-Treasurer. The second meeting was held at the home of William Bradshaw as provided by the by-laws. Bradshaw had been instructor (of the Junior Cricket Club) and for some time served in the same capacity (until 1855) for the members of the new club, while Thomas (Red Tom) Senior, who kept a Fruit and candy Store on 6th and Market Streets, became the first real Professional.[9]

PCC club colors were black, red and gold, representing "out of darkness through fire into light." These were the same colors as those of the I Zingari, founded in 1846. The I Zingari, founded in England, was

an amateur club, founded in friendship, benevolence and vintage port[, which] became the first and most famous wandering club in the world.... [It] was the idea of J.L. Baldwin and the Hon. F. Ponsonby, afterwards Lord Bessborough. The name I Zingari means "gypsies" in Italian. The club did a great service to amateur cricket by refusing to hire professionals to do their bowling.[10]

Both the I Zingari and the PCC attracted an aristocratic membership. The PCC employed professional bowlers and had an arrangement with the Kuhn family that allowed the PCC to play on their property in Camden with the proviso that the grounds would be vacated promptly when needed.

The ground was a square field of about three acres with the post and rail fence providing ample seating for the spectators. The ground was about three squares South of Federal Street, separated from the Delaware River by a row of frame houses, the last house in the road being the house of the Bradshaws. Mr. Bradshaw, an Englishman, had been quite a famous cricketer, but had grown quite old and stout by this time, while Mrs. Bradshaw was described as short and round, with a rosy but wrinkled face.[11]

The charter membership of the PCC comprised William Bradshaw and English-trained cricket internationals such as the Tichnor brothers. Philadelphia's leading families, including the Whartons, Biddles, Cadwalanders, Fishers, Harrisons, Lewises, Morrises, Wisters and Newhalls, also joined the PCC, attracted by the collegial atmosphere of the club. "By the end of 1855 the membership of the Club had increased to 84 and of these thirty-five had taken active part in play and practice. The ground was opened for play on April 22nd and practice continued on the good days as late as November 20th."[12]

On Bradshaw's departure to coach the Union Cricket Club in Cincinnati in October 1855, Tom Senior, a Yorkshireman, played for the PCC. The best English professional bowler in Philadelphia, Senior coached the Germantown Cricket Club. Senior's memorable qualities were "a sense of humour and ... his broad Yorkshire accent. He took a long run and habitually ploughed a hole in the wicket, bringing his foot down as he bowled with considerable force. In the days before overarm bowling was established, his action was quite unusual.... Tom loved the game for its sociability and enjoyed sitting in Mother Bradshaw's parlour, enjoying his pipe and pint and talking about the game."[13] Senior traded in his fruit stand on Market Street for part ownership of the Cricketer's Arms on Strawberry Hill. When not supplementing his income, Senior coached Walter Newhall to become an excellent batsman.

Neither the PCC nor the Germantown Cricket Club were welcoming to players under 16, so on November 9, 1855, five Newhalls and six Wisters founded the Young America Cricket Club of Philadelphia. According to YACC tradition, the club was founded after an apple barrage, as GCC cricketers playing in the Wister family apple orchards at Belfield denied the young Newhalls an opportunity to play cricket. The young Newhalls and Wisters expressed their disgust at being excluded by throwing apples at the older players playing on the Wister estate. Rotch Wister and the Newhall family helped organize the YACC and before long Wister was "known successively among the local fraternity as the 'father' and then as the 'grandfather' of American cricket ... remembered as a 'genial, sparkling, lovable' ... captain 'who urged on his men with cries of encouragement ... remarks, quips and cracks.'"[14]

The Wister and Newhall family interest in cricket was propitious for cricket because in 1855 the annual game between Canada and the U.S. was postponed after the British garrison sailed from Canada to fight the Crimean War. When the Crimean War ended in 1856, the international games resumed with the U.S. defeating Canada at Hoboken, New Jersey, by nine wickets. The return match at Toronto in 1857 was won by Canada. The U.S. organizer for these games was the St. George's Club in New York.[15]

On May 3, 1858, the National Cricketer's Association was organized in New York, but it did not acquire legitimacy as a central governing body for American cricket.[16] American cricketer members would not countenance players "revolving" between teams. Revolving players kept Americans from improving their cricket skills as they took team slots that might otherwise have given greenhorn players invaluable match experience. This tension between native players and English immigrants built up in annual matches played in New York. In 1860 there was a breakthrough for American-born cricketers when Frank Queen's *New York Clipper* was able to report that "seventeen Philadelphia cricketers (including six from Amsterdam, New York) defeated 11 English players in an All Star game[;] their average age was only 22."[17] The American victory augured well for cricket as there were 6,000 cricketers playing in the New York and Philadelphia area according to Porter's *Spirit of the Times.*

Philadelphia was not the only cricket success. Ten thousand cricketers played cricket in 22 states in more than 125 cities and towns in the United States before the Civil War.[18] By 1850 industrialization and urbanization created a need for efficient forms of exercise that could be calibrated in units of time. During this same period in Britain, cities quadrupled in size. The door for adults playing sport in America was opened in cities that gave an enthusiastic reception to Tom Hughes' *Tom Brown's School Days.* Cricket laid the foundation for team sport in America because it incorporated religion:

> It really is difficult to overstate this cross-fertilization between cricket and godliness.... The cricket cult revived the essence of Christianity as made intelligible to the middle and upper-class youth.
>
> The public schools and the universities churned out Anglican clerics ... and in many of the early county cricket sides were to be found parsons. To the Pauline texts of the race run straight and the well-fought fight were added the straight bat and the eighth deadly sin, "it's not cricket." Gone were the gaudy sky-blue coats and the nankeen breeches of the late Hanoverian MCC favours. Now all was virginal white, and the ritual was somber and rigid as any sacrament. Umpires, clad in long white robes, slowly walked in druidic procession to supervise the wickets, part altar, part cross.[19]

With so many Anglican vicars playing cricket in England, it did not take long for the clergy in America to recognize virtue in playing cricket. Dr. Higginson of Harvard preached the benefits of physical health in pursuing a righteous life. Cricket in America, with the health argument on its side, received the tacit endorsement of the church, though the expanding middle class increasingly played team sport on Sunday. It was the cricket-playing middle class that laid the foundation in America for the business of sport. This broad based American enthusiasm for cricket before the Civil War inspired Edmund Wilder, president of the National Cricketers Association, Robert Waller, who became president of the SGCC in New York on his departure from Philadelphia, and William P. Pickering of the Montreal Cricket Club to ante up £1,200 in gold for George Parr's All England Eleven of professionals to play a series of six games in Canada and America in October 1859. Pickering, who had been a cricket player and enthusiast all his life, both in England and Canada, "started correspondence with his friends in London in 1856 relative to bringing out an All-England XI to tour in North America and thus can be rightfully called not only one of the founders of two of England's most famous cricket elevens but 'Father of Cricket Tours' as well."[20]

Winter was setting in when George Parr's All England Eleven arrived in Philadelphia for a game played on October 10–12, 1859. Before arriving in the U.S., George Parr had succeeded William Clarke as captain of the AEE when Clarke died in 1856. Known as the Lion of the North, Parr, a crouching thumper of the ball, scored over a thousand runs in 1850, 1851, 1852 and 1855. At Trent Bridge, his home ground in Nottingham, a tree was known as Parr's tree because he hit it so frequently with his shots on the leg side. However, in America he only batted twice after he was injured in practice by English fast bowler Jackson, who hit him on the elbow in New York. Behind the stumps, Tom Lockyer was the finest wicket keeper the world had seen. Heathfield Harmon Stephenson of Surrey County was a ground bowler and opening batsman who would captain the first English team in Australia in 1862. The AEE team's openers, Hayward and Carpenter, were the mainstays of "Cambridge ... County.... Along with Richard Daft they had the best batting averages in England in 1861."[21] According to Henry Altham, "Hayward was best on a fiery wicket when his ability to keep down the rising ball was marked. His weakness was his poor run selection. In 1859, he scored 220, playing as a given man for the Gentlemen of Cambridgeshire against the University and twice scored centuries in the Players versus Gentlemen games at Lord's."[22]

In Philadelphia, Henry Chadwick was on hand to report the game for the New York press. He met the AEE team at the Girard House Hotel. Fred Lillywhite offered the most detailed report of the Philadelphia game in his classic father of all cricket tour books, *The English Cricketers' Trip to Canada and the United States in 1859*:

> SUNDAY, October 9 having been religiously kept (cricket never having been mentioned), all were "eager for the fray" on Monday, October 10. The ground is situate [sic] on the Carnac estate, about two miles and half from the center of the city, and is easily accessible per railway passing through the streets. Upon our arrival on the ground, we found that preparation had been made for the reception of the Eleven, quite equal to that of the St. George's Club at Hoboken. It had, however, been raining all night and during the morning, [and] the ground, therefore was dreadfully wet; so much so, that it appeared almost like a sheet of water, and it was past two o'clock before any of the English Cricketers could make their appearance, but it was even then too wet to proceed with the the contest.... Little of course was accomplished

that day — nine wickets only falling for 41 runs as the stumps were drawn at half past five o'clock.... WEDNESDAY, October 12 ... This was a splendid morning; the sun shone brightly, and with a blue sky, and the temperature just cool enough to realize what is called in England "a jolly cricketing day." At half past ten o'clock the English party ... upon arriving at the ground found a very large company to meet them, with a number of the young Americans practising in all parts of the ground; the band too, was playing "God save the Queen," as the English entered amidst most enthusiastic cheering. In two more hours the ground presented a most animated appearance. We never saw such a magnificent sight; about one thousand ladies were seated by themselves, and they appeared to be just as enthusiastic in their demonstrations of applause as if they had been versed in all the mysteries of the game.[23]

On October 12 Philadelphia's XXII went out to bat. William Rotch Wister batted third and was bowled by 4' 6" John Wisden for nine runs. Walter Newhall, Tom Senior's pupil, batted at number five and was bowled by George Parr for five runs. Hammond from Maidstone in Kent, an English professional on the Philadelphia side, made little impression with the bat as he was out for a duck (no runs). New York invitee Harry Wright did little better, going in number eight where he scored one run before Parr bowled him. His father, Sam Wright, a professional and groundsman for SGCC of New York, did better, scoring three runs. Tom Senior scored three and John Wisden scored 19 runs before he was run out. English-born cricket professional Gibbes was Philadelphia's top scorer, with 20 runs. Philadelphia scored 94 runs in their first innings. England replied with 126 runs, Harry Wright taking two wickets and Senior, six, including a hat-trick of Grundy, Stephenson and Lillywhite. In Lester's opinion, Wister's "selection of bowlers was poor as he took off Senior too early and kept Hallis, Waterman, and Gibbes on too long, resulting in over 60% of the runs being scored off them for 1 wicket between the three of them. American batting was not up to the bowling of Jackson.... The twenty American batsmen that faced the English bowling ... scored less than three runs each. Jackson took 10 wickets for ten runs in one match, Wisden took sixteen for 17 in another. Even on bad pitches wickets don't come as cheaply as that, and it is not reasonable to think of two hundred batsmen with any trained skill in defense being put out for 600 runs."[24]

At the Carnac estate in Philadelphia, the English opening batsmen, Hayward and Carpenter, showed what an opening partnership should be when they put on over 50 runs for the first wicket. In the second innings Philadelphia were out for 60 runs with Harry Wright scoring seven runs while John Wisden added five runs. England only needed 29 runs to win and they got them for the loss of three wickets, winning the match by seven wickets. Fred Lillywhite praised the Philadelphia XXII, noting that

they showed some excellent points in the way of fielding, and were justly applauded by their opponents for the skill they displayed.... It may also be stated, that the majority of the Twenty-Two were self-taught cricketers, being principally American, and great credit is therefore due, both to themselves and Hammond, their professional. They are excellent managers, will be good cricketers, and are really good and spirited fellows.... "Cricket in Philadelphia" has every prospect of becoming a national game.[25]

The Philadelphia cricketers parlayed their first international cricket experience into an excellence that came to dominate American cricket for the next 40 years. Just before the outbreak of the Civil War in 1860, there were enough cricket clubs in Philadelphia that the Union League was established.

The Germantown CC grounds and stands at Niceton became renowned throughout the cricket world as one of the finest settings in which to play cricket. Funded by higher society in Philadelphia, cricket survived the Civil War but leadership changed. The Wister family signed up for the Union cause in 1861when President Lincoln called for 75,000 Army of the Potomac recruits. There were major casualties. The eldest Newhall, Walter, was only 15 when he scored his first century against GCC for the YACC in 1851. He drowned in the Rippahannock River returning home while on leave from the Union Army.[26] After his death, cricket's leadership mantle in Philadelphia passed to his younger brothers, two competent first-class cricketers, George and Daniel Newhall, who continued to arrange matches between the GCC and the YACC on their Stenton ground. Dan Newhall launched a campaign to interest youngsters, and Germantown Academy became the most important Philadelphia cricket school. Afro-Americans in Philadelphia also played cricket at this time.[27]

After the Civil War, regular intercity cricket began when St. George's CC played the YACC at GCC's Niceton ground, to a tie of 99 runs each. Harry Wright opened for New York and scored 22 and 13 runs in both innings. Four Newhalls played on the YACC side and scored the bulk of the runs, aided by Rotch Wister, who scored one and four runs in both innings. Wister was out LBW to Harry Wright in the YACC second innings. Wright was the leading bowler with 13 wickets. Like his brother Harry, George Wright played out the Civil War as a cricket professional at PCC in 1864. On his Wednesdays off, George played baseball for the Olympics of Philadelphia.[28] Harry Wright had taken over from PCC's old professional from Bradshaw in 1860.[29] The Union Cricket Club in Cincinnati was "a social instrument governed by membership requirements and a constitution."[30] This cricket format proved to be ideal for raising capital for the Cincinnati Red Stockings in 1869. That such capital was needed to improve local playing conditions was amply demonstrated by a cricket field that beggared description as "a shabby field at the foot of Richmond Street called the Lincoln Park grounds."[31]

On the East Coast, cricket flourished in the elite atmosphere of the Ivy League colleges. University-trained cricketers from Harvard, Haverford and the University of Pennsylvania joined cricket clubs. The Longwood Cricket Club in Boston was popular with Harvard graduates. In Philadelphia, apart from the three major prewar clubs, the PCC, the GCC, and the YACC, the Merion Cricket Club opened in West Philadelphia during 1865 to accommodate greater numbers of college trained players.

When Edgar Willsher's team of English professionals arrived in America on September 13 for a six-week tour that lasted until October 24, 1868, the postwar readiness of Philadelphia cricket was put to the test.[32] Edgar Willsher was a cadaverous figure renowned in England for his left-arm, round-arm, above-the-shoulder bowling. Known as the Lion of Kent in deference to George Parr, from whom he inherited the mantle leadership of professional cricket in England, Willsher moved cricket forward after the MCC accepted his bowling action as legal on January 10, 1864. Willsher's team comprised four players from Surrey: Humphrey, Jupp, Griffith and Pooley — the wicket-keeper and successor to Tom Lockyer. James Lillywhite and Charlwood came from Sussex, Rowbottom and Freeman from Yorkshire, John Smith and George Tarrant from Cambridgeshire and Alfred Shaw from Nottinghamshire.

Shaw had started his professional cricket career with the Grantham CC in Lincolnshire in 1862. Grantham, a small industrial town in Lincolnshire, was surrounded by small villages that had grown rich in medieval times from sheep farming. Many of these farming villages such as Buckminster, and Woolsthorpe where Sir Isaac Newton was born, played cricket against the Grantham CC regularly in the summer. Shaw had just started his county cricket career at Nottingham when he was invited to tour America. His bowling action "was perfectly easy round arm. He could turn the ball both ways, particularly from the off, and he had consistent length. No more accurate bowler ever lived and to sheer accuracy he added considerable subtlety in pace and flight. He believed little in off theory and preferred to bowl directly at the wicket."[33]

He was the master of right-arm, medium slow, line and length bowling. His bowling accuracy remains unsurpassed. In his career as a cricketer, he "bowled 24,700 overs, 16,922 maidens, for 24,107 runs and 2051 wickets.... No bowler in the history of the game ... can claim a record of accuracy approximating this, in which more than half the overs bowled over a period of thirty one years were maidens, and the debit of runs is smaller than the total number of overs bowled."[34]

This was the first of three tours Shaw made to America. He is remembered in Australian cricket history for bowling the first-ever ball in an England-Australia test match when he opened the bowling against Charles Bannerman at the Melbourne Cricket Ground in 1877. Shaw was not only a great bowler but he was an innovator: "According to Ashley-Cooper in *Lord's and the MCC*, its was Alfred Shaw who first suggested the white washing of the creases instead of having them cut into the turf, as was the universal practice down to 1865."[35] When not on home turf, Shaw's penchant for travel help expand the game internationally. Shaw liked America. He remembered his first game for Willsher's team against the SGCC in Hoboken after a ten-day voyage from Liverpool. On defeating New York, Willsher's team played their next game in Canada. They stopped to view the magnificent Niagara Falls on their way to Montreal, in what had become almost as a mandatory stop by English cricket tourists since the days of George Parr's AEE visit in 1859.

After bowling out an All Canada team for 28 runs, Willsher's team visited Massachusetts. In Boston they played in swamplike conditions after all night rain on the pitch before traveling to Philadelphia. Willsher's team played a Philadelphia XXII on the GCC's Niceton pitch. In their first innings— on October 3–6 — the U.S. scored 88 runs. Charlie Newhall, bowling accurate yorkers for Philadelphia, caught Willsher's weak batting side by surprise. The 6' 1" Charlie Newhall had Willsher's team in trouble when he took 6 wickets for 34; then Willsher played a captain's innings to have his team finish with 4 runs more than the United States, with 92 runs in their first innings. By the second innings, the U.S. faced Humphrey and Freeman, the fastest opening bowlers in England. Fast bowling prevailed as the U.S. innings collapsed to 35 all out in their second innings. Freeman took 14 wickets for 15 runs, bowling 32 maidens in the process. Charlie Newhall again caused problems for Willsher's team in the second innings as they struggled to make the 33 runs required for victory, with only two wickets left after Newhall took 5 wickets for 21 runs. Newhall's haul of 11 wickets against England led to his recognition as the best bowler in America.[36] Following Willsher's close victory at Niceton, England easily defeated a United States XXII in a game at the same grounds for their fifth win of the tour. Again Charlie Newhall was not to be denied as he took 8 wickets for 57 runs in England's first innings and 6 for 30 runs in the second. With England's scores of 117 and 64, the U.S. XXII's batting proved too weak to secure victory as the U.S. were out for 47 and 62 in their two innings. England won by 72 runs. Crowds of over 5,000 spectators watched each day of the game. American umpiring was challenged by the English team but they were able to win all six cricket games on the tour. They failed to win at the three baseball games they attempted.[37] Lester noted that Willsher's tour "shows clearly, as they did in 1859, that our batsmen had yet to acquire the foundations of a sound and automatic defence. Indeed; a control of the instrument of play whether a bat or ball, had not yet been sufficiently learned. Willsher's side in the two matches bowled 2 wides and the Americans 24."[38] Thirty-four of the 38 English wickets that fell went to Newhall and Meade (the son of Union general Meade).

Four years later in 1872, Robert "Bobbie" Allen Fitzgerald, secretary of the MCC, led the first amateur team to visit America. Fitzgerald's tour reflected the MCC's increased control over cricket in England, which Fitzgerald—as the first paid secretary of the MCC—helped revive through improving the quality of MCC cricket. He encouraged the MCC's touring tradition with overseas matches in Paris and America. He was also instrumental in having W.G. Grace elected to membership at age 18, after Grace in his first major innings scored 224 runs for All-England against Surrey in 1866. Grace scored 2,000 runs in the 1866 season, becoming the first batsman to score 2,000 runs in a first-class season.

Fitzgerald published a lively account of the Gentleman's tour in the U.S. and Canada titled *Wickets in the West; or, The Twelve in America* (though the tourists barely went further west than Hamilton on Lake Ontario). Although the team nominally comprised amateurs, "the distinction was purely one of social class. The Twelve were as well remunerated as any professional touring team. *Scores and Biographies* states categorically that, in addition to having all their expenses including their travel, covered, 'For each match each gentleman cricketer received from their opponents 600 dollars in gold.' Fitzgerald, who as MCC Secretary was the arbiter of amateur status, clearly saw no contradiction in the arrangements and vehemently defended his men (all of whom were MCC members and therefore Gentlemen by definition)."[39]

Like Shaw, Grace made his visit to America early in his career. He demonstrated his revolutionary batting technique. Before Grace, "a man was a back player like George Giffen or a sticker ... like Harry Jupp. But W.G. was each and all at once, C.P. Fry's verdict in the Jubilee Book of Cricket. He revolutionized cricket. He turned it from an accomplishment into a science; he united in his mighty self all the good points of all the good players, and made ability the criterion of style."[40] In C.L.R. James' opinion, Grace's greatest strength was his lack of inhibition. Spectators watching Grace were passionate about their hero. In 1871 he played in three consecutive matches and scored 189 not out, 268 and 217 on wickets most cricketers would think too rough to play on today.[41] He drew large crowds to his games by the force of his personality, and "crowds ... roared as they saw his gigantic figure with the red-and-yellow cap and the black beard emerge from the pavilion to start an innings. The point is whatever his fatigue he could never take notice of it. The crowds and the people made of every innings a test innings."[42]

Other bachelors in the party were Alfred and Edgar Lubbock, A.N. "Monkey" Hornby, the Hon. George Harris, Arthur Appleby, W.H. Hadow, C.K. Francis, Francis

Pickering, W.M. Rose and C.J. Ottaway.[43] At Eton in the 1860s, Alfred Lubbock and Ottoway were two of the best batsmen in the school's history. Ottoway "was a most brilliant, all-round athlete who represented Oxford in cricket, Association Football, tennis, rackets and running…. Whilst still a boy he had an almost perfect defence, and his 108 in the 1869 Harrow-Eton match turned the tide in Eton's favour."[44]

England's accomplished amateur cricketers were accompanied on their trip to America aboard the SS *Sarmatian* by 100 children from a London orphanage sailing to the New World of opportunity. Lord's cricket ground had an orphanage adjoining its main ground in the place where the cricket school now stands, and Dr. W.G. Grace spent "most of his working life among the poor. In the great ship of Victorian society, Grace was naturally keen to secure a place for himself…. His star status lifted him above … demarcation lines Victorian snobbery guarded so jealously…. George Harris, who had worshipped him from afar at Eton, now found him a very congenial companion."[45] The Honorable George Harris became Lord Harris after the tour on the death of his father. Apart from Lord Harris and W.G. Grace there was one other future England captain on the squad, A.N. Hornby ("Monkey") of Lancashire, who opened the batting with Grace.

The players toured Canada first after docking in Quebec on August 7. They played their first American game on August 16 at Hoboken against a XXII selected by the SGCC. Simon Rae relates that "the team moved on from New York to play the most important match of the tour against Twenty-Two of Philadelphia. Philadelphia was the heartland of American cricket, and huge crowds thronged the German Town [sic] Cricket Club."[46] Grace took 9 wickets for 22 runs as the Philadelphia XXII scored 68 runs. The Englishmen then came up against the pick of the bowlers they met on the tour. According to Rae, Grace was impressed, noting:

> "[Charlie] Newhall, who was a right hand fast bowler, was one of the best … I ever played against; whilst Mead [sic], a medium pace left-hander, kept up a wonderfully good length." When Newhall bowled Grace for 14 the crowd responded vociferously: "I have heard many a great shout go up in various parts of the globe at my dismissal, but I never remember anything quite equal to the wild roar that greeted my downfall on this occasion." The two Americans bowled through the innings, dismissing the Twelve for 105. The Philadelphian second innings took the same course as the first, though this time Grace was replaced by Rose entirely and bowled throughout with Appleby. The game was watched with intense partisan interest. The ladies in the grandstand shrieked whenever a wicket fell, and the whole crowd cheered every single run as gradually the deficit was knocked off and the home team inched into the lead. In the end they made 74, with amateur fast bowler Appleby, taking 8 for 24 and Grace 11 for 46.[47]

With the pitch showing signs of wear, Grace believed runs would be hard to get. He was right. Facing 22 fielders and opening the batting as usual, Grace

> got off the mark with a single in Newhall's first over, but lost Ottaway to a fast delivery that sent his middle stump flying. Hornby made one good hit for three to leg, but then was snapped up at short leg. That brought Alfred Lubbock out to join Grace with the score at 8 for 2. Apart from a few high-risk short singles, the runs almost dried up. "Ball after ball was sent down, which we could do nothing beyond playing, and maiden over followed maiden over in unbroken monotony." After three quarters of an hour the total was fifteen. The wicket was crumbling, and getting worse and worse. Newhall's bowling rose dangerously, and Mead, as usual kept up a splendid length. First Lubbock went, and then Grace himself was caught in the slips. He had batted just under an hour and scored seven runs. "This is about

the slowest pace at which I ever remember scoring," he remarked. His fall again provoked wild jubilation. Hats and parasols were flung into the air and cheering and applause accompanied him all the way back to the pavilion. At 18 for 4 and with the great man gone, the Americans sensed a real chance of an astonishing victory. Hadow and Harris calmed the visitors' nerves with a steady partnership, and appeared to be steering to a comfortable victory when, with the score on 29 Harris slashed a lifter from Newhall and was caught at cover point for "a most valuable 9." Two more wickets fell on 29 and the tension mounted unbearably.[48]

Grace recalled,

> The excitement, which had been growing intenser with every moment, was now extraordinary. The atmosphere was electrical. I never remember seeing a team or crowd of spectators more excited. They were in rhapsodies, and could scarcely keep still. The quietude amid which each ball was bowled was almost deathly, and no wonder, for thirteen successive maiden overs had been bowled and not a single run had been secured for half an hour, during which time three wickets had fallen.[49]

Edgar Lubbock broke the maiden spell with a leg-bye which took the score to 30. Then,

> Appleby ... now produced the stroke of the day, a full-blooded off-drive which sped through the packed field all the way to the boundary, and the visitors were home by a whisker. Grace was greatly impressed with the fight the Americans had put up, and Lord Harris remembered the game as one of the best he had ever played in. He also noted that Fitzgerald's team was the only English side in forty years to win against the odds in Philadelphia, making the performance "very high class."[50]

The performance of the Newhalls in the game against Fitzgerald's team solidified their emergence as the premier cricket family in Philadelphia. A large family of nine boys, the Newhalls proved to be a first-rate cricket talent factory equal to the Grace family. By their performance against Fitzgerald's team, Philadelphia showed it played a higher standard of cricket than New York where, as Fitzgerald noted, baseball was likely to become America's sport of choice. New York had overtaken Philadelphia as America's premier port before the Civil War following the completion of the Erie Canal and the Hudson and Mohawk Valley Rail Road, which linked Manhattan to the Great Lakes. Boston challenged Philadelphia as the literary and intellectual capital of the United States, but proper Philadelphians were able to laud it over the Boston Brahmins in cricket. In 1873 Philadelphia was ready for greater competitive challenges and hosted the St. Louis Cricket Club as intercity cricket spread west to the Mississippi. The St. Louis CC defeated St. George's CC by 36 runs in Manhattan before traveling to Germantown, where they were beaten by the Young America CC.

Harry Wright had changed his job as UCC cricket coach to paid baseball manager following his Cincinnati Red Stockings tour of America in 1869. Wright knew the value of cricket tours for expanding the market since the days he first played against Canada in 1853. In 1874 he took baseball outside America for the first time. Fixtures for Wright's baseball tour in England were organized by Charles William Alcock, secretary of the Surrey County Cricket Club and the first secretary of the Football Association. From his office at the Oval in London, Alcock arranged the English fixtures for the Gentlemen of Philadelphia, Haverford College and Arthur Goodwill Spalding World Baseball tours of 1889. Wright's itinerary for 1874 created the template for the GOP, Haverford and Spalding tours to follow. The British Isles tour included a stop in Dublin, which Harry Wright felt was a good idea because of "all our Mc's and O's," members or the Philadelphia Athletics and the U.S. champion Boston Red Stockings whom Wright took on the tour.[51] One of the most memorable cricket games was a victory against the MCC ground staff in which Al Spalding of the Boston Red Stockings scored a match winning 25 runs for the Eighteen of America against an MCC XI.

> The MCC batted first, opening with Mr. Lubbock and Mr. Courtenay Edmund Boyle against H. Wright (medium, round) and McBride (fast underhand) "who took three strides and then let fly a tremendously fast grubber that rarely rose from the ground an inch after it was pitched." Play was suspended at five minutes past two when they retired for lunch. That was the signal for the ground staff to come on to the field and mark out a diamond shape for baseball. So it was baseball in the afternoon which Boston won. Then the cricket resumed at six o'clock. In the evening there was a dinner with the president of the club, the Marquess of Hamilton, supported by the treasurer, Mr. T. Burgoyne and the secretary Mr. R.A. Fitzgerald.[52]

The best shortstop on the England tour was George Wright, Harry's younger brother, who returned to the United States with tennis equipment, intent on introducing the new sport through his Boston shop of sporting outfitters, Wright and Ditman. Spalding was more ambitious and capitalized on his relationship with William A. Hulbert, the founder of the National League, by securing the right to provide baseballs for the league when it was established in 1880. By this time, Spalding owned the National League Chicago White Stockings. Cricket in Philadelphia stayed amateur. The amateur code was enforced by the leading cricket clubs that selected Philadelphia's cricketers. Cricket stressed its Anglo-Saxon roots as Philadelphia baseball flourished with Irish participation. According to Zoss and Bowman, "Irish-Americans were an increasing presence in the large cities of the North-East where baseball was definitely on the rise, the same cities where signs that 'Irish need not Apply,' were appearing. Some of the many editorials criticizing baseball for harboring rowdies and worse were probably thinly veiled attacks on Irish-Americans."[53] Anglican vicars' attraction to cricket was suspect in Roman Catholic Irish eyes. In Ireland curling was seen as the sport of the Gaels. In America, baseball was more lucrative than manual labor, in which the Irish navvy earned his Paddy nickname digging canals and laying tracks for the new railways. The cultural conflict between cricket and baseball was muted until the 1890s, when America's expansion of informal empire overseas in the Philippines and Cuba utilized baseball, as the British had cricket, in expanding their sphere of influence.

The imperial phase of cricket and baseball following the flag was made possible by improved rail links in the 1870s when cricket expanded in America with intercity competition between Philadelphia, Chicago and St. Louis. Philadelphia's cricket grew rapidly; the quantity of games played as the city's population doubled and the city's expanded middle class, created by the wealth that accompanied industrialization and urbanization after the Civil War, sought socially acceptable recreational outlets. Cricket fit the improving image of the middle classes aspiring to social acceptance by Philadelphia's elite. Philadelphia's cricket clubs proved ideal for fraternization between the upper and middle classes. Philadelphia's aristocracy, like their counterparts in England a decade earlier, realized that cricket and other sports were "not merely useful as substitutes for undesirable activities but might be used to inculcate positive virtues—loyalty and self-sacrifice, unselfishness, co-operation and *esprit de corps*, a sense of honour, and a capacity to be a 'good loser' or to 'take it.'"[54]

When the PCC received an invitation in 1874 from Captain N.W. Wallace of the 60th Royal Rifles quartered in the Citadel in Halifax, Nova Scotia, to a grand cricket tournament to be held in August, they accepted with alacrity.

Albert O. Outerbridge was named team manager for the Philadelphia 12 chosen by a committee comprised of one representative each from the four leading cricket clubs in Philadelphia. These clubs were the PCC, Germantown CC, Young America and Merion CC. The players selected included Daniel S., Charles A. and Robert S. Newhall of the Young America CC, Spencer Meade from the PCC, Francis Brewster from Germantown and the brothers George and Richard Ashbridge from Merion. Dan Newhall lead the tournament batting averages with 149 runs in three innings while his brother Charlie Newhall lead the bowling averages taking 17 wickets for an average 6.88.[55]

The tournament inspired the re-establishment of the Cricketer's Association of the United States (CAUS) in 1876, 14 years after it collapsed during the Civil War. It also provided the annual Philadelphia cricket trophy known as the Halifax Cup. Philadelphia's improved cricket competition was reflected in other large cities such as Chicago and St. Louis, where the best cricketers played on a regular basis with Philadelphia players such as W.P. Newhall. *The American Cricketer*, edited by Daniel S. Newhall began its 50-year publication run in September 1877 as intercity competition picked up.

Charles W. Alcock, the founder of modern organized sport. From his position as secretary of the Surrey County Cricket Club, Alcock helped Harry Wright and Arthur Goodwill Spalding organize their 1874 baseball and cricket tour of England. He was also the founding secretary of the Football Association in 1873 and organized the Gentlemen of Philadelphia tours in England. Source: *British Sports and Sportsmen.*

Daniel Newhall's cricket philosophy echoed that of the Reverend James Pyecroft, B.A. of Trinity College, Oxford, whose widely read *The Cricket Field; or, The History and Science of the Game of Cricket* noted that "there is no game in which amiability and an unruffled temper is so essential to success, or in which virtue is rewarded half as much as in the game of cricket. Dishonest or shuffling ways cannot prosper; the umpire will foil every such attempt — those two constitutional judges bound by a code of written laws and public opinion of a cricket club."[56]

In the Quaker City the umpire's authority was reinforced by a strong administrative body. The Associated Clubs of Philadelphia comprised members from Philadelphia's four leading cricket clubs: Germantown, Philadelphia, Merion and Belmont. The ACP's primary function was to organize tournaments, tours and international visits, although it also reviewed local cricket experiments such as the 8- and 10-ball over. Philadelphia's experimental cricket phase reflected optimism that cricket might be Americanized.

Local cricket skills in Philadelphia improved through immigration as well as local competition. The Canada-versus-U.S. games were restarted after the Civil War. In 1876, English-born John Hargrave and John Large put on a 220-run partnership against the Canadians.[57] This fine performance was followed by a greater one when first Australian cricket team to visit Philadelphia arrived on October 2–3, 1878, sparking great spectator enthusiasm. The *New York Times* noted that arrangements for Australia versus the New York XVIII to be played in Hoboken were dilatory, but in Philadelphia the 11 had been chosen and were regularly practicing against picked teams: "The Philadelphia team [will] be Messrs. E. Brewster, R. Nelson Cadweil, E.T. Comfort, John Hargrave, T. Hargrave, E. Hopkinson, Sutherland Law, and the four brothers Newhall."[58]

Philadelphia played with just 11 players as opposed to 18 for New York. The Philadelphian side was keen to test their mettle against Gregory's seasoned colonial team. The Australians had only lost 6 of 80 matches before arriving in Philadelphia. Pollard, describing the atmosphere in Philadelphia, noted:

> The Australians were dumfounded when the umpires applauded every run scored by Philadelphia and when Blackham had a stumping appeal rejected with the batsman three or four paces down the pitch, Dave Gregory led his players from the field in protest. In the dressing-room American officials told Conway (the tour organizer) the check they had given him that morning would be dishonoured unless the Australians continued the match. Gregory took the team back on the field, much to the relief of 10,000 spectators.[59]

After the game continued on the Germantown CC's Niceton pitch, Robert Stuart Newhall scored 84 runs against the finest fast bowler in the world, Demon Spofforth. Newhall's innings remains one of the finest ever played in Philadelphia. The four Newhalls on the team combined to score 131 of Philadelphia's 196-run first innings total. Philadelphia's run rate against the Australians was 4.2 runs an over and 11.4 per wicket. Australia fell behind Philadelphia by 43 runs as their first innings total score was 150 runs. In Philadelphia's second innings, Spofforth and Allan bowled unchanged, shooting Philadelphia out for 53 runs. Australia lost 4 wickets for 56 runs in their second innings before the game was called as a draw. Brothers Daniel S. and Charlie A. Newhall excelled in the bowling department for Philadelphia, taking 11 of the 15 Australian wickets.[60] After their close call in Philadelphia, the Australians played against an Ontario and Montreal XXII side which they defeated easily, scoring 319, with Charles Bannerman top-scoring for the Australians with 125 runs. Moving on to St. Louis' Peninsula Club XIX, Gregory's XI crushed the Midwesterners by an innings and 66 runs. The Australians played their last North American game of the tour in San Francisco before arriving in Sydney where they were given a glorious reception as national heroes.

Philadelphia reaffirmed its cricketing pre-eminence in America in 1879 when a combined Philadelphia and New York XI faced Lord Harris' team of English amateurs on their return from Australia, at Hoboken. Lord Harris' team crushed the combined Philadelphia and New York team by an innings and 113 runs.[61] Despite this overwhelming defeat, the United States chose only native-born Americans for the first time in the history of Canada-versus-U.S. play in 1879. Playing in teams of 12, the United States won the 1879 contest by five wickets even though Canada fielded no native-born players.[62] In September, English professionals captained by Richard Daft played in Philadelphia on a 12-game tour that visited Toronto, Hamilton, London (Ontario), Detroit, Syracuse, and Staten Island. At the same time as the Richard Daft tour, the Gentlemen of Ireland played 13 games in the United States and Canada and experienced their only defeat of the tour in Philadelphia on September 25 and 26 when they were crushed by an innings and nine runs.[63] The Associated Clubs of Philadelphia selected the teams that played in Philadelphia. This task required a permanent standing committee owing to all the international teams wanting to play in the City of Brotherly Love.

The ACP evolved out of the committee that organized the annual competition between the PCC, Merion CC, Germantown CC, and Young America CC, named for the Halifax Cup, starting in 1880. In Canada the selection of teams was made by the Ontario Cricket Association, organized by the Marquis of Lorne in 1880. One of the reasons that cricket was played with regularity in

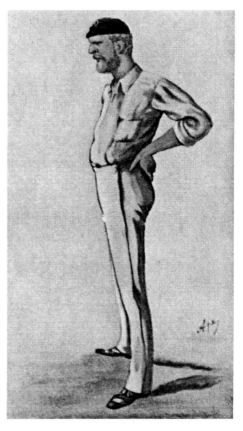

Charles Bannerman was the first Australian to score a century against England. He played in San Francisco in 1878.

Philadelphia was the expansion of the Philadelphia and Reading Railroad, the biggest employer in the city. With its new headquarters on Broad Street, the PRR developed real estate holdings on Chestnut Hill. In addition, large landscaped stations were built and given Welsh names. Haverford and Merion already existed, while Humphreyville was changed to Bryn Mawr.[64] As part of a plan to develop Chestnut Hill as a suburb for proper Philadelphians, PRR board director Henry Heston invited the Philadelphia Cricket Club to relocate on a ground opposite his 300-room hotel.[65] The PCC flourished on its new St. Martin's ground despite having a membership that was only 18 percent cricket-playing.[66] The strongest side at this time was the YACC. George Newhall still played for the YACC, and in a game versus the Baltimore Cricket Club, a three-generational team of Newhalls scored 357 runs with George making 180 not out.[67]

English teams loved playing in Philadelphia both for its money and its hospitality. Alfred Shaw's England XI that played at Niceton on October 7–10, 1881, was no exception. Shaw's team comprised nine of England's top professionals; George Ulyett, William Bates, Tom Emmett and Edmund Peate from Yorkshire, Richard Pilling and Roger Barlow from Lancashire, Bill Scotton and John Selby from Shaw's county team of Nottinghamshire, and Bill Midwinter from Gloucestershire. Midwinter was W.G. Grace's favorite batting companion beside Arthur Shrewsbury and achieved the unique distinction of playing international cricket for both England and Australia. Eight thousand spectators turned up on the first day of the game at Niceton to see Shaw put on a remarkable performance of line and length bowling that upset Philadelphia's batting as the home side went down to defeat by 132 runs. After the game, Shaw's Australia-bound professionals caught the train to California to play a California XXII in San Francisco.[68]

The following year on October 11,12 and 13, 1882, Murdoch's Australians took on a Philadelphia XVIII at Niceton. The Philadelphia side included Nottinghamshire-born A.M. Wood, John Thayer, three Newhalls, two Hargrave brothers and Howard MacNutt. The experienced Australian team comprised most of the players that had visited in 1878. Facing Demon Spofforth's, fast, variable pace and Boyle's leg breaks, the Philadelphia batsmen did not settle down and in both innings they were out for less than 100 runs. The highest score of the match was made by the Australian keeper Blackham, who scored 31 runs as Australia put on 106 runs in the first innings and won the game by nine wickets. Fast bowler Charlie Newhall had the best all-round performance for Philadelphia, taking 5 wickets for 47 runs in 44 overs. He also had the highest score in both Philadelphia innings; 14 and 18 runs respectively.[69] Aside from Charlie Newhall's outstanding all-round performance, Philadelphia's poor batting against spin bowling techniques was clearly demonstrated. It was determined that if Philadelphia were to stay on the cutting edge of world cricket, it should copy the Australian formula of touring England, the fountainhead of cricket, to toughen match capabilities through top-level competition. In 1884, Robert S. Newhall was appointed captain and $8,200 was raised to fund the GOP team's transport, accommodation, and games. Howard MacNutt recalled the momentous occasion for Philadelphia cricket in *Outings* where he wrote,

> last May 17th, eleven "Gentlemen of Philadelphia" cleared Sandy Hook outward bound. It was an English looking crowd this group of athletes clustered aft the deck of the City of Rome; tailor-made English look about them, but underneath the woolen checks and plaids there was a heap of American muscle which no tailor's art could add or conceal....
> The full representation of amateur ability in all-round sports which was embodied in these "Argonauts of '84," has never, to my knowledge, been estimated. It would have been difficult to name an outdoor sport without finding several skillful exponents among these eleven men who were picked to represent abroad the cricketers of the United States.[70]

The first game against 18 of Dublin was drawn. Five of the Irish side had played in Philadelphia on previous Gentlemen of Ireland tours of the United States. All the games played in England were against amateur Gentlemen teams. A confidence-building tour victory came against the Gentlemen of Cheshire in which Bob Newhall scored 126 runs. A close four-run victory, against the Gentlemen of Liverpool at the beautiful Aigburgh field, was followed by a loss to the Gentlemen of Scotland by five wickets. The GOP then beat Northumberland and moved onto Scarborough, a Yorkshire coastal resort with a beautiful cricket ground, where Storer scored another century for the GOP side. From Yorkshire the GOP descended on the famous fox hunting (the Quorn and the Pytcheley hunt) county of Leicester. Leicester was beaten by the GOP before the GOP lost by five wickets to a strong MCC side at Lord's. After a brief sojourn in London, the GOP met Major Wallace when they played Hampshire. Wallace had been responsible for Philadelphia's invitation to the first Halifax tournament in 1874 when he was stationed in the Halifax garrison with the 60th Royal Rifles. Major Wallace played for the Gentlemen of Hampshire, and he helped select a strong side as they won the game by five wickets. Then it was on to the land of Graces in Gloucestershire, where they beat E.M. Grace's Lansdowne Club at Bath. The GOP victory against Lansdowne was the prelude to a truly memorable match:

> They beat a Gloucester XI which included both E.M. and W.G. Grace on a day that both Clark and Charlie Newhall were bowling well. Grace was out to a brilliant catch by Thayer and he presented his bat to him in admiration — for the effort after the game. It took pride of place at Merion until both went up in smoke in 1896. Grace bowled unchanged and took all 14 wickets in both innings of 162 and 107 for 151 runs.[71]

After the game the Grand Old Man of Cricket, W.G. Grace, formed his opinion that the 1884 GOP team "gave a very fine batting display against second class teams. Three of them had an average of over thirty runs per innings and six more over twenty. Like the majority of amateur elevens, their weak spot was bowling, and some very heavy scores were made against them."[72] The best GOP innings of the tour was against the Gentlemen of Surrey in London at the Oval when Howard McNutt "joined Brockie at tenth drop with 75 not out to save the match for Philadelphia."[73]

In the cricket heartland of southern England, the GOP where overwhelmed by Sussex and Kent. The Kent side had the two hardest hitting batmen in England, the two Thornton brothers. Lord Harris captained the Kent side. He had visited Philadelphia in 1872 with Fitzgerald's team of amateurs. He later became president of the MCC on returning from India where he was governor of Bengal. Kent won the game played in Maidstone, by six wickets. Redemption for the GOP came against a United Services team when Scott and Thayer shared in a 160-run partnership that led to a final GOP victory for the tour. After the game there was a cricket dinner on board Admiral Nelson's HMS *Victory*.[74] The GOP's tour scorecard of eight wins, five losses and five drawn games was a superlative first effort in England. Lowry, the Merion CC bowler, "was the workhorse, taking 110 wickets for an average 12.72 during a summer of batting weather. The other eight bowlers took 176 wickets combined.... Thayer was the best all round cricketer, Clark a close third, and MacNutt fourth as he played the finest of all 317 innings played."[75] John Scott led the batting averages and George Patterson was second. On his return from England, George Newhall declared, "Cricket in America is a fact." Newhall advised those who felt the English were the sole purveyors of cricket to look to America's example:

> Brother Jonathan may enjoy this as sport heartily, but he makes more a study of it than his rival.... He, too, feels that cricket is a glorious, "noble" game, but it is no joke; it is preparation for a higher game of some sort. We have ... shown unusual traits in playing, and any innovations upon the sacred domain are resented on the bull-dog principle of rushing at all new-comers.[76]

Noting the game was expensive, as cricket grounds required five or six acres of ground manicured to look like the green on a billiard table for top-class cricket, Newhall observed that running a first-class club required an income of $2,500 a year, or $20,000 at today's rates. However, he strongly believed, "The game is worth what it costs. Of course we need a leisure class, not tramps in this country.... The credit of having raised the 'noble game' into—newspaper notice—must be conceded to Philadelphia, at present the head-quarters of cricket on this side of the Atlantic."[77]

The galvanizing effect on cricket of the GOP tour was soon demonstrated by the visit of E.J. Sanders' English side, which played eight games and lost their only game of the tour in Philadelphia, thereby becoming the first English team to lose in Philadelphia. Daniel Newhall led the scoring for Philadelphia as they racked up 200 and 178 runs against 147 and 122 per innings for Sanders' side. Sanders' second tour to Philadelphia the following year, in 1886, avenged the Philadelphia defeat when his stronger side won easily after scoring 325 in the first innings.[78] Philadelphia became a must-visit place for English teams, which started visiting Philadelphia annually from 1886. A link with the Caribbean cricket-playing islands was also established in 1886 when a team of white West Indian amateurs captained by Guy Wyatt (Georgetown CC) made a 12-game tour of Canada and the United States. Seven of the players on the West Indies team were from Jamaica, two from Barbados, and four from Demarera (Guyana). The West Indians had six wins, against the Halifax Wanderers, Ottowa CC, Toronto CC, Ontario Association XI, Merion CC and Longwood CC. They lost games to: Hamilton CC, Belmont CC and Staten Island CC; lost the return game against Merion CC; and drew the other two games against Montreal CC and the YACC. Two of the games they lost were in Philadelphia.[79] The standard of West Indian cricket impressed Philadelphian cricketers, and they lost no time in visiting the West Indies, where the GOP side defeated a strong West Indies side at Bourda in Guyana. Several GOP players on the West Indian tour were from the Haverford College Cricket Club.[80]

Play had improved at Haverford CCC since Dr. Lyons' days. When he restarted college cricket at Haverford in 1854,

> two runs at a time was almost a miracle; there was no such thing as "well held" and the "lost ball" was unheard of. A paper still preserved gives a diagram of the players in their positions in 1868. No "drives" argues no hard hitting; no third man in the slips shows that cutting was not much resorted to. A long stop to back up the wicket and a number of players on the leg side indicate bowling of a loose order. Fielding is yearly becoming a more important requirement in the selection of the team. The captain also must give more attention to the batting order; for he must adapt his men to one another as well as the varying conditions of the game.[81]

Haverford CCC first defeated Merion CC in 1869 but college faculty became concerned that high-level cricket might prove too much of a distraction for college athletes. Intercollegiate cricket was assured when Haverford beat the University of Pennsylvania in 1874. John Thayer suggested the founding of a university cricket league; this led to the founding of the Intercollegiate Cricket Association in 1874. The founding members of the ICA were Columbia, Princeton, Trinity College of Hartford, Connecticut, the University of Pennsylvania and Haverford CCC. Ohio State and Racine College in Wisconsin joined the league in 1882, but according to Lester their participation in the league did not last long because college cricket's vitality was centered in Philadelphia and they were too far away.[82] Harvard joined the league in 1887 and stayed in until 1905. Harvard attracted Haverford cricketers Brown and Scattergood when they did graduate work at the university.

Harvard's cricket schedule included Somerville, Chelsea, the Longwood CC in

Boston, Lowell CC, Haverford, the Boston Athletic Association at Longwood CC and the University of Pennsylvania, all played on Harvard's Holmes Field. Over half the cricket games were played on the American plan — a scheme adopted by the ICA at the suggestion of John Thayer, who recommended each batting side alternate after three wickets were taken. This innovation, borrowed from baseball, was designed to speed up the game. The innovation did not last because it undermined the dramatic intensity of cricket created by chasing large scores. This character-watching trait specific to cricket was one reason for cricket's popularity among British educators in the English public schools.

Robert D. Brown's cricket character combined with George Wright's versatile sporting skills as a veteran cricketer, professional baseball player and tennis coach put New England ahead of New York and second only to Philadelphia for quality cricket in the 1880s. George Wright played at Longwood CC in Boston from 1880 on, where he showed that he was "the same dashing batter and effective bowler of old.... It took the players of the New England clubs about two seasons to get the hang of his bowling."[83] With professional tennis player and cricketer Chambers tying batsmen down with his accurate bowling at the other end, George Wright was regarded as the best amateur bowler in New England. His bowling average for the seven years he played was 4.27 per wicket. Roffe, Longwood CC's wicket-keeper, said George Wright had a "very fast round arm, and when bowling around the wicket works for chances to the offside fielders.... Over the wicket he gets in some masterly work.... He is a dashing batter and for many years led the New England batting average. His 120 in 1888 against the Thorntons of Rhode Island, is the highest individual score in the New England States. As a captain he is a model, and he handles a team as but few men can."[84] The first innings total of 412 runs that Longwood CC scored against the Thorntons of Rhode Island set a New England innings record. George Wright scored 126 runs in the same game. When Young America CC visited Boston in May 1888 they beat Longwood CC by two runs after the YACC tour side had lost to Brooklyn CC and easily defeated Staten Island CC. Daniel Newhall made the highest individual score for the YACC in a low scoring game dominated by the bowlers.

> MacNutt led the Young America bowling with 5 wickets for 4 runs, and Geo Wright that of Longwood with 6 wickets for 28 runs. Rainy weather marred the pleasure of the contest.[85]

After winning at Longwood the YACC were defeated by Manhattan CC in Prospect Park but then easily defeated Staten Island in a second game at their Livingston ground. Brown, the best batsman in New England, was not available for the Longwood CC side defeated by the YACC, because he was captaining a Harvard ICA championship-winning team that comprised Quimby, Markoe, Dexter, Frost, Bulch, Hunnewell, C.F. Judson, Clyde, Myers, Paul, Norman, Keyes, Sullivan, Whiting, O.B. Judson, and Barnes.[86] Brown was selected for the GOP month-long July-through-August 1889 England tour. In the second game on July 8–9, Brown, the Harvard captain, "put on 99 runs with Storer in 37 minutes against the Gentlemen of Scotland."[87]

The tour record of the GOP was not quite as good as that of 1884. However, the second GOP team played more accomplished cricketers. They started the tour in Dublin where they played the Gentlemen of Ireland at Trinity College, then sailed the Irish Sea to Liverpool. They played in Scotland before taking on the Gentlemen of Liverpool on July 15–16; Gentlemen of Gloucester July 18–19; Surrey, July 22–23; MCC, July 25–26;

Kent, July 29–30; Hampshire, August 1–2; United Services, August 5–6; Sussex, August 8–9; and Cambridge. Henry Chadwick noted the Gentlemen of Philadelphia played

> 12 matches—won 4, lost 3, and 5 were drawn. Their batting average shows off to good advantage, as they made 4360 runs to 173 wickets lost, an average of 25.20 runs per wicket. The opponents lost in the aggregate 190 wickets, and made 4,614 runs, an average of 24.28 per wicket. The best bowling average is H.P. Bailey's, who bowled 133 overs and took 26 wickets for 371 runs, an average of 14.26 E.W. Clark, Jr., is second, with an average of 21.13, 43 wickets at a cost of 909 runs, and R.D. Brown takes third place with 22.37.[88]

Chadwick had the benefit of 40 years of first-hand experience in describing the quality of GOP cricket when he wrote,

> This much for the American exhibition of cricket in the British Isles in 1889. Now for a reminiscence of American cricket in 1859 by way of contrast.
> In 1859, being on the Tribune under Chas. A. Dana that year doing cricket for them, I was sent to Montreal to report of the first match of the All England Eleven under the veteran George Parr on the occasion of their advent as cricketers on the American cricket field. They played twenty-twos of Canada and the United States on their American tour, and of course won all their matches; but of that I have nothing to write about now. The only match I shall refer to is the one played at the old cricket field at Camac's, Philadelphia, on October 10th to the 13th, in 1859, in which they played the twenty-two of the United States.[89]

Four centuries scored by Philadelphia against tough English amateur teams was one less than the first 1884 tour, but they were scored against tougher teams. Playing for the GOP was an achievement that came from mastering well coached American Ivy League cricket, rigorous competition in the Halifax Competition, and a clear channel of promotion through the private cricket clubs.

An example of how the Ivy League university cricketers benefited from their interaction with the best players on the Philadelphia Cricket Club was provided by Patterson's captaining of Robert Brown at the Germantown CC. In 1889, Brown—who played for four teams, Harvard, Germantown CC, Longwood CC and the GOP—led the New England averages with 278 runs in 11 innings for an average of 30.88 per innings.[90] Brown's combined run production for all four clubs and the GOP in the 1889 season was over 1,000 runs. In 1890 he scored 190 runs for Harvard for average of 21.11 run per innings. Chadwick described Brown as a "fast over-arm bowler; he is a most aggressive batsman, taking every chance of making runs, but by good cricket."[91]

Harvard beat Haverford in 1890 in their best victory of the year. According to Chadwick,

> The bowling analysis in the first innings on each side showed that Garrett led for Harvard with five wickets for 18 runs, Brown getting four wickets for 19 runs. On the part of Haverford Baily took five wickets for 37 runs, and Firth five for 44. In the second innings Brown took five wickets for 12 runs and Garrett one for 16.[92]

When A.C. Garret took over the Harvard captaincy from Brown in 1891, Chadwick observed:

> Cricket this year at Harvard is flourishing, I am glad to see. Up to the middle of June Harvard's cricket team had won six of the eight games they had played. In these games the Harvard team made a total of 835 runs at a cost of the loss of 118 wickets, this yielding an average of 7.07 runs per wicket. Their opponents in the same games made but 479 runs, with

a loss of 110 wickets! An average of 4.35 per wicket. This is an excellent showing under the circumstances of the eleven having no proper cricket field of its own to train upon.[93]

Garret had played for Haverford before moving to Harvard where he also played for Germantown CC. When Garrett played for Germantown it had the best ground in Philadelphia since the Newhalls, veterans now, merged the YACC with Germantown CC, moving from their Stenton ground to Germantown CC's new ground at Manheim in 1890. Germantown CC's move from its old Niceton ground consolidated its position as the foremost cricket club in Philadelphia.

For the next decade, most international games were played at Manheim, where Daniel and George Newhall retained considerable influence. The Newhalls, seeking to extend their cricket careers that had started before the Civil War, went on to form the Philadelphia Veterans, a team that played regularly against the New York Veterans at the Columbia Oval in New York. The veterans' teams became a decided influence in maintaining cricket standards throughout the East Coast.

Garrett, a former captain of the Haverford CCC, represented the new generation of cricketers who had already made their mark. Chadwick reported that Garrett "was one of the Germantown team when they made 418 against the Young America Club.... On that day he made 30. He cuts well, using his wrists with great effect.... Medium pace round-arm bowler, with some break to leg."[94]

Harvard maintained its fine cricket program for the next 15 years. The Crimson won two more ICA tournaments in 1891 and 1892, giving up the championship silver ball to their archrival, Haverford, in 1893.

The strong link between the schools, universities and the four major cricket clubs in Philadelphia sustained the excellence of Philadelphia cricket for the next quarter-century. Philadelphia remained the only city in the U.S. capable of developing local cricketers free of expatriate notions and training. Philadelphia cricket developed its own unique talents and characteristics, just as did English and Australian cricket. Philadelphia's emphasis was on good play and good manners in the ballroom after the game. Philadelphia started the 1890s with a clear vision and young, well educated, internationally experienced players, capable of holding their own with all comers on the field and in the executive boardroom. On the field Philadelphia's top cricketers represented ultimate Victorian sportsman's ideal of grace under pressure. Their skills had been refined through competition; their talents were honed and made instinctive through regular practice. Like single malt whisky that had taken a decade to refine and mature, Philadelphia cricket was ready for the fine taste of success. The annual U.S.-versus-Canada match was not played in 1889 as GOP players were on the England tour. However, there was plenty of cricket played in Philadelphia that year, as the ICA competition became a proving ground for the new generation of cricketers. Patterson, Brown, Baily, Firth, and Garrett (who inherited the Newhalls' cricket mantle) developed first in ICA competition. The most renowned of these players, George Patterson, first played cricket with the Chestnut Hill Juniors in 1881 and graduated from Germantown Academy in 1886. The Germantown Academy was the most important Philadelphia cricket school. In 1887 it became a charter member of the Interacademic Athletic Association along with Haverford Grammar School, Penn Charter, and Rugby Academy.

The same year, Patterson scored 164 runs against the YACC for Germantown in the record-breaking innings of 418 runs on June 18, 1887, an American record. Four years earlier, on October 19, 1883, he had combined with Harvard player John Large (178 runs) in a partnership of 115 runs against the veteran Newhalls of the Young America team. Patterson was first selected for the all–Philadelphia team that played the Gentlemen of Ireland in 1888. He captained the University of Pennsylvania to the Intercollegiate Cricket Association championship in 1889. Then as captain of the Germantown Cricket Club from 1890 on, he established Philadelphia's bowling and then batting records.[95] Like Grace his cricket skills ripened slowly over six years. By 1886 Patterson consistently scored over 50 runs when he batted. Lester believed that

> when Patterson shuffled to the wicket a keen intelligence came with him. He was a batsman who wasn't going to get himself out; who could accommodate his defence to the state of the wicket; who already knew what was in your quiver, and how to shield himself against it. He presented you with a physical and intellectual problem as no other Philadelphia batsman did. He was a counterpoint for fifteen years for those batsmen in a hurry. He was a thorough workman when not scoring runs or getting wickets— deliberate, persistent, seldom brilliant, but always with a keen sense of the fine traditions of the game.[96]

George S. Patterson, through his fine example, guided Philadelphia cricket to a greatness that kept the cricket world knocking on the Quaker City's door.

4. Cricket in New York and New England from 1890 to 1920

IN AN 1890 ARTICLE TITLED "Cricket in the Metropolis" Henry Chadwick wrote optimistically of cricket's future in New York. He said,

> Not for the past twenty years has the noble game of cricket flourished in the metropolis as it did last season. Not only were there more cricket clubs in existence in the metropolitan district than ever before, but there was a marked improvement in the character of the play, as also in the personnel of the clubs.... For years the map of Central Park has been ornamented by a cricket field, but it has only been within a few years that the field in question has been allowed to be used by any club, and now that it is the clubs occupying it are obliged to put up with a very inferior condition of the field for cricket purposes, for the park officials will neither improve the turf themselves nor allow the clubs to do it at their own expense. At Prospect Park matters are very differently arranged by the Park Commissioners, as the splendid condition of the field of the Manhattan Cricket Club at the Parade Ground fully shows.[1]

Compared to Philadelphia cricket, Chadwick noted there had been two drawbacks to cricket in New York's metropolis: "One of these obstacles ... is the wearisome delays incident to its playing in the city; and the other is the 'revolving' which is connected with it; the former tires spectators, while the latter entirely destroys the esprit de corps which would otherwise prevail in the clubs."[2] In Philadelphia, games started on time as club membership was a social asset and nonpunctual cricketers were easily replaced. The New Jersey and Berkeley athletic clubs added cricket teams to those fielded in lacrosse, baseball, and football. The larger memberships of these two clubs enabled them to impose discipline on their cricketers in regard to punctuality, but most metropolitan cricket teams had no other sports memberships funding their operations and punctuality was difficult to enforce on players who relied on their jobs to fund their leisure time on the cricket field. The Metropolitan District League of New York proved its worth by punishing its member clubs with forfeiture of the game if their team was not in the field by 11:00 A.M.

In the 1890 season the Manhattan CC team, which played at Prospect Park in Brooklyn, was captained by the "redoubtable M.R. Cobb" who won the silver cup for best batsman and bowler as well as a gold medal and bat for the highest score of the season.[3]

The clubs of the Metropolitan Cricket League of New York for 1890 included the Manhattan, King's County, and Bedford of Long Island, and the New York and Cosmopolitan clubs of New York and the New Jersey Athletic Association.

The opening games of the league were picked eleven contests named East v West, the Long Island clubs comprising the eastern section and those of New York and New Jersey the western. There were two matches played on May 28, one being between the first elevens of the league clubs and the other between the second elevens. The eastern elevens won both matches, the first eleven winning theirs by 130 to 98, and the second eleven theirs by 111 to 28. The contests took place on the field at Prospect Park.

The outside clubs of the metropolis—those that are not in the league—are the St. George, Staten Island, Berkeley Athletic Club, Brooklyn, Amateur League, St. Austin's School and the Hamilton, Columbia College also has an eleven.[4]

At the end of the 1890 season,

the MANHATTAN C.C., by gaining the championship of the METROPOLITAN LEAGUE and inflicting a double defeat on the former premiers of New York, the STATEN ISLAND, showed conclusively that theirs was the first organization in the metropolis. The credit for their good record may be given to M.R. Cobb, the captain of the team.... Mr. Cobb ... is an extremely modest young man.... J. Rose, A. Wallis, B.C. Bloxsom, S.A. Noon, H.B. Coyne and F.J. Prendergast were the other members of the "M.C.C." who distinguished themselves, while Harry Tyers, the "pro," maintained his reputation, his work with the ball (30 wickets for 2.73) being an unusually brilliant performance.[5]

New York cricket tested its quality against other cities in 1891 when it participated in the Intercity League series

in which representative teams were engaged from the leading cricket centers of the country, viz: Philadelphia, Chicago, Boston, Pittsburgh, New York, Baltimore and Detroit. These seven contestants were divided into two lots: Chicago, Pittsburgh and Detroit representing the Western section, while Philadelphia, Boston, New York and Baltimore were entered from the East.... The Eastern series started with a surprise, Boston defeating New York in a game noteworthy only for the success of the bowlers.[6]

Boston's bowlers of Chambers and George Wright were more experienced than New York's players. They played for the Longwood Cricket Club in Boston, which became the foremost cricket club in Massachusetts under George Wright's influence. He and Chambers also coached tennis there. In the 1890 season, the American Cricket Annual noted that

Chambers, the popular pro., made quite a record for himself, his 122 wickets for 4.54 stamping him as one of the finest trundlers on the continent.

At HARVARD UNIVERSITY they won 7 games out of 10. Of course, R.D. Brown was the hero of the season....

At LOWELL, J.H. Comber, the captain of the team, was a host in himself, and did much to obtain the club's brilliant record.

The BROCKTON CLUB is another organization that shows energetic management....

In the PAWTUCKET CLUB, Killay has the proud distinction of being one of the few century scorers of the season. The club had a wonderful record, losing but 1 game out of 14 played.

They won the championship of the RHODE ISLAND LEAGUE, an organization that promises to do incalculable good too in the State....

The MYSTICS of Medford had a great tussle for the championship of the MASSACHUSETTS CENTRAL CRICKET ASSOCIATION ... confined to clubs within a 25-mile radius of Boston.... The fight for first place between the mystic and brockton was very close, the former winning by one point. The prizes for best batting and bowling averages presented to the Association by Mr. George Wright were won by J. Smith, mystic, and J. Kearney, CHELSEA.[7]

By 1891 there were three cricket leagues in Massachusetts. The Lawrence District League had a 16-game season between the Somerville, Fall River, Andover, Merrimac and Albion cricket clubs.[8] In the Western Massachusetts League, league teams were the Bay States of Northampton, Holyokes, and Springfields.[9] Massachusetts eastern and western sections played each other prior to taking on Rhode Island in an interstate match that Massachusetts won. Rhode Island's principal clubs were Saylesville, Ashton, Rumford, and Thornton. Other New England states with cricket teams were Vermont (Waterboro) and Maine (Sanford).

Outside New England, there was the Delaware Field Cricket Club and in Maryland, the Baltimore Cricket Club. The Baltimore CC was

> started by Randolph Winslow and John E. Carey in 1874, [and] has gradually grown, until at present it has 300 members, all of whom, with one or two exceptions, are native born. This Club deserves great credit for keeping up the game with the little opportunity they have for matches. L.K. Mallinckrodt won the batting prize last season ... while H.W. Brown was awarded the bowling trophy.[10]

By 1891, regular competition in and out of Massachusetts resulted in

> the Clubs ... playing better cricket than they realize, as ... that Club (under its new title of "Boston Athletic Association Cricket Eleven") is fast approaching the Philadelphia standard.... They successively defeated the Mystics, Brocktons, Harvards, Fall Rivers, Pawtuckets, Somervilles, twice each; and the St. Paul's, Chelseas, Lynns and Andovers, once. They also downed a strong picked Massachusetts eleven; defeated the New Jersey A.C., the Rosedales of Toronto, and the Brooklyns. Against the latter, Lott Mansfield made 132, not out, thus raising the New England record; the previous being 120, not out, by George Wright. Among so many good men it is hard to particularize, but the great success of the year was undoubtedly the bowling of Ralph Cracknell. Lott Mansfield made the excellent batting average of 29.33; Cracknell had 106 wickets at a cost of 4.03; George Wright 68 at 4.58; while the "pro" Chambers took 40 at 3.77.[11]

On September 16, 1891, Lord Hawke's England team visited North America on an eight-game tour to play six games in the United States and two in Canada. After losing its first game in Philadelphia and winning the second, Lord Hawke's team arrived in New York on October 5–6. The English team of accomplished cricketers

> contained only five who appeared regularly in first class cricket in 1891: the captain H.T. Hewett (Somerset), S.M.J. Woods (Cambridge U and Somerset), K.J. Kay (Surrey) and C.W. Wright (Notts). The remainder of the party consisted of Lord Throwley, the Hon. H.A. Milles, G.W. Ricketts, C. Wreford-Brown, K. McAlpine, J.H.J. Hornsby and G.W. Hillyard.[12]

Howard MacNutt (Germantown CC) who played on the 1889 Gentlemen of Philadelphia

Top: Lord Hawke's England team at Germantown CC in Philadelphia, 1891. Source: *Outings Magazine*, November 1890. *Bottom:* The gentlemen of Philadelphia team that played Lord Hawke's team at Germantown. The photograph was taken on the steps of the octagonal shaped cricket pavilion still used today at the Philadelphia Cricket Festival. Source: *Outings Magazine*, November 1891.

England tour, played for the Berkeley Athletic Club on his return. He played with Maxwell Cobb on the New York XVIII against Lord Hawke's team. Neither MacNutt nor Cobb excelled, as Lord Hawke's team scored 383 runs in their first innings. New York drew that match, scoring 122 and 168 for 5 in their second innings. After their drawn game in New York, Lord Hawke's tour moved on to Baltimore, which went down to a crushing defeat by an innings and 150 runs. On the fifth game of the tour against the Boston Athletic Association, which was dominated by Longwood CC players, Lord Hawke's team expected a challenge because the Longwood CC had a good 1891 domestic season.

Before playing the BAA on October 11–12, Lord Hawke had read "great reports about the bowling capabilities of Messrs Wright and Chambers, so we were scarcely taken by surprise when our first innings only produced 90 runs.... Wright displayed ... the finest cricket ... on the tour. While Lord Hawke still continued his sequence of double figure scores ... our 207 in the second innings, was the highest by an English team in Boston."[14] The Boston XII went down to a heavy 240-run defeat by Lord Hawke's XII after they scored only 29 runs in their second innings. Lord Hawke's team then went on to victory in Chicago and Ontario before returning to England on November 5.[15] Lord Hawke's North American team was stronger than the one he toured India with in 1889; that was captained by G.F. Vernon. Crowds were larger in India; 10,000 watched the first day of the most important game of the tour against the Parsis XI in Bombay.[16]

Crowds watching New York cricket were sparse in 1891 despite keen competition in the Metropolitan District League. The league was split into a first and second division of six teams each. Section one comprised Staten Island, New Jersey Athletic Club, Patterson, Manhattan, Brooklyn and Berkeley. Section two comprised King's County, New York CC, Harlem, Sons of St. George, Newark, South Brooklyn and the St. George Athletic Club. MacNutt's Berkeley CC won the league in 1891.[17]

In 1891 there was a trend for cricket clubs to reconstitute themselves as Athletic Clubs. The New Jersey AC, Staten Island CC and Baseball Club, the Longwood CC became the Boston Athletic Association and the Lowells became known as the Lowell Cricket and Athletic Association. With urbanization and industrialization representing progress, pressure for organized recreation of all forms increased amongst the rapidly expanding middle classes.

In New York, the Metropolitan District League remained the premier league though an additional New York League was established to accommodate additional teams that did not fit into the MDL schedule. William H. Thomson scored the only century in New York during 1891 with 103 for the Staten Island CC against Merion CC of Philadelphia.[18] New York's cricket future was enhanced by the emergence of the young Maxwell Cobb as a strong all-round player. Educated at Sutton Valence Grammar School in England, Maxwell Roger Cobb broke into New York cricket in 1889 just as the number of cricket games played in New York surged from 94 in 1887 to 234 by 1892. Cobb's top score in 1891 was 90 not out. During the rest of the 1890s, Cobb took 1,039 wickets for a 7.46 bowling average. Kelly, a good cricketer and future editor of the *Spalding Cricket Annual*, had the benefit of experience when he stated, "Mr. Cobb is undoubtedly the best all round cricketer in New York, having won the batting prize in the Metropolitan District Cricket League championship in 1890, 1891, 1893, 1899, and 1902, and the bowling prize in 1890, 1891, 1893, 1896, 1897, 1900, and 1901."[19]

Cobb's New York cricket career lasted over 20 years. In that time he scored 12 centuries for a first-class batting average (achieved against international teams) of 20.43 compared to 8.17 for Kelly. Both players participated in the same number of games: 18. Kelly's bowling average in these games was slightly better than Cobb's, being 17.77 per wickets with 45 wickets taken. Cobb took 44 wickets in the same number of games for a 20.15 average.[20] Between 1893 and 1912, Cobb played for five local teams: Manhattan CC, Berkeley AC, New Jersey AC, Livingston FC and the Knickerbocker CC, whose home ground in Bayonne was near the Rockefeller-owned Standard oil refinery, the largest in the world when it was built.

Founded on March 7, 1891, the New England Cricket Association also reflected the trend toward organized cricket, as it was established to coordinate competition between 15 clubs. *The American Cricketer* reported, "It was decided that it should embrace district leagues, each of which should arrange its own schedule, and the leading clubs in several districts should play against each other. George Wright, the well known ex–baseball player, was chosen president."[21]

Boston became the cricket hub of New England though cricket was also played extensively throughout New England and its adjacent states. The Makillrodt family were the backbone of the Baltimore CC, which beat the Philadelphia Cricket Club by an innings and 131 runs on June 29, 1892.[22] New Hampshire had the premier youth cricket program in the U.S. at St. Paul's School. Many St. Paul's players attended Ivy League universities where their cricket skills made them prized recruits for the Philadelphia country cricket clubs. Some of these players were on the New England XV that drew with the visiting Gentlemen of Ireland team on September 7, 1892, by scoring 120 runs to the GOI's two-innings reply of 84 and 41 runs.[23] Chambers of the Longwood Cricket Club got most of the wickets again, as he had the year before when he played for New England against Lord Hawke's English touring side.

In local 1892 competition, Boston defeated New York and performed admirably against Philadelphia as the Quakers scored 110 and 105 in their two innings compared to 83 and 93 for the Boston team.[24] Boston's strength was its bowling. The same was the case for the Manhattan CC, where Cobb ended the 1892 season with a 5.40 average, taking 32 wickets for 173 runs. Frederick Fitzmaurice Kelly was not far behind Cobb in the statistics once he arrived in New York from Chicago in 1893. Kelly succeeded Henry Chadwick as editor of *Spalding's Cricket Manual* after Chadwick's death in 1909. Like Cobb, Kelly learned his cricket in England before immigrating to the United States. Educated at St. Charles College in London's Notting Hill, Kelly took over 1,800 wickets between 1888 and 1912. In 1911 he played for the New York Veterans, taking 71 wickets for 8 runs a wicket. He had three centuries to his credit in 1897, with 100 for New Jersey versus Staten Island, 106 for the Knickerbockers versus SS *Etruria*, and 119 in 1913 for the New York Veterans versus the Philadelphia Veterans.

Outside New York cricket was also expanding. In Minnesota, the Minnesota, Como, Great Northern and Northern Pacific cricket clubs played each other. In Detroit, Michigan, the Detroit Athletic Club cricket team tied for the Detroit Association trophy with Chatham (Ontario). Ohio also sported cricket clubs located in Youngstown, New Castle and Jeanette.[25] Fred Bamford, who had played for Detroit, now captained the Los Angeles CC in southern California. Cricket's prestige as a sport attracted big patrons to the game at this time. In Pittsburgh, two of Andrew Carnegie's sons sat on the Pittsburgh CC board in 1892.[26] The cricket league in Pittsburgh organized games between four teams from East Liverpool, Glenshaw, Homewood and Wilkinsburg.[27] In Chicago, Philip Armour, a millionaire meat-packing pioneer, sponsored the Chicago Cricket Club while the Pullman Railway Car company raised $10,000 in stock to encourage organized sports participation among its workers. The Pullman Cricket Club was the most popular participant sport in Pullman and dominated cricket in Chicago as America's foremost blue collar team in the 1890s.

Intercollegiate cricket supplied recruits for senior cricket clubs. In Connecticut, Yale played against its state rival, Bridgeport, in 1891.Yale's best player and captain, Tibbetts, was educated at St. Paul's in Concord, New Hampshire.[28] In New York, *The American Cricketer* reported that "Columbia, too, has taken up the willow, and if the game thrives..., there is reason to believe that Princeton will fall into line."[29] Columbia took to cricket and played it for the next 20 years. Princeton took up cricket briefly in 1892. In New York the Metropolitan League organized games at Livingston Park (Staten Island), Prospect Park (Brooklyn), Central Park and Harlem (Manhattan Island), Paterson and Newark Bergen Point (New Jersey), Boston, and New Haven (Connecticut). Games held over this broad radius were made possible by the excellent New York and District rail system.[30]

The Gentlemen of Ireland, the first international side to tour New York in 1872, toured every two years. On their 1892 trip to America, their team was stronger than Lord Hawke's of the previous year.[31] Tours stimulated spectator interest and 1892 proved to be a banner year for sales of cricket goods by A.G. Spaulding and Bros.: "Shipments were made to Milwaukee, Duluth, Joliet, St. Paul, Minneapolis, Elgin, Paris, Texas and Iron, while their Denver house has demands from many small places."[32]

California cricket was flourishing and a cricket club had been started in Tacoma, Washington, by a Merion CC member that left Philadelphia. As cricket expanded out of its East Coast heartland, immigration to the West Coast made cricket an increasingly bicoastal affair. West and East coast teams did not play each other, preferring more affordable tours in their local hinterlands. On the West Coast, trips to Victoria and Vancouver had been made sporadically since April 1869. New York teams did not make tours of England like their Philadelphia competitors, though cricket teams in both cities had a tradition of playing against each other since 1846. As cricket expanded in the West and in Chicago, New York cricket teams became the first teams in the world to exhibit interracial sport, as West Indian immigrants took to the sport in large numbers. They played first at Prospect Park and then expanded to Cortlandt Park and the Boston area.

There were unique reasons why the West Indies became a haven for cricket. A West Indies team first toured the New York and Philadelphia in 1886. The Bermuda garrison had close links with Canada through the British armed forces and it was a mere 40-hour trip by boat to Bermuda from New York. By 1894 cricket was flourishing throughout the British West Indies, greatly encouraged by visits of English amateur teams. New York cricket at this time had expanded to 15 clubs in the Metropolitan District League and a second XI competition. The MDL's season opener at Weehawken in New Jersey was on May 6 between the Morris CC and Albion CC.[33] Albion lost to the previous season's MDL champions when they were crushed by the Staten Island Athletic Club on June 3. Snelgrove took six wickets for two runs as Albion CC were all out for 15 runs.[34] On the same day, the Electric CC First XI tied New York CC's Second XI with 32 runs each. The following week Maxwell Cobb scored 163 of 227 in the New Jersey Athletic Club first innings runs at Bergen Point in New Jersey.[35] Frank Prendergast was equally impressive on June 17 when he scored 101 not out for the Manhattan CC in Prospect Park as his home side declared their first innings closed at 198 for 4 wickets. On June 24 Cobb struck again, this time as a bowler taking five wickets for six runs while Clark did the same at his end as the Newark CC were bowled out for 14 runs at Bergen Point.[36] NJAC followed with another strong performance on July 4, when Yale University CC's archrivals, Bridgeport CC (Connecticut), were all bowled out for nine runs with Tyers taking seven wickets for four runs. Cobb finished the 1893 season with the best bowling average of his MDL career, taking 116 wickets for a 4.69 average. Cobb took over five wickets a game, breaking the coveted 100-wickets barrier in 1893. Cobb's bowling record was complemented by a brilliant batting performance. Against the visiting Elizabeth Club on August 17, Cobb and Tyers opened the batting, scoring 305 for the loss of no wicket. Tyers' (176) and Cobb's (126) opening partnership was an MDL and U.S. record. The Elizabeth CC was all out in reply for less than 60 runs in both innings.[37] Through the month of August, Cobb was unstoppable, scoring 63 and taking 7 wickets, all bowled, against Morris CC, the club he played for in the previous season.[38] Cobb's cricket won the league for the NJAC in his first season with the club. Victoria CC won the Second XI competition. With both MDL league competitions settled, the MDL selected the New York and District XVIII that played Australia at Staten Island following their arrival on the SS *Germanic* and their historic defeat by Philadelphia. When Australia, captained by wicket-keeper Blackham, played the New York and District XVIII at Staten Island on October 4–5, 1893, Hurditch, batting number 15, got the second highest score of 11 runs before he was run out in New York's first innings, of 103 runs. In the second innings, Cobb got New York's highest score with 35 runs. In the second innings, Hurditch was caught by Graham and bowled by Giffen for one run. Both Hurditch and Cobb played together on the New Jersey AC. Australia scored 216 in their first innings but the New York side managed to hold on for a draw, scoring 93 for 12. George Wright, Manhattan CC's professional at the time, also played with Cobb and Hurditch in the game, leading the bowling with 5 wickets for 76 runs in 27 overs. Cobb took 3 wickets for 43 runs in 25 overs.[39]

In the 1894 season, Frank Prendergast joined the NJAC and led the club's batting averages by season's end. Cobb took 94 wickets in 2,212 balls, almost double the 1893 average, with 8.30. Frederick Kelly, a good left-hand bowler, joined Cobb's team after his departure from Chicago a few months after the Chicago Exhibition ended. Kelly's arrival in Gotham was a boon for New York cricket, as statistics were more assiduously gathered by the keen Kelly who compiled them for Henry Chadwick (the successor editor to Jerome Flannery at the *American Cricket Annual* once A.G. Spalding and Bros. bought it). Kelly did not have much of a chance to make a strong impression against the 1894 Lord Hawke's side that visited North America in September to play five matches. Lord Hawke's tour was made at the invitation of the Germantown and Merion cricket clubs in Philadelphia, which had profited handsomely from the previous tour in 1891. Hawke brought a strong team with him to America:

> The side which was undoubtedly a first class one by English standards, consisted of Lord
> Hawke (Yorks), L.C.V. Bathurst, G.J. Mordaunt and G.R. Bardswell (Oxford U), A.J.L. Hill

(Hants), C.E. de Trafford (Leics), R.S. Lucas (Middx), G.W. Hillyard (Leics), J.S. Robinson and C.W. Wright (Notts), W.F. Whitwell (Durham) and K. McAlpine.[40]

The first game of Lord Hawke's tour in Staten Island was rained off after Lord Hawke's XII scored 289 runs in their first innings. New York did not get to bat so the game was drawn.

Except for this drawn game, Lord Hawke's team won all of its five matches. The last game, against the XV of Massachusetts at Lowell, resulted in a victory by an innings and 19 runs despite Joe Chambers 9 wickets for 77 runs, which kept Lord Hawke's first innings to 176 runs. Massachusetts' batting was weak as they were out for 53 and 104 in both innings. Hillyard took 9 for 15 for the visiting English team.[41] After his victories in North America, Lord Hawke was asked to lead the first England tour to the West Indies in January 1894. Lord Hawke was unavailable to lead another tour just three months after his trip to North America, so

> R.S. Lucas the Middlesex amateur led the party, the remainder of whom were R. Leigh-Barratt (Norfolk), R. Berens, F.W. Bush (Ex-Surrey), H.R. Bromley-Davenport, J.M. Dawson (Cambridge U), A. Priestley (MCC), R.P. Sewell (Essex), H.S. Smith-Turberville (MCC), W.H. Wakefield (Oxford U), J.H. Weatherby (MCC), M.M. Barker (MCC) and R.L. Marshall. The all amateur side was by no stretch of the imagination first-class by English standards. The trip was mainly a social one and the cricket was not taken too seriously. The team left Southampton on 16 January in the Medway and arrived in Bridgetown on 28 January.
>
> There was much interest in the opening match against Barbados and about 6,000 turned up to watch the play. A right-arm medium bowler, C. Goodman, bowled most effectively for the home side, who won the game by 5 wickets.... Travelling round the islands the team had easy wins over Antigua, St. Kitts and St. Lucia, but were beaten in a one day fixture at Vincent on a pitch totally devoid of grass.
>
> In Trinidad large crowds watched both matches, which were low scoring affairs. Trinidad won the second game, due to an innings of 77 by A. Warner, by 8 wickets. Two games were played against Demerara in Georgetown and again fair crowds watched.... The visit to Demerara was cut by three days when the boat was delayed and the team went on to Jamaica via Barbados. The passage from Barbados to Jamaica took four days.... The team arriv[ed] back in England on 1 May.[42]

The first England tour of the West Indies opened up a new frontier for cricket in the New World just as America was showing an increased love for professional sport.[43] With the MCC championing amateur sport, cricket found an American niche in what Mel Adelman defines as an area with premodern sport characteristics.[44] The slave based plantations of the West Indies had created sugar barons in eighteenth century England. Plantation culture with its feudal relationships remained intact even after the liberation of West Indies slaves in 1833. There had been no civil war forced by a rapidly industrializing North on a feudal South as in America. Cricket became the medium whereby potential conflict between the ex-slaves and the white plantation owners was resolved on the field. Resolution of potential conflict was more important, at this stage in West Indies cricket development, than money earned from professional sport. Baseball, now a fully modern sport — to use Mel Adelman's typology — with leagues, regular fixtures, paid players and corporate sponsorship had already overtaken cricket in terms of economic development. Cricket was better suited, with its premodern characteristics, to the evolutionary development of the British Empire's postmercantile economy. When the American-educated black Jamaican George Hedley was appointed captain of the West Indies team, the predominant influence of the white oligarchic plantation class in West Indies cricket was broken. C.L.R. James wrote of the psychological importance of this event and the sense of liberation black West Indians felt when it occurred. Hedley's appointment was the equivalent of the American Revolution in its liberating effect to the West Indies, without the bloodshed. Hedley became a working-class hero in the urban ghettos of Kingston, Jamaica, and throughout the whole Caribbean — ten years after Marcus Garvey, the Jamaican working-class leader of New York's black ghettos, was extradited from New York. The West Indians by 1930 played cricket in their own style and on their own terms, which reinforced the West Indian black identity as separate from that of the Afro-American. Afro-Americans colloquially referred to West Indians as King George blacks in a typology not far removed — except in the racial aspect — from the opposition of Loyalists and Rebels in the American Revolution. West Indians and Afro-Americans were cooperative in the face of the dominant white culture, but the sports they played came to reflect their different approaches to life. Cricket and basketball (invented in Indiana in 1898 by Dr. Naismith) would as the years passed prove to be similarly open to black athleticism. Both sports remain popular today within the West Indian communities of New York, Chicago, and Los Angeles and throughout the state of Florida.

West Indian players in New York and Boston carried the game forward in America once the white cricket establishment in the twentieth century, most notably in the exclusive club cricket of Philadelphia, switched to other sports such as tennis and golf. Aucher Warner (a member of the West Indian white oligarchy), who scored 77 runs in Trinidad's victory against the first England team in 1894, was the brother of Trinidad-born Sir Pelham Warner, who was soon to enjoy the social atmosphere of Baltimore and Philadelphia on his first English led tour of North America. The racial shift in North American cricket would not become obvious for another decade, as Philadelphia was much loved by English amateur teams. These teams, loaded with upper-class aspiring MCC players, basked in the social lionizing of Philadelphia's cricket clubs with their ballrooms and well established links to the Dance Assembly, put on so effortlessly as part of their summer social season.

It took a decade for West Indian teams to compete effectively against New York league sides, but once parity was achieved there was no setting back the clock. The expatriate English players — as opposed to the expatriate West Indian cricketers — in New York dominated the top levels of the game in New York through what Mark Twain labeled the Gilded Age, providing strong competition for the teams sponsored by the New York West Indian Benevolent Society. Each West Indian island had the opportunity to reaffirm its identity in the summer, playing cricket at Prospect Park for teams composed of players from St. Vincent, the Danish West Indies, Demerara (renamed British Guyana in 1910) and Jamaica. Hurditch, an MCC member, had fond memories of cricket games played in Demerara before he settled in 1893 for a decade's stay in the New York area.

Kelly, Cobb and Hurditch played on the 1895 NJAC side, which continued its strong batting performance from the 1893 season, scoring 210 for 4 in reply to Staten Island's 211 for 4 declared in the first innings before play ended in a draw. The 421-run combined total, made at Bergen Point, was scored in 4 hours and 15 minutes.[45] On July 24, Cobb scored 107 runs against St. George's AC at Bergen Point. Cobb's NJAC did not have it all its own way in 1895 as George Patterson, "America's W.G. Grace," scored 124 when the New Jersey side played the Philadelphia Cricket Club ground at Wissahickon. William Noble scored a century against the NJAC side on August 3. Nigel Druce of the visiting Oxford and Cambridge side also scored a century (121) on September 21 against an All New York side on which Cobb played at Staten Island.[46] Frank Mitchell, the honored secretary of the Cambridge University Cricket Club, started his ten-year North American touring career with the university tour. He led a side that comprised nine Cambridge men: "F. Mitchell, N.F. Druce, C.D. Robinson, W. McG. Hemingway, R.A. Studd, C.E.M. Wilson, W.W. Lowe, W. Mortimer, and H.H. Marriott; three from Oxford: F.A. Phillips, H.A. Arkwright, and J.C. Hartley; and two current county amateurs: V.T. Hill (Somerset) and F.W. Milligan (Yorkshire)."[47] The English team was considered first class, considerably stronger than the team that first visited the West Indies the year before. It left Southampton on August 24 aboard the SS *St. Louis* and then played its first game against a New York XII on September 3–4 at Staten Island. The Mitchell XII's first innings of 323 was built around Nigel Druce's 121 runs. Maxwell R. Cobb and Rokeby top scored with 73 and 66 for New York, who scored 112 in their first innings and 268 in their second. Mitchell's XII scored the required 58 runs for victory with the loss of 3 wickets, winning the game by 8 wickets.[48]

In 1896, cricket in New Jersey came of age with the formation of a separate New Jersey League comprising the following clubs: "Roseville CC, Union County CC, Forest Hills CC, Perth Amboy CC, Paterson CC, Kearney CC and Mile End CC."[49] The NJAC side stayed in the Metropolitan and District League. David Munro was voted president of the MDL and Cobb was elected to the executive committee. In 1896, a perpetual challenge cup was purchased and called the Cricket League Cup for the annual MDL champions. Victory pennants gave way to trophies at the MDL in a league that comprised Staten Island CC, New Jersey AC, Manhattan AC, New York CC and Crescent AC. The second tier of competition in the New York area was represented by the New York Cricket Association, which elected the Reverend W.S. Rainsford as their president.[50] The NYCA teams for 1896 were Harlem, St. George AC, King's County, Paterson, Brooklyn, Columbia, Manhattan and New Jersey AC. A resolution was adopted at the NYCA annual general meeting to prevent clubs with teams in either league from overlapping players for tough games. Elevens were required to declare their players' names to the secretary of the association so they did not overlap with those of the MDL. In this way the NYCA helped expand cricket experience in New York by protecting the environment for competition between lesser quality players than those found in the MDL. There was no protection for America's intercollegiate players (selected from Harvard, Yale, Columbia, and the University of Pennsylvania), who were easily defeated by a Canadian intercollegiate side in Toronto by eight wickets.[51]

Apart from Germantown CC and the NJAC sharing a victory each as representatives of the best teams in the Philadelphia and New York leagues, the big game of the 1896 season was against Australia. The selection for the New York team that faced Frank Mitchell's English university team in 1895 was made from the best players of the Metropolitan and District League. In 1896 policy selection policy changed. The NJAC team represented the MDL against the Australians at Bergen Point. It was clearly outclassed, *Outing's* commentator Arthur Inkersley noting,

The 1896 Australian cricket team which played in Philadelphia, Chicago and San Francisco. Harry Musgrove, who managed the side, also managed the first Australian baseball team to visit the United States in 1897. The Australian baseball tour failed to make an impact despite help from Arthur Goodwill Spalding after Musgrove mishandled the finances. Source: *British Sports and Sportsmen.*

> The home team started the batting, and with the exception of Tyers, the club's professional, the whole side played below their standard. The bowling of Jones, the Australian's crack trundler, was not of the quality that the local batsmen had been accustomed to, and his record, even for him, was remarkable. He took 8 wickets for 6 runs; the whole side were dismissed for 28 runs. [52]

In reply,

> The Australians were not long in putting together 253 runs, during the compilation of which Trumble, Trott and Darling gave a very good exhibition of their hitting powers, taking with equal ease all the bowling that the local players could produce: Balls were lost in the little wood just outside the grounds; others were sent sometimes over the fence, on the grand stand, and boundaries were particularly common.[53]

Australia scored 253 in their first innings after a strong opening partnership between Hugh Trumble (54) and Sam Gregory (25). Cobb clean bowled the Australian wickets' middle-order batting before Harry Trott and the left hander Joe Darling stopped the potential batting collapse with a century partnership. Kelly bowled Trott for the top score of 55 after he had mastered Cobb's bowling. Kelly was the more economical bowler of the two, taking 3 for 57 to Cobb's 3 for 68. In their second innings, the New Jersey XII faired better because "Jones had been left off the bowling list, and 126 were made, leaving the visitors easy winners by an innings and 99 runs."[54] Hurditch top scored in the NJAC second innings, with 28; Cobb scored 9 and Kelly, 27. Though Australia easily defeated New Jersey, Cobb, Hurditch and Kelly performed well enough against Australia to establish their prominence as New York's best three players in 1896. The NJAC won the inaugural Cricket League Cup in 1896, outclassing all local opposition.[55]

Strong NJAC play continued throughout the 1897 season. *Outing* reported, "The New Jersey AC have a good hold on the League Cup for another year, and at the present have an unbroken record of wins. The quality of the batting may be seen from the fact they have no less than nine batsmen with league averages of over ten runs."[56]

The NJAC margin of victory in two games against the second-best side in the MDL, Staten Island, was 100 runs or more in each game played. Cobb won the MDL bowling prize and his teammate H.C. Clarke won the batting prize for the 1897 season. The NYCA competition was less of a foregone conclusion. NJAC's second team did well, but Brooklyn CC won the association cup with an impressive 11 victories, one loss and two draws.[57] In nearby Maryland, the Baltimore CC toured Philadelphia during July in preparation for the arrival of Pelham Warner's English team.

Pelham Warner had led Lord Hawke's first tour to the West Indies in January 1897, where he topped the tour batting averages with 407 runs at 40.7 per innings. He scored 113 in Trinidad, his place of birth, much to the delight of his nanny, watching in the large crowd. The September 4, 1897, departure by Pelham Warner's team to North America was not the first cricket tour made by a West Indian–born Englishman. Warner's tour team sailed to New York on the USMS *St. Paul* out of Southampton.

The team was comprised mainly of county players including: Gilbert Jessop and W. McG. Hemingway (Gloucestershire), H.D.G. Leveson-Gower and Harry Chinnery (Surrey), H.H. Marriott and F.W. Stocks (Leicestershire), J.N. Tonge (Kent), Frank Bull (Essex), R.A. Bennett (Hampshire), J.R. Head (Middlesex) [and] A.D. Whatman (Eton Ramblers).[58]

Gilbert L. "Croucher" Jessop played cricket for Cambridge University and toured America with Plum Warner and Ranji in 1899. He was the hardest hitting English batsman of his era, his best innings coming against Australia in 1902, when he hit 104 runs in 72 minutes.

Jessop was one of three county captains on the side. The other two were Leveson-Gower of Surrey, and Warner. All three captains, Warner (Oxford), Jessop (Cambridge) and Leveson-Gower (Oxford) had won their blues at university. W. McG. Hemingway had made a previous tour of North America on Frank Mitchell's team. Hemingway was a contemporary of Jessop at Cambridge University they now played together on the Gloucester county team.

Warner's team played their first match at Livingston Park on Staten Island (New York's only club-owned cricket field), which was "rather small, but exceedingly pretty, while the pavilion and club house [were] most comfortable."[59] Turner, the *Outing* correspondent, reported that

> the visitors had matters pretty much their own way, and gained an easy victory by a margin of 244 runs. The Englishmen batted first, and finished their innings with a total of 196, Leveson-Gower heading the scores with a carefully played 42. The New Yorks were disposed of for 78, and narrowly escaped their follow-on. In their second turn at the bat the Englishmen were more at home, and a total of 249 was compiled. To this Head and Bennett contributed the lion's share, with 89 and 53 (not out) respectively. New York started their second innings with an uphill game before them. J.F. Curran (31) and M.R. Cobb (30) were the only players to make any stand, and the side were dismissed for 123.[60]

Playing Cobb for the first time, Warner rated the English expatriate as the second best all-round cricketer in the United States after John A. Lester. (George Patterson had retired during the 1896 GOP tour to England at age 34.)[61] Warner noted Cobb was "a capital bat with a very effective hook stroke, and a slow to medium right arm bowler. He is the type of bowler one would wish to see more of in America."[62] Warner saw Cobb as the main exception to New York's generally weak batting. For their part, the New York media were impressed by Gilbert Jessop's reputation as a long ball–hitter capable of striking the ball over 200 yards. After defeating the NYCC — led by the Old Carthusian Rokeby — by 244 runs, Warner's England team were dined at the Richmond Country Club. In his book *Cricket in Many Climes*, published three years after the tour in 1900, Warner wrote of how impressed by Kelly's left-arm bowling he was, and remarked,

> Cobb and Kelly bowled well for New York while Hurditch, Clark, Curran, Rokeby and Patterson batted fairly well. All round NYCC are by no means weak.... The cricket on the first day was distinctly in favour of the bowlers. Their fielding was good and Prendergast brought off two exceptional catches. On neither day did attendance exceed 800 ... a New York baseball match would attract 6–8000, especially Boston versus New York.[63]

Cobb, the leading wicket-taker for the NYCC, took seven wickets for 125 runs in the England XI's second innings, after taking five wickets in the first. He bowled the leading English batsmen of the day, Jessop and Warner, twice and Leveson-Gower the one time he was out. Cobb scored 11 and 30; Kelly, 8 and 1; and Hurditch, 19 and 7.[64] Cobb's fine play against Warner was duplicated for the NJAC team in 1897, when he took 48 wickets in the MDL season, for 525 runs and an average of 10.93.[65] Finishing his cricket career with NJAC, Cobb took 75 wickets for 649 runs for an 8.65 average in 1898, before he joined the Knickerbocker Athletic Club, which had its home ground at Bayonne, home to the world's largest oil refinery.

In Baltimore, the hospitality of the Maryland hostesses who danced the polka at lunch hour impressed Warner's team. Against the XVI of Baltimore Warner deployed all 12 of his players. Batting first, Warner's XII scored 252, Bennett contributing 64 and Hemingway 61. "All Baltimore were dismissed for 147 in their first innings. W.L. Sleeman (32), K. Mallinckrodt (29), L.K. Mallinckrodt (22), and H.M. Brune (150) were the only players to reach double figures. Stocks and Jessop did excellent work with the ball, their analyses being 8 for 29 and 5 for 28, respectively."[66]

After the Baltimore game Warner's team played twice more in Philadelphia before returning to England on October 6. Jessop and Marriott stayed behind in New York. Impressed by the standard of play in Philadelphia and great social activities in Baltimore — where aristocratic Englishmen were considered highly marriageable since the marriage of Consuelo Vanderbilt to the Duke of Marlborough and Jennie Jerome to Sir Randolph Churchill-Warner captained a second team to North America that played the NYCC at Livingston on September 21–22, 1898. Warner's second team did not have as many county players as his first, though Burnup of Kent and Frank Mitchell of Yorkshire had played previously in America. B.J.T. Bosanquet, Warner's new teammate at Middlesex, made the first of four cricket visits to the U.S. Bosanquet and John Ainsworth (Liverpool) rattled out the New York batsmen on the Livingston pitch for 49 in their first innings and 123 runs for their second innings in reply to the formidable English first innings total of 419 runs. Cobb and Kelly impressed Warner again by their bowling. Hurditch scored seven and nine and was caught and bowled by Bosanquet in both innings. Two New York players, Clark and Loehman, were brothers of famous Surrey cricketers. Loehman scored 11 and 16 runs.[67]

Cobb, Kelly and Hurditch did not have the opportunity to shine again until they played together on the New York XIV that faced the formidable Ranji's XI at Livingston Park on October 4–5, 1899. Ranji, captain of Sussex, brought Jessop, Bosanquet and Sir Arthur

B.J.T. "Bossie" Bosanquet played cricket in America four times and on both coasts. He tried out his trademark googlie ball in San Francisco before unleashing it on the Australian team that lost the Ashes to Plum Warner's team in 1903. The Australians still refer to the gogglie as a "bossie." Bosanquet played just seven times for England after graduating Oxford. He played for Middlesex on Plum Warner's team.

Priestley for return visits to the U.S.[68] Priestley had led the first English team to the West Indies, invited by Jamaica in January 1897. He refused to call off the tour after Lord Hawke let it be known he intended accepting the governor of British Guyana's invitation to play in the West Indies. Both the great Yorkshire captain and Cambridge University contemporary of Aubrey Smith (Lord Hawke) and the Lincolnshire MP (Sir Arthur Priestley) from Grantham proceeded with their tours as planned. Lord Hawke's started in

British Guyana. There were no financial losses to cover, as had been the case when Aubrey Smith and Hawke toured Australia from different cities in 1887, because players on both Priestley's and Hawke's teams were well-off amateurs. Ranji's tour to America was funded by the Associated Clubs of Philadelphia, founded in 1895 to assure that clashing schedules with visiting international teams to Philadelphia did not occur. International games in Philadelphia attracted large crowds and generated considerable profit for the clubs that hosted them. New York did not generate similar size crowds, but Staten Island CC (which Pelham Warner referred to as the NYCC in *Cricket in Many Climes*) proved able to host one international game a year from 1896 on, as the ACP organization in Philadelphia helped defray the cost of the event. Ranji's tour created a real stir in New York, because Ranji was seen as an exotic Indian prince like those portrayed by Rudyard Kipling, who had just published *The Jungle Books* at his temporary home in Brattleboro, Vermont. Ranji's side arrived in New York aboard the SS *Eturia*, where large crowds greeted him with a reception termed terrifying by one observer in this pre–pop star era. Ranji's ability to evade the press did not deter the wise cracks about the "Prince from Hindoo": "Within a day of his arrival it was announced he was searching for an American heiress, and most fantastic tales were being published about his riches and his Eastern background.... It was solemnly announced that whenever he made a century his 'royal father' sacrificed two slaves in gratitude to the Gods!"[69]

Ranji's full side comprised Bosanquet, Brann, Jessop, Llewellyn, MacLaren, Priestley, Robson, Robertson, Stoddart, Townsend, and Samuel Moses James Woods.[70] S.M.J. Woods, born near Sydney, played rugby 13 times England and cricket for Australia. Educated in England at Brighton College and at Oxford University, he played for Somerset County CC from 1888 to 1907 and captained the side in 1894.

> A player of great physique, cheery disposition, and unflinching courage, he was generally at his best against the strongest and never knew when he was beaten. Although essentially an all-rounder ... it is on his bowling that his fame will chiefly rest. He was fast an accurate and had at his command not only a deadly yorker but also a slow ball that was formidable and deceptive as any he sent down....
>
> Essentially a forcing batsman.... He used his reach, great strength and sure eye to hit at the pitch of the ball without leaving his crease. Often he knocked the most accurate bowlers off their length and he could cut any short ball with a swing of his massive shoulders and arms, sending the ball at tremendous speed past cover point.[71]

Woods had already visited America with Lord Hawke's side in 1891, toured South Africa with Hawke in 1897, and played on Sir Arthur Priestley's English West Indian side. After Ranji's game against the Philadelphia Colts was rained out, his team returned to New York. On Staten Island, the New York XIV's Maxwell Cobb scored a remarkable 77 in an opening partnership of 109 against the strongest English team ever sent to play cricket (judged a little below test quality) in America. Cobb's 77 represented over half the NYXIV first innings' total of 149, made against bowlers such as Gilbert Jessop, who proved devastating against all other New York batsmen, taking 9 for 17 in the first innings. Ranjitsinhji's XI scored 330 for 8 declared with Cobb taking 5 for 93. Cobb's brilliant bowling was made to stand up in the New York XIV's second innings as New York held on for a draw, making 132 for 11 when stumps were drawn.[72] Ranji played in three of the five games, scoring 42, 57 and 68.[73] Sir Arthur Priestley did not score many runs on the tour and was bowled for a golden duck on one occasion, but he earned his place as an after-dinner speaker who enthralled the audience, allowing the seasoned players to recuperate if they needed. As it turned out, Ranji's tour was the last before the outbreak of the Boer War, but this did not affect the prince's batting performance in county cricket, as he broke the 3,000-runs-in-a-season barrier on his return from North America. In New York, the tour represented the first time an Indian prince made headlines in sport. For the English team Stoddart headed the batting with an average of 58.50 and Jessop led the bowling with 24 wickets at the cost of 5.37 per wicket.[74] For New York, Cobb proved up to the task of batting against world class opposition; five years of competitive international games had given him sufficient seasoning to perform at the top level.

In 1900 Cobb joined the Livingston FC on Staten Island, which benefited his bowling average. Cobb's bowling average with the Knickerbockers of Bayonne in 1899 was 11.42. For Livingston FC in 1900 he took 78 wickets, for a 7.60 average.[75] The biggest cricket story of the 1900 cricket scene in New York was the improvement of West Indian batting performance. The *New York Times* reported a large crowd on hand to witness a match between the Manhattans and a picked team of West Indians at Prospect Park:

Andrew G. Stoddart batted well in San Francisco on an uneven pitch in 1881. He played for England and Yorkshire.

The West Indians had a strong batting side and succeeded in putting on 132 before they were disposed of. The light, which had been none too good all day, became execrable when the Manhattans went in to bat, and it was almost impossible to see the ball. They gave up all idea of run getting, and devoted themselves to holding up their wickets, with the result that when play eventually ceased they had scored 62 for the loss of seven wickets, and the game was drawn.[76]

The Manhattans' draw signaled the arrival of West Indian cricket on equal terms in the metropolis, though it would be another decade before it became dominant. In 1901 Cobb returned to the Knickerbockers, who played B.J.T. Bosanquet's North American

B.J.K. "Bossie" Bosanquet, inventor of the googlie. He introduced the googlie to the United States on a 1902 tour in San Francisco. Source: *British Sports and Sportsmen.*

tour team at their Bayonne, New Jersey, ground. Bosanquet's English team was considerably weaker than Ranji's 1899 North American touring side, but it contained the seasoned North American cricket tourists Frank Mitchell of Yorkshire, Arthur Priestley of Lincolnshire, and Robbie O. Schwartz, the great South African googlie bowler, who—learning at the hands of the master, Bosanquet—would become one of four googlie bowlers deployed by the South African cricket team in the first-ever triangular test tournament held in England in 1909. Frederick Kelly, who joined the Knickerbockers with Cobb and Hurditch in 1901, bowled well against Bosanquet's touring side, taking 8 for 56 in a vain effort to stave off defeat by seven wickets on October 2–3. Bosanquet's team were set 55 runs to win in an hour, which they scored in 45 minutes. The Knickerbocker XII's loss was soon avenged by a strong performance by Philadelphia in Bosanquet's fourth match of the five-game tour series, when Philadelphia overpowered Bosanquet's team with strong bowling performance by Barton King (6 for 74) and P.H. Clark (7 for 22) coupled with Lester's masterful batting.[77]

Cobb and Kelly did not benefit from touring England with strong teams like the GOP that toured England in 1903 under the captaincy of John Lester. New York cricket did not develop a touring tradition, a reflection of its more transient nature that was owing to its reliance on the largesse of the local park authorities rather than the solid financial membership found in the Philadelphia cricket clubs. In the annual New York versus Philadelphia game at Livingston Park in 1906, Philadelphia continued to dominate by their batting prowess, and Lester bowled Cobb for a duck in the July 19 game. Despite this uncharacteristic duck, Cobb and Kelly lead the white cricket establishment in New York for the next decade. Kent County CC, captained by Jack Mason and with Cuthbert James Burnup as the best batsman, easily defeated New York at Livingston on October 2–3 1903.[78] However, in 1905 Maxwell Cobb was on hand, for a strong performance against the visiting MCC side captained by Edward Mann. The MCC side was comprised entirely of university players. The fourth game against New York at Livingston Park was made close by Cobb taking 6 for 46 in the first MCC innings of 95. The MCC won by 50 runs keeping New York under 100 runs in both innings.[79] Starting in 1906, black West Indian players were selected for local international games. Cricket was perceived as a sport of enfranchisement by colonial British West Indians living in New York and in Boston. There were two black West India Cricket Club (A and B) teams, playing the New York leagues and in Boston. The West India Cricket Club won 11 of 22 games played in the Massachusetts State Cricket League, finishing third in 1906. Their best bowler, William Isaac, was the best bowler in the MSCL with a 3.96 average. The era of the West Indian quick bowler had already started on the East Coast before the First World War began. West Indian batting still needed to improve, and by the end of the decade it was on a par with the local English expatriate teams such as the NJAC.[80]

Hurditch did not play against the Australians on their next visit 16 years later in 1912, but both Kelly and Cobb did. The New York XV played the Australians on Staten Island at Livingston Park. The West Indian players in the side, John Poyer, Christopher Marshall and Frank Mahabir, showed themselves as the most capable batsmen. Columbia Oval veteran and Australian New South Wales player Arthur Hoskins also scored 10 of New York's 53 runs in their first innings. Cobb batted 11 in both New York innings and only bowled four overs, as Hoskins proved the most effective bowler with 4 wickets for 36. Kelly took 1 for 31 in 10 overs. Hurditch was still in California playing for the Santa Monica CC. He returned to the East Coast in 1913, where he founded a football team at the Belmont Cricket Club in the last year they had their grounds. By 1913 it was clear that the mantle of New York cricket leadership had passed to the West Indian community, as they scored most runs against the Australians. In 1913, when a stronger Australian side toured the United States and Canada playing 56 games, only Arthur Hoskins was selected for the combined United States and Canada team, which Australia defeated by 409 runs. Kelly and Hoskins did play together on the New York Veterans XIII that the Australians' side overwhelming defeated by 320 runs at Manor Field on August 4, 1913. Kelly scored 32 of New York's 144 to Hoskins' 17 runs.[81] A month later Hoskins and Kelly played a strong Incogniti CC from England — "about first-class." Captained by Col. C.E. Greenway, the side beat New York at Livingston Park by ten wickets on September 9–10. Arthur Hoskins was the best batman for New York, with 51 runs.[82] This last international game before the First World War in New York was remembered fondly by the Incogniti CC, which comprised mainly serving military men. It was a poignant reminder of the changed world after the First World War when they returned to play a nine-game tour in New York and Philadelphia on September 9, 1920. They arrived aboard the SS *Mauretania*, a sister ship of the SS *Lusitania*, which when torpedoed had been the *casus belli* for America's entry into the First World War on the side of the Allies in 1916. Cricket continued in New York throughout the First World War but the supply of expatriate cricketers from England and Australia was cut off during the war years. First-class cricket stopped in England because of the exigencies of war, when W.G. Grace proclaimed in 1915, that it was no longer patriotic to be playing while men were dying on the Front. The West Indian connection with cricket in New York was disrupted but not cut off, thereby establishing the new postwar reality that good cricket would be found in the nurseries of the British West Indies. These nurseries continue to supply the bulk of youngest cricketers to Florida, in the sugar cane cutting season, and to New York, where economic sinews between the Caribbean islands and the metropolis have been in place since before the American Revolution.

Top: The West Indian colored team in Prospect Park, New York, 1909. *Bottom:* Caribbean Cricket Club of Boston, 1909. Source for both: Spalding's Cricket Annual for 1909.

When baseball went nationwide through radio transmissions in 1920, American sports commentators such as Ring Lardner no longer felt any competitive pressure to mention cricket. America was triumphant and no longer a debtor nation. Cricket now flourished on the margins of American society, nurtured by its regular link with the Caribbean. As immigration patterns have changed, cricket has flourished since 1920 as a demonstration of ethnic pride, whether Indian, Pakistani, West Indian, English, Sri Lankan or, to a lesser extent, Australian. The ethnic minority cricketers in America perpetuate the same exclusivity English members of the St. George's CC did 165 years ago. They have not learned how to meld their separate cricket heritage with that of the American mainstream. Nevertheless, cricket, in being the first organized sport in America, created a unique template that has sustained it in urban environments such as New York's Prospect Park, the first of the publicly funded greenbelt areas to host the sport. Cricket has been played there, its continuity unbroken, since the end of Civil War. As an institution, cricket in New York retains its position because it played a vital role in enabling America to find its sports identity.

5. International Cricket Comes of Age in Philadelphia, 1890–1926

IN 1890 YOUNG GEORGE PATTERSON of the Germantown Cricket Club won the Childs Cup as the best bowler in Philadelphia cricket. Patterson first played cricket with the Chestnut Hill Juniors in 1881 and graduated from the Germantown Academy in 1886. The Germantown Academy was the most important cricket school in Philadelphia. It became a charter member of the Inter-Academic Athletic Association, founded in 1887, along with Haverford Grammar School, Penn Charter and Rugby. This was the year Patterson scored 164 runs in a team innings of 418 for Germantown CC versus Young America Cricket Club, an American record. Frank Bohlen (St. Paul's School) won the best batsman award in 1890.[1] According to John Lester, Frank Bohlen burst into the front rank of Philadelphia cricketers with an innings of 162 against the English Residents. In the opinion of *The American Cricketer* it was the "finest innings this side of the Atlantic." Bohlen scored his runs against professional bowlers. Also in 1890, Robert D. Brown had the best batting average in the Halifax Tournament, a tournament played between the five leading cricket clubs in Philadelphia: Germantown, Belmont, Merion, Philadelphia and Tioga.[2] Belmont CC won both the regular league and Halifax Cup competition in 1890, which was an upset because Germantown CC, having moved onto their Manheim ground for which they paid $90,000, were reckoned to have experience, tradition, organization and momentum on their side.

After sharing Germantown's Niceton grounds until 1877, the Philadelphia Cricket Club (PCC) acquired their ground at St. Martin's on Chestnut Hill when Henry W. Houston—a director of the Pennsylvania Rail Road (PRR)—arranged for the club to settle near his Wissahickon Gorge development in 1883. The real estate development was made possible by the laying of rail track into West Philadelphia by the PRR. Located opposite Houston's 300-room Chestnut Hill Hotel on West Willow Street, the St. Martin's cricket grounds became the new home of the PCC, incorporated in 1885. The mission statement for the club's articles of the corporation stated that the club was created for "the purpose of practicing and playing the game of cricket and tennis and the promotion of the health of the members ... by the exercise incident to the said game."[3] Witnesses to the establishment of the perpetual corporation were Charles Dana, A. Charles Barclay, Horace Magee and C. Stuart Patterson. The Patterson family, lawyers by profession, helped organize Philadelphia cricket, supplementing the efforts of the Newhall family, who joined Germantown CC when it merged with the Young America Cricket Club on March 17, 1890. When the Newhall family gave their loyalties to the GCC it attracted Philadelphia's top cricketers, including George Patterson. Designed by the architectural firm of McKin, Mead and Stanford White (the same firm that built the Newport Casino in Rhode Island in 1879), the Germantown CC clubhouse stood as a beacon of English country-house culture in the home of Republicanism. The PCC at St. Martin's emulated the Germantown CC in building a fine ballroom on the second floor, used for high-society weddings and balls. The balls were governed by the strict rules of the Dance Assembly, founded in 1746, and provided an opportunity for scions of successful families to strike up well considered marriages that coincidentally maintained family fortunes. According to Digby Beltzell, "The ideological rationale for the Anglo-American gentleman's right to rule was the club."[4]

The ability to play sports with effortless ease and incomparable style in a club setting became the epitome of upper-class elegance in the *La Belle Époque*. Cricket remained secure as the chosen sport of Philadelphia society when Henry James and Edith Wharton wrote on Anglophile themes in the Gilded Age. News that Philadelphia cricket was a good standard and played on some of the finest pitches in the world attracted the cricket world to its doorstep. Women sports enthusiasts who were knowledgeable cricket spectators became participants in the new sports of cycling and tennis. The American Lawn Tennis Association was founded in 1881 with support from local area cricket clubs including the PCC and GCC. In 1887, the PCC's manicured grass cricket grounds were chosen as the first site for the National Women's Lawn Tennis Championship; the event was held there until 1921 when it was moved to Forest Hills in New York. Horse shows also brought revenue to the grounds. Then in 1897 the PCC — reflecting the increasingly diversified sports interests of its members—became a founding member club of the Golf Association of Philadelphia.

The first cricket game at St. Martin's was between the Philadelphia Veterans and the Chestnut Hill Orphans' Home. The Veterans Cricketers' Association was the institutional memory for Philadelphia cricket where hallowed memories—such as of Walter Newhall's first-class century scored when he was 12 years old or Charlie Newhall's 84 against the Australians in 1878 — were passed down from one generation to the next. Though cricket had been played longer in America than in any country except England, cricket tradition remained stubbornly localized, with no national American cricket tradition or consciousness. Changing patterns of immigration and competition with new sports hampered the development of such a national consciousness, though it was not for lack of imagination, as a meeting in the GCC clubhouse on December 18, 1893, of the Philadelphia Veterans shows. At the meeting,

> the Secretary was instructed to invite the surviving members of the International Team of 1859 to be the guest of the Association at the next annual dinner and ... to collect dues of $1 per annum.

> A full statement was given of the condition of *The American Cricketer*, and the fact again

strongly emphasized that the paper did not receive proper support from the active players, the subscriptions thereto being mainly confined to the older cricketers, the result being the usual deficit at the end of the year, whereas with 500 prompt paying subscribers, all expenses could be met. [5]

George Patterson's bowling and batting performances gave the Veterans a lot to talk about. Following his 1887 record innings, he scored a century in the Germantown CC score of 631 against Rosedale CC, the first time 600 runs was exceeded in an American innings. By season's end in 1891, he took over 100 wickets and scored over 1,000 runs, becoming the first Philadelphia cricketer to achieve the "double." He led Philadelphia to the Inter-City Championship when his team beat Chicago in the final of the Inter-City Cup.[6] The competing cities included Milwaukee, Detroit, Chicago, Pittsburgh, Boston, Baltimore, and New York. Chicago had won their first match against Detroit easily:

> Batsmen of whom the East was already aware — Dr. E.R. Ogden, a former Canadian player; A. Macpherson, for some years one of the cracks of the Pittsburgh club; Bradley, the former Belmont professional; M.R. Cobb, of the Manhattans, then taking a brief residence in Chicago; and, among others, C.J. Self, J. Cummings and F.F. Kelly — combined to turn up the score to 202, to which Detroit replied with 51 and 59, being thus beaten by an innings and 92 runs. J. Horstead, Pickering, H.B. Wright and F. Bamford were the only Detroit batsmen to make much of a stand. Ogden and Kelly were the successful bowlers for Chicago. Of the latter, who in the second innings took 6 wickets for 11 runs, Philadelphia was to hear more.[7]

In the match between Boston and New York held in Boston, George Wright of Cincinnati Red Stockings fame and Chambers, the tennis professional at Longwood Cricket Club, limited New York to low totals of 45 and 50 runs:

> Thorpe, MacNutt, Fairburn and Chambers did the best batting for Boston. For New York Coulby and Lane alone got into double figures. The critics were not surprised to find Wright and Chambers performing well, as their effectiveness was known. Wright secured all ten wickets for 30 runs, and Chambers too 9 for 35.[8]

In Baltimore, Philadelphia sent down a strong squad for the June 12, 1891, game. The Baltimore Cricket Club, where the game was held, was founded in 1874, "but it was not until 1878 that the club, then quite small in membership, leased grounds at Mount Washington, also a suburb of Baltimore and situated about six miles from the city, on the Northern Central Railroad. The railroad runs numerous trains to Mount Washington, and the drive to the club, through Druid Hill Park, is a most pleasant one."[9] The Baltimore Cricket Club became the most prominent sporting club in the South, with over 200 members. Reflecting the social attitudes of the South, women had to be invited to join to the club. Once there, they earned a reputation for their great hospitality among visiting English cricket teams.[10] Philadelphia's strong batting side, which included Brockie, Bohlen, Ralston and Brewster, beat Baltimore with Cregar of Philadelphia taking 7 wickets for 27 runs. Tunstall Smith of Baltimore took 11 wickets for 90 runs.[11] After their successful visit to Baltimore, Philadelphia played Boston in Massachusetts. The game "was played on July 10 and 11 on the way to Toronto-Philadelphia sending to the Longwood grounds practically the same team that met all Canada for the international championship."[12] Philadelphia beat Boston by the small margin of 39 runs. The longer grass of the Boston outfield necessitated hard hitting, and the hard hitters were either players professionally such, or men who altered their style for the nonce, and went back instead of forward. G.S. Patterson, the Philadelphia Grace, did indeed score a hard earned 25 in the first innings against Boston, but from then on, in Toronto and Chicago, as well as Longwood, failed like his club mate Bohlen, to secure runs on a ragged wicket. For Philadelphia, A.M. Wood, Crawford Coates, Jr., N. Etting, H.C. Thayer, S. Welsh, Jr., and S. Law supplied nearly all the two totals of 110 and 105. Boston fell short with 83 and 93. The home eleven was very nearly the same as that which defeated New York, and again did Chambers prove his value, capturing 5 wickets for 35. Chambers, Wright, T. Pettit, the court-tennis champion, MacNutt and Comber did the best batting for Boston, and the match was in doubt throughout. Both sides played superbly but the Philadelphians were superior in team-work, and two magnificent one-hand catches in the second innings by A.G. Thomson and J.W. Muir, the like of which Longwood had not seen before, probably settled the matter.[13]

After defeating Boston, the Philadelphia clubs left nothing to chance in their pursuit of the cricket championship of the United States. Both Belmont and Germantown sent tours to Chicago before the championship game, and the Quaker teams found Frederick Fitzmaurice Kelly and Dr. Edward R. Ogden to be very effective bowlers. In a return visit to Philadelphia, Chicago thought they might upset the GOP side as they had defeated Germantown CC earlier in the year when they visited the Windy City. Dr. Ogden was not available for the September 11–12 game. The Philadelphia team, captained by George Patterson, comprised "F.W. Ralston, Jr., A.M. Wood, F.H. Bohlen, S. Law, C. Coates, Jr., P. Butler, F.L. Altemus, S. Welsh, Jr., H.P. Baily and H.I. Brown."[14] Chicago's team was composed as follows: "A. MacPherson (captain); C.J. Self, H.C. Wright, J.P. Dethier, J.A. Rogers, F.F. Kelly, J. Cummings, J.G. Davis, J. Langham, T. Dale and Bradley."[15] The game was played on Belmont CC's Elmwood ground. Philadelphia's more experienced players dominated their Chicago opposition, which did not have much experience playing regular two-day games:

> When the first century was passed, with only one wicket down, ... [Chicago was] already beaten, and not yet versed in the science of overtaking a long lead, allowed the lead to be made as long as the home batsmen chose.... The first three batsmen — G.S. Patterson, F.W. Ralston, Jr., and A.M. Wood — entirely broke down the bowling.... Philadelphia stayed at the wicket all day, and a little before the call of time had amassed 478 runs, the largest total ever made in a first-class match in America, and the largest number of runs ever hit off in this country in a single day. Kelly had secured 2 wickets, and those among the tail-enders for 71 runs.
>
> On the Saturday the Chicagoans took their turn to bat. The wicket had become bumpy, and greatly assisted Patterson, who was chiefly instrumental in retiring the side for 62, his average being 8 wickets for 18.... Philadelphia won the game by an innings and 359 runs.[16]

Philadelphia's crushing defeat of Chicago raised their expectations for a strong performance against the visiting English Amateur team. Philadelphia's confidence proved justified. Lord Hawke's first loss after three easy victories in North America was "a real surprise to them, and was accepted in England as betokening a gratifying advance in American cricket. When on the last day of the first match the Philadelphians were set 183 to win, the visitors had no fear of the result, and were astonished that the runs should be knocked off for two wickets. It was an equal surprise to the Philadelphians to fail so wretchedly in their second match."[17] Both games were held at Germantown CC's Manheim ground. The results were as follows: "First match, Lord Hawke's eleven, 259 and 171; Philadelphia, 248 and 183 — for two wickets. Second match, Philadelphia, 56 and 119;

Lord Hawke's eleven, 82 and 95 — for six wickets — a difference of 17 runs in the average per wicket."[18]

Following the financial success of Lord Hawke's tour, Robert Newhall became a determined advocate for international matches at Manheim, because over 22,000 spectators had turned out to see Lord Hawke's XI play two matches. Revenues from both matches improved cricket's infrastructure in Philadelphia. The Irish Gentlemen cricketers who toured in 1892 gave "glowing accounts of how they were entertained at balls and banquets, and escorted by guides to every place of interest to view the foreign sights, the most interesting being the falls of Niagara. When they arrived at Wissahickon, about six miles from the Germantown cricket club ... they were treated right royally. They were driven in carriages, drawn by four horses, to the cricket grounds each morning, and back again in the evening when the day's play was over."[19]

Working-class cricket also flourished in Pennsylvania. Three hundred miles away in Pittsburgh, the home of Andrew Carnegie's United Steel Corporation, there were four cricket teams in 1892. They played in a league against the nearby steel towns of Jeanette, New Castle, Youngtown and East Liverpool. John Schwartz was the recognized cricket dynamo in Pittsburgh and was voted president of the Western Pennsylvania League in 1892.[20]

School cricket was most developed in Philadelphia. By 1890, there were over 50 clubs playing within a 15-mile arc of city hall that took in the fairgrounds at Powelton and the junior clubs at North Broad Street near Carnac's Woods, where George Parr's All England Eleven had played in 1859.[21] Arthur Woodcock trained the Haverford College team to victory in the intercollegiate competition in 1893 over archrivals Harvard and the University of Pennsylvania, which had been unbeatable in 1890 when it had "such players of international fame as G.S. Patterson, F.H. Bohlen, A.G. Thomson, H.C. Thayer and Mac-Donald, the Australian."[22]

The 1893 college championship went to Haverford due to "the magnificent bowling of H.P. Bailey, who took 15 wickets for 29 runs.... This match was played to the so-called American plan according to which the sides change from bat to field every three outs.... Its baseball origin, however, was too evident for it to secure favor. Since this game the English custom of retiring the whole side has held its place unchallenged."[23]

Harvard won the 1894 intercollegiate cricket championship, "defeating Haverford in the final game 100 to 60. J.A. Lester alone held up the reputation of his college for a well played 38."[24]

Henry Chadwick was impressed by Harvard's cricket skills as they won 8 of 11 games played, with R.D. Brown leading the batting averages.[25] Brown's strong batting combined with that of "America's Grace," George Patterson, enabled Germantown CC to dominate the Halifax Cup. In the final, Bohlen and Patterson combined for 257 not out to defeat Merion and become the 1893 Halifax Cup champions: "Bohlen had scored 146 runs and Patterson 102 without a chance in the three hours that elapsed before the stumps were drawn, both then carrying their bats."[26]

Philadelphia cricket was deep with talent in the 1890s, as evidenced by Arthur M. Wood's individual batting record score of 228 runs set against a visiting Roanoke Virginia cricket team while playing for the Pennsylvania Railway Company XI on July 3, 1893. "Wood and McClure put on 188 runs in partnership for the fourth wicket. The inning was declared closed at the fall of the fifth wicket, the total then being 443."[27]

Wood followed up his success against Roanoke with 63 not out against a Philadelphia English Resident's side on July 28, a week after Philadelphia representative player Edward Cregar, playing for the Amateurs, scored 125 against the Philadelphia's Professionals.[28] The season of 1893 was one of prolific run scoring, with 53 centuries made in the United States and Canada, while in Philadelphia Edward Clark and George Patterson notched three apiece.[29] Brown also played that year for Longwood Cricket Club with George Wright and for the GCC in Philadelphia.

On September 29 and 30, 1893, Brown opened the batting with George Patterson when Philadelphia defeated Australia at Elmwood. Before the game, the Australian team captained by Blackham had been quarantined aboard the SS *Germanic* in New York, where "the following morning a tug was able to take the visitors off the steamer. A special train at Jersey City then conveyed the Australians directly to the new grounds of the Belmont Cricket Club, at West Philadelphia, where the opening contest of the tour took place."[30]

Philadelphia scored 525 runs in the only innings needed against Australia. This was the largest score ever against Blackham's Australians. The innings remains the highest ever scored by an American side in any international cricket game. Brown was out for 23 and Patterson run out for 56. Frank Bohlen continued his remarkable batting form by scoring 118. This remains the only American century scored against a visiting foreign team in an international contest. Only one player in the Philadelphia side scored less than double figures and that was William Scott with eight runs. Australia could only muster 199 runs in their first innings and 258 in their second, as they went down to defeat by an innings and 68 runs for their worst loss in America. King (playing in his first match against Australia) and Brown were the leading wicket takers, taking 11 wickets between them. The Australians played their next game in New York. The result was a draw against a New York and District XVIII in Central Park on October 4 and 5. Four great American players were on the New York side. They were George Wright, Maxwell R. Cobb (the first American based player to share in a 300-run partnership in 1893), Howard MacNutt (member of the 1889 GOP tour to England) and Charles Percy Hurditch. Hurditch was the only English county player on the side. He played wicket-keeper for Middlesex CC and later ushered in the golden age of Santa Monica cricket when he moved to southern California in 1909. Wright led the New York bowling with 5 wickets for 76 runs, while Cobb took 2 for 43. Cobb, New York's perennial batting champion for the decade starting in 1893, was New York's top scorer, with 35 not out in the second innings.

The Australians returned refreshed from their victory in Gotham City to beat Philadelphia at Manheim in a three-day match on October 6, 7 and 9 by 6 wickets. Bohlen was again the top Philadelphia scorer in both innings, with 33 and 54 not out in the second innings. Philadelphia scored 119 and 106 as the Australians coasted to easy victory, despite Bailey taking 7 wickets for 84 runs in the match.[31] The Australians then moved on to Boston where they played a Massachusetts XVIII in a very low scoring game at the Boston Red Sox grounds. Both George Wright and John Chambers of Longwood CC played. Chambers was the best bowler, with 7 wickets for 30 runs. The Massachusetts XVIII was out for 88 and 27 runs in each innings. They outscored the Australians (65 runs) in their first innings but collapsed in their second innings before the relentless accuracy of Giffen and Trott, who bowled unchanged for the whole innings. Next the Australians traveled to Toronto, where they defeated Canada by an innings and 70 runs before finishing off the brief tour in Detroit. The Detroit XVIII lost by an innings and 157 runs, in a game held at the Detroit Athletic Club. Opening the batting, Andrew MacPherson, who had played for the West of Scotland before joining the Chicago CC, was the best Detroit batsman, with 14 and 23. Frank Bamford, who later captained Los Angeles CC, made a pair of spectacles (two ducks or no runs in a row).

After the Australian visit it became clear to the four main Philadelphia cricket clubs that a permanent committee was needed to coordinate planning and share out the profits from charging gate receipts for the crowds of over 20,000 that watched the games. Robert Newhall, who would have preferred all international games to be held at Manheim, eventually relented and agree to sharing venues for international games between Elmwood (Belmont CC) Manheim (Germantown CC), St. Martin's (Philadelphia CC) and Merion (Merion CC). The Associated Clubs of Philadelphia (ACP) became the clearing house for international games and worked very effectively for the next ten years, as there was equal representation from the four clubs. This was as near as Philadelphia came to becoming the "Marylebone Cricket Club" of American cricket.

Cricket continued to draw large crowds in Philadelphia, as Patterson continued his torrid batting in 1894 when he scored 450 runs for one out from August 20.[32] On August 27 his George Patterson XI batted for two days for 689. This remains the highest domestic American cricket score and it was achieved during a fortnight in which Patterson scored 667 runs in three completed innings. On the basis of these batting performances it can be seen why George Patterson was called America's Grace. Patterson's achievements in Philadelphia inspired a new generation of cricketers, including John Ashby Lester, born in Ackworth in Yorkshire. On emigration from England, Lester started his American cricket career at Haverford College in 1892. In 1893 he won the Cope batting prize at Haverford with an average of 100.5 runs per innings. In 1895, he played for St. David's Cricket Club, scoring 119 not out against Belmont CC. In 1896 he played for Wayne CC where he earned a reputation as a reliable change bowler of variable place.[33] He later became Shakespeare Professor of English at Haverford. He was erudite; 50 years later, he wrote *A Century of Philadelphia Cricket*. In 1896 after winning the intercollegiate competition in May, Haverford College made their first English tour. Charles W. Alcock, who had organized the fixtures for Harry Wright's baseball tour to England in 1874, was entrusted with the fixture list. Haverford played the English public schools of Winchester, Rugby, Cheltenham, Harrow, Eton, Malvern College, Westminster and Charterhouse. The tour drew the attention of MCC president Lord Harris, who by way of encouragement to the Americans, wrote:

> I shall be out of the presidential chair of the MCC before your college team arrives, but it will be a great pleasure to me, in a humble way, to do all I can to assist in making their tour pleasant, and I shall amongst other things try to arrange at match with the MCC at Lord's. Marylebone Cricket Club always plays Eton and Harrow and other schools; so it would be quite natural for our team to play the club. Dr. W.G. Grace, Mr. R.A. Mitchell the headmaster of Clifton; Rev. M.G. Glazebrook, Headmaster of Weldon [and] Harrow; and Dr. Edmund Narre, Headmaster of Eton, are all taking an active interest in the arrangements.[34]

The experience gained from the Haverford College tour of England was invaluable for Henry Scattergood, the wicket-keeper, and Lester, who captained the side. Philadelphia-born Scattergood, who later became a lawyer, was the best wicket-keeper and certainly

John A. Lester (second from left, back row), as a member of the Ackworth Cricket Club in Yorkshire prior to immigrating to Philadelphia. Source: *British Sports and Sportsmen.*

the best connected player the Gentlemen of Philadelphia ever had on their seven tours of England. According to the *Haverford Biographical Catalogue*, Scattergood entered Haverford College in 1892, was a member of the football team and was treasurer of the tennis association in his second year. He became a member of the Haverford College First XI and won the Haines Fielding Belt as the best fielder in 1893. He was business manager of the *Haverfordian* and graduated Phi Beta Kappa with a degree in mathematics. After touring in England he attended Harvard University for a year before becoming a director of numerous business boards while president of the Union Insurance Company and the Insurance Company of the State of Pennsylvania from 1908 to 1911. Before embarking on his illustrious business career, Scattergood went to the Forsythe School, where he caught for the baseball team.[35] Scattergood's baseball skills were quickly adapted to cricket; he played on the same Haverford College team as Douglas H. Adams. Adams played on the Belmont Juniors and had one century to his credit before joining the Haverford England Tour side. He scored his 103 not out in 1896, against the Bank Clerks XI, and "was one of Haverford's representatives on the American College team, which played against the Canadian Colleges."[36]

The Haverford College Cricket team

landed in England on June 24th, and at the invitation of the Liverpool Cricket club availed themselves of two days' practice on the club grounds. After this, Captain Lester decided that his men were in sufficient form to undertake an extra match which had been arranged for them at Shrewesbury School....

> The opening match ... played on June 27th against Shrewesbury School resulted in a draw.[37]

The novelty of Haverford College's tour, the first of England by an American college, resulted in the players being given the royal treatment. At Lord's they watched Eton play Harrow and met the headmasters of 14 of England's finest public schools. Haverford College finished their 15 games with a record of four victories, four losses and seven drawn games. Their worst defeat was against Harrow on July 18, when Haverford were all out for 81 in their first innings as Harrow replied with 210 for 4 wickets, declared. Vebart and Dawson, the Harrow bowlers, then dismissed Haverford again in the second innings for a paltry 33 runs to win the game by an innings and 116 runs. Lester was the only batsman to post double figures in both innings, with 28 and 12 not out. The next game, the eleventh of the tour, went better; Haverford beat Charterhouse School at Godalming in Surrey by 92 runs. Drawing next with Eton, losing to Great Malvern, Haverford faced the Cambridge University Long Vacation XI for their last game of the tour. It was a grand finale in which "the Haverford innings brought ... splendid contributions from Lester, 136, and J.H. Scattergood, 88."[38] Haverford won the last tour game by 23 runs.

Philadelphia's senior cricket clubs also toured England in the summer of 1896. Prior to the tour, players selected for the senior tour side warmed up with intercity competition. Germantown CC visited

> New York on May 30th and played a match against a combined team from the Staten Island C.C. and New Jersey A.C. on the Staten Island grounds at Livingston. Germantown won the toss and started the batting. Until F.H. Bohlen came in their score was going slowly, but with his well played innings of 72 not out, the total was to raise to 138. This was not enough to secure victory for the visitors, and the home team put up 162 in their turn, winning by a comfortable margin. The best contributions toward the home total were C.P. Hurditch, 33; C. Byers, 24, and Lohman, 23.[39]

After losing in New York, GCC toured Halifax (in Nova Scotia, Canada) in July, where they beat the Halifax Wanderers. Their game against the Halifax Garrison was rained out. In the metropolis, Belmont easily won their first tour game against the New Jersey Athletic Club at Bergen Point by 175 runs. Then on July 17, BCC beat the Manhattan Cricket Club by 107 runs, with J. Barton King clean bowling all ten Manhattan batsmen for 20 runs. In their third and last game of the tour, BCC defeated Staten Island CC at Livingston Park by 75 runs due to a fine innings of 90 by Arthur Wood and King's fine bowling. Belmont returned to Philadelphia, where they played the visiting Staten Island Cricket Club at Elmwood on July 31 and August 1:

> Neither side were playing at full strength, but some good batting was done. Staten Island made a total of 213, Lohman playing a good innings of 97, and R.St.G. Walker gave an excellent exhibition for 51 not out. Belmont players scored well all through and ran up a total of 279, winning by a nice margin.
>   The second day the Islanders met the Germantown Zingari and had a great turn at leather hunting. Germantown kept the visitors in the field while they ran up 308 for the loss of three wickets and then declared. The Islanders were disposed of 117. The feature of the Germantown innings was the excellent score made by C.B. Warder, 140 runs.[40]

The cricket tours between New York and Philadelphia sides in the summer of 1896 were the prelude to selection for promising cricketers. Philadelphia had nine players selected for the United States side that played the Canadians in a three-day match, which might account for the smug tone of the New York–published September cricket report in *Outings* that noted:

> The principal event of the past month was the twenty-third annual match between the United States and Canada played at Philadelphia, September 4th, 5th, and 7th, and the result may have proved somewhat of a surprise to many cricketers on this side of the border, the Canadians winning by a margin of forty runs. Scoring was decidedly low throughout the match, particularly in the first two innings. Our friends in Philadelphia will need considerable brushing up before they meet the Australians. Their form shown in this match will leave them a long way behind against our visitors from the Antipodes.
>
> The Canadians started the battery, and were disposed of in fairly easy style for a total of 87. This gave the home team considerable confidence; but on going in to bat they found themselves at sea in playing the bowling of Laing and McGiverin, who disposed of them for the small total of 52. Laing took six wickets for 17 runs, and McGiverin 4 for 24. The Canadians in their second turn at the bat improved on their first innings, and a total of 117 was run up. The home team were left with 153 runs to get to, but against the bowling of Laing who was in remarkably good form, this was too much, and the team were dismissed for a total of 112. Laing in this innings took 8 wickets for 37 runs.
>
> The best bowling for the United States team was done by King and Patterson. In the first innings they took respectively 4 wickets for 38 runs and 6 for 23, and in the second, 6 for 41 and 3 for 40.[41]

Patterson, Arthur Wood, Frank Bohlen and King, the heart of Philadelphia's team, scored 43 runs between them in two innings against Canada. With just ten days to the game against Australia at Germantown, the prospects of Philadelphia putting on a good performance against the Australians looked bleak. The Australians were still smarting from the record 525 runs scored against them in 1893. *Outings* reported, "No less than eight of the team have passed the century mark once or more time during the tour.... Of the eleven who are familiar to cricketers here having played in previous matches, G.H. Trott, H. Tumble, S.E. Gregory, H. Graham, and G. Giffen are in the present team."[42] Philadelphia society did its part to soften up their Australian visitors by inviting them to balls and late night events at the Germantown, Merion and Philadelphia cricket clubs. *Outings* reported, "Dinners, dances and late hours do not tend to improve the eye, that all important organ to the first-class cricketer; though, when one thinks of the sixteen-weeks cricket that our visitors have passed through, a little diversion in the way of frivolity is most certainly excusable."[43]

King and Patterson were not in form when they played the Australians at Manheim on September 18, 19 and 21, 1896. Other members of the Gentlemen of Philadelphia had to carry the team, which lost to the Australians by 123 runs. *Outings* reported,

> Special credit is due to E.W. Clark for his two excellent not out innings. Without his help the Philadelphians would have made a sorry showing. G. Giffen gave a first class exhibition in the visitors' first innings; and in the second, J. Darling showed some of his hitting powers by placing the ball on the club house chimney; his innings of 69 included ten fours, two balls being lifted clean over the ropes. H.P. Baily and H.I. Brown shared the wickets of the visitors' first innings taking 5 for 61 and 5 for 45 respectively; in their second innings, E.W. Clark took 4 at a cost of 40. H. Trumble and G. Giffen disposed of the home team in their first innings at 4 for 50 and 5 for 67 respectively, and in the second innings G.H.S. Trott took the lion's share of wickets, 6 for 39.[44]

Australian left-hander Joe Darling's two shots over the boundary were made before the six-run rule was established. Until the rule change batsmen had to run six, which was difficult to do on the Manheim ground with its short boundary. Clark scored 38 and 35 not out as part of the GOP reply of 123 and 126 runs to the Australians' first effort of 192 and 180. Australian George Giffen accumulated the most runs in both innings with 62 and 42, though Joe Darling's second innings of 69 was the most entertaining innings, with its two chimney shots that were only given four runs apiece. After their victory, the Australians went by rail to Bergen Point where they defeated New Jersey XII before playing the GOP at Elmwood on September 25, 26 and 28. This time Giffen just missed his century when he was caught and bowled by Clark, after Iredale and Darling had opened the Australian innings with a 151-run partnership. The Australians built well on their foundation as their batsmen piled on 422 runs against Philadelphia. King led Philadelphia's bowlers taking 5 for 90 runs in 32 overs. In reply, Philadelphia was quickly in trouble when they lost both Patterson and William W. Noble for four runs. John Lester, promoted to the full Philadelphia side following his Haverford tour of England, faced a supreme test for a number three batsmen, and he buckled a little under the pressure but managed to take the score to 20 with his partner Edward W. Clark before he was beaten on the pads and out LBW to a fast ball from the world's fastest bowler, Ernie Jones. Clark tried to hold the innings together as he top scored for Philadelphia with 37. Philadelphia was all out for 144 runs and forced to follow-on. In the second innings Patterson and Noble failed again. Jones clean bowled Noble before a run was scored and Patterson made six runs before he was clean bowled by McKibbin. This time, however, Philadelphia's middle order all batted well. Lester scored a confidence enhancing 21 before he was caught hitting out to McKibbin's bowling.

The South African–born "Rattlesnake" Coates, also a recently promoted Haverford College player, scored 49 and Arthur Wood proved the value of his selection with the best Philadelphia innings of 58 before he was bowled by McKibbin. Despite the success of the new players, Lester, Wood, and Coates, this introduction of the youth movement to the senior Philadelphia side did not prevent the loss, as Philadelphia were all out for 207 in their second innings, losing the match by an innings and 71 runs. What appeared to be a devastating loss actually augured quite well for Philadelphia's third scheduled game against Australia, held at the Merion Cricket Club at Haverford on October 2, 3 and 5. This time Barton King and Percy Clark established themselves as the finest opening fast-bowling duo Philadelphia ever produced. They caught Australia by surprise, taking five wickets each as they tumbled Australia out for the low score of 121 runs. The fine bowling emboldened Patterson as captain, and he put on 91 runs with his new partner Arthur Wood who had been promoted from number seven in the batting order. Philadelphia batted confidently on the Merion wicket as their ability to handle fast bowling improved. Jones again took five wickets, but this time Philadelphia took an additional 50 runs off him as he ended his bowling analysis for the 282-run Philadelphia second innings, with 5 for 82 in 49 overs. In the Australian second innings, Edward Clark became the Philadelphia hero, taking 6 wickets for 24 runs in just 12 overs as Australia collapsed to 101 all out.[45] Philadelphia won the game by an innings and 60 runs in a wonderful confidence-building finish to the season, while Frank Iredale's Australians departed for games in Chicago and San Francisco.

The Philadelphia cricket season ended with the determination by the Associated Clubs of Philadelphia that

> with the vast improvement made in cricket at Philadelphia (and in fact everywhere in the country) since the last team visited England, there is every reason to expect very different showings will be made this year. Since the last team crossed the Atlantic the representatives of the Quaker City have laid claim to more than ordinary honors. In 1891 Lord Hawke's team suffered a defeat at their hands. In the following the year the Gentlemen of Ireland had to lower their colors when they met the Philadelphians. In 1893 the Australian team of that year lost in Philadelphia. In 1894 Lord Hawke's team was again beaten. The visiting Cambridge and Oxford team lost to home players in 1895, and in 1896 the Philadelphians gained their latest and most promising victory over the Australians.[46]

This time Philadelphia — captained by George Patterson — wanted to play the English counties to gauge their strength; it hoped this would "enable the cricket public to settle many differences of opinion with regard to the true standing of cricket in this country."[47] The team was made up of the following 14 men:

> G.S. Patterson, P.H. Clark, F.W. Ralston, F.H. Bohlen (Germantown Cricket Club), C. Coates, Jr., J.B. King, A.M. Wood, E.N. Cregar, Walter Scott (Belmont Cricket Club), H.P. Baily, H.C. Thayer (Merion Cricket Club), J.A. Lester (Haverford College Cricket Club), L. Biddle (Philadelphia Cricket Club), and F.H. Bates (Tioga Cricket Club). Patterson, Baily and Scott were on the team of '89.[48]

With the team duly selected, the 1897 cricket season in Philadelphia, New York and Boston opened on May 1. The GOP team practiced against the Philadelphia Cricket Club. Walter Scott dropped out before the tour to be replaced by H.L. Clark, who was a backup wicket-keeper for Ralston.

> The Philadelphia cricket team arrived in England June 2nd. After a few days' practice at Lords, the team made their way to Oxford for their first match against the Oxford University team, June 7th.... Owing to the heavy rainfall it was found impossible to finish even the first innings of the match, and the Philadelphians were left with 163 runs for the loss of 7 wickets. Lester had played a very fine innings of 72, not out, when game was stopped. He made a start in the right direction for repeating his great work of last season in England. His batting was very favorably commented upon by the Oxford cricketers. Ralston also came in for his fair share of praise for the fine work he had done behind the wickets. Speaking of stumpers, I regret that Dr. H.H. Brown was unable to accompany the team. The committee have done well, too, to have invited J.H. Scattergood, the Harvard stumper.[49]

Scattergood arrived in England after his Harvard CC side won the intercollegiate championship for 1897 defeating Haverford. The GOP needed help in batting in their second game against Lancashire CCC. They were all out for 86 in their second innings at Old Trafford in Manchester, for their first loss of the tour by seven wickets.

> The Lancashire captain took into consideration that the Philadelphians would hardly be in their best form so early in the tour, and dispensed with the services of Mold and Ward.... J.A. Lester again proved his ability as a batsman, with two very useful 24. H.P. Baily did the lion's share of the bowling, taking in the first innings six wickets for fifty-one runs.[50]

After their defeat at Old Trafford, the GOP team traveled to Cambridge where they came up against Gilbert Jessop, one of England's best batsmen. "The Croucher" was in for 95 minutes and scored 140 runs in an innings of 21 fours, two sixes and one five. Jessop punished King for 18 and Baily for 15 runs, in one over, outscoring Nigel Druce, a member of Frank Mitchell's 1895 Oxford and Cambridge team, which had been defeated by the GOP in Philadelphia. Druce played brilliantly, placing the ball at will for his 109, as he and Jessop scored over 200 runs in their partnership before Cambridge University were all out for 412 runs. In reply, the GOP was dismissed in both innings for less than 250 runs. Wood was the highest GOP scorer with 73, batting number two in the first innings. After their crushing defeat by Cambridge University, the fourth match of the tour brought a welcome victory.

> At Brighton (swept by ocean breezes), on June 17th, they opened their match against Sussex, a team which had among its members the celebrated Indian, Prince Ranjitsinhji, undoubtedly the foremost batsman of today.
>
> The Philadelphians batted first and compiled a total of 216 runs. Lester was again at the top of the batting list, and was well supported by King; the other did little toward swelling the total.
>
> When the Sussex team went to bat, King distinguished himself in a manner which will cause him to be envied by many another bowler who is getting his average reduced at the expense of the great Sussex bat, for he clean bowled Ranjitsinhji first ball and in short time the Counties' innings finished for the small total of 46 runs; King took seven wickets at a cost of 14 runs. Sussex had to follow on, but this time King's luck was not be repeated. Ranjitsinhji was not dismissed until 74 were placed to his credit by a beautifully played innings; W. Newham contributed 67, the innings finishing for a total of 252. This left the Philadelphians with 83 to get to win, and with Lester and Wood well set it was not long before the visitors were able to celebrate a victory by eight wickets.[51]

King took 13 Sussex wickets. John Lester, who captained him on two future GOP tours of England, believed the Sussex game marked the full emergence of King as Philadelphia's premier bowler.[52] The fifth game was at Lord's against Middlesex CCC on June 21:

> Middlesex went to bat first, and at the fall of the last wicket had run up a total of 234. Sir T.C. O'Brien was in very good form; Ford played with care, and Hayman and Webb both played an excellent innings. The visitors were not very much at home with the bat, and were disposed of for 117. In this innings Stoddart took 4 wickets for a small cost of 12 runs. The second day of the match being the Queen's Jubilee Day, everyone took a holiday, including the cricketers, and play was resumed on June 23rd. The visitors went to bat again, this time with much better results; a total of 270 was put up, Wood contributing a well-played innings of 80. Middlesex were left with 154 to make to win: this they got with the loss of three wickets, for Ford hit out in his old-time Cambridge form, and in seventy-five minutes had 112 runs to his credit.[53]

George Patterson did not play in the Middlesex game, and he dropped himself for the game against the Old Oxonians at the Oval, which the GOP lost by seven wickets though Coates had a brilliant second innings of 84. Patterson put himself back in the team for the game against Yorkshire, which was captained by his competitor of old, Lord Hawke. Philadelphia scored 225 in their first innings and had Yorkshire CCC in trouble after future England captain Francis Stanley Jackson was out for 4 runs. Rain intervened, resulting in a drawn game.

> From smoky Sheffield the Philadelphians went July 1st down to Bournemouth, where the fragrant odor of the pine trees and the morning dips in the ocean made three days of pleasure. Notwithstanding the fact their opponents, Hampshire, won the match by five wickets, the Philadelphians played good cricket and for the first time of the tour George Patterson got set playing in his old form for 88 runs; Lester also gave us another of his valuable contributions.

Had the Philadelphians held out as well in their second innings as in their first innings, Hants would have had their work cut out to win.[54]

The GOP traveled next to England's industrial heartland, the Midlands.

After three days' rest the Americans commenced the ninth match of their tour at Birmingham on July 8th against Warwickshire. This was one of the best matches of the tour, and resulted in a win (the second) for the Philadelphians by five wickets. Scoring was good on both sides, close to 1000 runs being made in the three days' play. Only one batsman in each innings left the wicket without scoring. These were undoubtedly Bohlen's days, for in both innings he scored and played well, and has considerably increased his average by adding 87 runs to his total without the loss of a wicket. Lester was once more at the top of the scoring list. King did fine work with the ball, taking twelve wickets in two innings.[55]

Philadelphia played Nottinghamshire at Trent Bridge where Patterson scored 164, the highest ever first-class innings by a Philadelphian in England. Wood scored a century (126 runs) in the same innings, as the GOP scored 421 in the first innings; the highest score of the tour. Nottinghamshire County followed-on before the game ended in a draw.

The tables were turned in the eleventh match when the Philadelphians met the county of "Graces," at Bristol on July 15th. The match finished in a victory for Gloucestershire, by an innings and 29 runs. The veteran W.G. was in fine form, and made his first hundred this season. Term being over at Cambridge, Jessop was with his county, and again treated the Americans to a century. Patterson did excellent work in both innings, in fact seemed to be quite true to his form at this time. Lester also continued his good work with the bat.[56]

Patterson scored two 50s against Gloucestershire and Lester, 62. Scattergood, fresh from his Harvard championship success, showed he could handle the pressure of playing with the senior GOP team. Batting last, he scored 13 in his first innings before he was bowled by Jessop. He was not out five in the second innings. The next game against Somerset CCC was drawn at Bath. Scattergood, the young Harvard stumper, came in for praise in the local papers, which reported that he "handled the ball so nicely that he was responsible for the dismissal of three of the Somerset team. Patterson kept up his good form to the extent of 52 runs, and Wood assisted with a carefully compiled 50. Of Somerset's total of 200, Palairet's 66 was the only good score, and this was made by first-class cricket."[57]

The remaining three games of the tour were near London. In their thirteenth match against the MCC and Ground at Lord's, the GOP were overpowered by a strong bowling side and lost the match by 227 runs. Patterson top scored with 64 before he was caught by Rawlins off Trott's bowling. Philadelphia scored 179 runs; Lester, 33; and King, 31 in reply to the MCC's 278 total. Frank Mitchell, who played on Lord Hawke's Yorkshire CCC side in 1894, scored 133 runs batting as opener for the MCC. A triple blue (rugby, soccer and cricket) at Cambridge, Mitchell had also played for Lord Hawke's England team in South Africa and for England six times at rugby, and then stayed in South Africa after fighting in the Yorkshire Dragoons during the Boer War. He returned to England as captain of the South African cricket team in 1904 and led his South African side in the Triangular Tournament with England and Australia in 1909. His cricket performances against strong Philadelphia cricket teams in the three tours he did of America in 1895 (as captain of a combined Oxford and Cambridge University side, which lost to the GOP), 1898 (with Pelham Warner), and 1902 (with Bosanquet) proved match-winning on two out of three occasions.[58]

In the scored innings the MCC total of 280 resulted in a commanding win as the GOP compiled 152 in reply. Lester scored 71. Patterson, who injured his left hand fielding a hard hit ball from Rawlins, was lost to the GOP for the last two games of the tour.

> The fourteenth match of the tour, played at Maidstone against Kent, finished July 28th, with a win for Kent, by an innings and nine runs. A previous rain had put the wickets in an easy condition, and Kent had the good fortune to run up a total of 454. By the time the Philadelphians got in, the crease was favorable to the bowler, and the Americans were all dismissed for 168; in their second attempt 277 runs were made.[59]

Lester, with four wickets against Kent CCC and two innings of 66 and 69, took over as GOP captain from Patterson. For the final game of the tour, organized by Surrey CCC secretary C.W. Alcock, the GOP returned to London's Kennington Oval to take on the Surrey County Cricket Club. Surrey CCC beat the GOP side on July 31 by 154 runs. Hayward and Abel's batting and Nice's bowling put Surrey in command. Thayer had the best innings for the GOP with 59. Surrey scored 273 and 372 and the GOP 233 and 258.

The tour was judged a success by the GOP though they only won two games, lost nine, and drew two. Playing cricket in the England accomplished the goal of improving Philadelphia cricket because the GOP had to raise the level of their game in playing more accomplished opponents. *Outings* noted,

> Although there is plenty of cricket in Philadelphia, it is all very much of the same standard, and not likely to improve a man's play, or teach him anything new after he has been associated with it for a few years. With so much inter-club cricket everyone becomes more or less familiar with the play of everyone else. Of course the international matches, which are played now almost every autumn, between the home teams and those from England, Ireland, and Australia, give us some new points; but to play the Counties on their own grounds is a far greater advantage; from an educational point of view, and particularly to play them as the games in this year's tour were arranged, with professionals included. Under the circumstances to gain a decided victory over Sussex and Warwickshire was a very creditable performance, but the match which showed the true value of the Philadelphia cricketers was undoubtedly the last of the tour, against Surrey. The exhibition they gave in this match would have been a credit to any English county....
>
> The total averages of the Philadelphians were considerably below the total averages of those men who played against them; and when one considers that only twice did their players past the century mark during the tour, and their ... opponents scored centuries ... nine times, it is not surprising there should be a difference?
>
> J.A. Lester returns the hero of the team; he made the most favorable impression in England, and deserves all the praise he got. A man who comes out of twenty-six innings with an average of 37.12 stamps himself as a first class cricketer, worthy of a place on any team. J.B. King's bowling performances were also remarkable; he took 72 wickets (twice as many as any other bowler on the team), at an average cost of 24.02.[60]

Patterson was second in the batting averages with 33.75 in 17 games; Arthur Wood was third, with 28.08. Patterson and Wood were the two centurions on the side, having both scored their centuries in the game against Nottinghamshire CCC. Cregar was second in the bowling average with 27.13, but he bowled 480 over less than King and took 23 wickets.[61]

The English tour proved to GOP players such as Lester, King, Wood and Cregar that they had the will to win at the top level. Lester improved his batting by learning from English players such as W.G. Grace, who scored 113 against the GOP playing for Gloucestershire. Lester was impressed watching Master in action. Fifty years after playing him, he wrote,

> What I saw was roast beef and Yorkshire pudding; the plain common sense that built the English constitution applied to the business of making a century....
>
> Three characteristics of the innings stand out in my memory. First was the solid base of impregnable defence on which all his scoring was founded. Between the straight bat that looked too wide for and gauge and the elephantine leg alongside, there wasn't a cranny for an off break to slip through ... then there was the uncanny placing of the balls on the leg wicket. And third was the profound respect that the old master showed when any bowler he did not know went against him. The respect lasted for perhaps an over or two overs; but W.G. had to know. He had to be satisfied what was in the bag before he ripped it open.[62]

Lester also observed Grace's bowling methods and was impressed by the variety of balls the champion bowled in an over. He kept all fingers on the ball before release but on occasion he would release a ball with the back of the hand showing to the batsman. He relied heavily on the leg break but would include a straight ball to keep the batsman on his toes. Lester considered Grace to be a googlie bowler six years before Bosanquet perfected the ball.[63] Match-winning confidence can only be obtained through playing top-level competition, and as Lester's observation of Grace showed, the lesson was absorbed by the GOP players. Philadelphia's cricket fans were keen to witness the English county

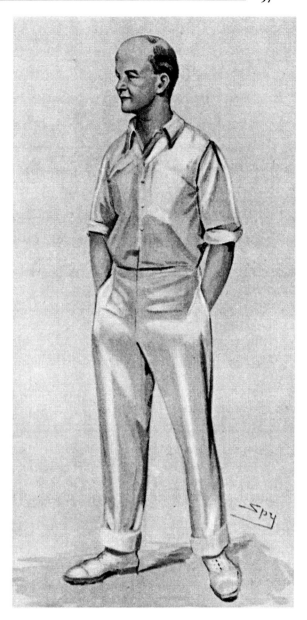

Sir Pelham "Plum" Warner captained English teams in the United States in 1897 and 1898. He was knighted for his services to cricket after becoming secretary of the MCC. During his playing career he captained Middlesex and England, returning with the Ashes Trophy from Australia in 1903.

players they had read about. Lord Hawke was not in a position to organize a team so George Patterson, at the request of the Associated Clubs of Philadelphia, invited Plum Warner, captain of Middlesex, to bring a team at the end the Philadelphia season.

Warner's team comprised A.D. Whatman (Eton Ramblers), John Reginald Head

(Middlesex), Harry Broderick Chinnery (Surrey) and Frederick George Bull (Essex), who was a canny, slow bowler who could make the ball break both ways. He took the most wickets— 43 — on the tour.[64] Henry Dudley Gresham "Shrimp" Leveson-Gower (Surrey CCC), like Pelham Warner, became a cricket institution unto himself. Later as an English test selector he helped organize and select teams for the Scarborough Cricket Festival in Yorkshire for 50 years. He was later knighted for his services to cricket. His early cricket career started

> at Magdalen College, Oxford, [where] he got his Blue as a Freshman in 1893.... A skilful right-handed batsman and a keen field, usually at cover-point or mid-off, he hit his biggest innings for the county, 155 against his former University at Oxford, in 1899, and he captained Surrey from 1908 to 1910.[65]

Prior to joining Warner's team, Leveson-Gower toured South Africa with Lord Hawke's team in 1896 to 1897. That fall, "during the American trip some of the newspapers experienced difficulty over Leveson-Gower's name and he found himself referred to in print as the 'Hyphenated Worry' and 'The Man with the Sanguinary Name.'"[66]

The wicket-keeper of the side was army captain Richard Alexander Bennett (Hampshire CC), a steady bat. William McG. Hemingway and Gilbert L. Jessop played for Gloucestershire CCC, and John Nigel Tongue for Kent CCC. Harold Henry Marriot was on his second trip to America, having first toured with Frank Mitchell's university side in 1895. After graduating from Cambridge, he played for Leicestershire CCC from 1894 to 1902.[67] Francis Wilfred Stocks was born at Market Harborough in the fox-hunting county of Leicestershire, home to the Quorn and Pytchley hunts. Stocks sported the running fox badge of Leicestershire CCC, where he was an adequate batman and fielder. According to Wisden, "His chief asset ... was left-handed, medium-paced, bowling. He had an easy delivery, and on ground which gave him any assistance was very difficult to play."[68]

The team arrived in New York on the evening of September 10 and defeated a New York representative side at Livingston on Staten Island, two days later. Warner's side then boarded the train for Philadelphia where they were met at the Broad Street Station by George Patterson, "the most famous of all Trans-Atlantic cricketers," who once he passed the bar exam and qualified as a barrister retired from cricket at 34. Warner — also trained as a lawyer — got on well with Patterson, noting in his autobiography that "G.S. Patterson, was a fine all round cricketer ... an outstanding lawyer, who was counsel for the Pennsylvania Railroad. He married a relation of Robert E. Lee.... As I knew my Stonewall Jackson, we got on well."[69]

Warner's team played their first game in Philadelphia against Robert Newhall's Philadelphia Colts XXII at Manheim. Warner reported that Robert Newhall — who was well known to cricketers around the world and founded the Colts to stem the wane of interest in cricket among the next generation —"conceived the idea of a Colts match as a means of instilling enthusiasm. ... Twenty-two fielders packed the boundary and a four was a rarity."[70]

In the second game against the GOP, 9,000 spectators turned up at the ground on the first day to see John Ashby Lester score a splendid 73 out of a GOP first innings total of 242. Thayer, Coates and William "Bill" W. Noble also scored well. The Philadelphia side took the field with light dimming and King bowled brilliantly to take nine wickets for 25 runs. King was the hero of the day when Warner's team was all out for 63 runs, in their first innings.

> The Englishmen in their follow-on showed true form, and a total of 372 was the result. Head (101), Leveson-Gower (63), Hemingway (56), and Captain Warner (51) all played a part in first-class style. The feature of the innings was the splendid work of the young Haverford wicket keeper. He was credited with no less than six dismissals, catching five and stumping one of the Englishmen. Philadelphia were left with 194 runs to get to win; this they did with the loss of six wickets, giving them a victory by four wickets.[71]

Percy Clark took 5 for 60 in the second innings, to help secure the GOP victory.[72] This victory was memorable to the Rugby- and Oxford-educated Warner because "the games were attended by great crowds, the country house set bringing large contingents; it reminded me of Eton and Harrow ... all the ladies in their smartest frocks."[73]

Having drawn over 13,000 paying spectators to the ground in two days, the Associated Clubs of Philadelphia paid for a Pullman coach to take the English team to Niagara Falls, which had been popular with cricketers since Lord Hawke and George Parr had visited decades earlier. Returning refreshed from the visit, Warner's team easily defeated Philadelphia by seven wickets when they scored 322 in their first innings with "Human Catapult" Jessop, scoring 88 runs in less than 45 minutes. Philadelphians had never witnessed such powerful hitting in all their years of watching international matches. Despite his prolific scoring, Jessop had most impact with the ball. He and Bull between them took 74 of the 100 wickets on the tour. Lester could not play for Philadelphia as he had exams at Harvard. Warner proposed a third game but Philadelphia, showing there were limits to the amount of time amateur cricketers could donate, were not able to raise a side after the longest and best schedule of international games ever played by Philadelphia cricketers.

With Philadelphia's best players doing battle against Warner's team, the Canadian team easily won the annual U.S.-versus-Canada game in 1897, by eight wickets. Stephen Goodman of New York took five of the 14 Canadian wickets but his services were temporarily lost to cricket in 1898 when he joined American forces fighting the Spanish.[74] The 1898 Halifax Cup was played at Manheim to Germantown and Merion's satisfaction where they tied for the cup. The U.S. beat Canada by an innings and one run at Merion CC. Under the presidency of Alexander Johnston Cassatt, the richest cricketer in the world, the Merion CC became a force to be reckoned with in Philadelphia cricket circles. Born in Pittsburgh in 1839, Cassatt was president of Merion CC from 1896 to his death in 1906. His estate was valued at 100 million dollars.[75] Cassatt's wealth brought him entrée to the aristocratic world of the Newhall, Patterson, Biddle and Morris families. Robert Morris' house, the biggest in Philadelphia during the American Revolution, was home to General William Howe, commander of British Forces in North America, and then to President Washington when Congress removed to Philadelphia in 1790. The Morris family was prominent in Philadelphia for over 250 years, starting from the time a Morris held the presidency of the First Federal Bank of the United States, located in Philadelphia. Christie Morris— scion of the Morris family and an excellent cricketer — gave his name to the C.C. Morris Library, the best cricket research library in the United States.[76]

Plum Warner enjoyed the aristocratic milieu of Philadelphia's cricket circles. He made an encore visit in 1898. His team left Liverpool on August 27 for Montreal, as Canadian venues were included in Warner's second tour of North America. Over half Warner's team were noncounty players but there some familiar faces in the side. Frank Michell's 133 for the MCC in an 1898 match at Lord's earned him a berth on Warner's side. He traveled two continents in 1898, as he went on Lord Hawke's South Africa tour before agreeing to Warner's Philadelphia trip. Recognized as one of Wisden's five cricketers of the year in 1901, he headed the Yorkshire CCC, batting with an average of 46.17 for an aggregate of 1,801 runs, including seven centuries — two of them not out — in consecutive matches.[77] Mitchell's teammate, six-foot-tall, Bernard James Tyndall Bosanquet of Eton and Middlesex, had not yet developed his trademark googlie ball. A powerful driver of the ball in true Eton style, Henry Altham was impressed by Bosanquet because "as a batsman, he was original. With his very short back-lift, his style was rough and unattractive, but few men could drive or hook harder, thanks to the great strength of his forearm and wrists. On difficult pitches he was particularly dangerous."[78]

Also from the Home Counties, Cuthbert James Burnup played for Kent CCC. He was one of the best opening batsmen in England. According to Wisden,

> He was a careful player who took few risks, he possessed strokes which enabled him to score on all types of pitches and he showed on occasion that he could force the pace. Eight times in a county career dating from 1896 to 1907, he exceeded 1000 runs, his best season being that of 1902 when he hit 2,048 runs including 6 of his 26 centuries, for an average of 39.38.[79]

South African–born Cyril Otto Hudson Sewell (Gloucestershire) was a hard hitting batsman and magnificent off-side fielder.[80] Vernon Tickell Hill (Somerset) was on his second visit to the United States, having played under Frank Mitchell's captaincy in 1895. He was "a left-handed batsman who drove with tremendous power and a man who could throw a cricket ball over 120 yards."[81] Barry (Middlesex) and Edward Cornwall Lee (Hampshire) rounded out the county players. Lee developed his bowling skills for Winchester and Oxford. He was selected by Warner on the strength of his 5 wickets for 57 against Cambridge University in 1898. A good tourist, he later traveled the West Indies in B.J.T. Bosanquet's side in 1902.[82] The county players were supplemented on the team by R.S.A. Warner (Oxford Authentics), E.F. Penn (Eton Ramblers) and J.L. Ainsworth (Old Marlborians). Warner's 1898 side faced a GOP side that did not have two of their top batsmen, Frank Bohlen and John Lester. Lester spent the summer playing cricket for the Santa Monica Cricket Club, which he reported for *The American Cricketer.*

Warner's first game in Philadelphia at the PCC's St. Martin's ground was against a Colts XVIII captained by John Thayer. Warner's team won the game easily by 9 wickets. After a break for a game in Baltimore, Warner's team returned to take on the GOP at Manheim where they played in front of 9,000 spectators during the three-day match. Percy Clark had the best bowling figures for the GOP with five for five in the first innings, but the tourists recovered to win the game by four wickets.[83] Warner burnished his reputation as a resourceful captain overseas, good in the clutch. American cricket had no one of Warner's ability to enhance cricket as an institution, though Henry Chadwick still provided a perspective on the game.

When Chadwick attended the New York and Philadelphia Veterans dinner, their captain John Green wrote in his October 1898 report, "With Chadwick present, whom so many of us remember as the official scorer of the grand old game away back before the war, in the columns of the *New York Clipper*, and with men around him who could recall every famous match that had been played for forty years past, the hours just flew by."[84]

As a commentator Henry Chadwick was unsurpassed in the cricket and baseball worlds. The visit of Prince Ranjitsinhji's XI was announced following an invitation by the Associated Cricket Clubs of Philadelphia. Chadwick was on hand to witness the press frenzy caused by the Prince's arrival in New York, when the team arrived aboard the Cunard liner SS *Etruria*:

> The team of amateurs he got together was the finest that had ever left England, and the only serious omission was that of C.B. Fry, who was unable to spend the time. It was composed of Ranji, Bosanquet, Brann, Jessop, Llewellyn, MacLaren, Priestley, Robson, Stoddart, Townsend and S.M.J. Woods.[85]

Ranji's team comprised the next generation of England's cricketers and they were in form. Ranji, coming off his first season as Sussex County captain, had become the first batsman to score over 3,000 runs in an English first-class season. Under Ranji's captaincy, Sussex "rose to fifth in the championship, winning seven of their matches. They were an immensely attractive batting side but with no reserve strength in their bowling."[86]

Ranji made up for his overdependence on Bland and Tate by adding Jessop, Bosanquet and S.M.J. Woods to the tour side. Inviting Arthur Priestley to join the side turned out to be a very wise move, as the member of Parliament for Grantham was a great after-dinner speaker. His services were much in demand in Philadelphia, for "he was discovered to be the only Englishman in America — perhaps in the universe — who could make after dinner speeches on equal terms with the American."[87]

Priestley lived at Hungerton Hall just six miles outside the market town of Grantham. He traveled extensively in the cricket world, captaining tours to the West Indies when he was not playing for Nottinghamshire CCC or representing his Lincolnshire constituency in the House of Commons. Priestley made the pilgrimage with the rest of the team to Niagara Falls, a welcome respite from the press corps in New York, who feasted on Ranji's exotic qualities as a "Hindoo" prince.[88]

On the field, Ranji's XI simply overpowered the opposition in New York, Philadelphia, Chicago and Toronto. Ranjitsinhji's XI played three games in the Friendly City but the first against the Philadelphia Colts XXII was rained out. C. Christie Morris played on the Colts side in his first representative game, scoring 0 and 1. In the second game played at the Merion CC on September 29–30 and October 2, the Gentlemen of Philadelphia went in to bat first, with King and Arthur Wood opening the batting. Jessop had the GOP 2 for 0 as he bowled King and Thayer for ducks. Wood then came together with Graves for a partnership of 63. Graves had recently been promoted from the Colts team, so his top score of 43 batting number four augured well for the future of Philadelphia cricket. The GOP was all out for 143. Jessop took 6 for 52 and S.M.J. Woods 4 for 53. Future England captain Archie MacLaren scored a scintillating 149 before he was bowled by Percy Clark. Brann and Townsend were dismissed for 0 and 28 which set the stage for Ranji who came in at number four with the score at 202 for 3.

> Terrific enthusiasm greeted Ranji's first appearance, although his swinging gait, so loved by the English crowds, was described by American newspaper observers as "rolling about like barrels on pins."[89]

Left: The Maharajah Jem Sahib of Nawanagar shown making his trademark leg-glance shot. As captain of the 1899 invitational side to Philadelphia, "Ranji" assembled the strongest team of English cricket talent ever to play in the United States. *Right:* Gilbert "The Croucher" Jessop. A member of Prince Ranjitsinhji's 1899 invitational side. Source for both photographs: *British Sports and Sportsmen.*

Ranji — who was not well on the trip as he suffered from asthma and was very seasick on board ship — set about the GOP bowling with gusto and put on 61 runs with his partner before he was bowled by Cregar for 57. After the maestro left, Stoddart scored 56, Jessop 64 and Bosanquet 42 as the score was run up to 435 runs. Cregar was the best GOP bowler, with 4 wickets for 47 runs in 13 overs. The GOP's second innings was worse than their first with only Graves offering any resistance before he was bowled by Stoddart for 36. The GOP were all out for 106. Ranji's XI won the game by an innings and 175 runs. That evening at the Merion Cricket Club Ranji's XI were entertained in the ballroom, where the "English team at any rate lived up to their blazers, which had been provided by Ranji. They were truly magnificent garments, in his own colours, each member having one for ordinary use and another in the form of a dinner jacket."[90]

For Ranji's team to make an impression with their blazers at Merion was a remarkable feat of showmanship in itself, because the thick green and red stripes of the Merion blazers were eye catching colors in themselves, much brighter than the Germantown black and royal blue. After dinner the English team prepared for their trip to Chicago, where they easily defeated the opposition before returning to Manheim to play the last game of the tour on October 6, 7 and 9. With Lester still unavailable for play the GOP, MacLaren opened with 52 before being bowled by King. Bart King also bowled Brann cheaply for three runs. Coming in again at number four, Ranji shared a 120-run partnership with Stoddart, scoring 68 before he was caught off Clark's bowling. Stoddart top scored for Ranji's XI with 74 runs. Ranji's XI were all out for 363 runs with Percy Clark having the best bowling figures with 5 for 77 runs in 31.2 overs. The GOP offered weak resistance as they were out in the first innings for 85 and scored 147 after following on with King top scoring for the GOP with 40. After his team defeated a Canadian side in Toronto, Ranji visited his friend Wilfred Laurier, the Liberal Party Canadian prime minister. Ranji then completed his second successive season as Sussex County captain in 1900, with another 3,065-run season, for a batting average of 87.57 per inning.

After the Ranji tour the Philadelphia cricket establishment knew they would have to improve the quality of their batting if they were to compete on level terms with international cricket teams in their prime. John Lester returned from California having evaluated cricket talent there, but it was homegrown Philadelphia talent that held the key to high quality play. The Associated Clubs of Philadelphia provided a cup for second tier competition not participating in the Halifax Cup. Teams such as St. David's, Radnor, Frankford and Ardmore improved with competition, and their better players were invited to play on the highly social but skilled teams that participated in the Halifax Cup.

John Barton King became the most respected amateur athlete in Philadelphia after George Patterson's retirement. Initially King earned his living in his father's linen and yard goods trade business, but later he sold insurance. Having well connected GOP team mates, such as wicket-keeper Henry Scattergood who married into the Morris family and later became an insurance company president, helped his career. From 1900 until his retirement in 1913, King was

> one of the finest cricketers of all time ... without question, the greatest of all of the many fine cricketers to have come from North America. He was one of the first half-dozen really great fast bowlers.... He was also a very fine batsman, not indeed world class, as was his bowling.... To this day his 344 for Belmont v Merion B stands as the North American record: he scored 39 centuries in his career and he topped 1,000 runs in a season six times, 4 of them also taking 100 wickets.... He scored 19,808 runs at an average of 36.47 and took 2,088 wickets at an average of 10.47.... He played for Tioga until 1896 when he joined Belmont, the Tioga being disbanded.... The nearest he came to cricket administration was to represent the Belmont club on the board of the American cricketer until 1912.[91]

One of Yorkshire and England's best all-time bowlers, George Hirst, credited King's "Angler," an in-swinger ball that curved late in the air, for improving his bowling. King imparted late swing by "complete relaxation and co-ordination in the absence of any tension in the arms, legs or shoulders."[92]

According to King, the Angler originated from the roundhouse pitch in baseball that was dropped by major league pitchers as it was slow and easy to hit.[93] King's innovation was the late break he imparted to the ball but saved for special occasions to offer variety from his more reliable off-break. He had C.B. Fry caught out in the slips after bowling the in-swinger to him in the nets. The second essential of King's bowling was the type of grip he used. In his own words:

> I delivered the angler from full height straight above my head, indeed at times from slightly over the left shoulder. I held the ball consistently with the seam just between first and second finger, with the thumb opposed. The third finger was just in contact with the ball, and the

fourth finger idle. It required only a slight adjustment of this grip to make the ball go straight without any curve, or to give it enough spin for a slight off-break. Control of the angler lay in the wrist and fingers.[94]

Lester remembered King's wrists and fingers being so strong that he could pinch the ball between his thumb and index finger, imparting an upward movement on the ball the height of a two-story building. King bowled fast for 20 years in a sport that generally burns out fast bowlers after five years. King credited his success as a bowler to the foil at the other end, most notably Percy Clark, who bowled off-swingers. Later he teamed most effectively with Ranji Hordern (Australia) who confused the batsmen with googlies while studying dentistry at the University of Pennsylvania.

In 1900 King remained an amateur, though professional cricketers were allowed to play in the Halifax Cup for the first time.

After not being able to muster a team for a third and deciding game against Plum Warner's XI, the ACP committee that acted as the governing body for Philadelphia cricket realized that to compete internationally professional cricketers would be needed to stiffen the ranks when amateur cricketers' workloads were heavy. Philadelphia's standard of play greatly improved when players were seasoned by overseas competition. Better cricket required more experienced umpires. Umpiring standards had to be improved as well. Robert D. Brown announced in *The American Cricketer* that umpires were to be paid from that time on and should forward their resumes to the ACP office in Germantown.[95]

The Haverford Cricket Club toured England in 1900. Locally, Philadelphia's senior cricket season started with an unblemished 178-run innings by Percy Clark batting for Germantown CC against Belmont CC. There were three intercity games against Baltimore, including one in which the whole Newhall family of 11 players took on Baltimore CC and won. One of the highlights of the 1901 Philadelphia cricket season was the opportunity to see the great Canadian player John M. Laing in action. A barrister by profession, the 6' 4" Toronto-based Canadian was the best all-rounder ever produced by Canada.

> During ten years from 1891, no team was representative without him. At a time when hundreds were completely rare he scored 11 centuries, and used his height ... as a very effective bowler. In nine matches for Canada against the United States, 63 wickets fell to him for 653 runs, his best performances being in 1895, seven wickets for 21 runs, [and] 1896, six for 17 runs and eight for 37 — 14 for 54 runs in the match. He played against many touring teams, including Lord Hawke's side in 1891 and 1894, Ireland in 1892, Australians in 1893, [and] Oxford and Cambridge in 1895. While living in Chicago in 1903, he scored 243 for Wanderers against Douglas Park.[96]

Bosanquet arrived in Philadelphia at the end of the season with a very strong bowling side that included England's most accurate bowler, Evelyn Rockley Wilson. A master at Winchester for 40 years, he was educated at Rugby and the universities of Oxford and Cambridge. Wilson preferred club cricket to county cricket so he could — as he stated — play three matches a week in the summer. He was pressed into service by Yorkshire CCC for the crucial closing summer months of the season. After visiting America, he also toured Australia, the West Indies and Argentina with the MCC. He bowled immaculate length and cleverly disguised variation of pace which made him difficult to punish. As a Wykehamist schoolmaster, he was renowned among schoolboys for his whimsical sense of humor.[97] One of the best amateur slow right-arm bowlers of his time, Wilson was paired with the great South African googlie bowler Reggie Schwartz, who learned the fine art of delivering the googlie by watching Bosanquet at work. Bosanquet's tourists won their first two games, beating the Colts XVIII and Haverford CCC but lost to the GOP by 229 runs in a game that saw R.D. Brown score a century against the visiting English amateurs.[98] King took 6 for 74 in the game and Percy Clark 7 for 22 runs. At the end of the 1901 season, King remained the best Philadelphia bowler, taking 52 wickets for 401 runs for an 8.86 per wicket bowling average. Edward Guest (Morristown CC), in the absence of John Lester who was pursuing his studies, led the batting averages with a 49.57 average from a total of 309 runs in nine innings with two not outs and a century to his credit.[99]

The Associated Clubs of Philadelphia called for another tour of England in 1903 as American cricketers proved unable to sink their regional differences and form a national organization.[100] John Lester captained the Gentlemen of Philadelphia team that arrived in England in June. A dedicated young cricketer, Christopher "Christie" Morris, who played his first international for the Philadelphia Colts XXII versus Ranji's XI, joined the GOP to strengthen the batting after the tour started. Philadelphia lost their first game to Cambridge University, in a three-day game, by six wickets at Fenner's Ground on June 10. The highlight of the game for the GOP was Lester's 96 and 41 batting number three, Bohlen's 54 and 63 as opener, and King's devastating opening spell in the second innings of 4 for 28 in eight overs. The big difference in the game was that Cambridge University batted well to number 11 and the GOP only had three batsmen capable of scoring over 50. Morris joined the team for the game against Oxford University on June 11, 12 and 13. He opened the batting with Bohlen scoring 30 in his first English game. After the GOP ended their innings with 214, King destroyed the Oxford University batting, taking seven cheap wickets as the Dark Blues were all out in their first innings for 87. Rain shortened play and the game was drawn. Traveling to Edinburgh in Scotland, the team founded the Philadelphia Pilgrims. Pilgrim membership was confined to veterans of international matches such as the Newhall family. George Patterson was universally acclaimed the first president of the Pilgrims before he returned to Philadelphia.[101] *The Grantham Journal* then reported:

> After concluding their two days' match at Edinburgh, on Tuesday, the Philadelphians traveled to Grantham on a sleeping-car; and arrived here about 5.00 A.M. on Wednesday. The car was shunted into a siding, and the cricketers were permitted to complete their night's rest. They rose shortly before seven o'clock, and received the warmest of welcomes from Mr. Arthur Priestley, who escorted them to the George Hotel; where a light breakfast was served. Then entering a break, the team were driven to Belvoir. Here they were shown around the principal rooms of the stately castle (owned by the Duke of Rutland) ... their only regret being that time did not permit a visit to the gardens.[102]

Priestley hosted the GOP at his Hungerton Hall residence. Prince Ranji stayed at Hungerton Hall on several occasions. It was located six miles outside Grantham, close to another famous Lincolnshire ancestral home, Woolsthorpe Manor, home to Sir Isaac Newton. Noting that GOP members all lived within ten miles of each other in Philadelphia and that only Wood (Nottinghamshire) and Lester (Yorkshire) were born in England, *The Grantham Journal* recorded the tour's progress and reported the Lincolnshire XVI game against the GOP:

They have won seven matches and lost only six; but as one of their victories was over Glam-organshire, which is only second rank, they have an even record.... They defeated Gloucester-shire by an innings and 26 runs, Nottinghamshire by 185 runs....

There was a good "gate" to watch the Americans, and the play was watched with intense interest. The home team went in first and made a really creditable stand against the rapid bowling and the clever fielding of the Philadelphians. Eventually, they were all out for 249, and half-an-hour before time (6.30) the visitors went to the wicket and played with a free-dom and confidence that compelled admiration. At almost every hit the ball went to the boundary, and in forty minutes the score had been carried to the respectable figure of 83 without the loss of a single wicket.[103]

The GOP players visited Harlaxton Manor that evening and Denton Manor in the morning, the home of Sir Charles G.E. Welby, Bart., CB, MP, before returning to the Grantham Cricket Club located on London Road where they picked up from the day before at 11:40 A.M.

King's fine cricket was the theme of general admiration. He began very carefully, and at length obtained complete mastery of the bowling, sending ball after ball to the boundary; but, as may be expected with such a hard hitting display, it was not without blemish, and he gave three rather easy chances, two with successive balls. His wicket did not fall until his score had reached a magnificent total of 178. At 443, Mr. Priestley declared the innings closed and the Lincolnshire men began their second innings.[104]

In declaring the innings closed, Priestley used his prerogative as honorary captain of the GOP side. The Lincolnshire XVI scored 220 runs for six wickets in the second innings to earn a draw. Gate receipts for the two-day game were 63 pounds sterling. King's 178 runs against Lincolnshire, though not considered a first-class game, was the highest score ever made by a GOP batsman in England. In their game against Nottinghamshire at Trent Bridge from June 18–20 the GOP scored over 400 runs (for nine declared) for the first time in all their tours of England. They won the match by 185 runs, thanks to a brilliant 164 runs by C. Christie Morris in the GOP second innings. Bowling was evenly shared with Percy Clark taking six to King's seven wickets. The GOP played the MCC next at Lord's on June 22–23. The MCC kept the GOP batsmen off guard, with Hearne and Mead bowl-ing unchanged as the GOP was all out for the lowest score of the tour, 65.

The second GOP innings against the MCC was little better as they were all out for 93 runs. Plum Warner and B.J.T. Bosanquet had recently returned from their two-game New Zealand winter tour with Lord Hawke's team, which beat the Kiwis by one innings on each occasion. Lord Hawke's XI played more games in Australia, but the games against New Zealand revealed that Philadelphia cricket was deeper in talent, New Zealand not becoming a test playing nation until after the Second World War. The two Middlesex County CC players, Warner and Bosanquet, were their side's leading scorers in both innings with 30 runs apiece as the MCC beat the GOP by five wickets. Against Kent, the key wicket was that of Burnup, who was dismissed cheaply for 12. Burnup had caused trouble for the GOP on their 1897 tour and when he visited Philadelphia with Plum Warner in 1898. He toured New Zealand with Lord Hawke in 1902. Now showing more confidence, the GOP beat Kent at Foxgrove Road in Beckenham on June 27, by 62 runs. They scored 311 runs against Kent in their first innings. Then King ripped through the tail end of the Kent batting order in their second innings as the GOP won by 62 runs. After their sec-ond victory, the GOP traveled to Old Trafford in Manchester where they defeated Lancashire

CCC on July 8 by nine wickets behind King's devastating bowling. King bowled Archie MacLaren for a duck in his first innings and took 9 for 62 in 25.5 overs, in the second innings. By the time the GOP arrived at Aylestone Road in Leicester they had developed into a formidable tour side. Lester scored a second century with 126 not out in the GOP first innings of 200. Lester carried his bat batting number three. King and Clark got five and four wickets between them in the first innings while Cregar picked up five in the second, as the GOP won by 101 runs. The penultimate game of the tour at the Kennington Oval saw the GOP compile another good score of 387 runs against Surrey County CC, as King scored 98 before he was run out after he mastered the world's finest fast bowler, Tom Richardson. Tom Hayward, one of the world's best batsmen, could not score enough runs to prevent the GOP winning by a 110-run margin. The GOP simply overwhelmed a strong Surrey CCC team behind the accurate bowling of King and Clark, who took five and four wickets between them in each innings. The GOP returned to America via Liverpool, with a fine winning record against county sides of five wins, two losses and one drawn. The tour's most lasting impact was on King, who transformed himself into a world class bowler, and John Lester, who proved himself a prolific batsman and excellent captain.

The 1903 tour of England was soon followed by a C.J. Burnup–led tour of Philadelphia. The first game was played at the Philadelphia Cricket Club ground at St. Martin's on Chestnut Hill on September 25, 26 and 28. Kent CCC arrived in Philadelphia without their ace bowler Hearne. The amateur Bradley proved a more than adequate replacement, taking 5 wickets for 56 runs in the first innings as the GOP were all out for 128. King scored most for the GOP, with 39 runs. Bradley mastered the GOP batting in the second innings as well, taking 4 for 70 runs, although this timer Lester, the GOP captain, mastered him, carrying his bat for 93 not out, out of a GOP total of 194. Burnup played a captain's innings in the Kent second innings, carrying his bat for one more run than Lester, scoring 94 not out. Burnup showed the rest of the Kent batsmen how to play King, who took seven Kent wickets for 39 runs in the first innings but in the second innings was restricted to 1 for 55. Following their captain's example, the remaining Kent batsmen batted solidly to knock off the GOP score with seven wickets to spare. In the second game against at the Merion Cricket Club on October 2, 3 and 4, the GOP had a disastrous first innings in which Bradley and Blythe bowled unchanged for Kent as the GOP were all out for 66 runs. Lester was the leading scorer (17 and 41) for the GOP (66 and 177) in both innings. Kent had a strong tail while Lester's team had only two other batsmen achieve double figures (A.M. Wood, 11, and P.H. Clark, 10).[105] The loss to Kent after the GOP had defeated them handily on tour was a disappointment, but the games marked the first time an English county team had played in Philadelphia.

The future of cricket in Philadelphia looked promising when the MCC in London took over the Advisory County Cricket Committee in 1904 to administer county cricket. Philadelphia's achievement in England during 1903 had earned the respect of English cricketers, and the GOP's relationship with MCC membership was generally close, so more county tours from England were anticipated. The two years between 1903 and 1905 were the high-water mark of Philadelphia cricket. Over 354 games were played in the season. Lester's *A Century of Philadelphia Cricket* graphs the dramatic drop from the peak. Cricket's decline occurred as baseball established itself as viable professional sport. The large crowds that watched the first World Series between the National (founded 1876) and American (founded 1900) leagues clubs in 1903 were from America's increasingly wealthy and rapidly expanding middle classes.

> Over the next decade, as baseball achieved an unprecedented popularity, Comiskey, Mack, and McGraw came to assume near legendary status in the emergent American mass culture. Baseball attendance doubled between 1901 and 1909, topping 7.2 million at the end of the decade. General prosperity, increased leisure time, expanded newspaper coverage, and improved urban transportation contributed toward the surge. The creation of the World Series in 1903, which pitted the champions of the two leagues in a season ending-spectacle competition, fueled further interest, producing an eagerly awaited spectacle that appealed to fans and non fans alike.[106]

In Philadelphia, Connie Mack understood his conservative fan base and he pandered to it by compelling "the Athletics to wear business suits on road trips to present a better image.... Mack, a teetotaler, 'clean as a hounds tooth,' according to the *American Magazine*..., symbolized the 'lace-curtain' Irishman, who had risen from rags to respectability."[107]

Baseball took a different path to expansion than cricket, which benefited from international rivalry as the hot climate countries of the West Indies and Australia developed cricketers used to playing fast bowling, while England's stickier wickets put the emphasis on impregnable defense and ball placement. The different topography of the pitch attracted literary men to cricket. Christopher Morley "darkling Prince Ranjitsinhji, delicate and devilish at the bat as any of Kipling's pathans. But I repeat, I know cricket only as a dream and poetry. For a hundred years cricket has been the only kind of poetry Philadelphia has really approved. And all year participants— Frankford, Germantown, Merion, and the University of Pennsylvania were poets without knowing it."[108]

On the first Haverford CCC England tour in 1896, Morley met fellow writer James Barrie, the creator of Peter Pan and the Allakbarries CC. Barrie found cricket poetic too, as he wrote how he loved "a rural cricket match in buttercup time with the boys at play, seen and heard through the trees; it is surely the loveliest scene in England and the most disarming sound."[109] Morley liked Philadelphia cricket for similar aesthetic reasons. To him cricket was

> a fairy tale. An excuse to get out into the afternoon air, the smell of apple pollen, the gentle chereography of the white pants in pattern on the turf, the batsman thumping down some pimple of sod, the bowler waving his field into some fanciful expertise..., the umpires in their long surplices.... The spectators, like professors of literature, can relish and sizzle in their membranes. These are part of cricket and part of Philadelphia.[110]

Cricket's rural and poetic idyll became past tense at Harvard in 1905 after its cricket feeder school, St. Paul's School in New Hampshire, stopped playing cricket. In Philadelphia the loss of young cricketers was not felt for ten years at the top level of Philadelphia cricket, as Pilgrim members Lester, Clark and King were still in their prime.[111] Baseball's impact was on the next generation of cricketers not steeped in the poetry of Philadelphia cricket. As baseball developed its own set of heroes it set about rewriting the history of baseball's origins. A commission created by Arthur Goodwill Spalding determined that major general Abner Doubleday was the founder.

> Spalding reveals in the final report of the commission, dated December 30, 1907, that among the motives for instigating the inquiry was a growing irritation at the "sneering comments"

he and the boys had been subject to in 1889 from English audiences in New Zealand, Australia, Ceylon, Egypt [and] England.[112]

Chadwick did not contest the findings of Spalding's commission. Chadwick edited *Spalding Baseball Manual* and starting in 1909, *Spalding's Cricket Manual*. Known as the Father of Baseball by this time in his career, Chadwick believed America needed to develop its own sporting heroes as surely as America's Founding Fathers had established America's unique republican form of government. The incorporation of baseball's founding myth into American cultural history occurred as baseball expanded its market throughout the United States.[113]

As baseball grew, Barton King added to his legend, in 1904 scoring four centuries. King won both the Childs' bowling and batting trophies for the first time since George Patterson did the double in 1890.[114] Christie Morris scored three centuries in the season, including two against Malvern and Winchester College in England on the 1904 Haverford CC tour of England. The MCC made their first official tour of the United States in 1905, the same year that Barton King established the highest individual scoring record in U.S. cricket history with 365 runs, playing for Belmont CC against the Merion CC B side.[115] Hamilton CC of Bermuda visited in 1905 with a side that included the Australians Kortlang and Bill Conyers, both first-class batsmen. In 1906, King scored over 300 runs an innings twice, including 315 of 572 runs against Merion CC B. Lester was equally prolific with six centuries. In 1907 Captain Vernon Hesketh-Pritchard, a master of underarm lob-bowling and friend of the writers Edward V. Lucas, Sir Arthur Conan Doyle and Sir James Barrie, led the second MCC side to Philadelphia; they drew both games. Hesketh-Pritchard played on Grace's London County CC at the Crystal Palace and opened the bowling for Hampshire CC. As a writer he became famous for his book *Through the Heart of Patagonia*.[116] South African googlie bowler Schwartz visited America again with Hesketh-Pritchard's side, which included Tom Hayward of Surrey CCC. Hayward endorsed a Spalding line of cricket bats made in Putney called "The Century" in same year as his American visit.[117]

Despite Harvard's withdrawal from the Inter-Collegiate Cricket Championship, competition between the remaining colleges in the cup was fierce in 1909 when the University of Pennsylvania CC toured England for the first time. The University of Pennsylvania fortunes rose with addition of accomplished googlie bowler Herbert V. Hordern to the team. "Ranji" Hordern had learned his cricket in Australia. Hordern excelled on the University of Philadelphia tour of Jamaica, becoming the leading wicket taker, following a Philadelphia season in which he took 213 wickets. He toured England with the GOP in 1908 and played for Australia versus South Africa in 1909. Hordern triumphed in the fourth and fifth tests against South Africa, taking 14 wickets and helping Australia to victory in both matches. He played in 33 first-class matches and took 217 wickets for a 16.79 average before retiring to concentrate on his dental practice in Sydney.[118]

The 1908 GOP England tour was the swan song of Philadelphia's greatest twentieth century players, John Barton King, John Lester and Herbert "Ranji" Hordern. The GOP tour was captained again by John Lester. Against Worcestershire CCC at the County Ground, New Road, Worcester, on July 9, 10 and 11, Lester made a rare duck in the first innings. But Philadelphia won the match by 95 runs after Hordern took 11 wickets for 108 runs. Arthur Wood scored a century in the second innings for the COP. The next match against Hampshire at Southampton was an easy win for the home side by an innings and 36 runs, with King taking 5 for 110 as Hampshire ran their first innings total to 463 runs. Hordern took no wickets in the game. Christie Morris showed early form with a well hit 74, Graves top scored with 76, and King opened the batting with 52. The GOP made a reasonable reply to a big score, finishing the innings with 275 runs, but their second innings fell apart as Llewellyn and Kennedy destroyed the GOP batting. Traveling to Lord's next to play Middlesex, the GOP were easily defeated when their batting failed again. They lost the July 20 game to Middlesex by seven wickets. A break in Ireland to play the national side resulted in a welcome victory as the GOP won by an innings and seven runs. Next was Derbyshire, in a game played at the County Grounds on August 17 and 18. King and Hordern overpowered Derbyshire in their first innings and they had them all out for 76. The GOP batted well in reply, scoring 247. Derbyshire scored 185 in their second innings to lose the game by nine wickets. King was the leading wicket taker with 12 wickets for 117 runs. Leaving Derbyshire's Peak District for the Midlands, the GOP played Nottinghamshire at Trent Bridge. GOP wickets fell rapidly to the combination of Wass and Hallam, as few GOP batsmen seemed capable of scoring. Nottinghamshire won the game by 130. This time there were no centuries against Nottinghamshire as there had been in 1903. After losing to Nottinghamshire, the GOP played Kent County on August 27, 28 and 29 at Canterbury and lost by four wickets. GOP nemesis Burnup was not playing for Kent on the occasion, but the GOP had a disastrous second innings in which Frank Woolley and Bill Fairservice bowled unchanged over 21 overs, dismissing the GOP for a lamentably low score of 37 runs. The game proved to be a good win for Kent as they had to overcome an 86-run deficit from the first innings as Lester took three of six Kent wickets to make the match exciting. The tour ended with King achieving an 8.86 average and taking over 100 first-class wickets. He finished the season atop the English bowling averages with a record that remained unbroken until 1958, when H.L. Jackson of Derbyshire beat it.

In 1909 the Gentlemen of Ireland toured Philadelphia. King clean bowled all ten of their players for 33 runs including the not out batsman, who survived because of a no-ball. This was the third time in his career that King took all ten wickets in an innings. However, King's brilliant success as a bowler did not result in an invitation to the first triangular tournament between South Africa, England and Australia, organized by the Imperial Cricket Conference under the chairmanship of Lord Harris. Philadelphia was not rankled by the exclusion, as Philadelphia teams received visits from the First All Bermuda team. In 1911 Germantown CC toured England in the summer. These games proved good preparation for the visit of the Australian test side in 1912.

The Australian side was weak as many of its best players had dropped out, refusing to accept the contract terms of the recently established Australian Cricket Board. The days of individual entrepreneurs organizing tours were over; revenues from international cricket games helped support county or state cricket development in South Africa, Australia, England and Philadelphia. The Australian Cricket Board persuaded "Syd Gregory, still battling the effects of his bankruptcy, to take over the captaincy of the 1912 team at the age of 42. The team Gregory took to England is widely recognized as the worst Australia has ever sent away, and had only nine wins in 37 matches."[119]

The Australian team's best batsmen, Macartney and Bardsley, returned directly to

Australia and did not play in a six-game tour of Canada and the U.S. The weakened Australian team lost by two runs to the GOP in a one-day match at Manheim: "The Philadelphians scored 185 and 74, Australia 122 and 135, in a celebrated victory for American cricket due largely to Barton King, who took 5 for 40 and 4 for 38 in both Australian innings."[120]

In the second game the GOP was beaten by 45 runs at Merion CC. King was the dominant player on the GOP side. Lester had retired from competitive cricket by this time and King followed him in 1913. He did not play against the much stronger Australian side that visited America and Canada in 1913 and played 58 games including three in Philadelphia, where they easily beat the best Philadelphia had to offer.

The 1913 Australian tour of Canada and America was unique because it was the first tour dedicated to playing the whole North America continent, including West Coast games in Vancouver (British Columbia) and California. The tour actually started in Vancouver and after crossing Canada started its American portion with three games against the Coloured West Indian team. Arthur Mailey, who was recommended by Victor Trumper — one of the finest Australian batsmen of all time — for a slot on the American tour, became the leading organizer of the 1932 Australian tour to America. The 1913 team comprised Austin Diamond as captain, Charlie Macartney, Arthur Mailey, Warren Bardsley, Syd Emery, Les Cody, Percy Arnott, Jack Crawford, Granville ("Jimmy") Down, Gordon Campbell, Herbie Collins and Edgar Mayne.[121] H.A. Furness' 106 not out against Australia at Manheim on June 21, 1913, for the GOP, was the only century scored against the Australians. Despite Furness' great innings, Australia won the game easily by an innings and 178 runs after Bardsley scored 117 runs in a first Australian innings of 521 runs.[122] Philadelphia scored 124 and 219 in their two innings. The Australians' only defeat of their 53-game tour came against Germantown after ten successive wins in Pittsburgh, Bermuda, Rhode Island, and New York.[123] The Australian players planned a second tour in 1914 because they enjoyed their romp across North America so much, but the Australian Cricket Board blocked it in favor of a South African tour that was cancelled once the First World War began.

Cricket continued in Philadelphia throughout the First World War, but starved of first-class competition and new recruits from the schools, the game lost its great personalities such as John Barton King and John Lester. Christie Morris still turned cricketing heads, and the strong Philadelphia cricket tradition kept the game alive until 1926 when the last Halifax Cup was played. The international first-class Philadelphia cricket tradition was sustained after the First World War when the Philadelphia Pilgrims faced the MCC and top English club teams such as the Incogniti CC. However, when the Australians dusted off their 1913 tour plans in 1932, Philadelphia's world renowned hospitality toward cricketers lay dormant in the teeth of the Great Depression, and the Australians headed for Hollywood instead.

6. A Century of Cricket in and Around Chicago, 1836–1936

CHICAGO, THE GEM OF THE PRAIRIE, started life as a stockaded trading post on marshy ground near Lake Michigan called Fort Dearborn.[1] The fort's small garrison was wiped out by an Indian attack during the War of 1812. When the village of Chicago was formally recognized in 1833 there were 100 inhabitants. Less than two decades after Chicago was incorporated in 1836, a local Kentish XI defeated a Chicago XI in 1850. During the 1850 decade Chicago cricket was played every year but not on a regular league basis. Chicago and Milwaukee played their first intercity cricket game in 1854 at Union Park. In 1857, a British Consul's XI was defeated by the Chicago Cricket Club, followed on June 25 by a victory against Captain Oldenshaw's XI. The CCC rounded off the season with a victory against the Union Cricket Club at Union Park in August. In 1858 the Prairie Cricket Club won city bragging rights in 1858 with a victory over the CCC at their ground located at the intersection of West Madison and Loomis streets. Both clubs combined in 1859 to defeat the visiting Cincinnatus Cricket Club on June 3 and Cleveland on June 22 and 23. In 1860 the Republican Convention that nominated Abraham Lincoln as candidate for president was held in Chicago. In background pieces about the convention, the *Chicago Tribune* reported that there was no baseball but the Prairie Cricket Club defeated St. Louis in St. Louis by 20 runs. Once the Civil War started, the Prairie Cricket Club kept cricket going in Chicago by playing "married" versus "nonmarried" games on May 25, 1861.[2]

Chicago's population had grown to 120,000 people by the time Anthony Trollope, traveling the U.S. by rail in 1862, noted that Cincinnati on the Ohio and St. Louis on the Mississippi and Missouri were larger towns, but Chicago was growing faster spurred by commodity sales of corn. Chicago supplied the gargantuan food needs of the Union Army during the Civil War:

> Twenty-one mainline tracks came into the city, and an average of 100 passenger trains and 120 freight trains left every day. More than 16,000 bushels of wheat passed each year through the massive elevators scattered along the banks of the river. The Union Stockyards had been

established ... on the southern outskirts and there were ... twenty-one packing houses in the city.[3]

Meat-packing pioneers such as Philip Armour became millionaires owing to their industrial innovations. Prairie Street, known for its cricket club, sprouted fine mansions overlooking Lake Michigan and became a place where Chicago's Corn and Meat Exchange elite could "look out on the wide lake which is now the highway for breadstuffs, and the merchant, as he shaves at his window, sees his rapid ventures as they pass away, one after another to the East."[4]

When the Civil War ended, Chicago had become known as the Queen City of the West, a robust symbol of country's expansion and wealth.[5] Just before the fire of 1871, Chicago had a population of 300,000, encompassing an area of six miles from north to south and three miles from the shores of Lake Michigan west.[6]

> In 1871, steam had not yet cut the masts from Lake shipping, so that on the city sky line would appear, above the rooks and down the streets to the river and the Lake, the delicate tracery of rigging....
> The [Chicago] river divided the city into three parts. It forked about half a mile west of the Lake, and its two branches ran northwest and south, forming a rough T shape, the base of which was the Lake shore.[7]

The 230-acre Lincoln Park on the lake shore became a refuge for people made homeless by the conflagration. The fire dramatically changed the wooden landscape and the streets of Chicago, which literally burned, being made of pine blocks in the muddier sections of the city. Few buildings were spared. The Chicago White Sox stadium in Dearborn Park was burned down.

> One of the businessmen who were not caught napping was George M. Pullman, inventor of the Pullman car, and President of the firm that made it. While the flames were still many blocks distant, he had gone with Charles W. Angell, the firm's secretary, to their offices on Michigan Avenue across from Dearborn Park. Although the danger seemed remote, Pullman directed those employees who showed up to load desks, chairs, books and papers, and supplies on a train and he moved them all down to his new stables on Eighteenth Street and the Lake.
> Pullman's company was one of the few able to resume business immediately after the fire.[8]

After the fire, cricket re-established itself in the city when a visiting Canadian XI was defeated by an Illinois XI at Union Park. The Ogden family, originally from Canada, organized the May 24, 1876, game that re-established the Chicago Cricket Club.[9] The Ogden family was the driving force behind the Chicago Cricket Club, and their influence helped make it the premier private club in the city. A member of the Chicago Historical Society, Dr. Edward J. Ogden was CCC president, insurance broker Mahlon D. Ogden was a director, and Dr. Russell Ogden was the CCC captain. In 1891, Edward and Mahlon Ogden were president and treasurer of the Canadian Club and the Chicago Historical Society, respectively. Chicago's top businessmen were found amongst 150 active and associate members. One of the three Ogden brothers, Mahlon Ogden, lived in a mansion on the north side of Chicago, which survived the fire.

> The three-story frame residence ... stood on Lafayette Place, facing Washington Park.... The grounds covered the entire block. The house had a wide front porch with a railing, and the fenced in yard held several outbuildings and many large elm trees. The house was twelve years old.[10]

Honorary CCC members included Philip D. Armour, the meat-packer millionaire, General Philip F. Sheridan, Mayor Carter A. Harrison and Marshall Fields, the department store magnate, whose ancestors came from Yorkshire.[11]

The same year that the Chicago Cricket Club was re-established, Arthur Goodwill Spalding pitched the Chicago White Stockings to victory in the first National Association professional baseball championship. Spalding became player-manager of the White Sox for a $4,000 annual salary, after coal magnate William Ambrose Hubert undercut Eastern cities' domination of league baseball by organizing the National Association of Professional Baseball Players in 1876. Ten dollars each team was all it took for Harry Wright's Boston Red Stockings, the Cleveland Forest City's, the Fort Wayne Kikiongas, the New York Mutuals, the Philadelphia Athletics, the Rockford Forest City's, the Troy Haymakers, the Washington Olympics, the Chicago White Stockings, and the teams of Cleveland's Forest City Club and Rockford's Forest City Baseball Club to become part of the National League. The league eliminated betting and drink at the games when overindulgence by the spectators threatened to ruin baseball. Spalding's book on baseball, *America's National Game,* published in 1911, depicts a hand labeled "drink" strangling an umpire by the throat. A strong president was needed to keep all the contending forces in line, so Sebenius Blakely of Connecticut, a future U.S. senator, became president of the National League.[12] During these contentious times in professional baseball, the Chicago Cricket Club played in Lincoln Park on Tuesdays, Thursdays and Saturdays in a season that extended from May 15 to October 1. As professional baseball flourished in Chicago, cross-pollination with local cricket proved beneficial for baseball: overhand pitching and the use of cricket pads by catchers, an innovation attributed to Peter "the Duke" Bresnahan, became part of America's pastime.[13] As baseball gained enormously in popularity in Chicago, the Pullman Athletic Club was incorporated in 1882 and sold $10,000 in stock to finance any sport that was requested by Pullman town residents. The Pullman Cricket Club became the most popular club in Pullman and produced enough players to field a second team that became known as the Wanderers' Cricket and Athletic Club in 1883. The Wanderers' home ground was located at the corner of 37th Street and Indiana Avenue in Chicago.

By 1884 when Pullman CC played Chatham CC in Canada, it was the powerhouse team of the cricket association. The team was named for George Mortimer Pullman, an ex–Colorado miner. Pullman left school at 14 and raised $80 million to build the town of Pullman. The founder of the Pullman Railcar Company knew from his mining days the social havoc drinking caused in the mining camps. The abstemious Pullman seized on the opportunity to build luxurious rail cars for the long journeys the miners were forced to make. Pullman cars utilized prodigious amounts of French glass, wood, iron, and a variety of other expensive materials that required highly skilled artisans to manufacture and assemble. Many of Pullman's workers came from England, Germany and France where the skills required for coach-work lined with mirrors and drapes were crafts with long established traditions. His desire to create an edifying atmosphere for his workforce extended to his personal choice of plays for the Pullman theater and selection of books in the library. He even told his workers who to vote for. Pullman believed fine living conditions would produce contented workers and therefore increase productivity. Idleness and drink were social scourges to be avoided by the rigorous playing of sport. "Men must play! Men will play!" was Pullman's credo. Pullman's sports facilities were located on the shores of Lake Calumet, 15 miles south of Chicago and linked to Chicago by the Central Illinois Railroad. Solon Spencer Beman and Nathan F. Barratt were the landscape architects who made Pullman's dream a reality. Conveniently located near the Central Illinois Railroad, the cricket and baseball grounds were created on 12 acres carved out of the banks of the Calumet River. The Playground, as the ball sports area was known, was linked by a bridge to an island in the river that was the site of a boathouse. The bridge made access easy to all sports venues. These sports included cricket, baseball, athletics, rowing, wrestling, gymnastics, and soccer. Cricket was the most popular sport played at Pullman, with 30 percent participation.[14] There were good sociological reasons for cricket's popularity. Fifty-three percent of the town's population were first generation immigrants and of these, one-third were from Northern England. Saltair, a planned community in Yorkshire, was one of the towns Pullman used as his model. Similarly, the Quaker chocolate maker Cadbury had already experimented in England with philanthropic housing. A quarter of Pullman's immigrants were bachelors who rented from families in the town. These bachelors were a ready source of sports talent. The combination of athletic competition with cricket games was popular in the 1890s. Events such as the cricket ball throw, the broad jump, and sprint races were popular with cricketers. The most famous of these Pullman cricketers was Paul Butcher, a Pullman clerk, whose greatest athletic achievement was his victory in the 100-yard race in the first AAU championship in 1888. He competed in track from 1882 to 1893 and played soccer from 1892 to 1893, indoor baseball in 1892 and cricket for seven years between 1882 and 1889. Pullman teams practiced hard and hired professional coaches to improve their play. Butcher's cricket teammate William C. Philpott remained a clerk-timekeeper throughout his tenure at Pullman. Frederick Wild played 11 years for the Pullman team in which time he rose in career from clerk to accountant. Harper, chief accountant of the Palace Car Company, played cricket and shot for the gun club in the early 1880s. A director and shareholder of the Pullman Athletic Club, he became its president in 1887. Many Pullman artisans and residents were from Yorkshire. Players were rarely selected from outside and had to be exceptional to make it onto the close knit, well financed Pullman Cricket Club side. Pullman attracted businessman cricketers from the adjoining towns of Kensington, Roseland and as far away as Hyde Park, located eight miles north of Pullman, halfway to Chicago. Their businesses including real estate, drug stores, coal dealerships, plumbing and hardware establishments, billiards halls and a saloon. Eight of the first 11 were white-collar workers. However, the Pullman Cricket Club was most popular with machinists and carpenters—18 of these skilled workers were club members.

The Reverend T.D. Phillips of the Chicago Cricket Club was not a resident of Pullman, but as a man of the cloth, he was welcome to play for Pullman teams. Phillips recruited for his congregation by playing cricket on several Chicago area league teams. These were the Wanderers, with 70 members; St. George's Cricket Club; and the CCC and Pullman which each had 150 members. The CCC had a wealthy membership while Pullman's was working class. The Reverend Phillips opened the batting for St. George's CC with Joseph G. Davis. Davis and Phillips developed into two of Chicago's finest batsmen, though it was not until he was 60 years old that Phillips scored his first century. In 1880 the Reverend Phillips was invited to play for Canada on tour to England. He took over the captaincy of the side when its captain, Thomas Dale, was arrested in a game against Leicester as a British army deserter. For Americans, the Episcopalian rector of Trinity Church should be cherished as the maternal grandfather of Ring Lardner, the great baseball writer.[15]

In 1887, Dr. Edward R. Ogden of the Chicago Cricket Club traveled to England as captain of an official Canadian cricket side that beat three county sides of Warwickshire, Leicestershire, Derbyshire and Ireland. Edward Ogden proved himself a first rate all-rounder on the tour, taking 9 for 83 against the MCC at Lord's, then scoring 132 against Hampshire and 98 runs against Durham.[16] Ogden's strong performance against English county sides makes the Pullman Cricket Club dominance of Chicago cricket by 1889 all the more impressive. They won seven of eight Arthur Goodwill Spalding championship trophies in ten years. Spalding, by then a sports magnate, sponsored the cricket league trophy, but his first love was baseball. In 1889 he organized a world baseball tour to promote the game. His Chicago White Stockings were captained by Cap Anson. For competition on the tour, an all-star team, selected from other National League teams and captained by John Montgomery Ward, were the main attractions, though diversionary entertainment was provided by "Professor" Bartholomew, the hot air balloonist, and Clarence Duval, the White Stockings Afro-American mascot. Ring Lardner dubbed the tour a "mission of instruction."[17] Spalding promoted his favorite sport, baseball, by restating the old chestnut that cricket was too slow and genteel for Americans: "England as the home of true sportsmanship ... had been for years sending their splendid cricketers to America, and now we would like to bring over a couple of baseball teams."[18]

William Alcock, the Surrey County Cricket Club secretary, organized the itinerary for the English part of the Spalding tour. Spalding met Alcock when on his first baseball tour of England with Harry Wright in 1874. On the 1874 tour the baseball players, selected from the Philadelphia Athletics and Chicago White Stockings, also played cricket. Harry Wright advised the American players to defend their wicket carefully. The supremely confident Spalding disagreed: "The first ball that threatened my wicket, I knocked over the fence.... The better and more accurately the Englishmen bowled, the more hits we would make, for such balls in our eyes were what we would term 'good balls.'"[19] Henry Chadwick credited Spalding as the most scientific ball hitter of his generation. He finished his professional baseball career with a .287 average. Commenting on the 1874 baseball team players' success at cricket, the *Field,* published in London, observed, "Baseball is a scientific game, more difficult than many. It is in fact, cricket of the America continent, considerably altered since its first origin, as has been cricket, by the yearly recourse to the improvements necessitated by the experiences of each season."[20]

Spalding's world tour arrived in England after games in New Zealand, Australia, and Ceylon (Sri Lanka). Lord Hawke, the captain of Yorkshire and England in Australia in 1887, attended the game at the Surrey Oval along with the lord mayor of London, the lord chancellor Sir William Webster, the duke of Beaufort and the American consul, Newton Crane. A total of 60,000 spectators watched games held in Bristol, Birmingham, Glasgow, Manchester, Liverpool, Belfast and Dublin. On the completion of the tour, Spalding's team arrived in New York where they were lionized at Delmonico's, located on 55th Street and 4th Avenue, by Theodore Roosevelt, Mark Twain and Walt Whitman. In reply to Twain's lauding of baseball as the game of the can-do American, Spalding noted that if it had not been for Cartwright's Knickerbocker team in New York trying to inculcate cricket's genteel ways, "the chances are there would have never developed a national game."[21] A pragmatic businessman, Spalding's love and promotion of baseball did not preclude him from building a cricket equipment factory on the River Thames near Putney. Spalding's sports equipment sales evolved into a highly profitable international business that helped defray the $50,000 he lost organizing the world baseball tour.

By 1890 baseball and cricket had been adopted by the American middle class in large numbers. Both cricket and baseball were bat and ball games, played without regard to the clock, conservative to innovation and languorous in application on the field.[22] George Wright remarked that where there had been one player now there were ten.[23] To accommodate the large numbers playing, cricket leagues were formed throughout the major cricket-playing cities in the United States: San Francisco, New York, Philadelphia and Chicago. Where cricket was not so prolific teams would travel on the new, efficient railway system to cities such as Milwaukee and St. Louis. Cricket flourished as English immigration to the United States peaked at 2.5 million people between 1880 and 1900. With America's population now over 55 million, interest in cricket by English immigrants improved the quality of play nationwide.[24]

Two teams were particularly strong as cricket's golden age dawned in Chicago. The Chicago Cricket Club rose to the Pullman challenge by practicing four days a week and incorporating in 1889, after raising $50,000 in stock. Games continued to be played at Lincoln Park until 1890, when seven acres were purchased at Parkside near the Central Illinois Railroad. The ground was shaped like the letter L. Four acres of the ground were dedicated to cricket and the remaining three acres to a cycle track. After the sod was laid, the pitch lay fallow for a year. The batting strip was a little sandy and was overlooked by a three-story clubhouse. The building was lined throughout with yellow pine. The ground floor was divided into five rooms, a cricketers,' a bicyclists,' a reception area, a wash area and a ladies' dressing room. The second floor was a long room used for luncheons and could be divided by curtains into separate rooms. The rear part of the long room was used for billiards, with the remainder used as a kitchen. The whole top floor was used for evening concerts and dances, and as a gymnasium during the day. The three-story clubhouse with a double verandah twelve feet offered an unobstructed view of the cycle track and cricket ground. After the sod was laid, the pitch lay fallow during 1889. When the strip was first played on, it was a bit sandy but did not hamper Chicago CC's rise to prominence as one of the best two cricket clubs in the Windy City in 1890.

The season of 1890 was the most competitive in the Chicago Cricket League's history. New sides kept joining the league. On June 28, Chicago CC won by an innings as F.F. Kelly and E.R. Ogden bowled unchanged in both innings, skittling St. George's out for 24 and 11 runs in each innings after Chicago scored 36 runs.[25] The following week, CCC administered a similarly lopsided defeat to Wanderers, who were shot out for 30 runs. On July 12, the Chicago Cricket Club kept their winning streak going against Pullman CC. They batted first with Dr. E.R. Ogden as their top scorer with 33 and Arthur Goodyear scoring 14 in an opening partnership of 50. Chicago was all out for 84 runs. Joseph Cummings was the leading wicket-taker for Pullman, with 5 wickets for 31 runs in 78 balls. Bowling unchanged for Chicago, Kelly took 6 for 33 and Dr. Ogden 3 for 96. Pullman was all out for 71 runs as they lost the game by 15 runs.[26] Pullman's July 12 loss to Chicago by 13 runs was their only defeat in 1890. The next week, on July 26, Albion CC, whose ground was located at the West Side Driving Park, had a tough introduction to a higher level of cricket scoring just 12 runs against the CCC, after Kelly top-scored for Chicago with 58 runs out of innings total of 156 for 6 wickets.[27] The following week, Chicago easily defeated the Wanderers by a score of 30 to 207 for 8 with Arthur Good-will capturing the batting honors before being bowled by Charles Self for 57 runs. Chicago with four wins in a row looked to be in a strong position to win the Spalding Cup but they lost to Pullman in their second game. In the third championship game held at the Playground, several thousand spectators saw Pullman declare at 129 for 8. Chicago scored runs aggressively in reply with Russell Ogden on 65 not out before bad light stopped play for a draw, with the Chicago on 97 for 6.[28] With one game drawn, Pullman and Chicago played another deciding match for the Spalding Cup. But before the big game with Pull-man, Chicago hosted St. George's CC at their Parkside ground and beat them easily by a score of 124 to 66 runs. Chicago reversed their batting order in the game, so the tail-enders who did not bat against Pullman in the drawn game the previous week, could get some practice. The following week saw the Chicago team in Milwaukee where they played the Cream City team on Saturday 30 at Bay View. Chicago won the low scoring game by seven wickets, thanks to a strong bowling performance by Frederick Kelly who took 8 wickets for 10 runs in the second inning. Chicago did not have Russell Ogden to for their visit to Milwaukee so Arthur Goodyear stood in as opener.[29] Coyne (21 and 11 in the sec-ond innings) was the top batsman for Chicago in its defeat of Cream City, powered by the strong bowling of F.F. Kelly who took 11 wickets for 26 runs in both innings. Cream City scored 39 and 53 while Chicago scored 61 in their first innings and needed only 33 in the second to earn the victory.[30] Chicago was not able to maintain the momentum from their Milwaukee victory and win the deciding game of the Spalding cup against Pull-man as the 1890 *Cricket Annual* noted.

> Cricket continues to boom in Chicago, and not withstanding the great improvement of the chicago's team, the pullman again won the Spalding Cup. The situation in Chicago is very similar to that in Philadelphia, the chicago and pullman bearing the same relation to each other as the germantown and belmont.[31]

Pullman's 1890 championship win completed a hat trick of successive Spalding Cup wins. In 1890 John Langham was Pullman's best player, with a batting average of 21.37. Dr. Ogden had the best league batting average and was regarded as the best all-rounder in the Windy City.[32]

Pullman's strength was their batting. Joseph Cummings became the best number-three batsman in Chicago's cricket history. Born in Durham on July 10, 1861, he arrived in Chicago during 1886 where his reputation as a punishing bat and good fast bowler earned him a mention in Wisden.[33] Joseph played first for the Wanderers, became the backbone of the Pullman CC team and received many invites to play on city sides, includ-ing Milwaukee for which he made his highest career score of 162 versus Racine College.[34] To have his cricket career listed in Wisden, the compendium of cricket statistics, was no small achievement as Wisden is generally dismissive of American cricket achievements owing to their lack of context and first-class designated matches. Russell Ogden, one of three cricket-playing brothers who had as much influence on Chicago cricket as the Newhall family had on Philadelphia cricket, was the most reliable opener for the CCC. Pullman's July 12 loss to Chicago by 13 runs was their only defeat in their 1890 Arthur

Goodwill Spalding championship trophy season. Pullman's 1890 championship win completed a hat trick of championship wins.

In 1891, after three consecutive Spalding Cup championship losses to Pullman, Chicago Cricket Club won the league "thanks to the phenomenal bowling of Bradley, who got five wickets for two runs; some fine wicket-keeping by Shaw, who made five catches, and an excellent innings by A. Macpherson."[35] Russell Ogden finished the 15-game season on top of the batting averages again, as he led the CCC to the league championship during a brilliant season in which the CCC lost only two of 15 and one out of nine games in the league championship. They won the Spalding Trophy due to the influx of new players and a greatly improved Parkside wicket: "In this latter respect the Chicago Club had every advantage, and much of the success is during the past season is traceable to the excellent facilities for practice and the benefit of professional coaching."[36] Frederick Fitzmaurice Kelly took the most wickets in 1891, with 69 for an average of

Maxwell Cobb and Frederick Fitzmaurice Kelly played cricket together in Chicago. Kelly later became editor of *Spalding's Cricket Guide* on the death of its editor Henry Chadwick. Source: *Cricket Magazine*, 1909.

6.13 runs per wicket. His batting improved to second in the batting averages, with 16.25 runs per innings. Arthur Goodyear played 17 innings for an average of 12.82 and showed promise as a bowler.[37] Joseph "Jos" E. Davis became secretary of the CCC after arriving from New York where he had played for the Manhattan Cricket Club of Brooklyn. In his first year with the CCC he captained the Second XI, which won the President's Cup competition, the championship for club second XI teams.[38]

Chicago's cricket performance was sharpened by visits on September 11 and 12 from Philadelphia's two strongest cricketing clubs, Germantown and Belmont. Germantown had just moved onto their new ground at Manheim in Philadelphia. The Chicago representative side beat the two Philadelphia teams with Charles Self scoring 28 runs for Chicago in the first game. Self died at the age of 24 a month after the game, from gastric fever. He had learned his cricket in Sussex. The Reverend Phillips, who had played with him on the Wanderers team, presided at his funeral.[39] Without Charles Self's county quality play, Chicago lost to a visiting Winnipeg team that won all its local fixtures except one. News of Chicago cricket reached England, where Lord Hawke organized a tour by England's top amateurs. They stopped in Philadelphia before defeating a Chicago All Star team by an innings on October 16 and 17.[40] In 1892, with Joseph Cummings dominating the batting averages, Pullman regained the Chicago Cricket Association championship. Cricket in Chicago progressed steadily until 1893 when cricket tours in the Midwest fell on hard times following the financial panic of 1893. Frederick Fitzmaurice Kelly moved to New York at the end of 1893 and played for several cricket clubs including the Staten Island Cricket and Baseball Club. A diligent statistician, Kelly was chosen by Spalding to be editor of the *Cricket Annual* following the death of its editor Harry Chadwick in 1909. Joe Davis was the *Cricket Annual* correspondent in Chicago. Writing in the *Cricket Annual*, Davis hoped the White City built for

> the Columbian Exposition would attract a few clubs from distant cities, but the widespread depression in trade nipped in the bud several projected visits. St. Louis was the only city that sent a team, and they proved quite unable to cope with the local elevens, losing all five games played. Their visit was marked by the compilation of two centuries, Dr. E.R. Ogden, of the Chicago Club, making 103 and J. Cummings, of the Pullman CC, 128, both being not out. Another century man turned up in Harry Watson, of the Albion Club, who put together 106 against the Chicagos at Parkside. Three centuries in one season give evidence of great improvement in the Chicago grounds, to say nothing of the advance in skill of the players.[41]

Pullman was in the forefront of domestic competition. The Spalding Cup became Pullman's in perpetuity in 1893, after they won it five times. The Pullman CC victory came as the Depression of 1893 took hold. The depression bankrupted 600 banks, 56 railroads, and 15,000 companies. The final game was held three months after the hugely successful Chicago Columbian Exposition. Pullman upset the Wanderers to win the Chicago Cricket Association championship on August 26, 1893. The Wanderers batted first and scored 89 runs. In reply,

> Pullman started badly, Ogden falling to Kelly in the first over. Cummings joined Goodyear and both played free cricket.... Then the champion (Cummings) gave an easy catch to Pugh at short leg — a great shout from the Pullman supporters arose as it fell from his hands.... Goodyear was out soon after the winning run had been made. His 27 was made without an actual chance and was worthy of much praise.[42]

As the depression deepened, unemployed workers marched on Washington from all points in the United States. Rail tycoon James J. Hill issued a warning from his fortress in St. Paul to President Grover Cleveland that 30,000 men had commandeered trains and were headed to the east. The actual number was 10,000 men. Seventeen armies of the unemployed marched on Washington. The most celebrated of these, under the leadership of "General" Jacob Coxey, a successful quarry owner and Populist, originated in Massillon, Ohio.[43] A California mystic wearing a sombrero and silver dollar buttons on his coat led the way with a banner which stated, "Death to interest on Bonds!" These Populist ideas later found voice in William Jennings Bryan, who declared that America would not be crucified on a "cross of gold." At this time it was believed by Senator John Percival Jones of Nevada that a currency backed by silver would make America less subject to economic fluctuations. In 1894, Coxey was more concerned about employment. His basic idea was that Congress should pay $1.25 per eight-hour day to unemployed workers. Coxey's economic stimulus ideas were not understood in this pre–Keynesian age, and he was arrested for trespassing on grass as the police in Washington, D.C., dispersed the marchers by attacking them with clubs and horses.[44] The Chicago mayor during these tumultuous political times was the Pullman cricketer John P. Hopkins, who had played on the 1889

Pullman team. He was a director of the Pullman Athletic Club and was elected mayor of Chicago in 1893.[45] George Pullman's workers were not happy, as they had their wages lowered a third. The typical family received 76 cents a day for food and clothing. On May 11, 1894, the Pullman workers petitioned for relief through the American Railway Union led by Eugene Debs. Once battle was joined, 120,000 rail workers supported a boycott in 27 states and followed union orders by going on strike. Democratic mayor Hopkins and Illinois governor John Peter Altgeld sympathized with the Pullman workers' demands and refused a Pullman request for state militia. The U.S. attorney general, Richard Olney, had seats on many railway boards and fresh from his success in breaking up Coxey's army, overrode Illinois' right to handle the Pullman strike as a state matter. Olney was determined to crush Debs, who had just won a successful strike against James Hill's Northern Railroad. Employing the Sherman Anti-Trust Act of 1890, the attorney general asked the courts across the country to declare the union in restraint of trade because the mails could not be delivered. The first injunction was issued on July 2, and President Grover Cleveland sent in troops on the grounds that the blanket injunction could be enforced. Two thousand soldiers arrived in Chicago, backed by 3,500 deputies paid by the railroads and described by the Chicago chief of police as thieves and ex-convicts. They helped the strikebreakers shoot railway workers; 34 died across the country in the resulting riots. The strike ended with a victory for the railways, as Debs went to jail in 1895 for contempt of court. The right to future strikes was put in question by the Sherman Anti-Trust Act's being first used against workers and not monopoly capitalists.[46] Pullman's benign image as a kind capitalist with his workers' interests at heart did not survive the rancor caused by the strike, and after five consecutive championships, the Pullman CC proved too distracted to retain its hold on the local championship.

There were five teams in the Chicago league in 1894: Pullman, the Wanderers, Chicago, St. George, and Albion CC. The Chicago Wanderers started their season in St. Louis, where they inaugurated a cricket ground on May 12 at Forest Park. The pitch was slow and heavy due to the newness of the turf and the recent rains, but this did not deter 700 spectators from watching the Wanderers defeat St. Louis by four runs. Jos Davis, now playing for the Wanderers, took ten wickets for 19 runs in a low scoring, two-innings game. The total number of runs scored by both sides did not reach over 100.[47] Returning to Chicago, the Wanderers beat Pullman by a wicket and 17 runs in the first league game of the season on May 19. On June 9, Pullman narrowly squeaked by against St. George's, and then they were easily defeated by the Wanderers in the second game of the season between the two clubs. On July 7, the Wanderers avenged an earlier defeat in the season by CCC, winning by one wicket when Keenan, Kelly and Davis combined to score more than half the winning total of 130 runs. On July 28, Butcher batted number ten in the last Pullman game of the season against the Wanderers. The batting champion of the 1893 season for Pullman, Joseph Cummings with an average of 35.33, was absent and the match was drawn. With two prior wins against Pullman in the 1894 season, the Wanderers won the championship for the first time. Emboldened by their league success they invited some of the best Chicago cricketers to tour Michigan and Canada with them in August. They lost the first game of the tour to Detroit, as Fred Bamford took 5 for 19 and was second highest scorer with 19. Detroit won by six runs on the first innings total. Veteran tour player the Reverend T.D. Phillips was the leading scorer, with 19 runs for the

Wanderers as opening bat. In the second game, against Hamilton in Ontario, Canada, the Wanderers drew after being set to score 244 runs. They made a game effort in reply with Phillips and Cummings scoring 56 and 74, respectively. The Wanderers' Chicago All Star team, with Phillips, Cummings, Davis, Keenan (CCC) and Henderson (Albion), won four of the five games. Frederick F. Kelly, who was a regular for the Wanderers by this time, did not make the tour. After the Wanderers' return to Chicago, Kelly was on the September 22 Wanderers team, which played a visiting Canadian team and lost by one wicket. *The American Cricketer* reported:

> Some fine cricket was witnessed at Thirtieth Street and Wentworth Avenue when the Wanderers team that recently visited Canada played other members of the club. The club was fairly represented, although weakened by the absence of Bailey, who was playing in Philadelphia against Lord Hawke's team.... Throughout the inning the Tourists' bowling was first class, Cummings, Goode and Henderson being in fine form. Against such a formidable attack the club did well to make 98. Kelly played the star inning of the game, while Keenan made his runs in excellent form. Eight of the wickets were clean bowled.
>   The home team were jubilant when they disposed of Cummings and Davis for small scores. Rev. T.D. Phillips, the grand old man of Chicago cricket, was in for over an hour and made the top score of the match, his 29 being made by faultless cricket.[48]

Several other games were played in September by teams testing the waters for future league cricket. These included the Ramblers and St. Lawrence. The Ramblers were easily defeated by Cicero at Ridgeland. Henderson, back playing for his old team the Albion, overpowered the St. Lawrence team as he took 7 wickets for 6 runs and 5 maidens.[49] The Pullman Cricket Club proved they were ready to put the nasty distractions of 1894 behind them when "Demon" Joseph Cummings led the league bowling with 2.80 runs a wicket. In batting, he led the averages for the fourth consecutive time, scoring 47.20 runs per inning.

According to Flannery, the league 1894 season was "one of the most successful ever known in Chicago. Favorable weather and fine creases resulted in high scoring and good attendance, while the matches with the Canadian and other visiting teams greatly increased popular interest in the game."[50]

Three new clubs joined the league, when three touring sides visited Chicago. The Chicago Cricket Club was not competitive in 1895 league competition, but one of their members, R.A. Helliwell, organized a successful tour of Ontario in Canada. Strengthened by Joseph Cummings, the Rev. Phillips, Henderson, and William Balster, the Chicago Wanderers team

> left the "Windy City" on Saturday, June 15th, for a week on the Bay of Quinte. Four of the eleven were with the Wanderers team that played in Western Ontario last year, and the whole eleven were conspicuous for their excellent fielding, with the other departments fairly well represented. They won all six of their matches with comparative ease, three of them in one inning, a fourth by 10 wickets, and the other two in the first inning by large margins.[51]

Games were played against Napanee, Kingston, Royal Military College, Picton, and a District XI hosted at the Napanee ground. The game against the Rosedale Cricket Club in Toronto produced the best cricket of the tour. Montgomery took seven Chicago wickets as Chicago scored 151 runs to Rosedale's 53. Cummings proved to be the best all-rounder on the tour. He and Henderson took five Rosedale wickets apiece, then Cummings scored 27, opening the batting. The following week, on July 4, the touring bug struck again as St. Louis took on the Wanderers in a high scoring game that saw the Chicago team defeated by 44 runs in the first innings. St. Louis had raised the standard of their game considerably since the previous year. In July, a strong Canadian team captained by C.S. Hyman won all five matches against R.H. Helliwell's Eleven, the Wanderers, St. George, Pullman and All Chicago.[52]

The Wanderers continued their annual tour tradition after the Canadian team visit and won six out of eight matches, defeating Chatham, Paris, Hamilton, Rosedale, Guelph, and Berlin. They drew with Toronto and lost to London in Ontario Province.[53] Many of the tour-seasoned players were then selected for a combined Chicago side, which played the visiting British Public Schools and Universities team at the Wanderers' Rosedale ground. "Demon" Cummings of Pullman CC (named for the great Australian, Demon Spofforth) led both the batting and bowling averages for 1895 with 47.20 and 2.80 per wicket.[54] After the Pullman strike was settled 12,000 residents remained in Pullman, where they stayed an average of four years. This continuity enabled the Pullman cricket teams to develop a core of reliable players that stayed together longer than any of the other local teams. Apart from the Chicago league, cricket at Pullman was played as part of local festivals generally held on national holidays such as Decoration, Labor and Independence days. The variety of venues and play helped cricketers retain their interest in the game. Of all the sports played at Pullman, cricketers had the greatest longevity as participants. Butcher played for 15 years. Three hundred of 329 athletes sampled were on a team for less than two years, with 200 lasting just a season. Athlete turnover was the lowest in cricket; over 60 percent of its players played at least two years while 23 percent played five years or more. Soccer also experienced a relatively low turnover rate.[55] Longevity playing cricket was dependent on broad based skills, some of which age better than others. For example, W.G. Grace's fielding contribution to his side diminished after age 51, when he could not bend and resorted to stopping balls with legs. Grace was still able to bowl effectively in his fifties and scored several centuries at age 50. Cross training with sports such as soccer helped cricketers retain their fitness and agility in both sports. Soccer kept the cricketers fit in winter and enhanced agility in the field for their summer game. In Australia, where soccer was not popular, Thomas Wills introduced Australian Rule Football to keep cricketers fit in winter. During the season, the CCC played cricket on Saturdays. The Pullman Cricket Club could also play on Saturday despite having a majority of working-class players, because skilled workers got Saturday afternoons off. Soccer was predominantly a working-class sport in Chicago; none of the elite Chicago athletic clubs played it. The Sunday kick-off times allowed broad based participation. The Pullman soccer team played teams from the mining districts of Carbon Hill and Braidwood. Pullman's broad based sports participation ensured a large pool of participants for all sports, but this unique sports experiment came to an end after George Pullman's death in 1897. As part of the Pullman estate settlement the Illinois Supreme Court decreed that Pullman should sell off all its assets in 1898. Athletic Island and the Playground, the scene of many glorious victories on the cricket field, fell into decay, and the grandstands were demolished and replaced by a railway roundhouse.[56] Pullman continued to play in the league — albeit with less success— after the city was dismantled. Despite its strong tradition of cricket success, Pullman was not a traveling club like the elite athletic clubs of Chicago

CC, the Detroit Athletic Club, St. Louis and the Cream City of Milwaukee. These teams met once a year in the Northwestern Cricket Association, founded in 1896 on a suggestion of the Winnipeg Cricket Club. In the four-game July tournament, All Chicago played a combined Omaha and Minnesota side. Chicago won the tournament with Minnesota second.

In 1896 Chicago league cricket was marked by club mergers. The Albion Cricket Club merged with the Oak Park Cricket Club to gain access to a good ground at Ridgeland. St. George's won the Walker Shield (which replaced the Spalding Cup). Pullman and St. Lawrence ended bottom of the table with one win between them in a ten-game season.[57] Intercity and international competition in 1896 created a lot of excitement in Chicago sporting circles. In September Toronto played three games in Chicago, as Edward R. Ogden topped the local Chicago batting and bowling averages in 1896 with 35.77 runs and 52 wickets. Cummings, playing for Pullman, was fourth in both averages. The Canadian tourists offered a tune-up for the stronger opposition provided by the 1896 visit of the Australian cricket team which had defeated England and won 20 of its 34 games in England. The great left-handed Australian batsman Clem Hill regarded his captain George Henry "Harry" Stevens Trott as one of Australia's truly great captains. Ranjitsinhji agreed, and the Wisden *Book of Cricketers Lives* noted that Trott, a Postman by profession:

> [He] overcame the disadvantages involved a lack of education, and won the warm regard of men with whom, apart from the comradeship of the cricket field, he had nothing in common. In managing his cricket team he owed much to his equable temper and innate tact.[58]

As a great cricketer, Trott was "one of the best ever point fieldsmen, sent back all of the best batsmen of his time with his leg breaks, and scored more than 1000 runs on all his four tours of England.[59]

On their return from England, the Australia team stopped first in America and New Zealand before docking in Sydney. The American part of the tour began in Philadelphia with three three-day games, starting at Germantown CC's Manheim ground on September 25 and 28. After losing one of the Philadelphia games the Australians arrived to play a Chicago XV October 8 and 9:

> Cap Anson one of the era's most prominent professional baseball players along with fellow Chicago white Stockings teammate Fred Pfeiffer signed on with the Chicago side and took a fine catch to oust the Australian captain Harry Trott.[60]

Chicago scored 105 in their first innings, with Joseph "Jos" Davis top scoring with 34 before he was bowled by bowler Hugh Trumble. Trumble had earned a reputation against England's team as a very effective variable pace bowler. Australia made 235 runs in reply as George Giffen top scored with 69 not out. Henderson and Wilmot took eight Australian wickets between them as Wilmot finished with the best bowling average — 17.66 — for his five wickets. In Chicago's second innings Wilmot scored only three runs as an opener. Woolwich-born William Balster scored only four runs as the number-three batsman in both Chicago innings. Pullman CC and the Chicago league's best batsmen for three years running, Joe Cummings held off the Australians with the highest second innings score of 27 runs, before he was bowled by McKibbin. Australia won the game by an innings and 37 runs before catching the train to San Francisco for the last game of their American tour.

In 1897, Edward Ogden led the averages again as Chicago cricket began to rely increasingly on knock-out tournaments to keep it going. The North-Western Tournament was held in St. Paul and was won by the Manitoba Association. Prest, an ex–Marlborough School captain, organized the Minnesota venue for the event, which was played on matting wickets. The Wanderers won the Walker Cup with Pullman second. The adjoining cities of St. Louis, Detroit and Milwaukee were down to one cricket team.[61] Fred Bamford, a stalwart of Detroit cricket for a decade, would soon head to California in 1898 to help found the Los Angeles Cricket Club. By 1899 the Chicago CC were an aging club with no new blood. Such players generally took up less physically demanding sports such as golf and yachting. They forfeited three of their games to Pullman and the Wanderers won the league again. The powerhouse players of the 1890s, Edward R. Ogden and Joseph Cummings, barely broke double figures during the ten-game season.

Ogden was not selected for the All Chicago team that played Pelham Warner's visiting English side on October 10–11, 1898. Warner's team played in New York, Philadelphia and Baltimore before catching the Ohio Rail Road out of Baltimore. The train passed through Cumberland, Berlin, Cornellsville, Pittsburgh, Newcastle, and Akron before Jos Davis met Warner's team in Chicago. Housed at the Wellington Hotel, the visiting English team stayed near the shores of Lake Michigan. The cricket field the teams played on was so small that a boundary was only given three runs. Chicago found their bowling inadequate as the English side scored freely in their first innings of 295 runs. Bosanquet hit 91, stopped just short of his century by Wilmot, who bowled him. Cummings and Davis had identical bowling figures, each taking 3 for 47. It was late in the afternoon when the Chicago players went in to bat. Only Beddon and Davis were able to master the Englishmen's bowling. Ainsworth and Bosanquet opened the bowling for Warner's team. Beddon went in first and carried his bat for 17 not out. Davis, with 16, was the only other Chicago batsman in double figures in Chicago first innings of 77 all out. Forced to follow-on, rain stopped play before Chicago resumed its second innings. The Chicago batsmen made a somewhat better showing, getting 83 runs for the loss of 7 wickets as they went down to easy defeat with a result made on first inning totals.[62] After the game, Warner's team were taken to visit Philip Armour's meat packing factories. Warner was oblivious to the fact that Armour had been an important patron of cricket in Chicago. On his return to England, Warner wrote that Chicago's local teams had a tendency to squabble amongst themselves. Warner wrote in his interesting book *Cricket in Many Climes* that he quite ruined his reputation as an orator in Chicago, "for I told my audience that the Chicago XV were quite the best we had faced, with the sole exception of the Philadelphians, the New Yorkers, the Baltimore XV, the Toronto XI and the Montreal XI, a list I then saw to my horror included all the teams we had played against."[63]

Cricketers in Chicago, like those in California, had difficulty against slow bowling that required proper foot placement. Such skills required regular practice. In Chicago, the amateur cricket establishment was not replenishing itself as baseball captured young recruits. While the cricket infrastructure deteriorated in America, there was always Canada, where Winnipeg hosted the annual North-Western tournament. Jos Davis reported:

> Too much praise cannot be given to the Winnipeg cricketers for their lavish hospitality. They spent nearly $1000 in entertaining us and I understand the City council voted $200 of this

amount. We were amply repaid for making the long trip of over 1000 miles and our visit was a source of great satisfaction to the Winnipeg men who like ourselves do not get sufficient outside cricket. You will doubtless laugh at the scores but the wickets were none of the best. The dragoon wicket was dreadfully fiery, while at times the ball shot.... We had at least 800 people out on Saturday.[64]

The big excitement for eastern cricket circles in 1899 was the visit of Prince Ranjit-sinhji's team to Philadelphia. Chicago had to be content with a visit from a strong Canadian team that included the great Canadian international John M. Laing. Laing, a barrister by profession, played nine consecutive matches against the United States, taking 63 wickets for 653 runs.[65] At Parkside in a two innings match, the Canadians were bowled out for 16 and Chicago then fell for 29 in reply. In the second innings the Canadians prevailed with stronger batting, scoring 119 as Chicago were out for 78.[66] The Canadians then easily beat the Wanderers before their final match against All Chicago on a fine warm day. All Chicago, with Cummings and Ogden playing on the same side, scored 176 in their first innings. The Canadians replied with 265. Cummings took the most Canadian wickets with 3 for 49. In the second innings Chicago scored 179 runs as Jos Davis led the batting with 69 runs. Laing and Fleury then knocked off the winning runs as the Canadians won by ten wickets.[67] As the Canadians took on Chicago, Cleveland took on Pittsburgh and Detroit. George Newhall of Philadelphia played for Cleveland but he was bowled for 9. For Detroit, the Bamford family of Fred and Frank G. still dominated the bowling.

In 1899, there were seven clubs in the league. Pullman and the Wanderers were joined by the suburban teams of St. Lawrence, Ridgeland, Douglas Park, Hyde Park and La Grange. Robert W. Fraser of the Wanderers was elected president of the Chicago Cricket Association, and the Northwestern Cricket Association tournament was slotted for Chicago.[68] The Wanderers leased the Parkside grounds formerly used by the CCC, as their ground on Thirty-Ninth Street and Wentworth Avenue was sold for baseball purposes.[69] The Wanderers remained the best organized club through 1900, when their secretary, Jos Davis, recorded that there were only three cricket teams left in Chicago and Pullman CC lost its ground. This left the revived Chicago team and the Wanderers as the two dominant teams. Both teams played at Parkside with the season reduced to eight games.[70] Davis led both the batting and bowling averages for the year with an average 42.50 runs per inning and 27 wickets for an average of 5.5. In 1902 and 1903 the Wanderers continued to dominate Chicago cricket while Manitoba won the North-Western Association knock-out tournament again. John M. Laing played for the Wanderers in 1903 and put on 313 against Douglas Park A. Laing scored 249 and Davis 103 before the Wanderers' innings came to an end with 385 runs on the board. The game held at Parkside on June 27, 1903, was played for the record books, as Douglas Park were all out for 26 in their innings.[71] Such a disparity in scores shows that Chicago cricket had reached the point of no return as far as developing first-class players was concerned. With the town of Pullman dismantled there was no nursery for first-class cricket left in the area, and established players had to travel to Philadelphia for first-class competition. William Balster of the Wanderers developed as Chicago's new reliable batsmen as Joe Cummings' prowess with the bat declined. The one bright spot in the 1903 season occurred when Chicago shared the North-Western Association title with Manitoba for the first time.[72] The Wanderers continued their domination of Chicago cricket through 1905 as the

Chicago Association expanded to seven teams again and annual fixtures increased to 16. The new sides in the league were Calumet and Metropolitan. Joe Cummings still performed well for Pullman, helped by F.F. Kelly. Balster scored the most runs in the season with 584, although J.G. Campbell led the batting averages with 48. Both batsmen played for the Wanderers.

After Minnesota CC lost their cricket grounds at the beginning of the 1907 season, a Middle-West Cricket League that included Detroit, Cleveland, Pittsburgh, Akron and Youngstown was established to promote intercity competition. In nearby Wisconsin, Kenosha had a fine cricket field and a Tri-City league. Horlicks CC, based in Racine and named for malt-beverage company, had financial staying power similar to Pullman CC during its golden years from 1887 to 1898. Horlicks players wore baseball uniforms with their names and numbers. Salt Lake and Denver cricket clubs wore traditional white flannels and were organized by John Walton. In Chicago, the Wanderers beat Hyde Park for the league trophy, greatly helped by the batting of William Balster, who scored the only century. He finished the season with 467 runs in nine innings for an impressive 66.71 average in 1907.[73] The Reverend Phillips played for a reconstituted Chicago Cricket Club, but his batting power declined as evidenced by his season batting average of four. William C. Jones' 31 wickets for 3.67 runs a wicket spearheaded a strong Hyde Park CC bowling side. Pullman CC had their worst game ever when their depleted side was bowled out for 0 with Jones taking 4 wickets for 0.[74]

In 1909 Henry P. Waller took over as top run-getter for the Wanderers. The leading club in Chicago for ten years, the Wanderers attracted the best players and used a professional coach. In 1909, Germantown CC of Philadelphia, Alameda CC in San Francisco and the Wanderers in Chicago were the best teams in America and a triangular tournament between the three city teams would have produced the most competitive cricket in America. By 1911, though, Philadelphia's cricket touring tradition came to an end with the retirement of John Barton King, America's best bowler, and the Wanderers lost their hold on the Chicago Cricket League title as they were challenged by the four-year-old South Park Cricket Club. South Park, founded from the remnants of the Kenwood Cricket Club, played on their home ground at Ogden Park.[75] Similarly, the Chicago Cricket Club that re-entered league competition in 1911 was formerly the Douglas Cricket Club. The borrowing of illustrious club names in U.S. cricket has become a common occurrence. The clubs have no capital value except for their established relationships with local authorities that regulate the use of public parks in Chicago. Therefore, there is significant value in keeping an entity name associated with a previous era of city growth, as elected officials were more likely to grant use of the park for cricket if they were presented with familiar names from the past. The Wanderers and Chicago CC kept their names intact because their grounds had strong lease or ownership rights; Pullman CC disappeared from the league schedule altogether in 1911, their grounds on the Calumet River having given way to rail yards. Cricket by 1911 had become a small businessman's game, while baseball attracted the corporate millionaires that had first supported cricket in Chicago before the turn of the century.

In 1912, the Pullman CC came back to life and won five out of nine games in the Chicago League using a mix of young experienced immigrant players and veterans. William Cummings, Pullman CC president for 1913, drew his father Joseph back into cricket with

The Chicago Wanderers, 1911. Number 13, William Balster, was Chicago's best batsman in the President Theodore Roosevelt era. Source: *Spalding Cricket Annual, 1911*.

winning results. *Spalding's Cricket Guide for 1913* reported Pullman's illustrious team of players included

> F. Wild [who] played with the western Association team in the successful tour of Philadelphia, in 1882, when they successively defeated Young Americans, Girard, Germantown and Merion teams. F. Wild, J. Cummings, and J. Langham all have played with teams representing the West vs. East. W.J. Kenny will be remembered as playing in 1896, [189]7, [and 189]8 for the Canadian International against America in both Philadelphia and Toronto. J. Armitage, veteran Yorkshire cricketer who went to Australia with J. Lillywhite's team in the 70's and who will also be remembered as playing professionally in Philadelphia in the early 80's and umpiring several important matches. A.T. Campbell learned his cricket in Melbourne and played for the Pittsburgh team some years ago.[76]

With veterans riding to the rescue of the Pullman CC, economic conditions improved in Michigan after a run-up in copper prices as the naval race between Britain and Germany began to get really serious. With Winston Churchill and Lord Battenburg now running the Admiralty in London, John Pierpoint Morgan began to corner the copper supply essential for armaments. The consolidation of the copper industry attracted British miners who played cricket. The Houghton County Cricket League was established in "Copper Country," following a meeting at the local YMCA in 1906. There were six founding teams in the league: Painsdale, Trimountain, Portage, Lake Atlantic, Tamarack and Kearsarge. Judge Norman Haire presented the league cup, which was won by Painsdale in the league's inaugural year. In 1907 J. Haldane Edwards became president of the Copper County Cricket League and a new team, Mohawk CC, won the Haire Cup. Wolverine Cricket Club (formerly Kearsarge) and Tamarack CC in Calumet County joined the Copper County Cricket League in 1910 as the league expanded from Houghton into four more Michigan counties with ten teams. The Chicago Wanderers' ex-captain Sam Davis recorded the highest score in the league during 1910 with 77 runs. In 1911 Hecla joined the Copper County league.[77]

The 1912 season started out cold and wet and got tougher when the Copper League's second vice-president Pollard (also president of the Wolverine CC) was killed in a copper mining accident.[78] Despite the loss of Pollard's executive talent, Wolverine CC won the Haire Cup for a second time due to Sam Davis' batting. He scored a century against Kearsarge CC and finished the season with a league-leading batting average of 24.40. Davis also led the bowling average with 74 wickets for 3.80 runs a wicket in a 12-game season. The same number of games were played in neighboring Chicago, but the batting averages for the Chicago League were considerably higher with newcomer Tom Smith scoring 61.90 an innings. The indomitable Joe Cummings of Pullman also finished high in the averages, with a 12.40 average. While veterans such as Cummings helped keep cricket going in Chicago, former Wanderers player Courtney Davis organized the Kansas Cricket County Club in 1912. The KCCC restricted membership to British subjects; 47 members signed up. Kansas competition was limited to an Anglo-American club and a country club. The KCCC colors, black and gold, were embroidered Old English style, and the club membership included "H.C. Davis, formerly of Dulwich College, Surrey, Eng., Sid Shaw, late of the Surrey Colts ... Baldwin late of the Kent Second Eleven; Ed Cartwell, Preston Grammar School, and a number of other[s]."[79]

Looking at the historical record of cricket clubs in America, 50 appears to have been the magical number of members to make a cricket club viable. This number did not have to be as large in areas where there were vibrant leagues, such as San Francisco, Philadelphia, New York and Chicago, as the pool of players was larger and migrated between teams when strong opposition was in town. The only strong competition provided in Chicago during 1913 was by the Australians, who played two games against a Chicago XVI and XV on August 27 and 28 at the Chicago White Sox stadium and a last one at Comiskey's Ball Yard on August 29.

The Australians arrived in Chicago on August 26, after defeating a combined Australia and Canada team at the Rosedale Cricket Club ground in Toronto by an innings and 147 runs. No Chicago or California players were selected for the U.S. side. The mission of the 1913 Australian team was to expand the quality of cricket played in the United States, but their arrival in Chicago came too late to save the Wanderers, who failed to field a side for the first time in their history; their grounds at Parkside were given over to lawn tennis following the retirement of Charles W. "Pop" Jackson who, after successfully handling the Wanderers' finances for 20 years, left the club for health reasons, after arranging for Wanderers players to join Pullman, he emigrated to Australia. Jackson had traveled to Australia with an England team in the 1880s. The remaining Wanderers players were distributed among the four remaining teams in the city: Pullman, Hyde Park, South Park and Chicago. The Wanderers' loss was Pullman CC's gain:

C.W. Jackson and William Balster, late of the disbanded Wanderers Cricket Club, cast their lot with the Pullman Cricket club, and ... the brilliant cricket of William Balster ... materially helped the Pullman Club. W.H. Dixon and J.P. Flinn, by a splendid display of batting pulled the Pullman Cricket Club to victory after the South Park Cricket Club considered the game won. Also William Balster, on another occasion, when playing against the Hyde Park Cricket Club in the deciding game of the season, compiled 19 runs and broke the bowling of the

Hyde Park Club, opening the way for V.J. Smeale to come in and win the game with a splendid 28 runs, which included five boundaries and eventually winning the match. In another game against the Chicago Cricket Club, William Balster made 62 not out.

F. Wild was chairman of the committee on arrangements for the Australian cricket team, and B. Govier, W.H. Dixon, W. Snowcroft, and A.T. Campbell of Pullman were picked to play against the Australians in their matches in Chicago.[80]

Frank Wild's term as Pullman president succeeded admirably, as his club won the league for the last time after his 30 years with the club. Joseph Cummings played cricket to the day of his death from heat-stroke, July 15, 1913. William Balster also finished his 25-year Chicago cricket career in style, by helping Pullman CC win the league and being selected to play for the *Chicago* team that played against Australia. In his heyday, Balster

had few superiors in the field. He was a good, all-round man, excelling as a batsman. He could hit brilliantly all around the wicket, but punished on the offside all loose balls. Before his accident, five years ago, while on a tour in Canada with the Wanderers, when he broke his shoulder bone, he was a good change bowler, while he was a brilliant fielder with no superiors.[81]

Before playing the Australians, Balster played only six regular games in Chicago and was second in the batting averages, with 26.00. By contrast, the Australian side that arrived in Chicago on August 27 had already played 25 games in Canada and America. With such a disparity of practice, there was little wonder American cricketers had difficulty facing international players of Charlie Macartney's caliber. Macartney, already extremely talented, played 50 first-class games a season, which in an average cricketer's lifetime of ten seasons meant a disparity of 450 games to 50 for a good Chicago player. The Australian team was captained by Austin Diamond and included future Australian all-time greats Warren Bardsley, Arthur Mailey and Charlie "Governor-General" Macartney. In the game prior to arrival in Chicago, Macartney scored 186 runs in Australia's first innings of 402 against the combined U.S. and Canada side at the Rosedale Cricket Club in Toronto. The "Governor-General" was a left-handed all-rounder who on a 1913 tour of America "reached such heights that he hit 2,390 runs and took 180 wickets, finishing at the top of both sets of averages. As a fieldsman, particularly at mid-off, he had few equals.[82]

Against such talent, the last three international cricket games played in Chicago before the declaration of the First World War were something of a foregone conclusion. In the first games against the Australians, the Chicago XVI scored 86 and 77 and the Australians scored 277 as they won by 191 runs in the first innings. In the second game Australia scored 372 runs as they won by 262 runs in the first innings. Australia won the third game at Comiskey's Ball Yard on August 29 by 209 runs. Andreas, Allen and Packenham had the best of games for Chicago. Henry Allen played for Schenectady CC in New York before taking 6 for 97 in the last Chicago game against the Australians. Andreas and Packenham (South Park) made the highest scores with 34 and 57.[83] Andreas was the only Chicago batsman to reach double figures twice. The lopsided Australian victories represented the finale for golden age cricket in Chicago. The curtain descended when Pullman pulled out of the league in 1914, the Parkside ground of the Wanderers was torn up for clay tennis courts, and William Balster died at age 50.[84]

Cricket continued in Chicago through the First World War and in the expanding suburbs of Chicago's South Side. In 1932 when Arthur Mailey, who had played for the 1913 Australian team, managed Donald Bradman's Australian tour of the United States and Canada, there were enough quality cricketers in the Windy City to challenge the Australia's at Grant's Park on a temporary pitch built for the occasion, adjacent to the Steven's Hotel.[85] The Chicago-versus-Australia games showcased the young Donald Bradman, chosen by Wisden, cricket's statistical guide, as one of the five greatest cricketers of the twentieth century. In the economic depression of the 1930s, there simply was no peer to Bradman, and England resorted to "bodyline" tactics to keep his prolific run rate in check. The prolific scoring and wicket taking of the Australians in the United States—they took over 1,000 wickets and scored over 10,000 runs—inspired the next generation of Chicago organizers to keep the game going.

Nottinghamshire-born bibliophile Karl Auty, who earned his living running the British-American Press in Chicago, became president of the Illinois Cricket Association in 1939. Just before the outbreak of the Second World War, Auty presided over an association that ran an 18-game season between 11 league teams: Chicago, Winnetka, Lake Forest, Washington Park, Lake Shore, Milwaukee, River Forest, South Park, Hyde Park and Oak Park. Chicago CC won the league in 1939 with Winnetka CC a close second. Batting was weak with the top batsman of the league, Len Cabral of River Forest, scoring 20.14 runs per innings. Catling of Chicago CC scored the only century. By this time cricket in Chicago depended on the Chicago Parks Board to supply and maintain cricket grounds. Two of the best cricket pitches were located on Wilson and Outer Drive, which was the home ground to both the Chicago CC and the Lakeshore CC. Hyde Park CC had a ground on Outer Drive and 48th Street. The century-old links with Canada were maintained throughout this period. Karl André Auty was educated at Nottingham University and the Sorbonne and was president of the Illinois Cricket Association when Chicago revived its touring tradition with Canada. A Chicago team toured Winnipeg in 1939 with a follow-up tour planned for eastern Canada in 1940.[86] All Chicago also played St. Louis in 1939, winning at home and losing in St. Louis.[87]

When the United States geared up for the Second World War, cricket and baseball were encouraged for maintaining morale and for fund raising. As Chicago's rail hub worked overtime for the war effort many more West Indian cricketers settled in the Windy City, grafting the rigorous shoots of New York's Caribbean cricketers to the carefully tended rose garden of British immigrant cricketers. Auty's enthusiasm for Chicago cricket remained undiminished for the next 20 years. When John Marder re-established the United States Cricket Association at a meeting of the Missouri Cricket Association in 1961, he recognized Auty's prodigious energy in maintaining cricket in the Midwest by naming the Canada-versus-U.S. challenge trophy for him when the test match series was resumed after a 50-year hiatus following the last game in 1913. Marder's research on the Canada-versus-U.S. games inspired a renewal of cricket throughout the United States. Marder, an American, was educated at McGill University in Toronto. Based in Beverly Hills as a public accountant, Marder assumed the presidency of the Griffith Park Cricket Association in Los Angeles. His cricket library was second only to Auty's in Chicago. United States cricket was fortunate to have two such like-minded individuals at the helm as Britain's brain-drain to southern California in the 1960s gave Southern California cricket an influx of public school trained cricketers. These scientist-players chased Sputnik during the week and the red leather ball during the weekend at Griffith Park and UCLA. In the process they laid the foundation for the renewal of international cricket in the United States. The Karl A. Auty trophy game between Canada and the United States was held at Griffith Park in 1966. This was the first time the test series was held in California. The game reflected the rise of California cricket since its early days when it was cut off from developments in New York, Philadelphia and Chicago. Chicago continued to remain a major cricket hub; however, the fortunes of United States cricket came to rest on California-based organizations. As international teams visited Los Angeles and San Francisco once jet travel smashed the barriers of distance, Californian cricket moved center stage.

7. Cricket and Baseball on the Western Frontier, 1852–1890

ENGLISH IMMIGRANTS TO AMERICA played cricket as a cultural reaffirmation of imported values in a new land. Cricket was played on the Wild West frontier before it was tamed in 1890.[1] The unincorporated lands that later formed the states of Utah, Iowa, Wyoming, South Dakota, Colorado, Arizona and California all hosted cricket matches on occasion. One in every three Mormon converts whom Brigham Young guided to the Great Basin area of Utah had British ancestry and they played "their cricket on dry and dusty grounds chilled by spring freezes or baked by summer heat waves. Yet play cricket those early settlers did, whatever the obstacles, determined to make their sport a rallying point for community vitality in an otherwise barren social landscape."[2] In Utah, cricket was popular before the new national pastime: "Cricket as a small town phenomenon spread throughout Utah well in advance of the nation's expanding baseball interest. The territory drew upon the large numbers of English converts and games were played in Sandy, Plain City, Wellville and Coalville."[3] In Butte and Livingston, Montana, Cornish miners introduced cricket of the most muscular sort during the 1850s when they started mining copper. The miners rarely passed cricket onto the second generation, as once their sons became Americans the need to play cricket as a cultural affirmation was lost.

In California, where there were also mining opportunities, when George Aitkin, the British Consul at San Francisco, supported the formation of the San Francisco Cricket Club in 1852. The *Alta California* reported on April 15, 1852, "A number of gentlemen of this city have organized a Cricket Club, and they have selected their sporting ground immediately south of Rincon Point. A number of interesting and exciting matches are expected to come off during the ensuing season."[4]

Rincon Point was a flat low-lying area adjoining San Francisco Bay where the Bay Bridge now stands, located near the Mission District. The Mission District was named for the Spanish mission of St. Francis d'Assisi, founded in 1776. The mission was the headquarters for 21 missions built north of Baja California and linked, a day's ride apart, by El Camino Real. Following the secularization of the missions in 1824 the area declined. Once in the heart of Yerba Buena, the Mission District became an integral part of San Francisco in 1849. By the time cricket was first played, San Francisco had become a cosmopolitan city of 30,000, with seven daily newspapers, 60 brick buildings, eight to ten first class hotels, and 107 miles of laid street, most of it planked. Over 1 million letters were written by these Argonauts.[5] The arrival of Virginian aristocratic families during the Gold Rush changed the area to a dynamic upper-class neighborhood that became home to the Charles Fairfax family, George Hearst, Harrison Randolph and Randolph William Botts, the son of Governor Botts of Virginia. Their liveried coachmen transported them in style up Rincon Hill with its beautiful views of the bay. Before Nob Hill was developed, cricket games were moved from Rincon Point to the Union Race Track.

Cricket games were important social events. The standard of cricket improved when East Coast American players such as George Stead, William Crossley and Harry Groom arrived on the West Coast to find their fortune. Both Stead and Groom had played cricket for St. George's Cricket Club in New York. Groom represented the United States versus Canada in 1846.[6] The *California Clipper* praised Groom's cricket prowess.[7] In San Francisco they played for the Pioneer Cricket Club, founded on March 23, 1857. The *Pioneer Cricket Club* had its club meetings at the British Benevolent Society, located in the British Consulate on 730 Montgomery Street, the first Tuesday of the month. The 63-member club elected Charles Boyer president, Joseph Powning secretary, and John Peel treasurer. Pioneer's archrival team from 1857 was the Union Cricket Club, founded with 56 members on June 14, 1857. The July 6, 1857, edition of *Alta California* reported that "an exciting cricket match came off on the ground adjacent to the Union Race Course, on the Saturday, between the Union and Pioneer clubs of this city. A large number of spectators were present. It was the second match between the clubs in each of which the Union came off victorious."[8] Groom was second highest scorer for Pioneer CC with 6 runs, and Stead got a pair of ducks—called spectacles in cricket—being bowled for zero in both innings. He did a little better with his bowling, taking one wicket to Groom's four. The Union CC won the game convincingly due to an opening partnership of 40 runs by the Anderson brothers, George and John. Union CC scored 186 runs in their innings while Pioneer CC was all out for 86 runs in their two innings. They scored 37 in their first innings and 25 runs in their second. A ball after the game was a good place for gentlemen to meet women in San Francisco; men greatly outnumbered women during the Gold Rush years.[9] At this time, the majority of San Francisco's 50,000 inhabitants were housed in a three-mile-square area and lived in tents. Fire was a constant threat at cooking time. Food and accommodation prices were subject to wild fluctuations so opportunities for entertainment were at a premium.

Connected to the rest of the world by rapid clipper ship communication — the *Morning Cloud* set a new record for the fastest voyage from New York around Cape Horn in 101 days in 1858 — San Francisco rapidly became a cosmopolitan city served by nine local papers and 27 foreign consulates. Poet Bret Harte became the voice of the gold rush miner, while Shakespeare plays were popular in mining towns. Many of the miners had good educations though few stayed more than two years. They helped speed San Francisco's transition from a frontier to a Blue Book society within a decade.[10] Cricket was a refining agent in San Francisco's frontier society as imported and tried methods of entertainment were needed in the predominantly male society. Cricket came with American aristocratic traditions associated with the Carolinas and Virginia's tidewater aristocracy. The Knickerbocker Cricket and Baseball Club, founded in San Francisco in 1855, stated in its articles of membership that the criteria for selection to the club was to be "To the Manor born." The Knickerbockers were founded around the time Alexander Cartwright, the originator of New York Knickerbockers Baseball Club, visited San Francisco, before he finally settled in the Sandwich Islands (Hawaii) and became one of King Kalakaua's financial advisors. The Knickerbocker Cricket and Baseball Club elected John P. Fox president in 1859. Albert L. Whitney was made secretary and Henry Bowie handled the finances.[11] The Knickerbockers' board of directors included R.C. Mayne, J.Y.F. Sullivan and H.J. Laselles, who were businessmen, bankers, and academics. All four San Francisco cricket clubs at this time — the Union, Pioneer, San Francisco and the Knickerbockers — selected their best cricketers for a game played on November 25, 1859, at the Union Race Track. The *Alta California* reported the game:

> George Anderson, back-stop for the Union Club, was severely hurt, three times by the ball striking him in the face. He maintained his post, however, and back-stopped admirably. Keller, of the Pioneer, and Howson of the Union also received severe hits, and were almost [in] fainting condition for five to ten minutes. Two heavy scores were made by Howson 11 and Anderson 26 against beautiful bowling. Howson made a splendid six strike. A good dinner and ball in the evening at Campbell's wound up the exercises of the day.[12]

Anderson and Howson were the only two batsmen to reach double figures, while Wilcox (Pioneer) and Kerrigan (Union) took the most wickets.[13] The game at the Union Race Track drew large crowds and showed there was a market for sport in the city just prior to the outbreak of the Civil War.

The Sacramento Baseball Club, founded on November 11, 1859, was California's first organized baseball team. It only lasted a year, not long enough to win the first California Baseball Championship in 1860, which was won by the San Francisco Baseball Club. The San Francisco Baseball club changed its name to the Eagles out of deference to one of their great New York players, Mervin Gelshen, who had played for the Eagles in New York. Gelshen played with John Fisher in California. John Fisher had played for the Empires in New York.[14] Better players required improved grounds. The Australian Hatton brothers spotted the opportunity and enclosed the Recreation Grounds near Portrero (Oil) Hill in the Mission District; both cricket and baseball were played there after the grounds opened. On big occasions entry fees could go as high as two gold pieces. As baseball and cricket drew large crowds in San Francisco, in the Sierra mining areas such as Grass Valley — the sixth largest town in California in 1860, with 3,000 inhabitants—cricket and baseball offered an organized alternative to pickup games of fargo in the saloons.

Cricket in the Sierra foothills was one of several sports played by the Cornish mining community of Grass Valley. Thomas Packard in his *History of American Mining*, stated, "The Cornishmen know better than anyone else how to break rock, how to timber bad ground, and how to make the other fellow shovel it, transport it and hoist it."[15] The Cornish were staunch Methodists. Fiercely independent, they introduced contract mining to the West Coast. They retained the fiercely independent spirit of the English artisans that played cricket in New York and Philadelphia during the 1840s. Cornish miners first immigrated to New World in the 1840s when copper was discovered in Michigan and Chile.

Emigration increased dramatically as a third of the tin mines were closed in Cornwall starting in the 1860s. Known in the Sierras as "Cousin Jacks" for their habit of reserving new jobs for their fellow Cornish "Cousin Jacks," by 1860 their brass bands and unique style of wrestling was supplemented by cricket. J.M. Days recalled that on July 4, 1861, an ill-tempered, low scoring cricket game was played in which American fielders, swarming like bees, held their experienced English-born opposition to a draw in a game held near the local racecourse a few miles from the Empire Mine.[16] The passion shown by American miners was contrary to cricket's ethos, which was about self-disciplined control before considered action. English — mainly Cornish — miners in the Grass Valley game were nonplussed by the invasion of the pitch. The 1861 game went to the core of the cultural bifurcation of the two games. Cricket remained the more cosmopolitan of the two games because of its international appeal, fostered by the growth of the British Empire. On America's Western frontier, the game expanded in Utah when, according to Melville, "the *Salt Lake Daily Telegraph*, in a declaration of war against the city's social lethargy, asked in 1869, "Can they not organize a baseball or a cricket club? ... Let us be more social, and when we have spare time, instead of moping around home, let us go to our clubs and organize matches."[17]

In San Francisco international sports competition was fostered by cricket when a team from Victoria in British Columbia played a California XI on April 18, 1869, at the Recreation Grounds. The California XI team included George Stead and Harry Groom. The game was close, exciting and attracted spectators of all nationalities, as California won by the close margin of 11 runs with California scoring 157 to 146 runs. Guerra almost won the game for the Canadians single-handedly and was undoubtedly the most valuable player in the two-game series. The cricket correspondent for the *Alta California* wrote inspired prose about Guerra's effort to triumph over seemingly hopeless odds:

> Guerra, a capital bat ... [struck] at every ball that afforded an opportunity for a run; his performance gave them new life, for he succeeded in sending the ball to the boundary on five different occasions, by which he scored four each time — then he made several runs of three.... Guerra must be got out or the game was lost to the Californians; but he had the eye of an eagle to see the ball coming and the strength of Hercules to knock it to the unprotected part of the field and seemed to give no opportunity to the field to put him out.... In this emergency Kohler designedly left an open place in the field to invite the stray ball from Guerra.[18]

Guerra was caught for 38 runs, more than twice as many runs as were made by California's best batsman, Gorman, who scored 15. Despite Guerra's heroics at the crease, several Canadian gamblers were upset by their team's defeat, as they lost large sums of money on the outcome. In the next game against California, held on April 24, California won more convincingly by a score of 47 to 108 runs. Guerra scored 30 of Victoria's 48-run total after Crossley put California in a commanding position by taking six quick wickets. Most of the California players were selected from the St. George's (which changed its name from San Francisco CC in 1867) and the Pioneer CC. The president of St. George's CC was William Lane Booker, the British consul-general at San Francisco and successor to George Aitken. The San Francisco CC only had 17 members when it was founded in 1864. St. George's CC meetings were held at the British Consulate residence on 531 Sacramento Street.[19] San Francisco tavern-keeper Samuel Foulkes was treasurer of St. George's and was elected president of the California Cricket Club, founded in June 1868. The San Francisco cricket team connection with Victoria was strengthened when the British Royal Navy shifted its Pacific Fleet home port from Valparaiso in Chile to Esquimalt harbor just outside Victoria during the Crimean War, when a hospital for wounded soldiers was built at the new port. Crew from two of the Pacific Fleet Royal Navy ships played occasional cricket games at their home port and against the miners of Fraser River, where gold was discovered in 1858.

Railway building brought cricket to Cheyenne in Wyoming and later to Northwest Iowa. Cambridge educated William Close set up a cricket club where members could

> relive their school day cricket heroics and toast the queen during post-match dinners as compensation for the alienation and isolation of the Iowa prairie. To that end they were persistent and wide ranging. The teams in the small Iowa communities of Le Mars and Sibley thought nothing of traveling as far as Minneapolis–St. Paul for their matches. Other immigrants, moving on to the more westerly lands opened up by Close, carried their cricket to such places as Omaha; Pipestone, Minnesota; and even up the Sioux River valley to the little South Dakota boom towns of Clark, Watertown and Waverly.[20]

With the completion of the Continental Railroad in October 1869, seven months after Guerra showed himself the best batsman on the West Coast, another U.S. cricketer, Harry Wright, brought the first professional baseball team — the Cincinnati Red Stockings— to visit San Francisco. Wright, a former Union Cricket Club of Cincinnati cricket coach, made the trip to San Francisco a year after his fine bowling performance against Edgar Willsher's All England Eleven in New York and Philadelphia. The *San Francisco Chronicle* reported that the Cincinnati Red Stockings was

> the wealthiest and most influential club in the United States. Its members number about 550, and are almost all businessmen. The President of the Club, A.B. Champion, is a prominent Cincinnati lawyer. The Vice President, Thomas G. Smith, is a wealthy iron merchant, Townley, the Treasurer-Secretary of a well-to-do Cincinnati insurance company, and J.P. Joyce Secretary, is a member of the firm of Joyce & Co., Cincinnati. Clearly, the Cincinnati Red Stockings are well financed as they bought the lease on the Union Cricket Club grounds where Harry Wright was the paid cricket club professional, and built the finest stadium in the land able to house 5000 seated in the Club House. The Club House [is] close to the railway lines thereby making it easy for spectators to see the players in action. What great players they were. George Wright was a powerful lead off and agile short stop while his brother Harry Wright was capable of hitting the ball over the fence whenever he came up to bat. Waterman was regarded as the hardest hitter on the team.[21]

Harry Wright received $1,200 as captain and manager of the Red Stockings. His players received $400 each. A jeweler by trade, Wright was comfortable with budget minutiae, tour itineraries and game promotion. He designed the baseball clothing that showed off their trademark red stockings. He exchanged the beaver or straw hats favored by the Knickerbockers for the pillbox hat used by cricketers of the period. Before arriving in San Francisco, the Red Stockings played university baseball teams such as Harvard as they traveled over 10,000 miles by rail, steamboat and stagecoach in 1869. Their unbroken 57-game winning streak left professional baseball squarely imprinted on the American psyche. Their 100 percent win rate was largely due to Wright's insistence that his players practice rigorously to improve and perfect their skills. Once Wright added the trade mark stockings showing the calf of the player's legs, there was could be no mistaking baseball players for cricketers.

The 1869 Cincinnati Red Stockings. The first professional baseball team in the United States, captained by Henry Wright (seated, center), played five games in San Francisco at the Recreation Grounds. George Wright is seated on Henry's left, wearing bow-tie. Source: *Harper's Weekly*, July 3, 1869.

It was San Francisco's cricketers playing for the Eagles who gave the Red Stockings their best competition on the West Coast. Games were played at the Recreation Grounds, located on 25th and Folsom Streets. Right fielder and cricketer John Aitken scored two of the Eagles' four runs in the lopsided 34-to-4 loss to the Red Stockings. In the second game Waterman, playing for the California Nine, was reported to have hit a ball four inches off the ground, "making what is called a 'Daisy cutter.'"[22] In cricket the daisy cutter was a bowler's delivery that stayed low enough to theoretically cut off the daisy heads on its way to testing the batsman's defensive skills.

Wright's team played cricket for their third game against a California XI selected from the Union, Pioneer, California and St. George's cricket clubs. U.S. international Harry Wright's swift round-arm bowling, introduced after he saw Edgar Willsher in action during an 1868 cricket match in New York, was too much for the San Francisco batsmen, whose batting techniques were not developed to bat against overhand bowling. After defeating the cricketers and the Pacifics, Atlantics and California Nines at baseball, the Red Stockings' finale in San Francisco was a fund raiser against the Fatmen's baseball team, a team not to be taken lightly. The team was composed of substantial men:

Captain and Pitcher William T. Douglas was a member of the San Francisco police force and weighed 295 pounds; Catcher Colonel Fritz better known as "Fat Boy," Short Stop Captain William Kentzel of the Harbor Police; First Base Uncle Jim Laidley, Harbor Commissioner,

275 pounds; Second Base J. Weiland of the Philadelphia Brewery, 235 pounds; Third Base Michael Reese, capitalist, 275 pounds; Right Field George Cofran, ex–Superintendent of the Public Streets, 240 pounds; center Field Adam Shupert of the California Brewery, 260 pounds; Left Field William Higgins, saloon keeper, 225 pounds; Scorer R.N. Torrey, Fire Commissioner; 230 pounds.[23]

The Red Stockings fattened their winning margin from a 34-to-11 tour average to 34-to-4 for California. Despite California's poorer showing, the Red Stockings' visit stimulated the growth of sport in San Francisco. The crossover spirit between baseball and cricket lasted 20 years longer on the West Coast than on the East Coast. Baseball players were used to strengthen the California XX that faced the Australians in 1878, the California XXII that played Alfred Shaw's England team in 1881, and the team that played the 1896 Australian side.

In addition to the symbiotic relationship between cricket and baseball in San Francisco, well trained American cricketers such as Harold Webster from Philadelphia increased the pool of sporting talent. Webster played cricket for the Merion Cricket Club in Philadelphia before he settled in San Francisco. He was elected secretary of the Occident Cricket Club in 1877. Webster was an energetic and enthusiastic secretary who used his new position effectively. In July 1878 he arranged two games against Her Britannic Majesty's *Shah* and HBM *Opal*. The two ships were the Royal Navy's Pacific Fleet on the West Coast. HBM *Shah* was the first ship to fire Whitmore torpedoes in the Pacific when it attacked the *Huclar*, a pirate ship off the coast of Chile in 1877.[24] Both games against the Royal Navy were played at the Recreation Grounds. The game on July 4

> excited much public interest. The attendance was large.... The grandstand was well patronized by a large gathering of fashionably attired ladies. Around the playing circle were several handsome equipages filled with fair admirers of the noble game. The *Opal* eleven were driven to the grounds in three carriages provided by the inviting team. Punctually at the appointed hour, Lieut. Henderson and Sanderson tossed for the choice of innings, and the former won, sending his opponents in to bat. Clark and Cross first wielded the willow for the Occidents. Cross played in his usual over-careful style, until Ward found a weak spot and sent him back to the tent for 1. Webster followed, but was unfortunately run out, making room for Powell, who with Clark ran the score to 30, when Ward sent Clark a trimmer that could not be denied. Clark's score of 17 was made in his best style, clean and hard hitting, and beautiful defence.... The byes were large, 25, and wides 4, making a century of the Occidents' total. Lunch followed, and Robertson and Stoddard opened the game for the *Opal*, the Occidents giving three cheers— a compliment which had been paid by the visiting team to the first batsmen of the O.C.C.[25]

After the first innings the *Opal* team was out for 51 with Cross taking 7 wickets. In their second innings the OCC's 49-run margin increased when Charles Brown scored 66 before being bowled by the *Opal*'s most effective batsman and bowler, Ward. The OCC went on to score 98 for 3 in their second innings before stumps were drawn and the OCC won the game based on the first innings score. After the *Opal* departed, a second cricket game was held at the Recreation Grounds between Base Ball Players and Cricketers. The Base Ball players won the game handily by a score of 139 to 87 in two innings. John Aitken, who had played against the Cincinnati Red Stockings, took seven wickets in two innings. Purdy was the best bowler for the cricketers, taking nine wickets.[26]

Across the bay in Oakland, cricket started on July 4, 1878. The *Oakland Times* reported the event:

The Oakland Cricket Club held an enthusiastic meeting Tuesday night, and a number of new members enrolled. It was resolved to play a match against some other club in August and all cricketers in Oakland and vicinity are invited to send their names at once to the secretary George F. Degen, 608 Sixteenth Street, in order that the best selection of players may be made.

The club will meet next Saturday afternoon at 1306 Telegraph Avenue, and proceed thence to the ground for practice.[27]

Following the meeting a constitution and bylaws for the club were drawn up ready for submission to the next club meeting.[28] Before the *Oakland Times* advertised the first game of cricket to be played in Oakland, on July 25, 1878, it reported that "a fine ground had been secured for practice, adjoining the Part Street Station, Brooklyn.... A fine supply of cricketing material which has just arrived from the East, was laid out for inspection, and called forth expressions of delight on all sides. The uniform adopted consists of white flannel shirts and trowsers, and red caps."[29]

The meeting was held at Degen's School. In the first intersquad game Gray captained one side, which was all out for 24, and McDougall the other, which scored 21 runs in two innings, going down to an ignominious defeat by an innings, at the hands of Gray's team.[30] After a year of practice games the Oakland side felt strong enough to take on Webster's Occident CC team. The *Oakland Times* announced a match on May 7 between an

eleven of Oakland and eleven of the Occident Cricket Club of San Francisco. Both clubs are strongly represented and a very close and exciting game is sure to be witnessed, probably the best ever seen on this coast, great interest being taken by both clubs and their friends. The Oakland eleven will consist of the following: Messrs. Powell, Clarke, Carvill, Scott, Sherott, McGrady, Johnson, McDougall, O'Connor, Cummings and Purdy, a very smart eleven in the field and also containing some fine batsmen and bowlers, and will undoubtedly uphold the honor of this side of the bay. The Occidents will have some sterling good men among them, including: Messrs. Webster, Sanderson, Brown, Waterman, Bell, Blakeley, Donohue, and Lachlan. For though perhaps they may be stronger in batting still they are inferior to their opponents in the field. All who can make it convenient to come should certainly do so, the ground itself looks attractive enough without the games for a quiet afternoon and a nice pavilion is being put up for the convenience of the ladies.[31]

Apart from cricket on both sides of San Francisco Bay, baseball-versus-cricketers games offered invaluable practice for the forthcoming game against the visiting Australian team. Fred Lange, one of the best baseball players in the Bay Area, remembers playing both cricket and baseball at a ground located on 12th and Market Streets. Lange judged Ed Taylor of the Pioneers baseball team as the most graceful fielder on the West Coast in 1875.[32] There were five salaried baseball teams in the National Association of Professional Baseball Players at this time, including the Boston Red Stockings managed by Harry Wright. Women were encouraged to watch these games to help enhance the moral atmosphere, because the Victorian underworld was still associated with the sport. Only ten percent of the spectators at baseball matches were women.[33] Cricket drew a much higher percentage of women as they could stroll around the oval while the game was in progress, which was more conducive to courting.[34]

Arrangements for the Australian team visit were initiated by Harold Webster in a meeting held at the Occidental Hotel, located in the heart of San Francisco's financial district on Montgomery Street. In *The American Cricketer*, Webster announced:

A rare treat will be afforded the public of San Francisco early next year, in an exhibition game of cricket between the famous Australian Eleven on the one side, and twenty-two of our local cricketers on the other. The game will be played under the auspices of the Occident Club.... En route they will give games here, in Salt Lake, in New York and in Philadelphia.[35]

Despite reports of David Gregory's Australian team having done extremely well in England, Webster remained optimistic about the prospects for the California XXII selected to play Australia in San Francisco. He believed "we have material for a fair eleven or twenty-two, should the Australian team pass through San Francisco."[36]

During their tour of England, the Australian team refined the 51 fielding positions into aggressive strategic positions. Boyle's mid–off position got its name from Australian cricket legend Harry Boyle after he fearlessly stationed himself six yards from the bat to "catch men out on defensive strokes to the off-breaks of Spofforth and Garrett."[37] Boyle's position became known as silly mid-off for the obvious reason that the position was a suicidal fielding position if bowling was inaccurate or short of a length. Webster's optimism did not account for the revolution the 1878 Australians had wrought in bowling to an aggressively set field.

In truth the 1878 Australians were a rough side, rough in their behavior, rough in their attitudes.... Dave Gregory was thirty-three years old. Most of his players were under twenty-five, but they were mentally tough and physically prepared for a tour which comprised 37 matches and numerous other events including single wicket contests and cricket functions.[38]

After getting off the train in Oakland following a week long journey across the United States, the Australians stayed at the 300-bedroom Victorian style Baldwin Hotel. Named for its owner Lucky Baldwin, who got his nickname after making his second fortune on the Comstock Lode in Nevada, the hotel was the finest in San Francisco at the time.[39] After their night at the Baldwin, the Australians played the California XXII at the Recreation Grounds on October 24–25. Batting first, the Australians put on a display of patience and power hitting not seen before on the West Coast. Their first innings of 302 runs was made in 146 overs. Charles Bannerman top scored with 78 runs. English-born John Purdy proved the most economical California XXII bowler, with less than 1.5 runs coming off each of his 41 overs. He bowled 14 maidens. John T. Cross paired with him at the other end, bowling 46 overs for 90 runs. In reply the California XXII did poorly, managing a total of 86 runs in both innings. None of the California batsmen were able to answer the pairing of fast bowler Demon Spofforth with left hander Frank Allan, who Spofforth said had "the greatest swerve he had ever seen, and secured his swerve by bending his knees and bowling the ball from 23 yards, thus giving it an upward curve and room for the air friction to operate."[40] Allan was a great bowler, but according to the *Home News* of Australia, Demon Spofforth was the best of them all: "His delivery is quite appalling; the balls thunder in like cannon shot; yet he has the guile when seemingly about to bowl his fastest to drop in a slow which is generally fatal to the batsman."[41]

Spofforth (7 for 14) and Allan (12 for 19) bowled unchanged in the first innings as they bowled out the California XXII for 63 runs in 38 overs.[42] In the California second innings the "quicks" were rested as Henry Boyle's leg breaks fooled the California batsmen into giving up 15 wickets for 34 runs. The local side went down to a crushing defeat by an innings an 134 runs. Malone, Aitken and Nagle were the only California cricketers to make double figures in each of their innings, and they were all baseball players. An

The 1878 Australian cricket team played a California XXII at the Recreation Grounds. Source: *New York Clipper*, October 5, 1878.

exhibition game between Harry Boyle's XI and Gregory XI after the match gave California players much needed experience playing alongside seasoned Australian players. The California players—Foulkes, Aitken, Purdy, Webster, Cross, Sanderson, Malone and Ford, benefited from the experience; they remained prominent in California cricket circles for 20 years.[43]

The Australians' departure left many enthusiastic San Francisco cricketers in their wake. Within a week Webster organized a Thanksgiving Day match between the Occident Cricket Club and the San Francisco Cricket Club. *The American Cricketer* reported the game came off "at the recreation Grounds in the presence of several hundred spectators":

> Great interest was manifested in the match, as the newly-organized San Francisco Cricket Club introduced two new aspirants to cricket fame in the persons of Brandon and Purdy, both young Englishmen who had earned reputations in the Old Country....
> The two captains (Mr. Cross of the Occidents, and Mr. Aitken, of the San Francisco CC) ... decided to send the San Franciscos to the wickets. This was a mistake ... as it allowed his opponents the best of the ground....
> Aitken and Foulkes opened the ball for their club.... Foulkes was given out under very peculiar circumstances. The bowler (Webster) bowled him a ball which struck him on the arm; the ball bounded into the air; the wicket-keeper, thinking that he had a chance of getting a catch, ran to make it, but failed, and the ball struck the wicket, knocking the bails off. The umpire decided the batmen was bowled and gave him out. The San Francisco Eleven felt a little sore over this decision.... They closed their innings at 139 runs, to which Purdy and Brandon contributed 28 and 31 (not out) respectively, and A. Knox added 26 in brilliant style. The batting of these three gentlemen deserves the highest praise; it was characterized by good defence, and fine, free hitting. Brandon carried his bat out [to] a perfect ovation.... He and Purdy fully realized the expectations I had formed of them. Mr. Cross handled his team in his usual clever manner, and with few exceptions the Occidents fielded well. Webster trundled very well indeed, and succeeded in taking the most wickets.[44]

Aitken captained the new San Francisco CC side to an overwhelming margin of victory in the first innings, with San Francisco scoring 139 runs to the Occident's 55, though the game was declared a draw as the Occident CC were not bowled out in their second innings follow-on. Sanderson was OCC's most effective bowler of the season and Ford their best batsmen. Ford had an innings of 80 runs in 1878, the first time a California batsman was recorded as having scored over 50 runs. Apart from the San Francisco Cricket Club, the Royal Navy also provided competition for the OCC.

The baseball fraternity was also inspired by their cricket experience against the Australians. Less than a month after the Australian departure, a match was held between nine cricketers who defeated eleven baseball players in two innings by 154 to 84 runs at the Recreation Grounds on November 20, 1878. The Occident Cricket Club provided most of the cricketers. Johnstone was the most effective bowler. Ford top scored with 34 in the cricketer's first innings.[45] Andy J. Piercy played in the game. Piercy honed his cricket skills with the OCC and by the end of the season he had become a useful bowler. In baseball he drew the attention of Carl McVey when he helped the McVey's Bay City Baseball Club (founded in 1879) defeat the visiting Chicago White Stockings. On the strength of his performance, Piercy accepted a contract to play for the White Stockings, becoming the first Californian to play in the National League as professional baseball player.[46] Piercy was on hand for the visit of Alfred Shaw's English team to San Francisco in 1881.

Shaw arrived in San Francisco at the peak of his illustrious cricket career. He was born in Burton Joyce, a village five miles to north of Nottingham on the River Trent in 1842. Along with Richard Daft, his captain at Nottingham County Cricket Club, his career spanned three generations of cricketers. Henry Altham elaborates:

> As to his accuracy we surely need go no further than the aggregate statistics of his whole bowling career.... In twenty seven seasons ... Shaw bowled in first-class matches 24,700 overs, of which 16,922 were maidens, for 24,107 runs and 2051 wickets. So far as I know no bowler in the history of the game ... can claim a record of accuracy approximating to this, in which more than half the overs bowled over a period of thirty-one years were maidens, and the debit of runs is smaller than the total number of overs bowled....
>
> His action was perfectly easy and natural round-arm; he could turn the ball both ways, particularly from the off, but his predominant characteristic ... was length ... to sheer accuracy he added considerable subtlety in pace and flight ... he believed little in off theory, but preferred direct attack on the wicket, and for his pace, a large number of his victims were clean bowled....
>
> Wherever he went, and especially in his long service at Notts, Shaw's name stood for hard work, clean living, and straight dealing.... It was Alfred Shaw who suggested the whitewashing of the creases instead of having them cut into the turf, as was the universal practice down to the year 1865.[47]

Alfred Shaw, captain of the first English team to play in San Francisco in 1881. Source: *British Sports and Sportsmen*, London: Longmans, 1907.

Shaw's San Francisco visit was his third to America. He first toured with Edgar Willsher in 1868 and then with Richard Daft in 1879. On Daft's tour he was phenomenal, taking 178 wickets for an average of 2.8 runs. In appearance, Shaw was the rotund epitome of a Victorian uncle with a small cap perched on the top of a rather large head complemented by a well trimmed beard. Shaw's non-athletic appearance did not deceive the California XXII, who knew they were up against one of the shrewdest players in the game. Shaw's tour cosponsors were James Lillywhite and Arthur Shrewesbury. Shrewesbury did not play in California, as he sailed direct to Australia where he organized the remainder of the tour. The players that visited California were George Ulyett, a Yorkshire CC professional who led the English batting averages in 1880; William Bates, Tom Emmett and Edmund Peate, three other Yorkshire professionals; Roger Pilling and Robert Barlow, Lancashire players; William Midwinter of Gloucestershire, teammate of W.G. Grace's; and William Scotton and John Selby, who played for Nottinghamshire with Shaw. It was an all professional side.[48] Some members of the side kept fit running alongside the train on the journey from St. Louis. The California XXII, captained by Sanderson of the Occidental Cricket Club, had a secret weapon in Piercy. He caught the England side off guard at the Recreation Grounds with his unorthodox bowling, taking five wickets for nine runs in six overs as England were all out for 93 in their first innings. English commentators blamed the pitch as this was an England team that had scored 277 to beat *Philadelphia* by an innings and 104 runs, 254 against St. George's CC at Hoboken for a draw, 114 and 166 against an America XVIII to win by 132 runs, and 144 for 5 in St. Louis before rain stopped play. [49] Wynne-Thomas noted, "The game in San Francisco was the low point of the tour — the venue resembled a stone quarry and the crowd was less than a hundred. The home team had little idea of the game and one of the few spectators who knew about cricket complained: 'This is a farce [of] the game; it's like obtaining money under false pretences.'"[50]

Local contemporary reports in *The Olympian*, the journal of the Olympic Club, saw the game quite differently and noted so in an article reprinted verbatim in *The American Cricketer*:

> Piercy is a baseball player and has held a prominent place in several California nines, and has recently returned from an engagement with an Eastern club. For several years he has at intervals, played cricket, and understands the game thoroughly. His bowling is really pitching only that the ball strikes the ground before hitting the bat. He gives the ball a puzzling curve in the air, and when it rises from the pitch its course is most uncertain and puzzling; the English cricketers have never stood up to such "bowling" before; and the pace being terrific and the ground very far from true, they were all at sea, and the wickets fell before the curling cannon balls like stubble before a scythe.[51]

Piercy's successful bowling against Shaw's England XI made the predominantly American crowd proud, and they clamored for his early return in the second innings after California were all out for 44. Sanderson was the only Californian to make double figures in the California innings. The buildup for the moment of truth was made more frustrating for the partisan crowd by the delay of bringing on Piercy to bowl, as "Happy Jack" George Ulyett went on the offensive and was well on his way to scoring the highest innings of the tour "at a venue that resembled a stone quarry." Wynne-Thomas' characterization remains puzzling, as San Francisco— according to commentators such as Robert Louis Stevenson — has always been noted for its unstable sandy soil. Granite for the San Francisco Mint building (built in 1878) had to be imported 80 miles from Rocklin, ten miles east of Sacramento. Pictures of the Recreation pitch at this time show it to be quite sandy, though the Australian team in 1878 had complained there was glass on the pitch. Sandy or quarrylike, the state of the pitch did not affect Ulyett, who was well set and on his way to 167 runs before Piercy was brought on to bowl. *The Olympian* noted,

> The second innings of the eleven began just before two— Barlow and Ulyett, as usual appearing first. Waterman and Purdy opening the attack ... Dean and Sanderson took the places of Purdy and Waterman, but the hitting became more vigorous.... The spectators complained that Piercy had not been tried. "Some stated that they had come to see the baseball player lower the England eleven's wickets. Not to look at duffers trying to bowl!" "He cleaned them out yesterday, why not let them do it again to-day?" [Quotation marks per original.] After lunch, all took their places on the field, and a general cheer went up when Sanderson handed

the ball to Piercy. In his first over Ulyett hit him to the fence for four, and both he and Bar-low kept up the merry game. When Piercy pitches them up they smote him hard, and when he dropped short they placed the ball for singles.[52]

Ulyett's innings was the first recorded century on the West Coast and was played just as baseball was becoming semiprofessionalized in San Francisco. The overwhelming display of batting prowess by Ulyett may have actually set back the thin roots of cricket in San Francisco just as they tried to expand to an American audience. Ulyett's innings

was faultless, not a single chance being offered throughout. It was a hard earned innings, too. He ran a great many sharp runs, and many of the boundary hits were run out. He never flagged for an instant and never asked for a second's breathing time, and he hit with as much vigor in his last over as at any time. He also made the hit of the match, a splendid 6 over the southern fence, which was applauded alike by the fielders and the spectators. His grand innings includes one 6, twenty-five fours, four 3's, four 2's and singles.[53]

Ulyett's innings was so dominating that on Saturday only 15 of the California XXII showed up to play. Piercy was tried again with no further luck. If Piercy had been successful in the second innings, cricket might have proved attractive to San Franciscans, who were used to striking pay dirt. Andy Piercy already operated a ballpark across the bay, oppo-site Neptune Beach on Alameda Island.[54]

Commentators showed intimate knowledge of the game in their newspaper reports. As events turned out, England declared at 367 for 2 in their second innings, with Aitken — another baseball player, who played for the defunct San Francisco Cricket Club in the 1870s— picking up one of the two England wickets. Shaw chose to let George Ulyett have his way with the bat as a demonstration of the finest batting technique England had to offer, and the California XXII did not have time to bat again in a second innings. Shaw's American cricket matches barely paid the freight for his team's onward passage to Australia and New Zealand. However, once on board ship, Billy Bates and Tom Emmet were invited to sing before the king of the Sandwich (Hawaiian) Islands, which resulted in an invitation to the King Kalakaua's palace in Honolulu. In Australia Shaw's team achieved a creditable record. They were

the sixth English team to tour Australia and won 8 of their 14 matches against the odds, lost three and drew three. Ulyett was the best of the English batsmen, with 1424 runs at 33.11, and Peate the best bowler with 264 wickets at 5.84. Pilling kept wicket economically....

The amazing Midwinter not only completed the tour for England, taking useful wickets and scoring handy runs, but he rejoined Victoria for inter-colonial matches in 1882–83! He told the Sydney *Mail* he objected to being called an Anglo-Australian and insisted he was Australian to the core, but the paper would have none of it. "Are we to endure another season of vagueness from this very slippery cricketer?" the paper asked.[55]

Cricket was the game that unified Australia. By 1880 most Australian bush towns boasted pitches of their own and the game had become the Australian pastime. Talent was color-blind if not Aboriginal. Sam Morris, "a colored batsman born in Hobart of West Indian migrants lured by the [Australian] gold rushes, scored 280 for Richmond against St. Kilda in Melbourne."[56]

Despite great social amenities in San Francisco, English and Australian teams by-passed California for a decade. Meanwhile, baseball sank deep roots into the sandy Cali-fornia soil. By 1885 there were three baseball parks in the Bay Area located at Central Park,

8th and Market and in Oakland at 13th and Market Street. Two baseball leagues were in operation, the California and the California State leagues. The former comprised the Stars, Haverleys and Pioneers of San Francisco and the Atlas of Sacramento. The California State League comprised the California of San Francisco and two teams in Oakland, the Damianias and the Greenwood-Morgan Baseball Club. Starved of professional cricketers, San Francisco cricket expanded its role as a classy sport in the newly established country clubs located on San Francisco's peninsula area to the south of the city. Some of the Occidental CC players joined the Merion CC based out of the fine facilities of the Olympic Club in 1884. In 1885 the Olympic Club moved its playing fields from the Oakland Baseball Ground to a new facility in Golden Gate Park. The new Haight Street Grounds, located at the eastern end of the park, featured private boxes and carriage parking for the city's elite, which included the publisher of the *San Francisco Chronicle*, De Young, and the Central Pacific railroad millionaires, Crocker, Huntington, Stanford and Hopkins. Ladies' Day was inaugurated at the ballpark on May 21, 1886. This may have been instrumental in helping curb the unruly behavior at baseball games. English traveler William Clulow wrote on his visit to San Francisco that "If one meets a man in the street with his arm in a sling, one broken leg, an eye out, it may be safely conjectured that this 'wreck of humanity' has been 'adjudicating at some recent big baseball match,' and has had to run the gauntlet of some two or three thousand infuriated lookers-on."[57] Clulow's comments might explain why "Gentleman" Jim Sullivan, the world champion boxer who trained at the Olympic Club, was invited to umpire important baseball games.

As more spectators paid to watch boxing and baseball, sport facilities for spectators improved. Overlooking the railway at Webster Street in Oakland opposite Alameda Island, the new Alameda Stadium had cushioned seats and housed Oakland's first professional baseball team, the Greenwood-Morgan Baseball Club.[58]

In the Sierras cricket was played more frequently (than during the Civil War) in the predominantly Cornish mining town of Grass Valley, home of the Empire Mine. The Empire Mine recruited the world's best engineers to design and upgrade mining equipment. With regular shifts, some of the miners had leisure time. Grass Valley was home to Cornish-born mine superintendent John Clift, who gave his name to the Clift Hotel on San Francisco's Nob Hill. The English-born Coleman brothers invested some of their profits from the Empire Mine in the narrow gauge Northern Central line they built from Grass Valley to Rocklin, where it connected with the Central Pacific line to Sacramento. From Sacramento, steamboats ferried baseball and cricket teams to San Francisco and Stockton. When baseball teams won a series of games they tied brooms to the handrails of the ships to signify a clean sweep to their supporters. In this era, of Thayer's "Casey at the Bat," set in Mudville (Stockton), the Grass Valley Union Cricket team plied the same route to take on the Merion Cricket Club in Golden Gate Park at the Olympic Club's Haight Street ground. In their first San Francisco game in 1883, the Grass Valley Union Cricket team was soundly defeated by Merion. There were only two Bay Area cricket clubs in the 1880s, after the Oakland CC folded, the Merion CC and the Occident CC, so competition from the Sierra foothill mining towns was encouraged by the city teams. In a 15-game season, Merion CC was the strongest side in California during the 1883 season, winning both the Harrison Trophy and the Olympic Cup.

The Harrison Trophy was donated by Illinois-born William Greer Harrison, the

Olympic Club's president. Ben S. Benjamin headed the Merion averages with 11.67 runs per innings and a highest score of 40. John Purdy, who played first for Oakland CC after his selection to the California XXII that played Alfred Shaw's England XI in 1881, led the batting for the Occident CC with an 8.80 batting average and a highest score of 26 runs. The California batting averages were far behind those achieved in Philadelphia. Sanderson, Purdy, Cross, Bristowe, Aitken and Stuart all played for the Occident CC. On June 4, 1884, they played a local Australian side at the Olympic Grounds located at the corner of Fourteenth and Center Street in Oakland.[59] The score was 94 to 41 for the Australians.[60] OCC played HMS *Swiftshire* in November.[61] Then Merion CC played in Oakland and beat the British mariners on July 19. Their next game, against the other San Francisco team, was also played in Oakland on July 26. The game resulted in an OCC victory over Merion as they won the Harrison Trophy in a four-game series. The OCC won the championship game on first innings totals of 71 to 54 by a 17-run margin. *The American Cricketer* declared that the final game between the two clubs in 1884 was "certainly the best ever played between the local clubs":

> Barney and Ben Benjamin, who were the first Merion representatives, started scoring very rapidly, 15 runs being registered after Purdy and Waterman had each sent down an over. This was too good to last.... G. Theobald now partnered Jacobs and the spectators were treated to some fine cricket; both batsmen played very carefully.... Jacobs succumbed to the veteran Philadelphian.... He certainly played Waterman in better style than any other batsman seen on the Oakland grounds. He will prove a valuable acquisition to the M.C.C.... Altogether the Merion lost the game by their bad fielding and bowling.[62]

San Francisco's cricketers owed a lot to the philosophical vision of Olympic Club president William Greer Harrison's belief that sport was essential for creating healthy and productive citizens. He encouraged the use of the Olympic Club facilities by the cricketers in Oakland. As the East Bay urbanized with the advent of the telegraph, shipping and railways, Oakland's rural aspect changed due to colorful real-estate promoters, such as German born Charles A. Klinkner, who "boomed" Klinknerville real estate located between Oakland and Berkeley. He sailed close to the law in his promotions. The San Francisco police blotter reported that Klinkner once was arrested wearing a jacket with "thirty-eight pockets and it was almost a days' work to search him."[63] Despite brushes with the law he was civic minded, supporting the local Klinkner's Baseball Club by providing them a ground on San Pablo Avenue close to the Oakland Trotting Park. The Oakland team played one of its last games in Klinknerville before it became the home ground of the Alameda Cricket Club just before Klinkner's death in 1893. Klinkner's Recreation Grounds were enclosed so the Alameda Cricket Club was able to charge entry fee to the spectators before it was forced to move to its Webster Street location as a result of Klinkner's death. The move to Webster Street was an upmarket one, as nearby Alameda Island became regarded as the healthiest city on the Pacific coast following the completion of its unique sewer system.[64] Oakland's first industrialist millionaire retreat, Alameda Island became renowned for its Richardson Romanesque and Queen Anne Victorian mansions. Norman Shaw, an English architect, developed the Queen Anne–style house, with its ornate drawing rooms designed for courting, in a period when East Bay industrialists' daughters married English aristocracy. General Kirkhams' daughter became Lady York-Buller and Maude Burke became Lady Burke-Cunard. According to Elinor Ruckley,

Alameda considered itself something of a Newport. Tennis courts and cricket fields abounded everywhere; the glistening bathing beaches on the unpolluted Bay were the finest....

Alameda was a magnet for yachtsmen. Its Encinal Club on the Southern Shore boasted the most imposing boat house in California. Among yachts moored in the Estuary was that of Frank M. Smith whose borax factory in Alameda was the biggest borax supplier in the world....

Alameda was the only municipality in the Bay Area where residences might be built right on the water. Many Northern Californians maintained week-end houses.[65]

This wealthy, leisured society nurtured the best cricket club in California for the next decade. The Alameda Cricket Club became the chosen club for many of San Francisco's best cricketers, such as Sanderson, Cross, Purdy, Theobald and Cookson, all of whom would make major player contributions to cricket in northern California for the next generation.

8. The California Cricket Rush, 1890–1914

CRICKET WAS PLAYED IN TEN of California's 59 counties by 1900. During this time, San Francisco was the hub of cricket activity in northern California. Harold Webster, an American-trained cricketer from Philadelphia, convened the inaugural meeting of the California Cricket Association in November 1891, held at the Occidental Hotel in the heart of San Francisco's financial district. *The American Cricketer* reported:

> Cricket is very much like real estate in this section of the country, booming in parts. The good work was commenced last year by the formation of three clubs in San Francisco, namely, the Alameda, Burnaby and Pacific Cricket Clubs. Of these, the Alameda was head and shoulders stronger than the other two.... The season of 1891 has started with five clubs in the field, viz, the California, Burnaby, Alameda, Oakland and Pacific. The first four named have formed themselves into a cricket association, to play for a pennant. These clubs play their competing matches on Sunday, and as the Pacific is a Saturday club it has not deemed it necessary to join the association. There are also country clubs at Santa Rosa, Lower Lake, Lakeport, Grass Valley and Los Angeles.[1]

Some of the southern California cricketers played for San Francisco when the opportunity arose. Irrigation engineer William Pedley lived near Riverside, 60 miles east of Los Angeles. He traveled north to San Francisco in 1892 and scored 22 runs opening the batting for the Alameda Cricket Club against the California Cricket Club. He took three wickets in the same game, a strong all-round performance.[2] There was no restriction on player movement between northern and southern California teams. However, California Cricket Association rules did restrict the movement of northern California players between teams. Amateur cricketers chose to follow the CCA rules for the betterment of the game. The CCA Charter laid out the following rules for cricket:

1. Clubs affiliated with the association cannot play against non-affiliated Clubs without the sanction of this Association.

2. No members of a Cricket Club represented in this Association can play with more than one club, except as hereinafter provided.

3. On or before September 6th, any member of an affiliated Club, can upon fourteen days' notice to this Association, and by showing good cause, be permitted to resign from his Club and join and play with any other Club.

4. On or before the 13th day of April in each year, the secretary of each affiliated Club shall furnish the Secretary of this Association with a complete list of the members of his Club, and shall further notify the Secretary of the Association of the enrollment of each newly elected member thereafter.

5. Any member of an affiliated Club, who may be in arrears or delinquent in his dues or assessments to his club, cannot play for another Club until such arrears or delinquency are paid up.

6. All scheduled matches must start punctually at 11:30 A.M. Half an hour allowed for lunch. Wickets drawn at 5:30 P.M. unless the Captains of the competing teams agree otherwise.

7. The penalty of infringing the foregoing rules shall be the forfeiture of the match in question [by] the Club offending.[3]

With the exception of Lake County, cricket's growth in California was largely dependent on immigration from Britain and Australia. Colonies settled by British residents were set up throughout the state in the 1890s as California settlement agencies actively searched for immigrants. Two of these colonies in northern California, at Burns Valley in Lake County and in Placer County next to the Central Pacific Railway line ten miles outside of Sacramento in the Sierra foothills, became very active cricket and sporting communities.

Lake County was located a day's journey north of San Francisco by rail to Calistoga and then stagecoach to Lower Lake.[4] Forty-five miles from Calistoga, rounded hills overlook Clear Lake's west shore where the city of Lakeport grew into the leading commercial and administrative center of Lake County. The 82-square-mile surface of Clear Lake marks it as California's largest inland lake, though smaller than Lake Tahoe which shares its shoreline with Nevada. From 1890 Clear Lake's paddle steamer service linked the three main towns of Upper Lake to the north, Lower Lake on the southernmost shore, and Lakeport located on the western shore to the north of Mt. Konocti. At 1,300 feet above sea level, in the late afternoon, west shore winds frequently whip down off Mt. Konocti's 4,000-foot symmetrical volcanic cone, stirring up waves on Clear Lake's fish rich waters. The whitecaps crash on the shore of promontories and small islands, named for local cricketers who for 20 years, from 1890 to 1910, turned Lake County into the best cricket-playing county in California. Baylis Point, Jago Bay and Beakbane Island were named after local cricket players.[5] Thomas Beakbane and his partner Herslet were real-estate promoters and insurance brokers for British fire insurance companies such as the London and Lancashire, Manchester Insurance and the Caledonian Insurance Company of Edinburgh. Beakbane and Herslet's real-estate promotion of Lake County land was helped by the fact that Lillie Langtry chose to buy Guenoc Ranch in Coyote Valley five miles from the Burns Valley settlement after one of her San Francisco performances in 1887. She kept the ranch until 1903. Langtry's amorous associations with Edward, Prince of Wales (later King Edward VII) and his first cousin, First Lord of the British Admiralty, Prince Louis of Battenburg (changed to Mountbatten during the First World War) enhanced Lake County's alluring appeal to British investors.

Charles Owen was one of these investors; he settled in Burns Valley a few miles from Guenoc Ranch in 1886. As a Lancashire cricketer, Owen was steeped in the industrial cricket tradition associated with the textile mills. Cotton financed cricket in Lancashire where, in 1888, it was organized into two major leagues. Each league had two divisions of 14 teams each, a total of 56 teams competing each season. The Saturday cricket league was run by the Bolton and District Cricket Association. Each club was allowed one professional. These professionals had a wide variety of cricket organizations to choose from in Lancashire;

> these have ranged from the ultra-ambitious and "wealthy" clubs to the most modest of teams.... In addition, many teams have been fielded by a wide variety of industrial and commercial organizations including ... a very sizable number of cotton mills, back-street chapels and mission-huts. Cricket players ranged in quality from the up-and-coming outstanding local lad, to County, State, and a sprinkling of Test players.[6]

Owen founded Burns Valley Cricket Club in 1887 and had little difficulty in attracting local British cricketers whom he melded into a high quality team.[7] One of the players, Percy Baylis, was a carpenter. His father was an English-trained surgeon who had homesteaded on Baylis Point where he was buried after drowning in a sailing accident on Clear Lake. Born in Burns Valley in 1871, Percy attended high school in Oakland then moved to Oregon where he worked briefly as a miner. After the mine closed, Baylis returned to Lower Lake where he became superintendent of the Wrey Ranch, one of the first commercial wineries in Lake County. Percy married Fannie Jago, the daughter of British major general Jago, who before retiring to Lake County had commanded the Gibraltar garrison. General Jago's son Louis owned Jago's Cash Store in Lower Lake, which enjoyed a popular local reputation among ranching customers because of its wide inventory, which ranged from needles to a threshing rig.[8] Another Burns Valley cricketer was attorney David Jones who ended his career as a judge and appears to have been well esteemed locally, as Jones Bay was named for him. When he played cricket for Burns Valley he lived next to the ranch of his fellow club member and realtor, Thomas Herslet, southeast of the Burns Valley School House. Initially, Burns Valley Cricket Club cricketers sharpened their skills with intersquad games between "Smokers" and "Non Smokers." According to Henry Maudlin's history of Lake County, "When the Englishmen came they brought with them a desire to continue a sport which they indulged in England — the playing of cricket. A place was set up near the present Garner Resort and it became a popular sport for the County."[9]

The Burns Valley Cricket Club pavilion and field with its convenient quay can still be seen at the Garner Resort. Visiting cricketers could disembark from the paddle steamer at the quay or travel around the lake by stagecoach. In 1889 the Pacific Cricket Club of San Francisco played their first three games against Burns Valley, which they won easily. The matches were well attended; the steamboats *Freda*, *Tabasca*, and the fastest of them all, the *Meteor*, ferried spectators across Clear Lake to the Burns Valley games. Many spectators came from Lakeport, and among them were wealthy American ranchers who enjoyed the social occasion and diversion from the loneliness of ranching in a lightly settled area.

Page Collier, who owned the *Meteor*, was an all-round American sportsman. Apart from winning the competition for the fastest boat on the lake, he became swimming champion of Lakeport in 1893.[10] His father, Captain William B. Collier, had settled on the northeast shore of the lake at Black Point in 1887. Prior to changing his career to that of horse breeder, he had been superintendent of the United States Warehouse for Indian Supplies in San Francisco. His son Page was raised on the ranch and became a very popular member of the Lakeport Cricket Club after it was founded by Herbert Keeling in 1889. Keeling had settled in Lake County just a year before. Schooled at Dover College in Kent, he played cricket in the Sussex leagues and played for Brighton Cricket Club on their home ground, which they shared with the Sussex County Cricket Club. Charles Aubrey Smith was Sussex County Cricket Club captain at the time, but there is no record that the two great California cricketers ever played against each other. Brighton Cricket Club played cricket against lower level cricket clubs with great cricketing tradition such as Arundel CC and Tunbridge Wells CC in Kent.[11]

Herbert Vincent Keeling, founder of the Lakeport Cricket Club. Source: Keeling Papers, Lake County Historical Courthouse Museum, Lakeport, California.

Though a little below County level standard, Arundel Cricket Club was one of cricket's oldest clubs, with a 300-year-old cricket playing tradition.[12]

Herbert V. Keeling's father, the Reverend William G. Keeling, had a family of nine children. Herbert was the youngest of the four boys. As a patron of the Brighton Cricket Club the Reverend Keeling encouraged his son Herbert to play cricket. Herbert carried the family cricketing tradition with him to California when he left England at age 20. Keeling settled first near the Hildebrand family ranch in Kelseyville, Lake County, after a brief stay in Santa Barbara where he found farming was not his vocation.[13] He found his true calling in Lake County as a lawyer after taking the bar exam in 1893. In the same year he became a lawyer he founded the Lake County Title and Abstract Company, which is still in operation today. Keeling's law and title insurance practice soon expanded into investment real estate. As his practice flourished so did his involvement in cricket, Masonry, and the local Episcopal church. Keeling became a Lakeport Mason's Lodge member, working his way to Master. As his Masonic career progressed he became a member of Odd Fellows, and attained the twenty-third degree of the Scottish Rite Temple. He later joined the Shriners and went with them to Hawaii a decade after his cricket days ended. He invested in a mine, named Sixes Mine, after the equivalent of a home run in cricket.[14] Lake County was mined for borax, sulphur, gold, silver, and cinnabar before ranching and horticulture became the leading industry. Cinnabar, used in gold refining, was mined at the New Almaden near San Jose starting in 1826, when California was still part of Mexico.

Converted to mercury, it was used in gold separating furnaces. Lake County's mining activity centered on Middleton, 12 miles to the south of Burns Valley, where Captain White was superintendent of the Sulphur Bank Mine. Louis Jago worked at the mine for Captain White before establishing his Lower Lake store.

Louis Jago became a useful player on the Lakeport Cricket Club team, founded by Keeling in 1889. Keeling communicated his enthusiasm for the game effectively as he recruited team members from the wealthiest American born landowners in Lake County. At first, the Lakeport Cricket Club confined its activities, like those of the Burns Valley Cricket Club across the lake, to intersquad games. In the first skirmishes between members of the Lakeport team, the Democrat side captained by Keeling defeated the Republican side by an innings. The *Lakeport Bee* reported:

> The lower ground was used for the first time this season and was far from good, this we believe was the case for poor play and we expect with improved grounds, to see better cricket all round.
> On the Republican side but little can be said of the batting, John Deputy standing out as a brilliant exception.[15]

In the second warm-up game, held in 1890, Keeling took ten Republican wickets as the Democrats won yet again. Scores were low, as Lakeport Cricket Club in eight attempts only compiled two innings that went over 50 runs. Lakeport's weak batting was typical of any side starting out. The New England cricketers Charles Hammond and the Rodman brothers played cricket at Harvard and Yale but did not join the Burns Valley Cricket Club that played the Pacific Cricket Club on September 8 and 9, 1890. Burns Valley CC won both games.

> The second match ... seemed at the commencement of the second innings all in favor of San Francisco, but the Lake county cricketers pulled an up-hill game out of the fire by superior play, while the all round fielding was exceptionally good. For the Pacifics Howell again did a grand day's work with the ball, while Balnaves at long stop fairly carried off the fielding honors.[16]

Howell took 23 wickets for 76 runs for the PCC. Keeling was Burns Valley's most successful bowler with 19 wickets for 88 runs.[17] Harold Ward and Arthur Theobald were the best PCC batsmen. Barry and Thomas Herslet scored the most runs for Burns Valley CC. Keeling and Baynton showed promise as an opening pair capable of starting the innings with a 20-run partnership on two of the four occasions they opened the batting during the two-game, four-innings series. The games against San Francisco teams were important for cricket in Lake County as they offered the opportunity for the best players on the Burns Valley Cricket Club and Lakeport CC to play together against strong opposition. Though BVCC beat Lakeport CC three times in the 1891, the sides benefited from the joint games. Keeling's batting and bowling against Burns Valley showed promise of greater things to come. The *Lakeport Bee* reported of one game, "The chief glory of the match belongs to Mr. Keeling, who succeeded in carrying his bat through both innings scoring altogether 82 runs out of the 140 made by the club. He was also instrumental in dismissing every member of the opposing side."[18] The *Lakeport Bee's* coverage of the matches was helped by Captain William Crump's membership in the Lakeport team; he briefly owned the *Bee* when it was published as the *Lakeport Democrat*.[19] In addition to securing news coverage Keeling received strong support from the Hammond, Edmands,

Rodman and Collier families. Hammond, Edmands and Rodman lived on adjoining ranches in Upper Lake. Keeling's records show that he did the legal work resulting in the subdivision of the 1,234-acre Hammond estate. Charles Hammond and his brother Gardiner bought the land in 1884. Grizzly-bear hunter William Hunter was the first American to settle in Upper Lake when he built a flour grist mill there in 1854.[20]

Before arriving in California, Charles Hammond went to St. Paul's School in Concord, New Hampshire, the best cricket and preparatory college for Harvard University. At Harvard, Hammond spent time with classmates Theodore Roosevelt and Owen Wister. After graduation he married Harriet Paine Lee, the sister of Theodore Roosevelt's first wife.[21] Apart from his excellent cricket skills, Hammond had a good career in state politics, being appointed an honorary lieutenant colonel in recognition of his service on California governor Gillett's staff in 1906. It was Hammond who successfully orchestrated Lake County community opposition to the Yolo Water and Power Company's attempt to buy up the water rights of Clear Lake for less than a million dollars and then divert them to water hungry San Francisco. This attempt occurred before the damming of the Hetch Hetchy Valley, opposed by John Muir. While Hammond fought political battles, his brother-in-law Bill Edmands, a Lakeport teacher, lived on the ranch next door. Edmands had met Hammond at Harvard where he was captain of the rowing team. After he arrived in Lake County in 1890, he bought land from Charles Hammond's brother, Gardiner, then purchased an additional 900 acres on which he planted olive groves and vines. On the swampy acreage overlooking Clear Lake's shoreline, he planted thirsty eucalyptus trees and willow trees to act as a wind breaks and drain the marshy land. Behind this ecological water barrier California oak trees flourished on the edges of a paddock grazed by sheep. This beautiful, tranquil setting by the lake was overlooked by a fine Victorian house with verandas on two sides, which became the clubhouse for the Lakeport Cricket Club when games were played on the cricket oval below starting in 1892. Edmands' Red Hill Ranch, still stands. To the west it overlooks Rodman Slough, which was where the steamboat *Freda* used to disembark its cricketers and spectators on game days.[22]

Robert Simpson Rodman was born in the cricket playing city of Pittsburgh in 1855 and graduated Yale University in 1879.[23] Rodman was the son of Union general T.J. Simpson. He was popular at Yale, where he was invited to join the Skull and Bones Society under one of its ten designations as the most socially adept member of his class. His brother, West Point graduate Arthur Rodman, later joined him on the Upper Lake Ranch. Arthur was a keen athlete who chose to bike around the lake to cricket games when they were played on the Black Point estate of the Collier family. Other club members were drawn from Lakeport's professional and business community. Greene, the wicket-keeper, owned a saloon, and had a street in Lakeport named after him. Allen and John Spurr owned the Lakeport Hotel. Judge Sayres was for a time Keeling's law partner. Sayres was a well known name in Philadelphia, where the Union Cricket Club — the precursor to the famous Young America Cricket Club — had first played their games on Mrs. Sayres' estate. The California Sayres became a judge and along with Charles Hammond was active in California state Republican politics. Both Sayres and Spurr kept their sporting options open. Apart from playing cricket, they owned sailboats. It may have been no coincidence that the boats were named the *Star* and the *Young America;* the YACC had been Philadelphia's best cricket team from 1855 until its merger with Germantown Cricket Club in 1891.[24] The

Young America Cricket Club was founded by the Wister family. Owen Wister, the great nephew of William Rotch Wister, the YACC founder, attended Harvard with Charles Hammond and was a great friend of Theodore Roosevelt. Keeling seized the opportunity to meld the well educated New England Yankee ranchers with the hotel owners of Lakeport, laying the foundation for 20 years of cricket in Lake County. Apart from cricket, Keeling had a broad range of interests. He enjoyed San Francisco theatre and accompanied his second wife, opera singer Gertrude Wells, on the violin. Despite his affinity for the rich cultural atmosphere of San Francisco in the Gilded Age, with its literary Bohemian Club frequented by Robert Louis Stevenson, the opera, the Mechanics' Institute, the Olympic Club, the Harvard Club and the Pioneer Society, cricket remained Keeling's primary recreational outlet until his forties. On his trips to San Francisco, Keeling played for the Pacific Cricket Club. At the time, the PCC was a Saturday club side, which meant it did not participate in regular Sunday league games organized by the California Cricket Association. Keeling's first game in San Francisco for the PCC was against the California Cricket Club in 1891. The CCC was captained by the Philadelphia-trained cricketer and secretary of the California Cricket Association, Harold A. Webster. The CCC won easily, but the *San Francisco Chronicle* gave the PCC credit for "a good fielding innings against sterling defense and under a broiling sun. The body of spectators present was not over large, but very observant, [and] had only words of praise for their sportsmanlike efforts.... H.V. Keeling of Lake County played for the P.C.C. and gave frequent examples of sharp fielding, which the city men might well have emulated."[25]

Webster, California's best wicket-keeper, persuaded William Roderick "Digger" Robertson to join the California Cricket Club in the CCA's inaugural season. Robertson was born in Deniliquin, New South Wales, on October 6, 1861, and died in Brighton, Victoria, on June 24, 1938. The known details of Robertson's career are precise because he was a first-class Australian player who played against Alfred Shaw's team for his home state, Victoria. He scored 33 and took 8 wickets for 82 runs in the match. On the strength of his performance for Victoria, Robertson was selected for the Combined Australia XI that played Shaw's English side at Adelaide in 1884. He batted number 11 and took no wickets.[26] Robertson played seven first-class matches in Australia, scoring 109 runs and taking 15 wickets before immigrating to California.[27] In 1887 Robertson clashed with his East Melbourne CC captain, Australian bowling legend Harry Boyle, in a game against England. The feud spilled into the columns of the *Australasian,* where Robertson denied that he had acted in an "uncricket-like" manner by refusing to bowl in a game between England and the EMCC. Robertson noted in his defense, "If my expression of opinion that our captain should not take himself off after taking three wickets for eight runs, to put me on could be construed into a refusal to bowl, I should be guilty."[28] Robertson took umbrage at "the offensive language made use of by our captain.... Towards the end of the first day's play he requested me, in most insulting terms, to leave the ground; and although I finished that day's play, I was certainly justified in not taking any further part in the match without some apology for language more becoming a bullock-driver than a gentleman cricketer."[29] Ultimately, the EMCC committee ruled that Robertson should make a written apology to Boyle. Boyle and Robertson did reconcile, though five months later the *Australasian* reported that Robertson "might give up cricket altogether, and play baseball."[30]

New South Wales' loss was California's gain. Robertson made his first impact as a bowler in San Francisco cricket. Then after three years he set batting records in CCA league play. He played first for the California Cricket Club. His second club was the San Francisco Cricket Club. With his last California cricket club, the Bohemian Cricket Club, he won the CCA championship in 1896. Playing for the CCC in 1891, he scored 136 runs, "head and shoulder above any other team," against the Alameda Cricket Club, in what the *American Cricketer* reported was "the finest score ever heard of on the Pacific coast."[31] Robertson's century — the first by an individual batsman in California since George Ulyett scored his century for Shaw's visiting England side in 1881 — was a portent for the future. In 1894, Robertson, playing for the San Francisco Cricket Club, scored 208 not out against the first team he played for in San Francisco, the California Cricket Club. This was the first recorded double century in California history. While CCA cricket went from strength to strength the Pacific Cricket Club benefited from its strong connections with the British Consulate in San Francisco and the Olympic Club. The Olympic Club, established by firemen in 1866, introduced the German turnverein tradition of exercise to keep fit for fighting fires. When William Greer Harrison became president of the Olympic Club for 13 years from 1886 to 1899 he turned his influence toward promoting English amateur sports because he believed they fostered the highest and best manhood in its membership. Illinois-born Harrison was a man of immense energy and charm. In 1891 when the CCA was founded he donated the Harrison Trophy and raised enough bond money, in harness with Senator Flood, to rebuild the old Olympic Club, which had burned down. He became president of the PCC with which the British consul-general in San Francisco, Walter Courtney Bennett, toured Lake County on the July 4th weekend in 1892. The annual game against Burns Valley Cricket Club proved more entertaining than usual. The *San Francisco Chronicle* reported:

> fires broke out in the dry grass and all the cricketers both local and foreign, had to turn to fight the flames. Next morning a dip in the cool waters of the beautiful lake restored the amateur firemen and the second match was played. In this the Burns Valley men completely turned the tables. Kelson, a new player, and Webber, the invariably useful trundler, bowled unchanged throughout the match, and their undeniable deliveries, taken with Bayton's grand score of 71, decided the match early in the day.... That night a dance was given in the Burns Valley Hall, and the scarlet and black cricketers attended in force and showed they could trip the light fantastic even if cricket at 90 in the shade was not their forte.[32]

The Burns Valley Cricket Club victory, the first in four years of competition, reflected an increasing parity between town and county cricket in northern California. Parity between clubs enhanced competition between them during the economic depression which hit California in 1893 and lasted until 1896. In California, the first sports casualty caused by the depression was the poorly run California Baseball League, which collapsed, ending professional baseball in California for seven years. Despite their amateur status, cricket and baseball represented different sporting constituencies in San Francisco in the 1890s; where baseball was a largely blue collar sport and cricket stuck to the Philadelphia mold and positioned itself as the sport of gentlemen. Robertson, as we have seen, could play both baseball and cricket, but he continued to focus on cricket. *The American Cricketer* reported in 1893 that "Robertson is one of the best amateur bowlers going, and Webster is truly up to professional form behind the wickets. He is also a fine steady bat, and yesterday carried his bat for a brilliant 56. For Alameda Ward and Pedley both played well, although they made no remarkable analysis."[33]

In northern California the Burlingame Country Club, founded in 1893 in San Mateo County, devoted itself to polo. Leland Stanford and James Flood, California multimillionaires and senators, lived in San Mateo County where Burlingame formed a cricket team that played Lake County at Calistoga in 1893.[34] Burlingame cricket did not make a strong impression in San Francisco where Robertson, playing for the San Francisco Cricket Club, raised the level of the game by hitting two consecutive centuries against his old club, the California Cricket Club, and the Pacific Cricket Club.[35] Robertson's remarkable batting improvement did not win the Harrison Trophy for the SFCC side because the Alameda CC quartet of Hogue, Ward, Sloman and Randall combined to overcome one star with a weaker supporting cast to win the CCA league in 1893.

In 1894 four teams played in the CCA: Alameda CC, California CC, Pacific CC and San Francisco CC. Strengthened by locally trained talent, the Bird brothers and Moriarty were baseball players who played an important role in Alameda's league championship victory in 1894. With no professional option available for California baseball players during the depression years from 1893 to 1898, cricket proved attractive to baseball players, who still fielded without gloves in the 1890s. Lange noted in his history of the Pacific Coast League that a majority of the California baseball players in 1881 played under assumed names to avoid causing parental disapproval of Sunday baseball.[36] Before the demise of the California League, crowds of 20,000 had attended games between teams such as the San Francisco Olympics and Oakland's Greenwood-Morgan team (later renamed the Oakland Colonels) at the Haight Street Grounds from 1889.[37] The Californian professional baseball players were "not known as heavy batsmen, [but] they were widely recognized as excellent fielders, base runners and pitchers."[38] Base running and moving the batsmen into scoring position by well placed hitting was fundamental to Golden Age cricket. This Henry Chadwick type of play remained a hallmark of California ball until well into the twentieth century. California's baseball and cricket scenes overlapped. The California openness to other races' playing baseball was a distinct contrast from New York. In 1888, black catcher Wilds played professionally in the California State League, two years after Cap Anson refused to play against black players in professional baseball on the East Coast.[39] Spanish names also featured on California baseball rosters. Cricket did not attract racially diverse players, as the sportsman's ethos propagated by the English public schools was still confined to making gentlemen of white people. It was different on the East Coast, where the West Indian community played regularly in the New York League.

In the Sierra foothills of Placer County, ten miles from Sacramento on the Central Pacific line, public schoolboy cricketers settled in a bucolic cricket wonderland:

> Within a few years the landscape of the Colony, which had been mostly a dense forest of oak and pine, began to be beautifully dotted here and there with young thriving orchards, attractive homes, and streets lined with palm trees.... Lands of the Colony extended north of Rocklin and eastwardly to Penryn, touching the Central Pacific railroad at three points, Rocklin, Loomis and Penryn. It was bounded on the north by high Boulder ridge, which made a sweeping half circle, and was crested with a thick pine forest ... just north of Loomis the lands extended to both sides of the railroad almost to Newcastle.... The view from numerous vantage points in the colony was magnificent. To the north could be seen the snow capped Sierra Nevada, to the west the Sacramento Valley; to the south a continual series

of rolling foothills…. The colony, organized into a corporation with seven stock-holders elected as a Board of Directors for a term of one year, was composed of ten thousand acres for which Whitney was issued ten thousand shares of stock at one dollar per share.[40]

Captain J. Booth Clarkson, formerly of the Third Royal Fusiliers, was the first president of the Citrus Colony Club when it opened on New Year's Eve in 1890. The first English colonist in Citrus Colony, Clarkson bought 100 acres of land where he earned a living as the resident manager for the English estate agents Scott and Jackson:[41]

> At its height, around 1893, there were about forty-three English families living in the Colony, approximately two hundred and eighteen residents. Actually, it was a "bit of old England" transplanted in the foothills.[42]

Major Turner of the Leicestershire Regiment had seven children and brought 50 acres near Captain Clarkson. Additional British military settlers included Colonel Watson, who had served 35 years in India where he became officer commanding the 24th Native Madras Infantry before his appointment as brigadier general in Bermuda. Apart from retired military personnel, several Oxbridge graduates chose to settle in Citrus Colony. Wallace Dewe, educated at Trinity College, Oxford, had a talent for drama as well as cricket. Joel Parker Whitney, an Anglophile with an English wife, visited England 26 times in his lifetime, and he proved right in assuming that excellent sports facilities would attract the gentleman class of English settler. To execute his plan, he bought a house and called it the Citrus Colony Club House. The clubhouse, on Boulder Ridge, overlooked the orange groves and attractive homes in the neighborhood. A flag of three orange C's on a white background fluttered at the club flagpole. Membership was 30 dollars. Club membership granted access to the two-story Norman style granite clubhouse, with its basement billiard room, reading room, large kitchen, two small rooms for breakfasting, a large bedroom with several cots and two double sleeping apartments for guests. Larger affairs of the colony were held in a room above the fruit house in Loomis overlooking the Central Pacific Railroad. The Citrus Colony's cricket facilities were unique and enabled them to host opposing teams, overnight, at the ground.[43] The players rode to the ground on their horses when Citrus Colony played the Pacific Cricket Club in the first game of a cricket festival held in the cooler autumn weather, on October 30, 1892. The *Citrus Colony News* reported:

> The Cricket Festival … was a brilliant success. The home team batted first, and put up 125 runs, Simmonds playing beautifully for 59, not out, and Godfrey Jackson hitting finely for 44. Paul and Turner dismissed the visitors for 72 leaving the county in a majority of 53 runs. In the second innings Simmonds made 18, and the Jackson brothers 43 and 37 respectively, both being not out when time was called. Placer thus won [both] of the first innings.[44]

In their first year, Citrus Colony changed the balance of cricket power in California as they easily defeated Santa Clara County and Lake County in their second and third games of the festival. The *Citrus Colony News* recorded:

> Lake batted first innings but failed to do themselves justice being put out for a very small score of 20. Placer made 195, the chief scorers being Turner 50, G. Jackson 40, Marsh-Brown 17 and Lannowe 16. Lake made a better showing in the second innings, but they were dismissed for 77 runs.[45]

Charles K. Turner — one of Major Turner's seven sons — settled in Penryn after completing his education at St. Paul's School in London.[46] The close contact British settlers had with England inspired their interest in English sports: cricket, soccer, tennis and horse paper-chases (in lieu of fox or coyote hunts). Remittance men and the third sons of aristocratic English families were recruited by estate agents Scott and Jackson. Educated in some of England's finest schools, the Citrus Colony colonists played sport to a high level. In the winter months the cricketers kept in condition by participating in athletic competition and soccer. Auburn and Placer regularly competed against each other under English Football Association rules. Brothers Geoff and Arthur Jackson and Chris Simmonds played halfback on the Placer team. Michael, one of seven Turner brothers, also played on the team.[47] The colonists also played American football, earning the reputation as the best team on the coast. Seven hundred admission-paying spectators attended one of their New Year's Day games in 1897 to watch Oakland play Citrus Colony. The next day a rugby game was played on Phalo field, near Rocklin. American residents of Penryn still speak fondly of their sporty English settlers. Local historian Barbara Pierce supplied me with all the newspaper clippings of "their" cricket team a century later when I came on the scene. Barbara also suspected playing sports may have been too much of a distraction from the day-to-day grind of running a ranch.[48] Richer ranchers relied on Chinese labor not susceptible to the local outbreaks of malaria. In retrospect, it appears the English colonists entertained themselves while trying to remain self-sufficient in the teeth of an economic depression that lasted five years, between 1893 and 1898. A puritan work ethic could do little to overcome elemental economic forces such as the low price of fruit that prevailed in Penryn and Loomis during the five-year depression. The depression lasted longer in California than on the East Coast because California's banking sector was still underdeveloped and relied to a great extent on East Coast–based banks, which held onto gold backed dollars thereby reducing liquidity for commercial activities out West. Financial hardship enhanced the intensity with which the Penryn's English colonists applied themselves to their sports. The English settlers became one of the top cricket teams in California from 1895 to 1897.[49] This sporting excellence was not just confined to cricket. The two best tennis players in the colony were Joel Parker Whitney's sons, James G. and John A. Whitney.[50] Joel Parker Whitney, one of the wealthiest men in California at the time, may have been related to the East Coast Whitneys, who were also educated at Yale. One of them, Harry Payne Whitney, became famous for the captaining the first American polo team to defeat an English side, at Meadowbrook in New Jersey in 1909. The Whitney sons participated in the Hotel Del Monte Tennis Tournament near Monterey, where George Wright, the famous American cricketer and major league baseball player, brought Harvard's best tennis players to compete against the Whitney's in 1895.[51]

Cricket was played regularly by the Citrus Colony Cricket Club from 1891 on. Apart from games with the local agricultural college run by Englishman Frank Karslake, CCCC played Grass Valley and Nevada City. Nevada City was a mining town, located in the California High Sierra, six miles from Grass Valley, home to the miners of the Empire and Northstar mines. The miners enjoyed the social occasion provided by playing the CCCC fruit growers. In April 1895, the *Grass Valley Union* reported:

> The Nevada City Cricket club, reinforced by a few players from Grass Valley, left for Penryn, Placer County on the evening of the 26th ... where, as they knew, they would be badly beaten.
> Notwithstanding their defeat, our boys enjoyed their visit exceedingly, as the CC club

proved themselves generous hosts.... Want of practice was the principal reason for our club's defeat, as the players had not handled a bat in several years. The batting of Messrs. Simmonds and Adler for the Citrus Club was indeed a revelation to our boys.[52]

In their next game, Placer County defeated the Pacific Cricket Club. Walter Courtney Bennett, consul general in San Francisco, was bowled by Chris Simmonds in the first innings, for a duck. In the second innings the consul was bowled by Charles Turner for one run.[53] Placer County won the game by an innings and 34 runs. The Citrus Colony Cricket Club was captained by Arthur Coates. The St. John's, Cambridge, man had learnt his cricket at Shrewesbury School. Coates, an engineer, chose to live in the Citrus Colony where he bought five acres and corresponded with his cricket hero, W.G. Grace.[54] Coates was a skilled cricketer and good organizer. He made arrangements for the American football game against Oakland, and his impact on Citrus Colony's cricket fortunes was immediate. Under his management Citrus Colony's team, with Simmonds, Alder, Butt, the Turners, the Jacksons, and Lannowe, became one of the finest teams in California. In 1895, they went undefeated in five games. Playing as Placer County, the county in which the CCCC was located, they scored 260 against Santa Clara and drew with Alameda CC, the strongest team in California. On May 18–19, the Citrus Colony team were "pitted against the Pacific Club, of San Francisco, one of the strongest organizations on the Coast":

> The visitors arrived on the night of the 17th, and slept at Rocklin, the hotel accommodation at Penryn being limited. The game began at 11 A.M. on Saturday, the Colony batting first, and with much success, as Simmonds and Jackson could not be separated for an hour, and did much to tire the opposition bowlers; Garnett, Butt and Coates also hit freely, and the score reached the respectable figure of 146 runs.
> The Pacifics could make no stand against the excellent bowling of Simmonds and Turner, and Butt, and were dismissed for 56 runs. Being so much in arrears, they balked a second time and were got out for 55 runs. Butt and Turner being very deadly with the ball. The Colony thus won by an inning and 35 runs. The team dined together at the club house on the conclusion of the match and a most delightful evening was spent. The Pacifics returned by the midnight train, much pleased with their trip to Placer County.[55]

Lake County's lopsided losses to Placer County in 1895 made Keeling determined to improve Lake County's batting through match practice. Red Hill Ranch became the preferred Lake County cricket venue in 1895 for both the Burns Valley and Lakeport cricket teams. The *Lakeport Bee* reported:

> Tuesday was certainly a Red Letter day in the history of Lake County cricket.... Messrs. Hammond and Edmands were the promoters of the match and they prepared a very good ground, the wicket perhaps favoring the bowler rather than the batsmen. The field presented an extremely pretty appearance, with two marquees and two flag poles in the foreground, one flag the "Stars and Stripes" and the other the "Union Jack" (the latter the work of Mrs. Hammond in honor of the visitors). The *Tabasco* with the Lakeport party were the first to arrive at the wharf and was followed soon after by Mr. Collier's pretty launch the *Meteor*, the *Freda* with the Burns Valley contingent being the last to reach port.[56]

Lakeport CC won the first Red Hill Ranch game against Burns Valley CC, by 20 runs. Webber was the best bowler for Burns Valley while Keeling and Spurr scored the most runs for Lakeport. The close matches between the two sides generated local interest, the *Clear Lake Press* noting in one of its match dispatches:

Lakeport CC versus Burns Valley at Red Hill Ranch, 1895. Source: Lake County Historical Courthouse Museum, Lakeport, California.

About two o'clock on Saturday afternoon of the past week, the little steamer *J.D. Stephens* left Lakeport carrying invited guests up the lake to Red Hill Ranch, where the annual two-days contest between the Burns Valley and the Lakeport clubs was in progress. It was three o'clock when the little steamer was drawn up to the temporary pier made necessary by the very low water. The guests were then carried overland from the landing past the beautiful homes of Red Hill ranch to the cricket field. Here the last half-day's game was being played. Guests of Lower Lake, Burns Valley, Upper Lake, Kono-Taye and Lakeport, were comfortably seated, well protected from the sun's rays. The game went on "Innings" "overs" and much other Choctaw was scored by the bright little secretary near at hand, and hieroglyphics was being bulletined on the board hard by. But though the writer was blind as a mole to these beauties, the beauties of her nature were intelligible enough. At the close of day ... with Lakeport the winner the guests were taken to Me-Tel Vineyard, the charming home of our host and hostess, Mr. & Mrs. C.M. Hammond, where the evening swiftly passed in conversation, feasting, dancing and general merry-making.[57]

The Hammonds represented the epitome of Anglo-American culture and hospitality in Lake County at the turn of the century. Their mansion, called Me-Tel, has since burned down but in its heyday it was a "happy combination of an elegantly appointed American home, with its broad vine shaded verandahs and its rich furnishings within the stately hall of an English gentleman."

Books in abundance, musical instruments, and scientific instruments betokened as significantly within, as did the highly developed and highly improved grounds that our host was a gentleman of education and energy holding the beautiful belief that one of the noblest employments the earth affords is the cultivation of the soil where an educated intellect, cultured taste and love complete the stature of the cultivator.[58]

Steeped in the classics, Lake County's pioneer cricketers were familiar with the Cicero, Ovid and Horace. Red Hill Ranch became Lake County's country house where local politicians mingled after the games to plan out the future of the new towns around Clear Lake.

In San Francisco, Illinois-born William Greer Harrison, simultaneously president of the California Cricket Association, the Pacific Cricket Club and the Olympic Club, was intent on building up the sporting infrastructure of the city. He invited Lake County to play. The *San Francisco Chronicle* outlined the historical significance of the Lake County CC trip, noting:

> In 1890 the Pacific Cricket club made the trip into Lake county and played two matches. Every year since the two clubs have met either in Lower Lake, Lakeport, or Calistoga; but this is the first time that an eleven has traveled to San Francisco.
> Mr. Keeling's team is particularly strong in bowling. The captain ... is a very fair trundler; and so is Webber, who used to represent Wellington School in his younger days. But the crack bowler of the team is supposed to be F.W. Kelson of Hurst College, England. He bowls a rapid left hand delivery, with a strong break from the left side, and has been particularly effective when bowling on turf....
> W.S. Baynton who used to be captain of Winchester College eleven during his school days is one of the most "correct" batsmen in Lake County. Of the other names Edmonds and Hammond are Harvard men; R.S. Rodman comes from Yale and his brother from West Point. So the leading schools of the two countries are represented in the visiting eleven.[59]

Lake County's cricketers traveled by stage coach and train, and prior to arriving in San Francisco elected Keeling captain in Pieta. According to the *San Francisco Chronicle* Keeling took his captaincy seriously, as he set an example by "the punctual way he went to bed every night and shunned the many charming and alluring attractions of the Bay city."[60] Keeling's virtuous example was not followed by the rest of the team, who stayed out late. According to the *San Francisco Chronicle*, Lake County's arrival in the City created quite a stir in local cricket circles:

> The grounds at Alameda were thronged with cricketers yesterday anxious to get a line on the bold players from Lake county who had come all the way from Lillie Langtry's adopted home to play a series of matches against the local clubs.... Keeling 31 and Baynton 10 ... were the first players on their side to show a liking for the fast concrete wicket. In the two innings, Lake county had run up a grand total of 116 runs. Pacific had therefore only 33 runs to get ... and thanks to the admirable work of Meyer, who served 18 not out, the scarlet and blacks exceeded that total by 6 runs with 7 wickets to spare.[61]

Other cricketers on hand to watch Lake County's first tour to San Francisco were "President Walter Welch and Captain George Brotch of the new Redwood City Cricket club.... Capt. Brotch an old Philadelphia player, who with Walter Welch, has pulled many hard fought inter-university games out of the fire by their brilliant work at the bat, put in an application for the association."[62]

After their defeat Lake County played the Bohemian Cricket Club in Klinknerville and lost by two runs. The following day, against the Alameda Cricket Club, they limited "the crack club on the coast" to 134 runs:[63]

> Kelson and Keeling were both in great form and kept the champions guessing.... Hood, who did not turn until somewhat late, carried his bat for 40. Sloman 24, Moriarty 22 and Price 19 made nearly all the runs.
> Lake County replied with 83, just 51 runs behind the champion's total. Kelson 21, Keeling 18, Bayton 16 and Edmands 10, all played good cricket for their runs, but the rest of the side did nothing.
> Alameda, therefore won by 51 runs.[64]

Next:

> Lake County played its third cricket match yesterday at Golden Gate, and after a rattling
> finish managed to gain a victory by the narrow margin of six runs.
> The visitors went first to bat, and their first representatives, Keeling and Renwick, by
> beautiful cricket [brought] the score to 85 before a separation was effected. Bayton and Kel-
> son continued the good work, and when the last wicket fell the telegraph board showed 158.
> To this total, Captain Keeling with 53 compiled in beautiful style, Renwick 38, Bayton 21 and
> Kelson 16 were the largest contributors.
> Robertson (not Digger but JC) and Seager were the first batsmen for the Presidio team and
> the pair put up a splendid game, no less than 61 runs being registered before a separation was
> effected. Seager was the first to go, soon followed by Townsley and McLaurin. Moran then
> became associated with Robertson and the score soon mounted up to 140, when Robertson
> and Moran both lost their wickets. No one else made any show of resistance against the
> bowling of Keeling and Webber, and the Presidio's total closed at 152. Just six runs short of
> the Lake county effort.[65]

With three (they lost a fourth game to Alameda CC) losses and one victory to their
credit in San Francisco, the Lake County team caught the train to Penryn where they
stayed in the Citrus Colony Club. The Loomis Cricket Festival in November 1895 attracted
teams from Lake County, Santa Clara, San Francisco, and Nevada County in California.
Lake County were without their best bowler, Webber, for the festival as he had injured
himself playing against Alameda and returned to Lakeport to run his bar. Placer County
played Lake County in the first game of the festival and scored 174 runs in the first innings.
In reply Lake County were 66 in their first innings and 136 in their second as Keeling
and Hammond tried gallantly to overcome a 210-run deficit after Placer County declared
at 100 for 2 wickets in their second innings. Keeling with 60 runs made the highest innings
of the tour and "Hammond's display was certainly one of the very best things of the tour
and too much praise cannot be given him and Keeling for their splendid effort to save
the game."[66]

In the next game, Placer County crushed Nevada County. Placer County scored 334
for 6 in reply to Nevada County's first innings total of 64 runs. Simmonds carried his bat
for 162 not out, supported by Harry Alder who scored 101, batting number seven, in what
must have been the fastest century of the season. Then Placer County defeated Santa Clara
by an innings and 106 runs in a game that saw Arthur Coates score 78 not out, his top
score in California. Placer County's batting in the 1895 festival was solid. Their top four
batsmen averaged over 40 runs per innings, with Coates leading the averages with 85.05
per innings. Simmonds scored the most runs in eight innings for 40 runs per innings.
Simmonds, Placer County's best all-rounder, opened both the batting and bowling for
Placer County in his six years with the club. Chris Simmonds' bowling average was 11.75
per wicket.[67] Placer County's most economical bowlers were Harry Alder and Harold Butt
with 8.75 and 9.75 per wicket. Charles Turner was Placer County's workhorse, taking 20
wickets in 524 overs for 201 runs and a 10.25 average per wicket.

Alameda CC did not participate in the festival held during the week, but the following weekend, they traveled to Loomis and beat Placer County by 27 runs on first innings
scores of 199 to 173. The close game against the CCA team, champion for four years in
a row, showed parity between town and country sides was improving. Placer were the
second best team in California behind Alameda CC, so it was no surprise when they easily

defeated Nevada City in their eighth and last game of the season. The third best team in California, the Pacific Cricket Club, played their last game of the season against San Jose, "the Garden City," a fixture the PCC maintained for the next three years. For Lake County, Keeling had the best batting average, with 27.42 per innings in 1895. Renwick and Charles Hammond were next in the Lake County averages with 18.0 and 17.0 runs per inning. Webber was Lake County's best bowler. Based on comparative averages between the top two country teams in California for 1895, Placer County was far stronger in all departments of cricket than Lake County.

After the winter break, Placer County's 1896 cricket season started out as the year before, with a fixture against Nevada City, but went down to a surprise defeat as Nevada City XVIII beat them by 13 runs. In a second game, played on September 9, Placer County defeated the Nevada City XVIII by 23 runs.[68] After the second game, five of the Placer County side were selected to play for the California XVIII against the visiting Australian test side.[69] Jackson and Turner played for both Auburn CC and Placer County. Chris Simmonds, Harold Butt and Harry Alder were Citrus Colony CC and Placer County players. An additional two "country" players were selected for a California XVIII from Lake County, Herbert Keeling and Chris Enderby. The Australian visit to San Francisco was the first since 1878. Four of the Alameda CC players selected for the California XVIII — Hood, Sloman, Hogue and Robertson — scored centuries in 1896 domestic competition. Simmonds was the only country player to score a century against Nevada City. On paper, the California XVIII looked capable of putting a large number of runs on the board against a strong Australian batting side that lost one of its three games in Philadelphia. On their train trip to San Francisco, the Australians stopped in Chicago where, according to the *San Francisco Examiner*, they "inflicted a very decisive licking to the ambitious 'Wanderers' of that city. Among the Chicago cricketers who did fairly good work the name Howell appears in the dispatches. This is probably Charlie Howell, formerly Captain of the Pacific cricket club of San Francisco, who removed to Chicago some years ago."[70]

Two thousand spectators turned out for the first day of play at the U.S. Army's Presidio ground. The pitch was concrete. John E. Aitken, California's top scoring batsmen against the 1878 Australian team, was one of the umpires chosen to preside over the game of the decade. Three of California's top batsmen, Charlie Laurence, David Hearfield and Harold Richardson, were prevented by the pressure of business from playing the midweek game on October 15–16. Earlier in the season, Richardson, playing for Alameda CC, had scored 208 not out against the California Cricket Club. Australian legends Harry Boyle (Robertson's nemesis when he played for East Melbourne CC), Alick Bannerman and Demon Spofforth stepped down from the 1896 side to make way for the new generation of players; left-hand opening batsman Clem Hill, fast bowler Earnest Jones, and captain Harry Trott. Harry Musgrove, the Australian team manager chosen from 31 applicants for the post, presided over arrangements that had gone very smoothly despite the loss of the Ashes by two games to one, to an English side captained by W.G. Grace.[71]

The Australian cricket team was met at the Sixteenth Street Station by Olympic Club president William Greer Harrison and two other CCA officers. They stayed at the Baldwin Hotel, where the 1878 Australians were lodged, and dined at St. George's Athletic Club on Mason Street. Next day, the Australians won the toss and batted first on the Presidio pitch. Bill Robertson drew first blood, bowling Harry Doonan, with just nine runs on the board. It was left to Giffen and Darling to save the Australian innings. They made a century partnership in the face of some very effective bowling by Digger Robertson, who ended the innings with 7 wickets for 71 runs. The Australians first innings total was 193 runs.[72] The San Francisco crowd sensed an upset, as the same Australian team had scored 422 runs in their second game against Philadelphia. This note of expectancy was soon dashed, however. California's lack of seasoned batting was quickly exposed by the fast bowling of Earnest Jones and Charles Eady combined with McKibbin's spin bowling. The *San Francisco Examiner* recorded the slaughter of California's batsmen on the second day:

> J. Myers, the not out of the previous day, opened the batting with H.A. Butt of Placer county. At the close of Wednesday's play six California wickets had fallen for twenty runs. McKibbin and Eady were the bowlers. Butt scored a couple, but the slow bowler took his off stump next ball 7–2–22.
>
> Keeling of Lake County then came to the wickets and gave the exhibition of the innings. He cut McKibbin for a couple, drove Eady for a single and then cut the slow twister again for a couple in the following over. Myers had not scored when caught in the slips off Eady, 8–2–23. Fane Sewell was immediately caught by the same bowler 9–0–28. Keeling was next clean bowled by Eady, 10–9–31.
>
> Billy Robertson, the hope of California cricketers, was next up, but he did not do much for his adopted country, being stumped off McKibbin after scoring four. No one else made any stand, and to the great disappointment of the spectators all seventeen wickets were down for 43 runs, leaving Townsley not out with three to his credit.[73]

More than 150 runs behind the Australian total, the California XVIII were required to follow-on and after lunch California batted again. Dr. Bowhill, a professor of veterinary science at Berkeley, opened the batting with his Alameda CC teammate, captain Hogue. Hogue scored the first boundary of the game for California. The opening partnership held up well against the Australian opening bowlers, Harry Trott and Harry Doonan, before Hogue was caught in the slips off Eady with 15 for the first wicket. Several wickets fell in quick succession until Keeling joined Butt with the score 6 for 29 runs.

> Butt was his partner, and Placer County and Lake County began to show the city players how to treat Australian bowling. Butt hit the boundary for four and then was stumped 7–5–38.
>
> Keeling brought forty on the board with a sharp cut. Then Bolwey retired, 8–1–42. Sewell came in, and only scored a single when Jones ripped out his middle stump 9–1–47.
>
> Sloman joined Keeling, who was showing by far the best form of all the California team, and played out the over. But a single by Sloman bought him up against Doonan who clean bowled him second ball, 10–0–48. Harold Ward followed but did nothing, 11–0–49. Same fate for Townsley, first ball 12–0–49. A drive by Keeling bought on the half century, and Dickinson, the newcomer faced Doonan, playing out the over. Keeling hit to leg for a couple, but after a maiden from the other end the same bowler got Keeling caught in the slips, 14–16–56. The Lake county representative was generously applauded on his return to the stand having made the only batting display for California.[74]

Digger Roberston was the last man in for California. He stayed in to preserve a technical draw for California with one wicket left in two innings of 103, in reply to the Australian first innings of 193 runs. There was no doubt, to those watching, that the Australians outplayed the local side. The *San Francisco Examiner's* verdict was clear: "It was a decided defeat for California."[75] After the Australian side sailed away on the SS *Mariposa*, the *San Francisco Call* noted that California's batting was a disappointment after Robertson's fine bowling kept the Australians' first innings below 200 runs:

Now that the Australians have come, conquered and departed, a few reflections of the local cricket event of the decade may be in order. That our eighteen strong team should have suffered defeat at the hands of such consummate masters of the game as Trott and his star combination was almost inevitable. But our Eastern brothers will surely comment on the fact that after disposing of so strong a batting aggregation for 193 runs we made so miserable a showing at bat. The visitors themselves were surprised at this, for the bowling of Robertson and Cookson and the fielding of Butt, Hogue, Robertson, Hood and others had led them to expect greater opposition when they took the field. How was their anticipation realized?

With the exception of Keeling of Lake County, who in both innings, made the top score, playing over after over of the deadly bowling with confidence and accuracy; of Bowhill, Simmonds (who shaped well) and Hogue, what account did all our reputed batsmen give of themselves? They fell like tenpins before the hurricane balls of Jones and the crafty breakers of Donnan and McKibbin.

The result of the big match seems to point out a very obvious moral, viz, that the batting practice hitherto indulged in has been wholly ineffective. It is no practice at all to stand at the nets and slog a few lobs and pitches all around the field. But how often have the men the chance, on a Thursday or Saturday afternoon, of getting anything better? It could be surely arranged that at least one of our best bowlers should be on hand on these occasions and do a little amateur coaching. Some say we may run to a professional ground bowler and systematized coaching but in the meanwhile an effort should be made to better the existing order of things.[76]

The Call's assessment was a challenge directed at the will of the players to lift their game by diligent practice and application of disciplined batting skills. In a cultural environment where cricket was played as an expression of ethnic identity, mere participation and going through the formalities of the game — especially the social aspects such as the tea break — were what mattered most. If cricket in San Francisco had been played like baseball, under intense local competitive pressure, there is little doubt that the quality of cricket would have risen, although perhaps not to the Philadelphia level where the game was treated as superior to its American cousin and played with serious competitive intent. Selection to the Gentlemen of Philadelphia side was recognized as the supreme honor by members of sports clubs in Philadelphia, where cricket careers started in early grade school. School cricket was not played in the San Francisco; the majority of cricketers were expatriates trained outside America. The Australian cricket team's visit inspired Placer County's "colonists" to take an ambitious six-game tour encompassing Lake, Alameda and Santa Clara counties. The Bohemian CC, captained by Robertson, had already won the Hunter-Harrison trophy in 1896, with Pacific Cricket Club runners-up and Alameda CC uncharacteristically in third place, when Placer County's best players— Simmonds, Butt, Jackson and Turner — were joined in San Francisco by the rest of the Placer County on October 19. Coates gave a first-hand description of the tour:

Starting on Monday by "No 4" we reached Calistoga on time, and thence traveled some thirty-five miles by stage to Burns Valley, near Lower Lake. Here we were met and entertained by the Burns Valley Club, and after a pleasant social evening, were glad to retire early after one long journey. Next morning was lovely, bright, sunny, and cheerful, and we began our first game in the best of spirits. Placer batted first, but were dismissed for the moderate total of 63 runs, of which Simmonds (9), Arthur Jackson (14), Turner (14) and Alder (15) made the bulk.[77]

Playing for Burns Valley CC, Keeling took 4 for 22 runs as Placer County scored 63 runs. Simmonds and Charles Turner bowled unchanged, retiring Burns Valley CC for 37 runs. The *Placer Herald* noted:

Lakeport and Burns Valley cricket teams at Burns Valley, 1896. H.V. Keeling, with bat, third from the left in the front row, has Bill Edmands on his right and Charles Hammond on his left. Source: Lower Lake Schoolhouse Museum, Lower Lake, California.

Burns Valley found themselves quite unable to cope with the bowling of Turner and Simmonds and were all out for thirty-seven runs. Placer then batted a second and put up eighty-nine, of which Simmonds made forty-four and Butt sixteen, the former playing fine cricket. In the second effort the local men showed better form and had run up a score of 107 when time was called leaving Placer victorious by twenty-six runs on the first inning.

The same evening the team left Lower Lake by steamer and after a delightful run along beautiful Clear Lake we were received in Lakeport by the hospitable portals of the Lakeport hotel.

The second match, against Lakeport, was the handsomest win of the tour. Going in first to bat, Placer put up the excellent total of 165 runs, of which Simmonds made eighty-four, achieving the rare distinction of being the first man to bat and seeing all the rest of the team dismissed while he remained unconquered. Paul (15), and Budgett (21) gave valuable assistance. Lakeport could do nothing with the bowling of Simmonds and Turner, and were put out for thirty-one in the first innings and fifty-six in the second innings, leaving us winners by in one innings by seventy-eight runs. Keeling made twenty-nine in the second innings for Lakeport and Arthur Jackson bowled well for Placer.[78]

Simmonds dominated the bowling, taking 6 wickets for 7 runs in Lakeport CC's first innings and 5 for 33 in their second. His partner Charles Turner bowled unchanged at the other end and took 3 for 14 in the first innings and 5 for 19 in the second innings. For their last and third game in Lake County, Placer CC played best players of BVCC and LCC which comprised the Lake County team:

Again we batted first, but could only score fifty-eight of which Turner made fourteen and Lannowe eleven, not out, but Lake county fared still worse, and were dismissed by Turner

The Citrus Colony Cricket Club playing in front of their clubhouse at Citrus Colony in Penryn, near Sacramento, California, 1896. Source: The California History Room, California State Library, Sacramento, California.

and Simmonds for twelve — the smallest score ever made in California in an important match. In our second innings Simmonds made twenty, Marsh-Brown eleven, Paul ten and Butt fourteen, the total being seventy-one. Our bowlers dismissed the Lake county men for ninety-one, to which Keeling contributed twenty-two and Hammond twenty-eight.[79]

Placer County won the close two-innings match by 26 runs. Keeling and Enderby were the best bowlers for Lake County, taking ten and five wickets respectively. Placer County's Turner took ten wickets and Simmonds eight. After three successful days of cricket in Lake County, Placer County celebrated:

Dinner at the hotel and a jolly social evening wound up our first visit to Lake County, but not we hope our last, for we enjoyed the delightful scenery, genuine hospitality, fine weather, and good cricket, and what more could be desired. The catching and fielding of our men was good all through.

Next morning we started betime and, after a picturesque but trying drive of forty-eight miles to Calistoga, we reached San Francisco the same evening quite tired out.[80]

After the grueling journey to San Francisco, Placer County faced Alameda CC on their home Webster Street ground the next day, October 24. The Alameda CC crushed Placer County after Hogue and Hood opened the innings with a century partnership. Hood top scored with 72 runs before he was caught and bowled by Paul. Building on the opening partnership, American-born Harold Ward, Jr. (61 not out), combined with baseball-trained

Harry Bird (24 runs) for a 90-run partnership as Alameda CC declared at 265 runs for 8 wickets. Simmonds' bowling was ineffective against Alameda CC on their concrete wicket. Turner took seven wickets while Butt, Paul, Jackson and Simmonds rotated the bowling at the other end, getting one wicket between the four of them. In reply, Placer County was all out for 67 runs, as Alameda CC won the match by 165 runs. After an excellent dinner with the ACC and PCC San Francisco clubs, Placer faced the PCC on the same concrete pitch that had confounded them the day before against Alameda CC. The result was predictable:

> The next day we met the Pacifics, the weather being milder, but dull and threatening still. Pacific batted first but were all out for 102, thanks to Paul's efforts. He dismissed five batsmen for seven runs—the best bit of bowling done so far by our team. Our total was fifty-four (A. Jackson 20) so we met our second defeat.[81]

After losing their second game of the tour to the PCC by 48 runs, Placer County traveled to San Jose for their last game against Santa Clara County. The October 25 game was cut short by rain and ended in a draw. With the tour complete the Placer County assessment of their performance was clear:

> What success we had we largely to Arthur Jackson, Simmonds, Turner and Paul, but the whole team did their best, and kept in good training; however, until we can get more practice we can hardly cope with the best City clubs, who begin playing in May and have at least one match game a week up to the end of October, while [we] can only play in the Spring and the Fall....
> Butt proved a very popular Captain, and his fame as a songster now extends for Nevada County to Lake, the City, and Santa Clara County.[82]

Placer County's season ended at home in Loomis where they crushed the Nevada City Miners by 18 wickets and had a 240-run balance. Placer County, seasoned by the tough tour, scored 294 runs for two wickets declared against a hapless Nevada City bowling attack. Simmonds scored 147 not out, ably supported by Arthur Jackson, 55 and Charles Turner, 67. The ten-game Placer County batting averages in 1896 were led by Chris Simmonds with 43.6 runs, having scored 350 runs in ten innings with two centuries and two not outs. Charles Turner finished the season with 66 wickets and a 27.1 bowling average.[83] Turner played more games. He played cricket against Australia for the California XVIII and Auburn CC, a team he founded in 1896 with Arthur Jackson. By comparison, Philadelphia's top batsmen in 1896 were W.W. Noble, who headed the batting table with 62.0 runs an innings in six games, and George Patterson, who was second with a 50-run average in eight games.[84]

In 1897, Queen Victoria's Diamond Jubilee galvanized local cricket activity in northern California. Cricket festivals were planned by both town and country sides. However, the first cricketer off the mark in April 1897 was Harry Musgrove. Flush from his success as manager of the Australian cricket team in 1896, Harry Musgrove returned to San Francisco (on the same SS *Alameda* used by Arthur Spalding's 1889 round-the world baseball tour) as the manager of the first Australian baseball team to tour the United States. The tour ran from April to September, 1897.[85] Musgrove had played cricket for East Melbourne CC and represented Australia once at cricket. His 1897 Australian baseball team was captained by Frank Laver, another East Melbourne CC cricketer, who played 15 times for Australia. All but one of the Australian baseball players were club level cricketers. After losing their first two games, the *San Francisco Chronicle* reported, the Australians

> played baseball like cricket. They stopped to think too often while men were flitting around the bases.... They are a lusty lot the kangaroosters— these Australians from the bush, but they can't play ball, that is— baseball. The Australians go into bat as if they were playing cricket but the cricket idea will have to be abandoned if the visitors really intend to tour the continent as baseball players.[86]

Their first victory came in the third game of the tour, when they defeated Stockton 13 to 10. This was followed by a close loss to the San Francisco Athletic Club by 26 to 25 runs. Completing the California leg of their U.S. tour after winning one and losing five games, the Australian baseball team crossed 46 miles of snow-covered High Sierras by the Cape Horn route, to take on the YMCA in Ogden, Utah. Other games followed in Denver, where the local press commented:

> The Australians have all the marks of good cricket players— run well and field well, either hand or both as the emergencies of the game demand. In fact, they did most of their fielding one-handed which created intense wonder in the baseball audience that was out to see the playing.[87]

Moving on to Iowa, the Australian baseball team played at Council Bluffs and then caught the train to Chicago where they met Joe Quinn, the first Australian to play in the major leagues in a long baseball career that spanned 17 years from 1884 to 1901. By June the team was in Pittsburgh, where they lost to the Duquesne Athletic Club. The team then moved on to Washington, D.C., via Baltimore and New York where Cap Anson, who had been on Spalding's world tour that visited Australia in 1889, organized a game at the famed Polo Grounds against nine players from Chicago and Brooklyn teams. After losing a close game, Spalding took the Australian baseball team to see a professional game between Cleveland and New York and then invited the team to visit his New Jersey estate near Atlantic City. Following the visit, the 47-year-old Spalding played in an old timers' game at Boston's South End Field, which attracted 500 spectators. The Australians' inability to draw large crowds put the tourists in a financial bind, and Harry Musgrove began paying himself first. The players called Musgrove to account and he left the tour. Still the tour continued, with games against Pawtucket, Rhode Island, Brockton in Boston, West New York, and against an All Philadelphia team. The *Sporting News* portrayed the foray of the Australian baseball players into the citadel of American cricket, which they lost by 9 to 2 runs, as marking a new era in baseball history. It was the first time a foreign baseball team played in Philadelphia, although English cricket teams made annual visits.[88] The Philadelphia baseball game, held in September, capped a remarkable 20-game odyssey across the United States that ultimately proved that Australians were best suited to cricket and probably set baseball back permanently as a contender to cricket in Australia. However, the tour did set a record in the number of games played throughout the United States that was not equaled by an Australian cricket team until the 56-game U.S. tour of 1913.

In California, the 1897 Australian baseball tour proved no distraction for Arthur Coates, who as one of the CCA vice-presidents organized the Diamond Jubilee celebrations. In *The American Cricketer*, Arthur Coates reported there would be "a 'Jubilee' match Town vs. Country. The country XI will be made up of four men from Placer County, as many from Santa Clara County, the rest from Lake County. It should be a good game, although the country players are under the disadvantage of not knowing each other's play."[89] The additional cricket matches held in honor of the Jubilee made the 1897 season a busy one. The season lasted from April 7 to November 7. Secretary of the CCA Arthur Inkersley, who lived at 508 Montgomery Street in San Francisco, announced that the CCA clubs for 1897 were "Alameda, Bohemian, California, Placer County, Pacific, San Jose, and Lakeport."[90]

In Placer County, the season started with a win by Auburn CC, which beat Citrus Colony by 16 runs on May 9, 1897. Charles Turner dominated the game, scoring 61 not out in Auburn's first innings total of 119 runs. He then took five Citrus Colony wickets to win the match. The following week on May 15, Placer County easily defeated Frank Budgett's XI at Loomis. Against Budgett's XI, Charles Turner (33 not out), played for Placer County. Simmonds (106 not out) carried his bat and Arthur Jackson (77) piled up 234 for 1 before Placer County declared. A third very low scoring game was held on May 22 at Loomis, when Nevada City were all out for a total of 16 and Placer County could only muster 48 runs in reply.[91] The Placer County games were excellent practice for the Country versus Town game held in San Francisco on June 20 at Golden Gate Park. Hogue's 72 and Arthur Dickinson's 45 laid the foundation for an overwhelming innings and 43-run victory as the Country side was only able to muster 123 runs in two innings in reply to the Town's first innings total of 186 runs. Digger Robertson took 12 wickets for 42 runs or 3.5 runs per wicket as he overpowered the Country side with his bowling. Paul (Auburn CC) had the best bowling analysis for the Country players, taking 5 wickets for 51 runs for an economy rate of 10 runs per wicket.[92] After Town's victory, the locus of cricket festival celebrations shifted to Citrus Colony where Queen Victoria's Diamond Jubilee was celebrated in true "Country" style. The walls of the colony club house were decorated by Union Jacks and Old Glory flags. General Hamilton was the guest of honor and Major Turner, the president of the club, made the first toast to President McKinley and people of the United States, "alluding in well-chosen terms to the respect all Britons felt for the President as Executive of a nation of 70 million free people, and expressing a hope that a 'wave of prosperity' would soon striketh the Placer fruit growers. The toast was drunk with much cheering."[93]

After the meal, toasts, and dancing, entertainment was provided on June 27, 1897, by a brass band from Roseville and a game of baseball between the nines of Loomis and Penryn.[94] In Lake County's first season game, Burns Valley CC easily defeated Lakeport CC as Chris Enderby took six wickets including Keeling for a duck. Enderby scored 56 in the third game of the season against Lakeport CC. The three games between the Lake County sides were good preparation for Placer County's visit. Without Coates as manager,

> the Placer county cricket eleven were decidedly not up to their best form at Lower Lake Tuesday in the match against Burns Valley.... Only one of their batsmen scored double figures, and the whole team was dismissed for 47 runs. The Burns valley eleven was not in particularly good batting form either, their total for ten wickets being only 74 runs. Webber and Keeling obtained all the Placer county wickets and Turner and Simmonds were equally successful with the ball against the Burns Valley dwellers.
>
> In the second innings, the Placer county team did a little better, scoring 63 runs, to which C. Simmonds contributed 19 and W. Pretherick 14 not out. The match was decided, however, on the first innings, and so was a victory for Burns valley by 27 runs.[95]

The Placer County players fared no better against Lakeport CC the next day:

> [They] met a more disastrous defeat than in their match the day before at Burns Valley, being beaten this time by twelve runs with eight wickets to spare. This game ... was witnessed by an unusually large number of spectators who took keen interest in the play, owing principally to the fact that, with the exception of Keeling, the captain, the team was composed of native-born Americans.
>
> Placer went first to the bat, but did not stay long at the wicket against the bowling of Keeling and Rose, who proved unplayable, and the whole side was retired for an insignificant 24. Lakeport did a little better, scoring 51 of which Keeling was responsible for 21 and the extra's column 12.[96]

Rose, Lakeport CC's new fast bowler, changed the balance of power between Placer and Lake counties. In their third game the colonists were beaten 39 to 17 runs, as none of the Placer County men proved capable of scoring double figures. Rose took 7 wickets for 7 runs in 20 balls.[97] The *San Francisco Chronicle* put its finger on the reason for change in Lake County's fortunes:

> The greatest improvement, undoubtedly, is in the bowling. Webber has always been a very useful and reliable bowler, and the same remark applies to Keeling, but a good fast bowler has always been sadly missed. Kelson and Enderby were both useful men in their day, but it has been left to the young Lakeporter, Rose, to supply the want and to astonish the cricket world of California by his marvelous ability. Possessed of plenty of pace, a natural and easy delivery, a strong active frame, and with youth on his side, he has all the materials of a first class bowler.[98]

After so many one sided defeats by Placer County, Keeling clipped the *San Francisco Chronicle's* report, which declared:

Lake County Men Defeat Colonists.

> The Placer county cricketers arrived in the city last evening after completing a somewhat disastrous tour through Lake County. The visitors speak very highly of the quality of cricket played there and note a wonderful improvement all round since their last encounter three seasons ago. Thursday was the last match of the tour in Lake County, when they played their third game against an eleven composed of the crack players of Burns Valley and Lakeport.
>
> The locals went in first and were disposed of by CK Turner and Simmonds for the comparatively small score of 39, Keeling with 11 being the only double figure. Placer was in high hopes of avenging the two previous defeats and regaining lost laurels. Their expectations were never realized, for it took Rose and Keeling just 50 balls between them to rattle the whole side out for just 17 runs, the smallest score of the season, not one of the Citrus Colony men reached double figures.
>
> Rose secured seven wickets for as many runs, a performance which stamps him a coming bowler.[99]

After their victory against Placer County, Lake County toured San Francisco in 1897. In San Francisco, Lake County continued their victorious ways, defeating their oldest nemesis, the Pacific Cricket Club, on their new home ground at the Haight Street facility in Golden Gate Park. Under their new Australian captain Arthur Dickinson, PCC were a strong side. They had already beaten the Bohemian Cricket Club — without Digger Robertson since his return to Australia — twice. They also defeated the CCA 1897 league-champion Alameda Cricket Club 207 to 109 runs. San Jose also developed as a force to be reckoned with in 1897 after showing surprising strength against the visiting PCC side due to William Howard, who took 6 wickets for 70 runs and scored 41 runs not out, on the July 4 weekend. Both sides had to be satisfied with a hard fought draw. PCC were all out for 166 as San Jose scored 131 for 6 wickets before stumps were drawn.[100]

Lake County's fortunes ascended as Placer County received three mortal blows in 1898. Placer County's cricket organizer, Arthur Coates, died in Los Angeles from an asthma attack at age 50.[101] This loss was compounded by a serious malaria infestation that, combined with four years of poor income during the economic depression, made many of the colonists return to England or depart for new lands in South Africa and other parts of California.[102] A minority of English colonists became American citizens. The Jackson family settled in Auburn and one became the agricultural commissioner of California. By 1900 Placer County ceased to exist as a British sporting colony. The colony's best cricketers found other teams. Edward Lannowe joined the Pacifics and Harry F. Elliot joined the Alameda CC. Chris Simmonds and his wife moved to Riverside in southern California where he and his son continued playing cricket for the Santa Monica Cricket Club until 1920.

The 1898 season was the last hurrah for Placer County's players. Newcomer Harry F. Elliot, led Placer County's batting averages for the season with 23 runs per innings. Regulars Edward Lannowe, Harold Butt, Chris Turner, Chris Simmonds and William Pretherick placed high in the 1898 CCA batting averages as the Alameda CC won the CCA league Hunter-Harrison Trophy for a fourth time. John Meyers, the Pacific CC captain, lead the CCA batting averages with 38.25 runs an innings. There were three centuries during the season. Apart from Hogue's century, two of the centurions were new names to the CCA, Croll and Baugh. Chris Simmonds was the best bowler in California in 1898, taking 23 wickets in nine innings for a 6.13 average. Lake County did not take part in CCA competition, but Rose ended the Lake County season with 44 wickets for 92 runs averaging 2.09 runs a wicket.[103] Following Digger Robertson's return to Australia to play for South Melbourne, the Bohemians CC folded. CCA cricket was lackluster in 1898 for several reasons. Harold Richardson — California's best batsman — had returned to England, where he played for Surrey County in the first half of the 1899 season.[104] Another Alameda CC player, Harold Ward, left California to try his luck in the Klondike in 1898. With Richardson, Robertson and Ward, three of the city's top players, gone from the San Francisco cricket world in 1898, Arthur Coates in his last report to the *American Cricketer* (published posthumously) mused,

> It is the dream of many of our enthusiasts to send a representative California team East to play Chicago, New York and Philadelphia clubs; but who shall say when the dream may be realized? Such trips would be an immense benefit to cricket in the state, but I fear there are insuperable difficulties in the way.
>
> There are some fifteen to sixteen clubs in the State, the most prominent being the Alameda and Pacific clubs of San Francisco and the Lake, Santa Clara, and the Placer county; these five being within reasonable distance of each other, are able to meet from time to time, and thus arises an amount of friendly rivalry which is helpful to the game.[105]

Arthur Coates' dream was realized a century later when competition between the four cricket regions of the United States—Central, South, East and West—was instituted in 1997 as part of the selection process for the United States team that took part in the International Cricket Council World Cup tournament held in Malaysia. League baseball got back on track in the Golden State, a century earlier, following the re-establishment of the California Baseball League in 1898. Fixtures were held at the enclosed Recreation Grounds on 8th and Folsom streets in San Francisco. Crowds of 5,000 paid to watch the games.

In 1899 there were just three regular CCA league sides: Alameda, Pacific and California. Lake County was an associate CCA member and did not participate in regular league play. Edward Brown from the Alameda CC was voted president of the CCA. The vice-presidents of the CCA were Captain Metcalf (Pacific), Robert Hogue (Alameda), William McGavin (California) and Herbert Keeling (Lake). Non-CCA teams also sent delegates: Thomas Beakbane (Burns Valley CC), Bill Edmands and Arthur Spurr (Lakeport CC) and Robert Truman (Mountain Copper CC). The CCA schedule for the 1899 season was flexible as the three San Francisco teams competed for the Brown Trophy. The season started on May 7 and lasted until October 8. The city teams played each other twice a month with the fourth weekend of each month set aside for nonleague games between such sides as Insurance versus Banks or Married versus Single. All games were played at the Alameda CC ground on Webster Street, located on the East Bay near Oakland. Golden Gate Park and the Presidio grounds were not available in 1899 as the areas were given over to military preparation for the Spanish-American War. As war clouds loomed in the Pacific, Placer County's players found new cricket teams as Citrus Colony dispersed. Charles Turner joined the Santa Cruz. Harold Richardson also played for Santa Cruz on his return from playing for Surrey County CC. Without Richardson's batting, Alameda CC lost the CCA league Brown cup in 1899 to the California Cricket Club.

In 1900 Alameda CC regained the championship after Richardson and Ward, fresh from the Klondike, rejoined the team. The Alameda side defeated the Pacific, California, Sacramento and Santa Cruz for the Brown Trophy in a 13-game season. Ward was the best CCA bowler, taking 52 wickets. Alameda CC won the CCA league again in 1891. The most significant cricket event of the year occurred when American-born cricketers defeated a CCA expatriate team by 277 to 107 runs. The Bird brothers, who played for Alameda CC, both scored centuries. This was a great accomplishment for the two ex–baseball players, who had been unable to score above ten runs an innings when they started playing cricket in 1890.

Stanford University's involvement in sports strengthened cricket in Santa Clara County. Stanford played Berkeley at rugby. The annual game between the two universities became one of the main San Francisco social events of the year. Both universities had cricketers on their staff. Lake County continued to attract teams from San Francisco. Harold Richardson scored the first century against Burns Valley Cricket Club on September 15–16. San Francisco scored 240 to BVCC's 95 runs. Chris Enderby was the top scorer for BVCC with 34 runs.[106]

In 1902, the Pacific Cricket Club won the CCA league championship, but the greatest excitement came at the end of the season when Lord Hawke's England touring team for New Zealand stopped in San Francisco to play a California XVIII on November 25–26. The *San Francisco Chronicle* reported that the CCA-selected team were all British expatriates. This was not entirely true, because Australian Arthur Hoskins had played for the New York Veterans based at the Columbia Oval, where he had played for the United States versus Canada; and he was selected for the California team. Lord Hawke's team was captained by Trinidad-born Pelham Warner, in the absence of Lord Hawke who sailed by the

Suez Canal route to New Zealand on a different ship. Warner's team stayed at the Palace Hotel, San Francisco's foremost luxury hotel, which had a unique atrium-style covered driveway and had been favored by famous English guests such as Rudyard Kipling and Oscar Wilde.[107] The *San Francisco Chronicle* covered in detail the preparations for what was the most important local cricket match since the visit of the 1896 Australians. On November 26 it reported:

> Walter Courtney Bennett, C.I.E., The Consul-General of Great Britain; Edward Brown, president of the California Cricket Association, and William Greer Harrison, president of the Olympic Athletic club formed the reception committee.... Mr. Harrison invited the visitors to a drive through the Park and an incidental view of the Cliff House and the seals.[108]

Harrison's renown in San Francisco sports circles made him well suited to greet the visiting English cricketers with Consul-General Bennett. Both officials had worked together on the Pacific Cricket Club since 1890. Along with Alameda CC and CCA president Brown, the three greeters met the England captain, Warner. This was Plum's first trip to California, after three to the East Coast where he had played in New York, Philadelphia and Baltimore.[109] Warner became secretary of the MCC and a close confidant of its president, Lord Harris, once his England and Middlesex County CC playing days were over.

Eton-trained B.J.T. "Bossie" Bosanquet introduced the googlie to cricket on this 1902 tour, and he bowled the new ball to great effect in San Francisco. Describing how to deliver the googlie, Bosanquet said, "The whole secret of it lies in turning the ball over in the hand by dropping the wrist at the moment of delivery, so that the axis of the spin is changed from left to right to left, thus converting the spin from an ordinary leg break to an ordinary off break."[110] Though Bosanquet's test career spanned only seven games he helped secure the Ashes for England with a devastating bowling spell against the Australians who named the ball the "bossie" in honor of its innovator. In California, Wilkes and Elliot became the most successful exponents of the googlie. The *San Francisco Chronicle* did not mention the googlie when it described the England team, beginning with

> C.J. Burnup ... another brilliant batsman with the wonderful faculty of forcing runs when his side is in desparate straits. Burnup first became really prominent when playing for Cambridge University. Kent County then claimed him and his career from the time of his joining the county cricket has been sensational. Burnup is in the front rank of English cricket in every department of the game.
>
> B.J.T. Bosanquet of Eton, Oxford, and Middlesex is another of England's most brilliant amateurs. He is an all round player, an effective batsman, and as a bowler may be described as a "mixer."
>
> T.L. Taylor, Uppinghman, Cambridge captain and Yorkshire, is the wicket-keeper of the team and one of the best bats in England to-day.
>
> E.M. Dawson, Harrow, Cambridge captain last year and now of Surrey, is a splendid left hand batsman and a punisher. Dawson made a great mark in county cricket this season.
>
> Hargreave, the Warwickshire professional, is considered one of the best slow bowlers in the world. This bowler met with wonderful success against the Australians during the English tour, and was absolutely unplayable on a wet wicket. Hargreave is a run getter in tight places and a reliable field.
>
> Thomson, the Northamptonshire professional is another good bowler, fields well and generally comes off with the bat when the runs are most wanted.
>
> With P.R. Johnson of Somersetshire and J. Stanning of Cambridge and Yorkshire, two splendid batsmen and fielders, there is formed one of the finest teams of cricketers that ever the left the shores of Great Britain seeking other fields to conquer.[111]

The California XVIII was captained by H.C. Cassidy (Pacific) and included veterans Keeling and Enderby (Lake County) from the 1896 game against Australia. Harold Richardson (Santa Clara) was available for his first California representative game as were the Elliot brothers, who had started their cricket career with Citrus Colony and now played for Sacramento. Arthur Wilding (Alameda) and David Jameson, who later played for Santa Monica CC, were two of the new promising California players. Five hundred spectators turned up at the Presidio grounds to watch the match that began at 10:00 A.M. It was agreed to decide the match in one innings as darkness came early in November. California won the toss and batted first. Harold Richardson (27) and Harry Elliot (14) put the California XVIII innings on a sound footing, scoring 33 runs for the second wicket. When Arthur Hoskins (10) was out to Hargreave, California's score was a credible 68 for 4 wickets. Unfortunately, Keeling and Enderby were out for ducks before Cassidy (11), Ward and Wilding took the score to 125 all out. The second highest scorer was "extras," which the *Chronicle* blamed on the rough state of the field. Bosanquet took 11 wickets for 42 runs in 32 overs. There were four stumpings by Taylor, the English wicket-keeper. In reply, England pressed to get the runs against Harold Ward's accurate bowling. He took three of England XII's wickets for 34 runs, in 18 overs. Harold Richardson bowled Warner for 52 and Bosanquet was 50 not out. England won the game by three wickets. Bosanquet's 50, which included six boundaries, was generally considered the finest innings in California that year. After the game, festivities were held at the California Hotel.

With the departure of the England team, which won all 18 games in New Zealand, cricket in northern California settled down to its familiar pattern, with regular realignments of teams and their members. Lake County players Thomas Beakbane and Herbert Keeling joined the California Cricket Club so they could participate in CCA league cricket, because Lake County continued to stay out of CCA participation. Executive cricket talent was at a premium in California in 1902. Brown became president of California's two most prestigious cricket clubs, the Alameda CC and the Pacific CC. The PCC was captained by American Clement Hill in a league season of 12 games between three CCA teams.

With professional baseball back in full swing there was less crossover of baseball players to cricket. In the improved economic situation, good local baseball players could earn professional contracts. The quality of baseball fields improved as an average 5,000 "kranks" (from the noise made by the payment turnstile) or paying spectators passed through the gates for baseball games at the Haight Street facility in Golden Gate Park or the Recreation Grounds at 25th and Folsom. Cricket did well to attract 500 nonpaying spectators to the CCA games. Cricket reaffirmed its elitist formula with the founding of the San Francisco County Cricket Club, captained by 32-year-old Harold Richardson in 1903. British consul-general Walter Courtney Bennett and Greer Harrison no longer had time for executive positions with the PCC. The country connection was maintained, with Santa Cruz replacing Sacramento, which was a member of the CCA in 1902. Brown remained president of the Alameda CC and took over as president of the California Cricket Club in 1903. Despite the executive shuffling the team to beat from 1903 was the SFCCC under Richardson's captaincy. Harold Richardson's batting dominated CCA cricket as he finished with a 146-run average in 1904, scoring 730 runs in 12 innings. In 1905, Richardson's average was 125 runs in 12 innings for a total of 626 runs. He also led the bowling, taking 27 wickets for an 8.44 average in 1905.[112] Richardson's domination of CCA cricket was unassailable, as the best Alameda CC batsman had an average of 18 with a total of 118 runs.

In 1905, the next best batsman was Arthur Jenkins of Santa Cruz CC, who compiled a 46 average in less than five games. For Alameda CC, Harold Ward developed into the premier CCA bowler. Keeling and Beakbane continued to play for the California Cricket Club. Under Brown's presidency they were vice-presidents of the 15-year-old CCA when the April 16 earthquake hit San Francisco at 5:15 A.M.[113]

The earth's crust slid sideways along the San Andreas Fault, creating a 200-mile-long zone of damage. Four hundred thousand San Franciscans felt the increasing intensity of earth tremors for 40 seconds. Once the shaking was done, the Queen Anne–Richardson style houses that composed the core of San Francisco's housing stock lay in ruins. The Nob Hill mansions of Central Pacific Railroad millionaires Leland Stanford, Collis Huntington, Charles Crocker and Mark Hopkins withstood the earthquake but became tinder for the fire that started several hours later. Numerous carriage and trolley horses were killed by falling debris. If it had not been for cars commandeered from prosperous San Franciscans, transport in the city would have been a serious problem. The San Francisco earthquake democratized the use of the automobile. Burst water mains compounded damage by the initial earthquake as the fabled San Francisco Fire Department was stripped of its major fire fighting weapon. The SFDP was left to fight fire with dynamite. Fire chief Dennis Sullivan's emergency plan could not be implemented after he was killed by the falling brick chimney of the California Hotel as it sliced his three-story house in half. Chief Sullivan was not the only commanding presence killed that day. Harold Richardson, 35 years old, California's greatest cricketer and batsmen, was one of 300 people killed by falling buildings.[114] Nearly a century later it remains hard to believe that a player of such commanding presence at the wicket could have been so easily been bowled out by fate with only 35 years on the board.

The British consul-general and PCC member Walter Courtney Bennett lived to tell his story. The facade of the British residence near Union Square collapsed, exposing all interior walls. Made homeless, Bennett pulled his wife and daughter from their beds. In his Foreign Office report to London, he gave a first-hand account of San Francisco's worst earthquake since 1867:

> Everywhere there was the noise, like thousands of violins, all at discord. The most harrowing sound one could imagine. All this as [an] earthquake two and three feet high undulated through the ground and the bell on St. Mary's Church still beat frantically — a harbinger of things to come.[115]

Britain's senior diplomat in San Francisco was happy to curl up under a blanket in Golden Gate Park with his head on his bulky briefcase — all that was left of the British Consulate's documents— his wife and child by his side and his memories of playing cricket in Golden Gate Park left to remind him of a more tranquil time.[116] Oakland and its neighbor Berkeley, the third and fourth largest cities in California, escaped the full impact of the temblors. Ninety miles to the north in Lake County, brick buildings— including Keeling's law office — were badly damaged in Lakeport. Damage was more severe to the south of San Francisco, where a series of tremors destroyed large parts of Hollister, Gilroy, Palo Alto and San Jose. In Palo Alto a redwood forest was turned to tinder and several Stanford University buildings fell down. In San Jose, 100 people were killed when part of St. Agnew's Asylum for the Insane collapsed.

President Theodore Roosevelt declared a federal emergency. Jack London and his wife Charmian caught an empty ferry to San Francisco to report the biggest story of his life for *Century Magazine*. Over 50,000 refugees found shelter in Oakland. Many of the refugees never went back to San Francisco; Oakland's population permanently tripled to 160,000 as a result of the earthquake. In San Francisco temporary camps were set up to house the homeless in Golden Gate Park. They were still there a year later. The playing of cricket and baseball stopped in San Francisco as an immediate consequence of the earthquake. It did not start again until 1908, by which time San Francisco's best cricketers found the opportunity to play in southern California. Edward H. Wilkes and Harry Elliot (Pacific) joined the San Monica Cricket Club, where they played cricket on the Old Polo Ground overlooking the ocean and at the Vineyard switching yard of the Pacific Electric, located at the intersection of San Vicente and Olympic Boulevards.

By 1908, Thomas Price of the Olympic Club was able to report to the cricket world that

> with new hope the California Cricket Association held its annual meeting in 1908 and at once procured two grounds. The three old clubs which constituted the Association in former years were reformed, and three new clubs, inspired by enthusiasm, entered the ranks. This gave a competition of six clubs, the veteran clubs being Alameda, San Francisco County and the Pacifics, while the new clubs were the Barbarians, the Wanderers and the Golden Gates. The Burns Valley club, as has been customary for several years past, affiliated with the Association but did not take an active part in the series; a new country club was formed in San Mateo, which although not taking part in the series, played several games with the city teams. While the games were forging ahead in San Francisco, things were looking brighter in Southern California, and under the leadership of several local enthusiasts clubs were formed in Los Angeles and Santa Monica.[117]

The Barbarian Club was primarily a rugby club that flourished during the heyday of Stanford versus Berkeley rugby games. The rugby background of the Barbarian players made them fit cricket players in the summer. Determined to win, they stuck with cricket, improving each year in CCA competition. The two new grounds Thomas Price referred to were located near Oakland, where the Alameda CC built a new clubhouse and concrete pitch, and in Golden Gate Park, which became the home ground of the Golden Gate Cricket Club in 1908. San Mateo's Burlingame Country Club proved a welcome addition to the CCA as they had a well maintained turf pitch. With new playing surfaces, the loss of Harold Richardson, and a new CCA president, Captain John Metcalf, Arthur Wilding as secretary-treasurer, and Harold Ward and Thomas Beakbane as vice-presidents, the CCA was well balanced. Teams were keen to play in 1908 after the two-year break. Thomas Price reported:

> In the championship series the games were closely contested. The result of the competition was in doubt right up to the end. Of the season, the Pacifics finally turning up winners with 14 points scored, closely followed by Alameda with 13, the Barbarians with 12. The leading batsman of the year was H.R. Elliot of the Pacific club, with an average of 46.10 and a high score of one hundred and twenty one not out. He also had the distinction of being the only man to obtain a century during the season. Wilkes, also of the Pacific club, headed the bowlers with an average of 4.08 for 35 wickets and was second in the batting with an average

of 25.80, closely followed by Stewart of the Barbarians, Renwick of San Francisco County and Moverly of the Barbarians, all of whom had an average of 24.

The bowlers had things all their own way. Johnson 4.61 for 17 wickets, Stewart 5.33 for 18 wickets, and Lyman 6.35 for 17 wickets, all members of the Barbarian club bowled in good form, while Renwick of San Francisco County, in obtaining 50 wickets at a cost of 6.94, did exceptionally well.[118]

Renwick was a former Citrus Colony player. In 1908, after its two-year earthquake induced hiatus, San Francisco could not get enough cricket. After the CCA league was decided, the cricket season was extended with a "Champion versus the Rest" match. In Lake County, Herbert Keeling's expanding business interests took more of his time and he phased out of cricket along with many of his team members. Charlie Hammond was serving on Republican California governor Gillett's staff, while Keeling was using the first motorbike to be purchased in Lake County to scout out new real-estate investment opportunities. He would later become mayor of Lakeport in 1924, where he encouraged the growth of Rotary Clubs once he determined they posed no threat to the freemasonry organizations close to his heart, the Scottish Rite Temple and the Shriners. William Hearn became president of the CCA in 1909. Six teams participated in the 1909 season. The Barbarians won the league with a record of nine wins and one loss. The Wanderers of San Jose, San Mateo County, Alameda, and the Golden Gates also participated in the league. Despite the loss of veteran teams such as the Pacific and the California Cricket Club, Thomas Price was adamant that the 1909 season was

> a very successful one ... and the closeness of the competition for the California Cricket Association Premiership Cup and Wolff Pennant was sufficient to maintain interest all through the summer and the crowds of spectators at every important match testified to their appreciation of the improved standard of play....
>
> The leading batsman of the year was A.R. Elliot of the Barbarians, who again showed his versatility by performing several splendid feats with the bat and made an aggregate of 354 runs in 8 innings in which he participated, finally winding up the season with a splendid average of 88.50.
>
> The bowling of Sid Stewart was a feature of the season's cricket, he easily heading the association records with an average 3.74 for 35 wickets, and also had the distinction of taking 10 of his opponents in one innings for 10 runs.
>
> The following is the "all star" team picked as being representative of the California cricket Association: A.R. Elliot, S. Stewart, H. Renwick, H.B. Ottersdessen, H.F. Elliot, Thos H. Price, E.M. Petersen, W.E. Moran, W. Nield, A.H. Moverly, S. Charlton.[119]

Five of the players listed by Thomas Price played for the Barbarians. These players were the Elliot brothers, Otterdessen, Price and Stewart. All the players mentioned were new to the league except the Elliot brothers. The old guard CCA players were found on the Alameda CC team, where Harold Ward remained president while his son Henry was secretary-treasurer of the club. Neither Ward's performance with the bat and ball merited attention in 1909.

The change of the old guard was confirmed in the 1910 season, which was won by San Jose, the first time a non–San Francisco team won the CCA since the founding of the association in 1891. The irreversible decline in San Francisco cricket set in as Peterson of San Francisco County won the batting prize with a 32.11 average, in contrast to Harold Richardson's 125-run average just before the 1906 earthquake. In 1911 Spalding's cricket annual reported:

Cricket in and around San Francisco was never in a more deplorable condition.... With five clubs the championship series arranged by the California Cricket Association should have been something to be proud of. Instead ... the players themselves showed lack of interest, could not or would not turn out to play, and in every way the series was a joke. Again I think the schedule ran on into the football months. Last season there was not one of the five clubs that turned up to keep its engagements with a full team. For the first two games full teams were in evidence, but were played with five or six men, and even less than that [per] side.[120]

The root cause of cricket's decline in San Francisco was the increased transience of the expatriate and immigrant populations following the earthquake. Greater employment opportunities opened in southern California following the shift from a rural to urban community, enabled by increased use of oil and importation of water via Mulholland's California Aqueduct, completed in 1913. Life in San Francisco sped up after the earthquake as the automobile became the ubiquitous vehicle of choice. Social change also accelerated in California following the earthquake; the Progressive Party of Hiram Johnson pushed women's suffrage through the California legislature, allowing women to vote for the first time. Johnson's administration also improved governance in California, requiring charters for the cities of Los Angeles and San Francisco. For the first time, recall elections were allowed along with the ballot initiatives, which enabled people and not politicians to select the legislative agenda. Mayor Schmidt of San Francisco had been corrupted by his close ties with the Southern Pacific Railroad, which dominated California politics for over 70 years. This corruption was depicted by novelist Frank Norris in *The Octopus*. The Progressive Party destroyed the Southern Pacific's financial stranglehold at the ballot box. Cricket was part of the old panoply of San Franciscan life and it was now time for the new. With William Harrison no longer president of the Olympic Club, Keeling and Hammond in Lake County becoming politicians and out of cricket, it was left to a more transient, less affluent, cricket population to keep the game alive. In 1913, rugby players lost influence at Cal Berkeley and Stanford when American football was reintroduced, reflecting the rapid growth of the uniquely American sport from coast to coast. Soccer became the sport of choice among cricketers. Walter Umack, writing in *Spalding's Cricket Manual for 1913*, noted that in California

practically every cricketer on this coast is a Soccer enthusiast, and as the first games of football start early in October and practice early in September, the Soccer has greater fascinations for the men than cricket. Football starts early in the State.... Last year a full round was chopped off the schedule over the preceeding years, but this was found inadequate.[121]

Soccer was the first sport in England to go fully professional. Rugby was still divided between the amateur Union players and the professional League players of Northern England. England's cricket captain still had to come from amateur ranks whereas in soccer, skill reigned supreme as spectators showed they were willing to pay in large attendance figures for a good game. Charles Burgess Fry, one of England's best batsmen, played soccer for England when international competition in soccer was limited to three countries, Scotland, England and Ireland. As soccer expanded rapidly in California, East Coast baseball increasingly relied on California players, both sports depleting the pool of sportsmen available for cricket in San Francisco. According to Umack, California cricketers in 1913 were a "very transient bunch":

Many a time a good cricketer is put into the game and shows real class. His team mates are congratulating themselves on securing such a fine batsman or bowler, and the opposition is rejoicing that with such a man "we shall have some good cricket," irrespective as to whether he is an opponent or not, when the following week he notifies his club he cannot play any more, as he leaves the state on Monday.... The San Francisco club fell all to pieces and this old club more than any other was low in players. It had enough members on its roll to form a team, but they failed to come out and showed lack of interest. The Barbarians were in something of the same fix as the San Francisco team, and in many of the games only three or four men were on hand.[122]

The Alameda Cricket Club, for 20 years the mainstay of San Francisco cricket, by 1913 was barely able to hold onto its Webster Street ground. Real estate development had encroached on the ground to the point that bowling was only possible from one end. This left Golden Gate as the only San Francisco team with their own ground suitable for playing cricket from both ends of the wicket. In the last CCA championship before the outbreak of the First World War, Henry A. Oxenham led the Golden Gate team to victory in the league prior to his permanent departure to Alaska on urgent business. Oxenham also captained the Golden Gate team that traveled to Los Angeles over the July 4 weekend, where they easily beat the Los Angeles Cricket Club on their home ground at the Vineyard.[123] The Golden Gates beat Los Angeles 105 to 61 runs. In their second game the Golden Gates declared at 177 for 3 and the LACC were only able to score 106 runs in reply. Los Angeles, Santa Monica and San Diego (founded in 1910) became CCA associate members in 1913, the year the Golden Gate team were truly California champions. The enthusiasm that made San Francisco the hub of cricket in California for 62 years, between 1852 and 1914, was absorbed by Los Angeles when the CCA ceased to exist.

9. Southern California's Cricket Pioneers, 1888–1913

CRICKET STARTED IN LOS ANGELES in 1888 when the Atchison, Topeka and Santa Fe Railway Company lowered its passenger fares to one dollar. Many immigrants headed west from Kansas City and cricket-rich Chicago to Los Angeles.[1] The Midwesterners found land cheap. Largely an expatriate affair, cricket soon spread to the citrus growing towns of Duarte, Azusa and Riverside in the San Bernardino Mountain foothills.[2] The Los Angeles Cricket Club played its first games in Agriculture Park, a mile from Sixth Street Park, where some of the first professional games of baseball were played in Los Angeles between teams such as the Nameless and Academy clubs.[3]

The Los Angeles cricket touring tradition started in 1891. Los Angeles cricketers organized a cricket tour the same year a regular league was established in San Francisco. The *Los Angeles Herald* believed the tour would result in victory for the local players as they had "good trundlers" (bowlers) and aggressive batsmen.[4] Competition between the two California cities was found worthwhile by local cricketers and in the 1893 *American Cricketer* carried a tour report.[5]

In southern California, cricket sank its deepest roots in Santa Monica. Real-estate entrepreneurs Colonel Baker and Nevada senator John Percival Jones platted the seaside town in 1875.[6] Both Jones and Baker were founding board members of the Santa Monica Improvement Corporation, which allocated $10,000 to build the Casino Club with adjoining tennis courts on Third and Washington. The Casino courts took their name from the home of tennis on the East Coast, the Newport Casino in Rhode Island.

By 1898 the "Orange Blossom Special" linked Santa Monica to Riverside with a two-hour ride rated one of the prettiest on the Pacific Electric Car system. In spring the red cars of the Pacific Electric passed through acres of the white citrus scented flowers remembered by Oscar Wilde for their perfumed fragrance from his visit to Los Angeles with the D'Oyle Carte Opera Company in 1881. The orange blossoms Oscar Wilde smelled generated more cash than all the gold mined out of the Sierras during the Gold Rush.[7] Santa

Monica provided recreation for the Riverside citrus elite. Many British sportsmen from Riverside were citrus growers and spent their summers in the cooler Santa Monica climate. Cyril Maud, James Bettner, his son Robert Bettner, William Pedley and George Waring were founding members of the Riverside Polo Club in 1892. Pedley was hired by the British owned San Jacinto Land Company as manager and chief engineer in 1889. Like many playing members of the Riverside Polo Club, Pedley learned polo while stationed in India. George Waring was managing director of the Arlington Fruit Exchange and Victoria Citrus Co-Operative, located in the Arlington Heights area of Riverside. In Santa Monica, Waring became vice-president of the Southern California Lawn Tennis Association when Abbot Kinney was its president. A regular visitor to the Miramar residence of the Jones family (a huge Richardson-Victorian mansion built on the coastal bluffs [palisades] overlooking the Pacific Ocean in Santa Monica), Waring became a confidant of Thomas Dudley, the English-born mayor of Santa Monica from 1906 to 1912 and 1914 to 1916.[8] His longevity as mayor was attributable to his creative vision for the city. Dudley believed that "the public should have access to the beach as a playground for all; that beauty ... should be the goal toward which the community should strive, and provision for recreation should be placed within the reach of all residents of Santa Monica at a low cost."[9]

Robert Bettner was born in St. Louis. A successful real-estate entrepreneur, he built the Rubidoux Estates in Riverside and leased land for the Riverside and Santa Monica polo grounds.

Cricket offered a sporting diversion for polo players. Bettner played with Charles Cochrane Le Bas on the first Santa Monica Cricket Club side, in 1898. C.C. Le Bas had played for the MCC and Ground when Wright made his baseball tour of England in 1874. Le Bas settled in Riverside in 1895, where he helped organize a cricket game for the Riverside Polo Club celebrations for the opening of their new grounds as part of the Chemawa Park.[10] The park was owned by the Riverside and Arlington Street Railway, built after Henry Huntington became an investor in the Mission Inn.[11] Both Young and Le Bas had played club-level cricket in England.[12] In 1901 the *Riverside Daily Press* announced:

> The cricket game on Thursday on the new park is arousing considerable interest. Many have not seen the national game of England, and it is safe to say that there will be a big crowd of the curious and the enthusiastic to witness the game. The admission will be 25 cents. The local team of eleven will be selected from the following fourteen players: C.E. Maud, W.E. Pedley, Thomson, H. Thomson, H.C. Cayley, H. Wilson, M.E. Flowers, M. Redmayne, W.L. Roberts, Mr. Roberts, Jr., R.H.H. Chapman, C.E. Orr, G.L. Waring. H. Hudson will act as scorer.[13]

On May 2, the *Riverside Daily Press* reported:

> A number of cricket enthusiasts have spent the day at the new park watching the game between the Riverside and San Luis elevens. The game of cricket is not well known in this country. There have been a few games played in Riverside, but not enough to initiate the general public into its fine points, which will probably account for the fact that there were not more in attendance today.[14]

Chris Simmonds (ex–Citrus Colony) opened for the Riverside cricket team with William Pedley (Alameda CC) and scored a third of Riverside's innings total of 35 with 12 runs. Despite the California Cricket Association league experience of Simmonds (he was selected for the California XVIII that played Australia in 1896) and Pedley, the Riverside cricketers were overpowered by the San Luis Rey team:

Riverside Polo Club members Cyril Maude and George Waring. Maude and Waring played for Riverside against the Del Rey Cricket Club from Oceanside in a cricket match held to celebrate the opening of polo grounds at Chemawa Park in 1902. Robert Bettner, second from the left, was the American patron of the team. His father leased the Santa Monica Polo Grounds in 1893, which became the home ground of the Santa Monica Cricket Club from 1896. George Waring played cricket for Santa Monica and helped found the first golf club there in 1906. Source: Riverside Museum Archives, Riverside, Ca.

When the visitors took the bat, it was soon seen that they were much stronger than the home team. At 3 o'clock they had 20 runs to their credit and only one man out with one wicket down. The names of the members of the San Luis Rey eleven are: F.R. Jeffrey, C.R. Boyeson, H. Bradley, T. Hay, H.C. Hargrave, W.S. Hargrave, J.H. Young, W.C. Lundie, C.G. Porteous, H. Thatcher and H. Evans. The bowlers for the Riverside team were W.E. Pedley and S. Simmonds and for the visitors, F.R. Jeffrey and E. Evans.[15]

Oxford University–trained John Young helped San Luis Rey compile an insurmountable winning total of 90 runs. Then,

Mrs. Gilliland, Mrs. Franklin Hall and Mrs. Robert Lee Bettner entertained at the Casa Blanca Tennis Club house in honor of the visitors who are here to attend the cricket match and polo game. The evening was passed in dancing and cards, and was an event long to be remembered with delight by the social side of the valley.

Several days had been spent by the hostesses and their lady friends in the decorating the club house.... The mantle was a mass of white roses, and from the ceiling were hung baskets filled with flowers. Out through the doorway could be seen the porch, which had the appearance of an eastern bungalow, with its low ceilings, Chinese lanterns, and heavy hangings.... Claret, punch and lemonade were served in huge cut-glass bowls in this room throughout the evening.[16]

In addition to Riverside residents, guests for the events came from Santa Barbara, Oceanside, Redlands, Los Angeles and Santa Monica. Riverside's social activities helped keep cricket alive in southern California during the Boer War, when the English population dropped by more than 50 percent to 2,700 from its 5,400 high in 1890.[17]

John Lester, the gold standard of Philadelphia cricket, arrived in southern California in 1898 to play cricket for the SMCC at the polo grounds on Eighth and Nevada streets in Santa Monica. Bordered to the west by a dense screen of eucalyptus and pepper trees planted to provide shade and break the strong on-shore breezes from the Pacific, the polo grounds were the venue for the SMCC when "an afternoon game meant a kind of gathering of the clans, with 'society' out in full force. The ladies took turns serving tea to the members and their friends and usually a delightful afternoon was had."[18] The Santa Monica Cricket Club, captained by Edward W. Barry, included Anthony Butcher, William Young, George Stearns, William Pedley, Edward Cawston and George Waring.[19] On September 16, 1898, a cricket tournament was held between the Los Angeles CC, the Santa Monica CC and a country team composed of citrus growers from Duarte, Azusa and Glendora. The LACC beat the SMCC in the final game to win the tournament by a score of 169 to 124 runs. A week later, strengthened by John Lester, the SMCC beat the LACC in a return match by 46 runs. According to a report in the *Santa Monica Outlook*,

> In batting Mr. Lester scored 29 points and his bowling was a "caution" being very effective and puzzling the Los Angeles team. A. Butcher, a Cambridge University man scored 18 and W.H. Young of Duarte made the score of the day with 53.[20]

After his return to Philadelphia's lush turf cricket pitches of the Belmont, Germantown, Philadelphia, and Merion cricket clubs, Lester wrote,

> Cricket in Southern California in midsummer, when the turf is everywhere brown and burnt, [and] the only green things are eucalyptus trees and orchards, would seem quite out of the question. But there are fifty thousand Englishmen in California, and many a thriving cricket club, keen to play though the weather be hot and the wicket brown. Many of the cricketers of Southern California have ranches within the prolific fruit belt, which neighbors Los Angeles.[21]

Lester, a Haverford University CC and Merion Cricket Club member, noted,

> The games were played on extensive polo grounds, devoid of turf, of course, but fairly level and true. The wicket, carefully prepared, rolled was laid with matting, and played well throughout.[22]

Lester assessed the quality of cricket players in southern California:

> The leading spirit in Southern California cricket is E.W. Barry, the son of the colonel of a crack English regiment. Barry is a good bat, a fair fast bowler, and an indefatigable captain. Among the other good cricketers on the three contesting teams was A. Butcher, an old Cambridge University man; W.H. Young, an excellent all round player; R.H. Chapman, an Uppingham boy of some years ago; H. Jones Bateman, captain of Charterhouse in 1884; and several other university and public school men. To judge from reports J. Scott is the best bat in Southern California, but he failed to come off in this year's tournament.[23]

Cricketers trained in the English public schools and the British army in India believed, along with Endicott Peabody, Theodore Roosevelt's headmaster at Groton in Connecticut, that

> Sport as conducted in England, provided health and moral education. The highest achievement of any game can be claimed for the national game of cricket, which is used as a measure of moral quality. Of some fine action, they will say: "That's cricket!" ... Final condemnation is found in the criticism, "That's not cricket!"[24]

By contrast, in America, Peabody observed:

> our first approach to a game is apt to be the quest for someone to beat.... Athletics in many cases is just plain business.... Worst of all, in consequence of the intense competition there has grown up in many schools the notion that any play is legitimate if it is not forbidden by the letter of the rules.[25]

Peabody clearly recognized that sport reflected the values of the society it was played in. He appreciated cricket as a moral mentor, but he preferred gridiron football as it reflected American values. In Santa Monica cricket reflected the inherently British political, social and economic climate of the town. Social capital acquired by performing admirably on the field might be translated into business relationships in the banquets that followed many of the matches.

Santa Monica played San Luis Rey. San Luis was located four miles inland from Oceanside where the San Luis Rey Mission dominated rich agricultural land. With the secularization of mission lands in 1834, land was subdivided after the 1851 California Land Act, which required owners of rancheros and mission lands to prove land ownership or have it escheat to the state. Large numbers of English immigrants bought San Luis Rey Mission land from 1890. As in parts of the British Empire such as South Africa, Rhodesia or Kenya, middle- or working-class English families who settled on cheap land found that they

> could lead the good old life of a country squire, riding to the hounds and that sort of thing. Quite a few Englishmen fell for the idea and so the colony sprang up. Most of them, however, found that in spite of the wealth of the land in San Luis Rey, it took a lot of work to run a ranch. Consequently many of them moved to Oceanside.... There were facilities down near the present Santa Fe tracks, for English sports, such as cricket.... Transportation was poor then.... In order to go from Redlands to Oceanside, a person had to take a train to Orange, then to Los Angeles, then wait for a train to Oceanside.[26]

The majority of San Luis Rey's English settlers came from Ealing in London, and many became members of the Oceanside Athletic Club near the Santa Fe rail tracks, which

> used to serve tea every Saturday afternoon.... It was a very old fashioned kind of club because men did all the voting and decided everything, and ladies served the tea. We didn't have any vote or anything at all!... Some of the Americans finally decided they wanted some cold drinks and I think we tried to persuade them that tea was much more cooling when you were playing tennis.[27]

The comment about the Americans was made by a pioneering English octogenarian resident of Oceanside, Gladys Young Van Deerlin, who lived in the San Luis area for over 50 years. American sociologist Leo Kuper in his groundbreaking book *Plural Societies* is adamant that America has never been a melting pot. Rather, America, Kuper believed, comprised an assembly of different ethnic groups vying for social position and hegemony within the power structure.[28] When cricket was adopted by the power elite in American cities such Philadelphia, San Francisco, or Santa Monica before the outbreak of the First World War, cricket attendance was popular because the social activities after the games were displays of social capital and political power.

Cricket and tennis matches in Santa Monica also provided a political platform for the women's rights movement in California. As Gladys Young Van Deerlin noted in her Oceanside interview, women asserted their independence in the West in ways they could

Del Rey Cricket Club of Oceanside in 1902. Source: Oceanside Museum Archives.

never have imagined back in Ealing: "They packed a gun for protection against strange men and rattlesnakes, not necessarily separate species. They took up tennis and cricket. They also became proficient swimmers at the Oceanside beach, in attire that consisted of bloomers, sleeve-blouses, caps, black stockings and bathing shoes."[29]

These English women were a world away from the polite society of Victorian and Edwardian London. Women took on men at their own power game on July 22, 1899, at the new cricket ground. The *Oceanside Blade* reported: "At the cricket match Saturday the ladies defeated the gentlemen 86 to 85. It is rumored that the gentlemen were hobbled and played left handed."[30] The ladies continued to defeat the Oceanside men at cricket on a regular annual basis. In 1903 the ladies had their best win, scoring 105 runs to the men's 75.[31]

After the Boer War ended in 1902, there was a dramatic increase in English settlement of southern California, and the British community increased eightfold, to 17,500 people. Many new British immigrants found life congenial in Santa Monica. A second generation of cricket players was organized by the mayor's son, Peter Dudley. A July 23, 1906, report in the *Santa Monica Outlook* announced that some Santa Monica boys had formed a cricket club at Mayor Dudley's house on Fourth and Arizona. The SMCC lost their first home game at the polo fields to the Los Angeles CC by 78 runs. In the second game, played at the Agricultural Park near Exposition Park, the LACC won easily again. Los Angeles then beat Santa Monica two more times on their polo ground pitch.[32] Charles Le Bas captained Santa Monica when they defeated the Oceanside team on August 25 at the South Oceanside ground. The *Oceanside Blade* reported:

The day was fine and the pitch in excellent shape. The game opened with J.H. Young and C.R. Boyson for Oceanside facing the bowling of Justice and Dr. Jessop. The innings closed at a total of 58. After an excellent lunch served by the ladies, Santa Monica went to the bat and after piling up 147, declared the innings closed.[33]

Harry F. Elliot top scored with 68 not out for Santa Monica. The Santa Monica team also included Mr. Baldridge, F. and H. Justice, Bannister, H. Little and F. Elliot.[34] Oceanside comprised "W.S. Hargrave, E. White, H. Palmer, G. Thatcher, H. Hargrave, E. Trevellyan, J. Young, C.R. Boyson, I.D. Schaffer, R. Pedley and F. Ramsay."[35]

The LACC, Oceanside versus SMCC games were welcome news in San Francisco, where no cricket was played for two years following the San Francisco Earthquake. As Bay Area cricket ground to a halt, the Los Angeles Cricket Club found a permanent home for the first time in its 20-year history when it leased ground located at the Vineyard Pacific Electric Station between San Vicente and Pico boulevards. Fayatteville Square on Victoria Hills was bounded to the south by Arlington Heights, which gave a hint of its citrus colony connections with Riverside's Arlington Heights. Before Hancock Park or Beverly Hills were conceived, the upscale housing development comprising two concentric circles of Victoria Hills Crafts Movement mansions had their upscale ambience enhanced by cricket matches viewed from the arched concrete bridge that spanned the tracks linking Victoria Hill with Pico Boulevard. The cricket ground was set up away from the switchyard that housed a large electrical plant with a cooling tower used for electrifying the San Vicente portion of the tracks. English cricketers to Los Angeles loaned their names (such as Cochran) to streets in the area. *The American Cricketer* reported:

It is proposed that an organization of Englishmen shall be permanently formed under the name of the Los Angeles County Club. A lease of fifteen acres belonging to the Los Angeles Pacific Electric Company has been secured at the junction of the Sawtelle, Venice and Redondo lines west of the city.

It is proposed to lay the grounds into a cricket field, football field, tennis and handball courts, lacrosse field, and such other sports as might be provided for. A clubhouse and grandstand are to be built, and games are to be played there the year around.

In addition to C.P. Hurditch, who has lately joined the club, from Staten Island N.Y., the two Milner brothers will play for Los Angeles this season. Both these men have rendered an excellent account of themselves in China, South Africa and Australia, and with some of last year's stars, Southern California should be enabled to put a first class team into the field this season.[36]

Four local sides started the 1908 season with a month-long, weekend, intramural cricket festival between teams calling themselves the I Zingari, the MCC, the Wanderers and the Pilgrims. The first regular 1908 season game was held on July 27 at the Polo Grounds, where LACC beat SMCC 163 runs to 87.[37] Hurditch (37) and LACC captain Tom Bamford (67) top scored for the LACC. Sweet (23) top scored for SMCC with Le Bas (3). William Meggett and Archie Mitchell took the majority of LACC wickets. Hurditch and Heavens took most of the SMCC wickets.[38] In the August 11 return game, the *Santa Monica Outlook* reported a lopsided Los Angeles win against Santa Monica, noting that

for Los Angeles C.P. Hurditch went in first and scored more than the Santa Monica side, a bad beginning in the way of disheartening the enemy. Tempest's three and Bamford's four were much below average for these batsmen, and the nicks by Barwell and J.S. Heavens were unfortunate but Packman hit up 16.[39]

Hurditch scored 73 of LACC's 131 runs. This was enough to beat SMCC, which scored less than 131 runs in both innings. Los Angeles won the match by an innings when Bhumgara destroyed the Santa Monica batting by taking eight wickets.[40]

Charles Percy Hurditch, a Middlesex County CC player and MCC member, strengthened the Los Angeles side in 1908. A successful businessman, Hurditch's credo, "Originality is necessary in many things," shaped his four-year effort to put southern California cricket on a broader footing. Hurditch had played cricket in New York and the West Indies— Jamaica, Barbados, Trinidad and Demerara (Guyana). His most memorable game in Jamaica was against the Asylum Cricket Club in Kingston. As Hurditch relayed the story:

> A member from the [Asylum] club was one of the patients[;] the poor fellow was to all intents and purposes fairly well, but was known to have an occasional outburst. As he was a very keen cricketer he took part in all the matches, invariably going in first. But his style was entirely original, as he refused to play or hit at any ball off the wicket, while those that were straight, were met by his bat firmly fixed in the block hole. Now I had kept wicket many times when he had been batting and knew his style well, and having instructed the bowler to keep them a bit short, managed to catch him in front of the wicket, literally taking the ball off his bat. When the poor fellow saw how he was out, his temper got the better of him, and, raising his bat he was about to hurl it at me when a Providential attack overcame him and he fell to the ground having to be carried off the field by the attendants. Though sorry for the poor chap, I could not but be thankful for the termination.[41]

Intrepid and confident, Hurditch epitomized the ideals of the golden age of cricket. American cricket writer Mike Marquesas could have been writing about Hurditch when he noted,

> In the Golden Age 1895–1914 style was supreme. The model amateur batsman combined timing and power, grace and aggression. His play looked "effortless," a telling adjective. The off-drive, transmuting the power of the bowler into its opposite through timing and footwork, was the consummate expression of this aesthetic. How you looked became as important as how you scored. The aesthetic was counterposed to the utilitarian.[42]

When he lived in New York, Hurditch played in the Metropolitan District Cricket League (MDCL) for the Staten Island Cricket and Baseball Club. He was selected for the New York and District XVIII against Harry Trott's visiting Australian test side on October 4–5, 1893, and scored the second highest innings of 11 runs before he was run out in the drawn game in Central Park. Three years later on September 23–24, 1896, he captained the New Jersey XII that faced Harry Trott's Australians at Bergen Point. Batting number three in the order, he was the best American batsman, with 30 runs in two innings. Australia easily beat the New Jersey XII by an innings and 99 runs. In the 1904 MDCL season he scored 555 runs and finished top of the batting averages ahead of the perennial batting champion M.R. Cobb.[43] When not playing for Staten Island, Hurditch played cricket for the Belmont Cricket Club of Philadelphia and the New Jersey Cricket Club before joining the Los Angeles Cricket Club in 1908. His international and extensive East Coast cricket experience made his observations of the California cricket scene pertinent. Arriving in Los Angeles two years after the San Francisco earthquake, he found southern California cricket to be stronger than the variety played in San Francisco. Hurditch recognized Herbert Marshall of the Santa Monica Cricket Club as "a magnificently free bat and excellent bowler [and] Pat Higgins ... as the Jessop [England's hardest hitting batsman] of America." He added that these, together with "C.P. Somerville, an old Cheltenham boy — all these playing for Los Angeles— and at least two from San Francisco [H.F. Elliot and E.H. Wilkes], would be a tower of strength to a representative [American] eleven."[44] Wilkes learned to bowl the googlie from its originator, Bosanquet, when he played against him for the California XVIII at the Presidio in 1902.

With three wins each for Santa Monica and Los Angeles, the 1908 southern California cricket Dudley Cup championship trophy, donated by the English-born mayor of Santa Monica, Thomas Dudley, midway through the season, was evenly poised. Then a summer recess was taken to play new competition from Clifton, Arizona. Clifton's cricket team came from a copper mining area in eastern Arizona's mountains. Clifton was one of those mining towns supplying the copper ore that found a ready market as electric wiring. Clifton's highly stratified

Charles Percy Hurditch. Source: *Cricket Weekly Record* XXVII, no. 804 (April 22, 1909).

social structure was typical of most mining towns at the turn of the century. Fresh from Scotland, James Colghoun arrived in Clifton to work for the Arizona Copper Mining Company two days after an Apache raid in 1883. Colghoun subsequently saved the company from bankruptcy by introducing more efficient ore extraction techniques and balancing the books. The managers' houses in Clifton were located in a separate cantonment next to the river that ran through the town. Harold Shortridge, a Clifton copper-miner, recalled

> many times peeking into the yards at night when garden parties were being held. The yard was festooned with Japanese lanterns and many beautifully dressed men and women were in attendance. Society in Clifton was formal. Women would make their calls in the afternoon wearing gloves and lovely clothes. If the lady of the house was not home the visiting lady would leave her calling card in the slot reserved for it.[45]

Shortridge quotes Sir Henry Newbolt's *Vitae Lampada* in his preface to James Colghoun's book on Clifton. The stanza he quotes was familiar to most British educated schoolboys:

> For when the one great Scorer comes
> To write against your name
> He writes not whether you have won or lost,
> But how you played the game.[46]

Clifton and Bisbee played the game and soon looked for new fields to conquer in cool Santa Monica by the Pacific.[47] The miners practiced for some time before traveling to Santa Monica. *The Copper Echo* reported that Bennie, the general manager of the Shannon Copper Co. Mine (one of the Arizona Copper Company mines), was Clifton's best player.[48] On August 19, 1908, Clifton's arrival was noted in the *Santa Monica Outlook*:

> Just before noon, Gregory's band arrived and played spirited music until 2 o'clock. Spectators were arriving constantly and this afternoon there was a good size crowd at the game.
>
> Lunch was served to the visiting team.... The platform erected in the eucalyptus grove was utilized as a dining hall, and decorated with potted palms and ferns. Long tables were set up on the platform and two large American flags waved above it. The second game will be played Friday at the polo grounds.[49]

The Santa Monica Cricket Club easily beat Clifton in their two games, but the defeated Clifton dwellers made friends, as the *Santa Monica Outlook* reported:

> Socially and in the real world of sport this has been a good week for the cricketers and their friends. Two games of cricket between Santa Monica and the Clifton men have drawn to the old polo grounds on Nevada Avenue a large crowd, and they have made the place such a center of interest as has not been seen since the polo club used to have big summer tournaments here.[50]

A social game organized by Mayor Dudley and William Pedley achieved a closer result. Clifton lost by 35 runs with four of their players making double figures: Cuthbert, Thomson, Liddell and Mason. Le Bas captained the social side for Santa Monica, and they would have been defeated if it had not been for a superb innings of 91 runs out of a total of 183 by Richard Justice.[51] Any hope Clifton may have had for a victory on their foray into southern California was thoroughly dashed the next day when they played a combined Southern California All Stars team at the Vineyard ground. Southern California knocked up 333 runs, a record innings total for them. Patrick Higgins (104), Archie Mitchell (82) and Hurditch (49) scored the majority of Southern California's runs. Clifton could only muster 66 runs in reply.[52]

After the excitement created by Clifton's visit to southern California, spectator interest in cricket reached fever pitch and was rewarded by a remarkable Dudley Cup championship match. Los Angeles batting first scored what appeared to be an insurmountable first innings total of 196 runs. Hurditch's (76) stabilized Los Angeles after both opening batsmen were dismissed for no score. Higgins (31) and Bamford (27) also made significant contributions for Los Angeles. In reply, Santa Monica was "not only sure but brilliant and H. Justice with 73, A. Mitchell with 81, W. Hunt with 51 and S.P. Cook with 36 gave them victory, and Archie Mitchell's 81 not out was applauded to the echo. This was the highest score of the day. The beach cricketers [were] winners by 4 wickets and 61 runs.[53]

The SMCC became southern California's best team though Hurditch led the season batting average of 57.55 per innings for the LACC. A post-cup game with Los Angeles resulted in another win for the beach cricketers by 15 runs.

Bhumgara, the second leading wicket taker for Los Angeles in the 1908 season, after Tempest, was a medium fast bowler from British Honduras (Belize). The first West Indian–born cricketer recorded as playing in California, Bhumgara started an enduring tradition of multiethnic sports in California. This multiethnic cricket was a distinct contrast to Anglo-Saxon dominated Philadelphia cricket and segregated baseball on the East

Top: All Southern California cricket team versus Clifton, Arizona, 1908. *Bottom:* Santa Monica Cricket Club, 1908. Their patron, Mayor Dudley, presented the cup for the winners of the southern California cricket championship. Source for both pictures: *Spalding's Cricket Annual,* 1909.

Coast. When the Jim Crow era of baseball (1886 to 1947) ended, it was California that set the trend when Jackie Robinson started playing for the Los Angeles Dodgers.

Excitement created by the hard-hitting, multiethnic cricket carried over into the 1909 season. In the first game of the season on July 6, Independence Day weekend, the *Santa Monica Outlook* reported "large numbers of spectators, especially women, taking lunch at 1:00 P.M. Bamford the Los Angeles captain won the toss and sent in Tempest to bat with Wilkes."[54]

Santa Monica won the first game of the season by three wickets. Hurditch, LACC's crack batsman, switched allegiances to SMCC in the off season and opened the SMCC batting at LACC's home Vineyard ground. With Hurditch on side, the SMCC won the Dudley Cup for the second year in succession in 1909. The LACC benefited from the intermittent addition of Wilkes in 1909, though he played regular league cricket in San Francisco for the Pacific Cricket Club.[55] In 1910 with Hurditch as captain, the SMCC elected Patrick Higgins vice-captain, and persuaded Wilkes to add his googlie bowling ability to the side.[56] All three players had lost respect for Bamford, the long serving LACC captain. It is likely that Bamford found himself outshone both in leadership and cricket skill on the field. The SMCC dominated the LACC in their first Vineyard game of the 1910 season, scoring 280 runs. Wilkes contributed an aggressive 95 runs comprising six sixes and eight fours to help win the match by 206 runs.[57] Wilkes and Harry Elliot played in two of the four Dudley Cup games for the SMCC in 1910. They were in Santa Monica for the second game held on August 1:

> With C.P. Hurditch out in reply to Los Angeles total, Elliot and Wilkes treated the spectators to some fine cricket, the pair knocking up 80 runs before they were separated. At 136 Elliot was beautifully caught on the boundary by the Los Angeles captain for 67. Thereafter Jamieson and Higgins together, some splendid slogging was indulged in, the Australian Jessop hitting a 6 and two fours in the over from Tyke, one of his strokes sending his ball onto the roof of the pavilion. At 185 Jamieson was run out and the side was all out for 210. Aspin carried his bat for 31.[58]

A more apt comparison for Higgins, who hailed from New South Wales in Australia, would have been Victor Trumper, rated the third best batsman of the golden age behind Grace and Ranjitsinhji by Charles Burgess Fry, Jessop's teammate on the England team. The SMCC batting proved too strong for the LACC under their captain Tom Bamford. In 1910, the SMCC won the Dudley Cup for the third consecutive time. Spalding's cricket manual noted that "The Los Angeles Cricket Club did not have a very successful season during 1910, losing the Dudley Cup to Santa Monica Cricket Club in three games. The two wins to their credit were from the Riverside Cricket Club and the Watts Cricket club. In no game were they able to place their full strength in the field."[59]

After the 1910 season the lack of parity and healthy competition between southern California's two leading cricket clubs lead to a search for an event that would continue the high level of spectator interest shown during three Dudley Cup seasons. Tennis provided the answer. It had achieved international recognition in Santa Monica as a result of May Sutton's (1904) and Marion Jones' (1907) victories at Wimbledon and the U.S. tennis championship held at Germantown Cricket Club. May Sutton, playing tennis with pink ribbon in her hair and with corset-less Gibson Girl freedom, spawned both a social and sporting revolution with her aggressive tennis style. Sutton's Wimbledon victory was the first by an American player in an English ball sport. It generated immense enthusiasm throughout America's cricket clubs, and wives and girlfriends of cricketers took up lawn tennis with alacrity. In 1910, Santa Monica's female tennis and international field hockey players were looking for new fields to conquer. They chose cricket. The *Santa Monica Outlook* announced in banner headlines:

Women Will Form Cricket Club at the Beach.

Women have gone for cricket, their first game to be played August 13th at the old polo grounds which are now being put into shape by the Santa Monica Cricket club. It will be the first time that cricket has ever been played by women in Southern California. May Sutton, the tennis champion will captain, also in the team, Mrs. Woodhouse of Los Angeles, Mrs. Hurditch wife of the men's team captain, Mrs. Elliot, Mrs. W.G. Cochrane, Mrs. Wiles, E.W. Bamford, Miss Jones and Mrs. Higgins (all cricketers' wives). The women will play Santa Monica Cricket Club which is considered one of the best cricket clubs in California.[60]

Along with Charles Hurditch, Mrs. Widdowson — formerly Miss Gladys Archer, a well known tennis star — was the main organizer of the event. Santa Monica society was definitely supportive. It was announced in the *Los Angeles Times* that

Mayor Dudley and a large contingent of society women and their escorts are to be present. This will be one of the social events of the season and the following women will preside at the tables: Miss E. Corson, Mrs. J.B. Proctor, Mrs. C.C. Le Bas, Mrs. Waring, Mrs. McConnochie, Mrs. F.A. Bundy (ne: May Sutton), Mrs. Hodgson, Mrs. C.P. Hurditch.

Most of the women who will participate in the match are members of the Santa Monica Hockey Club. Mrs. Farquhar (Miss Marion Jones) is a one time tennis champion.[61]

Social change came to California during the Progressive-era governorship of Hiram Johnson. Johnson supported women's voting rights in California. In August *The Santa Monica Outlook* reported:

Sunny California is to the fore once again, showing to the residents of other countries the way life can be enjoyed during the leisure hours. The fair sex famous for their many charms of personality and athletic achievement not content with what they have already accomplished in the way of tennis, golf and sports ... have entered the realm held sacred by men. They have thrown down the gauntlet with a vengeance with the result that the national game of Old England — cricket to wit, will be invaded by them some twenty strong on the grounds of the old polo field, Nevada Ave. and 8th Street. They will play the best team of the cham pions of this part of the Coast, ... numerous boxes of gloves and pounds of candy already have been wagered on the result, in which a political election occupies very much rear position.... Those who have been privileged to watch the many practice games these past two weeks are more than surprised at the lovely form shown by the ladies, who under the watchful eye of Captain Hurditch and Secretary Collins have found the boundary with surprising ease, performed "the hat trick" time out of number, chased the sphere with remarkable celerity and held fast to "flies" that would make an outfielder on the diamond green with envy.

Hockey and tennis at which all of them shine (some with international brilliancy) have rendered them particularly alert in the field. Pasadena, Covina and even Fresno are sending players and many applications for places on the team have come from a signal distance.

To mark the importance of the "maiden" match, the Santa Monica committee have generously consented to the cancellation of their usual program on the promenade at North Beach and bandmaster Gregory and his accomplished musicians will hold forth on the ground.

Rev. D.D.H. Brownston has been asked to umpire, a former Halifax (Nova Scotia) cricketer and minister thus again shows his love and interest in the game.[62]

Santa Monica Women's Cricket Team, 1909. Two of the Sutton sisters were on the team, their sister May Sutton was the first American Women's Champion at Wimbledon in 1905. Source: *Spalding's Cricket Annual*, 1910.

With such a deep well of sporting talent to draw on, the ladies defeated the Santa Monica Men's Cricket team, which played and fielded left handed for the occasion, by two runs. In "losing" their first game of the season, the Santa Monica cricketers drew over 2,000 spectators to the ground, a quarter of Santa Monica's population at the time. This was a larger turnout than achieved for the men's games, and so the event organizers succeeded spectacularly in their purpose of combining cricket and women's rights to create spectator interest and press coverage as far away as London. Santa Monica was put on the world map by the event and Hurditch's dictum that originality is necessary in many things was shown effectively in action. Following May Sutton's involvement in the Santa Monica women's cricket game, Mayor Dudley agreed to become president of the SMCC.[63] Despite the success of the women at cricket there were still political battles to be won. On March 9, 1911, Mrs. Emmeline Pankhurst, the English suffragette leader, visited Santa Monica to address the Political Equality League.[64] During Governor Hiram Johnson's Progressive Party administration, the California Legislature passed a law allowing women to vote in California.

In Los Angeles, the LACC captain Tom Bamford had to quell discontent over a third losing season at the club's Annual General Meeting. John Alton, the president of the LACC, set a dissenting tone as he opposed the wearing of white flannels as mandatory. Club members were not as wealthy as those in Santa Monica and some could not afford cricket uniforms. Bamford pointed out that only 27 members had paid dues the previous year. He believed that "cricket had not suffered through lack of management or a club house. You are never going to make a success of a club if players do not pay their dues. That is what killed cricket last year."[65] Peter Dudley, attending the Annual General Meeting on behalf of the SMCC, disagreed with Bamford, noting that team spirit and quality players were important. He declared, "Los Angeles has 100,000 to draw from and Santa Monica 10,000.... Our assets amount to a few pads and bats and [a] $150 building but we will play you any day and if we get killed then all the better for cricket."[66] One of the players, Cadamon, got to the core of the problem when he exclaimed, "It was simply murder playing Santa Monica last year."[67] The journalist attending the meeting noted dryly that Cadamon was still alive. The LACC's poor performance continued unbroken in 1911. On July 2 a cartoon in the *Los Angeles Times* lampooned the LACC for its dismal cricket performance. The cartoon depicted old or disabled Los Angeles cricketers ready for entry to the Old Soldiers Home in Santa Monica, which still housed Civil War veterans.[68]

Despite the LACC's decline, Patrick Higgins was recognized as the most consistent, hardest hitting batsman in California. Born in New South Wales, the Australian Higgins earned the nickname "Jessop of America" while he was the rugby coach at the University of Southern California. Higgins was a great swimmer, rugby and field hockey player. As a batsman, Higgins had a great variety of shots and was an extremely punishing hitter of the ball. Known as the Father of Cricket in California, Higgins' batting improved dramatically after the arrival of first-class player Charles Hurditch.

In 1911 San Diego and Fresno participated in the Dudley Cup Competition. Charles Pennington had migrated from the Pacific Cricket Club in San Francisco and helped found the San Diego Cricket Club with a pitch in Coronado. Jamieson, who played for SMCC, founded the Fresno Cricket Club in 1911. Both the SMCC and LACC clubs traveled to play San Diego CC in a triangular tournament with return matches held at the Polo Grounds and the Vineyard. Fresno CC challenged the winner of the triangular tournament, SMCC, to a match in August, initiating the first regular visit of a northern California cricket team to southern California. Santa Monica was up to the challenge and won the Dudley Cup outright in 1911 under Hurditch's captaincy. After winning the championship, Hurditch left southern California for Philadelphia, where he used his fine publicity skills to infuse energy into the moribund soccer program at the Belmont Cricket Club. There he instituted the Cricket League Cup for soccer and induced famous players such as Bossie Bosanquet, John Lester, Arthur Wood, C. Christie Morris, E.N. Cregar, John Thayer (the founder of the Inter-Collegiate Cricket Association in 1881), John Orton and several other American first-class cricketers to take up soccer.

In San Francisco cricket fell on hard times because of competition with soccer. Los Angeles was not soccer crazy in 1912. Marshall D. Taylor, the *Los Angeles Times* cricket correspondent, explained cricket's virtues to his readers on July 15. Echoing the cultural entropy of American observers who considered cricket a complicated game, Taylor feigned bemusement at baseball, noting:

> The spot designated for matches is called the diamond. To me, it resembled a huge compass, at the four points of which were placed half filled gunny-sacks. The pitcher acted as the pivot and around him most of the play centered.
>
> There were nine men on each side and a foreman to boss both teams. The foreman and one of the players who squatted on his haunches behind the batsman, each wore a muzzle....
>
> The foreman yelled: "Ball three." I am quite positive that only one ball was in use, because I distinctly saw the foreman fill his pockets before the game started, and his pockets still bulged.
>
> However, I was informed that Burrell was taking his base. He was doing nothing of the

kind. He did not even wait to take his bat, but threw the weapon carelessly to the ground and walked in a leisurely manner toward a little brown hassock in front of the cheaper priced seats. To be exact it was east on the compass....

A second player came forward and began to wave his bat from side to side as if trying to shake something from its point. Before he had time to accomplish this self-imposed task, the pitcher let fly a fast one, which broke from the off to leg.

The foreman snapped out: "Strike one!" Why I have not the remotest idea. The newcomer never touched the ball....

Single after performing a near Dervish dance, hurled the ball, with a great show of feeling toward what seemed to me to be his opponents head. Straight as a dart it came toward the batsman's cranium. Instead of driving the ball to the off, the batter deliberately tried to pull it to leg. Misjudging the angle and pace he skied the sphere high up into the slips.

To a cricketer it looked an easy single, but before the batter could even start to run, the foreman yelled "Foul." Here again I failed to see in what manner Hosp had fouled the ball.[69]

Los Angeles' budding Henry Chadwick needed time for a few more baseball games before he discovered that stealing a base did not result in court time. Taylor clearly demonstrated the gentle deprecation that the English overseas applied to games they did not control. Polo and tennis had become popular sports among the American upper class and baseball filled the niche that had once been filled by professional cricket in America. Amateur cricket in Los Angeles and Santa Monica, combined with its social activities, reinforced English identity as Anglo-American culture fastened itself on southern California's rapidly urbanizing landscape.

Cricket purported to follow chivalric ideals in this golden age, and Patrick Higgins' swashbuckling batting genius in 1912 was all that one might expect of Sir Lancelot riding to the rescue of his game. Higgins rode a brilliant batting streak that shattered all previous American and southern California batting records. Marking his return to the LACC as secretary following Hurditch's departure for Philadelphia, he began the season with 159 runs for a Los Angeles First XI versus a Los Angeles XXII. In July he scored two centuries against the Fresno CC. In August, the *Santa Monica Outlook* announced:

> A number of local players are joining the LACC players in to-morrow's match with the Mountain Ash Glee Club of Wales. W.G. Cochrane, P.J. Higgins, P.J. Dudley will play. This is not the strongest team Los Angeles has put on the field as many of the best players are businessmen and have to be in their office. But W.G. Cochrane who scored 102 not out last Sunday and P.J. Higgins, who has never made less than a hundred in any innings this season, are in form, and the Welshmen will get all that is coming to them in the way of leather chasing.[70]

Higgins scored 121 runs against the Welsh Glee Club. He continued his torrid pace in August scoring three more centuries against the Pilgrims and the Wanderers. Higgins piled up 1,085 runs in his nine innings in July and August, scoring seven consecutive centuries for an average of 180.83. His highest score was 240 runs not out against the Wanderers.[71] This eclipsed the previous highest southern California batting average of 71.50, achieved by E.H. Wilkes in 1911.[72] The international cricket press perspective on Higgins' achievement was clear:

Mr. P.J. Higgins, of California

> His friends call him "Pat." But such familiarity is not for me. I can only salute with wonder a man who plays practically every game, and plays them all like a master, as it is said P.J. Higgins does. That he is a very fine cricketer admits of no dispute; he also an expert at

hockey, golf, both codes of football (perhaps I should say all three codes for he has played the fearful and wonderful American variety), baseball and water polo. Moreover, he is a very fine swimmer ... "for strenuosity Pat has the recent T. Roosevelt whispering for help."

... His fielding is said to be wonderful and he is a good wicket keeper. His bowling is fast and varied. His batting powers are attested to by his deeds. Such good judges as C.P. Hurditch, H.F. Elliot, and E.H. Wilkes, all of them have had a lot of experience of cricket in England, are said to consider him a marvel.

Enthusiastic Californians proclaim Higgins the most wonderful cricketer in America. But to that dictum the eastern players are not likely to assent. Is there not Barton King, the man of many centuries against the Mountain Ash Glee Club, too, and a really good bowler? The Mountain Ash Glee Club, by the way, rather sticks in my gullet. Fresno, the Pilgrims, the Wanderers, Santa Monica, Phoenix—all these doubtless had bowlers and fieldsmen. Has the Glee club either. Was it not rather a slaughter of the innocent, P.J.H.? Were they worthy of your willow? But anyway, being there, it was up to you to make good (I partly understand American, and hope in time to be able to write it quite a piece)—and you did![73]

Patrick Higgins. Source: *Cricket Weekly Record*, May 1911.

Higgins' success was achieved when SMCC, after five years of unbridled success, could barely muster a team after Hurditch's departure. In September 1912, Santa Monica was devastated by a big fire, which spread from residences at the beach to Pier Avenue and burned most of Victorian Santa Monica south of the pier. The Fraser Pier was burned down and the Casino tennis club located near it was damaged. Fraser and Henry R. Gage, co-owners of the pier, sustained the heaviest losses, as they were not insured for fire. Fraser's extensive losses included the Decatour Hotel, the bathhouse, the pumping plant and the new brick plant in front of it on Marine Street.[74] Six years after he re-established the SMCC, Peter Dudley became president of the Santa Monica Chamber of Commerce in 1912. He called a meeting to review what could be done about the fire. In December, Santa Monica lost its leading social light and founder with the death of Senator John Percival Jones. Following his death the small businessman's support for cricket as a focus of social integration was undermined when inventor of the safety razor, King Gillette, bought Jones' Miramar estate for $125,000. The Santa Monica polo grounds went with the estate sale. Gillette added the Grisly block to this estate and then subdivided his new purchase into 570 housing lots marketed as Gillette's Regent Square, "housing lots without peer." Terms of the lot sales were 50 percent down with the rest paid at five percent over five years.[75] Cricket in Santa Monica had lost its political, financial and home base all in one year.

In Los Angeles, the pavilion built by John Brown of the LACC for $1,000 in 1908 burned down on May 28, 1913.[76] The Vineyard ground continued to be used by the cricketers despite the loss of their pavilion. It suffered severe neglect in the off-season and had to be cleared of debris in July 1913, when the supremely confident California cricket champions, the Golden Gate Cricket Club of San Francisco, under the strong captaincy of Henry A. Oxenham, challenged the LACC to two games over the July 4 weekend. Oxenham led the New York batting averages in 1907, but unlike C.P. Hurditch his impact on California was restricted to one year.[77] But what a year it was. The LACC warmed up with an intersquad game on July 1 between the Wanderers and Marylebone. Tom D. Bamford opened the batting for the Wanderers and his brother Frederick Bamford did the same for Marylebone. Dean dominated the bowling with six wickets and scored the most with 25 runs. Wilkes umpired the game, which Marylebone won easily by 70 runs. One game of practice was clearly not enough preparation to roll back a GGCC side that played regular CCA league cricket. The parlous state of southern California and lack of league practice was obvious to the *Los Angeles Times* reporter who declared,

> The Golden Gate Cricket Club ... simply smothered Los Angeles ... at the Vineyard, winning the match by ten wickets. The locals took to the field without having practiced once this season and accepted the challenge of the northerners as a mere matter of course. Cochrane and Higgins played the best innings for the home side. The latter drove Serjeant clean out of the field ... the first big drive of the match.[78]

Higgins was not up to his 1912 form. He was out for the top score of 19 runs as the LACC were bowled for 65 runs in their first innings. Tassell and Lewis scored the bulk of the runs for the Golden Gate in their first innings and Oxenham scored 54 in the second innings. Golden Gate beat the LACC by ten wickets in two innings.

Higgins' batting may have suffered because of the turmoil surrounding his tenure as rugby coach at the University of Southern California, which came into question when Stanford decided not to travel to southern California for the lucrative annual rugby match. Berkeley had phased in American football to replace rugby and Stanford followed their lead. Both the Olympic Club of San Francisco and the Los Angeles Athletic Club played rugby against Stanford and the University of Southern California, founded as a university for Methodists by W.P. Widney. The offer by the Olympic and Los Angeles Athletic clubs to field rugby teams in their respective cities was looked upon favorably by the *Los Angeles Times*, which stated,

> This is one of the best things that could possibly have happened. It means a boom for the game, a boost for the Trojans and, best of all, the establishment of regular club athletics on a big scale.... There is nothing in the world so good for a varsity team as regular competition and this is only found in match games. One reason for the superior development of California and Stanford ... has been the fact that these two universities had the benefit of very stiff competition at the hands of the Olympic Club and the Barbarians.[79]

The Barbarians were an excellent rugby team who had fielded the winning cricket side in the CCA in 1909.[80] In the *Los Angeles Times*, Owen Bird noted the reasons for rugby's resilience in the Southland:

True, there are many schools in the South playing Rugby, but the stronger, faster varsity men generally smash up their lighter high school opponents when in a practice brush.... Coach Pat Higgins says that he is going on a skill hunt for fast, snappy, full-backs this season.

"I want two of these birds on my team," said Pat yesterday, "and I'll tell you why.

"U.S.C. has always been weak in having only one good man for this position in the past and when he was hurt, it put the defense of the team on the outs. Now I am going to develop two, play one back there during the first half and let him attack as well as defend and also look for the weak spots on the other side, as a full can see more of this than any other man on the team.... It will be up to this second man to carry the ball on the attack, instead of kicking all the time. These Australian and New Zealand teams pull off this stuff all the time and we can do it as well."[81]

In the same article Owen referred to American football as having a following, especially in Whittier. Los Angeles high schools played rugby or American football but not cricket, which relied for growth on trained players immigrating from the British Empire. In 1913 the LACC were lackluster cricketers and the only Los Angeles cricket team. The *Los Angeles Times* cricket reporter Marshall Taylor was quite disparaging of the LACC, observing,

The Los Angeles Cricket Club which has been sound asleep since the San Francisco team smothered them at the Vineyard last month, has awakened to the fact that San Diego is bringing a team to play the locals on August 31. This is a one day match and will tax the locals to their fullest extent, as the borderers are exceptionally strong.

The locals, however, have been strengthened by the acquisition of A. Bingham, who has just arrived from Kent. Bingham has played for Kent County eleven and is a tremendously fast bowler and hard hitter. With such players as Palmer, Higgins, Sheppard, Hornidge, Megget, Bamford, Bingham, Packman, Cochrane, Barnes and Chancellor on the local line-up, San Diego will find worthy opponents.

Won't Practice

The whole trouble with the Los Angeles Cricket Club is that their players will not turn out to practice. No matter how

Los Angeles Cricketers Meggett, Hope, Higgins, Justice and Bhumgara in 1909. Source: *Spalding's Cricket Annual*, 1909.

good a player may be, it is impossible for him to take a bat in hand and slog out a big score or keep his length with a ball, unless he has practiced faithfully before an important match.[82]

After six years of intense cricket activity from 1907 to 1913, the Southland cricketers had not replenished their player pool from the schools as rugby did. In 1913, the nearest competition was found in San Diego and coaches were not teaching cricket in the schools. Major demographic changes were afoot. Southern California broke all building records, while Los Angeles expanded beyond its urban Midwestern roots, once water from the California Aqueduct opened the floodgates of growth. In Santa Monica after losing the polo grounds, cricket resumed at the newly built Santa Monica High School on Michigan and Fremont. Mayor Dudley, elected for a second term from 1914 to 1916, no longer needed team sport to encourage growth in his city. Golf offered a reasonable alternative and polo would become popular again at the new Riviera ground of the Los Angeles Athletic Club. Higgins moved to Santa Clara in 1914 to coach rugby after his rugby coaching days at USC came to an end with the adoption of American football in 1913. Higgins' batting legacy remains a strong testament to the quality of southern California cricket when Santa Monica, a beach city of 10,000, and Los Angeles, a town of 100,000 people, were still forging their urban identity in the southern California landscape.

10. The Hollywood Cricket Club and the Rebirth of Southern California Cricket

CRICKET DID NOT DIE IN SOUTHERN California with the purchase of the Santa Monica Cricket Club's polo field ground by King Gillette in 1913. Cricket reincarnated itself with the rise of the film industry in Hollywood. There were some good cricketers in Hollywood at the time. One was Australian silent actor Sydney Deane. Deane arrived in Hollywood in 1913, the year Owen Wister's novel *The Virginian* was made into a Western.

Before his arrival in Hollywood, Deane played first-class cricket in New South Wales, then moved to New York as an opera singer. In New York he played cricket with fellow Australian thespian Arthur Hoskins for the New York Veterans on their home ground at the Columbia Oval. Hoskins played against David Gregory and Austin Diamond's visiting Australian cricket teams for New York in 1912 and 1913.[1] Deane did not play in these games, but his New York Veterans cricket experience made it easy to adjust to playing for the Los Angeles Cricket Club at their Vineyard ground, one month before the outbreak of the First World War in Europe. Deane scored 23 runs, opening the batting for Wanderers versus Marylebone at the Vineyard on July 1, 1913. He also took 6 wickets for 21 runs.[2] Like his batting, Deane's early career in the silent movies was solid. His silver screen career started in 1914 when he made appearances in *Brewster's Millions*, *The Arab* with Rudolph Valentino, *No Man's Land*, and *The Last of the Mohicans*. During the war, Deane continued to hold the attention of the movie camera with his craggy features and robust frame. Deane played with English cricketer and actor Henry Pratt (Boris Karloff).

Pratt had been playing cricket for ten years before Aubrey Smith arrived in California. Born in London in 1887, Pratt left Merchant Taylor's Grammar School in 1903 for Uppingham Public School in County Rutland. Uppingham School's cricket coach was Heathfield Harmon "Spurgeon" Stephenson. A legendary figure in the cricket world, in 1862 Stephenson was the first to captain an English team in Australia. George Parr nicknamed

Stephenson "Spurgeon" on their tour of the North America in 1859. John Lester visited Stephenson on his first tour of England with the Gentlemen of Philadelphia in 1898. Uppingham had the largest unbroken stretch of playing fields in Britain, known as the Middle. Sports were played to develop self-confidence and self-reliance, important qualities for a distinguished family of Indian Service civil servants such as Pratt's. Pratt flourished at Uppingham, where he played cricket and field hockey for Firecroft House. He left England for Canada in 1909, where he adopted the stage name Boris Karloff. Arriving in Hollywood just before the First World War was declared, cricketer Pratt had a decade to play the game before his career started flourishing when he played Frankenstein in 1931. He played against Santa Monica CC which from 1919 used the Santa Monica High School field, conveniently located near the Elks Club, as their home ground.

Peter J. Dudley, a second generation SMCC player who had first played with the SMCC on their old Polo Grounds pitch in 1906, resuscitated the team after the First World War ended. He was the son of English-born Santa Monica mayor Dudley, who left office in 1916. A former president of the Santa Monica Chamber of Commerce, Peter Dudley was president of the Santa Monica Bank (owned by the Jones family — the cofounders of Santa Monica) with first-hand experience of cricket's ability to create a highly integrated social community. Deane joined Henry A. Bingham on the side. Bingham learned his cricket at Thanet College in Kent, where his batting average was 77.13 and 50.25 for the two seasons he was in the First XI. He represented Kent against Yorkshire and also played for the MCC and South Devon. An all-round sportsman, Bingham played hockey and soccer to a high level. Before joining the SMCC, Bingham debuted for the Los Angeles Cricket Club against the San Diego CC in 1910. Deane along with Chris Simmonds (ex–Citrus Colony) and fellow New South Wales cricketer Pat Higgins all played for the Santa Monica Cricket Club in 1919. Higgins returned from Santa Clara where he was rugby coach and was present when Deane scored 159 not out against the Overseas Cricket Club, on July 5, 1919. On September 21, 1919, Deane took all ten Los Angeles Wanderers wickets for 39 runs. Apart from the Wanderers there were three teams in the Los Angeles area: the Sons of St. George, the Overseas Cricket Club and in Pasadena the Alexandria, which played in Tournament Park opposite the Scroops Institute, which later became Cal Tech. Reviewing the 1919 cricket season in southern California, Frank P. Lee noted in *The American Cricketer:*

> The Santa Monica Cricket Club is entitled on their play this season to the championship of the Western States of America. The Club played thirteen matches.... In every instance, the superiority of the Santa Monica Club has been most marked in every department of the game and their brilliant play has led to a quite remarkable revival of interest in cricket in Southern California. In the event of an "All American" team being selected as customary on the season's form, Santa Monica could rightfully claim four representatives: Pat Higgins, Sydney Deane, H.P. Bingham, and A.R. Mitchell. Higgins is one of the best all round athletes in America. American cricket annals can show several records by Higgins. He is one of the most fearless batsmen in the world, rivaling G.L. Jessop or H.E. Trott. He is a brilliant field and excellent fast bowler. Sydney Deane formerly played for New South Wales for whom he kept wicket. He played for Australia against the England team captained by Aubrey Smith. He is a splendid bat and one of the best "googly" bowlers in America.[3]

Sydney Deane's film career faltered in 1920 when he failed to make the switchover to talking pictures. In his last game in southern California, the SMCC destroyed the combined efforts of the Overseas Cricket Club and Pasadena Cricket Club, with a first innings total of 294 runs. Deane was sorely missed in the next game when the SMCC lost to the Overseas Cricket Club on their turf wicket at Exposition Park. Ashley Cooper (the name of W.G. Grace's first biographer) scored 31 runs. Boris Karloff was out for one run. Rawlings took four wickets. The most exciting play of the day was the run-out of SMCC's last batsman, Fresco, who playing as a substitute for Deane. Fresco fell, "and although he tried everything in his power to beat the ball to the wicket and started up the pitch on his hands and knees— the ball traveled faster and Santa Monica lost by one run."[4] The SMCC played 15 games in the 1920 season with Deane leading the southern California batting averages with a total of 634 runs scored at the rate of 57.63 an inning. He was also second in the bowling, taking 30 wickets for an average of 7.26 a wicket. Pat Higgins' 1912 batting average of 180 dropped to 18.66 in 1920 when his best innings was 63. Archie Mitchell led the bowling averages for the second year in a row, with 47 wickets taken for an average of 5.46 runs per wicket.

Sydney Deane. Source: *Cricket Weekly Record*, July 30, 1913.

He also served notice that his batting skills were improving by finishing third in the batting averages with a score of 48.88 runs per innings.

After Deane left in 1921, three SMCC players defected to the Overseas Cricket Club.[5] Without these leading Santa Monica players, Pat Higgins had to carry the batting against a resurgent Los Angeles CC. He made a game effort but cricket died in Los Angeles until businessman Ernest Wright and the great sportsman Sam Milbourne gave the game younger leadership from 1924 until 1929 when C. Aubrey Smith arrived in Hollywood to start his third career with the Metro Goldwyn Mayer studio.

Actor Smith hit the ground running in Hollywood, his biographer Rayvern Allen noting that

> from the day that Aubrey saw off Alfred Aloysius to the African jungle in Trader Horn to the time he caught sight of stenographer Claudette Colbert on the park bench in the Gilded Lily was just over 4 years, and in that span Aubrey had taken part in nearly fifty films.... In most of the films he was a chief supporting player, a character role, lordly, avuncular.[6]

Smith had a clause inserted in his MGM contract that provided for visits to watch test matches in England. In the days before regular air travel this meant leisurely trips home on the *Queen Mary*. The former Sussex County and England cricket captain found his way to Hollywood by reprising his Broadway stage role as Sir Basil Winterton in an MGM movie opposite Marion Davies, *The Batchelor Father*.[7] Critics praised Aubrey Smith in the film. One said that having "all the virtues and idiosyncrasies of the real Englishman ... without ... conceit, he steps on stage and joins the scene with all the plasticity of a professional cricketer on a good pitch."[8]

Three years after his arrival in Hollywood, Aubrey Smith founded the Hollywood Cricket Club in 1932 at age 65. Smith was fortunate in his timing, as Noel Coward's play about the Boer War, *Cavalcade*, was being made into a movie that required 400 English accented actors in 1933. The resulting influx of English actors expanded the pool of cricket talent. According to Boris Karloff, this importation of new cricket talent came none too soon for cricket in southern California. Karloff recalled, "Aubrey Smith founded the Hollywood Cricket Club four years after UCLA's Westwood campus opened."[9] Karloff credited Aubrey Smith with finding new grounds, noting,

> Aubrey found us playing on rough fields under dangerous conditions. He at once went to see Mr. Moore at UCLA, Westwood, who with extraordinary generosity gave us the use of the campus for our Saturday and Sunday games, with the single proviso that we try to pull in a few students; a few of them came, looked, sniffed and departed. But little by little, the idea took hold, until this year, aided by Peter Kinnell and Eugene Walsh, the latter a brilliant cricketer from South Africa, and also the students at the University, Aubrey has been able to keep his word to the school, and any Tuesday or Thursday he may be found enthusiastically coaching twenty or thirty youngsters at the nets.[10]

Referring ironically to Aubrey Smith's age, Karloff observed that with Aubrey's arrival, "a change came over the spirit of the dream. A promising young cricketer named C. Aubrey Smith, better known as 'Round the Corner' Smith, came to Hollywood, and today, thanks to his untiring efforts, the game is on a firm footing for the first time."[11]

Some of Aubrey's disciples at UCLA made it into cricket's senior ranks, including several members of the Severn family. Dr. Clifford Brill "Doc" Severn, an immigrant osteopath from East London, South Africa, headed a clan of seven children. The eldest, Cliff, met Aubrey while playing for UCLA and at 80 still remains active in the sport. He and his younger brothers Winston and Raymond played for the United States and Cliff's father was an MCC member.[12] Doc was regularly seen at the Griffith Park cricket grounds in the 1970s, greeting the new generation of cricketers with a smile of achievement on his face, for he kept Aubrey Smith's dream going during the Second World War.

Smith's first allies in cricket were the Women's Field Hockey Association of Los Angeles, who joined him in requesting a hockey and cricket ground. In a May 1932 session of the Los Angeles City Council, Mrs. Sochet of the Park Board proposed to parks and recreation commissioner C.G.S. Williamson that grounds be set aside for these two popular English sports.[13] Griffith Park had been donated to the city in 1898 when cricket was flourishing in the city. Though nothing appears to have been written into the Covenant of Donation for Griffith Park, there remains a strong oral tradition that Henry Griffith, who donated the land for the park, requested that ground be set aside for a cricket field. Griffith lived in Santa Monica at this time, and cricket was taken very seriously in his social circle. City council records indicate that it took five carloads of English grass seed and cost $30,000 to build the cricket pavilion erected in Griffith Park. The pavilion still stands, devoid of its history since it became the Equestrian Center. The C. Aubrey Smith Cricket Grounds were officially opened with Claude King as master of ceremonies on May 21, 1933.[14] Now with its own cricket ground, the Hollywood Cricket Club became a force in southern California cricket. All previous club histories, even the storied Santa Monica Cricket Club, were pushed out of the limelight by Hollywood glitz.

Limelight attached to the Hollywood CC because Aubrey Smith's unique history spanned three cricket eras and three careers. At Charterhouse, where as a younger boy he fagged (did menial tasks) for Baden-Powell, Aubrey Smith began his cricket career in a public school with a very strong cricket tradition:

> The walls of the main cloister at Charterhouse are studded with memorials to half-forgotten campaigns, from Afghanistan to Omdurman, listing the names of hundreds of Carthusians who "played up, played up and played the game" and paid the price for doing so with their lives.[15]

Sir Henry Newbolt's *Vitai Lampada* (1897) lauds this Imperial theme, which had no better practitioner than Robert Stephenson Smyth Baden-Powell—"Stephe" to his friends—founder of the Boy Scout movement. As colonel of the First Bechuanaland Regiment, Baden-Powell became the archetypal product of playing-field imperialism nearly a century after Wellington credited the playing-fields of Eton in the defeat of Napoleon at Waterloo. In Baden-Powell's case, his moment of glory came 11 years after Aubrey Smith captained the first English team in South Africa, at Mafeking where he organized the defense of the town, which was liberated after a 207-day siege by the Boers. According to Niall Ferguson, "To Baden-Powell the siege was the ultimate cricket fixture. He even said as much in a characteristically light hearted letter to one of the Boer commanders: '...Just now we are having our innings and so far have scored 200 days, not out, against the bowling of Cronje, Snijman, Botha ... and we are having a very enjoyable game.'"[16]

While the British Empire expanded in South Africa, President McKinley presided over America's imperial expansion in the Pacific. McKinley appointed Judge Taft (later President Taft) governor of the Philippines. In both Cuba and the Philippines the United States introduced baseball and missionaries to spread the gospel of the Star Spangled Banner. With imperialism on the rise, the Boy Scout movement spread rapidly in the United States. The echoes of Newbolt's *Vitai Lampada* resounded through baseball in its imperialist role. Baseball writer and *Chicago Tribune* correspondent Ring Lardner's neighbor in the Hamptons, Grantland Rice transmuted Newbolt's *Lampada* into a baseball anthem during the 1920s:

> For when the one great Scorer comes
> To write against your name
> He writes not what you won or lost,
> But how you played the game[17]

Aubrey Smith played both life and cricket well. He earned his blue at Cambridge University in his freshman year of 1882, the same year he debuted for the Sussex County Cricket Club. Lord Sheffield (who donated the Sheffield Shield still competed for annually in Australia) was president of Sussex Cricket Club. At Cambridge, Smith was captained

1882 Cambridge University team. C. Aubrey Smith and Lord Hawke are standing on the top row, extreme left. Source: *British Sports and Sportsmen* (London: Longmans, 1907).

by one of the imperial cricket architects, the Right Honorable Martin Bliden (better known as Lord Hawke). When Bliden and Smith played against the MCC for Cambridge University in 1882, Smith took 5 wickets for 17 runs in 20.3 overs with 14 maidens. The summary of Aubrey Smith's cricket career at Cambridge University in Wisden notes:

> Four times he played at Lord's against Oxford and, by a remarkable series of coincidences, all of these matches ended with a decisive margin of seven wickets, Cambridge winning three of these encounters. In the 1884 match which Oxford won, C.A. Smith was not out 0 in each innings and took two wickets for 65 runs, but in the other three games he showed his worth. In 1883 he helped C.T. Studd dismiss Oxford for 55 and in the second innings he took 6 wickets for 78 and Oxford just equaled the Cambridge total of 215. He made 4 catches in the match. His last effort for the Light Blues brought 6 wickets for 81. His captains were the three brothers Studd and the Hon H.B. Hawke.[18]

The Studds still hold the record at Cambridge for captaining the varsity team as successive brothers. Charles Thomas Studd was the youngest and most famous of the trio (that also included John E.K. and George Brown Studd), scoring a century against the 1882 Australian team that defeated England and led to the creation of the Ashes.[19] George Brown Studd was on the Honorable Ivo Bligh's team that returned the Ashes to England. He moved to Los Angeles in 1891 after spending several years as a missionary in Indian and China, where he played for the Shanghai Cricket Club.[20]

Aubrey Smith's health was more robust than Studd's, who had been forced to leave England's damp weather for health reasons. As a member of the Sussex CCC side in 1885, Aubrey reveled in the English climate, taking five wickets for eight runs against his old Cambridge University side. Smith played against all the big names of golden age cricket in England, including W.G. Grace, who had this to say for Aubrey Smith's bowling abilities:

> I am not advocating the cultivation of a style merely for the purpose of distracting the attention of batsman, but I would point out the great success that has attended such bowlers as Messrs C.A. Smith, Spofforth, Giffen, and Ferris, who have peculiar deliveries. When Smith begins his run, he is behind the umpire and out of sight of the batsman; and I can assure you it is rather startling when he already appears at the batting crease. [21]

Pelham Warner first saw Aubrey Smith at Lord's in his prime. Fresh from Trinidad where he grew up, Warner recalled:

> The first time I saw Lord's was on Friday, May 20, 1887. Only recently arrived in England from the West Indies, I had as a boy devoured the pages of *The Field*, which in those days gave a great deal of space to cricket. ... It was therefore with a thrill of anticipation and delight that I passed through the main gate and watched the play from the seat in front of the ivy covered tennis court, with the great clock in the middle where the Mound now stands. I can recall vividly even now the first wicket I ever saw taken at Lord's— C. Aubrey Smith, from the Nursery end, clean bowling F.E. Lacey with what looked from the ring a very good one.[22]

In 1887 Smith captained Shaw and Shrewesbury's team to Australia. Smith's was not the only England team touring Australia that year, as his Cambridge University teammate Martin Bliden captained a second one. Bliden (the seventh generation descendent of Admiral Hawke) became Lord Hawke on his father's death during the tour. After Lord Hawke's early departure from Australia, Smith took cricket professionals Docker, Stoddart, Brann, and Newham to New Zealand to join a Rugby Union XV that included four English international rugby players. Shaw and Shrewesbury hoped to defray the $2,400 they had lost on the Australian leg of their cricket tour by extending the tour with rugby. However, in the teeth of an Australian banking depression, all the players were lucky to get boat fare home.[23]

Seasoned by a winter cricket tour, Smith had his best innings in first-class cricket, scoring 142 for Sussex at Hove against Hampshire in 1888. For the season, he accumulated an aggregate of 1,448 runs for Sussex, finishing with a season bowling average of 20.18. He was also selected to play for the Gentleman of England with W.G. Grace at Lord's, where "he and S.M.J. Woods dismissed the last four players for one run scored after A.G. Steel handed the ball to Smith. Each of the Cambridge fast bowlers took two of these wickets and the Gentlemen won by five runs. In the match Woods took 10 wickets for 76 and C.A. Smith 5 for 36.[24]

In 1889 the Australian major Wharton asked Smith to captain the first English team to South Africa:

> All matches were against the "odds" except two engagements called "English Team v XI of South Africa," but some years afterwards given the description "Tests." During the tour C.A. Smith took 134 wickets for 7.61 each, a modest achievement compared to 290 wickets at 5.62

credited to John Briggs, the Lancashire left-hander. Smith stayed in South Africa for a time in partnership with M.P. Bowden of Surrey, a member of the team, as stockbrokers. During this period he captained Transvaal against Kimberly in the first Currie Cup match in 1890, so initiating a competition which has done much to raise the standard of cricket in South Africa.[25]

The Sir Donald Currie Cup was named for the owner of the Union Castle shipping line, which linked England and South Africa via the Suez Canal. Smith, who read his own obituary after nearly dying of black water fever while in South Africa, resumed his first-class cricket career with Sussex County, which he had captained from 1887 to 1889. He played for Sussex CCC until 1896 when new stars such as Prince Ranjitsinhji and Charles Burgess Fry joined the club. Smith announced his final retirement from first-class cricket in 1902. Smith's cricket statistics were solid. He played 173 innings, scoring 2,724 runs for a 15.74 average per innings. His 230 first-class wickets were taken at a cost of 23.31 runs.[26] After 14 years in first-class cricket, Aubrey concentrated on his acting career, in which he put up equally impressive figures, appearing in 100 plays in Britain and the United States. Allen comments,

> Smith was not noted for his interest in theatre when attending Charterhouse. However, the school's great acting tradition — Henry Siddons, G.F. Kean, Sir Johnstone Forbes-Robertson, Cyril Maud and boy-scout founder, Baden Powell, were all Old Carthusians — may have influenced him to join the Thespid Society on entering St. John's College in September 1881.[27]

From 1902, when the recently married Aubrey Smith rented Avenue House in West Drayton from the Pankhursts of suffragette fame, Smith's theatre career flourished.[28] Before leaving for New York and Broadway, Smith's acting career centered on London's West End at the Garrick Theatre. He played opposite the 50-year-old Lillie Langtry as the Duke of Orme in *The Degenerates*. In *The Second Mrs. Tanqueray*, Aubrey was directed by Charles Frohmann and played opposite Mrs. Patrick Campbell. On the West End stage, Smith earned a good reputation. As "a reliable, pipe-smoking character actor with a tweedy countenance and rock solid principles, he found himself readily employable in Edwardian theatre ... [as it] revolved around drawing-room comedy ... easily definable types, who on the whole operated with tailor-made rules and limited compass."[29]

His first-class cricket career over after 1902, Aubrey Smith played in the Actors XI, whose team colors were white, green and magenta, the same as the suffragettes. Aubrey chose similar colors for the Hollywood CC, founded in 1932.

When not playing for West Drayton CC, Thespids, or the Actors XI, closer to London's West End, Aubrey played with the London and Provincial Actors side. In 1905, he played at the Oval, in a benefit for the Actors' Fund with H.B. Warner and minor-county player Oscar Asche.[30] In a second fixture held at Lord's, Aubrey captained the Actors against an Authors team led by Sir Arthur Conan Doyle. Captain Gordon Guggisberg of the Royal Engineers was selected for the Author's XI. (Guggisberg had written *Modern Warfare*, a groundbreaking work on the inevitability of war once mobilization was ordered.) Guggisberg scored 58 against Aubrey Smith's team.[31] In reply, the Actors XI opened the batting at Lord's with Gilbert Hare and H.B. Warner (a future Hollywood CC player) putting on a century partnership for the first wicket.[32] Conan Doyle's brother-in-law the Reverend Ernest William Hornung also played for the Writers on occasion. Like Doyle he was a member of the MCC. Hornung wrote *Raffles: The Amateur Cracksman* while

Aubrey Smith flicks the coin before coming to America for the Actors XI in 1909 as Oscar Asche looks on. Source: Guggisberg Collection.

teaching at Uppingham. Raffles the larcenous cricketer was brought to the screen by Samuel Goldwyn with David Niven in the lead role. David Niven recalled,

> At the tail-end of production we were doing a cricketing sequence — supposedly at some English county house which I was about to rob, and the [cricket] game in 110 degree heat was being photographed on a polo field in Pasadena.
> The director Sam Wood had been taken ill, and the great William Wyler had taken over. He knew nothing about cricket and had set things up like a baseball game, leaving me to unravel the shambles. Just as we got straightened out, a cry from the outfield, and the actors froze in unaccustomed white flannels. "Hey, hey, my buddy"... Scott Fitzgerald came tottering across the green turf like a stage drunk, weaving in great arcs.[33]

Both Scott Fitzgerald and William Hornung knew a little about the dark side of life. Raffles believed, "If you can bowl a bit your low cunning won't get rusty, and always looking for the weak spot's just the kind of mental exercise one wants."[34]

Conan Doyle's Sherlock Holmes detective novels also created employment for British actors in Hollywood. Sir Arthur Conan Doyle was a booster of baseball — as a young man's game. On a 1922 visit to the United States he said, "Baseball is a noble game. I enjoy watching it immensely and have even played it. I was once a member a member of an impromptu team of Americans, all in Switzerland at the same time. Our side won.... I was short stop on that occasion.... I know baseball is the game England needs.... It would not displace cricket ... as that is an old man's game."[35] Hollywood CC members Basil Rathbone and Nigel Bruce played Sherlock Holmes and Dr. Watson on the screen. Nigel Bruce resumed his acting career in Hollywood while the First World War still raged in Europe. Ronald Colman (gassed), Herbert Marshall (shot in the leg) and Nigel Bruce were all invalided out of the British army by 1917 .They were joined by a second wave of actors such as Cary Grant and Aubrey Smith, who arrived in Hollywood to reprise his Broadway version of *The Bachelor Father* opposite Marion Davis in 1929. It was not long before Aubrey Smith's "Round the Corner" ranch-style house at 2881 Coldwater Canyon Road became a stage apart from the studio's, where he

> looked as though he had just returned from a tour of Empire.... Otherwise known as California's Greatest Living Englishman, [Smith] presided regally over a company that included his cricketers augmented by Ronald Colman, Cedric Hardwicke, P.G. Wodehouse, Douglas Fairbanks Jr., Laurence Olivier, Stan Laurel, and other august Britishers, living permanently or passing through California. Amongst others in various years [came] directors James Whale, Alfred Hitchcock and David Butler; actors Charlie Chaplin, Clive Brash, Charles Laughton, Cary Grant, and George Arliss; actresses Merle Oberon, Vivien Leigh, Maureen O'Hara, Deborah Kerr and Ida Lupino; writers Hugh Walpole, J.B. Priestley and W. Somerset Maugham, together with occasional sojourners and permanent residents Christopher Isherwood, Aldous and Marisa Huxley and journalist Sheilah Graham.[36]

The Hollywood Cricket Club founders were Alan Mowbray, Stanley Mann, Herbert Marshall, Claude King, Philip Merivale, Reginald Owen, Noel Madison, writer R.C. Sheriff and Pat Somerset.[37] All were First World War veterans used to orders and military discipline. American-born Noel Madison was educated at St. Paul's in London. Harrow- and Sandhurst-educated Pat Somerset acted on Broadway before moving to Hollywood.[38] Aubrey Smith was voted president along with four vice-presidents, George Arliss, Ronald Colman, Lance Errol and Pelham. Grenville Wodehouse, who in 1931 arrived in Hollywood to write stories for Goldwyn in Culver City.

During his brief first stay in Los Angeles, Wodehouse lived at 10 Benedict Canyon Drive in Beverly Hills. Wodehouse played on his First XI at Dulwich College and fictionalized his cricket experiences as "Psmith" in *The Golden Bat*. Though Wodehouse was a county level cricketer, Hollywood CC was yet to be founded when he returned to Europe at the end of 1931, so his cricket career in Hollywood was very occasional following his return to Beverly Hills in 1936 when he lived at 1351 Angelo Drive. By this time, Bertie Wooster and his butler Jeeves, named for a Warwickshire county cricketer, far surpassed Psmith as popular fictional characters, and Wodehouse commanded one of the largest writing contracts in Hollywood.[39] Twenty-year-old Douglas Fairbanks Junior also played for the HCC while married to Joan Crawford. In playing cricket he was fulfilling his personal credo, "Do a little of everything and do it the best you know how."[40]

When the Australians visited Hollywood in 1932, both Karloff and Aubrey Smith used their star power to show the "invincible" Australian cricket team, managed by Arthur

Mailey, a great time in Hollywood. On Mailey's last major Australian tour of the United States in 1913, the Australians got no further west than Chicago. Recognized as the master of slow bowling, Neville Cardus wrote glowing of "the incorrigible Arthur Mailey, who bowled slows like a millionaire, indifferent to the general competitive currency and rates of exchange."[41] Mailey managed an Australian team that had a stated mission to revive cricket as a team sport in North America. The tour began in British Columbia at Cowichan on Vancouver Island. Donald Bradman scored 60 runs in the tour opener before getting caught. The recently married Bradman, already recognized as a prodigious talent in Australia, had yet to make his mark on the international stage, where

> for the next two decades [he] ... was to have a dominant role in tests, batting with unsurpassed reliability to score a century at an average more than every third time he batted. His batting was so proficient that many of his 16 first class ducks received more publicity than his centuries. No Australian has scored more centuries or come close to him for consistency. The astonishing deeds in the Bradman legend brought him 17 more lines than Stalin in Who's Who ... helped build entire grandstands on major Australian grounds, and left Australia with a superior won-and-lost record to any of the cricket nations.[42]

The Australian Board of Control approved Mailey's selection of players for the hundred-day tour, which attracted top Australian cricket talent during the Depression, which hit Australia particularly hard. Cricketers were happy to be selected as the alternative was generally unemployment. Vic Richardson was voted captain. (Richardson's nephew Ian Chappell captained Australia in 1975 for the Kerry Packer Organization. On a recent trip to Los Angeles to commentate on the 1999 India-versus-Australia A game held at Woodley Park in Van Nuys, he recalled the American tour was one of the highlights of his uncle's illustrious cricket career.) Other leading members of the team were Bradman, P.H. Carney, H. Carter, L.O.B. Fleetwood-Smith, W.F. Ives, Alan Kippax, Stan McCabe, R.N. Nutt, E.F. Rofe, E.K. Tolhurst and Dr. Rowley Pope as baggage master and scorer. After the second game in Vancouver, the local paper reported,

> The master batsman of cricket, in scoring 110 runs before returning undefeated at the wicket, gave a magnificent display of hitting. He showed in many ways he is a cricket genius and his performance was a treat to watch....
> He is a medium sized youth with a stern countenance.... Just look how he stands. His footwork is perfect and he seems to be always in position to hit any kind of ball.[43]

The Australians destroyed the Vancouver All Star side, getting all 18 players out for 64 runs after putting up a first innings total of 287 for 6.[44] The Canadian Pacific sponsors of the tour then transported their Australian passengers to Toronto, Guelph, Ridley College, Montreal and Ottowa before they entered the United States, 17 games later, to play in New York. Bradman scored eight centuries including two double centuries on the first Canadian leg of the tour. On his first tour of England in 1930, Bradman had scored three double centuries in the five-game test series against England for a test aggregate of 934 runs and an innings average of 139.14 runs. This remains a world record for any test series. His aggregate total score of 4,546 runs in 1930 remains the most runs by any Australian batsman on record.[45] In New York, the Australian team were met by several hundred American, British and West Indian cricket enthusiasts. Watched by over 2,000 spectators, the West Indian cricketers based in New York gave their Australian visitors the best competition of the tour. In New York's West Indian community cricket was played with a passion in several locations throughout the Big Apple, including Prospect Park in Brooklyn where cricket was first played in 1867.[46] Three games were played between the two teams. In the first on July 14, the New York West Indians batted first and were all out for 152 runs. Australia won by runs in the first innings, scoring 300 for 5 wickets in reply. In the second game the New York West Indian XI scored 222 runs and the Australians, buoyed by Bradman's 117, scored 276 runs for 7 declared to win by 54 on the first innings total. The last game, on July 16 against the New York West Indians, was drawn after the Australians made 206 for 6 wickets declared and the West Indians were 93 for 3 wickets in reply before stumps were drawn.

Bradman's reputation preceded him to Yankee Stadium, where he met the legendary Babe Ruth. *The New York Telegraph* noted:

> The Babe was surprised by Bradman's lack of size and weight. The greatest batsman that cricket has yet boasted is no bigger than Joey Sewell. Don weighs 145, is 24 years of age, and, according the cricket experts is a Willie Keeler rather than a Ruth — a scientist rather than a powerhouse. Bradman hits them where they ain't and has been known to score more than 1600 runs in a little more than fourteen days of cricket.... "Us little fellows can hit 'em harder than the big ones!" roared the Babe, and at once the proper spirit of comraderie was established.... "What's the big difference between baseball and cricket?" Ruth asked.... Bradman went on: "Our matches are prolonged for days and days. Only four or five batsmen may come up in an afternoon's play. There is more snap and dash in baseball."
>
> There was little conversation through the game.
>
> In the fifth inning the Australians were aroused when Frankie Croesetti drove a home run, with two on bases, to left center....
>
> "A beauty in the right spot," was Don's comment. "That was off a google ball," remarked Fleetwood-Smith star bowler of the visitors, who is quite a google thrower himself.... In the seventh inning the boys got up to stretch. "What's all this about?" asked Don. "Just an old American custom that takes the place of tea!" roared the Babe.[47]

Babe Ruth was injured when he talked to Bradman, but the gregarious attitude that endeared him to millions of American fans and saved baseball after the 1919 Chicago Black Sox match-fixing scandal certainly comes through in the interview. Like Grace and Bradman for cricket, Ruth drew the crowds in unprecedented numbers to baseball.

The Australians visited Detroit next, then Chicago, where Al Capone still held sway. In Chicago they played at Grant Park on a temporary pitch located adjacent the 5,000 room Stevens Hotel, the world's largest. At Grant Park, "the wicket was distinctly dangerous ... a police escort cleared the way for Bradman to bat. Fleetwood Smith has taken 150 wickets in a month."[48]

Mailey's decision to include googlie bowler Fleetwood-Smith in the place of the fast bowler Ironmonger proved inspired. With Errol Flynn's dashing looks, he was in like Flynn as a talented ladies' man, and was reputed to have had five dates a night on occasion. Some of the Australian players took to following Fleetwood-Smith around as his discarded ladies proved more attractive than their own. The Australians played four games in Chicago against four Illinois Cricket Association XVIII teams. The first game — on a treacherous temporary wicket — was drawn. The next three games played at Grant Park were comfortably won by the Australians who declared when they thought they had enough runs to win because of the dangerous state of the pitch. Next the second Canadian leg of the tour started in Winnepeg, before returning across the Canadian Rockies to British Columbia where Bradman noted:

After a farewell look at Vancouver, we journeyed to San Francisco and Los Angeles and played our final matches in Hollywood, where the Hollywood contingent [was] led by the doyen of British actors, Charles Aubrey Smith, ex–English cricketer of renown who was later knighted for his services to the film industry, where he resolutely kept the cricket flag flying.[49]

Arriving in San Francisco on August 20, the Australians crushed a Northern California All Star XV in Kezar Stadium located in Golden Gate Park. Declaring at 282 for 2 they scuttled out the hosts in two innings for 55 runs. Bradman and Tolhurst got centuries in the Australian innings. Stan McCabe took 13 Northern California wickets for 26 runs. The following day the California All Star XVIII fared little better when Australia won by 134 runs. Trenholm bowled Bradman for 29 and was the best batsman for Northern California. He top scored for his side in both games with 11 runs and took the only two Australian wickets. After beating Northern California the team traveled to Montecito, where they played Montecito at Peabody Stadium on August 24.[50] Bradman scored 121 runs as the Australians declared at 387 for 6 with the Montecito XVIII all out for 59. Next day at UCLA in Westwood, the Hollywood XVIII recovered to 99 runs in their innings as Hollywood's best batsman, Desmond Roberts (a Surrey County second team player) was bowled for a duck while opening the innings. Actors John Mills and Murray Kinnell were out for ducks as McKinnon top scored for the Hollywood CC XVIII with 19 runs. McCabe dominated the bowling with 12 wickets for 44 and top scored with 66 runs as the Australians declared their innings closed at 209 runs for 5 wickets. Canadian actor Ted Dudomaine bowled McCabe while Harper got Bradman out for 11 runs. After the match, Boris Karloff invited the whole Australian team to the MGM set of *The Mask of Fu Manchu*. A photograph taken on set shows Karloff as Emperor Fu Manchu, presiding over a group that includes director Charles Brabin, Lawrence Grant, Myrna Loy, David Torrence, and C. Aubrey Smith with the Australian team resplendent in their ribbon edged blazers, sitting in the foreground.[51] *The Los Angeles Times* reported:

An "Emperor" Meets His Master

A fearsome figure in the mask of Foo Man Chew, the huge Boris Karloff stood on the set in the Metro-Goldwyn-Mayer studio thundering out his commands in the voice of a powerful Oriental emperor.

Then came the fade out. The scene shifted to Hollywood's cricket field, and it was the same Boris, considered the best batsman in the movie colony's team, who a little later floundered about in a most undignified manner against the slows of Fleetwood-Smith.

The Australians spent the morning visiting the exclusive Metro studio, which resembles a great self-contained cosmopolitan colony.

They saw various pictures being made by Maureen O'Sullivan, Jean Harlow, Mary Astor, Clark Gable, the three Barrymores, Walter Huston, Mitchell Lewis, Marie Dressler, Myrna Loy, David Torrence and Boris Karloff.[52]

The visit to the set was also the occasion for the filming of a short called *Flickers* that starred Aubrey Smith and Australian batsman Alan Kippax.

Australia played the British-Born Film Stars XVIII on August 27, 1932, at UCLA's Westwood ground. As captain of the British-Born Film Stars XVIII, the 67-year-old Smith burnished his cricket legend by top scoring with 24 runs, going in at number 11. Smith's team included Mill Hill–educated Murray Kinnell.[53] Boris Karloff scored 12 as Fleetwood-Smith took 9 for 31. Stan McCabe was rested after taking two quick wickets

The 1932 Hollywood Cricket Club at UCLA in 1932. Pat Somerset, top row, third from right (before he became secretary of the Screen Actors Guild). Sitting: H.B. Warner, C. Aubrey Smith, Desmond Roberts (Surrey County Cricket Club) and Douglas Fairbanks, Jr. Front row: Bob Finlayson in wicket-keeping gear. Source: Jean Wong Collection.

of the top order batsmen for seven runs. Australia overtook the British Born Stars XVIII score with eight wickets in hand and with Bradman at 52 not out.

In the last and third game the Australians played in Los Angeles, actors John Mills, Ernest Wright, Ted Dudomaine and Boris Karloff scored nine runs between them for the Hollywood CC XVIII as Desmond Roberts finally showed his professionalism, scoring 67 runs of the 122 total. The Australians knocked off the Hollywood score with eight wickets to spare after Vic Richardson and Stan McCabe opened the batting with a century partnership. Ernest Wright, who had kept the Los Angeles Cricket Club going for ten years before Aubrey Smith's arrival in Hollywood, had the unique pleasure of taking Richardson's wicket in a three-game series that saw only nine Australian wickets fall.[54] Reviewing the cricket scores of the three Hollywood matches, one can discern cricket played in chivalrous mode. There was no attempt to bend the hospitable HCC stars to the Australian will. The Australians rested their "quicks" and put on their slower bowlers.

The Australian visit invigorated cricket in Los Angeles. There were ten teams playing in southern California when the Griffith Park grounds opened in May 1933. They were

Hollywood CC, Los Angeles CC, Venice CC, Canadian Legion CC, Pasadena CC, Pasadena Sons of St. George, Montecito CC, Santa Barbara CC and San Diego CC. To mark the beginning of the season the HCC held a dance in May at the Roosevelt Hotel. Boris Karloff fondly recalled Aubrey Smith, dressed in immaculate white flannels, cutting across the dance floor and whispering to the favored, "My house tonight—not a word—park on another street—come in the back door."[55]

The close social involvement between HCC members translated to political clout when Hollywood producers tried to cut actors' salaries by 50 percent, citing a decline in revenues from film theatres as a result of the Depression. Actors responded to the cut in income by forming the Screen Actors Guild. Kenneth Thomson, born in Pittsburgh and educated at the Carnegie Institute of Technology, was the first organizer of SAG, according to Boris Karloff. Karloff recalled:

> So far as I am concerned, it all started at a Hollywood Cricket Club dance at the Hollywood Roosevelt Hotel in May, 1933. Every year at the start of the cricket season we used to stage something of the sort to promote interest in the club and raise funds for the season just beginning. For some extraordinary reason Ken Thomson was there. As he is not too well known for his prowess as a cricketer, I suspect that he had been lured there in the hope of knocking him over for a small financial contribution to the cause of cricket—to be rewarded, of course, with a fancy card proclaiming him to be a non-playing associate, non-voting, dues-paying member of the Hollywood Cricket Club.
>
> Anyhow as the evening advanced and I was circumnavigating the floor in my customary slow and stately manner, Ken [Thomson] dropped anchor beside me and muttered in my ear the magic words. "Would you be interested in an autonomous organization for film actors with an affiliation with Actors' Equity?" Hastily scrambling off my unfortunate partner's foot, I practically yelled, "How ... when ... where?" At which he hissed, "Next Thursday, 8:00 P.M. my house ... don't park too close to the house," and practically vanished in a puff of smoke ... with his pocketbook intact, I trust. Well, I went, I listened and was conquered. Dear Ralph Morgan was presiding over a crowded meeting of perhaps half a dozen people. Ken Thomson, of course and his wife, Alden, Jim and Lucille Gleason, Noel Madison, Claude King...
>
> Anyhow, from then on it was a regular weekly event with one or two new recruits coming in.... Amongst the trickle were Sir Aubrey Smith, Ivan Simpson, Murray Kinnell, all members of the Cricket Club.... Among others who joined the group before the actual formation the Guild were Leon Ames ... [and] Alan Mowbray, whose personal check paid for the Guild's legal incorporation.[56]

In August 1933, HCC members Ivan Simpson and Kenneth Thomson wrote the SAG mission statement under the heading, "Statement of the Aims and Purposes of the Screen Actors Guild." Ivan "Simmie" Simpson was too old to take the field for the HCC, as he was among the first wave of English actors in Hollywood, having arrived in America in 1905. He served in the Canadian Field Artillery during the First World War and after it was closely associated with George Arliss' stage productions of *Disraeli* and *The Man Who Played God*. On the screen he appeared in *Sherlock Holmes* and the *Secret of Madame Blanche*. Simpson and Thomson convinced Aubrey Smith to join the fledgling organization, as member number 13. Karloff was number nine and Murray Kinnell, 37.[57] When Kinnell joined SAG and the HCC he was living with his wife at 6812 Arbol Drive in Cahuenga Pass, not far from the Hollywood Bowl in the upstairs portion of a house rented from Marilyn Monroe's mother.[58]

The Guild was incorporated on July 12, 1933. There were four HCC members, Claude

King, Alan Mowbray, Ivan Simpson and Aubrey Smith, among the original 18 founding members. Claude King, a stalwart Aubrey Smith supporter, was born in Northamptonshire and was promoted to the rank of major in the Royal Artillery by the end of the First World War. After his return to the U.S. in 1919 he started acting in silent pictures in 1920. Piper, his Dalmatian dog, spent a lot of time at the cricket field and shows up on several HCC photographs.[59] On August 7, 1933, the Guild adopted its motto, "He best serves himself who serves others." The Guild had no finances at this time, but Ralph Morgan, the first president, Kenneth Thomson, the first secretary, and SAG attorney Laurence Beilenson met at the Masquers Club where they agreed to back the organization financially.[60] At first the fledgling SAG organization was ignored by film producers. David Niven credits Aubrey Smith, who in his determination to "help the less fortunate than ourselves," inspired "Gary Cooper, Clark Gable, Spencer Tracy, Paul Muni, James Cagney, Robert Montgomery, Frederic March, Groucho Marx, and many other great stars to affix their names to the crusade which resulted in the producers' being forced to recognize the guild and to treat their highly profitable cattle more like human beings in 1935."[61]

Niven, an eligible bachelor, enjoyed sowing his wild oats and sharing a house with fellow prankster Errol Flynn. The swashbuckling Captain Blood and "Hat-trick" Niven lived in a Santa Monica beach house (rented from Rosalind Russell) which they named *Cirrhosis by the Sea*. Niven brought his "Hat Trick" nickname with him from Stowe School, located in Buckinghamshire, where he took three consecutive wickets (a hat trick) against Eton when playing for the Stowe second XI. An all-round athlete, Niven also boxed, fenced, and played for the Second XV at Rugby. Niven's father, a second lieutenant, was killed at Gallipoli. He was attracted to father figures such as Aubrey Smith and Ronald Colman who coincidentally provided the social focus of the Hollywood British Raj. Colman's Christmas parties were popular annual events in the British Hollywood community. Brian Aherne, George Sanders, Douglas Fairbanks, Jr., and David Niven were regular invitees. At the parties, the younger David Niven remained "respectfully silent because mostly they talked about the Great War: Colman had been gassed in it, Rathbone had won the Military Cross, Nigel Bruce had absorbed eleven machine-gun bullets in his behind, and Herbert Marshall had lost a leg."[62] David Niven had yet to fight his war, as he courted Indian-born Merle Oberon in 1935, who "was coming out of an unhappy affair with the introvert, intellectual Leslie Howard.... David Niven came as a welcome change. An outdoorsman with an uncomplicated attitude to sex and work, he provided an ideal partner on the tennis courts and in bed."[63]

With all his extracurricular activities, David Niven was not a regular player with the Hollywood Cricket Club. Screenwriter Philip Dunne recalls spending an afternoon in the Aubrey Smith pavilion at Griffith Park, where he was pleasantly surprised:

> Cricket is supposed to be an extremely dull game, at least to Americans, but I found it a delightful way to spend a Sunday afternoon in the smogless Los Angeles air. I also acquired some new friends, notably Boris Karloff, the famous Monster who was actually as kind and thoughtful an English gentleman as ever buckled on a pair of batting pads. He's also become something of a box-office draw at the cricket grounds, and fair sized crowds would show up for a glimpse of him. Once, [when] he strode out onto the field and the crowd was oohing and ahing at the sight of him, actor Alan Mowbray whispered to me "They don't know that what the Monster is really thinking is: 'Dear Jesus don't send me a catch!'"[64]

Karloff kept wicket and batted number five. His bandy legs frequently got in the way of the ball so he was often out Leg before Wicket. After one dubious LBW dismissal he was walking back to the pavilion when a spectator yelled, "Bad Luck! How d'you feel?" Replied Boris, "Oh, you know, fine and bandy!"[65]

Though quite a draw, the HCC was not the only sport in town to attracted celebrity attention. Polo was very popular in Hollywood during the 1930s. When U.S. international polo player Eric Pedley rode for the Midwick Country Club in Altadena, Hollywood watched. Claude King, writing in 1934, noted that "many movie folk were there — the John Cromwells, Leslie Howards, Freddie Marches, Bill Cowens, Spencer Tracy, Aubrey Smith and lots of others."[66] Polo continued to be popular in Los Angeles throughout the 1930s, where it enhanced the sportsman's image of effortless superiority so prized by the English public school. David Niven's first press notice, published in the *Los Angeles Herald*, blithely announced the impecunious Niven had arrived in Los Angeles to buy over 100 head of polo ponies.[67] On the strength of his self promotion Niven got invited to play polo by Darryl Zanuck, who was unseated from his polo horse when David Niven's novice mallet got wedged under Zanuck's saddle, much to the amusement of Douglas Fairbanks, Jr., who was watching. Nigel Bruce had little trouble persuading David Niven to play for the HCC after his miscue at polo. Niven remembered:

> The septuagenarian captain Smith still commanded respect both on field and stage as he was ... six feet four, ramrod straight, alert and vigorous. Never did he forget a line or misunderstand a piece of direction. Unfailingly courteous, kind and helpful, he was beloved by all.
>
> Every Sunday he ordered me to turn out for the Hollywood Cricket Club, I always called him "sir," and though dreading long hot afternoons in the field, I obeyed.[68]

When "Hat Trick" Niven started playing regularly for the HCC in 1936,

> There were twenty-two cricket clubs in California at that time. The Hollywood Cricket Club was deservedly the most famous, and crashes were frequent on Sunset Boulevard on Sunday afternoons when amazed local drivers became distracted by the sight of white flannel trousers and blazers on the football ground at UCLA.[69]

Laurence Olivier made a cameo appearance on the cricket field in 1936 after he found a note from Smith as he checked into the Chateau Marmont that proclaimed, "There will be net practice tomorrow at 4 P.M. I trust I shall see you there."[70] He showed up in cricket boots borrowed from Boris Karloff. The American-born Vincent Price remembers, "You have to remember that in those days the English colony really ran Hollywood. There was the old Harwicke-Smith guard up in the hills, and then down on the beach the young renegades, Niven and Flynn living at the house they called Cirrhosis-by-the-sea."[71]

H.B. Warner, Frank Lawton, Nigel Bruce, and Melville Cooper joined the HCC prior to their Vancouver trip in 1936, where they were photographed in front of the pavilion at Brockton Point in Stanley Park, Donald Bradman's favorite cricket ground. Sir Aubrey, depicted as the snobbish Sir Ambrose Ambercombie in Evelyn Waugh's *The Loved One*, was at his best on such tours, earning the respect of a third generation of cricketers through his open handed generosity and lack of bigotry. The usually punctilious Aubrey Smith was late for the game in San Francisco after he was found in a trench teaching an Afro-American laborer how to do the forward defensive shot with the laborer's own shovel. In Vancouver he tolerated Errol Flynn's playing for the team despite the Australian's complex nature:

> Errol was a strange mixture. A great athlete of immense charm and evident physical beauty, he stood legs apart, arms folded defiantly and crowing lustily atop the Hollywood dung heap, but he suffered — I think — from an deep inferiority complex — he also bit his nails. Women loved him passionately, but he treated them like toys to be discarded without warning for new models, and for his men friends he really preferred those who would give him least competition in any department.[72]

Australian actress Ann Richards, HCC's honorary mascot, crossed swords with Errol Flynn. She relates:

> Errol came to see me on the MGM lot where I was under contract. He was directed to an area where we practiced ballet and dueling. I was a fencer and used a foil. "Would you like a partner — I'll be very careful and gentle?" said Errol feeling sure I was not in his league. I replied, "If you want to duel with me you must wear a good protective canvas outfit like mine, plus a glove and mask." He said, "Oh little girl, come, come — you are sounding as if I have something to fear!" I replied with a giggle, "Only if you take me on without your protection. I'm a champion I want you to know!" ... In the count of three I whipped the foil out of his hand.... "It's all over — I win!" I said laughing. He was very gracious saying, "I salute you!" giving me the dueler's salute with his foil.[73]

The HCC were surrounded by glamour on and off the cricket field in 1937, and many top cricketers wanted to share in the glamour no matter what standard of cricket was being played. One of them was Eton-educated George Oswald Brown Allen. "Gubby" Allen replaced Douglas Jardine as English captain in Australia after Nottingham and England fast bowlers William Voce and Harold Larwood bowled at Bradman's rib cage with seven fielders positioned on the leg side to catch the deflected ball as he moved his bat up to defend his body. These bodyline tactics reflected the fascistic age of Mussolini and Hitler. Fast bowler Gubby Allen had refused to bowl to bodyline fields in 1933, which made him an acceptable face of English cricket in Australia. Allen's 1937 team lost the Ashes in Australia in a five-game series watched by a record 943,513 spectators.[74] The losing English side arrived in Los Angeles on April 17, 1937. Allen, Walter Hammond, and Charles Burgess Fry soon proved they could win in Los Angeles when they took on a combined Pasadena and Los Angeles team.[75] Four English captains, past, present, and future, were on the same field in Pasadena when Smith, Allen, Fry and Hammond took the field.

Off the field Fry tried to emulate his host, Aubrey Smith, with whom — on the surface — he seemed to have a lot in common. Though a brilliant classical scholar and all-round athlete at Oxford, C.B. Fry was a renowned batsman with six consecutive double centuries to his credit. His bowling career suffered after he was accused of throwing the ball once Lord Harris' MCC committee strengthened the straight-arm delivery rules for bowling in 1905. Smith was a bowler who batted well on occasion. Fry had the elusive flair that touches one cricketer a generation, though in his case his close friend "Ranji" inspired Fry to a greater level of achievement. Both players represented Sussex County less than a decade after Aubrey Smith's retirement from the club. In Hollywood, Fry was "encouraged by the high level demand for British character actors.... Like C.B., Smith had been a Corinthian footballer, a Sussex captain, an advocate of the national service and a cricketer who had toured South Africa as a member of the England side."[76] By 1937, Smith was earning well over $100,000 a year in Hollywood. This was a far cry from a professional cricketer's salary. Financially secure, Smith was more concerned about Neville

Hollywood Cricket Club and Screen Actors Guild players, 1937. Seated, front, left to right, Alan Mowbray, third left, Boris Karloff, Ralph Morgan (first SAG president), Noel Madison. Standing, second row: Kenneth Thomson (first SAG executive secretary). Leaning on the stair banister of the Masquers Club where the photograph was taken, extreme right, stands Claude King. Claude King was master of ceremonies at the opening of the Griffith Park Cricket Ground on May 23, 1933. Source: SAG Archives.

Chamberlain's appeasement of Hitler. While on the set of the *Prisoner of Zenda*, David Niven recalled that Smith's "great, craggy face was frequently creased by worry because he loved England very deeply."[77]

Fry soon realized he was outgunned when it came to performance on the Hollywood stage, but before he returned to England in May 1937, the 65-year-old Fry teamed up with septuagenarian Smith on a more familiar stage — the cricket pitch — provided by the HCC. Fry recalled

> "several first rate matches, in which neither Aubrey nor I failed as bowlers. Indeed, I record with delight that in the first match I had to be taken off because I was taking too many wickets too quickly."
>
> C.B.'s team mates were even more remarkable that the revival of his bowling career (after a thirty-five year break). In one match, as Benny Hill pointed out, in *A History of Cricket*, Fry found himself playing alongside A.J. Raffles (Niven), Sherlock Holmes (Rathbone), Dr. Watson (Bruce) and even Frankenstein's monster — better known as Boris Karloff.... William Henry Pratt ... had begun his acting career by producing plays at the Enfield Cricket Club.

The commitment that such players showed to the club ... was ... remarkable when one considers that many of them were not only rather old but had been badly injured in the First World War.... Rathbone had the dubious honor of being strafed both by Goering and Von Richthofen.[78]

Nigel Bruce hosted Allen in Hollywood and basked in reflected glory when Gubby "scored an undefeated 77 that, in Fry's view, was 'nearly as good as his innings in the test match in Brisbane' in the recent Ashes series."[79]

In 1937 David O. Selznick's production of *The Prisoner of Zenda,* a film that had the unique distinction of employing more HCC club members than any other filmed in the 1930s, went into production. HCC members who worked on *Zenda* included actors Ronald Colman, Douglas Fairbanks, Jr., C. Aubrey Smith, and Raymond Massey, and its director, John Cromwell. Film critics spread the credit amongst the cast members, noting, "Aubrey Smith comes right into his own as the faithful Captain Zapt and David Niven scores as the king's aide-de-camp."[80]

In *Zenda,* based on a novel by Andrew Hope, David Niven played Captain Fritz von Tarlenheim. Colman starred as Rudolph Rassendyll, the distant English cousin of King Rudolph of Ruritania. Madeleine Carroll as Princess Flavia falls in love with Rudolph Rassendyll while he is impersonating the king after the real King Rudolph is drugged on the orders of the scheming Prince Michael. The movie benefited from the American fascination with monarchy, which had been heightened by the abdication crisis over King Edward VIII and Mrs. Simpson. *The Prisoner of Zenda* had a similar fascination for Indian audiences of the subcontinent; 20 Bollywood versions have been made since the original 1937 version. Ashis Nandy believes the subcontinent was enthralled by double for King Rudolph, Rassendyll who satisfied

some of the criteria of European romanticism.... In the process ... [the story] established the continuity between traditions and modernity, and between the "intrusive," "hedonistic," "seductive" West and the "easy," "maternal," "moral" East. The continuity is established ... through the management of random events. As in cricket, you establish your "success" not through specific successes but through the way you negotiate a random set of challenges.[81]

The hedonistic West was certainly true to form in the American version of *Zenda.* Mary Astor, who played Antionette de Mauban in the film, was implicated in a divorce trial in which her diary had center stage:

Mary Astor, who looked like a beautiful and highly shockable nun, had a sweet expression and tiny turned up nose and made everyone feel she was in desperate need of protection. In point of fact she was by her own admission happiest and at her best in bed. She also, it turned out was highly indiscreet
... If "Dear Diary" caused a stir among the *Zenda* company, it was nothing to the upheavals and near heart attacks it perpetrated throughout the upper echelons of the film colony. Mary, it appeared, had been a very busy girl indeed, and her partners had been gleefully awarded marks in "Dear Dairy" for performance, stamina, et cetera.[82]

The indubitably discreet Aubrey Smith was made a Commander of the British Empire (CBE) in 1938 for his impeccable performance in cricket, Hollywood and for furthering Anglo-American relations. He visited England to receive his award and watch the Australians under the captaincy of Donald Bradman. Smith stayed at the George Hotel in Grantham, 26 miles from Nottingham where the first 1938 test was played at Trent Bridge from June 10 to14. In the game, Barnett and Hassett made "their Test debuts for Australia, and Edrich, Reg Sinfield, Doug Wright, Len Hutton and Dennis Compton."[83]

Walter Hammond captained the England team. England declared at 658 for 8 wickets in their first innings and had Australia at 194 for 6 wickets, when

> Stan McCabe produced one of the most spectacular displays of aggressive strokeplay cricket has known. Supported by three left-handed tail-enders, Barnett, O'Reilly, and McCormick, he cleverly retained strike, hooking and driving with devastating power and occasionally moving back to square cut balls to the fence.
>
> After McCabe reached his century in 140 minutes, fours sped from his bat. Three overs from Wright produced 44 runs and McCabe rushed to his second century in 84 minutes, the last 50 in 24 minutes. Bradman called his team-mates out of the dressing room to watch. "Don't miss a ball of this," he said. McCabe's timing and shot selection were flawless and his batting was so precisely controlled there was no hint of slogging in it, although he scored 72 of the 77 runs in 28 minutes for the last wicket. Fleetwood-Smith batted with him in this stand but had so little of the strike there was no chance to improve on his five not out.
>
> Of the last ten overs bowled at the Australians, McCabe managed to take the strike for eight overs, and in that period he hit 16 of his 34 fours, with almost all England's fieldsmen stationed near the fence. Neville Cardus called it "moving cricket that swells the heart," one of the greatest innings ever seen anywhere in any period of the game's history. Bradman called it the greatest innings he ever saw or hoped to see. When it ended with McCabe caught in the covers by Compton, trying to hit Verity out of the ground, McCabe had scored 232 out of 300 added while at the crease.
>
> McCabe was trembling like a thoroughbred race-horse after a classic win when he arrived back in the Australian dressing-room. It was the third majestic innings of his career, comparable with his 187 not out in the Bodyline series, and his 189 not out at Johannesburg in the Second Test against South Africa in 1935–36.
>
> McCabe's 232 run contribution at Nottingham took Australia to 411, not enough to avoid the follow-on, and Australia had to bat skillfully on the last day on a worn pitch to save the match.[84]

Aubrey Smith got to witness this great match while C.B. Fry, one of the most eloquent cricket commentators of all time, was his host in Grantham. He pressed Aubrey for his opinion of Reg Sinfield, who was one of Fry's cricket prodigies, discovered at Fry's nautical school HMS *Mercury* near Hambledon:

> "What do you think of him?" asked Charles Fry. "What do you think of my boy Reggie Sinfield?"
>
> "Well, Charles..." The shaggy eyebrows hunch together. The great jowls are massaged. The falcon's eye searches the sky for the phrase which will sum up Sinfield from now till the Day of Judgment. Here it comes. "Well, Charles, he's good ... And he isn't good." No elaboration of this pithy criticism could ever be wrung from him.[85]

From this exchange between the two great Sussex players one can discern that Aubrey Smith had the quality Romans called gravitas. When Aubrey Smith walked in the room cricketers listened as this was one man whose deeds exceeded his word; a definition of greatness. This greatness had a range beyond cricket. C.B. Fry, who had been asked by E.V. Lucas to take his place as host for Aubrey Smith at the George Hotel, recalled after fine food and wine, Smith asking whether anyone could repeat "Kubla Khan" from memory. Denzil Batchelor was up to the task:

> The mighty actor listened, musingly stroking the jowls that had so well adorned the Colonel of the Bengal Lancers, the flinty but marshmallow hearted Duke of Wellington, and the

Uncle of Little Lord Fauntleroy. When I, and Coleridge, came to an end in mid-air, he shook, between pity and admiration, that great eagle head which resembled not so much an eagle's poll as an eagle's eyrie. The clear blue eyes were lost beneath craggy tufts of eyebrow, and I could not tell whether they were twinkling.

"Good old Kipling," he intoned. "Nobody like him nowadays."[86]

As Aubrey kept his audience guessing in England, HCC members traversed new terrain in Hollywood. In 1938 Warner Brothers made *The Dawn Patrol* with David Niven playing opposite Errol Flynn in a First World War movie about the Royal Flying Corps going up against Baron von Richthofen's Flying Circus. HCC players Basil Rathbone and Michael Brooke were also in the cast. *Batchelor Mother* with Ginger Rogers, *Wuthering Heights* with Merle Oberon and Laurence Olivier, *Eternally Yours* with Loretta Young and Aubrey Smith as Bishop Peabody, *The Real Glory* with David Niven as Lt. McCool playing second fiddle to Gary Cooper as Dr. Bill Canavan were all movies made with HCC members. Niven's top billing *Raffles* was used by Samuel Goldwyn to entice Niven into signing a second seven-year contract with Goldwyn. This was the third time *Raffles* reached the screen; the earlier versions had been made with John Barrymore and Ronald Colman in the lead in 1917 and 1930.[87] Scott Fitzgerald was brought in to help update the *Raffles* script while Olivia de Havilland was chosen as Bunnie Mather's sister, Gwen. Dudley Digges played Inspector MacKenzie of Scotland Yard and HCC member E.E. Clive acted the part of Barraclough. Cricket's moment in Hollywood did not resonate much as Second World War clouds loomed. As Inspector MacKenzie closes in on Raffles, the script deviates from Hornung's patriotic redemptive ending, which had Raffles die while unmasking a Boer spy.[88] Not long after the movie was complete, David Niven was on board Douglas Fairbanks Junior's yacht moored in Avalon Harbor on Catalina Island when Laurence Olivier broke the news that Britain had declared war on Germany. Lord Lothian, the British Ambassador in Washington, persuaded older members of the British Hollywood film community to stay put, but the younger ones such as David Niven and Merle Oberon left for London. First World War veterans Aubrey Smith and Nigel Bruce bought tickets for fighting age British expatriates.

In 1939 Aubrey Smith was 75 years old when he played a lead role in *The Four Feathers*, scripted by Arthur Wimperis. Wimperis was a vice-president of the HCC and a long-time friend of Smith. His work included *Random Harvest* (1930), *The Private Lives of Henry VIII* (1933) and *Mrs. Miniver* (1942), for which he won an Oscar. Through his writing, Wimperis kept America's love affair with the British northwest frontier in Afghanistan going. William Randolph Hearst's keen news antennae drew a bead on the Hollywood English colony in 1940 when the *Los Angeles Examiner* accused Aubrey Smith, Ronald Colman, Cedric Hardwicke and Basil Rathbone of being well known Communists.[89] The HCC's role in forming SAG had not gone unnoticed by studio owner Hearst.

The Battle of Britain provided a distraction from Hearst's pro–German stance. Aubrey Smith proved his solidarity for Britain by digging up his croquet lawn and replacing it with a victory garden. Smith also wanted to close down the HCC in 1939 but energetic new member "Doc" Severn persuaded him to keep it going for the benefit of visiting servicemen. Charity cricket games were held in which HCC members Alan Mowbray, Murray Kinnell, Claude King, Ronald Colman, Sir Cedric Hardwicke, George Sanders, and Rod LaRocque helped raise money for war effort. HCC minutes reflect money being

raised for the Commando Fund. Boris Karloff, Atwater Kent, Cary Grant, Ann Richards, Frank Doyle and Henry Stephenson
were among those praised for their efforts.[90]
Ann Richards recalls HCC parties at Aubrey Smith's house during the Second World
War:

> On one visit, I noticed that Lady Smith
> had quite a number of chickens in a large
> coop in her back garden. Each of these
> birds was named by Lady Smith for each of
> Sir Aubrey's leading ladies! The Smiths also
> had a very large pig, lovingly called "Sir
> Francis Bacon."[91]

Fund raising for the war left the HCC
treasury somewhat depleted. Treasurer Frank
Doyle reported a balance of $202 at the
April 6, 1943, AGM. As a result of Doyle's
report, playing charges were raised from 10
to 50 cents a game. The HCC maintained
a close relationship with the British consul-
general in Los Angeles, Eric Cleugh, at this
time. Elsa Lanchester was a regular visitor
to the consul-general's house, where quite
a few games of cricket were hatched. The
consul noted that Aubrey Smith seemed to
have an uphill task, explaining cricket to
baseball players.[92] However, with the help
of Doc Severn and his seven children Aubrey Smith continued as president of the HCC.

Sir Aubrey Smith, drawn by Doc Severn.
Source: Jean Wong collection.

In England first-class cricket stopped for the Second World War and renowned
cricket grounds such as the Oval in London were turned into army depots. Just before
VE Day, the minutes of the HCC AGM held on April 2, 1945, noted that "with old time
enthusiasm and spirits, Sir Aubrey reviewed the past season. He was happy that games
had been provided for so many officers and men of the Allied Services."[93] RAF pilots ferried aircraft from Palmdale and Los Angeles manufacturing facilities back to England via
Newfoundland. There were enough of these crews to man two cricket teams in the league.
They played on the Smith and West fields at Griffith Park where Ernie Wright, Frank Doyle
and Bob Finlayson removed gophers to make the field safe for cricket. Gophers undermine cricket outfields with great regularity in southern California, creating ankle-
breaking holes for the unwary cricketer concentrating on high-hit balls descending rapidly
out of the blinding California sun. Gilmore Stadium (the home of the minor league Hollywood Stars team), adjoining Farmer's Market on Third and Fairfax, was another charity sports facility used by the cricketers. Aubrey Smith expanded the impact of such events
by going on the air with other British Hollywood stars such as Ann Lee. These radio events
were popular and effectively helped keep the plight of "Blighty" before the American

public. The British government showed its gratitude to Aubrey Smith for his war work by knighting him in 1944.

In 1948, Sir Aubrey died, still president of the HCC in Beverly Hills, at age 85. Sir Aubrey's ashes were spread at the scene of some his greatest cricket triumphs at Hove, the Sussex County ground. His life innings spanned four continents and three distinct cricketing eras: the golden age, the Depression, and post–Second World War cricket. Smith through his unique personality melded all three ages into one Golden Age for Hollywood cricket. His epitaph was written in film and at the Sir Aubrey Smith Cricket ground — the only one of its kind in the world, named after a cricketer — in Griffith Park. To paraphrase his friend C.B. Fry, Aubrey Smith's passing was like the parting of a reluctant sun that decides he must leave the "soft brilliance of California to a spell of velvet darkness." By 1948 regular air travel and the advent of television broke down the cultural isolation in which the Hollywood Raj had prospered. After five long war years first-class cricket resumed in Australia, England and India. Bradman took up the bat again. In London, Arsenal football star and cricket great Dennis Compton helped restore English cricket fortunes with his great hook shot and long innings. He represented an English side that was ready to adapt to cricket realities in a decolonized British Empire. Cricket in the United States was also ready for change.

11. Cricket for Americans

WHEN CRICKET MARKS ITS 300-YEAR HISTORY in the United States in 2010 there will be no hoopla or grand marketing extravaganza to mark the event. If the same milestone were reached in one of the United States' big three sports, baseball, basketball or football, no expense would be spared to celebrate the achievement before an adoring American public. Cricket may appeal to a pastoral past and decency but it does not radiate in any extreme sense of power, color or sex appeal. Cricket in the United States has had its day in the mainstream and has been relegated to the slipstream of America's automobile culture. Within the United States, total revenues raised from the membership of the 300 cricket teams that are members of USACA are a little over $100,000. The International Cricket Council also contributes $100,000. In the past four years this money has been spent flying USACA representatives to meetings and in funding the U.S. team's participation in international events. The most recent trips were to Malaysia and Argentina. No major sponsorship contracts have been signed, although Disneyland in Florida did explore the option of hosting cricket matches at its sports facility. Bobby Mascarenhas' World Tel organization did attempt to televise U.S. cricket for the Indian market, but the effort was given up in favor of televising an Australia A versus India A event held at Woodley Park in Van Nuys, California. Since Mascarenhas' untimely death in a car accident at age 44, no attempt has been made to televise interzonal games between the nine regions that are now represented on USACA's governing board. The advent of the Internet has improved communication between the nine U.S. cricket regions, but politics within each region remains ethnically based and does not translate well to national policy.

Despite regional drawbacks a national consensus has been achieved. It is agreed that senior cricketers need more competition and that school cricket remains essential if cricket is to flourish in the United States. Unfortunately, international event participation wipes out money for development of cricket at the grass-roots level in the United States. Support for cricket in the schools requires strong leadership away from the limelight inherent in international cricket. Moreover, as all regional organizations in the United States are dominated by expatriate politicians, the focus of cricket development is more toward interethnic games. Where there have been notable exceptions such as the USACA Under 13 tournament in Plano, Texas, held in September 2000, the selection process was biased in favor of those children whose parents helped organize the event. The selection process did not give the Under 13 players an opportunity to play one game of cricket. Without match experience, players' temperament under pressure — one of cricket's key tests — goes untested. Even if the players were topnotch there is no sustained funding to develop them. Moreover, as cricket is an amateur sport, athletes find most other sports in the U.S. more lucrative when it comes to college scholarship opportunities. U.S. cricket needs to develop funding for college scholarships so that good high school players might benefit from education at universities such as Haverford in Philadelphia or Harvard in Boston where cricket has a well established tradition on campus.

There are other sources of players. In September 1995 the Los Angeles Krickets recruited American players, and though they were homeless they achieved great results quickly because their baseball skills were well developed and translated quickly to fielding. Batting and bowling took a lot longer to coach, but the players mastered these skills, too, over a sustained six-month period of training. Over $50,000 — or half the USACA annual budget — was raised to train the team. One of the team's fund-raisers was headlined by comedian Drew Carey at the Improv in Los Angeles. The comedy showcase was attended by many friends of local cricket including Kris Sharma, president of the Southern California Cricket Association, and Steve Renahan of Section 8 Housing, who represented many of the homeless advocates in Los Angeles. The Australian and British-American chambers of commerce were represented by Ian Cesar and Dennis Storer OBE, the former UCLA rugby coach and British Olympic organizer for the Los Angeles Olympics. Chris Lancashire gave generously, as did actress Ali McGraw and BUM Equipment, which could not resist the wonderful tie-in the LA Krickets offered with their down-but-not-out players. David Williams of British Airways was a strong supporter and hooked the LA Krickets up with British Rail, which donated all rail transport for the team in England.

Starting with a clear mission that cricket skills would empower the homeless through improved self-esteem, Los Angelinos opened their hearts and pockets to the team. Over $50,000 was raised for a two-week tour of England. This was the same amount of money raised by the SCCA with 40 cricket teams and over 1,000 playing members. Even with their small budget, Jimmy Colabavala, treasurer of the SCCA, gained the board's approval to pay for passports used by team members that had never left their "hood." Conceived in the chaotic aftermath of the 1992 Rodney King riots and the 7.6 earthquake of February 1994, the LA Krickets benefited from a rare combination of experiences harnessed to unique circumstances. Homelessness became a key concern of British consul-general at Los Angeles, Merrick Baker-Bates, when Prince Charles of Wales came to town.

The building block of the tour was the British American Chamber of Commerce Cricket Club, founded in 1992. Richard Windebank, president of the BACC, referred a visiting delegation of South Coast Metropole leaders to me as my insurance business was located on Sunset Boulevard not far from downtown Los Angeles. The South Coast Metropole had arrived in Los Angeles to promote the benefits of doing business in Bournemouth, Poole, Southampton and Portsmouth. This just happened to be the area where cricket started on the South Downs of Sussex and Hampshire and the home of the Hambledon

Cricket Club, cricket's most famous eighteenth century team in England. After their lecture to a select audience of businessmen in the Biltmore Hotel, they hired a bus to view homelessness in Los Angeles with Ted Hayes as guide. I had met Ted Hayes and his executive assistant Katy Haber when helping Lord Alexander Rufus-Isaacs organize a CricketAid charity cricket match at Will Rogers Park in which England test players Robin Smith and Alan Lamb were the stars. Baltimore born African-American homeless activist Ted Hayes, in his 1994 pamphlet titled *The Other Side of the Pyramid,* explains that he was "the President and Founder of Genesis 1, Pilot Dome Village, part of a four phase comprehensive plan which address 'hard core' and hard to reach homelessness, through the implementation of the Exodus Genesis Incentive Plan (E.G.I.P). Its initial purpose is to uplift and empower the homeless by making them industrious and productive right where they are."[1] The domes, built from fiberglass and capable of housing three homeless people comfortably, were funded by a $250,000 grant from Atlantic-Richfield's President Lod Cook. The domes are still in operation at their location next to the Harbor Freeway in downtown Los Angeles. Called Justiceville by Hayes, the dome community was home to the homeless cricketers. The homeless Afro-American players were used to fighting prejudice and ignorance everyday, so they were the ideal standard bearers for a game that had been shorn from its American roots. The team derived its LA Krickets name as an ironic counterpoint to the ignorance of the average American about cricket, who when faced with the game would comment, "The only cricket I've heard of is the one that crawls under the door." These LA Krickets were different. They launched a publicity revolution in broad daylight which showed the pertinence of cricket as an antidote to American social ills with homelessness as chief among them. One of Justiceville's board members drew up the logo—a cricketer wearing a green hat with an insect cricket's feelers, holding a cricket bat astride a rampant L.A. symbol—that helped the homeless cricket players focus their energies to master a game many Americans found hard to understand.

By August 1995 the team was taking shape and John Hiscock was able to report in the *Sunday Express Magazine* that "The inhabitants of dome village ... have formed the world's first cricket team made up entirely of players with no real home."[2] The homeless players lived on general relief at Justiceville, which was where their training first took place on the asphalt track outside the domes opposite the United Parcel Service building. The homeless population Justiceville served was transitional and predominantly Afro-American. The transitional homeless had lost their homes in unexpected ways such as being thrown out naked on the street by an angry spouse, or ending on the streets after release from prison, drug use, or just bad luck. As the cricket coaching continued twice a week at the Domes it became clear that with Hayes' enthusiastic and charismatic leadership the cricket team would succeed. We instilled the belief that Justiceville players, like the aristocrat cricketers of the golden age, could learn cricket skills that represented the epitome of golden age style.

The cast of characters assembled by the LA Krickets included Australian pop star Jim Manzie. Off the field, Jim Manzie became team troubadour. As a veteran right-arm medium-pace bowler, Manzie played for the first-division SCCA Pegasus CC with Stephen Speak in Los Angeles. Manzie learned cricket at Melbourne Grammar School. While in school he had formed the Ole 55 pop group which had internal dynamics similar to the LA Krickets, in that the media tended to focus on the lead singer and not the rest of the group. He attracted the Australian media to the team using his experience as a touring musician. Manzie's easygoing manner endeared itself to Theo Hayes and Joe Jacobs, the two young dynamos on the LA Krickets. By far the best batsman on the side, Speak's cricket roots were those of the gritty Lancashire league with its no-nonsense approach to learning the game. Speak's club, Blackrod CC near Wigan in Lancashire, encompassed the push for excellence synonymous with Lancashire cricket. Speak made it to the Lancashire County Seconds before immigrating to southern California.

Leo Magnus, a 40-year Jamaican resident of South-Central, helped polish the players while on tour in England. A veteran of many cricket tours, Magnus at 80 still had the thumping heart of a Jamaican fast bowler at his best. A brooding presence fond of the camera, he proved the truth of Woody Allen's aphorism that 90 percent of life is just turning up. On a good cricket day Magnus rode the heavy roller at Woodley. He could be dangerous with the heavy roller. In an Ashes game on the Old Marder (named in honor of John Marder) field at Woodley, he was keen to participate in the three lunches available that day. It was a hard choice: Aussie pies, jerk chicken or curry. Distracted by one of Stephen Speak's boundaries, Magnus accidentally drove the roller into the drainage ditch as he crossed the bridge on the way to the jerk chicken lunch. He survived to have a calypso written about him by Jim Manzie.

Today Magnus' roller is bigger and has a roll bar on it. When he played on the UCC side in 1976 he sported a fine Afro hairdo. He vehemently opposed apartheid in its heyday. As the years went by, Magnus' bowling reflexes gave way to his role as the Delphic font to which many reporters migrated when they dug for clues about the alchemy of the LA Krickets. On his death of leukemia on May 16, 2004, it became readily apparent what an important touchstone Magnus had been for southern California cricket. As news passed along the cricket grapevine, all players observed a moment's silence at lunch break and set aside a plate for Leo at their respective lunch tables. The memorial held for him at Woodley drew all religions and was the largest crowd ever witnessed at Woodley on a noncricket day. His contributions and turns of phrase were unique. "How you're doing, partner," was how he uniformly greeted players. In his playing days on a tour of Canada in Toronto, Denis Stuart recalled Magnus missing a high catch, whereupon he exclaimed, "That ball went so high it had feathers on it!" Magnus' life innings will be passed down in cricketer's memories as he bound the old cricketers with the new. His last years were spent coaching young cricketers with Delores Sheen at Sheenway School in Watts. Father of five children, grandfather of 11, and great-grandfather of five, with Magnus' passing an irreplaceable father figure was lost.

Mustafa Khan was the first homeless player to join the side. An imposing, dignified presence at 6' 6", Khan had played professional basketball and once tried out for the world champion Los Angeles Lakers. In his early years Khan had another name, but prison changed all that as the black Islamic brotherhood spoke for the dignity of the drug- and alcohol-free Afro-American. To be one of the faithful required regular prayer discipline and forswearing intoxicants. Khan radiated a simmering dignity that demanded and received respect. After the cricket tour Khan was responsible for setting up the Sheenway cricket program with Delores Sheen. Today he still ambles out to the wicket in Watts as he fights off the lung cancer he feels he contracted from the second-hand smoke he inhaled in his parent's house growing up in Texas.

Ken Cheney, a plumber by trade, knew all the gang hangouts of South-Central. A true survivor, he survived Los Angeles gang life beyond its usual life expectancy of 38 years. Slick as well as smart, Cheney would have been a great second-hand car salesman in another life. Instead, he oscillated between jobs, crack and jail, where a good day was getting his paperwork done on time. Paperwork meant that if there was a roll call in jail you got off the toilet fast, doing your paperwork fast, to arrived on schedule to avoid extra chores. On arriving in London's Heathrow Airport it was Cheney who set the tone for the tour. In reply to an ITN reporter's query as to what it felt to be like to be in London, he piped up, "It's better than dodging bullets in Los Angeles." Cheney turned into an excellent wicket-keeper under the careful coaching of Guyana-born Mark Azeez of the Hollywood Cricket Club. Dexterous with quick reflexes, Cheney was the ham of the team. Asked in the early games by a Public Radio reporter what he thought of cricket, he offered the best insight of all: "This is not a game for sissies like a lot of Americans think. The ball is hard. When it hits you turn black and blue, but with us you can't see it!"

The 21-year-old Theodore Hayes was a trainee homeless advocate following in his father's footsteps with a strong mind of his own. The older brother of 100-meter 2004 Olympic gold medal hurdler Jennie Hayes, Theo spent time with the street gangs of Riverside where his social-worker mother, Arlene Hayes, brought Theo up after his father Ted devoted himself to homelessness. Riverside had changed from the ideal town of the 1890s citrus elite to a blighted neighborhood 60 miles from Los Angeles festering with all the social ills attached to poverty. In this environment, Hayes had the potential to become a gang banger, but he was just too talented to take the leap. Hayes was plucked by his father out of Riverside's gang environment and given responsibility for helping run Justiceville. When the cricket program began on the asphalt outside the domes, Hayes tentatively stuck his head around the fence to see what was going on. Was the sport cool? When he saw one of the best players was a homeless mother he did not think so. But then Khan started having a go with his lefties from a height of 6' 6" and Hayes saw that spin combined with bounce might be enticing. His full potential as a bowler could not be realized until we got to the grass three months after we started the project in April 1995. Then his natural athleticism kicked into full gear as he delivered quicker and quicker right-arm over-the-wicket deliveries, off a 12-step run-up. To run long, bowl fast, and deliver on a dime you need rhythm and Hayes had it. His natural bowling ability was infused with great agility on the field. His delivery stride did not quite affect the long arc of Australian ace Jeff Thomson. Thomson in his prime could touch the ground with the back of his hand before going full arc with a sideways cartwheel that rotated all the downward thrust to the pirouetting front foot before he hurtled the ball into the top (pitch), to rear up in the batsman's face. Hayes unceremoniously penetrated the best batsmen's defenses with his speedy bowling aimed at the block between bat and pad. He took the first wicket at Hambledon, then the second after consistently pounding away on a length for four overs. Hayes was part of an intimidating duo to batsmen when he combined with Vista volunteer Tom Fitzpatrick, fielding brilliantly with short-stop quickness at point. Their combination unsettled the opening batsman's confidence at Hambledon.

Tom Fitzpatrick, a broad stocky Irish-American with a solid baseball background, was employed by Justiceville to improve administration and outreach programs as a Vista volunteer. President Clinton encouraged the formation of the Vista Corps to work in America's inner cities. The Vista program was a domestic complement to President Kennedy's Peace Corps. Fitzpatrick's reliability was his hallmark both on and off the field. He backed up brilliantly and parried the sharpest blows cut from the bat. He kept the players in great heart while studiously avoiding the limelight, as he early perceived its corrosive affects on the sportsman's ego, integrity and libido.

None of these effects concerned 24-year-old Joe Jacobs. Fit and well proportioned by doing at least 100 push-ups a day in jail, Jacobs had strong shoulders and a temper that could flare, but which he learned to channel into an elegant batting style. At 5' 9" he had the frame of a soccer midfielder. Jacobs liked to hint of the tough life he had experienced in jail, caused by the unrequited anger at being raped and sodomized by an uncle at the age of eight. The experienced executive director of Justiceville, Katy Haber, reminded me that such sob stories should be taken with a grain of salt as survivors on the margins learn the arts of manipulating human emotions with great effectiveness. Jacobs' most memorable moment off the cricket field on tour came when he disappeared in London after a courtesy visit to the Phoenix Foster Home, where he precipitously fell for a long leggy blond. As we waited to board the train at Waterloo for Bournemouth, we kept waiting, missing one train, then another. Katy Haber had to call and tell the waiting Bournemouth mayor to send his welcoming brass band home. We had all given up hope when in the distance, bobbing up and down, a brown hat signaled that AWOL Joe was ready to rejoin the LA Krickets anxiously lined up for their Waterloo. Jacobs' broad, toothy grin, the gorgeous blond leaning on his arm and his empty condom hat pouch told the story. Once on the field at Hambledon, there was no denying Jacobs' catharsis when he hit another boundary. He hit boundaries with ease and regularity from almost the first day he picked up the bat. His instinct for getting behind the ball and positioning his feet to hit the ball with time to spare, spoke to the essence of all great batting, exemplified by Prince Ranjitsinhji and Sir Donald Bradman. We came to rely on Jacobs' batting to get us out of tough spots, and his strike rate was second only to that of Stephen Speak by the end of the tour. He outstripped the rest of the "ringers," though at Hambledon his brilliant boundary fielding with his characteristic baseball slide cut off many a complacent crack for four runs. This left the Hambledon batsmen hurrying to make up for lost runs.

Jacobs and Fitzpatrick were the two good reasons why a strong Hambledon CC side was confined to less than 200 runs. The day before in Poole Harbour, a CBS reporter knowingly looked at me in an interview and asked, sensing disaster, "Do you know what you're up against?" As captain I was confident of my men by this time. I knew they were set to turn the cricket world on fire. Jacobs proved beyond question that baseball players could become batsmen with a full range of shots, good defense and great fielding skills. Unfortunately, after playing four brilliant cricket games along with Fitzpatrick and Hayes for the Victoria Cricket Club in the Southern California Cricket Association, Jacobs lost contact after he reputedly found himself in jail again — nothing was heard of him until five years later when picked up his Disney check from Justiceville.

Spin-bowler Tom Weaver, the seventh son of a sharecropping family from rural Alabama, had a strong football background. How he had found his way to Justiceville no one knew, but he was the quiet man on the team. He showed an amazing dexterity with the cricket ball. He became the best right-hand finesse bowler on the team, teasing out his victims with a mild manner that masked an intense, craftsmanlike concentration on the delivery stride. Tom quietly maneuvered his way around the sharp edges of home-less politics and as his self-esteem grew with each successive game, he began to get back in shape again. He became a new man on the tour and he was one of those players you wanted to find a slot for in life. His best performance was 6 wickets for 21 runs against a very experienced Hollywood Golden Oldies side on our return from England. This moment perhaps was his greatest. He died not long after, from a drug overdose, after receiving his Disney money for the rights to the Los Angeles Krickets' story, which never made it to the screen.

Keith Hartog was the only Jewish, homeless person on the team. Hartog sold paint-ings for a living, but sales had become so slow that he found his way to the domes for a "temporary" stay that stretched into months. He kept his pride intact and continued to represent a famous artist between improving his batting skills on the field. Hartog was hard to teach at first, but he opened up to instruction when he realized all the other play-ers were learning too. Tentatively, he overcame his fear of the hard ball, and became the LA Kricket's first wicket-keeper. From his vantage point behind the stumps he had the perfect position to see the variety of spin, seam, and fast bowling that he later mastered as a reliable opening batsman. Hartog chopped down on any shooter with quick reflexes, intent on keeping his wicket as he was determined to stay in the game of life. Once he got off the plane in England he flowered into full glory as a batsman. He carried two large paintings with him on the London Underground and made sure they were hung prop-erly in the pavilion before he went out to bat. Some batsmen bat with heart; Hartog bat-ted with art. His finely tuned aesthetic sense came to the fore on Broadhalfpenny Down at Hambledon. The artist in him returned cricket to the community, made a sensory feast of the dappled light of the pine copse opposite the Bat and Ball pub and soaked in the Richard Nyren tradition celebrated by the granite obelisk monument familiar to all seri-ous cricketers.

The stone monument opposite the old Hambledon CC clubhouse — the Bat and Ball pub — was erected in 1910. It was where the LA Krickets sat on the shoulders of the giants of English cricket history: Jessop, Fry, Ranjitsinhji, Dennis Compton, Lord Colin Cow-drey — all the great cricket players had made the *haj* to the granite *mirhab* of cricket's Mecca. Secure in cricket's inner sanctum, and with pilgrimage fulfilled, Hartog went to bat at Hambledon with the same determination that Moses showed in leading the lost tribes out of Egypt. By the time he returned to the clubhouse, he had faced 51 balls, put on 17 runs, and kept the innings intact after the loss of two quick wickets. The glow on his face behind that fine square beard could have parted the Red Sea. The man had arrived and was whole again. His demons visited him just one time on tour and that was on the British Airways flight back to Los Angeles when the airline attendant cut him off at 33 beers. Hartog turned up at Woodley a year after the tour, introduced me to his new wife and told me proudly that he had founded a catering firm. Such is the confidence that cricket imparts to the once down and out businessman.

When Katy Haber's two forefingers started twirling her long auburn hair, we knew yet another great donation was coming to the program. Katy engineered the BUM Equip-ment deal, tapped her connections at the British Academy of Film and Television Arts

(BAFTA) and most important, proved the perfect hostess at each of the tour stops. Haber's fine working relationship with the British consul-general at Los Angeles, Merrick Baker-Bates, opened up crucial doors in London including that of Lord's, where the whole team trained prior to taking on Scotland Yard. Before taking on the Yard team of disadvantaged youth, the LA Krickets visited the London Metropolitan Police Headquarters where Joe Jacobs and Roger Simon tried out the cells and mused how much more pleasant an English jail was likely to be than one in America.

It was gang banger Roger Simon who was hardest to get out of the cell. We had had trouble getting Simon's passport organized in Los Angeles as he had delayed getting his photograph taken. Roger had disappeared the day before we left Los Angeles and returned to the Domes hours before departure with condom hats for the players. The khaki brown baseball hats with see-through condom pouches replaced the black BUM Equipment hats donated to Roger and Joe Jacobs. With his mother's support, Simon finally committed to the tour, where he proved to a favorite with Sky TV who just loved the way he drank in the English countryside. Simon was not hardened by his experience in South-Central; his mother if anything had protected him so well that he was too soft to survive the true gang bangers. Simon's sublime moment was when he lit the duck candle he was awarded to keep Mustafa Khan warm in the Ridlington CC club shed. Such remarkable scenes were made possible by an army of cricket supporters who piled in to help when and wherever they could.

After the first game of the tour, which the LA Krickets lost despite Stephen Speak's century against his old club, Blackrod CC, the Krickets bedded down in the clubhouse and after a fine breakfast were driven by Ridlington CC's captain from Lancashire to Rutland. The sound of thunderclaps and pouring, lightening-tinged rain greeted the LA Krickets on arrival in Ridlington in County Rutland, but the village team turned out to put on a fine game on a very sticky wicket near Uppingham School. Conditions were sticky, so was the wicket, and the mud was red. As the ball skidded off the wicket, the LA Krickets learned what a sticky wicket was all about and why cricket could be so different from baseball. The LA Krickets' usually athletic performance in the field was reduced to a series of pratfalls as the players skidded around in the mud in shoes without spikes. None of the players had cricket boots at the time, so we put in a call to Bob Cooke of Peak Sports, who was waiting for us at Hambledon with boots. Ridlington left us 113 runs to score in 25 overs. The reply was tentative and it took a brilliant batting effort by Speak to win the game on the last ball of the match with a six over the long on boundary. The hit seemed providential as we headed to London, where we ran out of funds to provide accommodation for the players. Ted may have known something I did not but I envisaged staying homeless in Hyde Park. Then the bus delivered us to the Bedford Hotel near Kensington, where we were told the Prince of Wales Trust had helped organize the accommodation for the three nights we needed to stay in London. Who the benefactor was that had opened the door for the homeless, we never really knew, and that was typical of the kindness we found throughout England.

London, as Dickens clearly showed, can be a tough city. Katy Haber found her bag had been stolen the next morning. Was it an inside job or an outside job? Collectively we moved beyond what could have become a crisis of accusation and caught the bus for Lord's, where the players got to try out the indoor nets and saw a picture of the 1868 Aborigines Tour to England in the MCC Cricket Museum. The Aborigine cricketers played 46 games and had a player die on tour.[3]

The LA Krickets played six games and developed a following in Los Angeles where the local news channels started following the LA Krickets' progress on the sports channels. Cricket had lost the media to baseball in the 1920s when Babe Ruth's charisma helped build Yankee Stadium just as America's corporations saw value in sponsoring baseball. With CBS, ABC and Sky TV now asking for our itinerary, Hayes became the fulltime communicator, while the team honed its skills to cover his unannounced departures from slips as he promoted cricket's beneficial effect on homelessness, to a larger audience.

On the field, Ted Hayes' departures from slips to do media interviews showed his priorities were limited by his higher calling. When he did connect with the media, it was like a cracking six over mid-on with not a chance of stopping the trajectory. Hayes had learned to aim for the stars after contemplating suicide at one of the low points in his life. The fact that he could contemplate suicide meant he had options. There are no suicides on skid row. After a redneck trucker told the nigger to jump, Hayes chose life. Anger turned the man around. He learned not to turn the other cheek. He had a life and a village to build. He was involved with the move from Riverside, civil rights marches, and the legal action using the law of eminent domain in favor of the homeless with Dan Stormer as his legal mentor. Social activism started the healing and roller-blading kept the hyperkinetic visionary in the zone. Always looking for the right platform, cricket presented itself as a new platform, and the message of homelessness used cricket as its medium.

What happened to the LA Krickets after they returned? Were the players empowered through self help? Harry Wright's Cincinnati Red Stockings lasted just a year as they put professional baseball on the map with a 61-game nationwide tour in 1869. Almost a century and half later, the LA Krickets brought cricket home to the American public. Their media presence attracted numerous invites. They played six overs against the visiting Sri-Lankan World Cup champions in 1995, then introduced cricket to South-Central on the Day of the Krickets in Carson, when many SCCA cricketers including U.S. cricket internationals Reginald "Regi" Benjamin and Hopeton Barrett coached young high school students under the solicitous gaze of Merrick Baker-Bates and the Samoan Chief of Los Angeles. Victoria Park in Carson remains home to Somoan-style cricket, played for over 40 years in Los Angeles. The LA Krickets' last game was near the banks of the River Jordan in Salt Lake City, Utah, against a team of Indian software engineer cricketers bent on victory. Merrick Baker-Bates invited the LA Krickets to demonstrate cricket in the land of the Mormons as part of the Utah–UK Festival in 1996. On a damp wicket where there had been October snow the day before, Hayes, now secure in media dominance, imperiously walked on the pitch and demanded the "ringers" step down and allow the homeless players to face the Indian finger spinners on a damp pitch. The slaughter lasted three overs and the LA Krickets were done. The self-esteem so carefully nurtured would have to find a new field for play. It was time to move on. We all returned to our lives. Jacobs claimed his Disney money. Cheney disappeared into South-Central, and Speak took up teaching and won the Southern California Cricket Association batting prize. Manzie re-established his music career. Azeez returned to his garage in Hollywood and with Leon Lamprecht and his brother, Kemal Azeez, continues to organize world cricket tours for the Hollywood Golden Oldies. Fitzgerald finished his Vista stint at the Domes and went into business. Tom Weaver became homeless again and died. Simon after being arrested at LAX on a warrant served his three-month jail sentence, where thoughts of Hambledon kept a smile on his face. He still had his cricket boots on when he came out of jail. His cricket credentials endeared him to Merrick Baker-Bates, who employed him as a gardener at the British Consulate in Hancock Park. Baker-Bates also arranged for the eye operation to remove cataracts that were first discovered when Simon kept missing balls at Third Man in the last game of the tour against Bournemouth CC. Hayes and Katy Haber began the Mom and Popz of Compton.

One of the first calls I received on my return from England was from Tom Melville, author of *The Tented Field*, which took as its premise that cricket in the United States was a cultural reject and would never go mainstream in America. He was right but for the wrong reasons. American cricket went out of its way to annex itself as a minority sport in America. It became the Ellis Island of all sports and opened the door of modernization and opportunity to the West Indian community following the imposition of racial segregation in major league baseball. The LA Krickets simply tapped cricket's tradition of being played by the underdog in the United States. When the team showed they were capable of playing on level terms with English gentlemen the Los Angeles public took the team to heart as they appeared nightly on Channel 5. The LA Krickets proved that for cricket to take off in America it needs local heroes.

A year after the tour, the Southern California Cricket Association raised enough funds under SCCA president Dr. Atul Rai and World Tel's Jimmy Mascarenhas to hire Malcolm Nash—the first cricket school coach appointed in the United States since 1926, when cricket was last officially played at Germantown Academy in Philadelphia. The SCCA-sponsored school cricket program started at Ivanhoe Elementary School in the Silverlake area of Los Angeles and was opened by Sir Richard Hadlee, 30 years after his father's visit to Los Angeles in 1966. Sir Richard's visit was sponsored by Air New Zealand as part of his rained-out visit to the Philadelphia Cricket Festival in 1995. Four of the six Southern California Junior Cricket Program coaches, Mark Azeez, Stephen Speak, David Sentance and Leo Magnus, honed skills coaching the Los Angeles Krickets. But the addition of Sherle Williams from Jamaica and Rodney Cutting from Barbados (the father of Fidel "Castro" Edwards—the current West Indian opening fast-bowler who took five wickets at age 19 in his first test-match against South Africa) has proved invaluable as they have obtained MCC-recognized coaching certificates. Malcolm Nash set ambitious goals. Within two years he trained and selected a United States Under XIII cricket team, captained by Bashi Kezar of the SCCA Victoria CC, which defeated Canada Under XIII at Larkspur Park in Marin County. Sir Gary Sobers, International Cricket Council ambassador at the event, recalled his world-record feat of scoring six sixes against Malcolm Nash (Glamorgan CCC) at Swansea. Sir Gary witnessed Keenan Fish from Colorado dominate as opening bowler for the United States against Canada. Fish has now moved into the senior cricket ranks in Colorado.

Public schools in Los Angeles are run in clusters through the administration of the Los Angeles Unified School District, which is the largest school district in the United States, catering to over 1 million students. The Southern California Junior Cricket program focused on the downtown school cluster, which included Hobart, Alessandro, Ivanhoe and now Micheltorena elementary schools. These schools, apart from Ivanhoe, have a predominantly Hispanic population, while Hobart, located near Koreatown, has a very active Korean community. We have found that the lower the economic group the more keen they are on team sports. The Hobart area has the greatest the density of people, five per room, in Los Angeles. Team sports are preferred in these poorer areas over more expensive individual activities such as music or gymnastics.

In northern California the ex–USACA treasurer Michael Miller set up the United States Junior Cricket Program to provide an umbrella 501c.3 status for cricket coaching programs that demonstrated an ability to train American students and not just expatriate children. New chapters have been added from Utah, Kansas, Seattle and Philadelphia. The Philadelphia junior cricket program has drawn on the century-old tradition of school cricket and has been well supported by the Philadelphia and Germantown cricket clubs, intent on reclaiming their old familiarity with the game. The Philadelphia school cricketers are fortunate to have a fine club setting for learning the game that engenders all that Americans feel is important about cricket; namely, its smart white clothing, its refined air and its emphasis on fair play and sportsmanship in an era when the large salaries of athletes have turned the business of sport into a zero sum game. With a 1 million dollar contribution, or less than one percent of the salary Alex Rodriquez earned from the Texas Rangers, cricket would lift itself out of its third world status in the United States— provided it hired a professional administrator immune from local and regional community pressure. Fair selection of players would be vital to the health of the game, poised as it is at an exciting crossroads, in the United States.

Dominated on the East Coast by the West Indian community, in Lauderhill, Florida, a community that is 60 percent West Indian, ex–West Indian test player Lance Gibbs has been appointed by the mayor to attract the next ICC World Cup in 2007 to the city with a 20,000-person stadium dedicated to cricket. Such promises have been made before. On the West Coast, Indian electrical engineers helped build America's new fiber-optic communications highway. Their enthusiasm for cricket inspired Bobby Mascarenhas' World Tel Media to put on a test match between the A teams of India and Australia at Woodley Park as part of his agreement with the USACA Board of Directors to promote cricket in the United States. Australia won the event handsomely. Played at Woodley Park in Van Nuys, total gate receipts for the event were $13,000, which barely put a dent in the $250,000 break-even cost required for the satellite coverage of the tournament, which was beamed to the Indian subcontinent, where American advertisers sought Indian markets for their products by paying for billboards for their product at an American-hosted test match. A ball-by-ball commentary by Ian Chappell and Michael Holding was carried by the local Indian Z channel and throughout the subcontinent. Though not a financial success, Mascarenhas' experiment with a new business model for cricket in America showed verve and nerve, which sadly was not to be repeated following his death in a car crash in India. The local Indian community will dominate cricket in California, Arizona — especially Phoenix and Tucson — and to a lesser degree New York for sometime to come. Hotel owners born in Gujerat, the western panhandle of India, vie for attention with electrical engineers and doctors educated in Bangalore.

The Bhaktas first arrived in the United States in 1947. Another 40 families settled in Panama where the dollar was the unit of currency. Agriculturalists by inclination, the

Bhaktas have bettered themselves through the ownership of motels along routes 10 and 40, located in the southwestern United States. From the first hotel owned in Hayward just outside San Francisco, Bhakta-owned motels and hotels represented by the Asian Hotel Owners Association now control over $60 billion in annual revenue. With the Bhaktas' support, cricket tournaments are well run. The Los Angeles Open was inaugurated in 2003 with $5,000 prize money to attract top teams from overseas such as Trinidad. In Los Angeles Jack Bhakta has been a significant contributor to the Hollywood Cricket Club, long since pulled from its English roots. The Hollywood CC no longer has its annual meetings and dance at the Roosevelt Hotel but in Diamond Bar located on route 10 thirty miles east of Los Angeles. The club, which once had the clout to help found the Screen Actors Guild, invited Indian cricketer Sunil Gavaskar to its seventy-second annual HCC banquet, last year.

Into the void left by the death of Sir Aubrey Smith in 1948 has stepped the Beverly Hills and Hollywood Cricket Club, founded by Eton-educated Lord Alexander ("Xan") Rufus-Isaacs and Baron Clement von Frankenstein.[4] Xan over the last decade has been involved in some memorable cricket matches in the park under the Hollywood sign. Julian Sands has played on the HBHCC side, as have Sir Mick Jagger and Hugh Grant. These cameo appearances have been enhanced by the excellent performances of public-school cricketers Simon Mathew and Dan Musgrave. In days past, the watering hole after the game was the Cat and Fiddle Pub on Sunset Boulevard, not far from the Roosevelt Hotel where the Motion Picture Academy Awards were held in 1924. The BHHCC exemplifies an English cricket tradition in Los Angeles that reached fruition as the Los Angeles Social Cricket League based in Erwin Park in North Hollywood.

Social cricket as opposed to the intense competition of SCCA league cricket received a boost in 1997 when the Lord's Taverners visited Los Angeles. In a trip initiated by Ashley Mote following his attendance at the SCCA 1996 banquet honoring Sunil Gavaskar held in the Furama Hotel located in Westchester, Ashley with his colleague John Price (England) put together an A-list of England cricket and entertainment talent that included: Sir Tim Rice (Jesus Christ Superstar and future MCC President), John Snow (Sussex and England), Mike Denness (Kent and ex–England captain), Brian Close (Yorkshire and ex–England captain), and Rachel Hahoe-Flint (ex–England Woman's Test captain). The Lord's Taverners visit resulted in an active pub league being founded in Los Angeles Southern California Social league that includes: the Fox and Hounds, the Springbok Pub, the Compton Cricket Club, Beverly Hills and Hollywood CC and the Mayflower Club. The new league provides less competitive cricketers a rare opportunity to develop their skills in a generally mature cricket environment where proficient cricketers from overseas would otherwise dominate local cricket. Trevor Roper and Matt Weston have run the league for eight years and it continues to attract stronger players. Unfortunately, few of these new players have been developed in the United States and the 300-year cultural gulf between indigenous and imported players still exists. Young imported players, still in the prime of their playing careers, have no intention of giving up their spot on the side for lesser players. Only the Compton Cricket Club, managed by Katy Haber and Ted Hayes, building on their Los Angeles Krickets experience, has shown the capacity for training American players from scratch. They have put the contacts they have made in England to good use. Several English county cricketers have visited to train the Compton Cricket

Club teams founded since the return of the Los Angeles Krickets from England in September 1995. These include Ed Smith of Kent, who notes in his book *Playing Hardball*:

> Cricket in Compton is the master plan of social activist Ted Hayes.... "Just think of the irony," Hayes told me as I left the Dome Village. "A group of homeless people are bringing the noble game of English cricket to the notoriously gang-infested ghettos of LA."[5]

United States Junior Cricket head coach Malcolm Nash is convinced that for cricket to take off in the United States it has to be taught in bulk. To that end he has met with California governor Schwarzenegger to gain his support for introducing a cricket curriculum to California schools through training the physical-education instructors in the colleges. Cricket organizers have been forced to change with the times and become deft administrators with the aid of the Internet and Cricinfo.com and USCricket.com. Most cricket teams have their own web page. The Internet remains a two-edged sword in cricket. While democratizing the sport, it has flattened the traditional hierarchical administrative order of the game. Club president and associations can be attacked without recourse to the civility of debates governed by Robert's Rules of Order. Cricket really needs a strong leader — a cricket commissioner — respected by all, to move to the next level. The American Youth Soccer Organization does offer a model. Parents get involved in coaching and have to take coaching courses. The trick is to make the game exciting for parents as well as juniors, and here cricket does have a strong advantage in being an international game. Tibetan monks play cricket as a Zen exercise. In Africa, South America and throughout Europe cricketers are welcome. School cricket trips might easily serve a broader educational purpose in breaking down America's xenophobic tendencies. Embraced by Islamic, Buddhist, Christian, Hindu and Jewish countries in this increasingly less secular world, playing cricket improves communication as exemplified by India-versus-Pakistan test matches.

Unfortunately, in the United States cricket has no common heritage to draw on because the individual expatriate histories of the game do not provide common ground. When an American talks of baseball he knows what Babe Ruth did on a certain day in the year. Every Englishman, Indian, Pakistani, or West Indian carries his own version of cricket history in his head. When these histories are supplemented by American cricket achievements on the field of play — when the new Bart King is found to emulate — then cricket will have arrived in the United States. Cricket stands poised on the edge of American sports history, and it would take just a very small percentage of what one baseball player makes to push it back into the mainstream of American sports culture. The challenge for cricket administrators in the United States is to make that happen by putting the growth of the game above local political concerns.

This process started with the founding of the Professional Cricket League in 2004, comprised of eight teams throughout the United States. Playing a 20 over format, found to be a big draw in England and several other cricket playing countries, United States cricket —funded by Indian entrepreneurs— seeks out a new market already carved out by baseball 130 years ago. This time around, cricket has strong links to the information revolution which transcends local support in favor of a global viewing audience. If local professional players do manage to connect with the local American public, a new sports revolution will be in the making. If that does not occur, cricket will played on local estates such as Jeneel Gupta's Palo Alto winery, where a beautiful cricket pitch has been built amid the vines of his 50-acre winery. In Los Angeles, Dr. Asif Khan, originally from Pakistan, has invested a million dollars of his assets in a pitch built for youth cricket in Fontana. The western frontier of cricket has now opened up and the third century of the cricket in America promises to be well financed. Christians marching as to war during the Muscular Christianity phase of the game prior to the Civil War have been increasingly displaced by religions newer to America, as Hindu temples in Orange County and mosques in Oxnard fund local teams. The east-facing imam, leading the faithful in prayer between innings, has become a regular occurrence on America's cricket fields. Reincarnated or not, every born-again or non–born-again cricketer looks for nirvana in the yogic present of a well timed shot. Cricket has become a game for clear heads, virtue and uniform values in a multicultural America.

12. Trends in Contemporary United States Cricket

THE ENGINE OF AMERICAN CRICKET for the century between 1890 and 1990 has been the West Indian community on both coasts and in Chicago. West Indian sailors were integrated in ship crews that sailed the eastern seaboard prior to the American Revolution. Herman Melville's *Billy Budd* was a black seaman.[1] When the British army left America in 1783, black Americans and West Indians migrated to Canada in the 100,000-person Loyalist exodus that secured Canada's future as an independent nation.[2] In the West Indian part of the British Empire after their emancipation in the British Empire in 1833, ex-slaves and West Indian Regiment garrison soldiers played cricket against the white plantation owners of the islands:[3]

> In *The Pickwick Papers* (1836) Dickens refers to a cricket match played in the West Indies by two officers. Trinidad became British only in 1797, yet in 1842, not ten years after the abolition of slavery, there was a well established Trinidad Cricket Club. By 1891 there was an inter-colonial tournament between Barbados, Jamaica, and what has now become British Guiana (Guyana).[4]

Writing in 1958, C.L.R. James explained the unique West Indian cricket topography:

> The islands are a scattered chain in the Gulf of Mexico stretching from Jamaica in the north, a few hours from Miami, Florida, to Trinidad in the south, a few hours from Venezuela. British Guiana (Guyana), on the mainland, is West Indian, in everything except geography. The islands differ widely from one another. Thus Jamaica is over 4,000 square miles in area with nearly a million people; Barbados is 166 square miles in area, and at one time had nearly 200,000 people, though the population is less today. Trinidad, nearly eighteen hundred square miles, about the size of Lancashire, has over 400,000 people....
>
> Apart from the Port of Spain in Trinidad (70,000), Kingston in Jamaica (35,000), Georgetown in British Guiana (55,000), most of the two million population live in small towns and villages. Even Bridgetown, the capital of Barbados, has only 13,000 people. Until the buses came transport was difficult. The organization of cricket on any extensive scale is therefore impracticable.[5]

After the American Civil War, cricket became easier for people of the West Indian Diaspora to play, as recreation and organized sports were encouraged in public parks. Playing cricket in New York for the West Indian community was both a political affirmation of cultural distinctiveness and a force for modernization. By joining local cricket clubs in the Bronx that played at Cortlandt Park, Prospect Park in Brooklyn or at Livingston Park on Staten Island, the West Indian cricketers gained a level of exposure to American white mores otherwise not available to the tenement dwellers of industrialized New York. West Indians played for the love of the game. They had no cricket professionals. Hard West Indian cricket pitches encouraged fast bowling. James wrote:

> In Barbados we get the fastest wickets in the world; in British Guiana and Jamaica there are good tropical turf wickets. Trinidad and some of the smaller islands use matting stretched on hard clay, which at least possesses the virtue of being ready for ordinary use with less than a quarter of an hour's preparation. The people are not keen to watch but they play.[6]

Cricket's inability to attract paying spectators did not deter the growth of the game on the East Coast, where it owed its resilience in the West Indian community to the fact that it was a bulwark against racial discrimination. As cricket teams played each other they helped integrate immigrants to the American mainstream. Referrals from established cricketers could change the quality of life. This process of modernization enhanced the American West Indian cricket teams' connections with their feeder clubs in the Islands. The West Indian's sense of cultural identity was based on the playing of

> cricket in a very definite sense. If Britain had Drake and mighty Nelson, Shakespeare, the charge of the Light Brigade, the success of parliamentary democracy, the few who did so much for so many — these constitute a continuous national tradition. Underdeveloped ... countries have to go back many decades, sometimes centuries, to find one.... The West Indies clearing their way with bat and ball, had made a public entry into the comity of nations. It had been done under the aegis of the men who more than any others created the British public-school tradition, Thomas Arnold, Thomas Hughes and W.G. Grace.[7]

The first English team to play in the West Indies landed in Barbados in 1895 and was captained by R. Slade Lucas. Slade Lucas's English team played in Barbados, Trinidad, British Guyana and Jamaica and lost three games. As a result of these West Indian victories,

> cricket leapt forward. In 1895–6 there was a yearly tournament in British Guiana. Jamaica sent a team to British Guiana early in 1896–7 to play two games, and then played Barbados on the way home. Late in 1896–7 ... two English teams toured the West Indies, one under Lord Hawke, and the other under the late Sir Arthur Priestley. Lord Hawke's team had P.F. Warner (born in the West Indies), H.D.G. Leveson-Gower, G.R. Bardswell, C. Haseltine and H.R. Bromley-Davenport. Priestley had A.E. Stoddart, S.M.J. Woods, R.C.N. Palairet and C.A. Beldam....
> For Priestley's team Stoddart was the outstanding batsman, making over a thousand runs. For Lord Hawke's team P.F. Warner fell short of that number only by 16.[8]

A team from Philadelphia visited a year later and won a close game against a West Indies side at Bourda in Guyana.[9] The standard of play against the English teams convinced Lord Hawke that a West Indian team could compete on even terms against English counties. The first West Indian team to visit England was led by the successful white businessman H.G.B. Austen, son of the bishop of the West Indies. Charles Augustus

Ollivierre of Jamaica and Learie Constantine of Trinidad stayed in England after the tour ended. Ollivierre played for the Derbyshire County CC and Constantine later accepted a contract as a professional for the Nelson CC in Lancashire.

In New York the West Indian Benevolent Association supported black West Indian cricket teams from 1893.[10] They competed against local New York teams such as the Manhattan Island and Staten Island cricket clubs. In 1906 the Jamaican Hinds scored a century against Manhattan CC.[11] Players such as Hinds were racial equality pioneers in America's Jim Crow society. The traditions inherent in English public school cricket were not available to American blacks. Excluded from professional baseball until Jackie Robinson played for the Brooklyn Dodgers in 1947, the Afro-American community organized the Negro Baseball Leagues.

> [The] entire experience of blacks in baseball in early twentieth century America exemplifies elements of Booker T. Washington's call for the development of separate economic spheres so that his race might prepare itself for inclusion in American life.... They strove to create viable enterprises that served their communities and simultaneously might win a measure of respectability in the broader society. These ventures would prepare them for the day on which, according to Dubois's vision, it would be "possible for a man to be both a Negro and American, without having the doors of Opportunity closed roughly in his face."[12]

West Indian–born cricketers in New York played in integrated leagues starting in 1893. Working-class Jamaicans inspired by the courageous leadership of Marcus Garvey — the founder of the United Negro Improvement Association, which later became the NAACP — were also at the forefront of the battle to integrate baseball. Effa Manley had Jamaican ancestry and was owner of the Newark Eagles. As a Negro Baseball League team owner,

> Effa Manley was an indefatigable campaigner against discrimination. In the years before she and her husband Abe purchased the ball club, Manley had achieved prominence in New York as the secretary of the Citizen's League for Fair Play, which waged successful campaigns against Harlem businesses that refused to employ African Americans. In Newark, Manley served as the treasurer of the New Jersey chapter of the NAACP and on several occasions held ballpark benefits for the organization. At one event the Eagles sold NAACP "Stop Lynching" buttons to fans. Manley also joined the "Citizen's Committee to End Jim Crow in Baseball Committee" created by the Congress of Industrial Organizations in 1942.... The Newark Eagles regularly raised money to purchase medical equipment for the Booker T. Washington Community Hospital. During World War 1 the Indianapolis ABC's and the Chicago American Giants played games on behalf of the Red Cross, and in the 1920's Hilldale played fund-raisers for war veterans. The first black baseball game at Yankee Stadium pitted the Lincoln Giants and Baltimore Black Sox in a 1930 benefit for the Brotherhood of Sleeping Car Porters.[13]

Raising funds for unions through sport benefits raised the political consciousness of the Afro-American community. In the early years of the Negro Baseball League white attendance was high, but this dropped off considerably after the First World War when Babe Ruth and radio helped lift white baseball to the forefront of the American consciousness. In Chicago, "the White Sox abandoned the 18,000 seat South Side Park in Chicago's Black Belt for the new Comiskey Stadium."[14]

Games between West Indian teams attracted to the area by railway jobs continued cricket's cosmopolitan tradition. West Indian cricket clubs developed cricketers, although a top-level standard of cricket was difficult to attain either in America or in the West Indies for several reasons:

The un-remitting concentration which becomes second nature to the county cricket batsmen or the players in high-grade club cricket in Australia is very hard for the West Indian
batsman to develop.... The best bowlers in the islands are snapped up by wealthy clubs to
bowl at practice, and local players are thus deprived of playing against these in inter-colonial
games. Furthermore, inter-colonial games are rare; many a batsmen gets one first-class
match a year; even when English teams come they play only two matches against island
teams, and a so-called test match. A batsman is keyed up for those brief occasions, but soon
slips back into easy-going habits. It is therefore a strain for him to score consistently against
the unremitting deadliness (comparatively speaking) of good first-class cricket....
It seems the habit of making long scores against first-class bowling like most other useful
habits owes much to the environment. Constantine ... agreed that you got into it after a time,
but complained that after a tour he dropped back into second rate club cricket and the habit-
ual concentration soon vanished.[15]

West Indian cricket in New York benefited from improved Island cricket. James notes
that between 1907 and 1911 batting in Barbados improved tremendously as Percy Goodman made two centuries in intercolonial competition in 1909 and "Tarilton, a white Barbadian, and George Challenor began to make their innumerable runs for Barbados....
Constantine was now at his very best. H.B.G. Austin was both stylish and reliable."[16]

When the University of Philadelphia CC played the English Public Schools in 1907,
Australian Herbert Vivian "Ranji" Hordern played for the University of Philadelphia
side. His dental studies precluded his touring with the Gentlemen of Philadelphia on their
1908 tour of England but Hordern was on the GOP team that visited Jamaica in 1909.
Ranji Hordern became one of the leading googlie bowlers of all time. When Australia played
the South Africans in 1910, "the South African team was loaded with googly bowlers and
Australia played South Africa at their own game in the Fourth and Fifth tests, by including the googly bowler Dr. Herbert Vivian ('Ranji') Hordern, who triumphed immediately.
His fourteen wickets helped Australia to victory in both matches."[17] Though the demands
of Hordern's dental practice cut short his test career, Johnny Moyes, a cricket commentator, wrote 37 years later that he was inclined to place Hordern ahead of Mailey and
Grimmett, Australia's two world-famous googlie bowlers, because of his better "control
of length, his disguised deliveries, his ability to flight the ball, and his clever fingers."[18]
Hordern played against New York teams while attending the University of Philadelphia.

In 1913, one of these New York teams, the West Indian Coloured team, took on a
strong Australia side captained by Austin Diamond with Warren Bardsley, Arthur Mailey, and Charlie Macartney at Celtic Park in Brooklyn on 8–9 August. The West Indians
were all out for 13 in their first innings, to which Australia replied with 213 runs. Richard
Cordice Ollivierre, from St. Vincent, took 7 Australian wickets for 57 runs, one of the
finest bowling performances against the Australians on their 1913 tour. Macartney, a devastating bowler for the Australians, took 17 wickets for 15 runs in both West Indies
innings. The West Indians performed better in the second innings, scoring 61 runs to
lose by an innings and 139 runs. By any standard the West Indian loss was a drubbing,
but it was clear that the West Indian Coloured team had made their mark on the New
York cricket scene.

New York cricket benefited directly from the improvement of cricket in the West
Indies, which supplied young recruits for the local New York and Boston area teams. The
Kingston Cricket Club was founded in Jamaica's capital city as early as 1844. After the First

Fields of dreams. Woodley Cricket Fields in Van Nuys with the Santa Monica Mountains in the background and Lake Balboa in the foreground. Source: Southern California Cricket Archives. Photographer: Michael Burke.

World War, Jamaican cricket achieved parity with that of its island neighbors, Trinidad, Barbados and St. Vincent. George Headley epitomized Jamaica's determination to lead cricket in the West Indies:

> When still only eighteen Headley had walked almost unannounced into big cricket in 1929, and scored 211 against one of the English teams which Jamaica has invited so frequently of recent years with such profitable results to her cricket.[19]

In the third test against England's team in 1930, Headley found a way to score runs off England's best bowler, Wilfred Rhodes, to win the match. Headley said,

> I had to do something. So I decided to get down to Rhodes as soon as he delivered the ball and hit the ball full pitch somewhere on the on-side boundary. Now I could not wait to judge the flight and choose the ball I would go down to. Rhodes was not giving the ball any air at all. I therefore had to make up my mind to depend upon his length, and periodically once or twice an over, as soon as the ball was out of his hand, I dashed and depended on his length for me to reach him full pitch. I did it all afternoon and we won.[20]

   Headley's improvisational batting technique stamped him as a unique cricket genius. He completely mastered Australia's best bowler, Grimmett, to score a double century. Headley knew it was an outstanding performance "because in those days the fielding side did not applaud.... But this day when Headley reached the century, Bradman, Ponsford, Kippax and the rest broke into spontaneous applause."[21] Headley restored cricket to the glamour of its golden era before the First World War, when batting was regarded as a dashing enterprise based on sound defensive technique. As the first black captain of the West Indies, Headley's batting skills were not lost on the West Indian community in the United States where his parents lived. Today, the West Indian community still fete George Headley with festival games played in his honor in New York, Miami and Los Angeles.

West Indian cricket flourished in New York through both wars and then expanded to Los Angeles in the late 1950s when air travel allowed direct travel to the West Coast from the West Indies. The four cricket-playing Durity brothers— Hollis, Herbert, Oscar and Anthony —from Trinidad, joined Earnest Wright's old team, the Los Angeles Cricket Club, where they played against cricketers such as Boris Karloff and Tommy Fairburn-Smith, who still played for Hollywood Cricket Club after the death of Sir Aubrey Smith. Oscar Durity joined the Durity family in Los Angeles after failing to make the great West Indian team captained by Gary Sobers. Sobers considered Oscar to be too slow a batsman despite Durity's scores of 97 not out and 101 against the Australian opening attack of Lillie and Thomson when he batted for Trinidad against the Australian test side. Roy Fredricks and Gordon Greenidge were preferred to Oscar Durity on the West Indian national side as they accumulated runs faster. Oscar joined his three cricket playing brothers— Herbert the wicket-keeper, and Anthony and Hollis, both fast bowlers— in Los Angeles. Between them the Duritys wrought a cricket revolution in southern California. The Los Angeles CC team won five successive Williamson Trophy knock-out competitions due to their prowess on the wicket in the 1950s. According to John Marder:

> Los Angeles became more and more the club of the West Indian cricketers and the club to which the cricketing immigrant naturally gravitated when he arrived from the islands, usually with his bats and pads. We owe a large debt to the West Indian immigration of the fifties which has given our cricket added excitement and skill.[22]

Wright's LACC team received strong opposition from the San Diego CC, which won the Williamson in 1953. After its initial success San Diego became dormant by 1962. The Britamer CC, founded in 1949 by Doc Severn, benefited from six cricket-playing Severn sons, three of whom, Cliff, Ray, and Winston, played for the United States. The Britamer CC won its first Williamson Trophy in 1955. While the Griffith Park ground, renamed the C. Aubrey Smith field after his death in 1948, remained the hub of southern California cricket activity through the 1960s, the growth of cricket required more fields and other grounds were found in "San Diego, Santa Barbara, Hermosa Beach, El Camino College, UCLA, El Salvador Field, Cal Tech, Henry Clay Junior High School, Pierce College, Milliken Junior Hugh in Sherman Oaks, Torrance West High School and in Marina Del Rey."[23]

Canadian interest in southern California cricket can be traced to the beginning of cricket in Los Angeles with teams such as the Canadian Legion. In 1955 there were visits from the "Toronto Ramblers, ... Calgary, Edmonton ... and Ottawa as a prelude to the revival of the match between Canada and the United States."[24] During the 1960s, John Marder, who had attended McGill University in Toronto before settling down to practice as a certified accountant in Beverly Hills, organized several tours to Canada.

Notable matches were also played locally. In a two-day match held in 1959, the Corinthians CC (founded in 1934 by Frank Doyle) played the Pasadena CC (founded in 1921) in a match celebrating the Corinthians' twenty-fifth anniversary. This was in the same year that "the Australian Old Collegians played Southern California, one of 68 games played during a world tour.... Southern California declared at 160 for six and put out the Australian XI for 125 to win the match."[25]

Los Angeles' secret weapon against the Australian XI was a strong West Indian cricketing contingent strengthened by the Beckford brothers, Audley and Linden, who mentored the recently arrived electrical engineer, Leo Magnus. In 1960 there were ten cricket teams in southern California: Britamer, Canadian Legion, Corinthians, Harlequins, Hollywood, Los Angeles, Pasadena, Santa Barbara, University and Venice. Many of the teams that played at Griffith Park benefited from the "British Brain Drain" to southern California as British trained engineers and doctors found good jobs in California when America geared up for moon travel after Sputnik was launched by the Russians. Pasadena CC became the dominant side in 1960, winning all three Griffith Park Cricket Association trophies: the C. Aubrey Smith (league), Williamson (knock-out) and the Marder Shield for the most wins in a season. In 1962 the newly formed Orange County CC won the Williamson Trophy in the first year of the club's existence.

After John Marder became president of the Griffith Park Cricket Association it was renamed the Southern California Cricket Association. Marder joined hands with a local Yorkshire-born cricket enthusiast, Tony Verity from Leeds, who immigrated to California to take up the professorship of neurosurgery at UCLA in 1959. They combined with Don King of the Canadian Cricket Association to resuscitate the Canada versus United States test match series after a 51-year hiatus. The collaboration bore fruit in the 44th United States versus Canada game held in Toronto in 1963. The Canadian team, captained by V.J. Walker of Toronto, easily defeated the U.S., which was all out for 117 runs in their first innings. Canada's Raymond Nascimento gave Canada an unassailable lead, scoring 176, the highest individual innings in the 123-year history of competition.

In 1964, the United States national side warmed up against a Midwestern All Star side at Forest Park in St. Louis. Bill Tatlock and Arun Mitra, both from the St. Louis CC, were selected for the United States side that played Canada. Cricket was played in 25 percent of Canada's schools, providing a greater pool of talent to draw on. The Canada versus United States game was played on September 6–7, 1964. Tony Clarke (Toronto CC), the Canadian captain, anticipated the U.S. players would have trouble against a spin attack and in a canny move brought on the spin-bowlers early while there was still some shine on the ball. The move succeeded brilliantly when Chris Bonadine took 6 for 7. Canada then batted well and declared after Raymond Nascimento and Frank Clark put on a fine stand of 116 for the second wicket. This left the U.S. to score 174 to avoid an innings defeat. Herbert Durity of Los Angeles stayed in two hours to fend off the Canadian spin attack, scoring 35 out of 63 as the U.S. was defeated by an innings and 94 runs.[26]

Though the United States were handily defeated by the Canadians, preparations for the test match breathed new life into United States cricket. In St. Louis, John Marder convened a meeting that established the United States of America Cricket Association (USACA) as the governing body for U.S. cricket. Not all was harmony, as New York only belatedly gave USACA their support, having been shut out of the initial deliberations. New York came on board in 1964 after they were invited to field a team against the visiting English County Champions, the Yorkshire CCC. John Marder's status as a U.S. cricket leader was reinforced when the MCC invited him to become a life member and the United States became a playing member of the Imperial Cricket Conference. Changed political realities in a postcolonial world resulted in the ICC being renamed the International Cricket Conference.[27]

There was great excitement in American cricketing circles when the Yorkshire County Cricket Club, English county champions, flew to New York from London on September 17 to start their American cricket tour in New York. The tour manager was Ron Roberts, a cricket impresario and member of the Somerset County Cricket Club committee. A veteran of five overseas tours, Ron played for the Cavaliers. The Yorkshire CCC was captained by Brian Close. The YCCC team had six England players on the side including "Firey" Fred Truman, the first bowler to take 300 wickets in test cricket. Known as a "bad boy" to the MCC authorities, his antics on test tours were occasionally confused with those of Dennis Compton who had an equally fine head of black hair in his prime. With his playing days over, Fred Truman became one of cricket's most sought after commentators. Brian Johnston recalls Truman played his cricket with "such astute tacticians and technicians as Hutton, Illingworth and Close.... He might have in fact made a great captain, and can at least be proud of his great achievement in 1968. In the absence of Brian Close he captained Yorkshire against the Australians at Sheffield and Yorkshire beat them for the first time since 1902 by an innings and sixty-nine runs.[28]

All the players mentioned by Johnston toured with Truman and Geoffrey Boycott. Boycott, one of the greatest modern opening batsmen, was renowned for his meticulous batting that led to consistently high scores. He scored 100 centuries in first-class cricket like W.G. Grace. The tour gave the opportunity for all the Yorkshire CCC players, on a team loaded with test-quality talent, to experience an overseas tour. The first game against the Brooklyn League proved tougher than anticipated. Without Boycott, who was in hospital following a strong reaction to a smallpox vaccination,

> Yorkshire turned out with only ten men against a Brooklyn Eleven composed of West Indians on Mount Vernon baseball park — the worst ground world traveler Trueman says he has ever played on — and finished up well on top of a drawn game.
>
> Batting first on a dishonest matting wicket that had the ball flying high over the heads of the six-foot-plus men like Dick Hutton or else keeping low or grubbing under the bat, Yorkshire hit a declared 217 for 8 in three and a half hours. Close set the pace with a sparkling 76 which included four 6's.
>
> Close used five bowlers before he was able to separate the second wicket pair Trevor Best and Tony King-then he learned that they had played for Barbados and Trinidad.
>
> The pair put on 95 before Don Wilson beat Best at 44 on 110 for 2. King went on to make 56, but once he went it would have been only a matter of time before Yorkshire bowled the rest out. Alas it became too dark at 130 for 4.[29]

Drawing the first game, Yorkshire CCC won their second game against the New York All Stars by 68 runs. Richard Hutton — son of the great Yorkshire and England player Sir Len Hutton — scored 46 and Phil Sharpe scored 22 when they opened the batting for Yorkshire. The third game of the tour was against a British Commonwealth Cricket Club in Washington, D.C. that "included players from a remarkable assortment of countries and who had as their scorer a gentleman called Ray Honda — an American of full Japanese parentage."[30] The Yorkshire players visited the Capitol after the game and presented "a cricket ball to Senator McCormack the No. 2 to the President while the vice-presidency was vacant. We were quite impressed with his New England 'old England' charm.

It was quite amazing to find a senior statesman in the greatest power on earth shaking each of the young cricketers warmly by the hand and immediately calling them by their Christian names."[31]

The humility of the Yorkshire champions was endearing to American and Canadian hosts. After their game in Washington, Yorkshire played three games in Canada with their last game played at Brockton Point in Stanley Park, Vancouver. A favorite ground of Sir Donald Bradman and many southern California sides, the ground has a "backcloth of pine-clad mountains ... and the tall tree encircled greenness that once was the Red Indian village of the Whoi Whoi tribe. Totem poles stare down at such as Freddie Trueman. Somehow all this is symbolic and significant—cricket where once they danced the war dance, willow bats now for whalebone tomahawks."[32]

Los Angeles provided a glitzy Hollywood contrast to the Northwest. A warm welcome was arranged by "America's Mr. Cricket, Bradford born Dr. Anthony Verity—no relation to Hedley Verity.... He is now secretary of the American Cricket Association [sic]."[33] Yorkshire CCC played two matches on the Sir Aubrey Smith ground at Griffith Park on September 27–30, 1964. Playing the first game on a blue matting pitch, Padgett was the leading scorer with 50, followed by Boycott (45) and Brian Close (40), as Yorkshire CCC defeated Southern California by a score of 250 to 78 runs. The hard hitting West Indian Linden Beckford put up the chief resistance, scoring 41 runs.[34]

In the second game against a Southern California All Star team, Yorkshire CCC were 369 for 9 declared with Ray Illingworth scoring his second century of the tour. The *Los Angeles Times* reporter Alan Thompson described the annihilation:

> In just 205 minutes the happy Tykes thrashed 326, and even the South Californians had to grudgingly admire the way their side was being hammered.
> Southern California could muster only 65 in an innings which stuttered along for 1 hr. 35 mins. And the greater part of those runs came from a man with a famous Yorkshire name, Tony Verity. He went in first wicket down and steadily claimed 23 before falling to Don Wilson.
> The slow left-arm turned in the tour's best analysis to date with a splendid six wickets for 11 runs in eight overs of which half were maidens.
> Southern California simply had no answer to him — or to Illingworth.[35]

After the game the Yorkshire CCC were entertained at the Roosevelt Hotel in Hollywood. In reporting the Yorkshire CCC visit, the *Los Angeles Times* revisited the story of Sir Aubrey Smith ordering his butler to bring him a new pair of glasses from his Rolls Royce after he dropped a catch. In 1964, 16 years after his death, the great character actor's presence in the Sir Aubrey Smith cricket pavilion at the Griffith Park cricket fields remained palpable. The *Los Angeles Times* described the Griffith Park ground as "this pretty little arena with an old fashioned pavilion with Sir Aubrey's own bat, ball and stumps in pride of place in the room."[36] Lady Smith, 92 years old, turned out to watch the Yorkshire CCC and recalled "Gubby Allen's team passing through on the way back from Australia in 1937."[37]

After he became president of the MCC, Allen recalled a brilliant catch by the 75-year-old Aubrey Smith at second slip to get him out when he played for Pasadena against Hollywood CC.[38] Having stirred memories and having created a little history of their own, Yorkshire CCC departed Los Angeles for Bermuda where their guest player Gary Sobers joined them as they overpowered the local sides. Brian Close achieved his objective of giving the non–MCC tour members on his side a 15,000 mile, three-week trip to remember, with a record of nine wins and no losses in 12 games. Thirty-five years later, when playing with the Lord Taverners in 1999, "Closey" still vividly remembered the hospitality of the Southern California Cricket Association when he stayed at the Sportsman's Lodge in Van Nuys. On that occasion, the revered England captain emphasized that cricket was a sideways game. Fred Truman also recalled his trip to California in his 2003 visit to the Philadelphia Cricket Festival as guest of honor, to a highly appreciative American cricket audience, in the ballroom of the Philadelphia Cricket Club.

News of Yorkshire's successful visit to the U.S. traveled fast on the English county cricket circuit with the result that in 1965, Ken Flavel of Worcestershire CCC decided to play his benefit year in Los Angeles, the same year that Worcestershire wrested the county championship from Yorkshire. As reigning county champions, Worcestershire CCC played a Southern California President's XI selected by SCCA president Claude Worrell. Five of the Southern California players had represented the United States against Canada. The team, captained by Jim Reid (Pasadena), included Chani Bains (Hollywood CC), Linden Beckford (Los Angeles CC), Hollis Durity (Los Angeles CC), Abid Hussain (Pasadena), Anil Lashkari (Pasadena), Leo Magnus (University CC), Ray Murdoch (University CC), Anton Perera (Orange County), and Cliff and Ray Severn (Britamer). Ron Roberts wrote in the *Daily Telegraph*,

> Jet travel is causing cricket — that dignified relative of baseball — to burgeon in California. One of the attractions is Griffith Park's unique cricket ground, named for the late English actor, Sir C. Aubrey Smith. Teams from major cricketing countries are making it their mecca in America.
>
> The Champions of England, Worcestershire will play at Southern California there Saturday in a 1 day, one innings game.... Worcester, which won 18, lost 3, and drew 7 in its 28 game schedule, has one of the world's greatest shotmakers in Tom Graveney. Tom is having a terrific world tour, compiling big scores in almost every game, with a top of 161 against Malaysia. His skipper Don Kenyon is another hard hitter.
>
> One of the fast bowlers, Ken Flavel, depends on overpowering speed. The other, Len Coldwell, uses pin point control of "swing" in either direction. Norm Gifford and Doug Slade provide a mixture of breaking balls which have furrowed the brows of the best bats in the business.
>
> California has a strong team, led by Jim Reid, Cliff Severn, Hollis Durity and Leo Magnus.[39]

The Southern California team performed well against a Worcestershire side that included the South African–born player Basil D'Oliveira. D'Oliveira left South Africa to play for England because as a colored player, apartheid laws precluded his participation on the South African team. Unfortunately, after their departure, Ron Roberts, who was involved in organizing both English county visits to the United States, died at the untimely age of 38. He left a cricket touring legacy in southern California, inspiring several southern California teams— notably Hollywood CC, Corinthians and University CC — to tour British Columbia and Mexico City, where the Reforma Club, located at 8,000 feet, was the venue used by the British Consulate for cricket.[40]

United States cricket was strengthened by matches between the U.S. and Canada and English county visits. A seasoned Southern California side toured Vancouver as a prelude

The four concrete wickets of Plano, Texas. Source: Public Relations Packet for U.S. Trials in 2002.

to its game against New Zealand. The New Zealand team was managed by the 1948 New Zealand captain Walter Hadlee, "a great figure in the game, a batsman of culture, class and achievement."[41] Walter Hadlee had six sons and three played for New Zealand. His son Sir Richard Hadlee, knighted for his services to New Zealand cricket, became the first test bowler to take 400 test wickets. The Hadlee sons were yet to break onto the international scene. Captained by John Reid, the New Zealand side included the great veteran left-hand batsmen Bert Sutcliffe, who had batted with Walter Hadlee when they played for Otago CC against the MCC captained by Walter Hammond in 1947.[42] The left-handed Sutcliffe held the world record of 385 runs playing for Otago versus Canterbury. An elegant batsman and graceful stoke player, he won an adulation uncommon before the era of sponsorship, television, and high pressure publicity. Tommy Freebairn-Smith reported in the *Los Angeles Times*, "The Anzacs come directly from a three game stop-over in England, where they won one and lost a pair. Before that they broke even in tours of India and Pakistan."[43]

In a coincidence, both New Zealand and Southern California were captained by two different Reids. The New Zealand John Reid "was an expert in all his field-batting, fielding, wicket-keeping, bowling fast-medium or off-breaks or off-cutters. He was without question the most successful all rounder in New Zealand cricket. He was a good, assertive captain."[44] The southern California Jim Reid had done much to improve the quality of southern California cricket by setting a no-nonsense tone of professionalism in the middle. Loath to cede momentum, Reid became renowned for his quirky bowling changes that often achieved the desired effect of trapping a batsman unawares, restoring game momentum to his side. In the New Zealand game, Southern California was not able to put enough runs on the board so it was the New Zealand John Reid that claimed victory. The young New Zealand side, which included future New Zealand greats Graham Dowling, Bevan Congdon, Richard Collinge, Frank Cameron and Richard Motz, returned home well seasoned, after games against India, Pakistan, the Swiss Cricket Association on their European leg of the tour, England and Southern California.

Cricket was thriving not only in Los Angeles in 1965 Jim Marwick, writing in the *Guardian*, noted that New York cricket also percolated with a

> standard of cricket ... higher than might be supposed. There are a handful of ex–first class players available and a fair percentage have played good club or university cricket. If American cricket is at all in the category of "coarse cricket" it is because of the difficulties inherent in playing the game at all, not through the lack of ability. The first problem is the finding of a place to play. The Staten Island club is particularly fortunate in that a piece of land was given to the New York Borough of Richmond by a Mr. Walker on the condition that on it cricket should have priority over baseball. The wicket is matting, and the team lays it before the game.... Such is cricket in New York, aggressively amateur but thriving. And Staten Island has an ace up its sleeve. It has in its possession the lease by which the Oval was transferred on January 11, 1864, to a Miss Mary Sheppard and her successors. One of the successors lost the document to the club because of its vice-president's superior skill at poker.[45]

The Sheppard lease granted grazing rights at the Oval. Sheep were hard to find in Hawaii when the North California Cricket Association selected a team to play the Honolulu Cricket Club in Hawaii in 1965. The Northern California team financed its own way to the islands where Honolulu CC won two of the three games. In Washington, D.C., the Commonwealth CC played a local Jamaican team under the watchful eye of their new patron Senator Leander McCormack. Cricket flourished throughout the United States in 1965 and John Marder, as president of USCA at a banquet honoring the West Indies cricket team hosted by the Northern Cricket Society in the Guild Hall Hotel in Leeds, was well positioned to capitalize on the enthusiasm. At the banquet, John Marder went so far as to make a plea for the West Indies, captained by Gary Sobers, to visit the United States and offer their coaching support in the schools. In his toast to Gary Sobers and his team, John Marder did not let his enthusiasm for the game undermine his sense of perspective when he noted, "American cricket will always be a minor sport but nonetheless significant on the world scene."[46]

Not long after John Marder's speech, a slag heap covered the mining village of Aberfan in Wales. A cricket game was organized in southern California as part of the disaster fund raising efforts. The inimitable Jack Smith of the *Los Angeles Times* reported $3,000 was collected at the match held at the Santa Monica City College stadium between a celebrity team and the Corinthian Cricket Club. He wrote:

> Hollywood's debonair British colony put on a rather improper cricket match Sunday in Santa Monica to raise money for Aberfan, the disaster-stricken Welsh village. Quite improper!
> First, the mayor of Santa Monica apologized for the weather. A faux pas. It was excellent weather, for cricket. Cold and gray, with a wind off the North Sea. Then the phonograph ran

down during the playing of "God Save the Queen." The match itself was a travesty. It should have been filmed and issued as "Carry on Cricket!"

Miss Joan Collins bowled the first ball for the all-stars— underhand; Miss Caroll Baker played a position called "square leg" if you can fancy that; Terry Thomas, the amiable cad, hissed at an umpire through the gap in his uppers; Milton Berle cheated; and a pair of Play-boy Bunnies served tea.[47]

Other stars involved in the event were Steve McQueen, James Mason, John Mills, Noel Harrison, Margaret Leighton, Sue Lyon, Lionel Jeffries, Ryan O'Neal, the Smothers Brothers, Jack Jones and Michael Callan.

On the serious side of the cricket ledger in 1966, a Southern Californian XI played the United States of America invitational XI at the Westminster High School in Orange County. This game was a prelude to the forty-ninth annual U.S. versus Canada test match, tied the previous year in Calgary. In that drawn game, Jim Reid was the U.S. top scorer with 57 and 19, while Dr. Alf Cooper of San Francisco took 6 wickets for 109 runs for the U.S. The Olympic Club of San Francisco helped players such as Dr. Cooper play to a higher level through their participation in the Price Cup league competition of northern California. The Price Cup got its name from Thomas Price, who was still actively involved in club affairs after leading his Barbarians team to the California League championship in 1913.

Over half a century later in 1966, Jim Reid led the California renaissance in cricket, captaining the United States to victory over Canada for the first time since the test series resumed. Larrier's spin bowling caught the Canadians by surprise in their second innings. The doyen of England's cricket correspondents, E.W. "Jim" Swanton, writing in the *Daily Telegraph*, was impressed by the win. He wrote:

I suppose one could catch most people by asking them which is the oldest of all international cricket rivalries. The answer not England versus Australia (which dates from 1876/77) but the United States versus Canada, who first played one another in New York in 1844....

The spiritual center is Southern California — not Philadelphia — when touring teams used regularly to visit England — and it is there that several famous visiting sides have been entertained. These include Yorkshire, Worcestershire, Canada and New Zealand.

Have a look at the atlas, calculate the distances involved, and one must take off one's hat to the Californians for their enthusiasm and for surmounting the practical difficulty of paying traveling expenses across their vast continent.[48]

While Swanton was writing about southern California's rise to prominence in American cricket he knew that Mike Brearley was studying at the two-year-old University of California Irvine campus in Orange County. England's future cricket captain had recently graduated from Cambridge University with a first in psychology. He played first-class cricket for Middlesex CCC before taking up psychology graduate studies in southern California. He had to be granted a leave of absence from his studies after he was appointed captain of England's Under 25 team to tour Pakistan in 1967 by the MCC. The *Los Angeles Times* reported:

Pakistan will be quite a change of scenery for London born and raised Brearley, who decided he wanted to continue his graduate studies in philosophy [sic] at UCI after having read Professor A.I. Melden's book, "Free Action," while in his first year of graduate work at Cambridge.

Dean Samuel McCullough, head of UCI's humanities, has granted Brearley a leave of absence....

McCullough, an Australian by birth, has outstanding cricket credentials himself. He played on the club team at UCLA from 1938–40 and then coached the UCLA cricket club team for three more years 1941–43 while a graduate student....

Brearley ... will be the only player on the team not considered a professional.... Mike played in the first class cricket league in 1966 and spent six months on a representative of the English team touring South Africa in 1964–65 and competed against top ranked cricketers in the 17 team league while an undergraduate at Cambridge.

Mike is not overly concerned because of his lack of practice since late September. "The cold and rainy weather in England this time of year make it practically impossible to practice outside anyhow," said Mike.

"The indoor practicing is marginal, since you can't work batting under nature's conditions. The outdoor grass has different types of breaks and bends and the pitched ball will react differently. It's very difficult to duplicate actual playing conditions indoors," Brearley concluded.[49]

Brearley played for Pasadena CC while attending UC Irvine. Pasadena CC was one of the few teams that predated the Sir Aubrey Smith era in southern California. Under the canny captaincy of Jim Reid, it had become the best team in southern California. Anil Lashkari opened the batting for Pasadena. Anil, a chemical engineer from Ahmedabad, was from a prominent textile family. His grandfather, Bechardas Ambavidas Lashkari, built the first textile mill there in 1865. Anil attended Leeds University in England and played for the Yorkshire Universities XI versus Yorkshire. Selected for All India versus Commonwealth, he sat on the bench as twelfth-man for India in 1954. In California, his apparently effortless, graceful, left-handed opening batting consistently compiled innings over 50 runs. These high opening scores were remarkable, as an English journalist covering Mike Brearley at Griffith Park pointed out, because on most cricket grounds in southern California

the grass in the outfield was so thick that the only way to hit a boundary was to lift the ball almost for a six. The most powerful cover drive on the ground produced only one run so that an individual score of 30 or so was quite extraordinary. But the most astonishing thing about the afternoon was the SMOG. Most of us associate California with sunshine and beaches, film stars and bathing beauties but L.A. certainly has one more claim to fame.... How the fast bowlers managed to continue I don't know, and for the batsman to run a three was to invite death by suffocation.[50]

Mike Brearley had a beneficial impact on cricket within the University of California system. UC Irvine was one of eight University of California campuses; cricket was played at three of them, Berkeley, Irvine and UCLA. Cricket was financed by the physical education department at UCLA, where the ubiquitous organizer Dr. Tony Verity was responsible — along with Dr. Peter Lomax, another British "brain-drain" immigrant to UCLA — for establishing the Art versus Science annual cricket fixtures played at Spalding Field adjoining the basketball stadium. UCLA Chancellor Murphy and his successor Chancellor Young attended the decade-long series of games as honorary guests. Such distinguished attendance at cricket games was sorely needed in 1967 because Mayor Yorty announced to the Los Angeles City Council that he planned to turn the Sir C. Aubrey Smith Griffith Park cricket fields into an equestrian center. To their credit the cricketers rallied quickly to protect their turf. The *Los Angeles Times* reported:

Protests against possible elimination of the Smith Field were carried to the commission by John Marder, United States Cricket Association president; Claude V. Worrell, president

Southern California cricket association, and Patrick Cooney, chairman of the grounds committee.[51]

Ironically — because cricket was first played by polo players on polo grounds in Santa Monica 80 years previous— it was polo players' lascivious eyes that wanted the grounds. At times they may have been tempted to do a cavalry charge on the flannelled fools at the wicket. Polo, unlike cricket, adapted to American needs after the First World War wiped out most of Britain's top polo players. Polo horses increased in height from 14 to 17 hands as polo became a millionaires' sport in the United States. Though they were arrayed against an affluent group, the cricketers rallied behind Mrs. Morton, president of the Recreation and Parks Commission, who pointed out that

> the city had pledged to find a new location for the C. Aubrey Smith cricket field and should deal most gently with the cooperating cricketers....
> The cricket association earlier protested that 3000 Los Angeles tax paying cricketers are being forced to make way for less than 11 tax-paying polo players.
> Association representative Claude Worrell told the commission that was the number of city tax payers among the polo players....
> William Frederickson Jr., general manager of the Department of Recreation and Parks, said that there was grassed playing field space available now in the Sepulveda Dam Basin....
> He said it might be advisable if the commission requests the cricket association to use its own funds to build a new club house in the Sepulveda Dam Basin.[52]

Barbados-born Claude Worrell's election as president of the SCCA was fortunate as he was a lawyer well versed in fighting discrimination in all its forms. Worrell was distantly related to one of the icons of West Indian cricket, Frank Worrell, the revered West Indian cricket captain from Barbados who was knighted for his services to the game. Claude Worrell numbered Congressman Mervyn Dymally (Compton) and Superior Court Judge Alvin Niles among his political allies. Niles was born in St. Vincent and Dymally was born in Jamaica. They were keen cricketers and members of the SCCA. Dymally became lieutenant governor of California under Governor Pat Brown. He became a key Afro-America leader in California after the Watts Riots in Los Angeles in 1965.[53] Well funded white polo players versus racially mixed cricket sides could have been a combustible mix in the political arena. It is to the credit of the Recreation and Parks Commission that they handled the turf battle so adroitly.

Claude Worrell's election as president of the SCCA reflected the increasing numbers of West Indian cricketers in southern California. Bhumgara (of Belize) was the first recorded West Indian cricketer playing in southern California, for Los Angeles CC in 1908. The Durity brothers— Hollis and Herbert — were pioneers of the major wave of West Indian immigration to Los Angeles which occurred when the Islands were directly linked to southern California by scheduled airline flights in the 1960s. Regular scheduled flights also revolutionized the MCC's contacts with the United States. Tours no longer needed to take over a month to allow for ocean liner transport at both ends. Two week tours of the United States became the norm. This was the case for the 1967 MCC tour of Canada and the United States, captained by David Silk. The British Embassy in Washington hosted the MCC on August 29 at the Rotunda. The tour was made as part of Canada's centenary celebrations. The four MCC games in the United States were played against the British Commonwealth Club CC and the Southern Zone — which comprised California players-at Potomac Park, Staten Island and the Brooklyn League at Red Hook Stadium in Brooklyn. The great West Indies and Barbados batsman Everton Weekes played for the MCC, which drew its game with the Staten Island CC and won the other three. Several of the players who played the MCC were selected for the U.S. side, which lost in Montreal to Canada by an innings and nine runs.[54]

The 17-man United States cricket team financed its own way to England in 1968. The U.S. team was managed by Dr. Tony Verity and had four southern California players: Hollis Durity, Anil Lashkari, Winston and his brother Ray Severn.[55] The skipper, Dr. Alf Cooper, and Kenneth Serpanchy were from San Francisco; Mike Stollemeyer lived in Washington, D.C.; and Les Fernandes was from Philadelphia. Both Stollemeyer and Fernandes were worthy heirs of West Indian cricketing families. A 17-fixture tour against English minor county (Triple A) competition was made less daunting by the beautiful accommodation provided by John Gardiner at his country house, "Plovers," in Kent. The first few games were played close to Gardiner's home. In a tradition usually reserved for visiting Australian test sides, the U.S. tour started on July 20 at Arundel in Sussex against the Duke of Norfolk's XI. The duke flew to the ground in his helicopter to watch his team, which drew the game. One-day games continued at Cranbrook against the Free Foresters, Kent CCC XI at Tonbridge Wells, and Sussex CCC at Hastings before the U.S. team moved to their new base, the Clarendon Hotel in London, to play Hertfordshire at Hitchin and the MCC. Gerard Dent, cricket correspondent for *The Observer*, captured the significance of the U.S. playing the MCC at Lord's:

> Yesterday the Stars and Stripes flew over Lord's for the first time for 96 years in honour of the first truly national American team to visit this country.
>
> This time it was cricket only and the MCC got their revenge for 1874. They fielded a strong team which included one Test and four first-class players and the American defeat by nine wickets was far from dishonorable.
>
> They batted first and after an early disaster, when their leading batsman, Fernandes, son of the West Indian Test player was run out, the lusty hitting of the brothers Severn from California, of Lashkari, the Indian opener from Los Angeles, and a Philadelphian Lancastrian, Brook, took them to 117.
>
> In the field the Americans stopped the ball uncertainly but threw it magnificently — low over the stumps and deadly accurate. They took only one wicket, but who can blame them with Saeed Ahmed striking the ball with his own special elegance and A.R. Day thumping a half-century? Thackhurdin was the best of the bowlers with a low, and very fast trajectory.
>
> The most important aspect of yesterday was that this match took place and the present tour is taking place; it means a great deal to American cricket.[56]

Not since Harry Wright and Arthur Goodwill Spalding took the Boston Red Stockings and Philadelphia Athletics to Lord's in 1874 to demonstrate baseball, then defeated the MCC and Ground in a game of cricket, had Americans played on the turf described by John Marder in the *The New York Times* as the Valhalla at Lord's. Arthur Spalding scored the most in the 1874 game, with 25 runs. In 1968 it was Alfred Brook, a member of the General Electric CC in Philadelphia, who scored 25 runs for the U.S. John Lee reported in the *The New York Times*:

> Of the 17 players in the touring side, three are native born Americans and most others have Commonwealth backgrounds. Six are from the West Indies, two from England, two from Ireland, and one each from Australia, Ceylon, India and Pakistan.

Their occupations range from biochemist to stevedore, and their average age is 28. They look rather natty in their blue blazers, encrusted with the team badge, an American eagle rampant over a horizontal bat.[57]

The *Daily Telegraph* noted that the strong MCC side needed only 117 minutes to dispose of the Americans, though brothers Raymond and Winston Severn stopped a total rout with a seventh inning partnership of 30 runs.[58] Of the heavy defeat at Lord's, Winston Severn in *Time* magazine offered this analysis: "We were a bit tight like an English team would be playing at Yankee Stadium for the first time."[59] Ted Clark's fast bowling simply overpowered the U.S. as he took 4 for 20 for the MCC while the U.S. dismissal was a run out. The MCC loss proved a test of character for the U.S. side, which traveled to Cleethorpes to play the Lincolnshire CCC minor county side. This was the first time a U.S. team had played Lincolnshire since 1903 when Bart King, on a team captained by Sir Arthur Priestley, scored 176 against a Lincolnshire XVI in Grantham. The Lincolnshire game was a draw.

The next game, against Nottinghamshire CCC at Trent Bridge, was played on a test wicket before the U.S. traveled to Northumberland where they earned the respect of local cricketers. Writing in the *Sunderland Echo*, Clive Page reported:

Two of the American side played entertaining cricket indeed. Lashkari, 12th man for India in 1956 [*sic*], and Fernandes who has played representative cricket in the West Indies, both gave the Northumberland attack a rough time.
Fernandes played the spinners beautifully and produced sweep shots off Norton and McNab that were a joy to see.
Wisdom who played many times for Jamaica contributed a chanceless 33, but these three found little support though Brook surprised everybody by walking down the wicket to Johnson repeatedly and driving him.... Lashkari and Fernandes took the score to 102 before Lashkari was bowled playing back to Greensword.[60]

Northumberland, scoring 267 for 5, declared as the U.S. held on for a draw with 200 for 9 wickets. Tough games were played against Durham, A.J. McAlpine's XI, Staffordshire, Worcestershire, Shropshire, Cheshire, Warwickshire, and Lancashire, before the U.S. played the Incogniti CC at Tonbridge on their return to John Gardiner's country house in Kent. Ford Motor Company sponsored the U.S. team's travel throughout the United Kingdom. The United States played the Incogniti CC at Tonbridge School where Colin Cowdrey first put bat to ball. Tim Heald in the *Daily Express* announced:

The mauve and gold and blue flag of the Incogniti fluttered from the flagpole, and above it the red, white, and blue of the Stars and Stripes....
A LARGE coach in the car park gave the game away completely. It had "U.S. Cricket Tour" on its side.... The current tour is the first ever staged by a full United States side, and it must be admitted that the players have not been as successful as the Gentlemen of Philadelphia.
Most of the matches have been against minor counties and of the 18 so far they have won only the one against Hertfordshire....
"QUITE FAIRLY I'll say we are just below minor counties standard," said the 60-year-old John L. Marder, president of the United States Cricket Association....
There are 150 clubs in the United States.... Most have to play in public parks as they are short of funds. All the equipment comes from England and there is a 20 percent import duty to protect non-existent American manufacturers....
The U.S. touring team returns soon for its annual match against Canada. It will be in Philadelphia and a crowd of 2000 is expected on each day.

> Before the team leaves here it is playing a Surrey team at the Oval and at the moment it is threatening to exercise a curious old right it has—"to graze sheep on the pitch there."

This right was won in 1870. In a game of poker.[61]

In organizing a fixture at the Oval, the 1968 U.S. tour of England emulated that of 1874, organized by C.W. Alcock of the Surrey CCC for Harry Wright. Such was the power of cricket tradition between England and the United States. After losing to a Surrey CCC side, the U.S. penultimate game was against Cambridgeshire; the team finished with a draw against Suffolk at Felixstowe. The progress of the U.S. tour had been closely watched in Philadelphia by the remaining members of the 1921 Philadelphia Pilgrims team that toured England. These members provided the last remaining link with American cricket in its Philadelphia glory days before the First World War.

The 95-year-old John Lester and Christie Morris were honored by the Merion Golf Club on March 15, 1969, at an event celebrating the opening of the C.C. Morris Library at Haverford College. The U.S. tour manager in England, Dr. Verity, was invited to this remarkable event in which the finest proponents of America's cricket tradition were on hand to pass the baton from one generation to the next. The C.C. Morris Library has continued to preserve the institution of cricket in America, providing protection — through historical relativity — from indifference and imposters who claim the sport for their own ego or political ends. Christie Morris entrusted the records held at the library to Dr. Howard Comfort, a Haverford University archaeologist, Haverford University cricket coach and a fine cricketer steeped in Philadelphia's cricket achievements. Ultimately, the U.S. cricket tour of England raised the quality of cricket in United States for another generation as competition between all the major cricket centers in the United States was enhanced. Dr. Verity noted that after 1968 many local cricket clubs felt they could organize tours, and they did so with increased regularity.

In 1969 Don Weekes, nephew to Sir Everton Weekes the great Barbados batsman, joined the University CC. A powerful hitter of the ball with immense forearms, Don Weekes arrived in Los Angeles from Barbados with solid West Indian batting credentials. He had the world record for the highest innings for a 15-year-old in first-class cricket, and he had earned the admiration of Sir Garfield Sobers, the West Indian captain, who said, "Don Weekes was the best cricketer never to play for the West Indies." Many cricketers who have made it to the cusp of international recognition, not quite to make it, suffer considerable psychological damage from having been so close to their ultimate goal, but Weekes' character was infused with a work ethic that enabled him to shrug off disappointment and move on to greater achievement. He played a brilliant decade with University CC, helping it win the SCCA league championship eight years in a row. He led southern California's batting averages in 1969, scoring a total of 672 runs in 16 innings for an innings average of 51.7. His highest score was 164 not out. On the strength of his batting he was selected to play for the U.S. versus Canada in the fifty-first game between the two countries, held at UCLA's Spalding Field in 1970. The *Daily Bruin* reported, "Don Weekes the star batsman ... was chosen to captain both the SCCA and U.S. teams."[62] The same article also reported:

> During the past two seasons the ... club has probably been the most successful team ever to play cricket in the area. The club has won the league championship, the knock-out competition, the six-a-side tournament and the league shield for total victories in both years. In

Cricket in front of the Hollywood sign. As cricket has expanded in the United States to over 10,000 players, cricket organizers have shown considerable imagination in finding new grounds to play on. This dog park in Hollywood offers a great setting for matches of the Southern California Cricket Social League, which now has been assigned a regular ground in Erwin Park, North Hollywood. Source: Sentance Collection.

many respects, however, the greatest achievement was in July 1970 when the team toured British Columbia and won the Victoria Centennial Cricket Trophy, against a side chosen from all the clubs on Vancouver Island, returning the trophy to Southern California for the first time since its inception in 1962.[63]

Opening the batting against British Columbia with Rick Bunsah, the University CC and U.S. captain, Don Weekes scored 201 not out as the UCC declared at 264 for 3. This was the first time — in over a century of cricket between the two regions— a double century had been scored against a British Columbian team by a southern California player.

"The Don's" presence attracted other good West Indian players to the UCC side, including the Jamaican Leo Magnus. Magnus joined Australian-born and baseball trained bowler Ray Murdoch (previously of the Hollywood CC) to form the UCC opening bowling attack, which lasted for a decade. Guyanese born Denis Stuart also joined the team. (Denis later became the West Coast representative for the Western Zone at USACA meetings.) Hasib Khan (who learned cricket in Pakistan) joined the team in 1972 prior to UCC's first England tour. The tour included fixtures against Guiness CC, Twickenham CC, Stoics, Circencester CC, Gloucester Club and Ground and Thornbury CC. Thornbury CC was near the Alveston home of W.G. Grace, which the UCC players visited. The Gloucestershire venues gave Leo Magnus the opportunity to play an invitational game for the Gloucester Seconds. Then using their credentials as a University of California side, the UCC players took on the English Public Schools Cricket Association which was defeated in a very exciting game with a winning four coming off the last ball of the match by Tony Verity. The remaining games of the tour were against the XL Club, John Gardiner's XI at Tonbridge Wells and Epsom CC. The 16-game UCC tour ended with 8 wins, 6 draws, 1 loss and 1 rain out. In the absence of Don Weekes, Anil Lashkari led the averages, scoring 654 runs for an average of 54.5. Denis Stuart was second with 31.6 while skipper Jim Reid averaged 27.92.

In 1971, two Orange County CC players, Jamaican born players, Basil Brown and Ray Mogg, were selected to play for the U.S. team that played Canada in Hamilton, Ontario. John Marder managed the team. Ray Mogg scored 50 in the U.S. first innings of 230 and Basil Brown scored 22. Canada made a bold declaration with 206 for 7 before the United States replied with 130, Ray Mogg again top-scoring with 31 runs. Basil Brown almost won the game for the U.S., taking 4 for 61 as Canada squeaked home by one wicket with 157 for 9. Basil Brown was at the top of his game in 1971. Later in the year, Dr. Peter Lomax (University CC) and Jean Wong (Orange County CC) organized a Southern California Cricket Association tour of Jamaica. Basil Brown's experience was invaluable in facing the Jamaican "quicks." Brown and Pablo McNeil (Los Angeles CC) were the best performers in the first Southern California team to tour Jamaica. The Southern Californians compiled a winning record of 9 won, 3 drawn and 3 lost in Jamaica. Ray Murdoch (then still playing for Hollywood CC) captained the side. In his opinion,

> success was largely due to the bowlers. Haseeb Khan bowled exceptionally, breaking through the opening batsman in nearly every game he played. Haseeb finished with 23 wickets for 257 runs, average 11.17. Basil Brown took over where Haseeb left off and spun out the remaining batsmen, especially against his old team Lucas, where he took 5 wickets for 10 runs. Basil took 5 wickets in an innings 4 times and finished with 35 for 417, an average of 11.91. Haseeb and Basil were ably assisted by Pablo McNeil, Denis Stuart, Jim Fleming and Leo Magnus....
>
> In general the fielding was very good; the catching, especially in the deep, was quite spectacular. Pablo McNeil took 4 catches with his back to the wall at Sabina Park. Anton Perera (O.C.), Haseeb Khan, Guy Fleming (Pasadena), Jim Reid and Leo Magnus all held good catches. Ray Mogg excelled in the field and proved to be the iron man of the tour playing in all 15 games. Don Weekes was a close second playing in fourteen games.[64]

The opening pair for the tour, Jim Reid and Ray Mogg, both found the Jamaican fast bowling intimidating, with Upton Dowe, the West Indies opening bowler, being adjudged the fastest bowler of the lot. Don Weekes scored fifties at Alcan and at Sabina Park against Kingston CC. However, it was the middle order batting, namely Jamaican born Basil Brown (O.C.) and Pablo McNeil (LA), whose familiarity with fast hard wickets proved invaluable to the success of the tour. Brown and McNeil led the team batting with over 300 runs each. Basil Brown's most impressive performance was as a bowler against a strong Jamaica Cricket Board of Control side which declared a 197 for 7 after Basil took 5 for 51.[65] The SCCA in Jamaica played Charley's Sporting XI, University of the West Indies, Lucas CC, Alcan, Jamaica Constabulary, Desnoes and Geddes, Richmond Sporting XI, Jamaica Cricket Board of Control, Metal Box Company, Kingston CC, Frome Estates Sporting XI, Montego Bay XI, Rankine XI, St. George's College Old Boys, and Snap-On Tools.

The success of the SCCA side in Jamaica spurred John Marder to arrange for the U.S. participation in the first ICC World Cup that took place in 1979, held at Birmingham in England. Locally, Tony Verity focused his energies on developing the University Cricket Club, which first saw light as the Westwood Cricket Club, founded by Sidney Albright in 1960. Anil Lashkari, Leo Magnus and John Mattingly from Pasadena helped put the University CC on the winning track in the 1970. Jim Reid joined UCC three years later. Reid and Lashkari had baseball playing sons—John and Neil—who showed great promise at cricket, and they felt the University CC would be the best team to teach them the true spirit of the game. As events turned out they were correct. Both John and Neil became young cricket stars and represented the United States in the inaugural 1979 ICC Trophy. University CC players continued to dominate a 12-team Southern California Cricket Team league, providing six U.S. players for the ICC tournament held in Birmingham. A rare father and son combination, Anil and Neil Lashkari, were joined by former Ranji Trophy player (equivalent of county level in India) Sri Nagesh, Jim Reid, Barbados–born fast bowler Stephen Jones and Haseeb Khan.[66]

Kamran Khan, a former Pakistani test caliber wicket-keeper and coach at Haverford College, kept the Philadelphia cricket tradition flowing, while Ophneil Larrier, who bowled the 1969 United States team to victory over Canada, headed the New York West Indian contingent along with Ian Atherly and William Boverill (Washington, D.C.). The United States won their first game against Israel at Blossomfield Cricket Club the ICC tournament. Thirty English police "bobbies" were on hand for the U.S. versus Israel game. ICC organizers took no chances after the recent war between in the Middle East. The United States fought their way to 126. Sri Nagesh and William Boverill put on 50 runs for the eighth wicket after the top of the batting order failed. The U.S. bowlers confined Israel to 85 runs as the U.S. coasted to a 41-run win. Stephen Jones took 3 for 16 for United States. John Kassell, the Israel captain and wicket-keeper, was appointed CNN correspondent for the Middle East when the ICC competition ended.

The United States played Sri Lanka next. Batting first, the U.S. openers Jim Reid and Anil Lashkari scored 47 for the first wicket. Neil Lashkari, batting number 3, was trapped by the off-spin of Dias de Silva for one run. According to Neil Lashkari, Dias—rated the best off-spin bowler in the world—spun the ball so much, you could hear it sizzle off the seam. Kamran Khan teamed with Bill Stuger for a 90-run inning partnership to stabilize the U.S. innings as they were all out for 168, three overs before their allotted 60. Sri Lanka, playing the U.S. on the Saints Ground at Northampton, caught the U.S. score in 40 overs anchored by Roy L. Dias' unbeaten 76 (though he admitted later in the pavilion he was caught behind first ball).[67] Sri Nagesh took his first wicket of the tournament while Boverell showed his all-round capabilities, taking 2 for 29 in the best bowling spell for the U.S. against Sri Lanka. The third game of the tournament against a strong Netherlands side at Leamington Spa was rained out. This meant that the U.S. game against Wales held at the Olton and West Warwickshire Cricket Club on June 4, 1979, was important. It turned out to be brilliant match. The United States squeaked by with a seven-run victory after Kamran Khan took off the wicket-keeping pads at his captain Anil Lashkari's request and surprised the Welsh on a damp wicket, taking 5 for 17 after all the regular bowlers had failed to make an impression. Two brilliant shoestring catches by Stephen Jones and the youngest player on the side, American trained John Reid, turned the match in favor of the United States. The United States' next opponent, Zimbabwe, was a very strong batting side destined to have two of the world's best batsmen within the next decade, the Flowers brothers. On this occasion at Moseley Cricket Club ground, two Zimbabwean players scored centuries as the African team finished their allotted 60 overs with the unassailable score of 336 runs. The U.S. team, with a changed lineup and new captain after Anil Lashkari stepped down for the game, could only manage 141 runs as they quickly fell the bowling of Hogg, Hough, Traicos and Rawson. Neil Lashkari opened the batting in place of his father and made his highest score of the tournament with 17 runs. His father Anil, also a left-handed opener, knew that for his son to develop against the finest bowling the world had to offer, he had to step aside and let his son get the first-hand experience he needed. Neil was a 19-year-old cricketer educated and trained in America, who really preferred baseball since his days at Burbank High School. Here was a canny father in action capturing the interest of his son by the heat of battle. Anil's timing was immaculate, as Kamran Khan and Neil Lashkari became the highest aggregate scorers for the U.S. in four ICC tournaments. There is room for visionary leadership in cricket. Anil Lashkari inspired selection set up U.S. cricket for another generation. Despite Anil "Pro" Lashkari's best efforts, the U.S. failed to qualify for the next round by the narrow margin of .016 as Sri Lanka squeezed through to the semi-finals and future greatness as a test playing nation.

In 1982, Kamran Khan of Philadelphia was elected captain of the U.S. team that participated in the second ICC Trophy in England. The U.S. team played a rigorous series of games before the tournament, starting with the Royal Household at Windsor Castle. The Queen was riding on her estate but did not visit the cricketers, who were not her subjects. The U.S. players loved the Windsor setting but not the pitch. Additional games against North Middlesex, Stourbridge, Whitecastle and Potter's Bar were part of the team's final preparations, which were taken seriously as Hong Kong had future England player and match winner Dermott Reeve. As events turned out, the four games against Gibraltar, Kenya, Papua New Guinea and Hong Kong were rained out and awarded two runs apiece as a draw. Then in the fifth game against old nemesis Canada, held at Sutton Coldfield, the United States went down to heavy defeat by a score of 233 to 95 as Stephens ripped through the U.S. batting, taking 4 for 26. The U.S. recovered their confidence against Israel, defeating them by 8 wickets. Neil Lashkari (76) and Kamran Khan (65) were both not out as they steered the U.S. past an Israel score of 157 runs. This time the Netherlands squeaked into the semifinals ahead of the United States. The U.S. team was less cohesive than the one in 1979, as it reflected the increased influence of Chicago in the selection process following the election of Nasir Khan from Chicago as USACA president.

Preparation for the 1986 ICC Trophy began with a triangular tournament in Bermuda that included Canada and the United States. Oscar Durity captained the side and made a hat trick against Canada for the second time in the storied history of matches between the two North American neighbors. Pakistani immigrants soon had a big impact on the quality of U.S. cricket, as Bobbie Raffae joined Kamran Khan on the U.S. team for the Bermuda tour. Raffae was not selected for the 1986 ICC tournament side. Southern California's contribution to the ICC Trophy U.S. team was restricted to two players in 1986. The majority of U.S. players were from New York. The institution of interzonal selection games between the four U.S. regions, West, Central, East and South, improved the selection process though players still had to pay their own way to England. Once in England, the ICC picked up the cost of hotel accommodation and local transportation. Preparations for the ICC tournament pitted East Coast against West Coast cricketers. Teddy Forster — who had moved to northern California from New York — and Neil Lashkari found themselves playing for English clubs against their East Coast teammates, who wanted to relegate the West Coast players to reserve status. In one game Neil Lashkari effectively countered the East Coast challenge and the English club he played for invited him to become their professional after the game was over. Sam Shivnarine, who had played for the West Indies, took over the captaincy from Kamran Khan and led his team to a convincing 72-run win over Canada on June 11 at Hinckley Town Cricket Club's field. Hubert Blackman joined veteran Neil Lashkari as opener, but they made an inauspicious start as the U.S. went 2 for 7 before Tim Mills from New York stabilized the innings with a well hit 40. Veteran Kamran Khan (19) with his new captain Shivnarine (26) provided solid middle order batting as the U.S. scored 151 in their innings. This was a low score, but fast bowler Miller (3 for 17) and off-spinner Kamran Khan (4 for 22) prevented Canada from establishing a solid partnership as they stumbled to 79 all out. The U.S. next defeated a determined Papua New Guinea side at Market Harborough. Lashkari (50) and Blackman (29) clicked as an opening pair as Kamran Khan (73) again led the batting with Shavnarine (47) and Smith the wicket-keeper (41) contributing a winning partnerships. They took the U.S. score from a beatable 177 for 5 to an insurmountable 263 for 6. The United States won by 49 runs; Papua New Guinea was all out for 234 as bowlers Prabhudas (3 for 69) and Foster (3 for 45) protected a large score. In the third game at Solihull Cricket Club, the U.S. were simply annihilated by the Netherlands in a 10-wicket loss with English county players; Bakker taking 5 for 20 and Lefebvre 3 for 2 as the U.S. batting collapsed to 88 all out in 34.2 overs. In Netherlands, artificial batting surfaces emphasized really fast bowling, which the U.S. proved unable to stop. In the fourth game, the U.S. did well to come back and win against a strongly favored Bermuda team at Stratford on Avon. The U.S. used seven bowlers to contain a hard hitting Bermuda attack led by Ricky Hill (58) of Baylis Bay CC. Hill was renowned in Bermuda for his hard, athletic hitting ability. The U.S. openers, Lashkari (29) and Blackman (37), fared well against Bermuda, opening the U.S. innings with a 50 partnership. Tim Mills (46 not out) and John Miller (23 not out) steered the U.S. to a 3-wicket win. In the fourth game against Fiji at Blossomfield Cricket Club, the U.S. won comfortably by 5 wickets after Neil Lashkari (104 not out) scored the first century by a U.S. player an ICC tournament since they began in 1979. Neil remembered the day as ideal for cricket. He felt comfortable at the wicket because he had played well against Israel on the same pitch in 1979. Experience counts.

Prior to Neil Lashkari's century in an international game, Furness scored 106 for Philadelphia against the Australians at Germantown CC in 1896. Ninety years between centuries is a long time to wait for a strong individual performance, but it certainly demonstrated the resilience of U.S. cricket. Kamran Khan and Lashkari combined for a record U.S. fifth-wicket partnership of 118 runs in an ICC tournament. The U.S. showed an ability to accumulate scores of over 200 in the fourth ICC Trophy tournament, the *sine qua non* for victory in one-day cricket. When the U.S. played Hong Kong at Leamington Spa, they were up against Miles, who had scored 176 in the previous game — the highest score of the tournament — but he was out early as Hong Kong stumbled to 143 all out in 54 overs. The U.S. overtook Hong Kong with five wickets to spare. In the sixth

Rendering of the Woodley Cricket Pavilion planned for the ICC World Cup in 2000. With the exception of the turn of the twentieth century pavilions built at Germantown, Merion, Philadelphia, and Staten Island Cricket Clubs, cricket pavilions are scarce in the United States. When the Hollywood CC (built in 1933) was turned into a wedding reception center in 1980, southern California's institutional memory suffered. Cricket in the United States needs a place to hang its pictures to combat ignorance of the game. Source: Pugh+Scarpa Architects, Santa Monica, California.

game, after winning the toss, the U.S. achieved a pyrrhic victory, by 8 wickets with Prabdhas taking 5 for 23 against Gibraltar at Aston Manor. The U.S. failed to score the 300 runs required for qualification to the next round. Two days later on June 27, the U.S. defeated Israel for the third time in ICC competition with Khan scoring 146 not out and Prabdhas spinning the U.S. to victory by 247 runs with another strong bowling performance of 4 for 34. Despite winning 5 of their 6 games the U.S. failed to make it to the next round. The Netherlands advanced from their group before eventually going on to win the tournament.

The ICC chose the Netherlands as the venue for the 1990 ICC Trophy. Both Kamran Khan and Neil Lashkari returned for a fourth series of ICC games. Arthur Hazzlewood and Leo Magnus were selected as managers of the U.S. side. Sam Shavnarine had the respect of the New York West Indian–born players on the U.S. side and captained again. There were just three new players on the U.S. squad, and one of them, Peart, a great left-handed opening bat from New York, scored a century in his first ICC game at Nijmegen against East and Central Africa. The U.S. scored 404 for the first time but the game was rained out. When the game was replayed at Nijmegen three days later, the U.S. won by five wickets after East and Central Africa were all out for 184 when Antiguan-born Reginald "Benji" Benjamin simply overpowered the hapless African players with his fast West Indian bowling. The U.S. took on and beat Denmark by 12 runs. With only 12 runs to go, Derbyshire CC player Ohte Mortensen (35 not out) teamed with Son Thomson (20) and looked set to win the match until Thomson was thrown out from the boundary by the baseball-trained Lashkari. Zahir Amin's (3 for 34) accurate, left-handed, off-spin bowling also contributed to the win.

In the next game held at Amstelveen grounds, the U.S. left-handed openers Peart (22) and Lashkari (18) blunted Kenya's fast-bowling attack led by the Odumbe brothers, with a 50-run opening partnership. After a solid start, and a captain's innings by Sam Shivnarine (30) and Ray Winters (26), the U.S. collapsed to 162 all out. Winters, a Jamaican opening bowler who had qualified for the U.S. team in New York, bowled both Kenya openers with 26 runs on the board. Winters and Benjamin were the fastest bowlers in the ICC tournament. Kenya was 3 for 34 when Earl Daley, the most accurate of the U.S. bowlers, picked up a wicket, before Odumbe and Tikolo came together to steer Kenya out of trouble to victory by 6 wickets. A similar pattern occurred in the game against Zimbabwe held at Nijmegen on June 16. The Flowers brothers were making their mark as the world's best batsmen though they had to work hard for their runs, taking 46 overs to catch the low U.S. score. The U.S. needed 300 runs to qualify for the next round and fell short with 131 runs. Zimbabwe won the match by seven wickets. The U.S. won their last game of the tournament against Papua New Guinea at Amstelveen by 67 runs, with Kamran Khan top scoring for the U.S. with 52 runs. Daley took 4 for 35 runs.

The 1990 tour was the last for Kamran Khan, Zamir Amin and Neil Lashkari, the only three players to have more than 20 caps for the United States in the twentieth century. Kamran Khan (623) and Neil Lashkari (502) are the only two players to have scored more than 500 runs apiece in aggregate. Peart (41.25) and Shavnarine (41.25) have higher scores per innings though Kamran Khan stands out as the best all-rounder, having taken off his wicket-keeping pads to become one of the U.S. all-time leading bowlers, with 21 wickets for 374 runs. Only Kallicharran (127.5) and Zahir Amin (183.5) have bowled more overs for the U.S. than Kamran Khan (112.2).

Kamran Khan fought hard to get the Philadelphia tradition back into U.S. cricket from his position as cricket coach at Haverford College. He helped found the United States Cricket Federation which was an organization founded by cricketers for cricketers. The USCF had sound ideas but never developed the political muscle to handle the long-established New York and Connecticut West Indian community polemical tradition that was an integral part of the West Indian cricket identity in the United States. The competition between USCF and USACA did not come to a head until the 1995, when immigration of young cricketers to the United States outstripped established cricket in California and New York. New York's teams tripled in number. Southern California jumped to 40 cricket clubs playing league cricket every weekend on ten different pitches located within a 150-mile radius centered Los Angeles. The circumference touched San Diego CC at the University of California San Diego and in the west, Victoria CC's ground at Balboa Middle School in Ventura. A similar geometrical growth has occurred in Boston; Broward County, Florida (especially around Miami); and northern California, where the big thirst of the hot Silicon Valley town of Sunnyvale for Indian-trained electrical engineers has really helped fuel the growth of the game.

With 50,000 new Indian families immigrating to the United States in 1995, cricket administration throughout the United States was increasingly influenced by the Laws of Manu, the instruction manual of Hinduism.[68] Most urban, educated Indians, when asked about the pervasive influence of the caste system on cricket in the United States, deny its impact. However, it is notable that many cricket teams in the U.S. carry a significant portion of identical surnames and that they outnumber cosmopolitan (multiethic teams) by a ratio of 3:1 nationwide. Top-level cricketers of any nationality remain the exception to this informal rule as they can get a berth on any team looking to win. For the majority of United States teams, cricket offers a snug fit with the Upanishads, where mastering the skills of bowling and batting give control over fate's arbitrary forces at the wicket. The intuitive wisdom of the sublimely masterful cricketers from Sunil Gavaskar to Salkin Tundulkar has gained them the same recognition from their legions of cricket fans as any minor Hindu god. They have been touched, in terms of Hindu cosmology, by the blinding light. Revered as gurus of their craft, they may not have achieved *moksha*, or eternal release from the endless cycle of existence known as *samsara*, but at the very least they have good *dharma*, which explains the deep devotion and financial commitment shown all international cricketers by the expatriate Indian community when they visit the United States. Sir Richard "Paddles" Hadlee when he visited Los Angeles remarked that he had never been so scared as when leaving Eden Gardens in Kolkota, as thousands of cricket supporters thronged the car trying to touch "the master." This devotion shown to cricket gods represents another major path to Hindu salvation, *bhakti* (devotion).[69]

In practical terms on the cricket field, a dicey LBW decision by an Indian umpire can be interpreted differently. There are six classical schools of Hindu philosophy, including yoga. The *Nyaya* school applies mostly to cricket. It is the source of most misunderstanding between Hindu and non–Hindu on the cricket field, as quibbling and disputations are two of the 16 categories of analysis in this system of logic. Ugandan Asians expelled by President Idi Amin rarely quibbled over umpire decisions when they settled in the United States after 1975. Some of the more recent Indian high-tech educated immigrants are adherents of the *Nyaya* school of philosophy, which lauds disputation techniques that can be counterproductive to harmony on the cricket field. On the West Coast, at league level, the implementation of Vedic cosmology can have the effect of locking in place the division structure throughout the league as decisions are influenced by "team dharma." Non-Hindu, Sri Lankan (Buddhist with some Hindu Tamil), West Indian, English, Pakistani, American or Australian players remain outside the caste system and therefore increasingly outside the power structure of the game on the West Coast. On the East Coast, the strong West Indian tradition prevails, while in the Midwest, Massoud "Chick" Khan strongly represented Pakistan's cricket traditions at the national USACA level when he served as president (1990–1998) prior to Dr. Atul Rai (1998–2002).

Indian Consulate statistics, for California alone, taken from the 2000 U.S. Census, indicate 24,500 Indians settled in Los Angeles, 26,500 in Sunnyvale and 5,500 in Riverside County in the year 2000. In southern California the old seniority system for earning a slot on the prestigious Woodley grounds has been undercut by teams of young players assuming the name of old clubs after voting out the old guard. Recent Indian immigrant team members tend to adhere to the beliefs of a good Hindu. For devout Hindus, "caste laws and mundane duties are more important than deities. What really matters [is] to eat properly, drink properly, marry the right person and act 'correctly' in keeping with the law."[70]

Celibate studenthood gives way to the second stage, that of the householder (*grhastha*) in which accumulating wealth and children eventually gives way to the third stage (*ashrama*) once the face of the grandson has been witnessed.[71] Victoria CC is representative of most teams in the Southern California Cricket Association that have changed chemistry considerably over the last decade as players have passed through the three stages of development. Teams that have achieved higher *dharma* through victory get better grounds. Where cricket clubs have an illustrious history that cannot be denied — such as the Hollywood Cricket Club — the answer becomes to envelop the team through democracy and then take it over through numbers. The Bhakta (devotion) clan chose the Hollywood CC as their club. They have powered it to heights — as evidenced by the winning of numerous trophies — the great Sir Aubrey Smith could never have conceived during his stint on the screen as a Colonel in *The Bengal Lancers*. Bhaktas love their cricket and have done more for the growth of the game in the last five years than any other cricket group. Strongly entrenched in the motel business, they too have felt the pressure from more recent Indian immigrants:

> India boarded the Internet and software express successfully in the 1990's, drawing on its 15–30 million-strong English speaking well educated middle class ... India's ... engineers ... became the principal source of skilled technicians for Silicon Valley.... In 2000, the total number of skilled workers in the U.S. approached 75,000, including more than one-quarter of the workforce at Cisco.... In wealth distribution terms, the result was yet another glamorous digirati ... the four major technological and financial concentrations of the region including San Francisco Bay and Silicon Valley along with the metropolitan areas of Boston, New York and Washington, S.C.[72]

In Sunnyvale; Plano, Texas; and in Broward County, Florida; where a 36-million-dollar bond issue will be used to build an international cricket stadium for 2006, local mayors have rewarded cricketers' electoral loyalty. An indication of cricket's importance in local communities can be measured by the height of the grass. Short grass means better cricket. Long grass means more political work to be done where soccer moms rule. Cricket moms are needed. Insurance liability laws also come into play as many insurers prefer at least two and half inch length grass to minimize sports injuries in American sports.

Despite the pressure on local cricket organizations, cricket touring by international sides has increased greatly, and the weak dollar will encourage more visits to the United States. The apex of English amateur cricket has been represented by the MCC tours of the United States. The MCC made two visits to the U.S. in the 1990s. In 1992, a Southern California XI side defeated the MCC. In 1999 they sent a stronger, younger team that

The joy of victory. Nasim Shirazi shares the joy of victory with fellow players Hasan, Ali Aijaz and Haidar Raza. Source: Southern California Cricket Association Archives — Amateur Athletic Foundation Library. Photographer: Michael Burke.

easily defeated Southern California by six wickets. The younger MCC side was needed since the great influx of Indian players from 1995 resulted in the average age of immigrant cricketers decreasing from 30 to under 25. Veteran opener Neil Lashkari batted for Southern California in both games against the MCC. Recent immigrant players Ali Aijaz and Joy Zinto have improved the quality of southern California cricket. All three U.S. players were chosen to represent Southern California against the ICC World Cup champions, Sri Lanka, in 1995. The Sri Lankan community in Los Angeles raised $25,000 at very short notice to make their world champions' visit possible. Local residents were given the honor of hosting individual world champions in their homes, based on the size of contributions made to toward the Sri Lankan players' fees. Lead by an Australian coach, the Sri Lankan team put on a marvelous display of attacking cricket and superlative fielding, which was truly appreciated by over 2,000 spectators housed under — just beyond the boundary — colorful tents displaying sponsors' banners. The Southern California side scored 164 runs, which included a powerful display of hitting by Jamaican-born U.S. player Hopeton Barrett. Barrett's innings of 24 runs in 24 balls included two overpowering sixes over long-on, off world-class bowling. Off-spinner David Martel also kept the Sri Lankan team in check with highly accurate bowling, although the Sri Lankan world champions won comfortably by six wickets.

Several North American cricket promoters have sought to establish a Sharjah Trophy series like that played in the Middle East. Funded by the Sultan of Qatar, the tournament has established a new level of compensation for players. Gold Rolex watches and Mercedes-Benz cars were given to the winning Qatar Emirates team after their ICC World Cup victory in Kenya in 1994 and their Sharjah Cup win in 1995. A similar event has been tried in Toronto at the hundred-year-old Toronto Cricket and Curling Club. Called the Sahara Cup, the test match level games were made financially viable by the revenues earned from beaming cricket between Pakistan and India to the subcontinent's 1-billion-person fan base.

American fans have yet to be attracted to cricket, though efforts have been made in that direction. Recent SCCA president Atul Rai invited Jamaica and Western India to play in a tournament at Woodley Park against the United States and Southern California for the Independence Cup in 1997. Independence was a coy reference to Indian independence from Britain by both Pakistan and India in 1948, not American independence in 1776. Limited for funds, the United States of America Cricket Association flew in six players from New York and one from Florida. Four SCCA players had played cricket professionally outside the United States. The captain Nazim Shirazi, a former member of the Bangladesh team, became used to playing before large crowds. In the United States, large crowds have never come out for cricket, so good immigrant players have a major adjustment to make.

For the West Indian communities in the United States, cricket continues to be a regular family affair in the park. Kirby Lee reported the July 4, 1997, game between Jamaica and the SCCA:

> Instead of U.S. flags, spectators danced to reggae music ... and dominoes was a common diversion during a match that lasted eight hours....
> For Jennifer Innis Stephen — a 1980 and 1984 Olympian for Guyana in the long jump and a member of the 1988 U.S. Olympic team in the 400-meter relay — watching cricket on July 4th has become a family tradition.... "I'm so used to watching it," Jennifer Stephen said, "Cricket is part of our culture."[73]

Ex-Jamaican (1984–87) and now U.S. fast-bowler Hopeton Barrett observed at the same match, "People in the U.S. don't realize how important cricket is and how much camaraderie it can bring between countries."[74]

Cricket in the U.S. does have a strong competitive side, which Kevin Modesti captured in his report:

> The U.S. batsmen overcame a slow morning to post 210 runs for nine wickets in 45 overs, then bowled over the top of the Jamaican order and looked like upset winners yesterday. At one desperate moment the visitors were 100 for seven wickets in 26 overs, well below the scoring rate they needed to win the 50 overs match.
> U.S. cricket officials were loving it because they remembered the confident statements of Jamaica's manager.... As one American said sagely, "In cricket you never underestimate your opponent."
> No sooner was that lesson dispensed than Jamaica demonstrated that although humility is nice, experience is better. Franklyn Rose, Jamaica's captain and number 8 batsman strode confidently to the wicket and rescued the favorites from an embarrassing defeat. The lanky Rose beat the U.S. fast bowlers like a steel drum and piled up a team high 59 runs.
> At the end of the nearly eight hour day, facing bowler Abdul Islam, Rose swept a ball to the leg side for a boundary four, giving Jamaica a victory with 214 for eight in 40 overs.
> Had the United States actually won the upset would have been compared [to] the U.S. soccer upset of England in 1951.
> It certainly would have been the biggest cricket accomplishment here since '79 when the United States nearly qualified for the sport's World Cup.
> "It would have been significant," said Don Weekes, a former Barbados test player, who called the Jamaicans a representative team of professionals.[75]

Ali Aijaz made 73 of the U.S. runs in the final game and was named batsman of the tournament. The strong performance of the U.S. weekend players against a professional team demonstrated that cricket in the United States has gone as far as amateur enthusiasm can take it—which is to say, to a high level. For sustained international competition United States cricketers will have to be paid for their services, as was proved by Aijaz' success with the U.S. team that finished first in a nation's match held in Dubai in December 2003. After the United States graduated—through their championship win—to playing cricket against the A level test nations of India, Pakistan, England, South Africa, New Zealand, Zimbabwe, Sri Lanka and Bangladesh, Ali Aijaz changed teams, on his return to Southern California, to second division on being offered $400 per game. The new age of professional cricket has dawned in the United States.

In 2004 a professional cricket league competition—funded by a successful Indian computer entrepreneur—was held with venues in Miami, New York, Chicago and Los Angeles. The same year, English businessman Gary Hopkins was appointed by the ICC to promote professional cricket in the United States. According to the SCCA,

> The CEO's primary task will be to secure the support of the ICC's Full Member nations to participate in a One-Day International tournament in the USA, and to co-ordinate the staging of any such. Any income from the international matches staged in the USA, will pave the way for investment in appropriate professional staffing, coach education, facility developments, competition structures and programs in the schools.[76]

At the annual Southern California Cricket banquet on November 20, 2004, CEO Hopkins unveiled Project USA. The United States of America Cricket Association, an amateur organization, will offer advice but their lamentable track record in servicing grassroots cricket has ensured that the ICC-USA will retain and review the disbursement of funds to cricket projects throughout the United States. The initial focus of Project USA's fund-raising efforts will be in Broward County, Miami, where a $36 million bond issue was passed by local taxpayers to fund an international cricket stadium. Ex-Australian captain Steven Waugh has been approached to lead the United States to the next level in international cricket. Steve Waugh's biography, *Respect the Past and Attack the Future*, should be appropriated as an apt motto for United States cricket. We have come a long way since the glory days of the Hollywood Cricket Club. Cricket's secular tradition in the United States has become a multicultural affirmation of civility against violent odds in a religiously polarized world. Cricket pioneered the secular sports movement in the United States, paving the way for the growth of baseball. Its near 300-year tradition of self-respect and tolerance in the United States makes it integral to the American Dream as the United States negotiates its identity as the twenty-first century world power.

Appendix: Chronology of Cricket in the United States, 1710–2000

Colonial Period, 1682–1776

1710 Oxford-educated William Byrd II plays cricket on the James River plantation in Tidewater, Virginia.

1739 New York papers advertise for cricketers.

1751 Cricket played a London XI and a New York cricket team using the revised rules of 1744. In Virginia "wicket" (old cricket) is still played.

1754 Cricket played in Maryland between a Cambridge XI and an Eton XI.

1763 First mention of cricket in Wales. Benjamin West's painting of the Cricketers depicts young South Carolinian aristocratic cricketers.

1776 American Revolution begins. British convict ships arrive in Botany Bay in Australia as white settlement starts.

1777 Hambledon CC, located in Hampshire County, beats an All England XI scoring 403 runs, helped by Tom Aylward's 167. First time a team score of over 400 is recorded in cricket and first time a century is recorded. Thomas Paine, writer of *Common Sense*, joined Hambeldon CC on his way to England from the ex-colonies.

____ Brooklyn CC plays Manhattan CC.

____ Prince of Wales is presented a cricket ball by Duke's, the first cricket equipment maker.

____ First reference to cricket in Lancashire and Cheshire.

____ First English cricket portrait portrays Lumpy Stevens, England's best opening underarm bowler.

____ First recorded game of cricket in Scotland.

____ Cricket club formed in Serigapatanum in S. India.

____ Leg guards, the precursor of pads, used by R. Robinson of Surrey for the first time.

1778 General Washington encourages the playing of wicket at Valley Forge. Cricket played regularly on Manhattan Island during the seven-year occupation of it during the American Revolutionary War.

1782 American lieutenant Feltman writes of playing cricket regularly in South Carolina.

1798 Jane Austen mentions baseball and cricket in *Northanger Abbey* (published posthumously in 1818).

After the American Revolution

1803 Engraving by George Tichnor depicts cricket played at Dartmouth College in New Hampshire.

____ Cricket played in New South Wales, Australia, for the first time.

1806 St. Anne's Cricket Club in Barbados established.

1809 Boston Cricket Club founded.

____ During the debate in the Continental Convention in Boston objection is made to calling the chief executive of the U.S. a "president" as cricket clubs already use the term for their elected club leader.

1810 An American traveler to England draws a sharp distinction between English cricket and that seen played in the U.S.

1814 Lord's third ground is opened on its present site using turf transported from two previous grounds.

1816 Wides first penalized; no distinction made from byes until 1827.

1818 First mention of cricket in Yorkshire.

1820 Cricket played in Gibraltar for the first time.

1821 First century in a Gentleman-versus-Players game. Cricket mentioned as being played in Charleston, South Carolina, for a long time.

1831 Union Cricket Club founded in Philadelphia. In Canada, cricket played in high school and clubs formed in Hamilton, Guelph and Toronto.

1836 Sam Wright immigrates to the United States.
____ Cricket first played in Chicago.

1837 Cricket played in South Australia for the first time.
____ New York CC founded.
____ Great Banking Depression hits New York.

1838 New York Cricket Club is renamed the St. George's Cricket Club.
____ Union Cricket Club re-established in Philadelphia.

1840 Carelton Cricket Club formed in Ottowa.

1842 Trinidad Cricket Club founded in West Indies.

1843 Intercollegiate sports starts at Yale with the founding of a boat club.

1844 First match in New Zealand.
____ April: First test match between Canada (Toronto CC) and America (St. George's—New York); U.S. wins.
____ September: Second test match between the U.S. and Canada. Canada wins.
____ Wister family play cricket in Philadelphia.
____ October 3: James Turner scores 120 for the Union Cricket Club of Philadelphia in a game against the St. George's CC in Manhattan.

1847 Knickerbocker Base Ball Club, founded by Alexander Cartwright, starts playing at Elysian Fields, Hoboken, New Jersey.
____ Harry Wright plays baseball with the Knickerbockers and cricket for St. George's CC.
____ All England Eleven of paid professional cricketers organized by William Clark of Nottingham.
____ Englishman Henry Chadwick, "father of baseball," begins covering both cricket and

baseball for Porter's subsequently Wilkes' *Spirit of the Times*.

1848 William Gilbert Grace born in England.
____ California Gold Rush begins after President Polk declares there is much gold to be found on the American River.

1850 Cricket in Lahore (later located in Pakistan) and at St. George's College in Jamaica.
____ California joins the United States under President Fillmore as a slavery-free state.
____ January 33: Knickerbocker Cricket Club meets at the Union Hotel in San Francisco.

1851 Gold discovered at Ballarat in Australia.

1852 April 15: Alta California announces cricket is to be played on a ground located south of Rincon Point in San Francisco.
____ United All England XI of paid professionals organized to compete against Clarke's All England XI.

1854 Philadelphia Cricket Club and Germantown Cricket Club founded in Philadelphia.

1855 Young America Cricket Club founded with American-born and -trained cricketer membership.
____ The Crimean War begins.

1857 Cricket fields included in winning "Greensward" plan for Central Park, New York, by English designer Calvert Vaux and American Frederick Olmstead.
____ July 6: Union Cricket Club v. Pioneers near Union Race Track in San Francisco.

1858 Black professionals leave San Francisco for Victoria after pro-slavery legislation passes California legislature.

1859 National Cricket Association founded in New York. George Parr's All England XI visits the United States and Canada in the first international sporting event of any kind. One of the games is played at the St. George's CC home ground on the Elysian Fields, located in Hoboken, New Jersey.
____ Henry Chadwick's first *American Cricket Manual* published.
November 25: California XXII Challengers v. Challenged at Union Race Track in San Francisco.
____ The Eagles baseball team established—first in San Francisco. It includes John Fisher, who played with the Empires of New York.

1860 Victoria Cricket Club formed in British Columbia, Canada.
____ Two thousand baseball clubs established nationwide according to Wilkes' *Spirit of the Times*. Twenty-five are in the San Francisco Bay Area.

___ Olympic Athletic Club founded in San Francisco with a focus on gymnastics.

___ Harry Wright becomes the professional at the Union Cricket Club in Cincinnati.

During and After the Civil War

1861 American Civil War starts.

___ July 4: Cricket played in the mining town of Grass Valley in the Sierra Nevadas.

___ William and James Shepherd play for the New York Knickerbockers at Hoboken and help establish the Pacific Baseball Club in San Francisco.

___ July 4: San Francisco Cricket Club founded.

___ Harvard University CC founded.

1865 Merion Cricket Club founded in Philadelphia.

1866 Pacific Baseball Convention promotes baseball championship at the Recreation Grounds at 25th and Folsom in San Francisco.

___ Caledonian Society founded in San Francisco, for Scottish-born members only.

___ Princeton University CC founded.

___ California Cricket Club founded with British consul P. Lane Booker as president.

1867 Prospect Park, designed by Vaux and Olmstead, opens in New York with cricket pitches.

1868 Edgar Willsher's six-game tour of Canada and the United States. U.S. team captained by George Morgan Newhall. In the last game at Hoboken, Willsher's team defeats a XXII of America by an innings of nine runs.

___ Australian Aborigines team plays 46 games of high-level cricket in England. They are the first Australian team to play cricket on tour in England. The first white Australian team follows ten years later.

___ San Francisco Cricket Club changes its name to St. George's.

___ November 28: Pioneer Cricket Club versus St. George's CC of San Francisco.

1869 April 18: First international cricket match in San Francisco, California v. Victoria at Union Race Track.

___ September 21: Continental Railroad links San Francisco to the rest of the United States.

___ New Recreation Grounds on 13th and Folsom set up by the Hatton brothers.

___ Occidental Cricket Club founded in San Francisco.

___ Cincinnati Red Stockings, with Harry Wright as manager and Aaron Champion as president, travel 10,000 miles and put baseball on the map in the U.S. as a professional sport.

___ Harvard baseball team beats the Philadelphia Athletics but loses to the Cincinnati Red Stockings.

___ Sacramento Baseball Club becomes California's first professional baseball club.

___ Baseball and cricket borrow players from each other throughout the 1870s. For lack of competition, 1870s college baseball teams on the East Coast routinely play professionals.

1870 Judge North founds the colony of Riverside in southern California with the help of the Southern California Colony Association.

___ The Chicago Fire. White Sox stadium burns down. Mahlon Ogden, one of the founders of the Chicago Cricket Club, saves his house.

1872 Robert A. Fitzgerald, secretary of the MCC, organizes the third English tour of America and the first by a team of amateurs; it includes W.G. Grace on his only tour to the North America. G.M. Newhall captains the Philadelphia team.

___ Belmont CC founded in Philadelphia.

___ British military play an American team for the Halifax Cup.

1874 The American team, comprised of Philadelphia players, brings home the Halifax trophy.

___ C.W. Alcock, Harry Wright and Arthur G. Spalding organize a professional baseball tour of England. Spalding scores 25 runs for the baseball team against the Lord's groundstaff at Lord's.

1875 Santa Monica founded by Senator John Percival Jones and Colonel Baker, husband of Mexican-American heiress Arcadia Bandini Baker.

1876 Chicago Cricket Club founded.

___ In Canada v. United States, John Hargrave and John Large score 220 in partnership for the U.S., the best performance ever by a pair of U.S. batsmen.

1877 Ranchero Marquez family of Santa Monica defeats an expatriate polo team in Santa Monica.

___ National Cricketers' Association organized in Philadelphia; it does not survive beyond the First World War.

1878 September 29–October 26: David Gregory's Australians play six games at Hoboken, Philadelphia, Montreal, and San Francisco. Philadelphia is the first team to play all American players against a foreign 11.

1879 March 15: Lord Harris' team beats the U.S. at Hoboken by an innings and 114 runs on their return from Australia and New Zealand where they played 14 matches.

_____ August 19–20: Second series of international contests begins between the U.S. and Canada, the rule being adopted that none but native-born Americans represent the U.S.

_____ September 10–11: Richard Daft's team of cricket professionals start their 13-game cricket and baseball tour in Canada, finishing with eight games in the U.S.

_____ First tour by Gentlemen of Ireland; Philadelphia beats Ireland.

_____ Record ninth-wicket partnership of 210 by Broughey (117) and Johnstone (100) in a minor game by a Philadelphia team in Canada.

_____ Olympic Club of San Francisco leases Oakland Baseball Ground.

_____ Oakland Cricket Club founded.

1879 Rudyard Kipling, aged 24, visits San Francisco and writes about the Bohemian Club.

_____ First tour of England by a Canadian team, led by Captain (later the Reverend) T.D. Phillips. Tour is abandoned after the team captain is arrested as a British army deserter at Leicester.

1880 George Morgan Newhall scores 180 not out for Young America CC v. Baltimore CC.

1881 September: Third Australian tour of England resulted in England's first home defeat, by a team rated the best Australian team sent to England in the nineteenth century.

_____ October 1–10: A team of English professionals captained by Alfred Shaw plays five games in the U.S. on their way to Australia. In the concluding contest against a California XXII in San Francisco, Yorkshire professional George Ulyett scores 164 not out, the first recorded century in California cricket history.

_____ Cap Anson's world champion Chicago White Sox defeated by a Bay Area Baseball IX.

_____ Robert Louis Stevenson writes about Lake County and Calistoga.

_____ Oscar Wilde visits San Francisco and Los Angeles.

_____ A.G. Brown (64) and G.W. Morris (133 not out) make a record breaking opening partnership against a Canadian XII.

_____ Canada tours England.

_____ Charles W. Elliot, president of Harvard, tries to ban college sports.

1883 *American Cricketer* became official organ of Cricketer's Association of the United States.

1884 First Gentleman v. Players game in Philadelphia. Six ball over used by Philadelphian cricket for the first time.

_____ Gentlemen of Philadelphia, captained by R.S. Newhall, tours England for the first time.

W.C. Lowry takes 121 wickets and J.A. Scott makes 1,054 runs, the first time both bowling and batting milestones are reached by American cricketers in England.

_____ West Indian team captained by L.R. Fife plays 13 games in Canada and the U.S. The book of the tour is the first published cricket book in the West Indies.

_____ C.L. Bixby tours West Indies for the first time.

_____ Digger Robertson plays cricket for Australia against England at Adelaide.

_____ Chicago Cricket Club gains strong support from the Ogden family. Philip Armour and Marshall Fields become patrons of the CCC.

_____ Dr. E.R. Ogden captains second Canadian tour of England.

_____ W.M. Massie scores 264 in a minor match in Florida, the first time over 200 runs are scored by a single batsman in the U.S.

_____ Lake County cricket starts with the founding of the Burns Valley cricket team, organized by Thomas Beakbane and trained by Lancashire cricketer Owen.

_____ The Olympic Club develops the Golden Gate Park athletic facility near Haight Stadium in San Francisco.

_____ Southern California Lawn Tennis Association founded in Riverside with James Bettner as first president.

_____ Second tour by Gentlemen of Ireland to Philadelphia. Philadelphia wins both matches.

_____ Cricket starts in Los Angeles.

_____ Six ball over officially adopted by the U.S. Leg Before Wicket (LBW) rule adopted but different from that suggested by the MCC.

_____ J. Cuddihy takes ten wickets in an innings in New York for the first time in the U.S.

1886 Philadelphia defeats a West Indies team in Bouda, British Guyana.

1889 Arthur Goodwill Spalding's All American baseball team tours the world and leaves San Francisco aboard the SS *Alameda*.

_____ Pullman Cricket Club founded just outside Chicago.

_____ E.N. Crane of the All American baseball team touring Australia throws a cricket ball 128 yards, 10 1/2 inches, winning a prize of £100 in Melbourne.

_____ June 19: A team of Philadelphia amateurs, captained by R.S. Newhall, leaves New York for a first-class cricket tour of Great Britain. Annual international contest between Canada and the United States is postponed on account of the Philadelphia tour.

_____ United States Cricket Association adopts the declaration rule for any time in any innings several years before the rule is adopted by the MCC.

____ C. Aubrey Smith captains the first England Cricket XI to visit South Africa.

____ H. Keeling starts the Lakeport cricket team in Lake County.

Leagues Start on Both Coasts

1890 Western Frontier declared closed.

____ In California, Charlie W. Laurence takes all ten wickets for Alameda CC versus Oakland CC.

____ Los Angeles Cricket Club founded.

____ Walter Chewiston, curator of Japanese artifacts at the British Museum, recommends Riverside to the Waterhouse family who then take an interest in the Gage Canal, leading to a strong British influence in the Riverside citrus industry.

____ Eight to ten ball over is adopted in Philadelphia.

____ Jerome Flannery publishes the first *American Cricket Annual*, taken over after his death by Frederick F. Kelly then published by Spalding until 1914.

____ March 7: The New England Association is organized, 15 clubs being represented. It embraces district leagues, each of which is to arrange its own schedule. Leading clubs in several districts are to play against each other. George Wright, the well known ex–baseball player, is chosen president.

____ The California Cricket Association is organized in San Francisco.

1892 April: The annual meeting of the Cricketer's Association in Philadelphia re-elects S. Newhall as president.

____ California Cricket Club re-established with Digger Robertson as captain.

____ May 3: In a game against Alameda CC, Robertson score 136 runs and takes 6 wickets for five runs, the first century recorded in California by a domestic player.

____ July 2–3: The Germantown Cricket Club scores 631 runs against the Rosedale cricket team of Toronto, the largest score in one inning yet recorded in America. F.E. Brewster (146 not out) and G.S. Patterson (135 runs) are the chief contributors to the Germantown total.

____ July 12: In San Francisco, Sloman scores 137 runs for the California CC against the Ashland CC.

____ September 11–12: The last and deciding game in the intercity league championship series (which excluded California) saw Philadel-

phia beat Chicago by an innings and 359 runs.

____ September 23: Lord Hawke's team of English amateurs (seventh English tour) arrives in Philadelphia to help inaugurate the new Germantown Cricket Club grounds, where they are defeated by eight wickets. Upwards of 30,000 people pay admission to the grounds during the three days.

____ September 27: Robert Hogue makes 141 not out for Alameda CC against Oakland CC.

1893 April 2: California Cricket Association annual meeting held in the Occidental Hotel, San Francisco.

____ President William Greer Harrison of the Olympic Club donates the Harrison Trophy to the CCA.

____ Four Bay Area teams participate in league competition.

____ Santa Monica Cricket Club founded.

____ Arthur M. Wood scores 201 not out for the Belmont Club of Philadelphia out of a total of 422, the largest recorded individual "first-class" score in America.

____ Third tour of U.S. by the Gentlemen of Ireland, captained by J.M. Muldon.

____ G.S. Patterson scores 1,748 runs in a season to gain the American record for most runs scored.

____ The North American record for the third wicket partnership, 267 runs, is established by A.M. Wood (182) and G.S. Patterson (132) playing for Germantown CC versus Philadelphia CC.

____ May 14: California opens its championship season.

____ Hood scores 124 not out for Alameda against the Pacific Cricket Club in San Francisco.

____ San Francisco Cricket Club, re-established by Berkeley Veterinary professor Dr. Bowhill, plays its first match against California, Webster scoring 114 not out in the victory.

____ Klinknerville Ground used by Oakland CC and Alameda CC.

____ Burlingame Country Club founded on the Peninsula. A Burlingame CC travels to Calistoga to play Lake County clubs for the first time.

____ Riverside and Santa Monica polo grounds leased by Robert Bettner. Santa Monica polo grounds, located at Sixth Street and Nevada (later known as Wilshire Boulevard) became the home ground of the Santa Monica CC.

____ Economic depression hits California starting with collapse of Riverside Bank. California Baseball League collapses in San Francisco Bay Area.

1895 Associated Cricket Clubs of Philadelphia organization set up to plan cricket in the city.

1896 May 27: John A. Lester's batting and bowling enabled the Haverford College XI to defeat St. Paul's School team. He scored 103 not out and took 5 wickets for 15 runs in the game, which was played in Concord, New Hampshire.

____ May 28: R. Hogue scored 108 runs of a total 166 for 6 wickets made by the Alameda CC in a game with the Wanderers of San Jose, played in San Francisco. E. Hood scores 152 for Alameda against the Pacific Cricket Club, to become highest individual scorer in California.

____ June 19: Haverford College under the captaincy of John A. Lester wins the intercollegiate cup by defeating the University of Pennsylvania.

____ September 28: Eighth Australian team to tour England visits U.S. Philadelphia beats Australia by an innings and 68 runs after compiling the highest ever score of 525 runs. F.H. Bohlen scored 118 of this total, the first ever century scored against any visiting cricket team to the United States.

____ First partnership of over 300 in North America when W.R. Cobb and H. Tyers of New York combine in a New York match for 305 runs.

____ Eight English trip to the U.S., captained by Lord Hawke, wins both matches against Philadelphia.

____ G.S. Patterson's XI makes 689 runs against an American West Indian XI to establish a North American record for runs scored in the first innings.

____ Alameda CC wins the California Cricket Association Championship Harrison Cup for the third successive time to become sole owners of the cup, with a record of 16 wins and 4 losses.

____ W.C. Robertson (206 not out) and A.D. Sheath (188 not out) score 340 not out for the Bohemians CC v. Robertson's old club, the California CC. U.S. and California record third wicket partnership.

____ Citrus Colony Cricket Club established at Penryn in Placer County.

____ The sixth wicket partnership record of 265 established by H.I. Brown (153) and E.W. Clark (106) in Philadelphia.

____ Hindu Gymkana Cricket Club founded in Bombay.

____ Ninth English team, captained by F. Mitchell, visits the U.S. and West Indies.

____ Alameda CC wins the Hunter-Harrison Cup.

____ Loomis Cricket Festival in Placer County. San Francisco and outlying county cricket teams compete.

____ Bohemian CC of San Francisco enters the CCA under captaincy of "Digger" Robertson.

____ Ninth Australian team visits U.S. and extends visit beyond the East Coast to Chicago and San Francisco. Australia plays a California XVIII at the San Francisco Presidio.

____ Haverford College visits England to play the Public Schools. This trip by Haverford College is made five more times before 1925.

____ Bohemian CC wins the Hunter-Harrison Cup. Bohemian CC captain Robertson scores 208 not out at Golden Gate ground v. Pacific CC.

____ Placer County CC visits Lake County CC for the first time. Lakeport CC bowled out for 12, lowest recorded score in California.

____ First attempt by women to get the vote in California fails.

____ In southern California the Henry Huntington Pacific Electric Car system links Riverside and Santa Monica with the Orange Blossom Express train. The rich growers of Riverside extend their social activities to Santa Monica.

1897 Queen Victoria's Diamond Jubilee.

____ Tenth English team to visit Philadelphia is captained by West Indian–born Pelham Warner.

____ *Cricket Club Life* is established; the magazine covers the game until it ceases publication in 1901.

____ G.S. Patterson captain the third Philadelphia team to tour England.

____ Alameda CC regains the Hunter-Harrison Cup.

____ Second Loomis Cricket Festival.

____ G.S. Patterson's side breaks the American record for the number of runs in one innings, scoring 689 runs against A.M. Wood's XI.

1898 Harold Ward (Alameda CC) joins the Klondike Gold Rush.

1899 Prince Kumar Ranjitsinhji visits the U.S. with an England team of amateurs including "Croucher" Jessop of Gloucestershire, renowned for his explosive batting, especially 102 runs against the Australians in 1902.

____ Alameda CC wins the Hunter-Harrison Cup.

____ Citrus Colony cricket ends at Penryn after malaria decimates the fruit growers in the area.

____ Professional baseball re-established in the San Francisco Bay Area.

____ Spanish American War begins.

____ Oceanside women's cricket team plays for the first time in San Diego County.

____ Boer War begins and several English cricketers from the Bay Area fight in South Africa in British regiments.

____ California CC wins the Brown Pennant.

____ Thirteenth English team visits Philadelphia, captained by B.J.T. Bosanquet.

____ California CC wins the Brown Pennant.

____ Sacramento CC and Santa Cruz CC join the California Cricket Association.

1901 Boer War ends. Death of Queen Victoria and the assassination of President McKinley. Theodore Roosevelt, first president to emphasize sport, founds National Collegiate Athletic Association.

____ Edward VII becomes king of England.

____ Lord Hawke's team, captained by Pelham Warner, plays California XVIII en route to New Zealand.

____ California XVIII puts on a strong performance. All out for 125 they had Hawke's team 155/8.

____ B.J.T. Bosanquet, originator of the bosey (in Australia) or googlie scores 50 runs in the game.

____ R.H. Brown scores 103 against Bosanquet's XI in Philadelphia.

____ Alameda CC wins the Brown Pennant.

____ First recorded ladies' match in the Bay Area.

____ July 27: Playing for Portland CC, Charlie Lawrence takes 10 wickets for 14 runs versus Tacoma, repeating the feat he achieved 21 years earlier against Oakland.

____ Riverside defeated by Luis Rey in southern California in a match held at the Riverside Polo Grounds.

1902 Lord Hawke's team, captained by Pelham Warner, plays a close game in San Francisco on its way to New Zealand.

____ Fourteenth England team, under Kent captain C.J. Burnup, visits Philadelphia.

1903 John A. Lester leads Gentlemen of Philadelphia tour of England.

____ Pacific CC wins the Brown Pennant.

____ "Cliff Dwellers" cricket team of Sausalito founded in Marin County.

____ North American fourth partnership record of 313 established in Chicago by Canadian J.M. Laing (299) and J.G. Davis (103) playing for Chicago Cricket Club.

____ San Francisco Cricket Club wins the championship Brown Pennant.

____ 375 cricket matches played in Philadelphia.

____ First MCC tour and fifteenth English tour of Philadelphia and West Indies.

____ J.B. King scores record high individual score of 315 and is involved in the record partnership for the second wicket of 339 with A.M. Wood, playing for Belmont v. Germantown CC.

____ Hamilton CC visits Philadelphia.

____ Philadelphia tours Bermuda.

____ San Francisco County Cricket Club beats Alameda for the championship Brown Cup.

____ Harold Richardson, who played eight games for Surrey CCC club in 1899, is the dominant batsman in northern California; he scores 730 runs for an 146 average per game and scores a century for U.S. versus Canada.

____ J.B. King scores 300 and 344 not out against Merion CC.

____ San Francisco County CC wins the California Cricket Association Cup.

____ C.K. Turner plays for Santa Cruz CC.

____ University of Pennsylvania tours overseas. "Ranji" V. Hordern, an Australian googlie bowler on the side, takes 213 wickets in a season for an American record.

____ Second MCC and sixteenth English tour of U.S., captained by H. Hesketh Prichard.

1904 May Sutton of Santa Monica wins Women's Singles at Wimbledon. First American to win Wimbledon.

1906 San Francisco Earthquake destroys San Francisco baseball headquarters in Golden Gate Park. Cricket and baseball move their operations to Oakland. Ex–Surrey County and California's best batsman Harold B. Richardson is killed in the earthquake.

____ Fifth Gentlemen of Philadelphia tour of England, captained by John A. Lester. The Philadelphia team proved long lived; eight of them lived until age 90 or above.

____ J. Barton King takes 87 wickets for an average of 11 runs per wicket. This record stands until 1958 when it is beaten by H.L. Jackson of Derbyshire CC. King becomes the only American cricketer to take 100 first-class wickets on a tour of England, taking 115 for 10.45 runs. He scores 26,730 first-class runs in his career, his highest score being 344 runs, and a total of 529 first-class wickets for an average 12.48 runs per wicket.

____ Santa Monica Cricket Club is reorganized.

____ Marion Jones, stepdaughter of Senator Jones of Santa Monica, wins U.S. Lawn Tennis Championship at Germantown CC.

1908 Thomas Dudley, mayor of Santa Monica, donates a loving cup as a trophy to be played for by southern California cricket teams.

____ Southern California All Stars with C.P. Hurditch, defeat Clifton (Arizona) after scoring a Southern California record 333 runs at the polo ground pitch of Santa Monica CC.

1909 Imperial Cricket Council founded with Lord Harris as Chairman. U.S. is not invited to join the ICC as South Africa and Australia join.

____ Fourth tour by Gentleman of Ireland of U.S., under captaincy of F.H. Browning.

____ J.B. King takes all ten wickets bowled in a match — a feat he achieved three times in his career.

____ Pacific CC wins the California Cricket Association Cup as league cricket starts again in California following the earthquake.

____ H.R. Elliot scores 121 not out for Pacific v. San Francisco.

____ Los Angeles Cricket Club secures lease at the Pacific Electric Vineyard station. Pavilion is built.

____ North American first innings partnership of 264.

____ Barbarians CC wins the California Cricket Association Cup. S.A.H. Moverly, the Barbarians' leading scorer, ends the season with 217 runs in 11 innings.

____ San Mateo CC join the CCA for the first time, providing a turf wicket on which their opening bowler Sid Stewart takes all 10 wickets.

1910 Los Angeles Cricket Club leading batsman C.P. Hurditch scores 633 runs in 12 innings to lead the southern California averages with 57.55. Australian Patrick Higgins is the second leading scorer, with 627 runs for an average of 52.25. Three Los Angeles players score centuries: C.P. Hurditch (137), Higgins (127) and N. Tempest (100). Best bowling is W. Meggett, 28 wickets for an 8.12 average; M.J. Bhumgara, 46 wickets for 8.35; and Archie Mitchell, 39 wickets for 9.78. Santa Monica Cricket Club averages are led by H. Justice, 454 runs for a 45.10; and W.R. Mitchell, 181 runs for a 30.16. SMCC best bowlers are F.E. Lee, 11 wickets for 8.90; and H. Justice, 37 for 12.02.

____ Santa Monica mayor Dudley presents the Dudley Club as the Southern California Cricket Championship cup. He does the same for tennis, seeing the importance of sport for enhancing the health image of Santa Monica real estate.

____ Santa Monica Cricket Club v. Los Angeles at the Polo and Vineyard Grounds.

____ Progressive Hiram Johnson elected governor of California.

1911 First All Bermuda tour to visit the U.S.

____ Wanderers CC wins the California Cricket Association Cup.

____ Women's cricket team defeats the Santa Monica CC (who were playing left handed). C. Percy Hurditch returns to Belmont CC from the Santa Monica CC. The quintessential English sportsman in Philadelphia, he focused his efforts on promoting soccer.

____ Women get the vote in California.

1912 Fourteenth Australian tour of England stops in Philadelphia on return to Australia.

____ Record ninth inning partnership in North America between O.D. Rasmussen (106 not out) and J.D. Cochrane (101 not out) in Los Angeles.

____ Patrick J. Higgins, the rugby coach at the University of Southern California, scores the American record of seven centuries, 159, 100, 100, 121, 182, 110 and 240 not out, for a total of 1,012 when playing for the Los Angeles Cricket Club, finishing the season with a 180.83 batting average.

____ Incogniti CC, first English private cricket club and seventeenth to tour America, captained by E.J. Metcalf, plays Philadelphia, Maryland and Long Island in New York.

1913 The most extensive Australian tour ever of North America results in 53 games including a loss to Germantown CC by four wickets.

____ Belmont CC folds.

____ J.J. Beecham scores 249 in British Columbia.

____ Los Angeles Cricket Club pavilion burns down.

1914 First World War.

____ Mrs. George Waring organizes a Santa Monica first aid group to knit socks for British soldiers as part of the British community response in California for British soldiers in the Great War.

1916 Sinking of the *Lusitania* brings America into the First World War on the Allied side.

____ Cricket played throughout the First World War in New York

Prohibition Era

1919 Volstead Act passed and Prohibition begins.

____ First World War revealed the nationwide need for a fitness program, so the secretary of war, Needham D. Baker, encourages the NCAA to continue the development of intermural sports in 1920. University of Michigan leads the way in 1921 when it requests all male students to take part in outdoor sports. By 1920, 90 percent play sports of the some kind.

____ B.J. Kortlang dominates New York cricket as a batsman.

____ Flu kills 2 million in the U.S. U.S. lost 150,000 in the Great War.

____ 300 lynchings of blacks in the South.

____ Incogniti CC second visit and eighteenth English tour to Philadelphia.

____ Professional golf begins to replace cricket as the sport of choice in Philadelphia.

____ Boris Karloff plays for the Overseas Cricket Club in Los Angeles. Hollywood impact on cricket begins in California.

1920 Sydney Deane, Australian silent actor playing for the Santa Monica CC, is the best cricketer in southern California.

1921 Philadelphia Pilgrims tour England — not treated as a first-class tour by Wisden.

____ Santa Monica Cricket Club dominates southern California cricket competition, with ex–New South Wales cricketer Sydney Deane as captain. The rapidly expanding movie industry brings many cricket-playing actors to California.

____ Oil industry takes off in California as Ford cars open travel to the masses.

____ Free Foresters tour Philadelphia, nineteenth English team to do so.

____ Santa Monica Cricket Club wins southern California tournament.

____ Santa Barbara Cricket Club founded.

____ Incogniti CC third tour of Philadelphia, the twentieth English team to visit.

____ Los Angeles businessman Ernest Wright helps keep cricket going in southern California, refounding the Los Angeles Cricket Club.

1926 Last Halifax Cup game played in Philadelphia.

1928 UCLA campus founded in the Westwood suburb of Los Angeles.

____ West Indies tour the U.S. — last visit to Philadelphia

During the Great Depression

1929 Stock market crash.

____ Golden Gate CC re-formed in San Francisco.

____ Ex-England cricket captain Cecil Aubrey Smith arrives in California to reprise his Broadway role in *The Batchelor*.

____ Third West Indies tour of the U.S.

1931 Nottinghamshire furniture millionaire Sir Julien Cahn leads an amateur cricket tour

of Bermuda and North America that bypasses Philadelphia in favor of New York.

1932 Hollywood CC founding member P.G. Wodehouse, formerly of the Dulwich School, becomes secretary.

____ Australian 56-game tour managed by Arthur Mailey in the U.S. and Canada. No games are played in Philadelphia for the first time, as cricket had been abandoned by the private clubs. Three games in southern California are played at Westwood. Donald Bradman scores 3,357 runs on the tour for an average of 108.

____ Prohibition ends.

1933 May 23: Dedicated cricket grounds and pavilion are opened at Griffith Park with Claude King as master of ceremonies.

____ Screen Actors Guild founded with four members of the Hollywood Cricket Club on the board, including Claude King and Boris Karloff.

____ Griffith Park Cricket Association founded in December.

____ *Cavalcade*, by Noel Coward, results in Hollywood hiring 400 English actors; cricket booms as a result.

1934 Frank Doyle founds Corinthian Cricket Club.

____ Cricket taught to UCLA students.

1936 Hollywood Cricket Club tours San Francisco and British Columbia.

____ Marin CC formed in San Francisco to play visiting Hollywood CC.

1937 England captains "Gubby" Allen, C.B. Fry, Walter Hammond and Aubrey Smith play for Hollywood Cricket Club and Pasadena CC.

____ Doc Severn starts playing regularly for the Hollywood Cricket Club.

1938 David Niven and Errol Flynn play for Hollywood Cricket Club.

During World War II

1940 Olympic Cricket Club in San Francisco wins the Price Cup and inaugurates Australia v. New Zealand cricket day.

____ Cricket played at Gilmore Stadium, site of the present Farmer's Market, to raise money for charity. The Hollywood Stars baseball team, owned by the Brown Derby founder and Bing Crosby, did the same.

____ America's greatest cricket statistician writes for the Illinois Cricket Association journal when Karl A. Auty is president.

____ Olympic Cricket Club are runners up in the Price Cup.

____ Doc Severn helps keep cricket alive in southern California during the war years by organizing games against visiting Australian and Royal ships or Royal Navy air force personnel.

1944 C. Aubrey Smith is knighted for his services to British-American relations.

Postwar through 2000

1948 Sir Aubrey Smith dies and his ashes are spread on the wicket at the Sussex County Ground in Hove.

____ Olympic Cricket Club wins the Northern California League.

____ Olympic Cricket Club wins the Price Cup.

____ The Hollis and Herbert Durity play for the Los Angeles Cricket Club as league cricket gets going again in California. The West Indian influence on the local game increases following the establishment of air service to the West Indies.

1949 Doc Severn founds Britamer CC in Los Angeles.

1950 Los Angeles CC becomes the team of choice for the West Indian community after the Durity brothers join the team.

1958 Harlequins Cricket Club founded and game against the Hollywood Cricket Club is televised.

____ John Haywood works the Los Angeles Skyhawks football broadcasts.

1959 Westwood Cricket Club founded by Sid Albright.

1960 Westwood Cricket Club changes its name to University Cricket Club.

____ John Marder becomes president of the Griffith Park Cricket Association.

____ John Marder founds and is elected first president of the United States of America Cricket Association (USACA). American cricket revived by USACA.

____ Jim Vivian elected president of the NCCA. Later dies in a San Francisco Bay yachting accident.

1964 September 27–28: Yorkshire County, captained by Brian Close and England's League Champions, plays at Griffith Park.

1965 Worcestershire CCC, County Champions, with Tom Graveney, Basil D'Olivera and Ken Flavel play at Griffith Park.

____ New Zealand, managed by Walter Hadlee, plays at Griffith Park.

____ Raisinland Trophy competition between northern and southern California starts. Trophy originated as part of the Raisinland festival in San Jose, at which Miss Raisin 1963 was British.

1966 Auty International Trophy (Canada v. U.S.) dinner held at Roosevelt Hotel. Mayor Tom Bradley and consuls from Britain, Canada, New Zealand and Australia in attendance.

____ Claude Vibart Worrell elected president of the SCCA.

1968 First United States team to play in England.

____ Rachel Heyhoe, English women's cricket team captain, plays in San Jose.

1969 September 21–24: Irish Union v. SCCA.

1971 Southern California Cricket XI tours Jamaica.

1976 University CC tours England.

1977 University CC tours England.

1978 University CC tours England.

1979 Six southern Californians represent the U.S. in the Prudential Cricket World Cup, held in England.

1982 Second ICC Trophy held in England.

____ Ian Botham plays at Woodley in Van Nuys.

____ Raju Patel, Redwood CC member, takes 73 wickets in a season.

____ Griffith Park Cricket Association grounds are taken over by equestrians after they overturn the cricketers' trust deed in court.

____ Queensland CC, captained by Australian captain Alan Border, visits California with fellow test cricketers Geoff Dymock and Robbie Kerr.

____ MCC, led by Tony Lewis and including test players Fred Titmus, Mustaq Muhammad, John Jameson and Nick Cook, struggle to beat a Northern California side on which former India test player Abid Ali scores 38 and Peter Musprat 64. Raju Patel, who broke the northern California bowling record in 1981, takes 4 wickets for 34 runs.

____ Northern California Cricket Association expands to two divisions.

____ Marin CC member Peter Musprat scores a northern California record 837 runs in a season.

1986 U.S. participates in the Third ICC Trophy, held in England.

1990 U.S. participates in Fourth ICC Trophy, held in the Netherlands. Neil Lashkari scores first first-class century for the U.S. v. Fiji since Furness scored 108.

____ Ventura Cricket Club founded.

____ Victoria Cricket Club founded.

1992 MCC visits California.

1994 Fifth ICC Trophy held in Kenya.

1995 Los Angeles Krickets, a homeless cricket team, tours England. The game at Hambledon makes CBS news. Local Los Angeles TV Channel 5 covers cricket on sportscasts for the first time in California history. The Krickets prove that there is an American audience for cricket with local players.

1997 Sixth ICC Trophy in Malaysia.

____ MCC visits California.

1999 Australia A v. India A at Woodley Park.

2000 ICC World Cup is awarded to Canada.

Chapter Notes

Preface

1. Ron Chernow, *The House of Morgan* (New York: Grove Press, 1990) p. 97.
2. Ibid., p. 171.
3. Ibid., p. 170.
4. Martin Williamson, "Commentary," .com, February 18, 2005.

Chapter 1

1. Tom Melville, *The Tented Field* (Ohio: Bowling Green Press, 1999), p. 3. Melville describes the evolution of wicket in the American colonies. For more on the literary evolution of America's identity read Malcolm Bradbury, *Dangerous Pilgrimages: Trans-Atlantic Mythologies and the Novel* (London: Penguin, 1995) p. 62.
2. William Byrd, *The Secret Dairy of William Byrd* (Richmond, Virginia: Dietz Press, 1941). According to Ron Yeoman, writing in the *Los Angeles Times* on the occasion of Yorkshire County Cricket club's visit to play the southern California Cricket association in 1964, the dairy manuscript kept from 1709–12 was in shorthand code. It was found in the Huntington Library in San Marino, California, in 1939, and decoded. It was found to be the shorthand code of a William Mason of London, who published a shorthand textbook in 1672.
3. Henry Wiencek, *George Washington: His Slaves and the Creation of America* (New York: Ferrar, Strauss and Giroux, 2003), p. 45. William Bird III squandered his father's inheritance on the gambling tables from 1760 to 1770 and fell from his rank as one of Virginia's wealthiest planters. Wiencek, p. 144.
4. John A. Lester, *A Century of Philadelphia Cricket* (Philadelphia: University of Pennsylvania Press, 1951), p. 5.
5. David McCullough, *John Adams* (New York: Simon and Schuster, 2001), p. 328.
6. David Underdown, *Start of Play: Cricket and Culture in Eighteenth Century England* (London: Penguin, 2001), p. 14.
7. Ibid., p. 69.

8. St. James developed during the reign of Stuart king James the First of England. A.L. Rowse, *The Early and Later Churchills* (London: Reprint Society, 1959), p. 126. The St. James neighborhood owed its existence to Henry Jermyn, who was granted the land by the Crown and built on it with his earnings at the gambling table. King James' mistress Arabella Churchill lived there along with many aristocrats close to the king, including the earl of Oxford and the earl of Feversham, who commanded James' army.
9. Tony Lewis, *Double Century: The Story of the MCC and Cricket* (London: Guild, 1987), p. 29. Lewis states:

> With money riding high on cricket, it was only to be expected that those that put the money up for the great matches should frame the rules and regulations: they had the most to lose. This explains why the aristocrats that drafted the 1774 code not only emphasized the gentlemanly qualities of fair play, but included regulations for the aspect of the game they had done most to encourage — gambling.
> Indeed, the Laws derived their authority from the prestige of the men who had made them. For example, the drafts of 1744 and 1774 were made by the London club and "committee of Noblemen of Gentlemen of Kent, Hampshire, Surrey, Sussex, Middlesex and London."

Ashley Mote, *The Game of Cricket*: privately published show rules written in 1744 and published in 1755.
10. George M. Trevelyan, *Illustrated English Social History* (London: Longmans, 1963), vol. 3, p. 112.
11. Niall Ferguson, *Empire: How Britain Made the Modern World* (London: Penguin, 2003), p. 86.
12. Steven Wells, "Cricket in America," *The Guardian*, July 27, 2004.
13. Wells.
14. Henry W. Brands, *The First American: The Life and Times of Benjamin Franklin* (New York: Anchor, 2000), p. 327. George III's ascension to the throne occured nine years after his father, Frederick, prince of Wales, died in Surrey after being hit by a cricket ball in 1751.

15. Carol Clark and Allen Guttman, "Art and Artist," *Journal of Sports History* 22, no. 2 (summer 1995): 85–90. West's student by correspondence, John Singleton Copley, became famous for his portraits of America's founding fathers. Both West and Copley were part of an American colony that stayed in London throughout the Revolution. West became the president of the Royal Academy and made his reputation with his paintings of *General Wolff's death at Quebec* and *General Clive's Victory in India*. West was patronized by King George III as he celebrated American victories with fellow expatriates in the London.

16. Gervase Jackson-Stops, ed., *The Treasure Houses of Britain: Five Hundred Years of Private Patronage and Art Collecting* (New Haven: Yale University Press, 1986), p. 509. The same page depicts Walter Hawkesworth Fawkes with a bat and two notched stumps, circa 1760.

17. Underdown, p. 70. Romney was still paid two guineas by the Sackvilles as a family retainer in 1768, long after his playing days were over.

18. Ibid., p. 72. London's population was 750,000 in 1780 — more than five times as large as Philadelphia, America's largest city at the time.

19. Ibid., p. 87. The English Civil War resulted in the Stuart King Charles I losing his head. Oliver Cromwell succeeded him as lord protector of the Puritan-dominated Commonwealth. Cromwell frowned on cricket. After he died, cricket was no longer frowned on as a frivolous waste of time in Charles II's reign.

20. Ashley Mote, *The Glory Days of Cricket: The Extraordinary Story of Broadhalfpenny Down* (London: Robson Books, 1997), pp. 87–88, 169–191.

21. Ibid., p. 87.

22. Ferguson, p. 85.

23. Lester, p. 7.

24. Ferguson, p. 85.

25. Edwin G. Burrow and Mike Wallace, *Gotham City: A History of New York to 1898* (London: Oxford University Press, 1999), p. 219, 247; see also George Kirsch, *The Creation of American Team Sports 1838–72* (University of Illinois, 1989) p. 13.

26. Lewis, p. 29.

27. Burrow and Wallace, p. 247.

28. Ibid.

29. Lester, p. 5.

30. "Order Book of General Peter Muhlenberg, March 26–December 20, 1777," *Pennsylvania Magazine of History and Biography* XXXIII (1909), pp. 262–263.

31. George Ewing, *The Military Journal of George Ewing (1754–1824): A Soldier at Valley Forge* (New York, 1938) p. 47. There are several theories of origin of the term "wicket" including that of being derived from *wicken*, Anglo-Saxon for a wicker gate used to pen sheep for the night. Shepherds on the Sussex Downs used their crooks to hit wads of wool in front of the wicken; this became synonymous in cricket with the wicket or set of stumps aimed at by the bowler.

32. Ibid.

33. Wiencek, p. 318; McCullough, p. 405.

34. Kenneth Kramer, "Notes from the Special Collections: Anyone for Cricket?" *Dartmouth Library College Bulletin*, April 1992.

35. Lester, p. 7.

36. Steven Wells, "What Goes Around, Comes a–Rounders," *Guardian*, July 22, 2004.

37. John Thorn, et al., *Total Baseball: The Official Encyclopedia of Baseball* (New York: Viking, 1997), p. 5.

38. Lester, p. 6.

39. Deb Das, U.S. editor of *Cricinfo*, "Cricket in Crescent City, New Orleans," June 6, 2005, www.cricinfo.com. The Crescent City Cricket Club remains merely a claim until documentary evidence is provided.

40. Moxley Sorrel, *Recollections of a Confederate Staff Officer* (New York and Washington: Neale Publishing, 1905), quoted in: Timothy Lockley, "The Manly Game: Cricket and Masculinity in Savannah, Georgia, in 1859," *International Journal of the History of Sport* 20, no. 3 (September 2003: 77–99.

41. Stephen Ambrose, *Nothing Like It in the World: The Men Who Built the Continental Railroad 1863–1869* (New York: Touchstone Books, 2000).

42. Op. cit., Steven Wells, "What Goes Around."

43. Edwin L. Doctorow, *Ragtime* (New York: Bantam, 1976) p. 266.

44. Op. cit., Wells.

45. Jonathon Yardley, *Ring: A Biography of Ring Lardner* (New York: Athenaeum, 1984), p. 66.

46. Yardley, p. 9.

47. Ibid.

48. Ibid., p. 11.

49. Ibid., p. 13.

50. Ibid.

51. Sir Derek Birley, *A Social History of English Cricket* (London, Acorn Press, 1999). Tragically, Kipling's warning that sport was not sufficient preparation for the carnage of modern warfare between equally equipped forces did not prevent the loss of Hornung's or Kipling's son and Barrie's foster son George Llewellyn on the Somme in 1916 during the First World War.

52. Douglas Booth, "Theory: The Foundation of Social Change," *Sports History Review* 34, no. 2 (2004). This article explores identity achieved through sport with a useful theoretical format.

Chapter 2

1. George B. Kirsch, *The Creation of American Team Sports* (Urbana: University of Illinois, 1989), p. 24.

2. Henry Chadwick, "Old Time Cricket," *Outing* XII, no. 5 (August 1888): 462.

3. Tom Melville, *The Tented Field*, p. 11.

4. Kirsch, p. 24.

5. George B. Kirsch, "American Cricket before the Civil War," *Journal of Sports History*, XI, no. 1 (spring 1984): pp. 38–42.

6. Ibid., p. 47.

7. Ibid., p. 47.

8. Ibid., quoting *Wilke's Spirit of the Times* article, August 12, 26, 1854.

9. Ibid., p. 34.

10. Tom Melville, p. 14.

11. Ibid., p. 80.

12. George Kirsch, "American Cricket: Players and Clubs Before the Civil War," *Journal of Sport History* 11, no. 1 (spring 1984): 38.

13. Burrows and Wallace, p. 733.

14. Ibid.

15. Ibid.

16. Fred W. Lange, *History of Baseball in California and the Pacific Coast League 1847–1930* (Oakland: self published, 1963), p. 7.

17. John Marder, *The International Series: The Story of the United States versus Canada at Cricket* (London: Kaye and Ward, 1968) pp. 36–37.

18. *The Sporting News*, June 1890.
19. Kirsch, *Journal of Sports History*, p. 38.
20. G.H. Lohmes, "Athletics at Cornell," *Outing*, March 1881, p. 453. For more on Tom Hughes experiences in America read Asa Briggs, *Victorian People* (London: Penguin, 1954), p. 174.
21. Kirsch, p. 210.
22. Ibid., p. 66.
23. Ibid., p. 63.
24. Ibid.
25. Christopher Devine, *Harry Wright: The Father of Professional Baseball* (North Carolina: McFarland, 2003), p. 14.
26. Ibid.
27. Ibid., p. 17.
28. Ibid.
29. Ibid.
30. Tom Melville, p. 13.
31. Ibid., p. 18.
32. Ibid.
33. Kirsch, p. 42.
34. Ibid., p. 48; *Clipper*, May 12, 1860, p. 31.
35. Marder, p. 43.
36. Ibid., p. 45.
37. Ibid., p. 48.
38. Ibid., p. 50.
39. Ibid., p. 55.
40. Ibid., p. 60.
41. Marder, p. 39.
42. Ibid.
43. Fred Lillywhite, Ed. Robert Marlar, *The English Cricketers' Trip to Canada and the United States in 1859* (London: Worlds Work Ltd., 1980), p. 32.
44. Ibid.
45. Marder, p. 34.
46. Lillywhite, p. 35.
47. Tom Melville, p. 52.
48. Ibid.
49. Kirsch, "American Cricket," pp. 40–45.
50. Tom Melville, p. 34.
51. "Championship Between the Excelsior and Atlantic Clubs of Brooklyn," *The New York Illustrated News*, August 4, 1860, p. 196.
52. Op. cit., Kirsch, *Journal of Sports History*, pp. 40–45.
53. Ibid., p. 34.
54. Ibid., p. 81.
55. Ibid.
56. Ibid., p. 85.
57. Ibid. Kirsch quotes Chadwick.
58. Alan H. Levy, "Myth Making and Hero Worship in Post Frontier American Society," in *The Cooperstown Symposium on Baseball and American Culture 2001* (North Carolina: McFarland, 2001), p. 55.
59. Ibid., p. 97.
60. "Yankee Slugger's Bat Still Has Clout," *LAT*, Friday, December 3, 2004, A24. Photographer Mathew Brady popularized the use of daguerreotypes during the Civil War.
61. Devine, p. 20.
62. Ibid.
63. M.M. Graff, *Central Park and Prospect Park: A New Perspective* (New York: Greensward Foundation, Inc., 1985), p. 107.
64. *New York Times*, 1865.
65. Kirsch, p. 42. On July 4, 1856, a few mechanics of the Ogdensburgh Railroad founded a cricket club at Rouse's Point, New York, composed mainly of natives.

The New Brighton Mechanics club was "principally composed of players whose livelihood is acquired by personal labor." To avoid confusion with the white-collar New Brighton Cricket Club, the Mechanics changed their name in 1858 to the Staten Island Cricket Club.
66. Tom Melville, p. 78. Arthur A. Outerbridge, the SICC president after the Civil War, played with the Philadelphia side in the first Halifax Cup competition in Nova Scotia in 1874, the same year that his sister introduced tennis from Bermuda to the cricket club. Mrs. Outerbridge has been credited with introducing tennis to America, but George Wright brought tennis rackets to Boston on his return from the Boston Redsocks and Philadelphia Athletics baseball tour of England in 1874. Either way, from the 1870s on, women played tennis in increasing numbers.
67. Ibid.
68. Lange, pp. 7–8.
69. "Great Baseball Match Between the Atlantic and Eckford Clubs of Brooklyn," *Frank Leslie's Illustrated*, November 4, 1865, p. 104–105.
70. Ibid., p. 104.
71. Charles Peverelly, *The Book of American Pastimes* (New York, 1866), p. 501.
72. Peter Wynne-Thomas, *The Complete History of Cricket Tours at Home and Abroad* (London: Guild, 1989), p. 17.
73. Lange, p. 7.
74. Ibid.
75. Tony Lewis, *Double Century: The Story of the MCC and Cricket* (London: Guild Books, 1987) p. 131.
76. Ibid., p. 110.
77. Ibid., p. 114. Rusy is quoted in Lewis' book.
78. Ibid., p. 125.
79. Gregory Gillespie, "Wickets in the West, Culture and Constructed Images of Nineteenth Century Canada," *Journal of Sports History* 27, no. 1 (2000): 55.
80. Thomas, *Complete History of Cricket Tours*, p. 18.
81. *New York Times*, July 20, 1873.
82. Ibid.
83. *NYT*, July 27, 1874, pp. 8–4.
84. *NYT*, July 18, 1875, pp. 7–16.
85. *TAC*, Nov. 28, 1878, p. 82.
86. *NYT*, July 18, 1875, pp. 7–16.
87. Will Roffe, "Cricket in New England and the Longwood Club," *Outing* XVIII, no. 3 (June 1891): 251.
88. *NYT*, September 15, 1878, p. 2–6.
89. Tom Melville, p. 66.
90. Tom Melville, p. 65.
91. Lewis, p. 100.
92. Wynne-Thomas, *Complete History*, p. 22.
93. Ibid.
94. Ibid.
95. Peter Wynne-Thomas, *Give Me Arthur* (London: Arthur Barker, 1985) p. 34.
96. Ibid.
97. Wynne-Thomas, *Complete History*, p. 23.
98. Ibid.
99. Jack Pollard, *The Complete Illustrated History of Australian Cricket* (Melbourne: Viking, 1995), p. 75.
100. Ibid., p. 69.
101. Alfred James. *Cricket Matches Played by Australian Teams in Canada and the United States of America 1878 to 1995* (Sydney: Private Publication, 1996).
102. Wynne-Thomas, *Complete History*, p. 28.
103. Ibid., p. 28.
104. *Outings* XII, no. 2 (May 1888): 186.
105. Ibid.

106. *TAC*, July 11, 1890, p. 85.
107. Lawrence Timpson, "American Polo," *Outing*, July 1896, pp. 30–332.
108. Tom Melville, p. 88.
109. Ashis Nandy, *The Tao of Cricket* (India: Oxford University Press, 2000), p. 61.
110. Mihir Bose, *A History of India* (London: Andre Duetsch, 1990), p. 33.
111. Ibid., p. 17.
112. Nandy, p. 1.
113. Joel Zoss and John Bowman, *Diamonds in the Rough* (Chicago: Contemporary Books, 1996), p. 84.
114. Nandy, p. 115.
115. Geoffrey C. Ward, *Baseball* (A. Knopf and Son, 1994), quoted by Ken Burns.

Chapter 3

1. John A. Lester, *A Century of Philadelphia Cricket* (Philadelphia: State University of Pennsylvania Press, 1951), pp. 16–47.
2. George B. Kirsch, "American Cricket," p. 33.
3. Ibid.
4. John Marder, *The International Series* (London: Kaye & Ward, 1963), pp. 13–16.
5. Kirsch, p. 33.
6. Ibid.
7. Tony Lewis, *Double Century*, p. 98.
8. Tom Culp, "Profile: The Philadelphia Cricket Club," *The CC Morris Quarterly*, winter 1998, p. 10.
9. Ibid.
10. Lewis, p. 98.
11. Culp, p. 10.
12. Ibid., p. 11.
13. Kirsch, *Creation of American Team Sports*, p. 218.
14. Ibid.
15. Ibid.
16. Ibid.
17. Ibid.
18. Ibid., p. 40.
19. Eric Midwinter, *The Illustrated History of County Cricket* (London: The Kingswood Press, 1992), p. 23.
20. Marder, p. 39, and Fred Lillywhite, Introduction by Robin Marler, *The English Cricketer's Trip 1859* (London: Windmill Books, 1980), pp. 1–2.
21. Henry Altham and E.W. Swanton, *A History of Cricket* (London: Unwin, 1963), p. 103.
22. Ibid.
23. Lillywhite, *English Cricketers' Trip to Canada*, p. 39.
24. Lester.
25. Lillywhite, p. 40.
26. Lester, p. 21.
27. Ibid.
28. Christopher Devine, *Harry Wright*, p. 26.
29. Ibid.; *CC Morris Quarterly*, winter 1998, p. 11.
30. Ibid., p. 30.
31. Ibid.
32. Lester, pp. 27–31; March scorecard, p. 34.
33. Altham and Swanton, p. 101.
34. Ibid.
35. Ibid., p. 102.
36. Lester, p. 28.
37. Wynne-Thomas, *Complete History*, p. 17.
38. Lester, p. 35.
39. John Mulvaney and Rex Narcourt, *Cricket Walk-about: The Australian Aboriginal Cricketers Tour 1867–1868* (London: MacMillan, 1988), p. 12.
40. Altham and Swanton, p. 133.
41. C.L.R. James, *Beyond the Boundary* (NY: Pantheon Books, 1963), p. 175.
42. Ibid., p. 181.
43. R.A. Fitzgerald, *Wickets of the West, or, The Twelve in America* (London: private publication, 1874), p. 113.
44. Altham and Swanton, p. 154.
45. Simon Rae, *W.G. Grace*, (London: Faber and Faber, 1998), p. 112.
46. Ibid, p. 124.
47. Ibid, p. 124.
48. Ibid, p. 125.
49. Ibid.
50. Ibid.
51. Joel Zoss and John Bowman, *Diamonds in the Rough* (Chicago: Contemporary Books, 1989), p. 234.
52. Rae, p. 125.
53. Zoss and Bowman, p. 389.
54. C.L.R. James, *Beyond the Boundary* (London: Phaidon, 1958), p. 162.
55. Lester, p. 45.
56. Arthur MacLaren, *Cricket Old and New* (London: Longmans, 1924), pp. 43–48.
57. *The American Cricketer*, Jan.–Feb. 1894, p. 5.
58. Roland Bowen, Cricket: *A History of Its Growth and Development throughout the World* (London: Eyre and Spottiswood, 1970), p. 160.
59. Pollard, *Complete Illustrated History*, p. 49.
60. Alfred James, *Cricket Matches*, p. 2.
61. *TAC*, Jan.–Feb. 1894, p. 5.
62. Ibid.
63. Ibid.
64. Owen Wister, *Romney* (Philadelphia: State University of Pennsylvania, 2001 ed.), p. 184.
65. www.ChestnutHillAcademy.org.
66. George B. Kirsch and J. Thomas Jable, "Organized Sport Comes to Philadelphia: The Rise of Cricket and Baseball," *Journal of Sporting History*, 1983, p. 26.
67. *TAC*, Jan.-Feb. 1894, p. 5.
68. Peter Wynne-Thomas, *Give Me Arthur* (London: Arthur Barker, 1985), p. 39.
69. Lester, pp.73–74.
70. Howard MacNutt, "Philadelphia Cricket Past and Present," *Outings* XII, no. 5 (August 1888): 457–459.
71. Lester, p. 83.
72. W.G. Grace, *Autobiography* (London: Longmans, 1902), p. 57.
73. Lester, p. 83.
74. Ibid., p. 82.
75. Ibid.
76. George Newhall, "Cricket in America," *Outings* V, no. 1 (1884), p. 48.
77. Ibid.
78. "Ancient History," *TAC*, Jan.–Feb. 1894, p. 6.
79. Hilary McD. Beckles, *The Development of West Indies Cricket: The Age of Nationalism*, vol. 1 (Georgetown: University of West Indies Press, 1998), p. 19.
80. Allan Curry Thomas, "Haverford College Cricket," *Outings*, p. 237.
81. Ibid.
82. Ibid.
83. Roffe, "Cricket in New England," p. 252.
84. Ibid.
85. "Cricket," *Our Monthly Record* XII, no. 4 (July 1888): 376; "Cricket," *Our Monthly Record* XII, no. 3 (June 1888): 283.

86. Henry Chadwick, "Cricket at Harvard," *Outings*, 1892, p. 425.
87. Ibid.
88. Ibid.
89. Ibid.
90. Roffe, pp. 251–253.
91. Chadwick, "Cricket at Harvard," p. 425.
92. Ibid.
93. Ibid.
94. Ibid.
95. Lester, p. 84.
96. Ibid., p. 85.

Chapter 4

1. Henry Chadwick, "Cricket in the Metropolis," *Outing*, August 1890, p. 43.
2. Ibid., p. 44.
3. Jerome Flannery, *The American Cricket Annual for 1891* (NY: C.J. Sabiston's, 1892), p. 10.
4. Ibid.
5. Ibid., p. 10.
6. *TAC* XV, no. 390 (Jan. 27, 1892): 1.
7. Flannery, *American Cricket Annual for 1891* (NY: C.J. Sabiston's, 1892), p. 21.
8. Ibid., p. 15.
9. Ibid.
10. Jerome Flannery, *The American Cricket Annual for 1892* (New York: The Week's Sport Co.), p. 10.
11. Ibid., pp. 12–13.
12. Wynne-Thomas, *Complete History*, p. 35.
13. Ibid.
14. "Lord Hawke in Boston September 1891," *The Cricket Field*, May 14, 1892, p. 25.
15. Wynne-Thomas, p. 35.
16. Ibid.
17. *TAC* XV, no. 393 (April 1892).
18. Ibid., p. 12.
19. *TAC*, August 15, 1903, p. 139.
20. "Two New York Veterans," *Cricket: A Weekly Record*, December 14, 1912, p. 593.
21. *TAC*, March 1894, p. 15.
22. *TAC* XV, no. 402 (June 29, 1892): 99.
23. *TAC*, September 7, 1892, p. 8.
24. *TAC*, March 1894, p. 15.
25. Flannery, *American Cricket Annual for 1891*, p. 13.
26. Flannery, *American Cricket Annual for 1891*, p. 107.
27. *TAC*, May 4, 1892, p. 35.
28. Flannery, *American Cricket Annual for 1891*, p. 14.
29. *TAC*, March 30, 1892, p. 24.
30. Ibid., p. 42.
31. "Personnel of the Team of Irish Cricketers." *TAC*, September 7, 1892, p. 160.
32. Flannery, *American Cricket Annual for 1893*, p. 102.
33. Ibid., p. 39.
34. Ibid.
35. Ibid.
36. Ibid.
37. Ibid.
38. Ibid.
39. James, *Cricket Matches*, Australia v. New York District XVIII scorecard, p. 13.
40. Wynne-Thomas, p. 39.
41. Ibid.
42. Ibid., p. 41.

43. Roger Norman Buckley, *Slaves in Red Coats* (New Haven: Yale Press, 1979), p. 5. As early as 1779, the Black Carolina corps was recruited from loyalists and free blacks. After the British surrender at Yorktown the corps was distributed among several British islands. On the eve of the French Revolution, it numbered 300 men and was quartered in Granada. Barbadian troops relieved Nevis and St. Kitts in 1666 and in King George's War (1740–48), black militiamen took part in expeditions to Nova Scotia, Quebec, Cape Breton, Florida, Havana and Carthagena. After the American Revolution, West Indian militia troops were used for defence. They were thought superior to white British troops in the tropics as they were less susceptible to yellow fever. Cricket became the game for the West Indian soldiers at the turn of the nineteenth century before it became the official game of the British army in 1841.
44. Melvin Adelman, *A Sporting Time: New York City and the Rise of Modern Athletics, 1820–1870* (Urbana: University of Illinois Press, 1986), pp. 20–44.
45. "Cricket Records of 1894," *TAC* XVIII, no. 473 (May 11, 1895), p. 5.
46. Flannery, *American Cricket Annual 1895*.
47. Wynne-Thomas, p. 42.
48. Ibid.
49. T.C. Turner, "Cricket," *Outing*, May 1896, p. 32.
50. T.C. Turner, "Cricket," *Outing*, July 1896, p. 57.
51. T.C. Turner, "Cricket," *Outing*, August 1896, p. 107.
52. Arthur Inkersley, "Cricket," *Outing* LXXIX, no. 2 (November 1890): 202–203.
53. Ibid., p. 203.
54. Ibid.
55. Arthur Inkersley, "Cricket," *Outing* LXXIX, no. 2 (August 1896): p. 108.
56. "International Cricket," *Outing* XXX, no. 6 (September 1897): 612–614.
57. "Cricket," *Outing* XXXI, no, 3 (December 1897): 306–7.
58. Wynne-Thomas, p. 46.
59. Pelham Warner, *Cricket in Many Climes* (London: Heinmann, 1900), pp. 83–85.
60. T.C. Turner, "Cricket," *Outing* XXX1, no. 2 (November 1897) 194–195.
61. J.A. Lester, *A Century of Philadelphia Cricket*, p. 54.
62. Warner, p. 91.
63. Ibid.
64. Ibid.
65. *TAC*, Aug. 15, 1903, p. 139.
66. *Outing*, November 1897.
67. Warner, p. 165.
68. Ibid.
69. Roland Wild, *The Biography of Colonel, His Highness Shri Sir Ranjitsinhji* (London: Rich and Cowan, 1934), p. 61.
70. Ibid., p. 62.
71. Benny Green, *The Wisden Book of Cricketers' Lives* (London: Queen Anne Press, 1983), p. 1000.
72. Wild, p. 51.
73. Alan Ross, *Ranji: Prince of Cricketers* (London: Collins, 1983), p. 114.
74. Inkersley, p. 326.
75. *TAC*, Aug. 15, 1903, p. 139.
76. "On the Local Creases," *New York Times*, September 9, 1900.
77. Ibid.
78. Ibid., p. 55.

79. Ibid., p. 58.
80. Arthur Goodwill Spalding, *Spalding's Official Cricket Guide 1906* (New York: American Sports Company, 1906), p. 87.
81. Ibid.
82. Ibid.

Chapter 5

1. Flannery, *American Cricket Annual for 1891*, p. 26.
2. Lester, *Century of Philadelphia Cricket*, p. 164.
3. Corporate Resolution and Club Charter hangs on the PCC dining-room wall.
4. E. Digby Baltzell, *Sporting Gentleman* (New York: The Free Press, 1995), p. 22. Randolph Churchill married into the Jerome family, who financed their horse racecourse at Jerome Park from mining wealth. The mining town of Jerome in Arizona was named for them. The Jerome marriage was the early part of a trend that resulted in 300 aristocratic British and Europeans marrying into wealthy American families as Europe's ailing aristocracies shored themselves up with wealth from the New World.
5. "The Veterans' Annual Dinner," *TAC*, Jan.-Feb. 1894, p. 5.
6. Bowen, *Cricket*, chronology section.
7. Thomas Wharton, "Inter-City and International Cricket in America," *Outing*, September 1891, pp. 138–140.
8. Ibid.
9. H.W. Slocum, Jr., "Lawn Tennis in the South," *Outing*, March 1895, p. 502.
10. Ibid., p. 503.
11. Thomas Wharton, "Inter City and International Cricket," *Outing*, June 1892, p. 177.
12. Ibid.
13. Ibid., p. 177.
14. Ibid., p. 178.
15. Ibid.
16. Ibid.
17. Ibid.
18. Ibid., p. 180.
19. *TAC*, Nov. 30, 1892, p. 187.
20. "Pittsburgh," *TAC* XV, no. 390 (January 27, 1892): 9.
21. Lester, p. 138.
22. "Haverford College Cricket," *Outing*, June 1895, p. 238.
23. Ibid.
24. Ibid.
25. Henry Chadwick, "Cricket at Harvard," *Outing*, June 1894.
26. *TAC*, April 1894, p. 174.
27. Ibid.
28. Ibid.
29. *TAC*, November 1894, p. 205.
30. *TAC*, April 1894, p. 175.
31. James, *Cricket Matches*, p. 14.
32. *TAC*, May 11, 1895, p. 25.
33. Op. cit., Thomas, "Haverford College Cricket," *Outing*, June 1896, No. 3, p. 239.
34. Ibid.
35. Ibid.
36. Ibid.
37. "Cricket," *Outing* XXVIII, no. 5 (August 1896): 106.
38. Ibid.

39. "Cricket," *Outing* XXVIII, no. 4 (July 1896): 82.
40. J. L. Turner, *Outing*, September 1896, No. 6, p. 140.
41. "Cricket," *Outing* XXIX, no. 7 (October 1896): 88.
42. Ibid., p. 89.
43. "Cricket," *Outing* XXIX, no. 2 (November 1896): 202.
44. Ibid., p. 203.
45. James, p. 13–16.
46. "Cricket," *Outing* XXX, no. 2 (May 1897): 189.
47. Ibid.
48. Ibid.
49. T.C. Turner, "Cricket," *Outing* XXX, no. 4 (July 1897): 414.
50. T.C. Turner, "Cricket," *Outing* XXX, no. 5 (August 1897): 507.
51. Ibid.
52. Lester, p. 156.
53. *Outing*, August 1897.
54. Ibid.
55. Ibid.
56. T.C. Turner, "Cricket," *Outing* XXX, no. 6 (September 1897): 612.
57. Ibid.
58. Wisden, p. 627.
59. T.C. Turning, "Cricket," *Outing* XXX, no. 7 (October 1897): 92.
60. Ibid.
61. Lester, *A Century of Philadelphia Cricket*, p. 158.
62. Ibid., p. 159.
63. Ibid.
64. Wisden, p. 123.
65. Ibid., p. 549.
66. Ibid.
67. Ibid., p. 593.
68. Ibid., p. 849.
69. Pelham F. Warner, *Long Innings: The Autobiography of Sir Pelham Warner* (London: George Harrap and Sons, 1951), p. 46.
70. Warner, *Cricket in Many Climes*, p. 97.
71. T.C. Turner, "Cricket," *Outing* XXXI, no. 2 (November 1897): 194.
72. Ibid., p. 194.
73. Warner, *Long Innings*, p. 45.
74. Ibid.
75. Benny Hill, *The Wisden Book of Cricketer's Lives* (London: Queen Anne Press, 1986), p. 149.
76. McCullough, *John Adams*, p. 441.
77. Wisden, pp. 626–627.
78. Henry Altham, *A History of Cricket* (London: Elm Books), p. 268.
79. Wisden, p. 128.
80. Ibid., p. 799.
81. Ibid., p. 426.
82. Ibid., p. 540.
83. Warner, p. 162. Warner followed Sir Arthur Priestley's 1895 tour to the West Indies, where he was welcomed as a local hero because he had been born in Trinidad where his father was Lord Chief Justice. Lord Hawke appointed him captain for his 1902 of New Zealand and Australia that stopped to play a game in San Francisco. In 1903 the MCC appointed him England test captain in Australia. The administrative skills he demonstrated were later put to good use for the MCC, where he became secretary once his playing days were over.
84. *TAC*, October 28, 1898, p. 124.

85. Wild, *Biography of Colonel, His Highness Shri Sir Ranjitsinhji*, pp. 61–62.
86. Ibid.
87. Ibid.
88. Ibid.
89. Ibid., p. 63.
90. Ibid.
91. "John Barton King," *Cricket Quarterly*, October 17, 1966, p. 61.
92. Lester, p. 168.
93. Marder, *International Series*, p. 157.
94. Ibid., p. 168.
95. "Umpires Wanted," *TAC*, April 30, 1900, p. 90.
96. Wisden, p. 529.
97. Ibid., p. 991.
98. Lester, p. 177.
99. *TAC*, November 15, 1901, p. 251.
100. Tom Melville, *Tented Field*, p. 108.
101. Lester, p. 208.
102. "Grand Cricket Match at Grantham," *Grantham Journal*, Saturday, August 14, 1903, p. 4.
103. Ibid.
104. Ibid.
105. Scores discussed here are in the score-card section of the book.
106. Jules Tygiel, *Past Time: Baseball as History* (New York: Oxford University Press, 2000), p. 54.
107. Ibid., p. 55.
108. Lester, introduction, p. xvii.
109. Birley, *Social History*, p. 196.
110. Lester, p. xvii.
111. Ibid, p. 83.
112. Zoss and Bowman, *Diamonds in the Rough*, pp. 39–41.
113. Ibid.
114. Lester, p. 211.
115. Bowen, p. 224.
116. Birley, p. 196.
117. *Spalding's Cricket Manual 1907.*
118. Pollard, *Complete Illustrated History*, p. 185.
119. Pollard, p. 194.
120. Ibid., p. 197.
121. Ibid., p. 201.
122. James, p. 41.
123. Pollard, p. 201.

Chapter 6

1. Robert Cromie, *The Great Chicago Fire* (New York: McGraw Hill, 1958), p. 1.
2. A.T. Andreas, *History of Chicago from the Earliest Period to the Present*, vol. 2 (Chicago: Andreas Publishing, 1885), p. 614; *Chicago Tribune*, May 7, 1860.
3. Cromie, p. 2.
4. Anthony Trollope, *North America* (London: Penguin, 1968), p. 99.
5. Cromie, p. 1.
6. Cromie, p. 2.
7. Ibid., p. 5.
8. Ibid., pp. 210–211.
9. Tom Melville, *Tented Field*, p. 81.
10. Cromie, pp. 228–229.
11. Stephen Birken, *Marshall Field III* (New York: Simon and Schuster, 1964), p. 19.
12. Joseph Durso, *Baseball and the American Dream* (Chicago: The Sporting News, 1986), p. 23.
13. Ibid., p. 116.
14. Duane Doty, *The Town of Pullman* (Pullman: T.P. Stackhauer, 1893), p. 150.
15. Yardley, *Ring*, p. 47.
16. Kevin Boller, "The Colourful History of Canadian Cricket," Canadian Cricket Association, www.canadiancricket.org/index.jsp?page_id=history|, 2001.
17. Zoss and Bowman, *Diamonds in the Rough*, p. 393.
18. Durso, p. 107.
19. Ibid., p. 111.
20. Dean A. Sullivan, ed. *Early Innings: A Documentary History of Baseball 1825–1908* (Omaha: University of Nebraska, 1995), p. xvi.
21. Ibid.
22. John Thorn, *Baseball: Our Game* (New York: Penguin, 1995), p. 54.
23. Tom Melville, p. 90.
24. www.census.gov/population/www/documentation/twps0029/tabox.html.
25. "Chicago in Cricket," *TAC*, July 17, 1890, p. 62.
26. "Chicago in Cricket," *TAC*, July 24, 1890, p. 69.
27. "Chicago in Cricket," *TAC*, September 11, 1890, p. 85.
28. Ibid.
29. Ibid.
30. Ibid.
31. Jerome Flannery, *The American Cricket Annual for 1890* (New York: Sports Publishing), p. 17.
32. Ibid.
33. Green, *Wisden Book of Cricketers' Lifes*, p. 199.
34. Ibid.
35. Ibid.
36. *TAC*, Nov. 25, 1891, p. 214.
37. Ibid.
38. Ibid.
39. Ibid.
40. Ibid.
41. J.G. Davis, "Cricket in the West," *The American Cricket Annual for 1893*, (New York: self-published, 1893), p. 77.
42. *TAC*, September 13, 1893, p. 181.
43. Harold Evans, *The American Century* (New York: Knopf, 1998), p. 33.
44. Ibid.
45. William J. Pesavento and Lisa C. Raymond, "Men Must Play; Men Will Play: Occupations of Pullman Athletes, 1880–1900," *Journal of Sports History* 12, no. 3 (winter 1985), p. 246.
46. Ibid.
47. *TAC*, May 24, 1894, p. 46.
48. *TAC*, May 24, 1894, p. 24; June 23, 1894, p. 53; June 24, 1894, p. 77; June 30, 1894, p. 85; July 28, 1894, p. 117; August 11, 1894, p. 134; September 1, 1894, p. 157; September 29, 1894, pp. 190–191.
49. *TAC*, Sept. 29, 1894, p. 190.
50. Flannery, *The American Cricket Annual for 1896* (New York: C.J. Sebastion, 1897), p. 63.
51. *TAC*, July 13, 1895, p. 103.
52. Flannery, *American Cricket Annual for 1896*, p. 67.
53. Ibid.
54. Ibid.
55. Pesavento and Raymond, p. 216.
56. Ibid.
57. Percy Williamson, "Cricket in the West," *The American Cricket Annual for 1896* (New York: C.J. Sebastion, 1897), p. 73.

58. Wisden, p. 900.

59. Pollard, *Complete Illustrated History*, p. 144.

60. Tom Melville, p. 65.

61. Joseph G. Davis, "Cricket in the West," *The American Cricket Annual 1897*, (New York: C.J. Sebastion, 1898), p. 64.

62. "Mr. P.F. Warner's Team vs Chicago," *The American Cricketer*, Oct. 28, 1898, p. 123.

63. Warner, *Cricket in Many Climes*, p. 167.

64. "Chicago Correspondence," *Cricket Club Life* (Cricket Club Life Publication Co.), September 23, 1899.

65. Wisden, p. 529

66. *TAC*, April 30, 1900, p. 90.

67. Ibid.

68. Ibid.

69. Ibid.

70. Ibid.

71. *TAC*, August 15, 1903, p. 139.

72. Ibid.

73. Davis, Jos G. "The Club of the West," *Spalding Official Cricket Guide 1907* (New York: American Sports Publishing Co., 1907), p. 55.

74. Ibid.

75. F.F. Kelly, ed., *Spalding's Official Cricket Guide, 1913* (New York: Sports Publishing Company, 1913), pp. 81–82.

76. Ibid.

77. F.F. Kelly, ed., *Spalding's Official Cricket Guide, 1910* (New York: Sports Publishing Co., 1910) p. 105.

78. F.F. Kelly, ed., *Spalding's Official Cricket Guide, 1913* pp. 81–82.

79. Ibid, p. 83.

80. Ibid.

81. Ibid.

82. Wisden, p. 576.

83. Ibid., p. 82.

84. "Club House Gossip," *TAC*, June 1915, p. 124.

85. Sir Donald Bradman, *The Bradman Albums: Selections from Donald Bradman's Official Collection, 1925–1949* (Bowral: Bradman Museum, 1963).

86. Marder, *International Series*, p. 271.

87. Karl A. Auty, *Illinois Cricket Association Manual* (Chicago: ICA, 1940), pp. 60–61.

Chapter 7

1. Frederick Jackson Turner at the 1893 World's Fair in Chicago postulated that the Western frontier was tamed after settlement averaged one person per square mile.

2. Tom Melville, "The Wild and Wicket West," *True West Magazine*, April 1995, p. 49.

3. Tom Melville, *The Tented Field*, p. 52.

4. *Alta California*, April 15, 1852, pp. 2–5.

5. John S. Holliday, *The World Rushed In* (New York: Simon and Shuster), p. 40. Holliday notes that 52,000 miners were at work by October 29, 1850, prospecting on the forks of the Yuba, Feather, Bear and American rivers. San Francisco's population increased from 2,000 to 30,000 by 1850, and there were 44 steamers employed in river trade with Sacramento. There were 12 ocean-going steamers connecting with Panama and mail was semimonthly. Thirty thousand gold miners came from France, Germany and England by 1852 and 25,000 from China. San Francisco became a cosmopolitan city overnight. (Holliday, pp. 411–13).

6. Marder, *International Series*.

7. Tom Melville, *Tented Field*, p. 39.

8. *Alta California*, July 6, 1857, p. 2–2.

9. Holliday, p. 455, notes the percentage of women went from 8 percent in 1850 to 30 percent by 1860. Twenty-four percent of the San Francisco immigrants were from foreign lands in 1850, and this percentage rose to 39 percent by 1860.

10. Franklin Walker, *A Literary History of Southern California* (Berkeley: University of California, 1950).

11. *San Francisco Directory* (San Francisco: Excelsior Steam Press, 1859).

12. Ibid.

13. "Cricket at Union Race Course," *Alta California*, November 25, 1859.

14. Paul Zigg and Mark Medeiros, *The Pacific Coast League* (Urbana: University of Illinois Press, 1994), p. 5.

15. Thomas Rodman, *History of American Mining*, quoted in Paul Friggens, "Cousin Jacks: Cornish Miners in the American West," *American West Magazine* XV, no. 6 (Nov.–Dec. 1978), pp. 55–72.

16. Tom Melville, "The Wild and Wicket West," *True West Magazine*, June 1995, p. 49. See also Tom Melville, *Tented Field*, p. 35. J.S. Holliday notes that quartz mining — the kind found at the Empire Mines in Grass Valley — first started at Fremont in Mariposa County when he imported Cornish miners to work his stake at the Bear Flag mine (p. 456). Quartz mines required better capitalization, and joint stock companies were used to raise this money at first from the East Coast and then later via the Pacific Stock Exchange located on Montgomery Street in San Francisco.

17. Ibid.

18. *Alta California* VIXXII (April 18, 1869): 1.

19. *San Francisco Directory* (San Francisco: Excelsior Steam Press, 1868).

20. Tom Melville, "Wild and Wicket West," p. 50.

21. *San Francisco Chronicle*, October 21, 1869.

22. Ibid.

23. Ibid.

24. Colin White, *Victoria's Navy: The Heydey of Steam* (London: Kenneth Mason, 1983), p. 70; Harry Williams, *The Steam Navy of England* (London: Allen and Co., 1903), p. 35.

25. *TAC*, II, no. 38 (July 25, 1878): 19.

26. Ibid., p. 20.

27. *Oakland Times*, July 4, 1878, p. 3.

28. *Oakland Times*, July 25, 1878, p. 3.

29. Ibid.

30. *Oakland Times*, July 30, 1878, p. 3.

31. *Oakland Times*, May 3, 1879, p. 3.

32. Fred Lange, *Memories and Musings of an Old Time Baseball Player* (San Francisco: private publication, 1934), p. 14. Lange mentions that the same Ed Taylor was the first baseball player to wear a glove, in 1886.

33. Gai Ingham Berlage, *Women in Baseball* (New York: Praegar, 1994), p. 3.

34. Ibid. Women's college baseball started at Vassar College in Philadelphia in 1866, at Smith College in 1879, and at Mount Holyoke in 1891 (p. 6). Women's baseball peaked in 1928 two year after the debut of softball in 1926 (p. 7).

35. *TAC*, October 11, 1877.

36. *TAC*, Jan. 24, 1878, p. 86.

37. Altham and Swanton, *History of Cricket*, pp. 144–145.

38. Pollard, *Complete Illustrated History*, p. 103.

39. Lucky Baldwin was a colorful character. After the

Baldwin Hotel burned down in 1898, he moved permanently to southern California where expanded his food growing ranch — which had supplied the hotel — into a racehorse training ranch at his Santa Anita home. The Santa Anita racetrack is still in operation today.

40. Pollard, p. 146.
41. Ibid., p. 103.
42. Ibid. In 1878, Spofforth took 281 prior to the tour, 326 wickets in England, 69 in the United States and then 88 during the run-down tour of Australia for a total of 764 wickets at a cost of 6.8 runs each (p. 104). On the same tour, Charlie Bannerman was the first Australian batsman to score centuries in England, New Zealand and Canada. When they returned to Sydney 20,000 turned out to greet them, about 10 percent of the city's population. The successful gates from the tour put the nail in the coffin of the English traveling elevens such as George Parr's and Edgar Willsher's and ultimately paved the way for county cricket in England. This was the first time a colonial side had beaten England at their own game in England, and from this moment baseball stood little chance in Australia, as victory in England had the same impact as winning the American War of Independence did to Americans; the difference being that with the Industrial Revolution having provided urban conditions necessary for the development of team sport on a competitive basis, cricket was substituted for war in the Australian psyche. Paul Johnston in *The Age of Liberalism* (New York: Harper Perennial, 1995, p. 50), makes the argument that the evolution of cricket after Waterloo allowed the members of the English aristocracy — most notably the duke of York and Lord Beauclerk — to substitute the game for dueling; whereas in France or Germany cricket was not played by the establishment and the Heidleberg scar caused by the nick of a rapier became a badge of honor in much the same way that skateboarders show off their injuries to each other today in America.

43. James, *Cricket Matches*, p. 6.
44. *TAC*, Dec. 27, 1877, p. 82.
45. *TAC*, October 1878, p. 83.
46. John Thorn, et al. *Total Baseball. The Official Encyclopedia of Major League Baseball, Fifth Edition* (New York: Viking, 1997). Look under 1881.
47. Altham and Swanton, *History of Cricket*, p. 102.
48. Pollard, *Complete Illustrated History*, p. 22.
49. Wynne-Thomas, *Complete History*, p. 23.
50. Ibid.
51. *TAC*, December 12, 1881, p. 265.
52. Ibid. *The Olympian*, published privately for members of the Olympic CXXX in San Francisco, is quoted in TAC, Dec. 12, 1881, p. 265.
53. Ibid.
54. Lange, p. 16.
55. Pollard, p. 68.
56. Ibid., p. 69.
57. William Clulow, ed. Peter Wynne-Thomas, *The Log of the "Old Un" from Liverpool to San Francisco* (1886; reprint, Exeter Press, 1994).
58. Zigg and Medeiros, *Pacific Coast League*, p. 6; Southern California Historical Society, *The Rise of Spectator Sports*, 1961, p. 298.
59. *Oakland Tribune*, April 19, 1884, p. 5:2.
60. *Oakland Times*, Tuesday, October 21, 1884, p. 3:4.
61. *Oakland Times*, November 28, 1884, p. 4:3.
62. *TAC*, July 28, 1884, p. 152.
63. "Charles A. Klinkner," *Journal of the Emeryville Historical Society* III, no. 3 (August 1992): 1–10.

64. Elinor Richey, *The Ultimate Victorians of the Continental Side of San Francisco Bay* (Berkeley: Harrell Books, 1970), p. 91.
65. Ibid., p. 109.

Chapter 8

1. *TAC*, November 1891.
2. Tom Patterson, *Riverside: A Colony for Southern California* (Riverside: Press Enterprise Co.,1971); *TAC*, November 1892.
3. California Cricket Association 1898 pamphlet, Keeling papers.
4. Robert Louis Stevenson, *From Scotland to Silverado*, ed. Bernard Bailyn (Boston: Belknap Press, 1966), p. 192, wrote about the area in 1881 when on his honeymoon with Fanny Osborne.
5. Henry Maudlin, *Clearlake Highlands and the Clear Lake Park Story* (unpublished oral history, 1975; Lake County Museum, Lakeport, California; Arthur Goodwill Spalding, F.F. Kelly, ed., *Spalding's Cricket Annual* (New York: American Sports Publishing, 1909), p. 10.
6. Roy Cavanagh, *Cotton Town Cricket* (Bolton and District Cricket Association, 1987), p. 3.
7. Maudlin, no. 287, note 7366.
8. Ibid.
9. Maudlin, no. 287, note 995.
10. Marion Greoble, *A History of Boating* (unpublished paper, 1968; Lake County Museum, Lakeport, California), p. 5.
11. Brighton Cricket Club fixture list for 1887, Keeling records (Lake County Museum, Lakeport, California).
12. David Underdown, *Start of Play*, p. 14. The Australians played their first game of each English tour on the Duke of Norfolk's ground at Arundel.
13. Keeling records, Lake County Museum.
14. Ledger, Keeling records, Lake County Museum.
15. *Lakeport Bee*, April 1890 (Scrapbook; Keeling papers, Lake County Museum, Lakeport, California).
16. Ibid.
17. Ibid.
18. Ibid.
19. Aurelius O. Carpenter and Percy H. Millberry, *A History of Lake County 1881* (reprint, Lake County Publishing, 1988), p. 161.
20. Ibid., p. 378.
21. Maudlin.
22. Oral interview with the present owners, Ralph and Barbara Wilcox, of Meteor (formerly Red Hill) Ranch.
23. Maudlin.
24. Greoble, p. 7.
25. Keeling scrapbook, Keeling papers.
26. Green, *Wisden Book of Cricketers' Lives*, p. 767; Pollard, *Complete Illustrated History*, p. 46.
27. Alfred James, personal communication with the author.
28. "EMCC V English Eleven," *Australasian*, March 26, 1887.
29. Ibid.
30. *Australasian*, August 10, 1887, research by Alfred James.
31. *TAC*, 1891.
32. *San Francisco Chronicle*, July 7, 1892.
33. *TAC*, 1893.
34. Ibid.

35. *TAC*, 1893.

36. Lange, *History of Baseball*, p. 11.

37. Henry Splitter, "Los Angeles Recreation: The Rise of Spectator Sports," *Historical Journal of Southern California Quarterly* XLII, no. 2 (June 1961): 301; Peter Filichia, *Professional Baseball Franchises: From Abbeville Athletics to the Zanville Indians* (1993), p. 209.

38. *History of Placer County* (unpublished MA thesis, Penryn Museum, Placer County, California), p. 166.

39. Lange.

40. Samuel E. Gittens, The Foundation of Places County Horticulture 1850–1900: Unpublished MA Thesis, Sacramento State College 1958, p. 164.

41. "Little Bit of England," *Sacramento Bee*, Sept. 18, 1896, p. C6.

42. Ibid., p. 166.

43. Op cit. Gittens, p. 166.

44. *Citrus Colony Journal*, October 30, 1892.

45. Op cit. Gittens, pp. 91–92.

46. Ibid. Charles Turner was born in Reading, England, in 1871. After settling in Placer County in 1892 he bought 40 acres with his brother A.G. Turner at Edgewood. After planting plums and peaches they shipped the fruit to the Pioneer Fruit Company in Auburn for marketing. In 1915 Charles Turner was appointed Placer County horticultural commissioner. He joined the lodges of the Knights of Pythias, the Ancient Order of Foresters, and was a member of Miami Tribe No. 55 and the Independent Order of Red Men. The Red Men lodge in Nevada City owned Red Man Park in Nevada City, where cricket was played on occasion.

47. "Local Kickers, Interesting Game between Auburn and the Colony," *Citrus Colony News*, Feb. 13, 1897.

48. "Little Bit of England," *Sacramento Bee*, Sept 18, 1966, p. C6.

49. "Champion Football," *Placer Herald*, June 18, 1896.

50. Riverside Museum archives has the photo of H.P. Whitney. Barbara Pierce supplied the newspaper cuttings from which this information is gleaned.

51. Patricia Yeomans, *A Hundred Years of Southern California Tennis Champions* (Los Angeles: private publication, 1987).

52. Keeling papers.

53. *Placer Herald*, May 25, 1895.

54. *TAC*, 1895.

55. *Placer Herald*, May 25, 1895.

56. *Lakeport Bee* cutting in Keeling scrapbook, dated 1895, Keeling papers.

57. "Visit to Red Hill Manor," *Clear Lake Press*, Saturday, 21, 1898.

58. *Clear Lake News*, September 8, 1898.

59. "Lake County Athletes: A Team of Cricketers from Clear Lake Comes Down to Play the British Game," *San Francisco Chronicle*, October 20, 1895.

60. Keeling papers.

61. Ibid.

62. Ibid.

63. "A Victory by Seven Wickets," Keeling papers.

64. "The Champion Alameda's Win the Cricket Match," Keeling papers.

65. "Lake County Scores a Win," Keeling papers.

66. Ibid.

67. "Cricket Festival in California," *TAC*, May 1896, p. 14.

68. Arthur Coates, "Season's Summary of the Placer County Cricket Club, California," *TAC*, Dec. 1896, p. 80.

69. "California Cricket," *TAC*, Nov. 1896, p. 72.

70. "Named to Play Cricket," *San Francisco Examiner*, October 12, 1896.

71. Pollard, *Complete Illustrated History*. England's second game against Australia at Old Trafford in Manchester was notable for the selection of Prince Ranjitsinhji over the objections of Lord Harris, a future president of the MCC and for five years governor of Bengal Province in India. Ranjitsinhji made a brilliant debut in the second game scoring 61 runs in the first innings and the fastest century in a test match in the second innings, when he scored 113 runs before lunch. At the end of the innings the Indian prince from Rajastan was 154 not out. As we have seen, Ranjitsinhji's career was an illustrious one.

72. James, "Cricket Matches."

73. *San Francisco Examiner*, October 16, 1896.

74. Ibid.

75. Ibid.

76. *San Francisco Call*, November 1896, Keeling scrapbook, Keeling papers.

77. "A Jolly Time: The Tour of the Placer County Cricket Club," *Placer Herald*, Oct. 31, 1896.

78. Ibid.

79. Ibid.

80. Ibid.

81. *Citrus News*, Oct. 31, 1896.

82. Ibid.

83. Ibid.

84. Arthur Coates, "California Cricket," *TAC*, December 1896, pp. 79–80.

85. Joe Clark, "The Australian Tour of America 1897," in *Time and Game: The History of Australian Baseball* (privately published), p. 14. www.australian-baseballhistory.webcentral.com

86. Clark, p. 4.

87. Ibid., p. 5.

88. Ibid., pp. 5–10.

89. "California Cricket," *TAC*, June 1896, p. 103.

90. *TAC*, June 1897, p. 102.

91. Ibid.

92. "California Cricket," *TAC*, August 1897, p. 129.

93. "Jubilee Festivities at the Citrus Colony Club," *Citrus Colony News*, June 26, 1897.

94. Ibid.

95. *San Francisco Chronicle*, May 1897, Keeling papers.

96. Ibid.

97. Ibid.

98. Ibid.

99. Keeling papers.

100. *TAC*, August 1897, p. 129.

101. *American Cricketer*, 1898. Harry E. Butler, one of the founders of Citrus Colony and the president of the Penryn Fruit Company, financed the first successful mosquito eradication program in the United States under the auspices of Professor B. Hems of the University of California. By 1912 agricultural production was regionalized in California. Southern California became known for its oranges, Fresno for its grapes and raisins, the San Joaquin and Sacramento valleys for peaches, apricots, and cherries, and Barlett pears became synonymous with Lake County.

102. Oral communication with the Stellenbosch Cricket Team at Vancouver's Golden Oldies Cricket Tournament, 2000. One of the Pixton family members playing on the Stellenbosch team still grew Bartlett pears at Stellenbosch near Cecil Rhodes' residence in Cape

Colony, South Africa. Bartlett pears flourished in Stellenbosch soils in South Africa after their introduction by Placer County settlers following their hybridization at Barlett Springs in Lake County.

103. Keeling papers, 1898.

104. Wisden, 1899.

105. Arthur Coates, "California in Cricket," *TAC* XXI, no. 519 (July 15, 1898). On May 5 against Derbyshire, Harold Richardson scored 45 in an innings of 345 runs. Surrey was a strong side that included four England test players: Tom Hayward, Leveson-Gower, Robert Abel and William Lockwood. On May 29, Harold Richardson was run out for one run in the largest innings ever scored at the Oval. Abel carried his bat for 357 runs, the second largest individual score of all time in first-class cricket. Hayward scored 158 runs as Somerset were set target of 811 runs by Surrey. On August 10 and 11, Richardson played for Surrey against Sussex. With Sussex in trouble Ranjitsinhji teamed with George Bran putting on 325 runs for the fourth wicket. Ranji's effort was not enough to avert the follow-on, and in the second innings it was left to former England captain and Cambridge Blue Charles Aubrey Smith and his partner Joseph Vine to stay in for two hours to save Sussex from certain defeat. Aubrey Smith scored 51. After August, Richardson left Surrey, but his brief stay on the team had given him invaluable experience with international cricketers. Surrey County Cricket Club's home ground, the Oval, was where Charles William Alcock, Surrey's secretary from 1872, had his office. Alcock was well informed about American cricket, having organized Wright's and Spalding's baseball tours of England, and the Gentlemen of Philadelphia and Haverford College tour fixtures in England from 1884 to 1908.

106. "California Cricket," *TAC*, November 15, 1901, p. 254.

107. See David Lavender, *Nothing Seemed Impossible: William C. Ralston and Early San Francisco* (Palo Alto: America West Publishing Company, 1976), p. 336 for more on the Palace Hotel.

108. "Champion Cricketers of England to Play To-Day," *San Francisco Chronicle*, November 26, 1902, p. 7.

109. Warner, *Cricket in Many Climes* (London: Heinmann, 1900), p. 82.

110. Michael Rundell, *The Dictionary of Cricket* (London: Oxford University Press, 1995), p. 82.

111. Ibid.

112. *TAC*, Feb. 1, 1906, p. 30.

113. Ibid.

114. Henry Altham, *Scores and Biographies* (London: Unwin, 1958), p. 159.

115. Gordon Thomas and Max Morgan, *The San Francisco Earthquake* (New York: Dell, 1971), p. 66.

116. Ibid., p. 159.

117. Jerome Flannery, ed., "Cricket in the West," *Spalding's Official Cricket Guide for 1908* (New York: American Sports Publishing), p. 95.

118. Ibid.

119. Thomas H. Price, "Cricket in California," *Spalding's Official Cricket Guide for 1910* (New York: ASPC Publishing, 1910), p. 95.

120. Walter Umack, "Cricket in and Around San Francisco," *Spalding's Official Cricket Guide for 1912* (New York: ASPC, 1912), p. 33.

121. Ibid.

122. Ibid.

123. "Golden Gate Beat LACC," *Los Angeles Times*, July 6, 1913.

Chapter 9

1. Robert Glass Cleland, *California Pageant: The Story of Four Centuries* (New York: Alfred Knopf, 1950).

2. Splitter, "Los Angeles Recreation 1846–1900, Part 2," *The Historical Society of Southern California Quarterly* XIII, no. 1 (June 1961): 67–69.

3. Ibid.

4. *Los Angeles Herald*, November 1891, p. 5.

5. Jerome Flannery, *American Cricket Annual, 1893* (New York: Sports Press, 1893).

6. Walter Crawston, *History of Santa Monica* (Santa Monica, 1963), p. 84; David Lavender, *Nothing Seemed Impossible* (Palo Alto: America West Publishing Co., 1975), p. 321. Percival Jones was born in Herefordshire, England, and immigrated to California. He was elected sheriff of Trinity County in 1866 before making his fortune as superintendent of the Crown Pointe Mine on the Comstock Lode in Virginia City. Jones became famous for saving miners by taking a breathing hose beyond the point of a fire in the Yellow Jacket Mine fire of April 1869. He was elected Junior Senator of Nevada and served for 30 years. A key advocate of the Silver Standard, Jones was appointed by Republican president Benjamin Harrison to a commission studying currency in the Hague. After moving to Santa Monica, he kept his position as senator. He developed the Independent Railroad with a pier in Santa Monica Bay in an attempt to undercut the Southern Pacific's plans for a Los Angeles harbor built on the Phinaes Banning's property in El Segundo. After the railway venture failed, Jones founded the Santa Monica Bank and continued mining for silver in the Panamint and San Bernadino mountains, where he had some success. Jones' daughter Marion became California and U.S. tennis champion at the 1907 Tennis Open Championships held at the Germantown Cricket Club. When Jones died in 1912, the year English tea magnate and America's Cup participant Sir Thomas Lipton visited Santa Monica, Jones left a big void in the political and economic firmament of the beach city, just as it became a major player in the southern California urban environment.

7. Dr. Vince Moses, curator of the Riverside Museum, provided this information. Dr. Vince Moses book on orange wealth is in the final stages of publication.

8. Crawston, p. 69. Thomas Dudley was educated at Wyggeston in Leicestershire and arrived in California in 1890. He spent several years in Kern County as part of a colonization scheme before he became a naturalized American citizen in 1895 and moved to Santa Monica in 1896. In 1902, he went into the banking business. He became partners with Abbot Kinney after marrying Francis G. Ryan, the widow of Kinney's first partner. Kinney and Dudley were board members of the Santa Monica Improvement Association (1888), responsible for the subscription drives that funded the first tennis courts in Santa Monica at Washington and 3rd and the Casino Courts where Senator Jones' daughter played before becoming Pacific Coast Champion in 1897. Marion Jones went on to become National Champion in 1900 on the Germantown Cricket Club tennis courts in Philadelphia.

Dudley and Ryan tried to duplicate the successful sports infrastructure built in Santa Monica in Venice, where they built a clubhouse, golf course, tennis courts, and a racetrack. This infrastructure was soon replaced by the Venice canals as Kinney developed his European vision for the sand pile south of Santa Monica. Santa Monica had a diverse sport infrastructure from its inception, which made it resilient in the face of changing fads and interests in sports. As one of the first regular polo players in Santa Monica, Dudley played on the same team as George Waring (Riverside) and Roy Jones (son of J.P. Jones). Off the field, Dudley was regarded as the dean of Bay City bankers and was elected to the Santa Monica City Council in 1901, where he served as its president from 1902 to 1907 until he became mayor.

9. Ibid. The enduring monument to Dudley's vision was the laying out of Palisades Park, the lawn covered, palm-tree dotted brow overlooking the majestic Santa Monica Bay with Malibu to the north and Redondo Beach to south. This left Santa Monica, with its sponsorship of cricket, tennis, dancing and swimming, as the premier resort in southern California.

10. Tom Patterson, *Riverside: A Colony for Southern California* (Riverside: Press Enterprise Co., 1971), p. 222. The Riverside Polo Club was founded in 1892 with the help of James Bettner. Mathew Gage, manager of the English-owned Riverside Trust Company, became president; other founding members included C.E. Maud, George L. Waring, and William Pedley.

11. Ibid.

12. "Chas Le Bas Dies of Heart Trouble," *Oceanside Blade*, July 25, 1925. The obituary refers to Charles Le Bas as being a cousin of the Duke of Roxburgh but a letter from the present Duke in answer to my query elicited no connection. Le Bas owned a ranch in Hollywood in 1918 where he devoted his time to war gardening for the Red Cross. He was quite a keen tennis player, too. *Oceanside Blade*, Oct. 12, 1918.

13. "The Cricket Team," *The Riverside Press*, April 30, 1901.

14. Ibid.

15. "In Social Circles," *Riverside Press*, May 3, 1901.

16. Ibid.

17. U.S. Census for 1900.

18. *The Santa Monica Outlook,* April 1898.

19. Santa Monica Outlook, September 18, 1898.

20. Santa Monica Outlook, September 25, 1898.

21. John A. Lester, "Cricket in the Far West," *American Cricketer*, October 28, 1898, p. 127.

22. "Local Team Wins," *Santa Monica Outlook*, September 9, 1898.

23. Lester, p. 127.

24. E. Digby Baltzell, *Sporting Gentlemen* (New York: The Free Press, 1995), p. 30.

25. Ibid.

26. "Two Old Timers Return to Oceanside and Note Many Changes in Values," *Oceanside News*, September 9, 1948. Includes interview with Gladys Young Van Deerlin. Material supplied by Oceanside Historical Society archivist Kristi Hawthorne.

27. Ibid.

28. Leo Kuper, *Plural Societies* (London: Oxford University Press, 1963).

29. "Two Old Timers Return," p. 10.

30. *Oceanside Blade*, July 22, 1899.

31. *Oceanside Blade*, July 18, 1903.

32. *Santa Monica Outlook*, July 23 to September 27, 1907.

33. "Cricket Match," *Oceanside Blade*, Sept. 1, 1906. All *Oceanside Blade* references were provided by the Oceanside Historical Society, PO Box 125, Oceanside, CA 92049.

34. *Oceanside Blade*, August 25, 1906.

35. Ibid.

36. *TAC*, April 1908.

37. "Los Angeles Won in Cricket Match," *Santa Monica Outlook*, July 27, 1908, p. 1.

38. Ibid.

39. Ibid.

40. Ibid.

41. Charles W. Alcock, "Charles Percy Hurditch," *Cricket Weekley Record*, April 22, 1909, p. 67.

42. Mike Marquesas, *Anyone but England: Cricket and the National Malaise* (London: Verso, 1994), p. 14.

43. Spalding, *Spalding's Cricket Annual*, 1904.

44. *Santa Monica Outlook*, August 13, 1908.

45. Harold T. Shortridge, *Childhood Memories of a Mining Camp, 1915–1926* (Clifton: self published, 1951) p. 24.

46. Quoted in James Colghoun, *The Arizona Mining Copper Company* (Bisbee: Bisbee Publishing, 1899), p. 24.

47. *History of the Phelps-Dodge Corporation*. Bisbee's town hall has a photograph of cricket played in the area when copper was worked there by the Phelps-Dodge Corporation. Like the Pullman Corporation in Chicago, Phelps-Dodge encouraged all forms of recreation under their legendary Scottish president James Douglas.

48. James M. Patton, *History of Clifton* (Greenlee Chamber of Commerce, 1977), p. 96.

49. "The Cricket Grounds Are a Lively Place," *SMO*, August 21, 1908, p. 1.

50. "Close Game of Cricket Played," *SMO*, August 8, 1908, p. 6.

51. "Santa Monica Play Los Angeles at the Vineyard in the First Round of the Dudley Cup," *Santa Monica Outlook*, July 6, 1909, p. 1.

52. Ibid.

53. Arthur Goodwill Spalding, *Spalding's Official Cricket Guide 1909* (New York: American Sports Publishing Company, 1909), p. 111.

54. "Cricket Team Re-Organizes," *Santa Monica Outlook*, July 6, 1910, p. 1.

55. "Local Cricketers Won Its Return Match at the Vineyard by 206," *Santa Monica Outlook*, July 10, 1910, p. 1.

56. "Santa Monica Wins Again," *Santa Monica Outlook*, August 1, 1910, p. 1.

57. Ibid.

58. Ibid.

59. Arthur Goodwill Spalding, *Spalding's Official Cricket Guide 1910* (New York: American Sports Publishing, 1911), p. 115.

60. "Women Will Form Cricket Club at the Beach," *Santa Monica Outlook*, August 1, 1910, p. 1.

61. "Women Choose Team Captain," *Los Angeles Times*, August 19, 1910, p. 8, col. 3. Though May Sutton loaned her name to the original publicity she did not play cricket. In her place, she encouraged her mother and sister Florence to represent the Sutton family. The four tennis-playing Suttons grew up on their English father's ranch in San Marino, where they would have become familiar with cricket as it was the MCC that helped Wimbledon get organized tennis as a competitive sport in England from 1876. Captain Sutton's ranch was located at the opposite end of Allen Street from the Henry Huntington residence in San Marino.

62. "Interest in the Game Is International," *Santa Monica Outlook*, August 19, 1910, p. 4–5.

63. "California Cricket," *Spalding's Cricket Manual 1910* (New York: New World Sports Publishing).

64. *Santa Monica Outlook*, August 1, 1910, p. 1.
65. "Disturbance in Cricket Circles," *Santa Monica Outlook*, March 24, 1911, p. 1.
66. Ibid.
67. Ibid.
68. "How Los Angeles Cricket Eleven Looks in the Eyes of Santa Monica Players," *Los Angeles Times*, July 2, 1911, p. 15.
69. Marshall Taylor, "Cricketer's View of Baseball," *Los Angeles Times*, July 15, 1912, p. 3.
70. *Santa Monica Outlook*.
71. *Spalding's Official Cricket Guide 1913*, (New York: American Sports Publishing Co., 1914), p. 90.
72. *Spalding's Official Cricket Guide 1911*, (New York: American Sports Publishing Co., 1912), p. 85.
73. "Mr. P. Higgins of California," *Cricket: A Weekly Record of the Game*, July 5, 1913, p. 384.
74. "Fire Devastates Santa Monica," *Santa Monica Outlook*, September 4, 1912, p. 1.
75. *Santa Monica Outlook*, May 28, 1913.
76. "Cricketers Lose Los Angeles Pavilion to Fire," *SMO*, May 28, 1913, p. 5.
77. *Spalding's Cricket Manual for 1913* (Chicago, 1914).
78. "Golden Gate Cricket Men Are Easy Winners," *LAT*, July 6, part 3, p. 4.
79. "Owen Bird, Local Rugby Situation Cleared Up by L.A.A.C," *LAT*, PV August 14, 1913, p. 2.
80. *Spalding's Cricket Manual for 1913*.
81. "Owen Bird," *LAT*, 1913, p. 2.
82. Marshall Taylor, "Los Angeles Cricket Club plays San Diego," *LAT*, August 12, PIV, p. 3.

Chapter 10

1. James, *Cricket Matches*. Batting number three, Hoskins made ten runs and a duck being bowled both times by Whitty when he played for the New York XV on October 1 and 2, 1912, at Livingston Park. In 1913 Hoskins was selected to the combined United States and Canada side that played Australia at Manheim on July 4, 5 and 7, 1913. Playing for the New York Veterans XIII at Staten Island, he made 17 runs, batting number three against the Australians at Manor Field in Livingston Park on Staten Island.
2. "At the Wicket, Wanderers Lose Match," *Los Angeles Times*, July 1, 1913, p. 6.
3. Frank P. Lee, "Santa Monica Wins," *TAC*, 1920, p. 24.
4. Ibid.
5. *TAC*.
6. David Rayvern Allen, *Sir Aubrey Smith* (London: Elm Books, 1982), p. 96. In the five years before cricket found its new permanent home in Griffith Park, Aubrey Smith's acting career was highly productive. He made eight films in 1932 including *Trouble in Paradise*. The same was true for Boris Karloff. In Lionel Barrymore's *The Unholy Night* (1929), Karloff put his film career on a firm footing as he tapped into his Anglo-Indian roots to portray a Hindu character. Then in 1931 the big break came for Karloff with his portrayal of Frankenstein for Universal in a film produced by Laemmele. After *Frankenstein*'s success, Karloff was signed to a $750 per week contract, half the $6,000 a month Goldwyn paid Ronald Colman.
7. Ibid., pp. 132–144. Davies was the mistress of Saint Simeon and William Randolph Hearst. In Hearst's central California coast castle, perched on the brow of the smooth, undulating Cambrian foothills with a spectacular view of the Pacific Ocean, Marion Davis surrounded herself with the glitterati of the time including England's most eminent men, Sir Winston Churchill, Randolph Churchill, George Bernard Shaw and Charlie Chaplin. Both Davies and Aubrey Smith were favorite actors of George Bernard Shaw, who made his only visit to Hollywood in 1933.
8. Ibid.
9. Boris Karloff, "Cricket in California," *The Screen Player*, May 15, 1934, pp. 6–7.
10. Ibid.
11. Ibid.
12. Wisden, p. 709.
13. *Proceedings of the 1933 Los Angeles City Council*, Los Angeles Archives.
14. Ibid.; Scott Allen Nollen, *Boris Karloff: A Gentleman's Life* (Los Angeles: Midnight Marquee Press, 1999), p. 7; Mike Eberts, "Griffith Park History Project," Glendale Community College, Community College.org.
15. Ferguson, *Empire*, p. 262.
16. Ibid., p. 277.
17. *Sports Illustrated* desk calendar, Dec. 1, 2004.
18. Green, *Wisden Book of Cricketers' Lives*, p. 824.
19. Ibid., p. 860.
20. Ibid., p. 860; *TAC*, 1909.
21. W.G. Grace, *Cricket* (London: J.W. Arrowsmith, 1891), p. 240.
22. Lewis, *Double Century*, p. 147.
23. Ibid.
24. Green, *Wisden Book of Cricketers' Lives*, p. 824.
25. Ibid.
26. Green, *Wisden Book of Cricketers' Lives*.
27. Allen, *Sir Aubrey Smith*, p. 98.
28. Ibid.; *SMO*, July 10, 1910. The Pankhurst's suffragette daughter Emily visited Santa Monica as a guest of the Women's League in 1910. She advocated women's rights as California women fought for the right to vote.
29. Allen, *Sir Aubrey Smith*, p. 98.
30. R.E. Wraithe, *Sir Gordon Guggisberg* (London: Oxford University Press, 1967), p. 105.
31. Ibid. Guggisberg had a productive year in 1905, as he married actress Decima Moore in the registry-office with Arthur Conan Doyle as witness.
32. Ibid. George du Maurier's batting was not required for the Actors, as Smith's side coasted to victory on the strength of the century opening partnership. Du Maurier's daughter Sylvia married Richard Llewellyn Davies; George, the eldest of their five sons, was the inspiration for James M. Barrie's Peter Pan. Du Maurier played for the Barrie's cricket team. George Llewellyn Davies—Du Maurier's grandson—also played on the Allahkbarries in the same year he captained the Eton XI to victory over Harrow at Lord's in 1912. Barrie's team was established in 1893 but did not acquire its *nom de guerre* until Masailand explorer James Thomson came up with "Allahkbarries" as the rough translation for "Heaven help Barrie's lot!"—as in another dismal performance. Performances improved when Arthur Conan Doyle and A.A. Milne, the inventor of Winnie the Pooh, joined the *Allahkbarries*. "Phantom Bowler" Milne met "Round the Corner" Smith when Milne founded Minerva Productions in 1920. The company was to produce silent comedies written by A.A. Milne, with Brunel directing, and a cast that included Aubrey Smith and Leslie Howard. Unfortunately, the Minerva Films venture did not produce more than the four silent comedies now preserved in the National Archives in England.

33. David Niven, *Bring on the Empty Horses* (New York: G.P. Putnam and Sons, 1975), p. 103. The polo ground David Niven referred to was the Midwick Polo Club, a popular with Aubrey Smith and Claude King at the time when Eric Pedley (the son of William Pedley, the Riverside and Alameda Cricket Club member) was a regular player. Eric Pedley played polo for the United States.

34. Ernest William Hornung, *Raffles: The Amateur Cracksman* (London: Wordsworth Classics, 1994), p. 41.

35. Zoss and Bowman, *Diamonds in the Rough*, p. 392.

36. Kevin Starr, *The Dream Endures* (London: Oxford University Press, 1997), p. 282.

37. John Hayward, *Sixty Not Out! Hollywood Cricket Club Diamond Anniversary* (Los Angeles: Hollywood Cricket Club, 1992), pp. 7–12.

38. "News from the Screen Actors Guild," April 20, 1974, p. 1.

39. P.G. Wodehouse, *Author!* (New York: Sribners), pp. 161–165. Wisden notes, "Percy Jevees (Royal Warwickshire Regiment) was killed on July 22, 1916. In 1913 he did brilliant work for Warwickshire as a bowler and batsmen. He was chosen for the Players versus Gentlemen in 1913 and his brilliant bowling helped the Players win." Green, *Wisden Book of Cricketers' Lives*, p. 495.

40. Douglas Fairbanks, Jr., Obituary, *Los Angeles Times*, May 8, 2000, B4.

41. Neville Cardus, *English Cricket* (London: Collins 1945), p. 34.

42. Pollard, *Complete Illustrated History*, pp. 250–251.

43. Bradman, *The Bradman Albums*, vol. 2, p. 293.

44. Ibid.

45. Pollard, pp. 255–269.

46. Zoss and Bowman, *Diamonds in the Rough*, p. 136. Cricket dealt with racial prejudice earlier than baseball and for that reason cricket has always had inherently political overtones for Black West Indian players. Sir Learie Constantine was the first black West Indian player taken to heart by the white working-class community of Nelson in the Lancashire League. From 1920, Constantine made converts of English spectators, showing that cricket skill had no racial boundaries. Constantine converted his hard won prestige, gained from his prowess as a great cricket all-rounder in Lancashire factory towns, into financial and intellectual support for West Indian nationalists and intellectuals such as George Padmore and C.L.R. James. James rewarded his patron with the best cricket book ever written on cricket as a social ameliorating agent: *Beyond the Boundary*. Cricket was one of the lenses through which the West Indian community focused their identity and apart from their color, made them distinct culturally from their baseball-playing white Irish working-class competitors, on the lower rungs of American urban society.

47. Bradman, p. 298.

48. Bradman, p. 307.

49. Ibid.

50. Alfred James, *Cricket Matches*.

51. Mike Coward, *Sir Donald Bradman* (Australia: PanMacMillan, 1998), p. 38.

52. Quoted in Bradman, *Tamed by a Googly!* p. 311.

53. *Standard Casting Directory* (Hollywood, February 1933) pp. 32–46. Kinnell was wounded twice during the First World War before returning to the London stage. He entered the U.S. in 1923 and soon connected with George Arliss in *Old English*. Some of his other film credits were *Grand Hotel*, *The Painted Woman*, *The Match King*, *Rasputin*, and *Today We Live*.

54. Sheriden Morley, *Tales from the Hollywood Raj* (New York: Viking, 1984), p. 141; Boris Karloff, "Oaks from Acorns," *Screenplayer*, Oct.–Nov. 1960, pp. 9–11.

55. Ibid.

56. Ibid.

57. Valerie Yaros, e-mail, June 29, 2000.

58. Donald H. Wolfe, *The Last Days of Marilyn Monroe* (New York: William Morrow and Co., 1998), p. 118. The book accuses Murray Kinnell of molesting Marilyn Monroe, but this seems unlikely as none of Kinnell's children claim to have been molested and his grandson Peter, living in Cincinnati, vehemently denies the possibility. Peter has Sir Aubrey Smith's 1882 Cambridge University blue blazer.

59. *Standard Casting Directory*, pp. 33–46.

60. Laurence W. Beilenson, "For the Record," *Screen Actor Magazine*, June 1937, p. 18. The Masquers Club was a place for Los Angeles actors to meet. Its bar now resides at the Mayflower Club on 1111 Victory Blvd. in Van Nuys.

61. Ibid.

62. Niven, *Bring on the Empty Horses*, p. 184.

63. Sheriden Morley, *The Other Side of the Moon: A Biography of David Niven* (New York: Harper and Row, 1985), p. 63.

64. Philip Dunne, *Taking Two: A Life in Movies and Politics* (New York: McGraw-Hill, 1980), pp. 18–19. Excerpted from Valerie Yaros' "Screen Actors Guild Chronology."

65. Christopher Reed, "Hollywood Bowl," *Manchester Guardian*, July 8, quoted in Hayward, *Sixty Not Out*, p. 5.

66. Claude King, "An Appreciation," *The Screen Player*, March 15, 1934, p. 6.

67. Morley, *Other Side of the Moon*, p. 50.

68. Niven, *Bring on the Empty Horses*, p. 197.

69. Karloff, "Cricket in California."

70. Ibid.

71. Morley, *Tales from the Hollywood Raj*, pp. 138–139.

72. Gerald Garrett, *The Films of David Niven* (London: LSP Books, 1975), p. 45.

73. John Hayward, *Hollywood Cricket Club: 70 and Still Going* (Los Angeles: Private Publication, 2002).

74. Pollard, *Complete Illustrated History*, p. 308.

75. E.W. Swanton, ed. *Barclay's World of Cricket: The Game from A to Z*, (London: Collins, 1980), p. 119. This also contains a great photograph of all three captains and SAG members Boris Karloff, Pat Somerset, George Duckworth, Bob Wyatt and Nigel Bruce.

76. Iain Wilton, *C.B. Fry: King of Sport* (London: Metro, 2002), p. 394.

77. Niven, *Bring on the Empty Horses*, p. 197.

78. Wilton, *C.B. Fry*, pp. 396–400.

79. Ibid.

80. Garrett, p. 117.

81. Ashis Nandy, *The Tao of Cricket, Game of Destiny* (India: Oxford University Press, 2000), p. 45.

82. Niven, p. 204.

83. Pollard, p. 315.

84. Pollard, p. 317.

85. Wilton, p. 402.

86. Ibid., p. 403.

87. Morley, *Other Side of the Moon*, p. 98.

88. Niven, p. 111.

89. Niven, p. 297.

90. Hayward, p. 12.

91. Haywood.

92. Ibid.

93. Ibid.

Chapter 11

1. Ted Hayes, *The Other Side of the Pyramid* (Los Angeles: Charlie Chan Printers, 1994).

2. John Hiscock, "Bats out of Hell," *Sunday Express Classic*, September 15, 1995, p. 31.

3. Mulvenny and Harcourt, *Cricket Walkabout*. The Aborigines were coached initially by Frank Wells, a visionary Oxford-trained sportsman. Wells was credited with introducing Australian Rules football to keep Australian cricketers fit in the winter months. An alcoholic, Wells did not make the Aborigines tour, but his players performed admirably, winning the respect of the English public — who thought they were turning out to see Aborigines a second time when the first white Australian team toured England nine years later with Demon Spofforth in 1878.

4. Pelham Warner, *Long Innings: The Autobiography of Sir Pelham Warner* (London: Harrap and Co., 1951), p. 45. Sir Pelham Warner, who trained as a lawyer at the Middle Temple, had a great respect for the judicial skills of the Beverly Hills and Hollywood captain's grandfather, the First Marques of Reading, noting, "There were many great figures in the temple in those days.... Rufus Isaacs was surely the model to follow, he never overstated his cases."

5. Edward T. Smith, *Playing Hardball: A Kent County Cricketer's Journey into Big League Baseball*, (London: Abacus, 2002), pp. 179–181.

Chapter 12

1. Herman Melville, *Billy Budd* (New York: Ventura Books, 1980).

2. Ferguson, *Empire*, p. 100.

3. C.L.R. James, *Cricket* (London: Allison and Busby, 1986), p. 121.

4. Ibid., p. 119.

5. Ibid., p. 121.

6. Ibid., p. 14.

7. C.L.R. James, p. 124.

8. Ibid., p. 16.

9. Deb Das, www.Cricinfo.com.

10. Thomas Melville, *Tented Field*, p. 16.

11. *American Cricket Manual 1909*.

12. Tygiel, *Past Time*, p. 117.

13. Ibid., p. 120.

14. Ibid.

15. C.L.R. James, p. 23.

16. C.L.R. James, p. 24.

17. Pollard, p. 185.

18. Pollard, p. 201.

19. James, p. 32.

20. James, p. 198.

21. James, p. 199.

22. John Marder, *Southern California Cricket Annual* (Unpublished, C.C. Morris Library, 1971), p. 3.

23. Ibid.

24. Ibid.

25. Ibid.

26. Marder, *International Series*; Tony Verity scrapbook.

27. C.L.R. James, *Nkrumah and the Ghana Revolution* (London: Allison and Busby, 1977).

28. Brian Johnston, *Chatterboxes: My Friends the Commentators* (London: Star Book, 1986), p. 193.

29. Alan Thomson, "Boycott Feels His Jabs," *Los Angeles Times*, September 21, 1964.

30. "U.S. Cricket" in Tony Verity's scrapbook. Ray Honda was scorer from the U.S. tour of England in 1968.

31. Ibid.

32. Ibid.

33. *Los Angeles Times*, September 15, 1964.

34. *Los Angeles Times*, September 30, 1964.

35. Alan Thomson, "A Dashing 'Ton' by Illingworth," *Los Angeles Times*, September 30, 1964.

36. Ibid.

37. Ibid.

38. Ibid.

39. Ron Roberts, "It's Cricket Saturday: English Champion Worcester to Battle Southern California Squad," exclusive to the *Los Angeles Times* from the *Daily Telegraph*, September 15, 1965.

40. The Reforma Club in Mexico City has a long tradition of encouraging English sports, which started when Cornish miners introduced soccer to Mexico at El Pachuco after the Spanish left in 1825 and the local silver mines flooded, requiring the use of the Cornish water pump. One of the rooms in the Reforma Club, la Casa Inglis, has a photograph of Emperor Maximilian in cricket gear standing with a cricket team at Chapultepec Park in Mexico City two years prior to his execution in 1867 by the forces of Benito Juarez. Robert E. Quirk, *Mexico* (New York: Prentice-Hall, 1971), p. 77.

41. Dick Brittenden, *The Finest Years: Twenty Years of New Zealand Cricket* (New Zealand: A Reid Book, 1976), p. 168.

42. Ibid.

43. Tommy Freebairn-Smith, "Hollywood Letter," *Los Angeles Times*, August 19, 1965.

44. Brittenden, p. 162.

45. Jim Marwick, "Slip Catchers in the Rye," *Manchester Guardian*, July 29, 1965.

46. "U.S. would like tour by West Indies cricketers." *Yorkshire Post*, July 30, 1965.

47. "Jack Smith, cricket's Dr. Strangelove," *Los Angeles Times*, November 27, 1966.

48. E.W. Swanton, "American Enthusiasm," *Daily Telegraph*, September 1, 1966.

49. "Irvine Student Leads British Cricket Team," *Los Angeles Times*, January 7, 1967.

50. Tony Verity's scrapbook.

51. "Cricket Clubs Assured Field to be Provided," *Los Angles Times*, September 17, 1967.

52. "Cricketers Run into a Sticky Wicket at Field," *Los Angeles Times—Valley Edition*, Friday September 29, 1967, p. 8, 11-f.

53. James A. Fisher, "The Political Development of the Black Community in California 1850–1890," *California Historical Quarterly*, September 1971, p. 256.

54. Marder, *International Series*.

55. John Woodcock, ed., *Wisden, Cricketers Almanac* (London: Queen Anne Press, 1983), p. 1256.

56. Gerard Dent, "MCC v. USA: A Yank Eleven at Lord's," *The Observer*, July 28, 1968.

57. John M. Lee, "U.S. Cricketers Soundly and Politely Trounced at Lord's," *The New York Times*, July 28, 1968.

58. "MCC Thrash Americans," *Sunday Telegraph*, July 28, 1968.

59. "Cricket: And Now the Colonials," *Time*, August 2, 1968.

60. Clive Page, "Americans Show They're Serious," *Sunderland Echo*, August 2, 1968.

61. Tim Heald, "Cricket Yankee Style," *Daily Express*, August 17, 1968.

62. "URA Clubs. Cricket — What's It All About," *Daily Bruin*, November 11, 1970. Don died during the writing of this book on November 29, 2003, two days after attending the annual SCCA Cricket Banquet where he talked with Wes Hall, the honored guest. As opening bowler for the West Indies test side, Wes Hall was a dominating fast bowler for the West Indies in his prime. Don Weekes faced and hit him hard on several occasions as a batsman and Don retained Wes' respect as a cricketer to the end.

63. Ibid.

64. Marder, p. 5.

65. Ibid.

66. Stephen Jones died of a brain tumor in November 2004.

67. Anecdote from Neil Lashkari interview on January 4, 2004.

68. Stanley Wolpert, *A New History of India* (New York: Oxford University Press, 1977), pp. 41–43. See also Tom O'Neill, "India's Untouchables," *National Geographic*, June 2003, p. 15.

69. Wolpert, p. 81.

70. Wolpert, p. 83.

71. Ibid.

72. Kevin Phillips, *Wealth and Democracy* (New York: Broadway Books, 2002), p. 271.

73. Kirby Lee, "Cricket Attracts a Foreign Crowd," *Daily News*, Saturday July 5, 1997, p. 7.

74. Ibid.

75. Kevin Modesti, "U.S. Cricketers Nearly Make History," *Daily News*, July 6, 1997.

76. Southern California Cricket Association 2004 Award Banquet program, p. 4.

Bibliography

Primary Sources

Board of Park Commissioners of the City of Los Angeles. Annual Reports, 1932–1938. Los Angeles Archives.

Early Days in California, Australia. Manuscripts, after 1852. Pp. 18 99/44c. Berkeley: Bancroft Library.

Keeling Papers. Lakeport Museum, Lakeport, California.

Maudlin's Oral History of Lake County. Lakeport Museum, Lakeport, California.

Minutes of the Riverside Polo Club 1892. Riverside Museum, Riverside, California.

Rudyard Kipling's letter from San Francisco. San Francisco: Colt Press, 1949.

Van Deeling, Gladys Young. An interview transcribed by Kristi Hawthorne. Oceanside Historical Society.

Secondary Sources

Adelman, Melvin. *A Sporting Time: New York City and the Rise of Modern Athletics, 1820–1870.* Urbana: University of Illinois Press, 1986.

Allen, David Rayvern. *Sir Aubrey Smith.* London: Elm Books, 1982.

___. *Sir James Barrie and Allahkbarries.* London: Elm Books, 1982.

Altham, Henry. *Scores and Biographies.* London: Unwin, 1958.

___, and E.W. Swanton. *A History of Cricket.* London: Unwin, 1936.

Ambrose, Stephen. *Nothing Like It in the World: The Men Who Built the Continental Railroad 1863–69.* New York: Touchstone, 2000.

Andreas, Andrew T. *History of Chicago from the Earliest Period to the Present.* Volume 2. Chicago: Andreas Publishing, 1885.

Auty, Karl A. *Illinois Cricket Association Manual.* Chicago: Illinois Cricket Association, 1939.

Baltzell, E. Digby. *Sporting Gentlemen.* New York: The Free Press, 1995.

Barclay, Thomas, and Peter Wynne-Thomas. *Who's Who of Cricketers.* London: 2003.

Bateson, Charles. *Gold Fleet for California:' 49 Convoys from Australia and New Zealand.* East Lansing: Michigan State University Press, 1964.

Beaufort, the Duke of. Edited by Alfred T. Watson. *The Badminton Library of Sports and Pastimes.* London: Longmans and Green, 1889–1920.

Beckles, Hilary McD. *The Development of West Indies Cricket: The Age of Nationalism.* Vols. 1 and 2. Georgetown: University of West Indies Press, 1998.

___, and Brian Stoddart. *Liberation Cricket.* Georgetown: University of the West Indies Press, 1992.

Beilenson, Laurence W. "For the Record." *Screen Actor Magazine,* June 1937.

Berlage, Gai Ingham. *Women in Baseball.* New York: Praeger, 1994.

Biecles, Hilary M. *The Development of West Indies Cricket: The Age of Nationalism.* Georgetown: University of West Indies Press, 1998, Vol. 1 & 2.

Birken, Stephen. *Marshall Field III.* New York: Simon and Schuster, 1964.

Birley, Derek. *A Social History of English Cricket.* London: Acorn Press, 1999.

___. *The Willow Wand: Some Cricket Myths Explored.* London: Simon and Schuster, 1989.

Black, Clinton. *A New History of Jamaica.* London: Collins, 1973.

Boller, Kevin. "The Colourful History of Canadian Cricket." Canadian Cricket Association. www.cricinfo.org. 2001.

Booth, Joseph. "Theory: The Foundation of Social Change." *Sports History Review* 3, no. 2 (2004).

Booth, Keith. *The Father of Modern Sports and the Life and Times of C.W. Alcock.* London, 2003.

Bose, Mihir. *A History of Indian Cricket.* India: Oxford University Press, 1983.

Bowen, Roland. *Cricket:A History of Its Growth and Development throughout the World.* London: Eyre and Spottiswood, 1970.

Bradbury, Malcolm. *Dangerous Pilgrimages: Trans-Atlantic Mythologies and the Novel.* London: Penguin, 1996.

Bradman, Sir Donald. *The Bradman Albums: Selections from Donald Bradman's Official Collection, 1925–49.* Bowral: Bradman Museum, 1963.

Brands, H.W. *The First American: The Life and Times of Benjamin Franklin.* New York: Anchor Books, 2001.

Brechin, Gary. *Imperial San Francisco: Urban Power and Earthly Ruin.* Berkeley: University of California Press, 1999.

Briggs, Asa. *British Sports and Sportsmen.* London 1917.

____. *Victorian People: A Re-assessment of Persons and Themes.* London: Penguin, 1967.

Brittenden, Dick. *The Finest Years: Twenty Years of New Zealand Cricket.* New Zealand: A Reid Book, 1979.

Bronson, William. *The Earth Shook. The Sky Burned.* New York: Pocket Books, 1971.

Brownlee, Methuen W. "A Chat about Cricket W.G. Grace." *Outing,* October 1886, no. 1, pp. 16–20.

Bryson, Bill. *Notes from a Small Island.* London: White Knight Production, 1968. Vol. 2. A Tour of Britain. Video.

Buckley, Roger Norman. *Slaves in Red Coats.* New Haven: Yale Press, 1979.

Burrows, Edwin G., and Mike Wallace. *Gotham: A History of New York to 1898.* London: Oxford University Press, 1999.

Byrd, William. *The Secret Diary of William Byrd.* Richmond, Virginia: Dietz Press, 1941.

Cardus, Neville. *English Cricket.* London: Collins, 1945.

Caren, Eric C. *Baseball Extra.* New Jersey: Edison, 2000.

Carpenter, Aurelious O. and Percy H. Millberry. *History of Lake County 1881.* Reprint, Lake County Publishing, 1988.

Cavanagh, Roy. *Cotton Town Cricket.* Bolton: Bolton and District Cricket Association, 1995.

Chadwick, Henry. *American Cricket Manual.* New York: Robert De Witt, 1873.

____. *Beadle's Dime Book of Cricket.* New York: I.B. Beadle & Co., 1860, 1866.

____. "Cricket at Harvard." *Outings,* 1892, p. 415.

____. *De Witt's Baseball Guide 1869–1885.* New York: De Witt, 1886.

____. *The Reliable Book of Outdoor Games.* New York: F.M. Lupton, 1893.

Chandler, Arthur. *Old Tales of San Francisco.* Dubuque, Iowa: Kendall/Hunt Publishing Co., 1977.

Chestnut Hill Cricket Club, Reports and Papers, 1878–1880. Philadelphia Library of the Historical Society of Philadelphia.

Cleland, Robert Glass. *California Pageant: The Story of Four Centuries.* New York: Alfred Knopf, 1950.

____. *The Cattle on a Thousand Hills: Southern California 1850–1880.* San Marino: The Huntington Library, 1950.

Cleugh, Eric. *With Let or Hinderance: Reminiscences of a British Foreign Service Officer.* London: Cassel, 1960.

Clulow, William. Wynne-Thomas, Peter, ed. *The Log of the "Old Un" from Liverpool to San Francisco.* 1886. Reprint, Exeter Press, 1994.

Cole, Lesley. *The Life of Noel Coward.* London: Penguin, 1979.

Colquohn, James. *The Arizona Mining Company.* Bisbee: Bisbee Publishing, 1899.

Conrad, Earl. *Errol Flynn: A Memoir.* New York: Harraps, 1992.

Coward, Mike. *Sir Donald Bradman.* Sydney: Australia: Pan Macmillan, 1998.

Crawston, Walter. *History of Santa Monica.* Santa Monica: self-published, 1963.

Davis, Joseph G. "Cricket in the West," *American Cricket Annual, 1893.* New York: Sports Publishing Co., 1893.

Dent, Gerard. "MCC v. U.S. A Yank Eleven at Lords," *The Observer,* July 28, 1968.

Dhondy, Farrukh. *C.L.R. James: Cricket in the Caribbean and World Revolution.* London: Weidenfeld & Wilson, 2000.

Dimbeleby, David, and David Reynolds. *An Ocean Apart: The Relationship Between Britain and America in the Twentieth Century.* New York: Random House, 1987.

Doctorow, E.L. *Ragtime.* New York: Bantam, 1976.

Doty, Duane. *The Town of Pullman.* Pullman: T.P. Stackhauer, 1893.

Down, Michael. *Is it Cricket? Power, Money and Politics in Cricket Since 1945.* London: Queen Anne Press, 1986.

Druxman, Michael B. *Basil Rathbone: His life and films.* South Brunswick, N.J.: A.S. Barnes, 1975.

Dunne, Philip. *Taking Two: A Life in Movies and Politics.* New York: McGraw-Hill, 1980.

Durso, Joseph. *Baseball and the American Dream.* Chicago: The Sporting News, 1986.

Evans, Harold. *The American Century.* New York: Knopf, 1998.

Evans, Henry R. *A History of the York and Scottish Rites of Freemasonary.* Silver Spring, Maryland: The Masonic Service Association of the United States, 1924.

Ewing, George. *The Military Journal of George Ewing (1754–1824): A Soldier at Valley Forge.* New York, 1938.

Ferguson, Niall. *Empire: How Britain Made the Modern World.* London: Penguin, 2003.

Fitzgerald, Robert Allan. *Wickets in the West; or, The Twelve in America.* London: Tinsley Brothers, 1873.

Flannery, Jerome. *The American Cricket Annual for 1891.* New York: The Week's Sport Company, 1892.

____. *The American Cricket Annual for 1892.* New York: The Week's Sport Company, 1893.

____. *The American Cricket Annual for 1895.* New York: The Week's Sport Company, 1896.

Foner, Philip S. *The Life and Major Writings of Thomas Paine.* New York: Citadel Press, 1993.

Friggens, Paul. "Cousin Jacks: Cornish Miners in the American West," *American West Magazine,* XI, no. 6 (November 1978).

Frith, David. *The Golden Age of Cricket, 1890–1914.* London: Omega Books, 1984.

____. *Wisden Cricketers' Almanac.* London: Queen Anne Press.

Garrett, Gerald. *The Films of David Niven.* London: LSP Books, 1975.

Gittens, Samuel Evans. *The Foundation of Placer County Horticulture, 1850–1900.* Unpublished MA Thesis, Sacramento State College, 1958.

Glassock, C.B. *Lucky Baldwin: The Story of Unconventional Success.* New York: A.L. Bart Co., 1933.

Grace, W.G. *Cricket.* London: J.W. Arrowsmith, 1891.

Graveney, Tom. *Cricket Over Forty.* London: Pelham Books, 1970.

Green, Benny. *The Wisden Book of Cricketers' Lives: Obituaries from Wisden Cricketers' Almanac.* London: Queen Anne Press, 1983.

Greoble, Marion. *A History of Boating.* Unpublished paper, 1968. Lake County Museum, Lakeport, California.

Guha, Ramachandra. *A Corner of a Foreign Field: The Indian History of an English Sport.* London: Picador, 2002.

____, ed. *The Picador Book of Cricket.* London: Picador, 2001.

Guttman, Allen. *From Ritual to Record: The Nature of Modern Sports.* New York: Columbia University Press, 1978.

Harris, Baron George Robert Canning. "The Philadelphian Visit to England 1884." *Cricketer's Annual.* London: James Lillywhite, Frowd & Co., 1884. pp. 45–68.

Hart, James D., ed. *Robert Louis Stevenson, from Scotland to Silverado.* Cambridge: Belknap Press, 1966.

Harte, Chris. *A History of Australian Cricket.* London: Andre Deutsch, 1993.

Hawke, Lord. "Lord Hawke in Boston, September 1891." *The Cricket Field,* May 14, 1892.

Hayward, John. *Hollywood Cricket Club: 70 and Still Going.* Los Angeles: P.H. Printing, 2002.

____. *Sixty Not Out! Hollywood Cricket Club Diamond Anniversary.* Los Angeles: Hollywood Cricket Club, 1992.

Hine, Robert V. *The American West: An Interpretative History.* New York: Little Brown and Co., 1984.

History of Lake County. Reprint, Fresno: World Dancer Press, 1993.

Hobsbawm, E.J. *Captain Swing.* London: Pelican, 1976.

____. *Industry and Empire.* London: Pelican, 1980.

Holliday, John S. *The World Rushed In: The California Gold Rush Experience. An Eyewitness Account of a Nation Heading West.* New York: Simon and Schuster, 1981.

Hordern, H.V. *Googlies.* Sydney: Angus and Robertson, 1932.

Hornung, E.W. *Raffles: The Amateur Cracksman.* London: Wordsworth Classics, 1994.

Hutchinson, Tom. *Niven's Hollywood.* Boston: Salem House, 1984.

Inkersely, Arthur. "Cricket." *Outing.* August 1896.

James, Alfred. *Cricket Matches Played by Australian Teams in Canada and the United States of America 1878 to 1995.* Sydney: private publication, 1995.

James, C.L.R. and Anna Grimshaw, eds. *Beyond the Boundary.* London: Phaidon, 1958.

____. *The Black Jacobins: Touissant L'Ouverture and the Santo Domingo Revolution.* New York: Vintage Books, 1943.

____. *Cricket.* London: Allison and Busby, 1986.

____. *Nkrumah and the Ghana Revolution.* London: Allison and Busby, 1982.

Johnston, Brian. *Chatterboxes: My Friends and Commentators.* London: Star Book, 1986.

Johnston, Paul. *The Age of Liberalism.* New York: Harper Perennial, 1995.

____. *A History of the American People.* New York: Harper Perennial, 1997.

Jones, Bernard. *Freemason's Guide and Compendium.* Exeter: Barnes and Noble, 1986.

Jordan, David Starr. *California and the Californians: The Alps of the King Kern Divide.* San Francisco: Whitaker Ray Co., 1903.

Kahn, Roger. *The Boys of Summer.* New York: Perennial Classics, 1987.

____. *The Head Game: Baseball Seen from the Pitcher's Mound.* San Diego: A Harvest Book, 2000.

Karloff, Boris. "Cricket in California," *The Screen Player.* May 15, 1934.

King, Claude. "An Appreciation," *The Screen Player.* March 15, 1932.

Kirsch, George B. *The Creation of American Team Sports.* Urbana: University of Illinois, 1989.

Knight, Stephen. *The Brotherhood: The Secret World of the Freemasons.* New York: Dorset Press, 1984.

Koltz, Esther. *Adobes, Bungalows and Mansions.* Riverside: Riverside Museum Press, 1973.

____. *Riverside and the Day the Bank Broke.* Riverside: Rubidoux Press, 1972.

Kramer, Kenneth. "Notes from Special Collections: Anyone for Cricket?" *Darmouth Library College Bulletin,* April 1992.

Kuper, Leo. *Plural Societies.* London: Oxford University Press, 1963.

Lange, Fred W. *History of Baseball in California and the Pacific Coast League 1847–1938.* Oakland: self published, 1938.

Lardner, William R. *A History of Nevada and Placer County.* Berkeley, 1924.

Lavender, David. *Nothing Seemed Impossible: William C. Ralston and Early San Francisco.* Palo Alto: America West Publishing Company, 1976.

Leake, Wilkie B. *A Short History of the Riverside Polo Club.* Senior Thesis, University of California at Riverside, June 1966.

Lee, John M. "MCC Beat Americans at Lords," *Sunday Telegraph,* June 1, 1968.

Lester, John A. *A Century of Philadelphia Cricket.* Philadelphia: University of Pennsylvania Press, 1951.

____. "Cricket in the Far West." *The American Cricketer*. October 28, 1898.

Lewis, David Levering. *W.E.B. DuBois: Biography of a Race*. New York: Henry Newholt and Co., 1993.

Lewis, Tony. *Double Century: The Story of MCC and Cricket*. London: Guild, 1986.

____. *MCC Masterclass*. London: Guild, 1982.

____. *Taking Fresh Guard: A Memoir*. London: Headline, 2003.

Lillywhite, Fred, and Robert Marler, eds. *The English Cricketers' Trip to Canada and the United States in 1959*. London: New Works, 1985.

Lindsay, Cynthia. *Dear Boris: The Life of William Henry Pratt*.

Lockley, Timothy. "The Manly Game: Cricket and Masculinity in Savannah, Georgia, in 1859." *International Journal of the History of Sport* 20, no. 3 (September 2003): 77–99.

London, Jack. *The Cruise of the Dazzler*. Oakland: Jack London Museum, 1992.

____. *People of the Abyss*. Oakland: Star Rover Press, 1904.

Lord, Walter. *The Good Years*. New York: Harper Bros., 1960.

MacLaren, Arthur. *Cricket Old and New*. London: Longmans, 1924.

MacNutt, Howard. "Philadelphia Cricket Past and Present." *Outings* XII, no. 5 (August 1888) pp. 457–459.

Mahan, Alfred Thayer. *The Influence of Sea Power upon History*. Boston: Little, Brown and Company, 1889.

Marder, John. *The International Series: The Story of the United States versus Canada at Cricket* (London: Kaye and Ward, 1968.

Marquesas, Mike. *Anyone but England: Cricket and the National Malaise*. London: Verso, 1994.

Maudlin, Henry. *Clearlake Highlands and the Clear Lake Park Story*. Unpublished oral history, 1981. Oral History Project, Lake County Museum, Lakeport, California.

McCullough, David. *John Adams*. New York: Touchstone, 2000.

McCullough, David. *John Adams*. New York: Simon and Schuster, 2001.

McKenzie, John. "Another Little Patch of Red," *History Today*. 2005, vol. 55(8): p. 23.

McWilliams, Carey. *Southern California: An Island on the Land*. Salt Lake City, Utah: Peregrine Books, 1973.

Melville, Herman. *Billy Budd*. New York: Ventura Books, 1980.

Melville, Tom. *Cricket for Americans*. Bowling Green, Ohio: Bowling Green Press, 1985.

____. "'De Gustibus Non Est Dispitandum.' Cricket at St. Paul's School. A Note on the Structural Character Debate in American Cricket." *International Journal of the History of Sport* 9, no. 1 (1992), pp. 105–110.

____. *The Tented Field*. Bowling Green, Ohio: Bowling Green Press, 2000.

____. "The Wild and Wicket West," *True West Magazine*, June 1995.

Michener, James A. *Sports in America*. New York: Random House, 1976.

Midwinter, Eric. *The Illustrated History of County Cricket*. London: The Kingswood Press, 1992.

Morley, Sheriden. *The Other Side of the Moon: A Biography of David Niven*. New York: Harper and Row, 1985.

____. *Tales from the Hollywood Raj*. New York: Viking, 1984.

Morris, Edmund. *The Rise of Theodore Roosevelt*. New York: The Modern Library, 1979.

____. *Theodore Rex*. New York: Random House, 2001.

Morris, George. *Errol Flynn*. 1975.

Mote, Ashley. *The Glory Days of Cricket: The Extraordinary Story of Broadhalfpenny Down*. London: Robson Books, 1997.

Muhlenberg, General Peter Gabriel. "Order book of General Peter Muhlenberg, March 26–December 20, 1777," *Pennsylvania Magazine of History and Biography* XXXIII (1909), pp. 262–263.

Mulvany, John, and Rex Harcourt. *Cricket Walkabout: The Australian Aboriginal Cricketers Tour 1867–1868*. London: MacMillan, 1988.

Nadeau, Remi. *The Silver Seekers*. Santa Barbara: Santa Barbara Press, 1999.

Nandy, Ashis. *The Tao of Cricket, Game of Destiny*. India: Oxford University Press, 2000.

Newhall, George. Cricket in America, *Outings* V, no. 1 (1884), p. 48.

Niven, David. *Bring on the Empty Horses*. New York: G.P. Putnam and Sons, 1975.

____. *The Moon Is a Balloon*. New York: G.P. Putnam and Sons, 1972.

Nollen, Scott Allen. *Boris Karloff: A Gentleman's Life*. Los Angeles: Midnight Marquee Press, 1999.

Nordoff, Charles. *Northern California, Oregon and the Sandwich Islands*. 1874. Reprint, Berkeley: Ten Speed Press.

Oborne, Peter. *Basil D'Oliveira. Cricket and Conspiracy: The Untold Story*. London: Time Warner Books, 2005.

Oslear, Don. *Wisden: The Laws of Cricket. The 2000 Code and Its Interpretation*. London: Ebury Press, 2000.

Outerbridge, Albert A. "Cricket in America." *Lippincott's Magazine*, May 1873.

Packard, Thomas. *History of American Mining*. San Francisco, 1939.

Padwick, E.W. *A Bibliography of Cricketers*. London, 2000.

Palmer, Harry Clay. Introduction by Henry Chadwick. *Athletic Sports in America, England and Australia*. Philadelphia: Hubbard Bros., 1889.

Patterson, George S. "Cricket in the United States." *Lippincott's Magazine* (via *American Cricketer*, Nov. 30, 1892).

Patterson, Tom. *Riverside: A Colony for Southern California*. Riverside: Press Enterprise Co., 1971.

Patton, James M. *History of Clifton*. Greenlee Chamber of Commerce, 1977.

Pesavento, William J. and Lisa Raymond. "Men Must Play; Men Will Play: Occupations of the Pullman

Athletes, 1880–1900." *Journal of Sports History* 12, no. 3 (winter 1985).

Phillips, Kevin. *Wealth and Democracy*. New York: Broadway Books, 2002.

Pier, Arthur S. *St. Paul's School*. New York: Scribners, 1934.

Pollard, Jack. *The Complete Illustrated History of Australian Cricket*. Melbourne: Viking, 1999.

Praegar, Arthur. *The Mahogany Tree: An Informal History of Punch*. London: Hawthorne Books, 1979.

Pyecroft, James. *The Cricket Field; or, The History and Science of the Game of Cricket*. Boston: Mayhew & Baker, 1859.

Quirk, Robert E. *Mexico*. New York: Prentice Hall, 1971.

Rae, Simon. *W.G. Grace*. London: Faber and Faber, 1998.

Ranjitsinhji, Kumar. *Jubilee Book of Cricket*. London: Badminton Press, 1910.

Richey, Elinor. *The Ultimate Victorians of the Continental Side of San Francisco Bay*. Berkeley: Harrell Books, 1970.

Robinson, Leigh Burpee. *Esquimalt: "Place of Shoaling Waters."* London: Hollingsworth, 1947.

Rodman, W. Paul. *A Victorian Gentlewoman in the Far West*. San Marino: Huntington Library, 1992.

Roffe, Will. "Cricket in New England and the Longwood Club." *Outings* XVIII, no, 3 (June 1891): 232.

Ross, Alan. *Ranji, Prince of Cricketers*. London: Collins, 1983.

Rowse, A.L. *The Early and Later Churchills*. London: Reprint Society, 1959.

Rundell, Michael. *The Dictionary of Cricket*. London: Oxford University Press, 1995.

San Francisco Directories, 1868–1920.

Shortridge, Harold T. *Childhood Memories of a Mining Camp, 1915–1926*. Clifton: self published, 1951.

Sinclair, Jack. *A Biography of Jack London*. London: Pocket Books, 1977.

Slotkin, Richard. *Gunfighter Nation: The Myth of the Frontier in the Twentieth Century*. New York: Harper, 1993.

Smith, Edward. *Playing Hardball: A Kent County Cricketer's Journey into Big League Baseball*. London: Abacus, 2002.

Sorrel, Moxley. *Recollections of a Confederate Staff Officer*. New York and Washington: Neale Publishing, 1905.

Spalding, Arthur Goodwill. *America's National Game*. Chicago, 1911.

____, and Henry Chadwick, eds. *Spalding's Cricket Annual*. Chicago, 1904.

____, and F.F. Kelly, eds. *Spalding's Official Cricket Guide 1910*. New York: American Sports Publishing Co., 1909.

____, and F.F. Kelly, eds. *Spalding's Official Cricket Guide1911*. New York: American Sports Publishing Co., 1912.

____, and F.F. Kelly, eds. *Spalding's Official Cricket Guide 1913*. New York: American Sports Publishing Co., 1914.

Splitter, Henry. "Los Angeles Recreation 1846–1900, Part 2." *The Historical Society of Southern California Quarterly* XLII, no. 1 (June 1961): 167–169.

Starr, Kevin. *The Dream Endures*. New York: Oxford University Press, 1997.

____. *Inventing the Dream*. London: Oxford University Press, 1985.

____. *Material Dreams: Southern California through the 1920s*. New York: Oxford University Press, 1990.

____. "The Sporting Life," *California Quarterly* 63, no. 1 (winter 1984), 26–31.

Stevenson, Robert Louis. *From Scotland to Silverado*. Ed Bernard Bailyn. (Boston: Belknap Press, 1961).

Sullivan, Dean A., ed. *Early Innings: A Documentary History of Baseball 1825–1908*. Omaha: University of Nebraska, 1995.

Sunkist Growers. *A Heritage of Gold: The First Hundred Years of Sunkist Growers Inc. 1893–1993*. Los Angeles: Sunkist Publishing, 1993.

Swanton, E.W., ed. "American Enthusiasm." *Daily Telegraph*, September 1, 1966.

____. *Barclay's World of Cricket: The Game from A to Z*. London: Collins, 1980.

____. *Gubby Allen: Man of Cricket*. London: Hutchinson/Stanley Paul, 1985.

Taylor, Marshall. "Los Angeles Cricket Club Plays San Diego." *Los Angeles Times*, August 12, 1913, p. 3.

The Tour of the West Indian Cricketers, August and September, 1886. Demarara: The Argosy Press, 1887.

Thomas, Allan Curry. "Haverford College Cricket," *Outings*.

Thomas, Gordon and Max Morgan. *The San Francisco Earthquake*. New York: Dell, 1971.

Thorn, John, Peter Palmer, Michael Gershman, and David Pietrusza. *Total Baseball: The Official Encyclopedia of Major League Baseball, 5th ed.* New York: Viking, 1997.

Trelford, Donald. *W.G. Grace*. Stroud: Sutton Publishing, 1998.

Trollope, Anthony. *North America*. London: Penguin, 1968.

Trueman, Fred, and Don Mosey. *Champion Times: Yorkshire CCC 1959–1968*. Skipton: Dalesman Publishing Co., 1996.

____. *As It Was: The Memoirs of Fred Trueman*. London: MacMillan, 2004.

Turner, Frederick Jackson. *History of Western Frontier*. Chicago, 1893.

Turner, T.C. "Cricket." *Outing*, August 1896.

____. "International Cricket in America." *Harper's Weekly*, August 19, 1905, vol. 49, p. 1, 192.

Tygiel, Jules. *Past Time: Baseball as History*. New York: Oxford University Press, 2000.

Underdown, David. *Start of Play: Cricket and Culture in Eighteenth Century England*. London: Penguin Books, 2001.

Verlag, Bernard and Graefe. *Kriegsschiffe der welt 1860 bis 1905*. Band 1. (Koblenz: Grossbriannien/Deutschland, 1993).

Walker, Franklin. *San Francisco's Literary Frontier*. New York, 1939.

Warner, Pelham E. *Cricket*. The Badminton Library series. London: Longmans, 1930.

____. *Cricket in Many Climes*. London: Heinmann, 1900.

____. *Long Innings: The Autobiography of Sir Pelham Warner.* London: George Harrap and Sons, 1951.

____. *Lords 1787–1945.* London: Harper & Row, 1947.

Waugh, Evelyn. *The Loved One.* London: Laurel Edition, 1948.

Weaver, T.B. *Amusement and Sports in American Life.* Chicago: University of Chicago Press, 1939.

Webster, Ray (comp.) and Alan Miller (ed.), *First Class Cricket in Australia,* vol. 1850–51 to 1941. Australia: Glen Waverly, 1991.

Wells, Stephen. "Cricket in America." *Guardian,* July 27, 2004.

Wharton, Thomas. "Inner-City and International Cricket in America." *Outing,* June 1892, no. 3, pp. 172–180.

White, Carl. *Santa Monica Community Book.* Santa Monica: A.H. Cawston, 1953.

White, Colin. *Victoria's Navy: The Heyday of Steam.* London: Kenneth Mason, 1983.

Wiencek, Henry. *George Washington: His Slaves and the Creation of America.* New York: Farrar, Strauss and Giroux, 2003.

Wild, Roland. *The Biography of Colonel, His Highness Shri Sir Ranjitsinhji.* London: Rich and Cowan, 1934.

Williams, Harry. *The Steam Navy of England.* London: Allen and Co., 1903.

Williamson, Percy. "Cricket in the West." *American Cricket Annual.* New York: Sports Publishing Co., 1896.

Wilton, Iain. *C.B.Fry: King of Sport.* London: Metro, 2002.

Wister, Jones. *A "Bawl" for American Cricket Dedicated to American Youth.* Philadelphia, 1893.

Wister, Owen. *Romney.* Philadelphia: State University of Pennsylvania, 2000.

Wister, William Rotch. *Some Reminiscences of Cricket in Philadelphia before 1861.* Philadelphia: Allen, 1904.

Wolfe, Donald H. *The Last Days of Marilyn Monroe.* New York: W.H. Morrow and Sons, 1998.

Wolpert, Stanley. *A New History of India.* New York: Oxford University Press, 1977.

Wraithe, Richard E. *Sir Gordon Guggisberg.* London: Oxford University Press, 1967.

Wynne-Thomas, Peter. *The Complete History of Cricket Tours at Home and Abroad.* London: Guild, 1989.

____. *Give Me Arthur.* London: Arthur Barker Limited, 1985.

____. *The History of Cricket from the Weald to the World.* London, 2003.

Yardley, Jonathan. *Ring: A Biography of Ring Lardner.* New York: Atheneum, 1984.

Yeomans, Patricia. *A Hundred Years of Southern California Tennis Champions.* Los Angeles: private publication, 1987.

Zigg, Paul J. and Mark Medeiros. *The Pacific Coast League, 1903–58.* Urbana: University of Illinois Press, 1994.

Zimbalist, Andrew. *Baseball and Billions.* New York: Basic Books, 1992.

Zoss, Joel, and John Bowman. *Diamonds in the Rough: The Untold History of Baseball.* Chicago: Contemporary Books, 1989.

Newspapers and Magazines

Actor Magazine
Alta California
Arizona Weekly Journal
Australasian
Chicago Tribune
Citrus Colony News
Clearlake News
Copper Echo-Clifton, Arizona
Daily Encinal
Field
Frank Leslie's Illustrated Magazine
Grantham Journal
Harpers
Hollywood Citizen News
Hollywood Variety
Lakeport Bee
Los Angeles Herald
Los Angeles Times
Manchester Guardian
Nevada Daily Transcript
New York Illustrated News
New York Times
Oakland Times
Oakland Tribune
Oceanside Blade
Outing
Philadelphia Enquirer
Placer Herald
Placer Times
Riverside Daily Press
Riverside Enterprise
Riverside Magazine
Sacramento Bee
San Francisco Chronicle
San Francisco Examiner
Santa Monica Outlook
Savannah Republic
Screen Actor Magazine
Screen Player
Screenland Magazine
Sporting News
Sunday San Francisco Examiner and Chronicle
Sunderland Echo
Times
Westways
Yorkshire Post

Cricket Periodicals

The American Cricket Annual, 1891–1906. Abbreviated as *TACA* in the notes.

American Cricketer, abbreviated as *AC* in the notes, was published weekly during the April to October cricket season and monthly from November to March. Devoted to the Noble Game of Cricket, *AC* was published for over 50 years (in Philadelphia, from June 28, 1877, to April 1929). The complete set of periodicals is available at the CC Morris Library at Haverford College and at the Philadelphia Library of the Historical Society of Pennsylvania.

C.C. Morris Quarterly
Cricket: A Weekly Record of the Game
Cricket Field (London)
Cricket Quarterly
Cricketer (London)
Cricketer's Annual (London)
Illinois Cricket Association Year Book, 1940. Karl A. Auty, editor.
Spalding's Official Cricket Guide, 1907–1913, abbreviated as *SOCG* in notes. The *SOCG* was edited first by Henry Chadwick. In 1909, F. Fitzmaurice Kelly took over as editor.
Wisden

Journals

British Colonist
British Columbia Historical Quarterly
California Historical Quarterly
Dartmouth Library College Bulletin
Historical Society of Southern California Quarterly
International Journal of the History of Sports
Journal of Sports History
Journal of the Emeryville Historical Society
Pennsylvania Magazine of History and Biography
Spalding Official Cricket Manual
Sports History Review

Encyclopaedias

Encyclopaedia of Sports. New York: A.J. Baines and Co., 1968.

Correspondence

Green, Stephen. MCC Library, London. Information on Gilbert Jessop, Patrick Higgins, Charles Hurditch, and Maxwell Cobb
James, Alfred. Australian Scorecards. 1999.
Webster, Ray. Digger Robertson. November 12, 1998.

Web Sites

www.AAFLA.org
www.Australianbaseballhistory.webcentral.com.
www.CanadaCricket.org
www.Cricinfo.org
www.Lauderhill.net
www.Lord's.org
www.SCCAcricket.com
www.USACA.com

Index